CLASSIC DATA STRUCTURES IN C++

CLASSIC DATA STRUCTURES IN C++

Timothy A. Budd
Oregon State University

Addison-Wesley Publishing Company

Reading, Massachusetts • Menlo Park, California • New York
Don Mills, Ontario • Wokingham, England • Amsterdam • Bonn
Sydney • Singapore • Tokyo • Madrid • San Juan • Milan • Paris

The procedures and applications presented in this book have been included for their instructional value. They have been tested with care but are not guaranteed for any purpose. The publisher does not offer any warranties or representations, nor does it accept any liabilities with respect to the programs and applications.

Library of Congress Cataloging-in-Publication Data

Budd, Timothy.
Classic data structures in C++ / Timothy A. Budd.
p. cm.
Includes bibliographical references.
ISBN 0-201-50889-3
1. C++ (Computer program language) 2. Data structures (Computer science) I. Title.
QA76.73.C153B83 1994
005.7'3—dc20 93-21664
CIP

2 3 4 5 6 7 8 9 10-MA-959493

PREFACE

A programming language is usually envisioned merely as a notational tool to be used in the description of computer programs. In a lecture he gave upon receiving the annual Association for Computing Machinery Alan Turing Award in 1979, the computer scientist Kenneth E. Iverson discussed computer languages in a talk entitled "Notation as a Tool of Thought."[1] I enjoyed the title (as well as the paper) because I have always held to the idea that computer languages are not simply a mechanism of description but also a vehicle of conception, cogitation, and analysis.

The field of computer science exists because there are problems that, for one reason or another, are best addressed using the mechanism of an electronic computer. We have countless reasons for using computers: the necessity for speed (the reason computers are used in the electronic ignition of our automobiles), for accuracy (the reason they are used in bookkeeping or in the generation of mathematical tables), and for convenience (the reason they are used to create spreadsheets and word processors); the need to deal with environmental conditions (the reason they are used on unmanned space probes), and large quantities of data (the reason why they are used in graphics and in large simulations, such as weather models), among others. But in each case, problems arise out of *human* experience. Problems are originated, conceived, analyzed, and developed in the way that human beings deal with problems. This is often a complex combination of intuition, pattern matching, guesswork, heuristics, sweat, and good luck.

An electronic computer, on the other hand, is a true *idiot savant*. It is a machine able to do only very simple things, but able to do them very quickly. If problem solutions are to be processed using such a machine, they must be expressed in terms that the machine can understand—a combination of simple logical, arithmetic, and symbolic instructions.

Thus a major problem in computer science is to bridge the gap between *problems*, which are developed in characteristically human terms, and solutions in the form of *programs*, which can be executed by a computer. The mechanism we use to bridge this chasm is computer language, and,

1. Iverson's paper is reprinted in [Ashenhurst 87].

more specifically, the creation of high level tools expressed in that computer language.

The first computers, developed in the 1940s and early 1950s, required programmers to work directly in the basic machine code of the device. Thus the programmer was responsible for making the transition from problem to program. It was usually the case that far more time was spent in trivial coding details, such as remembering how certain registers were being used or what values were associated with specific memory locations, than was spent actually thinking about the problem to be solved.

In response to the frustrations generated by the difficulty of programming, high level languages—beginning with Fortran, Cobol, and Algol-60—were developed in the late 1950s and early 1960s in an attempt to free the computer user from some of the tedium involved in coding computer programs. The key insight here was that the computer itself was capable—indeed, more capable than the human programmer—of performing many of the bookkeeping tasks involved in coding computer programs. Using high level languages, programmers could be less concerned with *how* a specific task was to be accomplished and more concerned with *what* task was to be performed. The computer itself could perform a translation from the high level language to machine language, and then execute the machine language program. Since then, the development of computer languages has been largely driven by the competing goals of creating language features that are more expressive, in which complex ideas can be more easily and correctly described, and creating language features that can be easily and efficiently translated into forms the computer itself can understand. The goal of expressiveness is moving the language toward the human side of the bridge, while the emphasis on efficient translation is moving the language toward the computer side of the bridge.

One of the most recent developments in programming language design has been the concept of object-oriented programming. I fully believe that object-oriented programming is popular because the metaphor on which it is based, which is a universe of interacting but largely autonomous objects, is similar to the way people view the real world. In this way, programming in an object-oriented language is closer to the human experience side of the bridge, and programmers can bring to bear real-world experience in the solution of software problems (something not always possible with other programming paradigms). The C++ language is by far the most popular object-oriented language developed to date.

In addition to more closely matching a common way of viewing problems, object-oriented programming also provides a number of mechanisms for the reuse of existing software components. We are starting to see the realistic possibility that in the future a program will not be laboriously handcrafted from the first line to the last but will instead be developed largely out of off-the-shelf standard components. Software reuse is emphasized, and object-oriented concepts are used throughout the present text.

Because the goals of ease of use and efficient translation are almost necessarily antithetical, programming languages almost always represent a technical compromise. The C++ language is no exception. It is often criticized as being large and complex, forcing programmers to work at a low level of abstraction (closer to the machine side than to the human side of the abstraction bridge). C++ is indeed large, but the features of the language are all useful in solving common problems. An understanding of the problems that a language feature is used in solving is thus a requirement in learning how to make effective use of the language. What about working at too low a level of abstraction? Here, too, the criticism is misplaced. It is true that the C++ language *permits* the programmer to work at a very low level of abstraction. But C++ is preeminently a *tool-building* language. By developing a repertoire of useful and reusable abstractions, programmers can raise the level of abstraction in their problem solutions. This book is foremost about the development of useful programming abstractions.

Background Assumed

The primary intent of this book is not to teach C++. I do not, however, assume that the student will have had prior experience with the language before embarking into the material presented here. It is sufficient for the student to have had exposure to concepts such as statements, expressions, and functions in some language, such as C or Pascal. At Oregon State University, where this book was developed, students will have started to learn C, but will not even have encountered arrays or structures before they reach the point where this text picks up.

Having said I do not assume the reader to be an expert in C++ prior to an examination of the material here, it is also important to note that it is my sincere hope that after having studied the material in this book the student will, by the end, be reasonably proficient in the language. So somewhere along the line I assume the student will be learning about programming in C++. However, for our purposes the acquisition of this skill is secondary to the development of an understanding of the process of solving problems on the computer, and in particular to an approach to problem solving that emphasizes the creation and utilization of reusable software tools, use of good software engineering principles (including object-oriented programming techniques), a knowledge of common and classic data structures, and a basic understanding of the principles involved in comparing and analyzing algorithms.

In line with this philosophy, I do not feel obligated to present all the arcane details of the language (and C++ is a language *rich* in arcane details). My exposition will flow in a more narrative and less encyclopedic fashion, and features of the language will be introduced as they pertain to the problems at hand. This type of presentation allows readers to encounter repeatedly the most important and frequently used aspects of the language. In an encyclopedic approach the reader is often hard-pressed to distinguish what is important from what is incidental. On the other hand, it is frequently useful to convey at certain points in the discussion additional information that does not easily fit into the narrative being developed. In these cases I have usually resorted to placing this information in a sidebar, or box. These boxes can almost always be ignored on first reading, and I would encourage students to do so. On subsequent readings they will enrich and reinforce a student's grasp of the material. Thus the goals of this book can be described as follows, in roughly decreasing order of importance:

- Introduce the classic data structures that are found in almost all computer programs.
- Instruct the student in the use of analysis techniques with which to evaluate algorithms.
- Provide examples of modern software engineering principles and techniques, including object-oriented programming.
- Introduce the proper use of various features of the C++ programming language.

Outline of Presentation

This book is divided into two major sections and four appendixes. Part I, entitled "Terms, Tools, and Technology," introduces the terminology we will use in our exploration of computer abstractions. This involves details of the computer language, as well as a language for discussing the analysis of computer programs, and a few ideas on problem-solving techniques.

Chapter 1 presents material that, in an initial impression, might appear to be only loosely related to the remainder of the book. This is not the case. An appreciation for many of the features of the C++ language is only possible with at least some understanding of the difficulties of programming in the large. Ideas such as software components, interface and implementation, and information hiding have only little applicability in small programs, but they possess critical importance in any significant software project. The responsibility-driven design exercises described in this chapter are intended to help the student acquire an intuitive understanding of these topics *before* the particular syntax used by C++ is introduced.

Chapter 2 introduces the general notion of an abstract data type. In this chapter we start to see some of the features of the C++ language that support the development of higher level programming abstractions. I explore some of these in the course of developing a new data type that corresponds to the abstract idea of a rational number. I introduce briefly the concept of stream-based input and output.

Chapter 3 presents material that can be given greater or lesser emphasis, at the discretion of the instructor. Some instructors feel that invariants, proofs of correctness, mathematical induction, and asymptotic analysis should be a fundamental component of the first year data structures course, while other instructors prefer to delay the presentation of this material until later courses. In practice, the induction proofs and asymptotic analysis we will deal with in the remainder of this book are all relatively simple and should present no difficulty to the student.

Part II, "Analysis, Algorithms, and Abstractions," is the heart of the book. Here we investigate high level software abstractions that are found in almost every computer program written in practice. We investigate strings, vectors, lists, trees, heaps, queues, sets, tables, graphs, and the problems of searching and sorting.

The `string` data type analyzed in Chapter 4 is used largely as a vehicle for introducing data structuring facilities in C++. By the end of this chapter, almost all the features of classes that we will make use of in the book will have been introduced. The optional last third of the chapter, on pattern matching, presents a nontrivial application of strings, and also illustrates to the student that even seemingly simple problems can have interesting and unusual solutions.

Chapter 5, which is extremely short, simply introduces the general categories of data structures we will investigate in the remainder of the text. No programs are presented, and no new data structuring facilities are introduced in this chapter.

In Chapter 6 a number of data abstractions are built on top of the primitive array facilities provided by the C++ language. Vectors, lists, and trees are the three fundamental structures out of which almost all complex data structures are constructed. Equally important with the introduction of the concept of a vector in this chapter is the development of variations on the vector data type to illustrate the two major techniques for software reuse: inheritance and composition. Finally, the chapter introduces a trio of algorithms for sorting, and the analysis of these algorithms is used as a vehicle to discuss algorithms.

Chapter 7 expands on one of the fundamental concepts of object-oriented programming: the development of new components through the use of inheritance. I discuss the motivation and various uses for inheritance. The concept of an iterator for a collection is introduced. Iterators permit the definition of operations on collections that are independent of the various implementation techniques used for collections. Such functions are polymorphic, a term introduced in this chapter.

Chapter 8 introduces the concept of a linked list, as well as the more general idea of dynamically allocated data structures. Several variations on the linked list are explored. One of these, ordered lists, leads naturally to an associated sorting algorithm.

The abstract ideas of the `stack` and the `queue` are explored in Chapter 9. Stacks and queues can be implemented in a number of ways, using either vectors or lists. The use of stacks and queues in searching is briefly outlined. A common use of stacks is in the simulation of calculators. An important idea introduced in the latter portion of this chapter is the notion of a framework. A framework is a class that provides a generic solution to a category of problems. Specific problems are then solved by specializing the framework using the mechanism of inheritance.

Trees, and in particular binary trees, are introduced in Chapter 10. Along with vectors and linked lists, trees are a fundamental tool used in the creation of higher level abstractions. The chapter presents some simple analyses of binary trees, and illustrates the use of trees in several applications, including parsing text in order to generate expression trees. Unlike the data structures that preceded this chapter, trees do not have an obvious linear ordering. Various possible orderings can be used to visit each node in a tree. I present four different tree traversal algorithms.

Chapter 11 is concerned less with a specific data structure and more with a problem domain—namely, searching a collection of values to determine if a particular element is present. The binary search algorithm is presented. Various data structures that facilitate the fast execution of search algorithms are then discussed. One of these data structures naturally leads to the first efficient (less than polynomial time) sorting algorithm developed in this text.

Another problem domain is discussed in Chapter 12. A priority queue is useful when the most important task performed by a collection is the selection and removal of the smallest element. Various data structures that can be used to implement priority queues are discussed. The use of priority queues in sorting is investigated, leading to heap sort, the most efficient general purpose sorting algorithm presented in this text. A classic example of the use of priority queues is in discrete event-driven simulation. A framework for such simulations is developed. Along the way this chapter discusses random numbers and the problems involved in generating random numbers on a computer.

Chapter 13 presents a classic data structure as its central theme: the hash table. Hash tables provide very efficient execution, at the expense of requiring the user to supply a function, the hash function, that will randomly distribute values over an integer range.

In Chapter 14 the abstract concepts of a set and a bag are developed. These high level data structures can be implemented in a variety of different fashions. I illustrate this, and provide several applications of the concept.

Another high level data structure, the dictionary or table, is presented in Chapter 15. A dictionary, which is a generalization of the vector data type, is an extremely general and useful data structure.

Although not exactly data structures in the same sense as the other abstractions discussed in preceding chapters, graphs are nevertheless commonly encountered in a wide range of problems. Chapter 16 presents several graph data structures and algorithms that can be used to manipulate these structures. Most importantly, the development of graphs as data structures illustrates how high level abstract concepts can be built on a foundation of the other data structures we have presented.

Finally, Chapter 17 discusses files as a data type. Files are not limited by available memory, and they can thus be used to store large quantities of data. In addition, information stored in files will continue to exist even after a program has finished execution.

There are four appendixes following the main text. Appendix A simply summarizes and reviews the behavior of each of the data structures developed in the text. Appendix B summarizes the rationale for and use of various features in the C++ programming language. This can be used by the student as a quick reference manual for these values. Appendix C summarizes in a tabular fashion the execution timings for the various sorting algorithms discussed in the text. Several exercises scattered throughout the text refer to this data. Appendix D simply presents values in tabular form for several functions. As with Appendix C, the chief use of these values is in conjunction with the solution of many exercises.

There is enough material presented in this text for a typical two-term sequence in data structures and advanced programming. To cover the material in one term would probably necessitate omitting almost all optional sections and ignoring some of the later chapters. The text has been designed with both possibilities in mind, and a great deal of flexibility is possible.

Obtaining Source Code

The C++ code used as examples in this text makes extensive use of templates. These are a relatively new addition to the C++ language, and not all compilers yet recognize them. The code has been tested using both the AT&T and GNU C++ compilers on Unix systems, and using the Borland Turbo-C++ compiler on the PC.

Source code for the data structures and applications described in this text, as well as overhead slides and other associated material, can be obtained by electronic mail. For those having Internet networking capabilities, the source can be obtained through a mail server by writing to `almanac@cs.orst.edu`. The author can be reached by electronic mail at `budd@cs.orst.edu`.

Acknowledgments

The following people have made a major contribution toward the creation of this book. From Oregon State University, my colleagues and students: Alice Albin, Marcus Beaman, Curtis Cook, Paul Cull, Aaron Drenkhahn, Dennis Foote, Mike Johnson, Tim Justice, Ted Lewis, Phat Ly, Eldon Metz, Tatsuo Natsukawa, Rajeev Pandey, Ignacio Perez, Jay

Reidy, Michael Schuyler, Grant Suehiro, Justin Varner, Brad Williams, Jesse Wiseman, and Nabil Zamel. A number of people outside of OSU have also viewed various early drafts of the manuscript and have provided useful criticisms and suggestions. These include William Allen (UCLA), Joe Gilray (Hewlett-Packard), Lindsay Marshall (University of Newcastle), Xiannong Meng (Bucknell University), Doug Moore (Rice University), Richard Pattis (University of Washington), John Skaller (Maxtal Pty Ltd.), Rick Zaccone (Bucknell University), and a number of anonymous reviewers. Finally, invaluable advice, support, and direction have been provided by my editor at Addison-Wesley, Lynne Doran Cote, and by the production and marketing personnel there, including Helen Wythe, Andrea Danese, Denise Descoteaux, and Peter Harris.

CONTENTS

* Section headings followed by an asterisk indicate optional material.

CLASSIC DATA STRUCTURES IN C++

PART I

TERMS, TOOLS, AND TECHNOLOGY

CHAPTER 1

Engineering Software

THIS BOOK is primarily concerned with data structures, algorithms for manipulating data structures, and the applications and uses of data structures, yet we cannot ignore the fact that the selection and manipulation of data structures are just one small part of the larger software development process. The mechanisms employed in the creation of data structures in the C++ language have been designed specifically to assist in the development of large software systems. By large software systems we mean programs consisting of tens or hundreds of thousands of lines of code and requiring the efforts of several members of a programming team. The term *software engineering* is often used to describe the development of such applications.

The student taking a data structures course at the level of the material presented here will often have had little experience in the creation of large systems, and thus will have minimal appreciation of the difficulties involved in software design and development, as opposed to the problems of mere coding. In order to better understand the relationship of data structures to this process, and the importance of the mechanisms provided by the C++ programming language, we will step back in this chapter and discuss the broader issues of software development. Subsequent chapters will then be much more narrowly focused on issues related to specific types of data structures.

The approach followed in this chapter will be to intertwine our exposition of software engineering concepts with a hypothetical case study in software design. The software development technique we describe here, called *responsibility-driven design*, is an iterative process of directed software evolution, and is applicable to the creation of both large and small software applications. The basic idea is to start with a general description of the problem at hand and simultaneously to evolve and refine the description (or specification) and lay out successively more detailed approaches to implementation. As the process continues, activities naturally progress from problem analysis to program solution, eventually resulting in a completed working software application.

In addition to describing a specific technique of software design, a major

Programming in the Small vs. Programming in the Large

The difference between the development of individual projects and more sizable software systems is often described using the terms "programming in the small" and "programming in the large." Briefly, programming in the small characterizes projects with the following attributes:

- ▲ Code is developed by a single programmer, or perhaps by a small group of programmers. A single individual can understand all aspects of a project, from top to bottom, beginning to end.
- ▲ The major problem in the software development process is the design and development of algorithms for dealing with the problem at hand.

Programming in the large, on the other hand, characterizes software projects with features such as the following:

- ▲ The software system is developed by a large team of programmers. Individuals involved in the specification or design of the system may differ from those involved in the coding of individual components, who may differ as well from those involved in the integration of various components into the final product. No single individual can be said to be responsible for the entire project, or even necessarily to understand all aspects of the project.
- ▲ The major problem in the software development process is the management of details, and the communication of information between diverse portions of the project.

Although the beginning student will initially practice programming in the small, aspects of the C++ language are best understood as responses to the problems of programming in the large (see, for example, the sidebar "Who Is Information Being Hidden From?" on page 17). Thus some appreciation of the difficulties involved in developing large systems is a helpful prerequisite to understanding the C++ language.

Increasingly, even beginning students are experiencing some aspects of programming in the large through the use of software frameworks. A software framework, such as a graphical user interface system (GUI), may handle a significant portion of the functionality involved in using a windowing system. The user of a software framework seldom understands the details concerning how operations are effected, instead merely needing to know how their new software component connects and interacts with the framework. Thus even relatively simple programs are generated as a component connected to a larger system.

goal of this chapter is to encourage in the reader the view that a computer program can be thought of as consisting of a collection of interacting, but largely independent, software components. Programs developed in this fashion are called *object-oriented*.

1.1 RESPONSIBILITY-DRIVEN DESIGN

We will illustrate the principles of responsibility-driven design by means of a case study. Imagine you are the chief software architect in a major computer firm. Your boss one day walks into your office with an idea that, it is hoped, will be the next major success in the product line handled by your company. Your assignment is to develop an interactive intelligent kitchen helper. The task given to your software team is stated in very few words (written on what appears to be the back of a slightly used dinner napkin, in handwriting that appears to be that of your boss).

Briefly, the interactive intelligent kitchen helper (IIKH) is a PC-based application that is a modern replacement for the index card box for recipes found in the average household kitchen. But more than simply maintaining a data base of recipes, the kitchen helper assists in the planning of meals for an extended period—for example, for one week. The user of the IIKH can sit down at a terminal, browse the database of recipes, and interactively create a series of menus. The IIKH will automatically scale the recipes to any desired number of individuals. The user of the IIKH can print out menus for the entire week, for a particular day, or for a particular meal. Additionally, the IIKH will print an integrated grocery list of all the items needed to satisfy the recipes for the entire time period, or for any shorter period (a day, a single meal, or a single recipe).

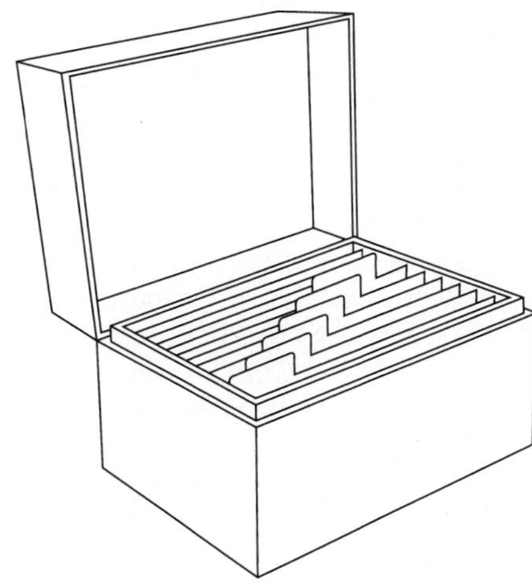

As is usually true with the initial descriptions of most software systems, the specification for the IIKH is highly ambiguous on a number of important points. It is also true that, in all likelihood, the eventual design and development of the software system to support the IIKH will require the efforts of several programmers working together. Thus the initial goal of the software team must be to clarify the ambiguities in the description and to start to outline how the project can be divided into components that can then be assigned for development to individual team members.

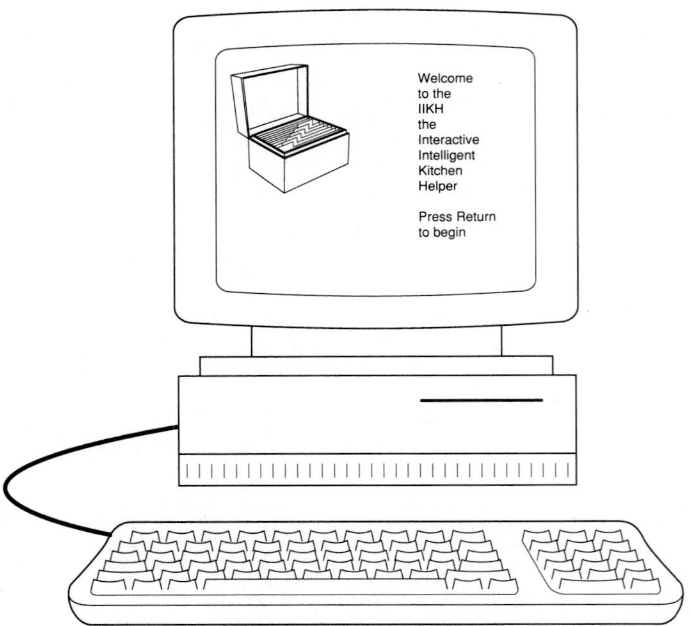

The fundamental cornerstone of the object-oriented style of programming encouraged by the C++ language is to characterize software in terms of *behavior*—that is, in terms of actions to be performed. We will see this repeated on many levels in our description of the development of the IIKH. Initially, your team will try to characterize, at a very high level of abstraction, the behavior of the entire application. This will then lead to the development of a description of the behavior of various software subsystems. Only when all behavior has been identified and described will the software design team proceed to the coding step. In the next several sections we will trace the tasks your software design team will follow in producing this application.

1.1.1 Working Through Scenarios

The first task is to refine the specification. As we have already noted, initial specifications are almost always ambiguous and unclear on anything except the most general points. There are several goals for this step. The first is to get a better handle on the "look and feel" of the eventual product. This information can then be carried back to the client (in this case, your boss) to see if it is in agreement with the original conception. It is likely, perhaps inevitable, that the specifications for the final application will change during the creation of the software system, and it is important that the design be developed in order to accommodate change easily, and also to note potential changes as early as possible. Equally important, at this point very high-level decisions can be made concerning the structure of the eventual software system. In particular, the activities to be performed can be mapped onto components.

The engineering of a complex physical system, such as a building or an automobile engine, is simplified by dividing the design into smaller units. So, too, is the engineering of software simplified by the identification and development of software components. A *component* is simply an abstract entity that can perform tasks — that is, it can fulfill some responsibilities. At this point, it is not necessary to know exactly the eventual representation for a component, or how a component will perform a task. A component may ultimately be turned into a function, into a structure or class (a type of software abstraction we will encounter in the next chapter), or into a collection of other components. At this level of development there are only two important characteristics of components:

- A component must have a small, well-defined set of responsibilities.
- A component must interact with other components to the minimal extent possible.

We will shortly discuss the reasoning behind the second characteristic. For the moment, we will simply be concerned with the identification of the responsibilities of components.

CRC CARDS — RECORDING RESPONSIBILITY In order to discover components and their responsibilities, your team proceeds by walking through *scenarios*; that is, the team acts out the running of your application, just as if it already possessed a working system. Every activity that must take place is identified and assigned to some component as a responsibility.

As part of this process, it is often useful to represent components using 4-inch by 6-inch index cards. Written on the face of the card is the name of the software component, the responsibilities of the component, and the name of other components with which the component must interact. Such cards are sometimes known as CRC cards, which stands for Component, Responsibility, and Collaborator. An index card is associated with each software component. As responsibilities for the component are discovered, they are recorded on the face of the index card.

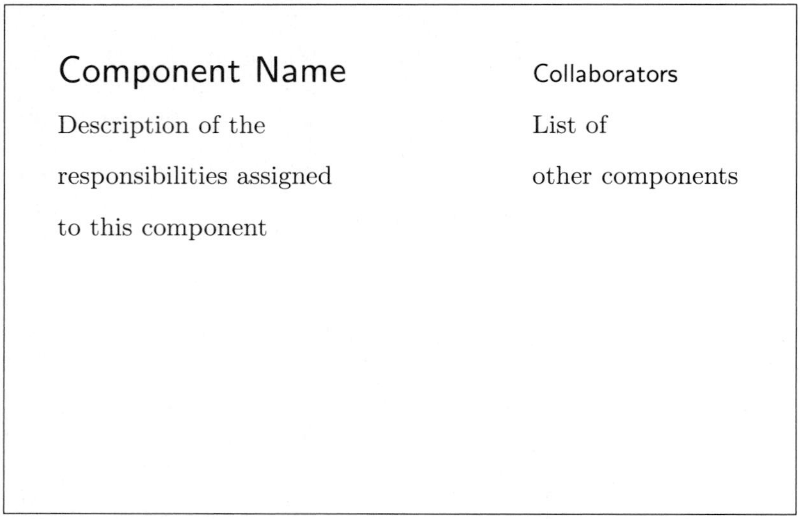

Component Name	Collaborators
Description of the	List of
responsibilities assigned	other components
to this component	

During the process of working through scenarios, it is useful to assign different CRC cards to different members of the design team. The person holding the card representing a component is charged with the task of recording the responsibilities of the associated software component, as well as with acting as the "surrogate" for the software during the scenario simulation. The design team member describes the activities of the software system, passing "control" to another design team member when the software system requires the services of another component.

The advantage of index cards is that they are widely available, inexpensive, and erasable. This encourages experimentation, since alternative designs can be tried, explored, or abandoned with little investment. The physical separation of the cards encourages an intuitive understanding of the importance of the logical separation of the various components, helping to emphasize the concepts of cohesion and coupling (which we will shortly describe). The constraints of an index card are also a good measure of approximate complexity. A component that is expected to perform more tasks than can fit easily in this space is probably too complex, and effort should be expended to find a simpler solution, perhaps by moving some responsibilities elsewhere to divide a task between two or more new components.

THE WHAT/WHO CYCLE As we noted at the beginning of this section, the identification of components is performed during the process of imagining the execution of a working system. Often this proceeds as a cycle of what/who questions. First, the programming team identifies *what* activity needs to be performed next. This is immediately followed by answering the question *who* is the agent that performs the action. In this manner, designing a software system is much like organizing a collection of people, such as a club. Any activity that is to be performed must be assigned as a responsibility to some component. (There is a currently popular bumper sticker that asserts, in slightly more colloquial terms, that a certain phenomenon can spontaneously happen. We know, however, that in real life this is seldom true. If any action is to take place, then there must be an agent assigned to perform the action.)

DOCUMENTATION It is at this point, as well, that the development of documentation should begin. There are two essential documents that should be part of any software system: the user manual and the system design documentation. Work on both of these can commence even before the first line of code has been written.

The user manual describes the interaction with the system from the user's point of view, and it is an excellent means of verifying that the conception of the application held by the development team matches that of the client. Since the decisions made in creating the scenarios will closely match the decisions the user will be required to make in the eventual application, the development of the user manual naturally dovetails with the process of walking through scenarios.

The design documentation records the major decisions made during the process of the software design, and it should thus also be produced during the process of design when these decisions are fresh in the minds of the creators, not after the fact when many of the relevant details will have been forgotten. It is often far easier to write a general global description of the software system early in the development. Too soon, the focus of concentration will move to the level of individual components or modules. Although it is also important to document the module level, excessive concern with the details of each module will make it difficult for subsequent software maintainers to form an initial picture of the larger structure.

CRC cards are one aspect of the design documentation, but many other decisions are also important and are not reflected in the CRC cards. Arguments for and against any major design alternatives should be recorded, as well as factors that influenced the final decisions. A log or diary of the project schedule should be maintained. Both the user manual and the design documents are refined and evolve over time in exactly the same manner that the software is evolving and being refined.

COMPONENTS AND BEHAVIOR To return to the IIKH, your team decides that when the system begins, the user will be presented with an attractive informative window. The responsibility for displaying this window is assigned to a component called the GREETER. In some as yet unspecified manner (perhaps by pull-down menus, perhaps by pressing a button or key, perhaps by using a pressure sensitive screen), the user can select one of several actions. Initially, you identify just five actions. These are:

1. Casually browse the *database* of existing recipes, but without reference to any particular meal plan.
2. Add a new recipe to the database.
3. Edit or annotate an existing recipe.
4. Review an existing *plan* for several meals.
5. Create a new plan of meals.

These activities seem to naturally divide themselves into two groups. The first three actions are associated with the recipe database, while the last two are associated with menu plans. As a result, your team next decides to create components corresponding to these two responsibilities. Continuing with the scenario, your team elects to ignore the meal plan management for the moment and to move on to refine the activities of the RECIPE DATABASE component. Figure 1.1 shows the initial CRC card representation of the GREETER.

Broadly speaking, the responsibility of the recipe database component is to simply maintain a collection of recipes. We have already identified three elements of this task. Namely, the recipe component database must somehow facilitate the user browsing and editing from the library of existing recipes, and it must also permit the inclusion of new recipes into the database.

There are a number of decisions that must eventually be made concerning how to best let the user browse the database. For example, should the user be presented first with a list of categories, such as "soups," "salads," "main meals," and "desserts"? Alternatively, should the user be able to describe keywords to narrow a search, such as providing a list of ingredients and seeing all the recipes that contain those items ("Almonds, Strawberries, Cheese"), or a list of previously inserted keywords ("Bob's favorite cake")? Should scroll bars be used, or simulated thumbholes in a virtual book? While these are fun to think about, the important point to realize is that such decisions do not need to be made at this point (see "Preparing for Change," page 12). Since these affect only a single component and do not impact the functioning of any other system, all that is necessary in order to continue the scenario is to simply assert that by some means the user can select a specific recipe.

Each recipe will in turn be identified with a specific recipe component. Once a recipe is selected, control is passed to the associated recipe object. A recipe must contain certain information. For example, a recipe consists of a set of ingredients and a description of the steps needed to transform

Greeter	Collaborators
Display informative initial message	Database manager
Offer user choice of options	Plan manager
Pass control to either	
Recipe database manager or	
Plan manager for processing	

Figure 1.1 CRC card for the greeter

the ingredients into the final product. In our scenario, the recipe component must also perform certain other activities. For example, the recipe component will display the recipe interactively on the terminal screen. The user may be given the ability to annotate or change the recipe, either the list of ingredients or the instruction portion. Alternatively, the user may request a printed copy of the recipe. All of these actions are the responsibility of the RECIPE component. (For the moment, we will continue to describe the RECIPE in the singular form. During design, we can think of this as a prototypical recipe, that stands in place of a multitude of actual recipes. We will return to a discussion of singular versus multiple components in a later section.)

Having pursued the actions that are the consequence of the user wishing to browse the database, we return to the recipe database manager and now pretend the user indicated a desire to add a new recipe. The database manager somehow decides in what category to place the new recipe (again, the details concerning how this is done are unimportant for our development at this point), requests the name of the new recipe, then creates a new recipe component, permitting the user to edit this new blank entry. Thus the responsibilities needed to perform this new task are a subset of those we already identified, in permitting users to edit existing recipes.

Having explored the browsing and creation of new recipes, we return to the GREETER and investigate the development of daily menu plans. The PLAN MANAGER is charged with this task. In some way (again, the details are unimportant here) the user can save existing plans. Thus the plan manager can either be started by retrieving an already developed plan or by creating a new plan. In the latter case, the user is prompted for a list of dates for which the plan is being developed. Each date is associated with a separate DATE component. The user can select a specific date for further investigation, in which case control is passed to the corresponding DATE component. Another activity of the plan manager includes printing out the recipes for the entire planning period. Finally, the user can instruct the plan manager to produce a grocery list for the entire period.

The DATE component maintains a collection of meals, as well as any other annotations provided by the user (indications of birthday celebrations, anniversaries, reminders, and so on). The DATE component prints information on the display concerning the specified date. By some means (again unspecified), the user can indicate a desire to print all the information concerning a specific date or to explore in more detail a specific meal. In the latter case, control is passed to a MEAL component.

The meal component maintains a collection of augmented recipes, where the augmentation refers to the fact that the user may indicate a de-

Preparing for Change

It has been said that all that is constant in life is the inevitability of uncertainty and change. The same is true of software. No matter how carefully you try to develop the initial specification and design of a software system, it is almost certain that changes in the user's needs or requirements will sometime, during the life of the system, force changes to be made in software. Programmers and software designers need to anticipate this, and plan accordingly.

- Maintain your primary objective: that changes should impact as few components as possible. Even major changes in the appearance or functioning of an application should be possible with changes to only one or two sections of code.
- Try to predict the most likely sources of change, and isolate the effects of such changes to as few software components as possible. The most likely sources of change are features such as interfaces, communication formats, and output formats.
- Try to isolate and reduce the dependency of software on hardware. For example, the interface for recipe browsing in our case study may depend in part on the hardware on which the system is running. Future releases may be ported to different platforms. A good design will anticipate this change.
- Reducing coupling between software components will reduce the dependence of one upon another, and increase the likelihood that one can be changed with minimal effect on the other.
- Maintain in the design documentation careful records of the design process and the discussions surrounding all major decisions. It is almost certain that the individuals responsible for maintaining the software and designing future releases will be, if not entirely different, then at least partially different from the team of individuals producing the initial release. The design documentation will help future teams identify the important factors behind a decision, and it will prevent them from spending time in discussions of issues that have already been resolved.

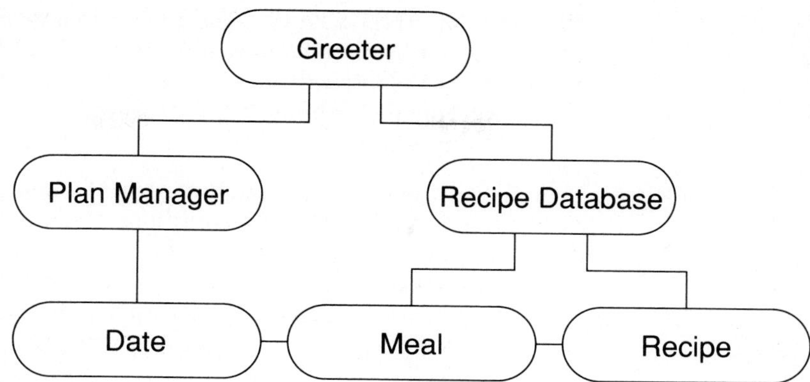

Figure 1.2 Communication between the six components in the IIKH

sire to double, triple, or otherwise increase a recipe. The meal component displays information about the meal. The user can add or remove recipes from the meal or can ask that information about the meal be printed. In order to discover new recipes, the user must be permitted at this point to browse the recipe database. Thus the meal component must interact with the recipe database component.

The design team will continue in this fashion, investigating every possible scenario. The major category of scenarios that have not yet been developed here involve exceptional cases. For example, what happens if a user selects a number of keywords for a recipe and no matching recipe is found? How can users cancel an activity, such as entering a new recipe, if after they begin they decide not to proceed? Each possibility must be explored, and the responsibilities for handling the situation assigned to one or more components.

Having walked through the various scenarios, your software design team eventually decides that all activities can be adequately handled by six components (Fig. 1.2). The GREETER needs to communicate only with the PLAN MANAGER and the RECIPE DATABASE component. The PLAN MANAGER needs, in turn, to communicate only with the DATE component, and the DATE agent only with the MEAL component. The MEAL component communicates with the recipe manager and, through this agent, with individual recipes.

1.1.2 Software Components

In this section we will explore in more detail the concept of a software component. As is true of all but the most trivial ideas, there are many different aspects to this seemingly simple concept.

BEHAVIOR AND STATE We have already seen how components are characterized by their behavior—that is, by what they can do. But components may also hold within them certain information. Let us take as our prototypical component a RECIPE structure from the IIKH. One way to view a component is as a pair consisting of *behavior* and *state*.

- The *behavior* of a component is the set of actions that the component can perform. The complete description of all the behavior for a component is also sometimes called the *protocol* for the component. For the RECIPE component, this will include activities such as editing the preparation instructions for the recipe, displaying the recipe on an interactive terminal screen, or printing a paper copy of the recipe.
- The *state* of a component represents all the information held within a component. For our RECIPE component, the state will include the table of ingredients and the list of preparation instructions. Notice that the state is not static and can change over time. For example, by using the ability to edit a recipe (a behavior) the user can make changes to the preparation instructions (part of the state).

It is not necessary that all components maintain state information. For example, it is possible the GREETER component will not have any state since it does not need to remember any information during the course of execution. But most components will consist of a combination of behavior and state.

INSTANCES AND CLASSES The separation of the concepts of state and behavior permits us to clarify a point we avoided in our earlier discussion. Note that in the real application there will probably be many different recipes. An important issue to note, however, is that all of these recipes will *perform* in the same manner. That is, the behavior of each of the recipes is the same; it is only the state—the individual lists of ingredients and instructions for preparation—that is different between individual recipes. In the early stages of development our interest is in characterizing the behavior common to all recipes, and the details particular to any one recipe are unimportant.

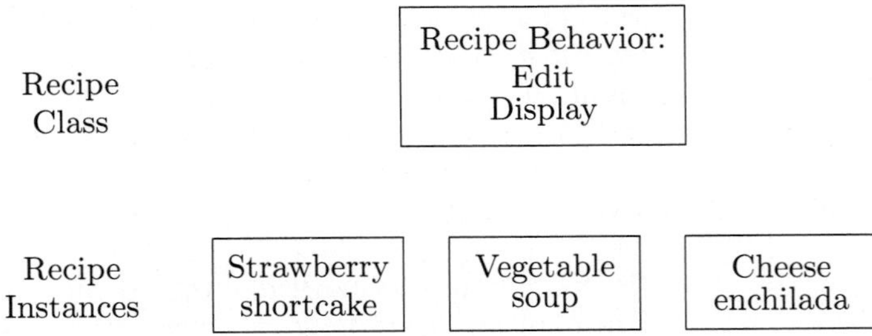

The term *class* is often used to describe a set of objects with similar behavior. We will see, in the next chapter, that the idea of a class is also used as a mechanism in the C++ language. An individual representative of a class is known as an *instance*. It is important to note that behavior is associated with a class, not with an individual. That is, all instances of a class will respond to the same instructions and perform in a similar manner. On the other hand, state is a property of an individual. We see this in the various instances of the class RECIPE. They can all perform the same actions (editing, displaying, printing) but use different data values.

COUPLING AND COHESION Two important concepts to understand in conjunction with the design of software components are the ideas of coupling and cohesion. Cohesion is a description of the degree to which the responsibilities of a single component seem to form a meaningful unit. High cohesion is achieved by associating, in a single component, tasks that are related in some manner. Probably the most frequent way in which tasks are related is through the necessity to access a common data area. This is the overriding theme that joins, for example, the various responsibilities of the RECIPE component.

Coupling, on the other hand, describes the relationship between software components. In general, it is desirable to reduce the amount of coupling as much as possible, since connections between software components inhibit ease of development, modification, or reuse.

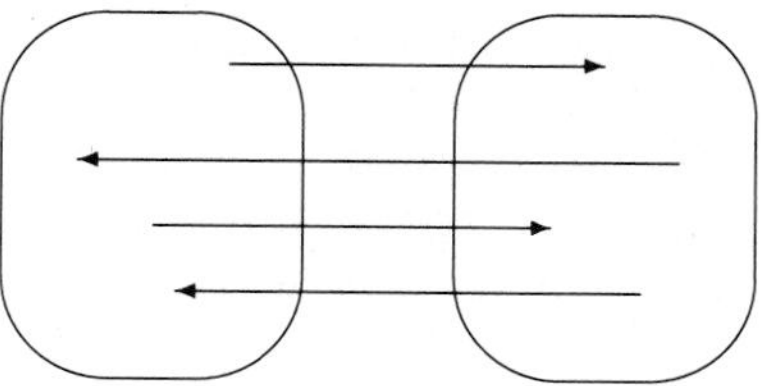

In particular, coupling is increased when one software component must access data values—the state—held by another component. Such situations should almost always be avoided, in favor of moving a task to be performed into the list of responsibilities of the component that holds the necessary data. For example, we might conceivably first assign the responsibility for the task "edit a recipe" to the RECIPE DATABASE component, since it is during the course of performing tasks associated with this component that the need to edit a recipe first occurs. But if we do so, the recipe database agent would then need the ability to directly manipulate the state (the internal data values representing the list of ingredients and the preparation instructions) of an individual recipe. It is better to avoid this tight connection by moving the responsibility for editing to the recipe itself.

INTERFACE AND IMPLEMENTATION—PARNAS'S PRINCIPLES The emphasis on characterizing a software component by its behavior has one extremely important consequence. It is possible for one programmer to know how to *use* a component developed by another programmer, without needing to know how the component is *implemented*. For example,

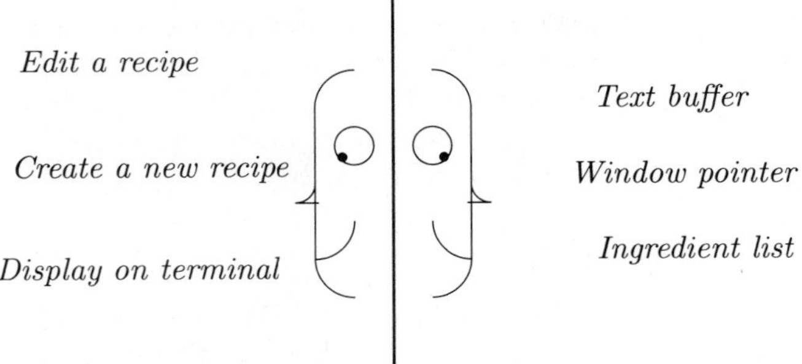

Figure 1.3 Two views of a complex system

suppose each of the six components shown in Fig. 1.2 is assigned to a different programmer. The programmer developing the MEAL component needs to be able to allow the IIKH user to browse the database of recipes and to select a single recipe for inclusion in the meal. To do this, the MEAL component can simply invoke the *browse* behavior associated with the RECIPE DATABASE component, which is defined so as to return an individual RECIPE. This description is valid regardless of the particular implementation used by the RECIPE DATABASE component to perform the actual browsing action.

The purposeful omission of implementation details behind a simple interface is known as *information hiding*. We say the component *encapsulates* the behavior, showing only how the component can be used, not the detailed actions it performs. This naturally leads to two different views of a software system (Fig. 1.3). The interface view is the face seen by other programmers. It describes *what* a software component can perform. The implementation view, on the other hand, is the face seen by the programmer working on a particular component. It describes *how* a component goes about completing a task.

The separation of interface and implementation is perhaps *the* most important concept in software engineering. Yet it is also often difficult for students to understand, or to motivate. As we discuss in the sidebar "Who Is Information Being Hidden From?" (page 17), the concept of information hiding is largely meaningful only in the context of multiperson programming projects. In such efforts, the limiting factor is often not the amount of coding involved in a project but the amount of communication required between the various programmers and between their respective software systems. As we will describe shortly, software components are often developed in parallel by different programmers who are in isolation from each other. Increasingly, there is also an emphasis on the reuse of general purpose software components in multiple projects. For both of these to be successful, there must be minimal and well-understood interconnections between the various portions of the system. These ideas were captured by computer scientist David Parnas in a pair of rules, which are known as *Parnas's Principles:*

- ▲ The developer of a software component must provide the intended user with all the information needed to make effective use of the services provided by the component, and should provide *no* other information.
- ▲ The developer of a software component must be provided with all the information necessary to carry out the given responsibilities assigned to the component, and should be provided with *no* other information.

A consequence of the separation of interface from implementation is the fact that a programmer can experiment with several different implementations of the same structure without impacting other software components. We will subsequently see that many data structures have a variety of different implementations, each optimized for a different purpose (faster execution, use of less space, and so on).

1.1.3 Formalizing the Interface

We continue with the description of the development of the IIKH. In the course of the next several steps the descriptions of the components will slowly be refined. The first step in this process is to formalize the patterns and channels of communication.

A decision should be made as to the general structure that will be used to implement each component. A component with only one behavior and no internal state may be made into a function. An example might be a

Who Is Information Being Hidden From?

Beginning students often have a difficult time understanding information hiding, for the simple reason that they often do not see who information is being hidden from. Consider the development of a software application small enough to be created by a single programmer. In this situation, there are two "protagonists." These are the programmer and the computer. Now certainly information is not being hidden by programmers from themselves, and on the other hand the computer must know all relevant details in order to create the executable application.

The situation is only slightly less confusing if we consider a threesome composed of a programmer, the computer, and the user of a software application. The third player, the user of the application, need not even know in what language the software system was written. So information hiding is complete in this case.

Seen in this light, the concept of information hiding is most meaningful in the context of a multiperson software project. In such a system, one programmer is viewed as a "user" of a software component that is developed by another programmer. This sense of "user" should not be confused with the final "user" of the software application.

component that simply takes a string of text and translates all capital letters to lowercase. Components with many tasks are probably more easily implemented as classes. Names are given to each of the responsibilities identified on the CRC card for each component. These will eventually be mapped onto function or procedure names. Along with the names, the types of any arguments to be passed to the function are identified. Next, the information maintained within the component itself should be described. All information must be accounted for. If a component requires some data to perform a specific task, the source of the data, either through argument or global value, or maintained internally by the component, must be clearly identified.

Careful thought should be given to the names associated with various activities. As Shakespeare claimed in *Romeo and Juliet,* a change in the name of an object does not alter the characteristics of the entity being denoted, but it is certainly not the case that all names will conjure up the same mental images in the listener. As government bureaucrats have long known, obscure and idiomatic names can make even the simplest operation sound intimidating. Thus the selection of useful names is an extremely important task, as names create the vocabulary with which the eventual design will be formulated. Names should be internally consistent, meaningful, preferably short, and evocative in the context of the problem at hand. A considerable amount of time is often spent finding just the right set of terms to describe the tasks being performed and the objects being manipulated. Far from being a barren and useless exercise, the proper selection of names early in the design process greatly simplifies and facilitates later steps.

The following general guidelines have been suggested for selecting names:

- Use pronounceable names. As a rule of thumb, if you cannot read a name out loud, it is not a good name.
- Use capitalization (or underscores) to mark the beginning of a new word within a name, such as CardReader or Card_reader, rather than cardreader.
- Examine abbreviations carefully. An abbreviation that is clear to one person may be confusing to the next. Is a TermProcess a terminal process, something that terminates processes, or a process associated with a terminal?
- Avoid names with several interpretations. Does the empty function tell whether something is empty, or empties the values from the object?
- Avoid digits within a name. Digits are easy to misread (0 and O, 1 and l, 2 and Z, 5 and S, and so on).

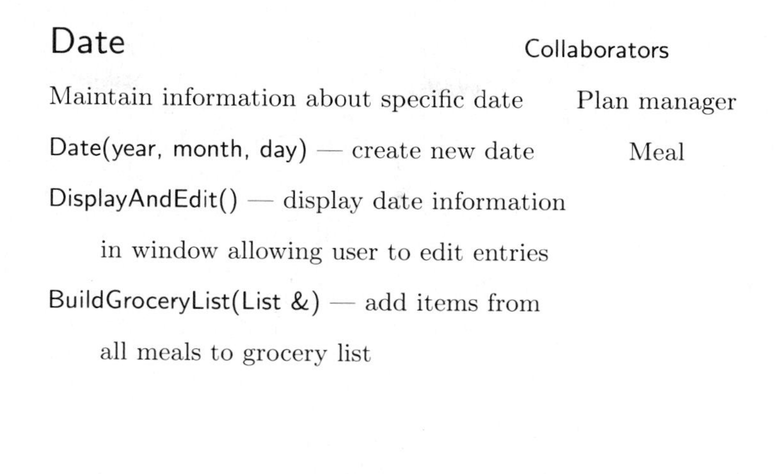

Figure 1.4 Revised CRC card for the DATE component

- ▲ Name functions and variables that yield Boolean values so as to describe clearly the interpretation of a true or false value. For example, "PrinterIsReady" clearly indicates that a true value means the printer is working, whereas "PrinterStatus" is much less precise.
- ▲ Extra care should be taken in the selection of names for operations that are costly and infrequently used. By doing so, errors caused by using the wrong function can be avoided.

Once names have been developed for each activity, the CRC cards for each component are redrawn, with the name and formal arguments of the function used to elicit each behavior identified. An example CRC card for the DATE is shown in Fig. 1.4. What is not yet specified is how each component will perform the associated tasks.

Once more, scenarios or role-playing should be performed at a more detailed level in order to ensure that all activities are accounted for and that all necessary information is maintained and made available to the responsible components.

1.1.4 Designing the Representation for Components

At this point, if not before, the design team can be divided into different groups, each responsible for one or more software components. The task now is to transform the description of a component into an implementation of a software subsystem. The major portion of this process is to design the data structures that will be used by each subsystem to maintain the state information required to fulfill the assigned responsibilities.

It is here that the classic data structures that we will spend the rest of the book exploring come into play. The selection of data structures is an important task, central to the software design process. Once the data structures have been chosen, the code used by a component in the fulfillment of a responsibility is often almost self-evident. But data structures must be carefully matched to the task at hand. As we will see, some data structures are better suited for processes such as searching for a specific element, while others are better suited for merging collections together and still others are better suited for placing values in sequence. A wrong choice of data structure can result in complex and inefficient programs, while an intelligent choice can result in just the opposite.

It is also at this point that descriptions of behavior must be transformed into algorithms. In Chapter 3 we will describe some of the features of algorithms. These include an accurate specification of the input and a description of the result or effect of each process. These descriptions should then be matched against the expectations of each component listed as a collaborator, in order to ensure that expectations are fulfilled and necessary data items are available to carry out each process.

1.1.5 Implementing Components

Having laid out the design of each software subsystem, the next step is to implement the behavior desired for each component. If the previous steps have been correctly addressed, then each responsibility or behavior will be characterized by a short description. The task at this step is to implement in computer language the desired activities. In a later section we will describe some of the more common heuristics that are used in this process.

If they have not been determined earlier (say, as part of the specification of the system), then it is at this point that decisions can be made on issues that are entirely self-contained within a single component. A typical decision that we were faced with in our case study was determining how best to let the user browse the database of recipes.

Note that as multiperson programming projects become the norm, it is increasingly rare that any one programmer will work on all aspects of a system. More often, the skills a programmer will need to master will be the ability to understand how one section of code fits into a larger framework, and the capability to work well with other members of a team.

Often, in the implementation of one component it will become clear that certain information or actions might be assigned to yet another component that will act "behind the scene," with little or no visibility to users of the software abstraction. Such components are sometimes known as *fa-*

cilitators. We will see examples of facilitators when we discuss strings in Chapter 4 and again when we discuss lists in Chapter 8.

An important part of analysis and coding at this point is to characterize and document the necessary preconditions a software component requires in order to complete a task and to verify that the software component will indeed perform correctly when presented with legal input values. This is establishing the correctness aspect of the algorithms used in the implementation of a component. We will discuss this in more detail in Chapter 3.

1.1.6 Integration of Components

Once software subsystems have been individually designed and tested, they can be integrated into the final product. Often this is part of a larger process, not a single step. Starting from a simple base, elements are slowly added to the system and tested, using *stubs*, simple dummy routines with no behavior or with very limited behavior, for the as-yet unimplemented parts.

For example, in the development of the IIKH, it would be reasonable to start integration with the GREETER component. To test the GREETER component in isolation, stubs are written for the recipe data base manager and the daily meal plan manager. These stubs need not do any more than print an informative message and return. With these, the component development team can test various aspects of the greeter system (for example, that button presses elicit the correct response). Testing of an individual component is often referred to as *unit testing*. Next, one or the other of the stubs can be replaced by more complete code. For example, the team might decide to replace the stub for the recipe database component with the actual system, maintaining the stub for the other portion. Further testing can be performed until it appears that the system is performing as desired. (This is sometimes referred to as *integration testing*.) The application is finally complete when all stubs have been replaced with working components. The ability to test components in isolation is greatly facilitated by the conscious design goal of reducing connections between components, since this reduces the need for extensive stubbing.

During integration, it is not uncommon for an error to be manifest in one software system, and yet to be caused by a coding mistake in another system. Thus testing during integration often involves the discovery of errors, which then results in changes to some of the components. After these changes have been implemented, the components should be tested again in isolation before attempting to reintegrate the software once more into the larger system. Reexecuting previously developed test cases following a change to a software component is sometimes referred to as *regression testing*.

1.1.7 Maintenance and Evolution

It is tempting to think that once a working version of an application has been delivered the task of the software development team is finished. This is unfortunately almost never the case. The term *software maintenance* is used to describe activities that take place subsequent to the delivery of the initial working version of a software system. A wide variety of activities can be placed into this category:

- ▲ Errors, or *bugs*, can be discovered in the delivered product. These must be corrected, either in *patches* to existing releases or in subsequent releases.
- ▲ Requirements may change, perhaps as a result of government regulations or standardization among similar products.
- ▲ Hardware may change. The system may be moved to different platforms. Input devices, such as a pen-based system or a pressure-sensitive touch screen, may become available that were not previously present. Output technology may change—for example, from a textual based system to a graphical window based arrangement.
- ▲ Users' expectations may change. Users may expect greater functionality, lower cost, easier use. This can perhaps occur as a result of competition with similar products.
- ▲ Better documentation may be requested by users.

A good design recognizes the inevitability of change and plans an accommodation for change activities from the very beginning.

1.2 PROGRAMMING FROM REUSABLE COMPONENTS

Two themes running through our description of responsibility-driven design have been the characterization of software components by their behavior, and the development of components that are as independent as possible from each other. To the degree that it is possible to achieve these goals, it should then be possible to carry a software component from one software project to the next.

There are obvious technical and financial benefits that can accrue from the reuse of general purpose components:

- ▲ A component that can be reused does not have to be rewritten. The programming time that would have been spent on developing the equivalent software in the second project can then be employed for other purposes.
- ▲ The incremental cost in reusing a component is considerably less than the cost of redeveloping a component.

- ▲ The use of standard components makes programs easier to read and maintain, since large portions of the code may be common to several applications.
- ▲ A software component that has been used on multiple projects is likely to be more thoroughly exercised, and more thoroughly debugged, than code that is used on any one project alone. If errors are tracked and corrected in all applications, then several projects will benefit.

The recent emphasis on the development of reusable components in the computer programming community is often likened to the historical progression in the industrial revolution of the nineteenth century. In the past, computer programs were created entirely from scratch, each line of code being developed for each new application. This is similar to the way in which farm implements or machines were once handcrafted by a blacksmith or other artisan. Just as the development of reusable and interchangeable components revolutionized the way machines were developed, so the development of interchangeable components will change the way software is created. In large part, this book can be seen as a compendium of simple reusable software components, components that are a part of almost all computer programs.

1.2.1 Mechanisms for Reuse — Composition and Inheritance

Although general purpose software components may be important, they must almost always be modified or customized before they can be utilized in any specific application. We will briefly describe the two most common mechanisms for this customization: composition and inheritance.

Composition simply means that one component may use another component to define part of its data area, or state. The RECIPE component, for example, could very well use a linked list, a subject to be discussed in Chapter 8, to hold the list of ingredients. Similarly, the GREETER component might hold the entire recipe database as part of its state.

The mechanism of inheritance is more subtle, and in many ways much more powerful. It is often the case that one type of component can be seen as a simple variation on another type. In such a case, the new component can be created as a specialized form of the original structure. We say the new form *inherits* from the original form. The inheritance relation means that everything known about the original structure — all data areas, all behavior — is also available to the new component. In addition, the new component may define its own data fields and new behavior.

An analogy is often made between inheritance and the genus-species-family classification of living organisms. The class ANIMAL can be described by the general behavior (respiration, for example) common to all

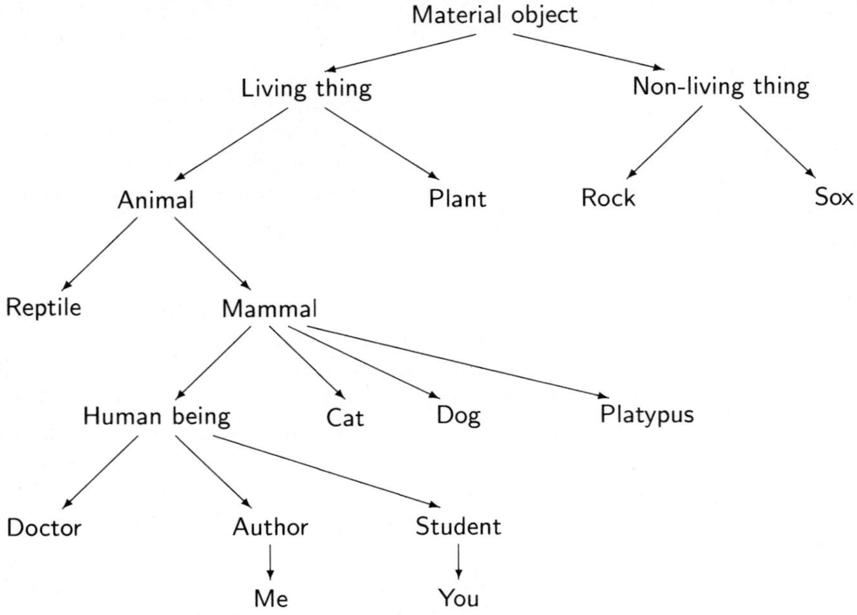

Figure 1.5 A typical inheritance hierarchy

animals. The class MAMMAL is a more specialized form of ANIMAL; nevertheless, everything known about animals is also true about mammals. The class CAT is yet a more specialized subclassification of mammal. At each level new information is added, but characteristics derived from higher levels in the classification system are also applicable to the new categories.

In Chapter 6 we will return to composition and inheritance, and explore in more detail how these mechanisms are used in the development of software systems.

1.3 PROBLEM-SOLVING HEURISTICS*

In Section 1.1.5, we discussed the task of taking an informal description of a software responsibility and converting this into a working software subsystem. In this section we will investigate several heuristics that are frequently useful in the completion of this task.

*Section headings followed by an asterisk indicate optional material.

1.3.1 Top-Down Design and Stepwise Refinement

The process of starting from a general abstract description of a task and iteratively refining this into a working program is sometimes referred to as *top-down design* (since we start at the *top*, the problem description, and work down to the *bottom*, the actual code). This process is also often described as *stepwise refinement*, since at each step some portion of the problem is being refined into a more complete description.

The following sections illustrate several of the ways in which refinement can occur.

1.3.2 Division into Steps

Popular folk wisdom tells us that the longest journey begins with a single step. The many tasks involved in complex operations can also be simplified by dividing them into a sequence of smaller, individual tasks. For example, in Chapter 4 we will consider the problem of substring replacement. The task to be performed is to take a string of characters and to generate a new string in which some subportion of the original has been replaced by a different string, which can be either smaller or larger than the segment being removed.

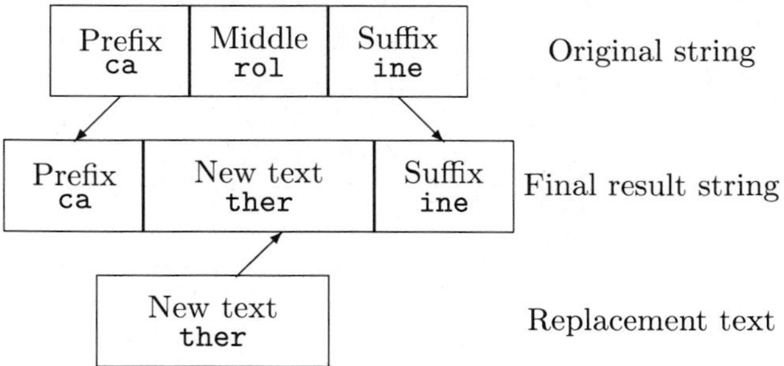

This task is accomplished by a sequence of four steps:

1. Allocate a new string of sufficient size to contain the result.
2. Copy into this new string the initial prefix, those portions of the original string that precede the section being replaced.
3. Copy into the new string the replacing text.
4. Copy into the new string the portion of the original string that followed the text that has been replaced.

Each of these new steps is then a further problem that can be subject to refinement until finally a complete solution to the problem is uncovered.

1.3.3 Separation into Cases

What often appears to be a single task at one level of abstraction can be more easily thought of as a selection from a number of special cases when viewed at a more detailed level of abstraction. We will see an example of this when we describe the printing of an integer in Chapter 3. To the client, all integers are the same with respect to the printing operation. In the actual implementation, however, it is useful to divide the task into three cases:

- Negative values
- Integers greater than or equal to zero and less than 10
- Integers greater than 10

The solution of a larger problem is then reduced to the solution of three simpler problems. In the course of this process, the solution of one case can often seem to involve the solution to other cases. We will see this in the printing example, where the printing of negative numbers will be accomplished by printing a leading minus sign, followed by the printing of the positive component. Thus the first case is reduced to the other two. Similarly, the third case, printing numbers larger than 10, will be addressed by repeatedly expressing the solution in terms of the second case. In this manner, a separation into cases can also often involve a search for commonality (discussed below).

1.3.4 Dividing and Conquering

Sometimes, even when no special cases can be identified, a problem can be addressed by dividing a task into two roughly equal portions, then solving each portion separately. For example, in Chapter 5 we will examine the problem of sorting a vector of values. One approach, known as *merge sort*, will be to take a list of n values and simply divide the list in half, resulting in two lists of $n/2$ values. Each list is then sorted separately, and the results combined back to form the sorted list. (We will discuss a variation on merge sort in Chapter 17.)

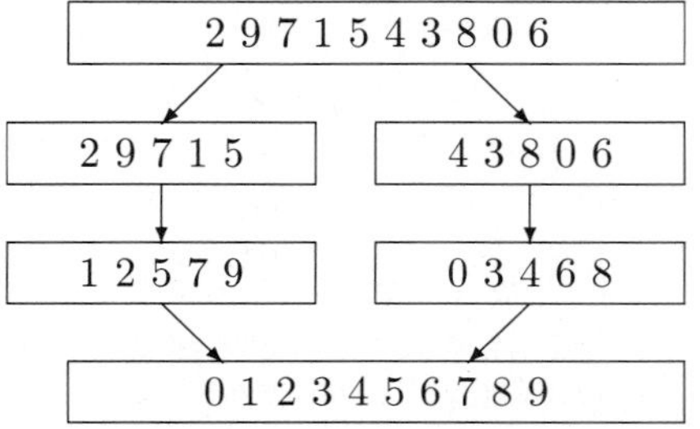

This general approach to problems—solving a problem of size n by dividing it into two problems of size $n/2$, solving the smaller problems, then combining the results—is known as *divide and conquer*.

1.3.5 The Search for Commonality

Situations that might appear on the surface to be different can often be seen in another light to have common features. For example, in the design of the IIKH we noted that it was possible for the user to view and edit individual recipes. It was also desired to let the user create new recipes. If it is possible to create an "empty recipe," then the latter process can be seen to be a combination of the two steps: (1) create a new empty recipe and (2) edit the empty recipe. Thus the actions of editing a recipe are common to the two different behaviors of the recipe object, and they should be combined into one function.

1.4 CHAPTER SUMMARY

Key Concepts

- Responsibility-driven design
- Software component
- Characterization by behavior
- Behavior and state
- Instance and class
- Interface and implementation
- Reusable component
- Coupling and cohesion
- Parnas's principles
- Software testing
- Software maintenance
- Composition and inheritance

The major purpose of this chapter has been to describe how software applications can be structured, not as single monolithic units but as a collection of interacting, loosely coupled, software components. Components can be viewed as consisting of two aspects: behavior (the actions the component performs) and state (the data the component maintains). Every component is described by an interface, a characterization of the behavior for the component, and an implementation, the code that actually performs the actions required to realize the behavior.

We have introduced a design technique that emphasizes the early identification of components and encourages the characterization of components in terms of their behavior. Characterization by behavior is a fundamental tenet of object-oriented programming.

An important aspect of modern software development is the reuse of existing code, through the utilization of general purpose software components. New components can be built out of existing components in a variety of ways. The most common form is composition. Here one component simply uses another component to maintain part of its state. Another form is inheritance. Using inheritance, a new component is described as a more specialized form of an existing component.

In this chapter we have described more or less the philosophy underlying the Object-Oriented programming technique. In the next chapter we will start to explore the actual mechanisms used in C++ to create software components.

References

Although the mechanisms used in object-oriented programming can be traced back to the early 1960s in the language Simula [Birtwistle 79, Kirkerud 89], the ideas first gained popularity with the work of Alan Kay and Adele Goldberg and their group at Xerox PARC (Palo Alto Research Center) and the language Smalltalk-80 [Goldberg 83]. A collection of papers describing Smalltalk and object-oriented programming in the August 1981 issue of *Byte* did much to capture the popular imagination. Interestingly, the problem that originally inspired Kay [Kay 77]—namely, the creation of a powerful programming language that could be used by non–computer literate individuals—seems today to be an area of relatively little work.

CRC cards were first described by Kent Beck and Ward Cunningham [Beck 89]. The term *responsibility-driven design* is from Rebecca Wirfs-Brock et al., who described the idea in a conference paper [Wirfs-Brock 89] and subsequently expanded on the idea in a book [Wirfs-Brock 90]. I have also discussed the idea in my own book on object-oriented programming [Budd 91]. More recently several other books describing object-oriented design have appeared [Coad 90, Coad 91, Mullin 89, Rumbaugh 91]. The guidelines for naming objects described on page 28 are adapted from Keller [Keller 90]. The concepts of coupling and cohesion are adapted from Stevens et al. [Stevens 81].

David Parnas actually first described his principles, in [Parnas 72], in terms of modules. They were subsequently extended to all types of software systems.

The analogy between reusable software components and the development of interchangeable parts in industrial applications is made by Brad Cox [Cox 90, Cox 91].

Exercises

1. Describe an organization with which you are familiar in terms of components and responsibilities. Develop a CRC card for each component.

2. Suppose you are designing a software component that represents a deck of cards. What operations should you provide? Would it make sense to divide the task into two separate components, one for the deck and another that represents an individual card? What are the responsibilities of each?

3. Explain and contrast each of the following pairs of terms: (a) behavior and state (b) instance and class (c) interface and implementation (d) coupling and cohesion (e) composition and inheritance

4. Develop CRC cards for the remaining portions of the IIKH.

5. Suppose that your firm decides to support two versions of the IIKH, one mouse-based and one keyboard-based. What components contain features that would likely need to be changed?

6. Suppose your software team decides to change the way in which the user browses the recipe database—for example, allowing the user to specify keywords. What software components need to be aware of this change? (That is, what

components would probably need to be modified to accommodate the change?)

7. Consider the problem of scaling a recipe. Some ingredients, such as eggs, come in only discrete amounts—that is, quantities that you cannot easily produce, such as 2.7 eggs. What difficulty does this cause for the software that must deal with the scaling? What components must be aware of these difficulties?

8. For the next software release, the president now proposes a facility to permit the inclusion of predefined files of recipes. Using this, the company could sell copies of popular cookbooks in electronic form. Recipes would be copied from the file into the recipe database. What portions of the application would need to be modified to support this feature?

9. Your boss one day decides it would be great if users of the IIKH could plan meals independent of dates. That is, the user could sit down and plan a collection of hypothetical festive feasts but not associate any meal with any specific date. Subsequently, the user could browse the collection of meals and select one for a specific date. Describe how the application would need to be modified to accommodate this change.

10. The next day your boss comes in and announces that if selling electronic cookbooks is a great idea (see exercise 8), then selling cookbooks along with preplanned meals is an even better idea. Since you already have the facilities to include meals not tied to any specific date (see last question), adding this new feature should present little difficulty. Explain how the application could be modified to provide this function.

11. Using CRC cards, design a software system to support an automated teller machine.

12. Using CRC cards, design a software system for a video store. The software system should allow users to browse lists of titles, perhaps first narrowing the search by selecting categories of movies. Once a title has been selected, the user should be able to view a short video clip of the movie. The software records the selections chosen by the user, printing a summary list at the completion of the transaction.

CHAPTER 2

Creating Software Components

In Chapter 1 we presented the idea that a program can be viewed as a loose collection of interacting, but independent, software components. By developing programs that utilize reusable general purpose components, new applications can be more quickly and more reliably constructed. In this chapter, we will explore the mechanisms available in the C++ language for the creation of such components.

For the purposes of illustration, the software component we will use in this chapter corresponds to the mathematical notion of an integer fraction, or rational number. We assume that most readers will be familiar with fractions and operations on fractions (Fig. 2.1), and thus there is little in the nature of algorithms that will be new in the material we present. Instead, our purpose will be to use this example to introduce features of the C++ language.

The term *abstract data type*, or ADT, is sometimes used for what we have up to this point been calling a software component. The term is intended to suggest an analogy to system defined data types, such as integers or floating point numbers. As with a component, data types are often characterized by their behavior. To make use of floating point operations, for example, it is only necessary to know the meaning of the functions and operators involved. It is not necessary to have a detailed understanding of the underlying bit representation, or how the bits are actually manipulated to

Operation	Calculation
$\frac{a}{b} + \frac{c}{d}$	$\frac{a \times d + b \times c}{b \times d}$
$\frac{a}{b} - \frac{c}{d}$	$\frac{a \times d - b \times c}{b \times d}$
$\frac{a}{b} \times \frac{c}{d}$	$\frac{a \times c}{b \times d}$
$\frac{a}{b} \div \frac{c}{d}$	$\frac{a \times d}{b \times c}$
$-\frac{a}{b}$	$\frac{-a}{b}$
$\frac{a}{b} == \frac{c}{d}$	(a == c) and (b == d) *if both proper form*
$\frac{a}{b} < \frac{c}{d}$	$(a \times d) < (b \times c)$ *if* $b > 0, d > 0$

Figure 2.1 Definitions of operations on rational numbers

produce result values. The term ADT is most appropriately used for components for which we expect to have a large number of instances, such as the rational number data type, or the RECIPE component in Chapter 1. Although still technically correct, the term seems less appropriate for components that have only a single instance, such as the `Greeter` component in Chapter 1.

We can summarize the behavior of the rational number ADT as follows:

- ▲ We should be able to easily create new instances of the rational number abstraction.
- ▲ We should be able to use arithmetic operations to manipulate rational numbers, yielding new rational number results.
- ▲ We should be able to assign a rational number value to a rational number variable.
- ▲ The modification forms of assignment (+= and the like) should be supported.
- ▲ We should be able to compare one rational number with another.
- ▲ We should be able to perform input and output operations with rational numbers.

2.1 CLASSES

The primary C++ mechanism we will use to create rational numbers—indeed, to create almost all the software components in this text—is the *class*. Figure 2.2 shows the class description for our rational number abstraction. The majority of this chapter will be spent in discussing features of this class description.

```
//
//   class rational
//        rational number data abstraction
//

class rational {
public:
    // constructors
    rational        ();
    rational        (int);
    rational        (int, int);
    rational        (const rational &);

    // accessor functions
    int             numerator      () const;
    int             denominator    () const;

    // assignments
    void            operator =     (const rational &);
    void            operator +=    (const rational &);

private:
    // data areas
    int             top;
    int             bottom;

    // operation used internally
    void            normalize      ();
};
```

Figure 2.2 A typical class description

2.1.1 Interface and Implementation

In the last chapter, we made the distinction between component interface and component implementation. In classes, this distinction is manifest on two levels. First, the code associated with a component is normally separated into two files. The interface file simply describes how to use the component—the name of the component, the names of operations, the argument types to be used with operations, and so on. A second file, the implementation file, contains the actual code to perform the actions. A class description, such as that shown in Fig. 2.2, would be found in the interface file.

Second, the class description itself is divided into two parts. The fields following the `public:` keyword denote, in a manner we have yet to describe, those behaviors and data fields that users of the data abstraction can access. The fields following the `private:` keyword, on the other hand, denote behavior and fields that are accessible only within the component and are "off-limits" to other users.

2.1.2 Data Fields

A class description is in many ways similar to a structure, or record, in other programming languages. Like a record, a class description can declare *fields* that hold data values. These data values represent the internal state of the component. The rational class declaration declares two fields. These appear near the bottom of the class structure. Both fields are declared as holding integer values. The first, named `top`, will maintain the numerator portion of the rational number. The second, named `bottom`, will maintain the denominator.

We can visualize a structure as a box or a container. Each data field is a compartment within the container. Only the data fields require space in the box; the functions declared in the class description do not occupy any space.[1] The rational number structure has two compartments, each holding an integer value. It is possible to deal with the container as a single entity, or with the contents of each compartment individually.

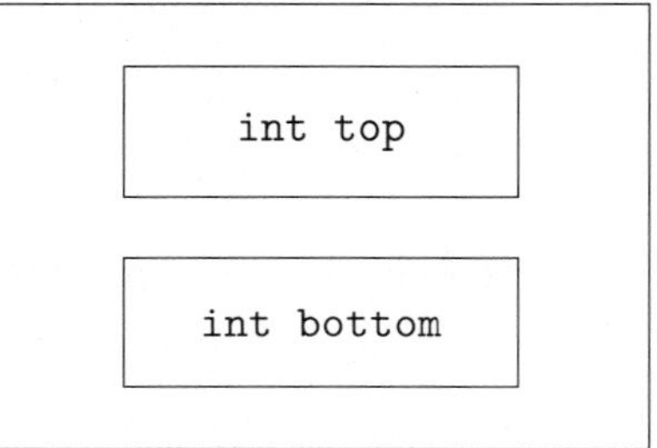

Note that, in the rational class declaration, both fields are declared to be private, and they are thus accessible only within the component. It is perfectly legal to declare publicly accessible data fields, and we will do so in some of our later data structures.

---

1. This is a slight misstatement. The use of a feature called virtual functions, which we will encounter in Chapter 7, will cause the generation of an additional pointer field in each data value.

2.1.3 Declarations

The logical place to start in our explanation of the behavior associated with the rational number component is with a discussion of how new rational numbers are created. As with all data types, the most common way to create a new rational number is through the use of a declaration statement. A simple declaration statement merely asserts that the programmer wishes to allocate and manipulate a new variable. The following statement, for example, creates a new variable named `x`:

```
rational x;
```

However, this leaves unspecified the question of how we should go about initializing the rational number to a specific value. Noting that any rational number so declared will automatically be set initially to zero alleviates this problem only slightly, since a problem will often require the number to be initialized with other values. Instead, C++ allows the programmer to provide arguments with a declaration statement that will be used to set the initial values of the data fields. A single integer argument creates a rational number with denominator 1, while two integer arguments specify both the numerator and denominator fields.

```
rational y(3);
rational z(2,3);
```

Because the implementation of this idea, called a *constructor*, is more complex than this simple description would suggest, we will leave a discussion of the details until later in this chapter, after we have established a framework for some of the more basic concepts.

2.1.4 Behavior — Member Functions

Having created a rational number, what can we do with it? That is, what is the behavior associated with the rational number abstraction?

Fundamental to all operations on the rational number data type is the ability to access the numerator and denominator fields. These data values are obtained via a pair of functions that are named, appropriately enough, `numerator` and `denominator`. As we noted in Chapter 1, a single class, such as the class `rational`, may often have many instances. To invoke these functions, therefore, we need to specify which instance — that is, which rational number — we wish to manipulate. This is accomplished by naming the instance, followed by a period, followed by the function to be invoked for that instance. The value to the left of the period is known as the *receiver* for the function.

To illustrate, suppose `left` and `right` are rational numbers. The following expression would perform the calculation, described in Fig. 2.1, to determine the numerator in the sum of the two values:

```
left.numerator() * right.denominator() +
    right.numerator() * left.denominator()
```

A function defined as part of the behavior of a class is called a *member function*. The declarations of the member functions `numerator` and `denominator` can be seen in the class description shown in Fig. 2.2. (Occasionally data fields are referred to as *data members*, and member functions as *function members*.)

The declaration of every member function must be tied to an implementation. The implementation of a member function looks very much like any other function. One difference is the name. The member function name specifies both the name of the function and the name of the class. This is analogous to the use of both first and last names to specify an individual. The completely specified name is referred to as a *qualified name*.

```
int rational::numerator() const
{   // return the numerator field of a rational number
    return top;
}

int rational::denominator() const
{   // return the denominator field of a rational number
    return bottom;
}
```

The `const` keyword following the argument list in both the class declaration and in the function implementation specifies that the function is *constant*. This means the function does not alter the value of the instance to which it is applied. Any value can be declared as constant in the C++ language. If a rational number is declared as constant, then only constant operations can be performed on the value, as only constant operations are guaranteed to not alter the state of the component.

2.1.5 Operators

We would like to be able to treat instances of our rational data type as mathematical objects. For this reason, the major class of operations used to manipulate rational numbers are the normal arithmetic operations of addition, subtraction, multiplication, and division. In C++ these operations can be defined by declaring *operators* to be used with our rational numbers.

Although they are written in an infix (in the middle) format, operators are in fact treated in the C++ language in much the same manner as functions. It is common in programming languages for the meaning of operators to be *overloaded*. This means that multiple function definitions are described by the same name, and they are disambiguated by the type of arguments used with the operation. For example, in most languages the symbol + is used to indicate both integer and floating point addition, depending upon the type of values used as arguments. In C++ all functions, including operators, can potentially have overloaded meanings. The only requirement is that a new definition of an existing name must not be ambiguous. This means the definition must not require arguments that match any existing definition. This requirement is easily achieved if one or both arguments are a new data type, since no existing definition can be using these types.

To illustrate, the following example shows how we might define the meaning of the + operator when applied to two rational numbers. Recall the definition of addition from Fig. 2.1. The body of the operator-function uses a declaration statement to create and initialize a new rational value. This value is then returned as the result of the function. Other operators can be similarly defined.

```
rational operator + (const rational & left, const rational & right)
{   // return sum of two rational numbers
    rational result (
        left.numerator() * right.denominator() +
            right.numerator() * left.denominator(),
         left.denominator() * right.denominator());
    return result;
}
```

The ampersand (address operator) in the argument list indicates that the left and right values will be passed *by reference*. A reference parameter is merely an address, a pointer to the actual argument value. The alternative, pass *by value*, is the default if no ampersand is specified. When pass by value is used, a new copy of an argument is created for each function call. For large structures, this can incur a significant cost. Thus, for most types of values, pass by reference can be executed much more efficiently than pass by value. The `const` keyword indicates, as before, that the function will not alter the parameter value.

Note that an operator is not a member function; it is merely a function that takes rational numbers as arguments. Having defined the arithmetic operators, expressions can then be written to manipulate rational quantities. For example, the following expression performs a calculation using three rational variables (`x`, `y`, and `z`) and places the result into a new rational number called `w`.

```
w = x + y * z;
```

The definition of an operator would normally be found in an implementation file. The associated interface file would merely include an indication that such an operation is available. This information is provided by a function *prototype*. A prototype simply lists the function names and the types (and, optionally, names) of any arguments. A list of prototypes for the arithmetic operations might be given as follows:

```
// prototypes for arithmetic operations, including unary
negation

rational operator + (const rational &, const rational &);
rational operator - (const rational &, const rational &);
rational operator * (const rational &, const rational &);
rational operator / (const rational &, const rational &);
rational operator - (const rational &);
```

Another set of operators that should be defined for our rational number data abstraction is the comparison operators. The following illustrates how one of these, the "less than" operator, might be defined. Notice that

Parameter Passing Mechanisms

The C++ language provides three different types of parameter passing mechanisms: pass by value, pass by reference, and pass by constant reference.

The default mechanism is called pass *by value*. This is the mechanism used, for example, in the constructors that take integer arguments. The characteristic of pass by value is that a *copy* of the formal argument is created and placed in the parameter area of the function. Changes to the parameter within the function will effect only the copy, and will have no effect on the formal argument.

When user-defined data types, such as our rational number abstraction, are passed as argument using pass by value, the copy is created using the copy constructor. Since the creation of a copy could potentially be a costly operation, pass by value parameter passing should normally be used only with simple data types, such as integers, characters, or floating point values.

An ampersand following the type designation in an argument list indicates pass *by reference*. In the rational number ADT we have used this parameter passing mechanism in the stream input operator. The ampersand is often referred to as the address operator, since it yields the address of its argument when used as a unary operator. Remembering this makes it easier to recollect that when pass by reference is used, it is the *address* of the formal argument that is passed to the procedure. Changes to the parameter value within the procedure will automatically and immediately be reflected in changes to the actual argument value. This is a very useful facility when it is desirable to have a procedure make changes to values in the caller's environment, as in the stream input operator, or when a procedure needs to return values that will change two or more variables. (We will see an example of the latter in Exercise 21 at the end of this chapter.)

The keyword `const` preceding a type designation indicates the parameter value is constant, and changes to the argument value are not permitted from within the procedure. When combined with pass by reference, the result is a parameter value that is passed *by constant reference*. We have used this mechanism extensively in the declaration of the mathematical operations in the rational number ADT. This combination has the advantage of efficient execution provided by pass by reference, with the guarantee that no changes will be made to the formal argument value as a result of invoking the procedure.

the return type is declared as integer, whereas the return type of the arithmetic operations given earlier was declared as rational.

```
int operator < (const rational & left, const rational & right)
{   // less than comparison of two rational numbers
    return left.numerator() * right.denominator() <
        right.numerator() * left.denominator();
}
```

2.1.6 Functions

Ordinary functions can be defined with arguments that are new user-defined data types. Unlike member functions, these do not have a receiver and are invoked by a simple function call. Ordinary functions cannot access the internal (private) structure of any class. However, the names of ordinary functions can be overloaded, just as we overloaded the names of operators.

To illustrate, we will provide a definition of the absolute value function when used with a rational number argument. The function definition could be given as follows:

```
rational abs(const rational & num)
{   // return the absolute value of a rational number
    int newtop;
    int newbottom = num.denominator();

    // get non-negative numerator part
    if (num.numerator() < 0)
        newtop = - num.numerator();
    else
        newtop = num.numerator();

    // create and return result
    rational result(newtop, newbottom);
    return result;
}
```

A further point to note concerning this example is the fact that the declaration of the variable `result` occurs in the middle of the function body, at the point where the variable is first required. In many other programming languages, declarations must all appear at the beginning of a procedure. The C++ language makes no such restriction.

2.1.7 Member Function Operators

Some operators are defined not as simple functions but as member functions. The most common situation in which this occurs is the definition of assignment and the various different forms of assignment permitted by the C++ language. By defining these operators as member functions, they are permitted access to the internal fields of the left argument, something that is not permitted by ordinary functions.

Figure 2.2 illustrates the declaration for assignment and for the addition increment form of assignment as a member function. Note that when a binary operator is declared in this fashion, the left argument is the instance and is thus not declared; the declaration is only needed for the right argument. Note also that in C++ assignment is an operator, not a statement. To indicate that no "result" is produced by the assignment operator, the result type is declared as `void`. The implementation of assignment could be given as follows:

```
void rational::operator = (const rational & right)
{   // simply copy values from right hand side of assignment
    top = right.numerator();
    bottom = right.denominator();
}
```

The addition assignment operator is similar. One problem is that, as a consequence of an addition, the result may no longer be in lowest denominator form. This would occur, for example, in the addition of 3/8 to 1/8, since the result should be 1/2, not 4/8. Since this problem will be common to all the arithmetic operations, we provide a single function to place the result into normalized form:

```
void rational::operator += (const rational & right)
{   // modify by adding right hand side
    top = top * right.denominator() + bottom * right.numerator();
    bottom *= right.denominator();

    // normalize the result, ensuring lowest denominator form
    normalize();
}
```

The `normalize` function is simply a member function, part of the behavior of the rational number ADT. In Fig. 2.2 note that the normalize function is declared as private. This means it can be invoked only from within other member functions in the rational number component. Another feature to note is that when one member function is invoked from within another member function the receiver does not need to be named and is assumed to be the same as the current instance. We see this in the call on `normalize` in the addition assignment operator.

The `normalize` function is shown in Fig. 2.3. The routine first checks the sign of the proposed top and bottom values, ensuring they are both nonnegative and storing the sign of the result in the variable `sign`. The proposed values are then converted to the canonical form by dividing by their greatest common divisor. The function `gcd`, which is not shown, is used to compute the greatest common divisor of two integer values. (We will examine one definition of the `gcd` function in the next chapter.)

An additional feature of the `normalize` routine is the use of the `assert` function. This procedure is provided as part of the C++ run-time library. The function takes a single Boolean condition, and it will generate an informative message and halt execution if the condition is not satisfied. Note that without the assertion a denominator of zero would eventually cause a division by zero error. The call on `assert` does not prevent the error but pinpoints more accurately the source of the error. We will consistently use the `assert` facility to check for conditions that must be satisfied in order to ensure the correct functioning of a particular section of code.

2.1.8 Initialization Using Constructors

One of the major objectives of the component view of software development is to simplify and minimize the details with which the user of a software service need be familiar in order to use a component. The creation of a new data value is almost always followed by a certain amount of initialization of the value. For example, the declaration of a new rational number would invariably be followed by an assignment statement or

Operators — Functions or Methods

A few operators, such as the various forms of assignment, are required to be defined as member functions. For most operators, however, the programmer has the choice of defining the operator either as an ordinary function, or as a member function.

To decide which option is preferable, there are basically two points to keep in mind:

- ▲ An ordinary function is normally not permitted access to the private portions of the class, whereas a member function is allowed such access. (The phrase "normally" is used, since we will encounter in Chapter 8 a mechanism to override this restriction.)
- ▲ Implicit conversions, say from integer to float or integer to rational, will be performed for both right and left argument if the operator is defined in functional form, but only for the right argument if the operator is defined as a member function.

Thus the member function form is preferable if the left argument is modified, as in assignment. The functional form is preferable if the left argument is not modified, or if conversions are permitted on both arguments.

```
void rational::normalize()
{   // normalize rational by:
    // a) moving sign to numerator
    // b) making sure numerator and denominator have no common divisors
    int sign = 1;    // sign is 1 if non-negative, -1 if negative
    if (top < 0) {
        sign = -1;
        top = - top;
        }
    if (bottom < 0) {
        sign = - sign;
        bottom = - bottom;
        }

    // make sure we are not dividing by zero
    assert(bottom != 0);

    // find greatest common divisor
    int d = gcd(top, bottom);

    // move sign to top and divide by gcd
    top = sign * (top / d);
    bottom = bottom / d;
}
```

Figure 2.3 Normalizing a rational number

some other action to establish the initial numerator and denominator values. This situation is common to most software components; creation is almost always followed by initialization.

Since these two operations, creation and initialization, are so tightly coupled, it is dangerous and defeating to the purposes of reliable software to keep them separate. It is defeating the purposes of abstraction because the user of a software component is required to remember two different operations, when in fact only one abstract idea is involved. It is dangerous because the user may inadvertently fail to initialize a value (for example, fail to assign a number to a rational value), or initialize a value twice (which is often just as bad).

The C++ language eliminates this problem by introducing a new type of function, called a *constructor*. A constructor is intimately tied to a class, a situation indicated by the fact that the constructor and the class share the same name. The syntax for declaring a constructor is similar to that used to declare a member function. The difference is that the constructor must have the same name as the class, and a constructor does not declare a return type.

As is the case with all function names in the C++ language, a constructor name can be overloaded with multiple definitions, as long as the argument lists are sufficiently distinct to permit the compiler to differentiate between individual function invocations. In Fig. 2.2 there are four different constructors listed near the beginning of the class definition.

Constructors are invoked implicitly as part of the execution of a declaration statement. The syntax is very much like the syntax used to invoke functions. For example, the following declaration statements create three new variables holding rational values. The first is initialized to the value 3/1; the second will be initialized with the value 3/4 and the third with the value 1/2. The last statement illustrates a feature of constructors, and of rational numbers—namely, that numbers are maintained in lowest denominator form:

```
rational a(3);
rational b(3, 4);
rational c(2, 4);
```

A single argument for a constructor can also be written by using a slightly different syntax. The argument can be given on the right side of an assignment token. For example, the following declaration is equivalent to the first declaration given above:

```
rational a = 3;
```

It is important to note that even though the assignment operator token is being used in this statement, this is not an assignment statement. The assignment statement operator we have defined previously will not be invoked. The assignment operator used within a declaration statement merely indicates an initialization. The same token is used for two entirely different purposes, depending upon context.

CONSTRUCTOR IMPLEMENTATION The implementation of constructors looks much like the implementation of other member functions, with two exceptions. First, a constructor does not declare any return type. Second, the procedure heading for a constructor declaration can be followed by a sequence of initializations. To illustrate, the function body for the constructor that takes a single integer argument can be given as follows:

```
rational::rational(int numerator) : top(numerator)
{   // by default initialize the denominator to one
    bottom = 1;
}
```

Following the argument list for the constructor is a colon and an *initializer*. The initializer is the name of a data field, followed by a value in parentheses, that will be used to initialize the data field.

The constructor body is similar to a function body—a sequence of C++ statements enclosed in a pair of curly braces. In this case the function body consists of just a single assignment statement.

In order to illustrate both features in this particular case, we have used both an initializer and an assignment statement within the body of the constructor. We could in fact have used either initializers for both or assignment statements for both. The following illustrates these two alternative possibilities:

```
rational::rational(int numerator) : top(numerator), bottom(1)
{
    // no further initialization necessary
}

rational::rational(int numerator)
{   // assign both top and bottom data fields
    top = numerator;
    bottom = 1;
}
```

Although initializers may seem unnecessary and redundant, we will subsequently encounter situations where values cannot be initialized by assignment statements, and they can only be bound to an initial value using an initializer.

The constructor with no arguments, declared with just an empty pair of parentheses, is used to initialize values in declaration statements where no arguments are provided. A constructor with no arguments is often called the *default constructor*, since it will be invoked by default if no arguments are provided with a declaration statement.

```
rational::rational() : top(0), bottom(1)
{
    // no further initialization necessary
}
```

The reader should be warned of a common programming error. By analogy with declaration statements that provide arguments to constructors, programmers sometimes want to use an empty pair of parentheses in a declaration statement in order to make sure the default constructor is invoked:

```
rational x();    // WARNING – An Error!!!
```

This is not correct. The statement written above is interpreted by the C++ compiler as a prototype that declares x to be a function that requires no arguments and returns a rational value. The proper declaration statement, as we showed earlier, uses no parentheses when no arguments are required. Nevertheless, the default constructor will still be invoked.

We turn now to the constructor that takes two integer arguments. The constructor will first initialize the values of the top and bottom data fields using the arguments provided. The function `normalize`, described earlier, will then be invoked in order to ensure the values are in our canonical form.

```
rational::rational(int numerator, int denominator)
        : top(numerator), bottom(denominator)
{   // make sure fields are in normalized form
    normalize();
}
```

COPY CONSTRUCTORS The last form of constructor given in the class declaration in Fig. 2.2 deserves special mention. In addition to being invoked in response to a declaration statement, a constructor will also be invoked when it is necessary to *copy* a data value from one location to another. In our examples this occurs when the system must copy the value yielded by an arithmetic function onto the execution stack of the caller. By default, such copies are performed simply by copying each field from one structure to another. On many systems, however, compiling the functions as we have written them will produce a warning message to the effect that "bitwise copy is being used" for this operation. We can eliminate this message and gain slightly more control over execution by defining yet one more type of constructor, the *copy constructor*.

The argument to a copy constructor is a reference to the same type as the constructor is producing. In this case this would be a constant reference to a rational value. The copy constructor, in effect, performs an assignment of the argument to the newly produced value. Most often, this is a trivial operation, such as the following:

```
rational::rational(const rational & value)
    : top(value.numerator()), bottom(value.denominator())
{
    // no further initialization required
}
```

It is good practice to provide copy constructors for any newly created data structure.

CONSTRUCTORS USED FOR CONVERSION In addition to their use with declaration statements, constructors are also used implicitly by the C++ language to define conversions. Consider the following sequence of statements:

```
rational x, y;
...
x = y * 3;
```

In order to provide a meaning to this expression, the integer constant 3 must be converted into a rational number, since only a rational number can be multiplied by another rational number. The fact that such a conversion is possible is indicated by the constructor that takes a single integer argument. The actions performed by that constructor will be used to implicitly create a new temporary rational number, which will then be used as the right argument in the multiplication. Following the execution of the statement, the temporary value will be discarded.

Temporary values can also be created directly by the programmer, by invoking the constructor as if it were an ordinary function. The following statement illustrates this, where the programmer has created a temporary value to hold the rational number 3/4:

```
x = y * rational(3, 4);
```

2.2 STREAMS

A significant omission in our discussion of the rational number data type has been any consideration of input or output. To better understand the problems involved, let us review some of the possible approaches to output used in computer languages.

The technique used in conventional C programs—and since C++ is descended from C, the approach still used in many C++ programs—is to employ the function `printf`. The `printf` function takes a variable number of arguments, the first of which must be a character string containing formatting directives. Formatting directives are written in the form of a two-character sequence, where the first character is % and the second character indicates the type of value to be printed. For example `%d` is used to print integer (decimal) numbers, `%s` to print character strings, `%c` to print individual characters, and so on. The following statement prints the value of the two integers `n` and `m` and their average:

```
printf("n %d m %d average is %d\n", n, m, (n+m)/2);
```

The problem with this approach is that the meaning of the formatting directives is fixed when the `printf` function is defined. If a new data type is created, such as our rational number data type, it is not possible to add a new formatting directive to indicate how formatting should take place. To print a rational number, we would need to directly access the numerator and denominator fields to print them as integers; but this conflicts with the protected status of these fields, as well as with our desire to treat the rational number abstraction as a single entity.

A solution that offers better possibilities for extensibility is to use the ability to overload function names in C++. For example, assume that the system provides a single function, say `print`, that can be used to print values on an output device. Various implementations of `print`, each differing in the type of argument they take, could be provided to print characters, integers, floating point values, and so on. When a new data type is created, such as our rational number abstraction, it would only be necessary to add yet another overloaded version of the `print` function. This solution will work; the only difficulty is that it is somewhat clumsy to print long sequences of values combined with literal text. For example, to produce the output corresponding to the single `printf` statement given previously would require the following sequence of seven statements:

```
print("n ");
print(n);
print(" m ");
print(n);
print(" average is ");
print((n+m)/2);
print('\n');
```

Nevertheless, the use of overloading seems to be a useful mechanism provided by the language that permits a programmer to easily define output for new data types. The key to overcoming the clumsy nature of the overloaded `print` function is to observe that perhaps what we want is the ability to overload *expressions*, not statements. To do this, C++ introduces a new data type, the *stream*, and in particular the data abstraction `ostream`, which stands for "output stream." One can think of streams as representing a file, although it is more accurate to say that it is possible for a stream to copy onto a file.

Next, the operator <<, which for integer arguments is used to produce a left shift, is redefined to indicate data flowing onto a stream. Assume that when the second (right) argument is a character, the single character value is copied to the file associated with a stream. (The details of how this is done are implementation dependent and will be ignored here.) We can overload the << operator to print a variety of other data types by reducing the problem to that of printing individual characters. Figure 2.4 illustrates the printing of signed and unsigned integer values.

The fact that each of these operator functions returns a pointer (reference) to the `ostream` value is significant. Since the << operator is left associative, complicated formatting can be written as a single expression. On many systems the global variable `cout` (for "common output") is the stream associated with a standard common output device. Thus the following expression can be used to print the value of two numbers and their average:

```
cout << "m " << m << " n " << n << " average " << (n+m)/2 << '\n';
```

More significantly, it is an easy matter now for a programmer to provide formatting capabilities for a new data type. For example, to output rational numbers, the programmer need only define the following operator:

```
ostream & operator << (ostream & out, const rational & value)
```

```
{   // print representation of rational number on an output stream
    out << value.numerator() << '/' << value.denominator();
    return out;
}
```

The output function should return the value of the first argument.

2.2.1 Stream Input

There is a corresponding data type `istream` for input streams. Just as the global variable `cout` represents the standard output, on many systems the global variable `cin` represents a standard input device. A characteristic of stream input is that "white space" characters (spaces, tabs, and newlines) are ignored during input. If `intval` is declared as an integer variable, the expression:

Why <<?

An obvious question is why the designer of C++ decided to use the left-shift symbol << for output. The answer is actually simple and illustrates some of the features (and problems) of using operator overloading in C++. To start with, it is not possible to invent a new binary token to represent output. The C++ language has a fixed set of operators, and no more. Thus the possibilities are somewhat limited.

The assignment operator was one possibility. Input could be specified using `cin` on the right side of an assignment, as in:

```
intvar = cin;
```

and output indicated by an "assignment" to `cout`:

```
cout = intvar;
```

However, this would mean that the same symbol would be used for both input and output, potentially causing confusion. Furthermore, the equal sign associates the wrong way; the expression `cout = x = y` means `cout = (x = y)`, not `cout = x; cout = y`. Worse, assignment can be described only by member functions. Thus the creation of a new data type would require adding a new member function to the user-defined class in order to perform input and to the `stream` abstraction in order to perform output.

Early versions of C++ tried using the operators < and >, but most people then confused input and output with the more conventional comparison meanings of these operators.

The operators << and >> do not appear to cause the same type of confusion. Their use as shift operators is relatively rare in programming, and thus most people readily accept a new interpretation. They are asymmetrical and thus suggest data flowing "to" and "from." They associate left to right, thus allowing sequences of operations to be performed end-to-end. Finally, their predefined precedence is low enough to allow arithmetic expressions to appear in output without using parentheses, as in:

```
cout << "a + b * c is " << a + b * c
    << '\n';
```

The left shift operator with its conventional meaning can be used in an output statement, by surrounding it with parentheses:

```
cout << " a left shift by 3 is "
    << (a << 3) << '\n';
```

```
ostream & operator << (ostream & out, const int value)
{   // print signed integer values on a stream

    unsigned int usvalue;
    if (value < 0) {
        // print leading minus sign
        out << '-';
        usvalue = - value;
        }
    else
        usvalue = value;
    // print non-negative number
    out << usvalue;
    return out;
}

char digitCharacter(unsigned int value)
{   // convert non-negative integer digit into printable digit
    // assume value is less than nine
    assert (value <= 9);
    return value + '0';
}

ostream & operator << (ostream & out, const unsigned int value)
{   // print unsigned integer values on a stream
    if (value < 10)
        out << digitCharacter(value);
    else {
        out << (value / 10);      // recursive call
        out << digitCharacter(value % 10);  // print single char
        }
    return out;
}
```

Figure 2.4 Various overloaded versions of the << operator

```
cin >> intval;
```

reads an integer value into the variable. As with the << operator, the >> operator returns the value of the left argument. When used in situations where a Boolean value is expected—for example, in `if` or `while` statements—the Boolean result generated is used to indicate end of file. Thus a loop that would read values repeatedly from the input until end of file

```
istream & operator >> (istream & in, rational & r)
{   // read a rational number from an input stream
    int t, b;

    // read the top
    in >> t;

    // if there is a slash, read the next number
    char c;
    in >> c;
    if (c == '/')
        in >> b;      // read bottom part
    else {
        in.putback(c);
        b = 1;
        }

    // do the assignment
    rational newValue(t, b);
    r = newValue;

    // return the stream
    return in;
}
```

Figure 2.5 A function to read rational numbers

was reached could be written as follows:

```
while (cin >> intval) {
    // process intval
    ...
    }
// reach this point on end of input
...
```

Input for user-defined input types is usually built out of input for the component parts. Figure 2.5 shows a function to read rational numbers. The input is expected to be an integer, which can optionally be followed by a division sign and a second integer. The function `putback` returns an unwanted character to the input stream. The next input operation subsequently performed will yield this character.

An easy way to remember the stream I/O operations is to visualize them as arrows. The input operator, $>> x$, points data into x, while the output operator, $<< x$, copies data out of x.

2.3 CHAPTER SUMMARY

Key Concepts

- Class declaration
- Interface file and implementation file
- Data field and member field or function
- Public access and private access
- Receiver
- Operator
- Constant value
- Constant member function
- Pass by reference
- Pass by constant reference
- Pass by value
- Function prototype
- Member function operator
- Assertion
- Constructor
- Initializer
- Default constructor and copy constructor
- Conversion
- Stream
- `cin` and `cout`

In this chapter we have introduced the idea of a *class*, which is the major mechanism used in C++ programs to create software components.

Class declarations are divided into public and private sections. The public section describes attributes that are accessible to users of the software abstraction, while attributes declared in the private section can be used only within the implementation of the component.

The data, or state, of a data structure is allocated by declaring data fields. Data fields can be given in either the private or public sections of a class declaration.

The behavior of a class is defined by the use of member functions. A member function must always be invoked *on* or *to* a specific instance of a class, called the *receiver*. The receiver is given first, followed by a period, followed by the member function. (An exception to this rule occurs when a member function is invoked inside the implementation of another member function. In this case the receiver is not given and is assumed to be the same as the receiver of the current method. We saw an example of this when the `normalize` routine was invoked inside the += method, and again when the same method was invoked inside a constructor.)

Operators, such as addition or subtraction, can be overloaded to have new meaning when used with user-defined data types. Operators can also be defined as member functions. This is preferable when the effect of the function is to change the value of the left argument. The most common operators used in this fashion are assignment and the various forms of arithmetic assignment.

Constructors are functions that are automatically invoked when a new instance of a data type is created. Constructors can take arguments to assist in the initialization of the newly created object.

Flexible input and output is achieved through the ability to overload operators. The shift operators << and >> can be defined to provide input and output operations when used with a new class of data types called *streams*.

There are three parameter passing mechanisms used in C++ programs:

- ▲ Pass *by value* is the default, used if no other specification is given. When an argument is passed in this fashion, a copy of the argument is created. Changes to the parameter value made inside the function will have no effect on the argument value when the procedure returns. When a user-defined type is passed as argument, the copy of the value is created using the copy constructor. Because the creation of a copy can be a costly operation, pass by value should be used only for simple data types (such as integers or floating point values).
- ▲ Pass *by reference* is indicated by placing an ampersand after the type designation in the argument list. When an argument is passed in this

fashion, the address of the actual argument value is passed to the procedure. Changes to the parameter value made inside the function will immediately be reflected in changes to the argument value, and they will persist even after the procedure returns.

- Pass *by constant* is indicated by placing the keyword `const` before the type designation in an argument list. Usually this is combined with pass by reference, to form pass *by constant reference*. The `const` keyword guarantees that no changes can be made to the parameter value. Thus this form has the advantages in efficient execution of the pass by reference, with the guarantees of pass by value that the argument will not be changed.

References

The definitive description of the C++ language is provided in the two books written by the designer of the language, Bjarne Stroustrup [Ellis 90, Stroustrup 91]. The first book, authored jointly with Margaret Ellis, is more technical in nature, whereas the second has more of a tutorial format. Hansen [Hansen 90] provides extended expositions on the answers to exercises given in Stroustrup's book. The *C++ Primer*, by Stanley Lippman [Lippman 91] also provides a well-written explanation of the features in the language. The book by Russel Winder [Winder 91] is useful reading in that it is less a description of the language and more of an exposition of how to develop software using the language. While a language manual can provide information concerning the legality of programs, it does not usually provide information on good programming style. An analysis of style in C++ programs is provided by Cargill [Cargill 92]. Coplien [Coplien 92] describes a number of more advanced and complicated uses of the C++ language.

A more complete explanation of streams can be found in Stroustrup [Stroustrup 91].

I have elsewhere written several hundred pages attempting to explain classes and object-oriented programming [Budd 91]; thus it is natural, I expect, that I feel the quick overview provided in Chapters 1 and 2 is something less than complete. Other explanations more tailored to C++ can be found in the previously mentioned books by Stroustrup or Lippman.

It is important to note here, rather early in this text, that a conscious decision has been made to present merely a subset of the C++ language, not the full language. Furthermore, it is common in the C++ world for programmers to have an overriding (and unnecessary) obsession with efficiency, usually to the detriment of clarity. For example, the absolute value function we defined in Section 2.1.6 could be more succinctly given as follows:

```
inline rational abs(const rational & x)
{   // return the absolute value of a rational argument
    return rational(x.numerator() < 0 ? x.numerator() : - x.numerator(),
        x.denominator());
}
```

Although shorter (and probably, faster), this form lacks some of the simplicity of the original. I have tried throughout this book to strive for clarity. In many cases the algorithms presented could be coded so as to execute slightly more quickly by avoiding the creation of unnecessary local variables or using conditional expressions or other features, but in practice clarity and simplicity are usually more important than raw execution efficiency. Meyers [Meyers 92] gives a good analysis of appropriate and inappropriate techniques for improving efficiency in C++ programs.

Meyers also suggests that assignment operators should always be defined so as to permit their use in nested (multiple) assignments. In general his arguments are convincing, and we should point out that the only reason we have not defined assignment in this manner is to avoid introducing the idea of a function returning a reference, which at this point in our discussion is unnecessary and confusing to the student.

Exercises

1. Explain the difference between a member function and an ordinary (nonmember) function. Explain the concept of a receiver.
2. Explain the difference between a data field and a member function (or member field).
3. Explain the difference between public and private access to data fields and member functions.
4. Explain the purpose of a function prototype.
5. Explain the difference between an operator defined as an ordinary function and an operator defined as a member function.
6. Write the implementation of the operators for subtraction, multiplication, and division of rational numbers.
7. Write the implementation of the operator for unary negation of a rational number. Notice this operator requires only one argument.
8. Write the implementation of the operators for equality testing (==) and inequality (! =) for rational numbers. Give as well the prototype declaration of this operator.
9. The text described the implementation of the "less than" relational operator. Write the implementations of the remaining three relational operators (<=, >, >=). Give as well the prototype declarations of these operators.
10. Write the implementations of the remaining arithmetic-assignment operators for rational numbers. These are $*=$, $-=$, and $/=$. Add the prototype declarations for these operators to the class description, given in Fig. 2.2.
11. The obvious implementation for the $/=$ operator is as follows:

```
void rational::operator /
     (const rational & right)
{
    // do cross multiplication
    top *= right.denominator();
    bottom *= right.numerator();

    // normalize the result
    normalize();
}
```

Using the following example, explain why this implementation will not produce the correct result, then explain how this difficulty can be avoided.

```
rational x(3,4);

x / x;
```

12. For a floating point value, the procedure `floor` returns the largest integer value smaller than the argument. Write a similar function that takes as argument a single rational number. (*Hint*: Integer division already does most of the work for you, although you may need to check how integer division is handled if one argument is negative. The language definition permits compilers to either round toward zero or round toward negative infinity in this situation.) Give as well the prototype declaration of this operator.

13. For integer values, the remainder function, %, is defined by the equation:

```
a % b == a - floor(a / b) * b
```

We can use this definition to implement the remainder operator for rational numbers. Using the `floor` function you wrote for the previous exercise, write this implementation. Give as well the prototype declaration of this operator.

14. Consider the following short sequence of statements:

```
int i = 1;
int j = 2;
i = test(j);
cout << "i: " << i << " j: " << j << '\n';
```

Which of the following definitions of the function `test` would compile without errors? For those that do compile, show what value would be printed. For those that do not compile, indicate the source of error.

a.

```
int test(int x)
{
    x = 4;
    return 5;
}
```

b.

```
int test(int & x)
{
    x = 4;
    return 5;
}
```

c.

```
int test(const int & x)
{
    x = 4;
    return 5;
}
```

15. Explain why the argument to the copy constructor must be passed by reference. (*Hint*: Consider how copy constructors are invoked implicitly in the language.)

16. Although the syntax for constant pass by value parameters is perfectly legal, the concept has little practical value. Explain why.

17. Write a stream expression to print the values of two rational variables x and y and their average.

18. Develop an ADT for complex numbers.
    a. The internal state of a complex number should be represented by a double precision floating point value for the real part, and a similar floating point value for the imaginary part. Give the class description for your abstraction.
    b. Implement three constructors. The default constructor takes no arguments. A constructor with one double precision argument sets the real part and assigns the value zero to the imaginary part. A constructor with two double precision arguments sets both fields.
    c. Define a pair of member functions to return the real and imaginary portions of a complex number.
    d. Using these, define the arithmetic operations of addition, subtraction, and multiplication.
    e. Define a stream output operator for complex numbers.

19. The absolute value of a complex number is defined as the real value representing the distance of the number from the origin. For a complex number $x + yi$, this can be computed as $\sqrt{x^2 + y^2}$. Write the `abs` function for the complex number ADT developed in the last exercise. Note that this function takes as argument a complex number but returns a double precision value.

20. For a complex number z that represents $x + yi$, the square root is a complex number with real part defined by $\sqrt{(abs(z) + x)/2}$ and imaginary part defined by $sign(y) * \sqrt{(abs(z) + x)/2}$, where $sign(y)$ indicates 1 if $y \geq 0$, and -1 if $y < 0$. Write the function that computes this value.

21. Using the function you developed in the last exercise, write a function that takes three double precision values a, b, and c as arguments and that computes the roots of the quadratic equation defined by $ax^2 + bx + c = 0$. You will recall that the roots of a quadratic equation are given by:

$$x = \frac{-b \pm \sqrt{b^2 - 4ac}}{2a}$$

The roots should be returned in the final two arguments to your function, which are passed by reference. That is, the prototype for your function is as follows:

```
void quadratic(double a, double b, double c,
        complex & root1, complex & root2);
```

Note that the roots can be complex if the quantity under the square root is negative.

CHAPTER 3

Algorithms — Descriptions of Behavior

Software components, no matter how they are structured or defined, must perform actions in order to be useful. In Chapter 2 we saw that such behavior is usually implemented by means of member functions or operators. In either case, the heart of the action is a sequence of computer instructions to be executed under certain circumstances. Such a sequence is known as an *algorithm*. In this chapter, we will consider some of the properties of algorithms and the techniques that can be employed in the analysis of algorithms.

An *algorithm* is a set of instructions used to solve a specific problem or, more commonly, to solve a general class of similar problems. Terms that have a similar meaning include *process, method, technique, procedure, routine*, and even, as we will investigate in a moment, *recipe*.

Once we have developed an algorithm for a problem, the discovery of a solution is simply a matter of executing each instruction of the algorithm in turn. If this process is to be successful, there are in general several properties that an algorithm must possess. Among these are the following:

- *Accurate specification of the input.* The most common form of algorithm is a transformation that takes a set of input values and performs some manipulations to yield a set of output values. An algorithm must make clear the number and type of input values, and the essential initial conditions those input values must possess in order to achieve successful operation.
- *Definiteness of each instruction.* Each step of an algorithm must be precisely defined. There should be no ambiguity regarding the actions to be carried out at any point. As we will see shortly, algorithms presented in an informal descriptive form are often ill-defined for exactly this reason, due to the ambiguities in English and other natural languages. In order to avoid this problem, the majority of algorithms we discuss will be presented in C++. Since C++ is a formally defined computer language, the interpretation of each step can be made clear by referring to the definition of the language.
- *Correctness.* An algorithm is expected to solve a problem. For any putative algorithm, we must demonstrate that the algorithm will in fact solve the problem. Often this will take the form of an argument, mathematical or logical in nature, to the effect that *if* the input conditions are satisfied and the steps of the algorithm executed *then* the desired outcome will be produced.
- *Termination.* It must be clear that for any particular input values the algorithm is guaranteed to terminate after a finite number of steps. We will postpone until later a more precise definition of the informal term "steps." It is usually not necessary to know the exact number of steps that an algorithm will require, but it will be convenient to provide an upper bound and argue that the algorithm will always terminate in fewer steps than the upper bound. Usually this upper bound will be given as a function of some values in the input. For example, if the input consists of two integer values `X` and `Y`, we might be able to say that a particular algorithm will always terminate in fewer than `X + Y` steps.
- *Description of the result or effect.* Finally, it must be clear exactly what the algorithm is intended to accomplish. Most often this can be expressed as the production of a result value having certain properties. Less frequently, algorithms are executed for a *side effect*, such as printing a value on an output device. In either case, the expected outcome must be completely specified.

This chapter will examine a number of different algorithms describe how we can evaluate each in terms of the properties given.

Lemon Soufflé

1 envelope unflavored gelatin
$\frac{1}{4}$ cup cold water
6 egg yolks
1 cup sugar
$\frac{2}{3}$ cup lemon juice
1 tablespoon grated lemon rind
4 egg whites
$1\frac{1}{2}$ cups heavy cream

1. Soften the gelatin in water. Beat egg yolks and sugar until thick and light. Stir in lemon juice and cook over low heat, beating steadily with a whisk until thickened and hot but not boiling (10–15 minutes).
2. Pour mixture into large bowl. Mix in gelatin until dissolved, then add lemon rind. Stir occasionally until cool.
3. Beat egg whites until stiff but not dry. Fold into lemon mixture, then whip the cream and fold in. Pour into a two-quart soufflé dish (or large bowl) and refrigerate at least 12 hours.

Figure 3.1 A recipe for lemon soufflé

3.1 RECIPES AS ALGORITHMS

Probably the most common form of algorithm the reader is likely to have encountered previously is a recipe. A recipe is a structured set of instructions used to transform an input (the ingredients) into a finished product (the edible). Consider the recipe for lemon soufflé shown in Fig. 3.1. Let us evaluate this recipe with respect to the properties of an algorithm we described in the last section.

- *Input.* The recipe begins with a list of ingredients. These define the basic set of initial conditions required before the steps provided by the recipe can be undertaken. Note that input conditions consist of both a set of input objects (gelatin, water, eggs, sugar) and a set of conditions (the water must be cold, the cream heavy).
- *Result.* The primary result of the recipe is usually described by the name—in this case *lemon soufflé*. Incidental consequences of executing the recipe procedure (such as producing a messy kitchen) are usually of little interest and are left unstated.
- *Correctness.* It takes a talented cook to be able to simply look at a recipe and decide whether the outcome will be tasty or even edible if the recipe is correctly followed. For most people, it is a matter of experimentation. As the saying goes, the proof of the pudding (or soufflé) is in the eating.

- *Termination.* It is somewhat difficult to guarantee from a mere examination of the steps involved in a recipe that it can actually be carried out in a finite amount of time. In step one, are we guaranteed that when beating the egg yolks and sugar they will eventually become thick and light, or that when the result is cooked over a low heat it will always become thick and hot? What if it never becomes thick? Perhaps in realization of this possible problem, the author of the recipe has provided an estimated amount of time this operation should take. If the time estimate is greatly exceeded and the desired outcome has not yet been achieved, then the cook knows something is wrong.
- *Definiteness.* It is in the area of definiteness that we see perhaps the greatest weakness of a recipe as an algorithm, and the significant differences between preparing a set of instructions for a human being to follow versus preparing instructions for a computer. What exactly is "thick and light" in step one? Does light refer to light in texture or light in color? How long should the mixture be whipped in step three? The success of the operation will depend upon answers to questions such as these, but the details are simply not found in the recipe itself. Instead, good cooks rely on experience and intuition to fill in missing information. Computers, on the other hand, do not have prior experience or intuition. Thus a "recipe" for a computer to follow requires a much more complete description of each step.

3.2 PRINTING INTEGERS

The first formal algorithm we will investigate is the procedure used to print a decimal textual representation of an integer value on the standard output device. We saw how this was accomplished using stream operators in Fig. 2.4 (page 49). We will assume as a primitive operation the ability to print a single character on the output. The goal of our algorithm, therefore, is to reduce the problem at hand (printing an integer) to the easier problem we have already assumed is solved (printing a character).

The most common technique used in the solution of a problem is to divide a task into steps, as was done in the lemon soufflé recipe. Another general technique is to ask if a task can be divided into *cases,* into two or more groups of values that are handled in a different fashion. If so, then each case can then be addressed as a separate problem. For example, a moment of reflection on the problem of printing integers will show that it can be easily reduced to the problem of printing positive (unsigned) quantities:

- If the number to be printed is less than zero, immediately print the leading minus sign, then print the negation of the number (which must be positive).

- If the number to be printed is not less than zero, then it must already be positive.

We see this division into cases reflected in the code. The stream operator for an integer checks the sign of the argument. Either the leading minus sign is printed or it is not; in either case, the positive component of the argument is assigned to an unsigned integer variable. We have thus reduced the problem of printing an integer to the easier problem of printing an unsigned (strictly positive) integer.

```
ostream & operator << (ostream & out, const int value)
{   // print a signed integer value on a stream

    unsigned int usvalue;
    if (value < 0) {
        // print leading minus sign
        out << '-';
        usvalue = - value;
        }
    else
        usvalue = value;
    // print positive component
    out << usvalue;
    return out;
}
```

The printing of unsigned integers as well illustrates the concept of dividing the input values into categories. In this case, there are again two types of values:

- The number to be printed is greater than or equal to zero but less than ten. In this case, we merely need to print the corresponding character representation of the value.
- The number is greater than or equal to ten.

We will assume the ability to convert a number between zero and nine into the character value representing the digit. This will be performed by the function named `digitCharacter`. With this, the first case is relatively easy to handle. The second case is more problematical.

A useful technique employed when approaching the solution of a problem that has been expressed in terms of cases, such as those identified here, is to try to find a means of taking the general case and rewriting it in terms of the simpler cases, or in terms of a simpler version of the general case. In this particular problem we solve the general case, where the number is greater than 10, by printing the number divided by ten, followed by printing the single character that corresponds to the remainder after the number has been divided by ten. Since the latter is only a single digit, we can use the same technique we developed for the printing of small numbers:

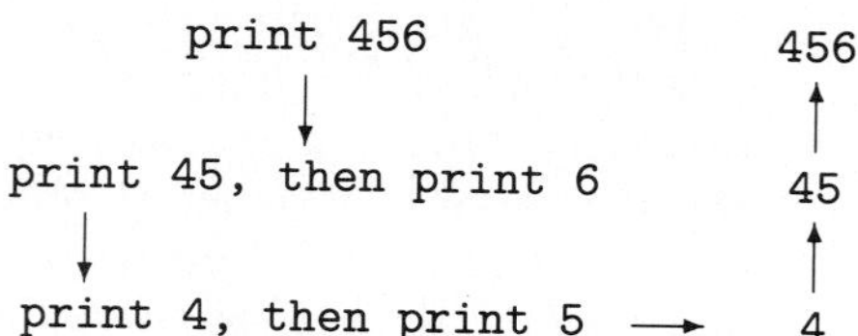

A procedure that during execution invokes itself with slightly different argument values is called a *recursive* procedure. The recursive procedure to print unsigned integer values is as follows:

```
ostream & operator << (ostream & out, const unsigned int value)
{   // print an unsigned integer value on a stream
    if (value < 10)
        out << digitCharacter(value);
    else {
        out << (value / 10);                  // recursive call
        out << digitCharacter(value % 10);    // print single char
        }
    return out;
}
```

Recall that space is allocated for parameters and variables declared locally within a procedure at the time the procedure begins execution. Such variables are discarded, and the space recovered, when the procedure is finished with execution. The same is true of recursive procedures. Each new invocation of the procedure is allocated new and separate copies of parameter values and local variables. Consider the execution of a procedure with the integer value 456. One set of values for the parameters will be created holding this value. When the recursive procedure call occurs, a *second* set of parameter values will be created, holding the value 45. Finally, a *third* set of values will be created for the execution of the procedure with value 4. Each of these three executions of the procedure will use their own data values. These data areas will be discarded as the procedures return, in reverse sequence from the procedure calls.

Let us now analyze this algorithm in terms of the characteristics we identified in the first section.

The input to the algorithm is clearly specified as an unsigned integer value. The purpose of the function is indicated not only by the function name itself but by a comment following the function body. Each step in the function is a simple C++ statement, and so there can be little doubt about the actions to perform. Thus what remains are the three more complex questions: How can we know for certain the algorithm will terminate? And even if it does terminate, how can we know for certain that it will perform the desired action? Finally, even if it does terminate and produce the correct answer, can we describe exactly how long it will take to execute? In order to have confidence in our algorithm, it is necessary to provide an argument, or *proof*, to answer each of these questions.

3.2.1 Proving Termination

By far the most common technique used to prove termination of an algorithm when it is not immediately obvious is to identify a property or value that possesses the following three characteristics:

- ▲ The property or value can be placed in one-to-one correspondence with integer values. (Most commonly, we simply use some integer quantity that appears in the problem; in other cases it is necessary to construct a mapping from some quantity in the problem to the integers.)
- ▲ The property or value is non-negative.
- ▲ The property or value decreases steadily as the algorithm executes. (We often say that such a quantity is *monotonically decreasing*.)

If we can discover such a quantity, then the argument for finite termination can be expressed as follows: This quantity must begin with some value (even if we don't know precisely *what* that value might be). Over time, the quantity is always decreasing. Since it can never be negative, the algorithm must necessarily terminate before the quantity is reduced below zero.

In this particular case the quantity we need to reason about is the magnitude (or absolute value) of the number being printed. To show monotonicity, it is necessary to consider only the general case, since we have already argued that the first case (numbers between zero and 10) can be executed at most once. In the general case the number passed as argument in the recursive call is necessarily smaller (by a factor of 10) than the current argument. Thus for any positive integer argument, we must eventually reach a single digit value and the execution of the algorithm will stop.

3.2.2 Proving Correctness

The proof of correctness for our algorithm follows almost directly the case analysis we used in developing the algorithm.

Case 1: Assume that the input is an integer greater than or equal to zero and less than ten. Execution will proceed to the statement following the `if`, and the correct result will be printed (assuming, of course, that the function `digitCharacter` performs correctly).

Case 2: Assume that the input is an integer greater than or equal to ten. Here it is necessary to discuss *how much* larger than ten is the input value. We will use a *proof by mathematical induction* to show that no matter how large this integer value is, the correct outcome will be produced.

Like the proof of termination, a proof by mathematical induction requires the identification of a discrete quantity in the problem that changes over time and that can be associated with an integer value. As in the termination proof, this quantity may or may not actually occur in the algorithm itself. In this case we will frame our proof in terms of a quantity N that represents the number of digits in the decimal representation of the argument value. A proof by mathematical induction then consists of two parts:

- A *base case* proof. This argument must show that if the quantity N is some finite value (usually, zero or one), then the algorithm produces the correct answer. Our first case, above, provides our base case since

Zeno's Paradox

The most nonintuitive of the three properties we require for proving termination is the first—that the quantity or property being discussed can be placed into a one-to-one correspondence with a diminishing list of integers. To illustrate the necessity of this requirement, consider the following "proof"—that it is possible to share a single candy bar with all your friends, no matter how many friends you may have. Take a candy bar and cut it in half, giving one half to your best friend. Take the remaining half and cut it in half once more, giving a portion to your second best friend. Assuming you have a sufficiently sharp knife, you can continue in this manner, at each step producing ever smaller pieces, for as long as you like. Thus we have no guarantee of termination for this process. Certainly the sequence here ($\frac{1}{2}, \frac{1}{4}, \frac{1}{8}, \ldots$) consists of all non-negative terms and is decreasing. But a one-to-one correspondence with the integers would need to increase, not decrease.

In the fifth century BC the Greek philosopher Zeno used similar arguments to show that no matter how fast he runs the famous hero Achilles cannot overtake a tortoise, if the tortoise is given a head start. Suppose, for example, that the tortoise and Achilles start as shown below at time A. When, at time B, Achilles reaches the point from which the tortoise started, the tortoise will have proceeded some distance ahead of this point. When Achilles reaches this further point at time C, the tortoise will have proceeded yet further ahead. At each point when Achilles reaches a point from which the tortoise began, the tortoise will have proceeded at least some distance further. Thus it is impossible for Achilles to ever overtake and pass the tortoise.

```
Achilles  A ——→ B ——→ C ——→ D
Tortoise        A ——→ B ——→ C ——→ D
```

The paradox arises because of an infinite sequence of ever smaller quantities, and the nonintuitive possibility that an infinite sum can nevertheless result in a finite value. By restricting our arguments concerning termination to use only a decreasing set of *integer* values, we avoid problems such as that typified by Zeno's paradox.

this showed that if our algorithm is given a single digit number it produces the correct outcome. (A number cannot have zero digits, since the numerical value zero produces the single character 0.)

- An *induction step* proof. This argument must show that if we *assume* the result holds (that is, the algorithm produces the correct result) for quantity N, *then* the result must also hold for quantity $N + 1$. To prove this second part in our particular case, let us assume the input is a positive number greater than 10 and possessing $N + 1$ digits. The recursive call passes as argument a number with only N digits, but our assumption tells us that this number will be printed correctly. To print the new number, it is necessary to print only the low-order digit (the digit yielded when computing the remainder after dividing by 10). Therefore the number with $N + 1$ digits will be printed correctly. Because we made no assumptions about this number, we can therefore conclude that any number with $N + 1$ digits will also be correctly written.

Since we can argue that the result holds for our base case, and for the base case plus one, we can apply the induction step twice and argue that the result must be true for the base case plus two. We can similarly argue that it must hold for the base case plus three, and so on. We can therefore conclude that the result holds for any positive value of N—that is, for any number of digits in a positive number.

In using mathematical induction to support an argument, it is important that both portions, the base case and the induction step, be presented. Failure to include one or the other can lead to incorrect results.

MATHEMATICAL INDUCTION The dictionary defines induction in logic as the process of reasoning to a conclusion about all members of a class from examination of only a few members of the class. Thus we might infer, for example, that all elephants are gray based on the observation of large numbers of gray elephants and the absence of evidence to the contrary. Of course, induction in this sense is a weaker form of reasoning than deduction, which is based on reasoning about conclusions that must necessarily be true if the assumptions are true and valid rules of inference are followed. For example, albino (all white) elephants are rare, but they do exist.

In contrast, *mathematical induction* is actually a form of deduction. A conclusion verified by using mathematical induction rests on just as strong a foundation as the reasoning behind the classic syllogism:

All people are fallible.
The author of this book is a person.
Therefore the author of this book is fallible.

The validity of a proof based on mathematical induction is perhaps best illustrated using the technique of proof by contradiction. In this technique, we assume the negation of the assertion we are trying to establish is true, and then show that this necessarily leads to a contradictory situation. If we assume that the proof by induction we gave was not valid, then there must be some smallest value N for which the result is not true. We need not know or care what the value of N really is, but let us assume it is, for example, 37. Thus the assertion is false for value $N = 37$. Our base case showed that the assertion was valid for $N = 1$. The induction step showed that if it were true for some value $N - 1$, then it must be true for N. If we apply the induction step 37 times, we arrive at the conclusion that the assertion must be true for $N = 37$. But no assertion can be both true and not true.[1] This is our contradiction, and the only solution is to reject our initial hypothesis that there is a smallest value for which the assertion is false.

Induction arguments are common in the development of computer algorithms, and it is important that the student has some familiarity with their form. We will explore a few more examples.

Theorem 3.1 The sum of the integers from 1 to n is $\frac{n(n+1)}{2}$.

To establish a base case, we note that for $n = 1$ the fraction becomes $1(2)/2$, which is 1. If we think this is too simple, we can try the next case, which is $1 + 2 = 3 = 2(3)/2$.

To establish the induction step, we consider the sum $1 + 2 + 3 + ... + n$. This can be written as $(1 + 2 + ... + (n - 1)) + n$. Our induction hypothesis tells us that the parenthesized sequence is the same as $(n - 1)n/2$ (substitute $n - 1$ for n in the formula). The result is therefore $\frac{(n-1)n}{2} + n$, which is $\frac{(n-1)n}{2} + \frac{2n}{2}$, or $\frac{(n-1)n+2n}{2}$, which can then be simplified to $\frac{(n+1)n}{2}$, and we are finished.

Another example is suggested by the following observations:

$$1 = 1^2$$
$$1 + 3 = 4 = 2^2$$
$$1 + 3 + 5 = 9 = 3^2$$
$$1 + 3 + 5 + 7 = 16 = 4^2$$

Theorem 3.2 For all values n greater than or equal to 1, $1 + 3 + ... + (2n - 1) = n^2$.

Our observations will work for the base case. To see the induction step, we simply note that $1 + ... + (2n - 1) + (2n + 1)$ is the same as $n^2 + 2n + 1$, which is the same as $(n + 1)^2$.

The most difficult part of using mathematical induction is often discovering exactly the formulation of the conjecture you wish to verify. In

---

1. This is the law of the excluded middle, or as computer scientist David Gries calls it, the law of the excluded miracle.

many cases this is simply a process of taking a few good guesses after examining the pattern formed by the base cases, and then trying to prove the induction step using your guess.

Occasionally, it is necessary to discover an upper bound for some quantity. To do this, we can use mathematical induction with a relational test, rather than an equality. To illustrate, consider the famous Fibonacci numbers, which are defined by the equations:

$$\begin{aligned} \text{Fib}(0) &= 0 \\ \text{Fib}(1) &= 1 \\ \text{Fib}(n+1) &= \text{Fib}(n-1) + \text{Fib}(n) \end{aligned}$$

Theorem 3.3 For all nonnegative integer values n, $\text{Fib}(n) < 2^n$.

It is easy to verify that the conjecture is true for values 0 and 1, since $2^0 = 1$ and $2^1 = 2$. For the induction step, we consider $\text{Fib}(n+1)$, which we know to be equal to $\text{Fib}(n-1) + \text{Fib}(n)$. Since we can bound $\text{Fib}(n-1)$ by 2^{n-1} and $\text{Fib}(n)$ by 2^n, we know $\text{Fib}(n+1)$ must be less than $2^{n-1} + 2^n$. We can manipulate without falsifying a less than relation by adding nonnegative quantities to the right side, or by multiplying values on the right side by values greater than 1. Thus, for example, we know that $2^{n-1} + 2^n$ is less than $2^n + 2^n$. But this is equal to 2^{n+1}. Therefore $\text{Fib}(n+1)$ must be less than 2^{n+1}, which proves the induction step, and thus the theorem.

3.2.3 Analyzing Execution Time

The arguments presented in the preceding two sections are also the key to discovering the execution time for our algorithm. As we have seen, for positive values the number of digits printed (and thus the number of times the algorithm will recursively call itself, since it prints one additional digit on each recursive call) is exactly the number of digits in the base-10 representation of the argument value. But this quantity can be described as the smallest integer greater than the logarithm (base 10) of the argument value.

It is obvious that if we are executing the algorithm on a particular machine, the code executed prior to a recursive call (if there is one) will take a certain constant amount of time, and the code executed after a recursive call will similarly take a certain constant amount of time. Furthermore, the code executed in those cases that do not make a recursive call will also take a certain constant amount of time. It is also obvious that it is difficult to say exactly how much time this will be, since the exact figure will depend upon factors such as the machine that the algorithm is running on, the quality of the assembly language generated by the compiler in use, and so on. But we will show that the exact *value* of these constants is usually unimportant; it is only necessary to know that such constants exist.

To see this, let us represent by c the largest of the constant values described in the last paragraph. We can therefore say that the execution time of the printing algorithm will never be larger than $c * (\lceil \log_{10} |value| \rceil)$, since the left term in the product is the maximum time taken at any step and the right term is the maximum number of steps. Here the $\lceil ... \rceil$ represents the "ceiling" function that returns the smallest integer greater than or equal to the argument value. Since we do not really care about the constant value, we can simplify things somewhat. For example, it is conventional when describing algorithmic bounds to use base-2 logarithms, rather than base-10 values. But $\log_2(n) = \log_{10}(n)/\log_{10}(2)$, so this simply changes the constant factor somewhat. Next we can eliminate the ceiling function, since if the argument to the ceiling function is greater than 2 (and we can assume this with no great loss of generality), then doubling the constant value will more than compensate for the removal of the function. If we finally express the running times in terms of the magnitude (that is, absolute value) of the argument, instead of the argument itself, then we can assert that there exist constants c_1 and c_2 such that the running time of our algorithm is bounded by $c_1 + c_2 \log n$, where n is the input value.

We now want to assert that we can ignore the c_1 term. As n increases, the $\log n$ factor will continue to increase, and the significance of the constant term becomes increasingly less and less important. By simply increasing the constant c_2 slightly, we can more than offset the effect of the c_1 term, which means that it can safely be ignored.

It might seem that with all the fudging and overestimation we have been doing, the significance of the final result we have obtained would be almost nothing. To understand why this is not the case, we must understand the concept of *asymptotic behavior*. Consider the functions graphed in Fig. 3.2. The addition of a constant to any one of these functions would merely raise the values along the y-axis. The multiplication of a function by a constant will merely change the rate of growth, but not the basic shape, for that function. The assumption behind considering asymptotic behavior is that in the long run, neither of these changes will make any difference. That is, for *any* constants c_1 and c_2, if we have two functions $c_1 n \log n$ and $c_2 n^2$, eventually it *must* be true that the latter function will be larger than the former, *regardless of the constants involved*. A large value for c_1 and a small value for c_2 may delay the point where the two functions cross for a time, but the inevitable must surely occur at some point. This is illustrated by the graphs shown in Fig. 3.3, which compare the two functions $200 + n \log n$ and $n^2/4$. The large constant added to the first function ensures that for a time it is larger than the second, as does the small constant multiplier on the second function. Eventually, however (in this case, around 30), the quadratic behavior of the second function dominates all else, and despite the constants involved, the first function yields smaller values.

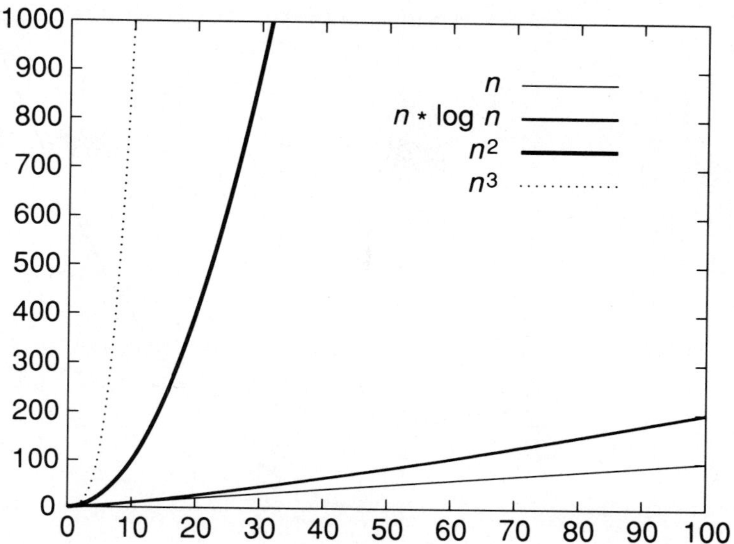

Figure 3.2 Asymptotic behavior of several functions

A common phenomenon illustrates this idea. Consider a drop of water on an inclined plane. Gravity is pulling the water down, and this is being resisted by the surface tension between the drop and the plane.

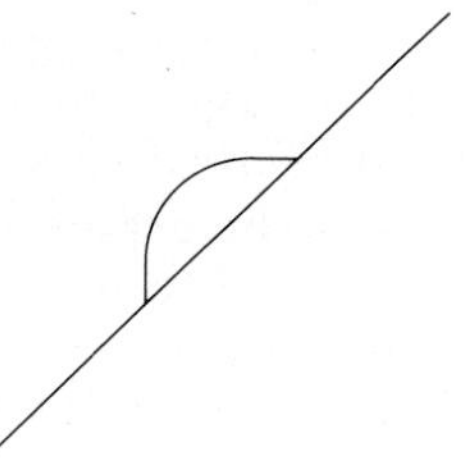

We can idealize the situation slightly and consider the drop to be a perfect hemisphere. If r represents the radius of the drop, the surface area between the drop and the plane is πr^2. Gravity, on the other hand, operates on the entire volume of the drop, which is proportional to r^3. Thus the force of gravity can be described by $c \times r^3$, for some unknown constant c, and the force of surface tension is similarly described by $d \times r^2$, making use of some unknown constant d.

The observed phenomenon is that small drops will remain on the surface. This is the situation when the force of the surface tension is greater than that of gravity. As drops get larger, their radius increases. Eventually, no matter what the constants may be, a cubic (r^3) function will always become larger than a quadratic (r^2) function. Thus we would predict that

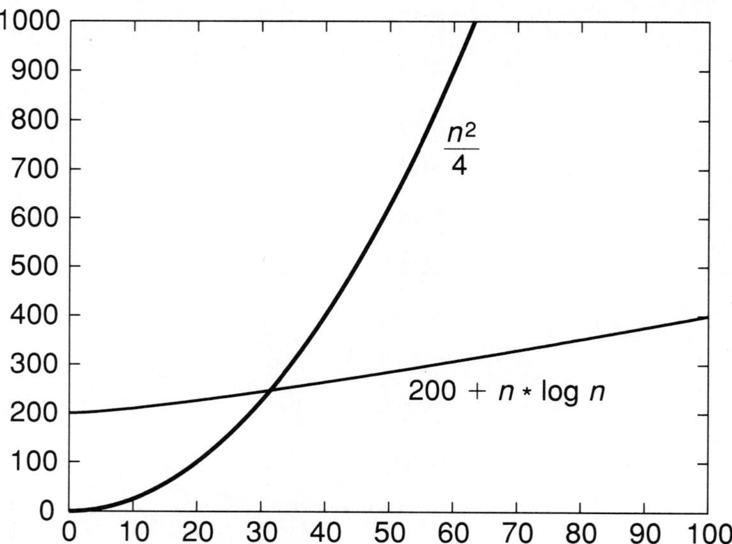

Figure 3.3 Comparing $n \log n$ and n^2 growth

large drops must always fall off the surface, as gravity prevails over surface tension. This, of course, matches what we observe to occur.

The idea that we can predict the long-term behavior of functions without specific knowledge of the exact constants used in describing the function allows us to ignore, within reason, constant factors in an analysis of execution time. Instead, we merely state the function that in the long run dominates the expression. The notation used to describe this is called *big-oh notation.* If we state that the running time of our integer printing algorithm is $O(n \log n)$, what we mean is that there exists some constant c such that the running time of the algorithm is always less than $c\, n \log n$. Of course, it follows from this definition that an algorithm with a running time of $O(n \log n)$ can also be said to have a running time of $O(n^2)$, or even $O(n^3)$, since these other functions are all asymptotically greater than $O(n \log n)$ (see Fig. 3.2). In order to make meaningful comparisons, we will always use the smallest big-oh expression we can.

Many of the algorithms we will examine later in this text are said to be *sublinear,* which means that their running time is asymptotically faster than $O(n)$. We could not graph these on the same axis as Fig. 3.2, since for these functions sublinear values would not be noticeable even at the far end of the graph. Since sublinear functions grow so much more slowly, this implies that an algorithm that runs in sublinear time is enormously faster than one that runs in time proportional to any of the functions

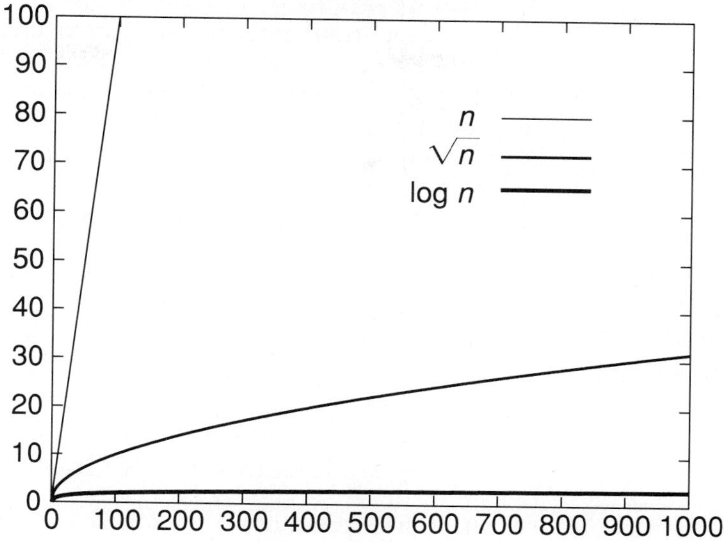

Figure 3.4 Sublinear asymptotic behavior

shown in Fig. 3.2. The graph shown in Fig. 3.4 illustrates the values of several typical sublinear functions. Notice we have changed the limits on the x and y axis from the earlier graphs. The linear function $y = n$, which is given in both figures, appears in Fig. 3.2 to be an exceedingly slow-growing function. In contrast, in Fig. 3.4 it appears to grow very rapidly in comparison to the functions $y = \sqrt{n}$ and $y = \log n$.

Another way to visualize the importance of the dominating function in execution time is to consider some values for various functions on large values of n. Assume, for example, that we can perform one operation every microsecond (that is, 10^6 operations per second). Table 3.1 illustrates how long it would take to perform a task, assuming various different running times. The multiplication of the dominant function by a constant will, of course, change the running time. This is insignificant when compared to an algorithm with a more expensive asymptotic running time. For example, an algorithm that runs in $8n$ steps will require 0.8 seconds to execute. If we are comparing this to an algorithm that runs in $n\sqrt{n}$ time, the 0.8 seconds are still far better than the 31.6 seconds for the second algorithm. Similarly, this chart illustrates why we can ignore additive terms other than the dominant function. If we have an algorithm that runs in $n^2 + n \log n$ time, then the $n \log n$ factor will add an insignificant 1.2 seconds to the 2.8 hours of execution time we would estimate by considering only the quadratic term.

Since we usually ignore everything but the dominating function in analyzing execution time, we also often use very general terms when describing execution behavior. An algorithm is said to be *logarithmic* if it is $O(\log n)$. A *polynomial* algorithm is one with a polynomial order execution behavior. Varieties of such algorithms include *linear* $O(n)$, *quadratic* $O(n^2)$, and *cubic* $O(n^3)$. An *exponential* $O(2^n)$ algorithm is an algorithm with an exponential function as a dominating factor. As Table 3.1 indicates, exponential algorithms are seldom realistic for any but the smallest input values.

Comparisons of the asymptotic running times of two algorithms must always be understood as statements about long-term behavior, not binding for small inputs. It is possible for a function with running time $O(\log n)$ to

Asymptotic Execution — A Grain of Salt

It is important to understand the significance of the limitations of asymptotic running times. Sometimes such figures need to be taken with a grain of salt. The following are a few situations in which the asymptotic running time may not be the most important factor in selecting an algorithm:

1. If the program is to be executed only a few times and then discarded, the cost of writing and debugging will likely dominate the cost of executing. Simple algorithms that can be easily validated are preferable in this situation to complex, but potentially more efficient, algorithms.
2. If the inputs are always small, then the asymptotic behavior is not a good predictor for execution time. For example, theoreticians know of an integer multiplication algorithm that is asymptotically faster than the more conventional algorithm, yet it is never used in practice since the leading constants are so large that the improvement in execution behavior would not be significant for any realistically sized values. In choosing between the two algorithms shown in Fig. 3.3, the quadratic algorithm might be preferable if the value n was never larger than 20.
3. A complicated algorithm may be undesirable if it cannot be easily explained or documented. Software is almost always eventually examined and modified by individuals other than the original author. It is important that the working of a software system be easily understood from a simple examination of the code.
4. Faster algorithms often achieve their speedup at the expense of using additional memory. This is sometimes called a *time/space tradeoff*. If the memory requirements are prohibitive, then no matter how fast the algorithm promises to execute, it cannot be used.
5. The asymptotic analysis may fail to consider factors that will eventually dominate execution time. An example factor easily overlooked is excessive memory usage, causing extensive and repeated swapping of a program from main memory to disk.
6. Finally, in many numerical algorithms issues such as accuracy and stability under perturbation may be just as important as asymptotic efficiency. Nobody really cares how fast you can compute the wrong answer.

Table 3.1

Function	Running Time
$\log n$	1.2×10^{-5} seconds
$\sqrt{n}$	3.2×10^{-4} seconds
n	0.1 seconds
$n \log n$	1.2 seconds
$n\sqrt{n}$	31.6 seconds
n^2	2.8 hours
n^3	31.7 years
2^n	More than a century

be slower than an $O(n^2)$ algorithm for very small values of n. If n is never expected to be very large—for example, if n is the number of digits in an integer—then more careful analysis may be required, as might happen if we had to choose between two algorithms (see again Fig. 3.3). If n is expected to be smaller than 30, then the algorithm with asymptotically worse performance may in practice be faster.

Similarly, asymptotic analysis will tell us nothing about how to choose between two different algorithms with the same running time, say between two $O(n^2)$ algorithms. For these reasons we will often also use actual running times of algorithms as a means of comparison. However, asymptotic analysis has proven to be a very good general guideline in comparing algorithms. In general, if we have an $O(n^2)$ algorithm and an $O(n \log n)$ algorithm, then we expect that, for sufficiently large n, the latter will perform significantly faster than the former.

3.3 INTEGER EXPONENTS

The next algorithm we will consider involves raising a double-precision floating point value to a positive integer exponent. Consider the function shown in Fig. 3.5. The program takes as input a double precision base and an unsigned integer exponent, and it computes the base raised to the exponent power. Note that the algorithm makes the assumption that the result will not overflow the maximum value that can be held in a double precision value. Since the only way to check for overflow is to compute the answer, this assumption cannot be validated prior to execution, and thus it is merely stated as an assumption in a comment and not tested by using the `assert` facility.[2]

Because the proof that the result produced by this algorithm is correct for all legal input values is relatively simple, we will use this algorithm to introduce the concept of a program *invariant*. An invariant is simply a statement that makes an assertion concerning what must be true when execution reaches a point in the program during the course of execution. Because invariants need not be computable expressions, it is not always possible to use the `assert` mechanism to test an invariant condition. For this reason, we will write invariants simply as comments. An argument

2. Some computers possess the ability to detect arithmetic overflow conditions when they occur. Such ability is not required by the C++ language, and thus we ignore this possibility here.

Logarithms

The definition of the logarithm function is tied to the concept of exponentials. Specifically, if x is the logarithm base b of a positive number n (written $x = \log_b n$), then b^x must be n.

In mathematics logarithms usually use as a base the value 10 or the value e, an irrational number approximately 2.72. In computer science it is more convenient to use logarithms with the base value 2. Hereafter, when we use the log function, we will mean the logarithm function with the base 2, unless specified otherwise.

One of the more important uses of the log function is to give a description of the size, or magnitude, of a positive value. To see this, consider the chart opposite, which shows powers of two in both binary and decimal form.

Now consider an arbitrary positive value, such as 14. The binary representation of 14 is 1110. Since 14 is between 8 and 16, we know the logarithm of 14 must be between 3 and 4. More importantly, since 14 is smaller than 16 (which in binary is a 1 followed by four zeros), we know the binary representation of 14 requires four or fewer digits. This observation can be generalized. For a positive value n, the number of digits in the binary representation of n is no larger than the ceiling of the logarithm of n.

This observation permits us to see how it is possible to construct a loop that executes a logarithmic number of steps. If we start a loop with a positive value n and iterate by repeatedly dividing by two (or, alternatively, by shifting right by one), then at each step the loop value is losing one binary digit of significance. If we begin such a loop with the value 14, the steps will be 14, 7, 3, 1, and 0. (You should write these values in binary and note the pattern.) The loop value will remain nonzero for at most a logarithmic number of steps.

n (decimal)	n (binary)	$\log n$
1	1	0
2	10	1
4	100	2
8	1000	3
16	10000	4
32	100000	5
64	1000000	6
128	10000000	7
256	100000000	8

```
//
// power - raise a double to a positive integer exponent
//    assumes result does not overflow

double power(double base, unsigned int exponent)
{   double result;

    result = 1.0;
    // inv: result holds base raised to 0
    for (int i = 0; i < exponent; i++ ) {
        // inv: result holds base raised to i
        result = result * base;
        // inv: result holds base raised to (i+1)
        }
    // inv: result holds base raised to exponent
    return result;
}
```

Figure 3.5 Integer exponentiation, first version

that the program is correct then proceeds by joining together the invariants, which together then constitute the proof of correctness.

Invariants can often be discovered by asking "what" questions. That first question is "what is this procedure intended to do?" The answer to the question should then be the invariant that appears immediately before the end of the procedure. For each statement, the programmer should ask the question "what does this statement do?" For example, the `for` loop computes the result by using repeated multiplication. Thus, after one execution of the loop, we will have computed $base^1$, after two executions we will have computed $base^2$, and so on. To argue the general case, we need to express this in terms of the variable `i` that controls the loop. Prior to starting the loop, we have computed $base^0$ and placed this value into the variable named `result`. Each iteration through the loop changes the value of the variable `result` by multiplying it by `base`. The consequence is that, at the point the value of the variable `i` is being tested (following the loop increment), the value held in the variable `result` is the quantity $base^{\mathtt{i}}$. The loop will terminate when the value of the variable `i` is equal to the `exponent`, and thus the variable `result` holds the correct value.

In subsequent algorithms in this book we will frequently provide invariants for procedures involving loops but will usually omit arguments for correctness, or leave such arguments to be developed as exercises.

We go on to consider the running-time efficiency. The most significant time used in executing this algorithm will be spent performing multiplications or divisions. Thus we will count as our "step" in measuring time the cost of a single multiplication. The time spent in execution of a loop

```
//
// power - raise a double to an integer exponent
//     assumes result does not overflow

double power(double base, unsigned int exponent)
{
    if (exponent == 0)
        return 1.0;
    else if (even(exponent))
        return power(base * base, exponent / 2);
    else
        return power(base * base, exponent / 2) * base;
}
```

Figure 3.6 Integer exponentiation, second version

is, of course, the product of the number of iterations of the loop and the time spent performing each iteration. Thus it is not difficult to see that if `exponent` is positive we will perform `exponent` multiplications. If we let n represent the exponent, then we can say that this is an $O(n)$ algorithm.

It is not difficult to discover a more efficient algorithm. Consider the following two observations:

$$x^{2n} = (x^2)^n$$
$$x^{2n+1} = (x^2)^n x$$

We can use these observations as a basis for a new algorithm, as shown in Fig. 3.6. Here there is one special case, namely the exponent zero. For positive nonzero values, the base is squared while the exponent is halved prior to a recursive call. To compute x^{53}, for example, the following sequence of multiplications takes place: $x^{53} = x * (x^2)^{26}$, $x^{26} = (x^2)^{13}$, $x^{13} = x * (x^2)^6$, $x^6 = (x^2)^3$, $x^3 = x * (x^2)^1$, $x^1 = x * (x^2)^0$. Since at each recursive step of the algorithm the exponent is halved, and since at most two multiplications are performed at each step, the number of multiplications is at most $2 \log n$, where n represents the magnitude of the exponent (see "Logarithms," page 74).

To illustrate the difference in the rates of growth in the running time between the $O(n)$ algorithm in Fig. 3.5 and the $O(\log n)$ algorithm in Fig. 3.6, we can compute the value 5^n for various values of n. Table 3.2 describes the number of multiplications involved as well as the actual running times in seconds on a certain machine to perform 1000 executions of the algorithm.

The algorithm in Fig. 3.6 works fine for integer exponents but not for floating point exponents, although we usually think of the exponential function as being defined for both integers and floating point values. Just as the symbol + is used for both integer and floating point addition, C++

Table 3.2 Comparison of running times for exponent algorithms

n	Execution Time Algorithm 2.8	Execution Time Algorithm 2.9	Multiplications Algorithm 2.9	Execution Time Algorithm 2.10
10	3.2	3.2	6	6.0
20	5.8	3.8	7	6.0
30	8.5	4.0	9	6.0
40	11.1	4.5	8	6.0
50	13.7	4.6	9	6.0
60	16.4	4.6	10	6.0
70	19.0	5.2	10	6.0
80	21.6	5.1	9	6.0
90	24.2	5.3	11	6.0

allows the programmer to provide multiple meanings for the same function name, as long as the arguments are different. This process is called *overloading* the function name, and such functions are said to be *overloaded*. Consider, for example, the exponential function shown below. This function uses the `exp` and `log` functions of the standard math library in order to compute noninteger powers, using the fact that $\log a^b$ is $b \log a$.

Of course, floating point operations are not as efficient as integer operations. For comparison, we also provide the running time of this algorithm in Table 3.2.

```
// power - floating exponentiation.
//     assumes overflow and underflow do not occur

double power(double base, double exponent)
{   // log function only works for positive values
    assert((base > 0) && (exponent >= 0));
    return exp(exponent * log(base));
}
```

3.4 GREATEST COMMON DIVISOR*

The last algorithm we will investigate in this chapter is in some ways the first. Donald Knuth, the computer scientist who originated the term

*Section headings followed by an asterisk indicate optional material.

"analysis of algorithms" and who has done a great deal of research into the history of algorithms, has claimed that the sequence of operations presented in the third century BC by the Greek mathematician Euclid in Propositions 1 and 2 of Book 7 of the *Elements* is the earliest known nontrivial completely specified mathematical algorithm. The algorithm is intended to discover, given two positive integer values n and m, the largest positive integer that evenly divides both values.

Rather than simply presenting the algorithm as a finished accomplishment, let us investigate the facts that might lead us to the discovery of the algorithm. Assume that we have two positive integer values: n and m and $n >= m$. The first fact we might observe is that any value can be divided into zero. Thus if $m = 0$, the greatest common divisor is n. Next we might note that if n is equal to m, then they divide each other and each must be the greatest common divisor. Finally, we might note that any divisor of both n and m must also divide $n + m$, but that would seem to be leading *away* from a solution (since the numbers are getting larger) rather than toward an answer. However, the opposite might be useful. In particular, let us consider $n - m$. If d is a divisor of both n and m, then $\frac{n}{d}$ must be an integer, as well as $\frac{m}{d}$. Therefore $\frac{n}{d} - \frac{m}{d}$ must be an integer as well, but this is the same as $\frac{n-m}{d}$. Thus d must be a divisor of $n - m$.

Conversely, if d is a divisor of m as well as a divisor of $n - m$, then d must also be a divisor of n. (If $\frac{m}{d}$ is integer and $\frac{n-m}{d}$ is integer, then $\frac{n}{d}$ must be integer.)

We can rewrite these observations as the following facts:

$$\begin{aligned}
gcd(n, 0) &= n \\
gcd(0, m) &= m \\
gcd(n, m) &= n, \qquad \text{if } n = m \\
gcd(n, m) &= gcd(n - m, m), \qquad \text{where } n >= m \\
gcd(n, m) &= gcd(n, m - n), \qquad \text{where } m >= n
\end{aligned}$$

These lead directly to the algorithm shown in Fig. 3.7. For example, if we were to use this algorithm to calculate the greatest common divisor of 40902 and 24140, the intermediate values would be 40902 − 24140 = 16762, 24140 − 16762 = 7378, 16762 − 7378 = 2006, and so on, until eventually we discover that the GCD of 40902 and 24140 is 34.

It can be easily seen that the sum of $n + m$ is constantly decreasing each iteration of the loop, and thus termination of the algorithm is ensured. (Note that this would not be the case if we had not already checked to make sure the values of n and m were nonzero before entering the loop and were not equal on each iteration of the loop.) If one of the inputs is very large and one very small but relatively prime, then the values will change very slowly. For example, if n is 199 and m is 2, then n will cycle through all the odd numbers before we discover that the gcd is 1. On the other hand, we can do no worse than this, and so the algorithm is $O(n + m)$. (We

```
unsigned int gcd(unsigned int n, unsigned int m)
{   // compute the greatest common divisor of two positive integer values
    if (n == 0)
        return m;
    if (m == 0)
        return n;

    while (m != n) {
        if (n > m)
            n = n - m;
        else
            m = m - n;
        }
    return n;
}
```

Figure 3.7 Euclid's greatest common divisor algorithm

can, in fact, improve this performance to logarithmic time. The technique to do this is explored in the exercises.)

What remains, then, is to show the validity of the algorithm by presenting a proof of correctness.

3.4.1 Loop Invariants

Although we have already argued informally for the correctness of the GCD algorithm presented in Fig. 3.7, we will repeat a more complete argument here and use the opportunity to present an analysis technique that is invaluable when arguing about programs containing loops. The technique

Loop Invariants and Mathematical Induction

To turn a proof based on invariants inside a loop into a proof using mathematical induction, we simply let the *number of times execution has passed through the loop* be the induction value. If the loop is executed zero times, then n must be initially equal to m and hence both n and m are equal to the GCD. This is our base case.

For our induction step, we assume that execution has taken us through the loop N times, and that when we reach the loop condition it still remains true, and thus we cycle once again $N+1$ times. But we know that each time we modify n or m, then we have not changed the value of the GCD. Hence by the end of the loop on the $N+1$ time we will not have changed the value of the GCD for n and m, even though the values n and m will themselves have changed. Thus no matter how many times the loop is executed, it must be true that the invariants we have specified are valid when execution reaches the associated location in the program.

```
unsigned int gcd(unsigned int n, unsigned int m)
{   // compute the greatest common divisor of two positive integer values

    if (n == 0)
        // if n is zero, then the gcd must be m
        return m;
    if (m == 0)
        // if m is zero, then the gcd must be n
        return n;
    while (m != n) {
        if (n > m)
            n = n - m;
            // after changing n, the gcd has not changed
        else
            m = m - n;
            // after changing m, the gcd has not changed
        }

    // m is equal to n, and hence the gcd must be n
    return n;
}
```

Figure 3.8 The GCD algorithm augmented with invariants

is often known as the development of *loop invariants*. The loop invariant technique is simply a special application of mathematical induction, but often it is easier to phrase a proof in terms of loop invariants than it is to develop the more general induction proof.

As we have noted already, an *invariant* is simply an assertion that we expect to hold true when execution reaches a particular point in a program. The input assertions discussed previously are examples of invariants, since they describe properties of the input values that are expected to be true prior to execution. Unlike an input assertion, an invariant need not be something that the computer can check. For example, we might phrase an invariant in terms of the output values, rather than the input values. Similarly, we will often introduce quantities that occur only in the invariants. The purpose of the invariant is simply to provide fixed points in a program from which we can build a proof of correctness. In Fig. 3.8 we have annotated our version of the GCD algorithm with invariants.

Even though we do not know the value of the GCD, our approach will be to argue that as *n* and *m* change, the GCD of the *current* values of `n` and `m` is the same as the GCD of the *original* values of `n` and `m`. This follows directly from the observations we made earlier.

3.5 CHAPTER SUMMARY

Key Concepts

- Properties of algorithms (input specification, definiteness, correctness, termination, result)
- Proof of termination
- Proof of correctness
- Mathematical induction
- Analysis of execution time
- Asymptotic analysis
- Big-oh notation
- Invariants

An algorithm is a set of instructions used to solve a specific problem. To be useful, an algorithm must possess certain properties:

- ▲ It must accurately describe the input values.
- ▲ It must be completely specified at each step.
- ▲ It must be correct.
- ▲ It must be guaranteed to terminate on all input values.
- ▲ The result, or effect of the algorithm must be completely characterized.

An argument that an algorithm must terminate for all input values can be provided by finding an integer quantity that is non-negative, and that decreases steadily as the algorithm executes.

An invariant is a statement that describes the state of computation when execution reaches a particular point in a program. Invariants can be used to structure arguments as to the correctness of an algorithm.

When the execution time of an algorithm is not constant for all input values, then mathematical induction may be necessary to prove correctness or termination.

On a coarse level, algorithms can be compared by their asymptotic growth. The asymptotic growth characterization of an algorithm is often given by a "big-oh" expression. This expression characterizes the behavior of the algorithm as input values grow ever larger.

References

The study of algorithms, as well as the term "analysis of algorithms," was popularized by Donald Knuth in his three-part series [Knuth 73, Knuth 81, Knuth 75]. The characteristics of algorithms described at the beginning of this chapter are adapted from volume 1. A discussion of Euclid's GCD algorithm appears both in volumes 1 and 2.

Since the 1970s the study of algorithms has emerged as an important subdiscipline within computer science. More recent descriptions of the field can be found in the works by Sedgewick [Sedgewick 92], Cormen et al. [Cormen 90], or Harel [Harel 92].

When discussing the property of definiteness with regard to algorithms, we asserted rather casually that once we have presented an algorithm in C++ each step will have been adequately defined, since the C++ language has been formally defined. In fact, the definition of C++ is exceedingly complex, and language-lawyers can still find ample opportunities to disagree on various issues. The most readily available more-or-less complete description of C++ is contained in the book by Margaret Ellis and Bjarne Stroustrup [Ellis 90].

The technique of using loop invariants is usually associated with the idea of "proving programs correct." Program proofs treat computer programs as mathematical objects and try to prove mechanically the validity of these objects. Such proofs tend to be more complex than the proofs we develop. A good introduction to program proving can be found in the book by David Gries [Gries 81]. Another prominent advocate of program proving is Edsger Dijkstra [Dijkstra 76].

The "grains of salt" given on page 72 are adapted from the book by Aho, Hopcroft and Ullman [Aho 83].

I acquired the lemon soufflé recipe from a Belgian graduate student when I participated in an international dining club during the time of my dissertation studies at Yale University. Some would argue that no soufflé algorithm that uses gelatin can be considered correct, but the results are generally satisfactory.

Exercises

1. Examine a recipe from your favorite cookbook. Evaluate the recipe with respect to each of the properties described at the beginning of this chapter.

2. Use mathematical induction to prove that a common multiplier can be factored out of a summation. That is, for any constant c and non-negative integer n:

$$\sum_{i=1}^{n} c \times f(i) = c \times \sum_{i=1}^{n} f(i)$$

3. Prove, by mathematical induction, that the sum of powers of 2 is one less than the next higher power. That is, for any non-negative integer n:

$$\sum_{i=0}^{n} 2^i = 2^{n+1} - 1$$

4. What is wrong with the following induction proof that for all positive numbers a and integers n, it must be true that a^{n-1} is 1. For the base case we have that for $n = 1$, a^{n-1} is a^0 which is 1. For the induction case let us assume it is true for 1, 2, 3, . . . n. To verify the condition for $n + 1$, we have

$$a^{(n+1)-1} = a^n = \frac{a^{n-1} \times a^{n-1}}{a^{n-2}} = \frac{1 \times 1}{1} = 1$$

So the conjecture must hold for $n + 1$ as well.

5. Prove that the following formula describes the Fibonacci numbers:

$$\text{Fib}_n = \frac{1}{\sqrt{5}}\left[\left(\frac{1+\sqrt{5}}{2}\right)^n - \left(\frac{1-\sqrt{5}}{2}\right)^n\right]$$

a. Verify that the formula works for the values 0, 1, and 2.

b. Show that $(\frac{1+\sqrt{5}}{2})^2$ is the same as $1 + \frac{1+\sqrt{5}}{2}$, and similarly that $(\frac{1-\sqrt{5}}{2})^2$ is the same as $1 + \frac{1-\sqrt{5}}{2}$.

c. By substituting the formula, verify that $\text{Fib}_{n+1} = \text{Fib}_{n-1} + \text{Fib}_n$. (*Hint*: Rewrite $(\frac{1+\sqrt{5}}{2})^{n+1}$ as $(\frac{1+\sqrt{5}}{2})^{n-1} \times (\frac{1+\sqrt{5}}{2})^2$, then use the property you verified in the previous step.)

6. Show that each of the three properties identified in Section 3.2.1 is necessary to assure termination of an algorithm. Do this by exhibiting three algorithms that each satisfy two of the three properties but nevertheless do not terminate.

7. Critique the following argument that purports to show that all horses gathered in a single corral are the same color. Suppose there is one horse in a corral. Thus we have a base case, since for N equal to one (this one horse) all horses in the corral are the same color. Let us assume this color is black. Now let us consider the induction step by adding a new horse, of unknown color, to the corral. The corral still contains the black horse, so let us remove it. We now have a corral containing N horses and by our induction assumption they must all be black. But the horse we removed is also black, therefore when we return it to corral we will have $N+1$ black horses. We can continue in a similar manner adding horses one by one, and thus no matter how many horses we add to the corral they must all be black.

8. Suppose by careful measurement we have discovered a function that describes the precise running time of some algorithm. For each of the following such functions, describe the asymptotic running time in big-oh notation.

a. $3n^2 + 3n + 7$

b. $(5 * n) * (3 + \log n)$

c. $\frac{5n+4}{6n}$

d. $1 + 2 + 3 + 4 + ... + n$

e. $n + \log n^2$

f. $\frac{(n+1)\log n}{2n}$

9. For each of the following program skeletons, describe the asymptotic execution time as a function of n. You can assume the remaining portions of the loops require only constant execution time.

a.
```
for (int i = 0; i < n; i++) {
      ...
      }
for (int j = n; j >= 0; j--) {
      ...
      }
```

b.
```
for (int i = 0; i < n; i++) {
      for (int j = 0; j < n; j++) {
            ...
            }
      }
```

c.
```
for (int i = 0; i < n; i++) {
      for (int j = 0; j < i; j++) {
            ...
            }
      }
```

d.
```
for (int i = n; i > 0; i = i / 2) {
      ...
      }
```

e.
```
for (int i = 0; i < n; i++) {
      for (int j = 0; j * j < n; j++) {
            ...
            }
      }
```

f.
```
for (int i = n; i > 0; i = i >> 1) {
      for (int j = 0; j < n; j++) {
            ...
            }
      }
```

10. Prove the correctness of the algorithm presented in Fig. 3.5, assuming that numeric overflow does not occur.

11. Prove the correctness of the algorithm presented in Fig. 3.6, assuming that numeric overflow does not occur. (*Hint*: Give base cases for several small values, such as 0, 1, and 2, then divide the induction step into two cases, depending upon whether the value n is even or odd.)

12. Complete the loop invariants for the following procedure that sums the values of an array. Using your invariants, give an argument as to the correctness of the algorithm.

```
//
// sum the elements of a double array
//

double sumArray(double data[ ],
     unsigned int size)
{
     double sum = 0.0;
     // inv:
     for (int i = 0; i < size; i++) {
          // inv:
          sum += data[i];
          // inv:
          }
     // inv:
     return sum;
}
```

13. Complete the loop invariants for the following procedure that computes the factorial function for an unsigned integer argument. Using your invariants, give an argument as to the correctness of the algorithm.

```
//
// compute the factorial of an integer value
//

double factorial(unsigned int val)
{
     double result = 1.0;
     // inv:
     for (int i = 1; i <= val;  i++) {
          // inv:
```

```
            result *= i;
            // inv:
            }
        // inv:
        return result;
    }
```

14. Appendix C tabulates values for various functions. Using these values, answer the following questions.
    a. Suppose we have a program that implements a particular algorithm. By careful measurement, we have discovered that for inputs of size n the program will take $5n^2$ seconds to execute. We have a second program that uses a different algorithm to perform the same task. This algorithm requires $1000 \log n$ seconds for inputs of size n. Approximately how large must n be before the second algorithm is faster?
    b. Suppose the second algorithm requires $10,000 \log n$ seconds for inputs of size n. How large must n be before the algorithm is faster.
    c. Answer the same question, assuming the second algorithm requires $100,000 \log n$ seconds on values of size n.
    d. Consider another pair of algorithms for a different task, the first requiring $5n^2$ seconds on inputs of size n and the second $300n \log n$ seconds. At approximately what value of n will the second algorithm start to be faster?
    e. A third pair of algorithms requires $\log n$ steps and $\sqrt{n}$ steps. Will the first algorithm always be faster? Under what conditions will the second algorithm be preferable?

15. In Chapter 6 we will encounter an algorithm named `bubblesort`. It is claimed that bubblesort is an $O(n^2)$ algorithm. Appendix B gives actual timings for the bubblesort algorithm for various input values. One way to test the hypothesis that this algorithm is indeed $O(n^2)$ is to try to compute the coefficient in front of the leading term. That is, the hypothesis is that:

$$time = c\ n^2$$

for some value of c. We can approximate c by computing the quantity $time/n^2$ for each of the data points, where n is the size of the vector input. Because its values are so small, it is convenient to scale the values and actually compute $(time \times 1000)/n^2$. Compute this quantity for each of the values in the column labeled `bubble` in the first table in Appendix B. The table of functions supplied in Appendix C may be useful. Do the results seem to indicate that `bubblesort` is indeed an $O(n^2)$ algorithm?

16. Perform the same analysis as described in the previous question for the column labeled `selection`. Does the result indicate that selection sort is an $O(n^2)$ algorithm?

17. Perform the same analysis as described in the previous question for the column labeled `insertion`. Does the result indicate that insertion sort is an $O(n^2)$ algorithm?

18. Perform the same analysis as described in the previous question for the column labeled `list`. Does the result indicate that list insertion sort is an $O(n^2)$ algorithm?

19. Perform the same analysis as described in the previous question for the column labeled `tree`. Does the result indicate that tree sort is an $O(n^2)$ algorithm? Try using $(n \times \log n)$ in the denominator. Is it more likely that tree sort is an $O(n \log n)$ algorithm?

20. Using the techniques described in the previous questions, determine whether heap sort (described in the column labeled `heap`) is more likely an $O(n^2)$ algorithm or an $O(n \log n)$ algorithm.

21. Explain what problems will occur if the recursive calls in the algorithm in Fig. 3.6 replace the expression `base * base` with `power(base, 2)`.

22. Explain why you would not want to rewrite the recursive calls in the algorithms shown in Fig. 3.6 as

```
power(base, exponent / 2) * power(base, exponent
/ 2)
```

23. Finish tracing the intermediate values that demonstrate the greatest common divisor of 40902 and 24140 is 34.

24. Give an argument that explains how the inner loop of the GCD algorithm will still remain correct if it is changed to the following:

```
while (n != m) {
    if (n > m)
        n = n %  m;
    else
        m = m % n;
    }
```

25. Show that for any integer constants n and m, if $n > m$, then $n \% m < \frac{n}{2}$. (*Hint*: Divide the proof

into two cases corresponding to $m < \frac{n}{2}$ and $m >= \frac{n}{2}$.)

26. Explain how the result you produced in the last question can be used to show that the revised GCD algorithm given above produces a result in $O(\log n)$ steps. (*Hint*: Consider the sum $n + m$ and show that after *two* iterations of the loop this value can be no larger than half its original value. This then shows that the number of iterations of the loop is at most $2 \log n$.)

27. Write a recursive version of the GCD algorithm. Give a proof, using mathematical induction, showing the correctness of your algorithm.

PART II

ANALYSIS, ALGORITHMS, AND ABSTRACTIONS

CHAPTER 4

Strings — An Example ADT

NEXT TO NUMBERS, individual characters and strings of characters are perhaps the most common data values used in programming. Almost any application that must send or receive textual information to or from a user will use character values. Yet the C++ language does not provide a string type as a primitive, building instead rudimentary strings out of pointers and arrays of characters. For this reason, a string class is a logical candidate for development as an abstract data type.

In this chapter we will investigate a string data type, using the creation of this abstraction to again illustrate the techniques used in the implementation of a new data type, and as a vehicle to introduce a number of features of the C++ language.

4.1 PRIMITIVE STRINGS

In C++ a character is simply treated as a type of integer value. Integer operations are used to manipulate character quantities. We have seen this already in the function `digitCharacter` (Fig. 2.4, page 49), used to convert an integer value into a character equivalent. Relational tests are also useful with character values. The following procedure, for example, returns true if a character argument represents an uppercase (capital) letter:

```
int isUpperCase(char c)
{   // return true if c is an uppercase letter
    return (c >= 'A') && (c <= 'Z');
}
```

Even more unusual is the following expression, used to convert an upper case letter into lower case.

```
c = (c - 'A') + 'a';
```

In the basic C++ language, the closest concept that corresponds to the intuitive idea of a character string is simply a pointer to a sequence of characters. String literals, sequences of characters surrounded by double-quote marks, are treated by the compiler as though they represent an array. The address of the array is then implicitly converted into a character pointer. Thus in a pair of statements such as the following:

```
char * p;
p = "hello world!";
```

it is a mistake to think that any movement of characters is being performed. Instead, the address of the unnamed array of characters that holds the text "`hello world!`" is being assigned to the pointer `p`. The value of the literal is the address in memory where the characters are maintained.

Pointers can be subscripted in C++ (see "Pointers on Pointers" on p. 91). The expression `p[0]` yields the character "`h`," and `p[6]` returns the character "`w`." A subscripted pointer is a legal target for an assignment. Consider the following statements:

```
p[0] = 'y';
p[5] = p[6];
p[6] = ' ';
p[8] = 'i';
p[10] = '\?';
```

The effect of this sequence of assignments will be to change the text array into "`yellow oil?!`." C++ provides no checks on the validity of subscripts applied to pointers. Thus it is possible (but rarely useful) to subscript a pointer with a negative value, or a value larger than the size of the array of characters being pointed to. In our case, doing so will yield unpredictable values.

By convention, strings are terminated by a null character—a character with value zero. Thus the unnamed string representing the text "`hello world!`" actually contains 13 characters, the last character being the null character indicating the end of a string.

Pointer values can be assigned to pointer variables. This can result in two pointers referring to the same data area. For example, the following sequence results in the modification of the value referred to as `q[2]`, which is the same value referred to by `p[2]`.

```
char * q;
q = p;
q[2] = 'x';
```

If a buffer to hold string values is desired, it is declared simply as an array of characters. Such a buffer can be initialized with a string constant, which must have a length smaller than the number of elements declared in the buffer, as in the following:

```
char hellobuffer[20] = "hello world!";
```

Although the declared size of the array is 20 characters (meaning it can hold a maximum of 19 characters and the null character), only the first 13 positions are initialized. The values of the remaining seven positions are undefined.

Since a primitive string is simply an array of characters, we can use

Pointers on Pointers

A pointer is simply a variable that maintains as value the address of another location in memory. Because memory addresses have a fixed limit, the amount of storage necessary to hold a pointer can be determined at compile time, even if the size or extent of the object to which it will point is not known.

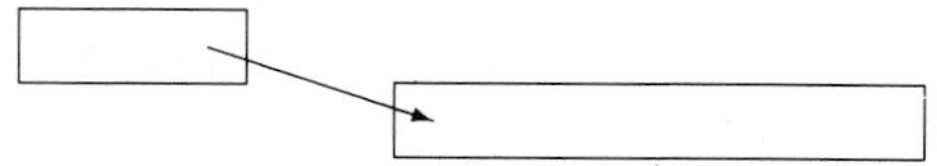

A *null* pointer has value zero and should not be considered to point to any valid object. A pointer with nonzero value is said to be non-null.

There are three principle mechanisms used to access the values pointed to by a pointer.

- ▲ A pointer variable can be subscripted. This is useful only if the pointer addresses an array of objects, as in the `string` data structure. The subscript index is used to determine the element accessed by the expression.
- ▲ A pointer can be explicitly *dereferenced* using the unary * operator. If p is a pointer to a value of some type, then *p is the value addressed by the pointer.
- ▲ A pointer to a structure, or class, can combine pointer dereferencing and member field extraction using the pointer operator. If p is a pointer to a value of a class type that contains a member field x, then p->x is the same as (*p).x.

A pointer should be distinguished from a *reference*, such as that generated using the pass-by-reference parameter passing mechanism. While internally they are implemented in much the same manner, they differ in three important ways:

- ▲ A reference can never be null; it must always refer to a legitimate object.
- ▲ Once established, a reference can never be changed so as to make it point to a different object.
- ▲ A reference does not require any explicit mechanism to dereference the memory address and access the actual data value.

The manipulation of pointers can be tricky and is one of the most common sources of programming errors. For this reason, we will encapsulate, for the most part, manipulation of pointer values within a class and use few explicit pointer values in our example programs.

array operations to manipulate the string. For example, the following simple procedure computes the number of non-null characters contained in a string value.

```
int CstringLength (const char * str)
{   // compute number of non-null characters in a C string
    int i = 0;
    while (str[i] != '\0')
        i++;
    return i;
}
```

4.2 THE STRING DATA ABSTRACTION

The description in the last section of the primitive string facilities provided by C++ indicates a number of ways in which a higher-level abstraction could make improvements:

- Better bounds checking on subscripting, string copies, and string catenation.
- Assignments that result in copies, not sharing data areas.
- Comparisons performed using relational operators, such as <= and ==.
- High-level operations such as substrings, pattern matching, and so on.

In this section we will outline the characteristics of our string data abstraction as viewed by a user. In the remaining sections of this chapter we will then describe in more detail how this functionality is implemented.

Instances of the data type `string` can be declared, and initialized either with a size for the string buffer or with an initial value.

```
string a;
string b("one two");
string c = "three four";
string d = 'x';
string e(27);
string f = c;
```

A string value can be assigned either a C++ character string constant or another string. The variable on the left of the assignment symbol is assigned a copy of the string represented by the expression on the right side. Subsequent changes to variables appearing in the right side will have no effect on the assigned variable.

```
b = "five six"; // destroys old value
d = c;
```

Subscripting can be used to access individual characters in a string. A subscripted expression can be used as the left side of an assignment, to change an individual character:

```
b[0] = 'h'; // b is now "hive six"
```

Subscript indices are checked for validity. Thus indexing values such as b[−1] or b[8] will produce an error.

Two string values can be compared using any of the six relational operators. A string is lexicographically equal to another string if all strings are the same length and all characters are equal. If they are unequal, the comparison of characters in the first location where a difference occurs indicates the relationship. This is similar to the order in which words are listed in a dictionary. For example, the following assertions are all valid:

```
string anne = "anne";
string allen = "allen";
string alfred = "alfred";
string annette = "annette";
string betty = "anne";

assert(anne == anne);
assert(alfred < allen);
assert(annette >= anne);
assert(anne == betty);
```

One string value can be concatenated onto the end of another using the assignment operation +=. For example,

```
betty += "sue";
```

results in the variable `betty` holding the value `annesue`. The binary operator + by itself is used to concatenate two strings yielding a new string, without modifying either argument.

Substrings of a string can be produced by noting the index of the first character and length, using the parentheses operator. Thus, `alfred(2,4)` yields the string "`fred`".

Substrings can also be used as a target for an assignment, in which case the substring is replaced by the string on the right side of the assignment operator, which can be of any length. For example,

```
allen(2,2) = "a";
```

results in the variable `allen` holding the value "`allan`." Notice that two characters in the original string have been replaced by a single character.

Finally, we will introduce a new data type that can be used to search a string for occurrences of another string.

4.2.1 Creation

There are several methods of initializing a new string. As with the rational class, each method invokes a corresponding *constructor* to perform this initialization. Figure 4.1 shows the class description of our string abstraction and illustrates these constructors.

Internally, our string abstraction maintains information using a pair of values. A character `buffer` maintains a primitive array of characters. As we saw in the last section, the physical length of this buffer may have little relation to the logical length of the string being maintained. An unsigned short integer maintains the physical length of the data area. Part of the task of string operations will be to ensure that access to the underlying buffer never exceeds the bounds of the physical data area.

The character buffer used in implementing the string abstraction is unlike data values we have seen up to this point. Most variables are associated with storage that is *automatic*. This means that space for the variable is allocated when the procedure containing the variable is entered, and it is freed when the enclosing procedure is finished. (We noted this in the discussion of the number printing algorithm in the last chapter, and will discuss this point again in more detail as one of our examples in Chapter 9.) Furthermore, automatic variables must have a fixed size; it is not legal to declare an array with a bound that depends upon a computation performed at run time.

In our string abstraction, on the other hand, the space required by a string changes as we perform operations. Appending one string to another, for example, may necessitate the creation of a larger buffer. Thus we need a mechanism for *dynamically* allocating space as statements are executed. In C++ this dynamic allocation is accomplished using the operator `new`. To illustrate, the constructor that provides an initial size for the string value is implemented as follows:

```
string::string(int size)
{   // create a new string with a buffer of the given size
    // make sure size is non-negative
    assert (size >= 0);

    // hold one addition char for null value
    bufferlength = 1 + size;

    // allocate buffer, check allocation was successful
    buffer = new char[bufferlength];
    assert(buffer != 0);

    // initialize to all null characters
    for (int i = 0; i < bufferlength; i++)
        buffer[i] = '\0';
}
```

```
class string {
public:
    // constructors
    string          ();
    string          (char);
    string          (int);
    string          (const char *);
    string          (const string &);

    // destructor
    ~string         ();

    // assignment and catenation
    void            operator =      (const string & right);
    void            operator +=     (const string & right);

    // substring access
    substring       operator()      (unsigned int start,
                                     unsigned int length);

    // input of an entire line of text
    istream &       getline         (istream &);

    // number of characters in the string
    unsigned int    length          () const;

    // access to a single character
    char &          operator [ ]    (unsigned int) const;

    // compare - used in relational operators
    int             compare         (const string &) const;

    // conversion to ordinary C string
    operator        const char *    () const;

private:
    // data fields - character buffer and length
    unsigned short int  bufferlength;
    char *              buffer;
};
```

Figure 4.1 Interface for the class `string`

The `new` operator is used to allocate the array of characters that will hold the actual values used in our string abstraction. This operator returns a null pointer if there is insufficient memory remaining to allocate the desired object. Thus we use `assert` to check that the allocation was successful. It is good defensive coding practice to always check in order to ensure that an allocation request was successful.

In a similar manner the constructor that takes a literal character pointer uses the function `CstringLength` we presented earlier to compute the length of the initial buffer, and then copies the values from the string into the buffer. Note that the argument is declared as `const`, indicating for the pointer references a value that will not be changed by the procedure.

```
string::string(const char * initialtext)
{   // create a new string and initialize with argument
value
    // length is length of text, plus null char
    bufferlength = 1 + CstringLength(initialtext);

    // allocate buffer
    buffer = new char[bufferlength];
    assert(buffer != 0);

    // copy values into place
    for (int i = 0; initialtext[i] != '\0'; i++)
        buffer[i] = initialtext[i];
    buffer[i] = '\0';
}
```

The copy constructor, the constructor that takes a string argument, is almost identical, accessing directly the buffer in the argument string. The C++ run-time system uses copy constructors to generate temporary values when class arguments are passed as value parameters. For this reason, a copy constructor should always be written for every user-defined class. The copy constructor for our `string` data type is as follows:

```
string::string(const string & initialstring)
{   // create a new string, initializing with copy of argument
    // length is length of text, plus null char
    bufferlength = 1 + CstringLength(initialstring.buffer);

    // allocate buffer
    buffer = new char[bufferlength];
    assert(buffer != 0);

    // copy values into place
    for (int i = 0; initialstring.buffer[i] != '\0'; i++)
```

```
        buffer[i] = initialstring.buffer[i];
    buffer[i] = '\0';
}
```

The constructor that takes as an argument a single character allocates a buffer of length 2, large enough to hold the character value and a null character.

```
string::string(char c)
{   // create a string with a single character
    bufferlength = 2;
    buffer = new char[bufferlength];
    assert(buffer != 0);

    // initialize with single character
    buffer[0] = c;
    buffer[1] = '\0';
}
```

This constructor is not only useful but necessary to avoid a subtle potential programming error. Without it, the declaration that initialized a string value with a character constant would not, as the programmer might reasonably expect, initialize the string to the value of the character. Instead, the value of the character would be implicitly converted into an integer value, and a string with an uninitialized buffer would be allocated using the constructor that takes an integer argument.

Finally, the *empty*, or *default*, constructor (the constructor with no arguments) allocates a buffer that contains only the null character.

```
string::string()
{   // create a string with no characters
    // length is one, holding just null character
    bufferlength = 1;

    // initialize buffer with null pointer
    buffer = new char[bufferlength];
    assert(buffer != 0);

    // initialize to null
    buffer[0] = '\0';
}
```

THE DELETE OPERATOR Since dynamically allocated memory is not freed automatically by the system, it must be freed by the user. Once freed, memory is "recycled" by the run-time system for use in subsequent allocations. Removal of memory is accomplished by using the operator `delete`. There are two forms of the delete operator. The form shown here is used when deleting an entire array. If only a single value is being deleted, the square brackets are omitted.[1]

To facilitate actions that must be performed when variables are released, such as dynamic memory management, C++ provides a feature called a *destructor*. A destructor is in a certain sense the opposite of a constructor. It is called implicitly by the system whenever a variable is about to be deleted, either automatically when the procedure containing the variable declaration is being exited, or as a result of an explicit operation by the programmer. A destructor is written as the class name preceded by a tilde. A destructor for our string abstraction could be defined as follows:

```
string::~string()
{   // called implicitly when a string is about to be deleted
    // free the memory associated with the buffer
    delete [ ] buffer;
    // set the pointer variable to null
    buffer = 0;
}
```

An example will help illustrate the relationship between destructors and the delete operator. Imagine a simple procedure containing a string as a local variable, such as the following:

```
void readInformation ()
{    int i;
     string prompt = "name:";
     double size;
     ...
}
```

When the procedure is invoked, space will automatically be created for local variables in an area called the *activation record stack*. The activation record stack grows and shrinks as procedures are entered and as they exit.

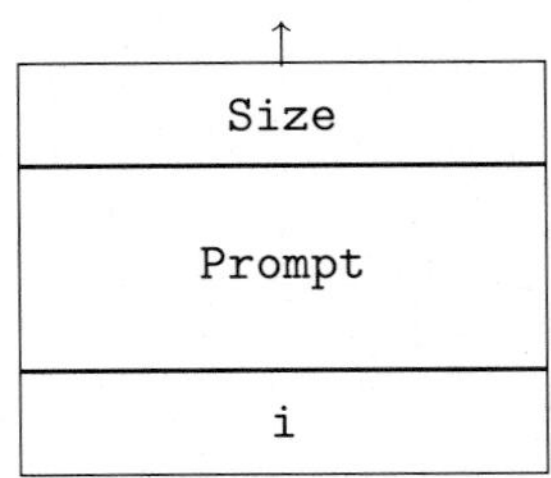

1. An earlier version of C++ required that the size of the array being deleted be provided between the square brackets. Some compilers still insist on this information.

For the string variable, the stack contains only the space declared in the class description itself. This consists of two fields, the size field and a pointer field. During execution of the constructor for the string, memory for the character values associated with the string will be dynamically allocated. This dynamic memory occupies a different portion of computer memory, and is independent of the stack.

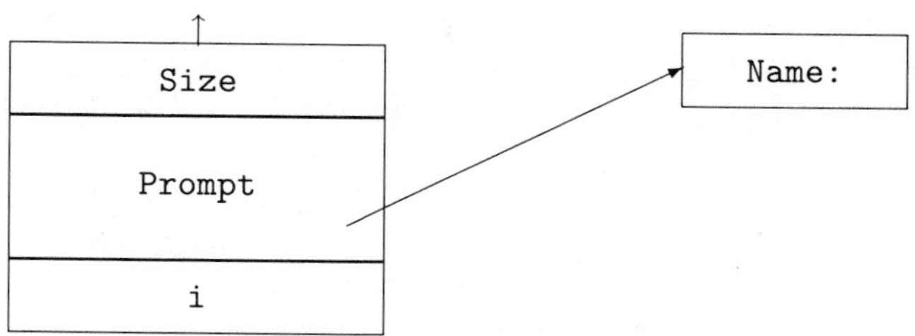

When the procedure exits, space for local variables will automatically be recovered. This space includes only the size field and the pointer field. Further action is required in order to also delete the dynamically allocated storage for the character buffer. This is provided by the destructor for the class `string`. Immediately before the space for the string `prompt` is deleted, the string destructor is invoked. The string destructor deletes the dynamically allocated character buffer, thus freeing this space for reuse by subsequent allocations.

Destructors are almost never directly invoked by the user; instead they are implicitly called by the run-time system. Note that this destructor is invoked when the `string` is to be deleted. Dynamic memory is freed only by using the `delete` operator. Without the destructor, the dynamic memory allocated to the buffer would still be considered "in use" by the run-time system. Repeated operations on strings would then eventually result in an assertion failure when memory becomes exhausted.

4.2.2 Implementing Behavior with Member Functions

Recall that functionality is defined for an ADT through the mechanism of a member function. We will describe the implementation of the various member functions associated with our string abstraction.

LENGTH OF STRING The first member function we define for our string abstraction simply returns the number of non-null characters held in the string. To accomplish this, it invokes the `CstringLength` function on the underlying buffer. Because this operation does not change the string itself, the function is declared as constant.

```
unsigned int string::length() const
{   // compute the number of nonnull characters in a string
    return CstringLength(buffer);
}
```

ASSIGNMENT Recall that assignment is an operator that is defined as if it were a member function. An implementation of this function needs to check to see if the value being assigned fits in the current buffer. If not, the old buffer must be deleted and a new, larger buffer must be allocated. Once this is accomplished, the value of the old string can be copied into the new buffer area. This implementation could be given as follows:

```
void string::operator = (const string & right)
{    // copy values of right argument into string
     const int rightLength = right.length();

     // if it doesn't fit, make a new buffer
     if (rightLength >= bufferlength) {
          // delete current buffer
          delete [ ] buffer;

          // allocate the new one
          bufferlength = 1 + rightLength;
          buffer = new char[bufferlength];
          assert (buffer != 0);
          }
```

Who Cleans Up?

Destructors are mainly used for housekeeping tasks, such as the release of dynamically allocated memory. Care must be taken, however, in ensuring that the memory being released is not being used by some other value. As we noted earlier, the implementation of strings in simple C++ allows two character pointers to denote the same buffer, as in the following diagram:

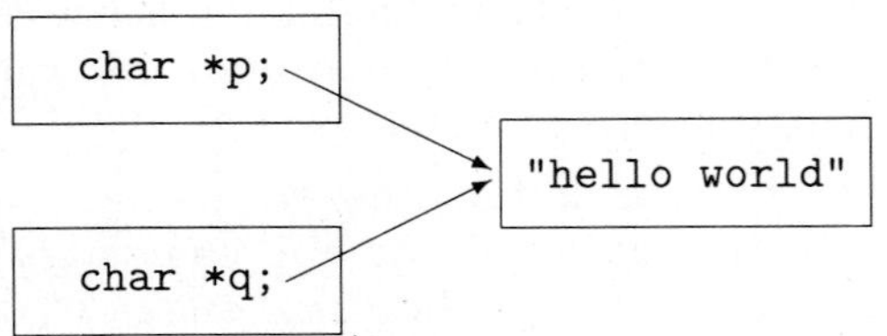

The picture is symmetric. Which value "owns" the memory area, and thus should be in charge of deleting it? There are twin problems to be avoided here: not deleting the memory and deleting it more than once, both of which will likely lead to eventual error.

In our string abstraction we will avoid this problem by adhering to the principle that every string maintains its own private data area that is not shared, and every string is responsible for deleting its own data area. When one string is assigned to another, it will copy the contents of the old string into the new, rather than sharing a common buffer.

In more complex situations sharing is an important part of memory usage. In these cases deciding how to perform memory management can be a complicated problem. In basic terms this usually comes down to a simple question: Who is in charge of cleaning up? Some of the books cited in the reference section present more information on this issue.

```
        // copy into buffer
        for (int i = 0; right.buffer[i] != '\0'; i++)
            buffer[i] = right.buffer[i];
        buffer[i] = '\0';
}
```

As we have noted already, another form of assignment occurs when call-by-value parameters are used on `string` values. A nameless temporary variable is created to hold the parameter value. This value is then initialized using the copy constructor. The temporary value will be deleted once the procedure returns from the call.

Temporaries and Conversions

The assignment operator is defined only for strings on the right side. However, values that can be *converted* into strings may also appear. That is, the following is valid:

```
string sam;
sam = "mark twain";
```

The literal character string "mark twain" will be first converted into an unnamed temporary string using the constructor function described earlier. This string will then be assigned to the variable `sam` using the assignment operator. Finally, the unnamed temporary will be deleted, which among other things will invoke the destructor function, freeing up the space used by the buffer in the temporary value.

There are several important points to note in connection with this process. The first is that this process of creating a temporary just for the purposes of assignment might seem very wasteful of computer resources. This is correct. One solution is to overload the assignment operator so that it can take a character argument directly, as is done in Exercise 11. Another possibility is to change our memory allocation strategy, so that the temporary variable and the left side of the assignment can share the same buffer. Some of the works cited in the reference section give more insight into how to do this.

The second point is that the steps involved in performing this task are very different from the steps involved in an assignment statement that appears as part of a declaration. That is, an expression such as

```
string sam = "mark twain";
```

invokes the constructor for string values once. No temporaries are created, no assignment statement is executed. The *initialization* described by an assignment operator in a declaration statement is not the same as an assignment statement.

A final point is related to the dual use of constructor functions as both initializations for declaration statements and as conversion functions. It is legal for the right side of an assignment statement to contain anything that can be converted into a string. This in turn is partly determined by the list of single argument constructors for the class. The following statement is legal, but obscure.

```
sam = 20;
```

The statement does not make the string `sam` contain the text "20," nor does it even have a character with ASCII value 20. Instead, it creates a new string temporary of size 20 (but uninitialized) then assigns the (empty) value of this string to the variable `sam`.

SUBSCRIPTING The subscript operator is considered to be a binary operator, despite the fact it does not use the infix notation as do other binary operators. The left argument is the object being subscripted, and the right argument is the index value. As with the assignment binary operator, the subscript operator is defined as a member function, and thus the declaration of the left argument is omitted. Note that the index is declared as an unsigned integer, and therefore will always contain a non-negative value.

Subscripting is somewhat complicated by the fact that it can be used both in an expression and as a target of an assignment statement. The requirements for these two uses do not exactly match. When used as an expression, we want to return the null character. For example, the most common technique used to loop over the characters in a string requires this behavior:

```
for (int i = 0; str[i] != '\0'; i++)
    ...
```

On the other hand, although we want to permit programmers to modify any character position using the subscript operator, we do not want to allow them to overwrite the null character.

To be legal for use on the left side of an assignment, the subscript operator must return an *lvalue*—that is, an address. The most convenient way to do this is to return a reference. (When returning a reference, care must always be taken to ensure that the object being referred to is not destroyed during the process of procedure return.) By returning a reference to a global variable for out of range index values, we ensure that the programmer will not be able to overwrite the null character at the end of the buffer. Since we can do nothing to prevent the modification of this value, it is reassigned to null each time it is used. (The programmer can assign to the value returned by this operation, but the character value that is modified will be the global variable, and the null character in the string buffer will not be modified.)

```
char nothing;     // global variable holding null character

char & string::operator [ ] (unsigned int index) const
{   // return the character referenced by the index value
    // first see if the index is in bounds
    if (index >= CstringLength(buffer)) {
        // not in bounds, return null character
        nothing = '\0';
        return nothing;
        }
    // otherwise it is a valid index, return character
    return buffer[index];
}
```

If it is desired that the subscript operator be used only in expressions, and not as a target of an assignment, then the subscript operator can return a nonreference, or a reference declared as constant.

CONVERTING WORDS TO ONE CASE The following useful function converts all capital letters in a word to lowercase. A companion routine can be written to convert to uppercase. The procedure uses the fact that arithmetic can be performed on character values just as if they were integers.

```
void toLower (string & word)
{   // convert all capital letters in word to lower case
    for (int i = 0; word[i] != '\0'; i++)
        if (isUpperCase(word[i]))
            word[i] = (word[i] - 'A') + 'a';
}
```

EXAMPLE APPLICATION—COUNTING VOWELS As an example of the use of string operations, the procedure shown below takes as argument a string and computes the number of vowels that appear in the string. It does this by testing each character in turn, incrementing a count for each vowel. After counting the number of vowel letters, an output indicating the ratio of vowel to nonvowel characters is printed.

```
void vowelcount(const string & str)
{   // count the number of vowels in the argument string
    double count = 0;
    int max = str.length();

    for (int i = 0; str[i] != '\0'; i++)
        if ((str[i] == 'a') || (str[i] == 'e') || (str[i] == 'i') ||
            (str[i] == 'o') || (str[i] == 'u'))
                count += 1.0;

    cout << "the word " << str << " has " << count
        << " vowels; ratio of vowels to nonvowels is "
        << (count / max) * 100.0 << '\n';
}
```

The output from the program would indicate, for example, that the ratio of vowels to nonvowels in the word "`sequoia`" is 71.4 percent, and in a word like "`glyph`" or "`crypt`" the ratio is 0 percent.

4.2.3 Comparison Operators

The six relational operators (<=, <, !=, ==, >, and >=) are implemented as true operators, not as member functions. That is, the left argument has no more special status than the right argument. There are, in fact, benefits to this arrangement. In particular, it is possible to perform automatic conversions on either the left or right argument. If sue is a string variable, then both the following expressions are legal:

```
sue > "sammy"
"allan" <= sue
```

Because the six relational operators are so similar, it is useful to factor out the common task into one operation. (This is an example of the "search for commonality" we discussed in Chapter 1.) Each of the six individual operations will then be implemented as a call on this common function.

We will define the common operation as a member function, which we will call `compare`. This function will perform a lexicographic comparison of two string values:

```
int string::compare(const string & val) const
{   // compare the buffer to the argument string value
    char * p = buffer;
    char * q = val.buffer;

    // loop as long as both have characters and are equal
    while ((*p != '\0') && (*p == *q)) {
        // inv: up to *p buffer and val are equal
        p++; q++;
        }

    // by subtracting the values referred to by the pointers,
    // we yield a negative value if the first string is smaller
    // than the second, a zero value if they are equal,
    // and a positive value if the first is larger than the second
    return *p - *q;
}
```

The compare function loops over the characters in the two strings, using a pair of pointer values. As long as both pointers yield nonempty characters, the characters are compared. If they are unequal, then the comparison can halt. The loop exits either when an unequal pair of characters is encountered, or when both character pointers encounter a null character. If both strings terminate simultaneously, both pointers will point to a null value and zero will be returned. If only the first string terminates, since the null value is zero a negative result will be generated, indicating that the second string is larger. Conversely, if only the second string terminates, a positive value will be generated, indicating that the first string is larger.

Having defined `compare`, the six relational operators can be easily defined. The following illustrates the declaration of the "less than" operator. The other operators are similar:

```
int operator < (const string & left, const string & right)
{   // test if left string is lexicographically less than right string
    return left.compare(right) < 0;
}
```

COMPUTING SMALLEST AND LARGEST WORDS To illustrate the use of comparisons, consider the program shown below. This procedure reads individual words from the standard input (we will explain the input and output procedures in more detail in Section 4.2.5) and discovers the lexicographically smallest and largest words.

```
void words()
{   // count the largest and smallest words in standard input
    string largeword;
    string smallword;
    string wordbuffer;

    // initialize both largest and smallest to first word
```

Inline Functions

Encapsulation mechanisms such as class definitions often lead to a proliferation of functions with trivial implementations, such as the six relational operators. In some cases the overhead of execution for performing a subprocedure call exceeds the execution time spent executing the body of the procedure. Overall execution time in these situations can be reduced by declaring the functions as *inline*. An inline function is simply a pattern; instead of generating an actual function, the compiler replaces calls on an inline function with the code produced by the body of the function.

An inline function is indicated by the keyword `inline` preceding the body. The definition of an inline function is also given in the interface file, normally in place of the prototype description, instead of being found in the implementation file. An example is the following:

```
inline int operator > (const string & left,
                        const string & right)
{   // test if left string is lexicographically
    // greater than right string
    return left.compare(right) > 0;
}
```

Since the code for the function is duplicated at every place the function is invoked, inline functions should be used only for functions that have very simple function bodies. A good rule of thumb is to use inline functions only when the body of a function is a single return expression or a single assignment statement.

It is also possible, using a similar syntax, to declare inline function methods.

```
    cin >> largeword;
    smallword = largeword;

    // now loop over all remaining words
    while (cin >> wordbuffer) {
        if (wordbuffer < smallword)
            smallword = wordbuffer;
        if (wordbuffer > largeword)
            largeword = wordbuffer;
        }

    // now print results
    cout << "smallest word is " << smallword << '\n';
    cout << "largest word is " << largeword << '\n';
}
```

If input consisted of the following:

```
it was the best of times,
it was the worst of times.
```

the result would indicate that the lexicographically smallest word was `best`, and the lexicographically largest word was `worst`.

4.2.4 Catenation — Reusing Operations

The string append operator, which we will implement by using the addition assignment operator +=, adds one string to the end of another. If there is insufficient space in the buffer of the target string for the new characters, the contents of the current buffer are copied into a new larger data area, and the old values are copied into the new area.

```
void string::operator += (const string & val)
{   // append argument to end of current string

    // if there isn't space, make new buffer
    int combinedLength = length() + val.length();
    if (combinedLength > = bufferlength) {
        char * newbuffer = new char [ 1 + combinedLength];
        assert (newbuffer != 0);

        // copy over old values
        for (int i = 0; buffer[i] != '\0'; i++)
            newbuffer[i] = buffer[i];
        newbuffer[i] = '\0';

        // delete old buffer and reset pointer
```

```
            delete [ ] buffer;
            bufferlength = 1 + combinedLength;
            buffer = newbuffer;
            }

        // catenate val on end of current string
        int i = CstringLength(buffer);
        for (int j = 0; val.buffer[j] != '\0'; j++)
            buffer[i++] = val.buffer[j];
        buffer[i] = '\0';
}
```

We use the append operation to illustrate a general programming principle. Often one task can be most easily implemented by making use of the functionality provided by another task. By reusing the first task, coding effort is reduced and reliability is increased.

In this case, the more general problem is to concatenate two strings together, producing a third and leaving the arguments intact. This is easily implemented by making use of a copy constructor and the append operator. The constructor produces a copy of the left argument. The right argument is then appended to this copy, and the copy returned as the result of the operator.

```
string operator + (const string & left, const string & right)
{   // concatenate two strings, leaving arguments unchanged
    string result(left);
    result += right;
    return result;
}
```

To illustrate the use of concatenation, consider the following example, which shows as expected that one plus two equals three:

```
string one("th");
string two("ree");
string sum;

sum = one + two;
cout << "one + two equals " << sum << '\n';
```

4.2.5 Input Output

We have seen in earlier chapters that stream output is defined for literal C style character pointers. The easiest way to implement output for our string ADT is to provide a mechanism to convert a string into a character pointer. Because we do not want to encourage programmers to manipulate the string through the resulting pointer—which is in preference to manipulating strings using the string operations we have provided—we declare the value the pointer accesses as constant.

We have seen already how constructors are used by the C++ system to perform conversions. Thus characters and literal strings can be converted into instances of the `string` ADT since they are permitted as arguments to constructors. It is also possible to explicitly define operators to convert an instance of an ADT into another type. To do this, the name of the target type is used as the name of the operator. As with constructors, no result type needs to be provided in this case. Such an operator is referred to as a *conversion operator*.

The method used to convert a string into a pointer to a constant array of characters is the following:

```
string::operator const char * () const
{   // convert string value into char pointer value,
    // by returning access to the underlying C buffer
    return buffer;
}
```

When a string value is printed by using the stream operator, this function will be used to change a string value into a pointer value. The existing stream operator that takes as an argument a character pointer will then be invoked.

For character pointers, the string input operation is defined to return the next white space terminated word. We can copy this into a temporary buffer (declared large enough so as to not be likely to overflow), then use the assignment operation to modify the argument string. Notice that the second argument is here not declared as `const`, as it is being modified as part of the input operation.

```
istream & operator >> (istream & in, string & str)
{   // perform string input,
    // read next white-space separated word into string
    // implementing using existing character input facility
    char inbuffer[1000];

    in >> inbuffer;
    str = inbuffer;
    return in;
}
```

We have seen an example of input and output already in the program that computed the lexicographically largest and smallest words.

It is occasionally necessary to read from the input an entire line, and not simply a single word. This is accomplished by the function `getline` in the stream I/O package. We can incorporate this feature into our string package with the following method:

```
istream & string::getline(istream & in)
{   // read an entire line of input into string
    in.getline(buffer, bufferlength);
    return in;
}
```

The getline function will read until the end of a line is encountered or until a specified number of characters have been read, whichever occurs first. It is thus necessary for the user of this method to ensure that the string buffer is declared with a sufficiently large number of positions.

4.2.6 Substrings — Facilitators*

We will override the parentheses operator, sometimes called the function call operator, to provide the ability to access subportions of strings. The parentheses operator is unique among the C++ operators in that it does not have a predefined fixed number of arguments. In our case, it is convenient to use two arguments.

There are two common notations used to indicate substrings. The first specifies a substring using a left and right index. The second notation, the one we will use, specifies a substring using a left index and a count of characters. The following examples illustrate the substrings indicated by a pair of expressions:

elizabeth(1,3)   e[liz]abeth

alfreda(2,4)   al[fred]a

If substrings were used only in expressions and not as the target of an assignment, then the implementation of the substring operation would be relatively simple, as shown by the following:

```
string string::operator()(unsigned int index, unsigned int count)
{   // simple implementation of subscript operation
    int buflen = length();

    // if index out of range return empty string
    if (index >= buflen)
        return "";

    // convert count, if necessary
```

*Section headings followed by an asterisk indicate optional material.

```
    int numberleft = buflen - index;
    if (count > numberleft)
        count = numberleft;

    // make the new string
    string newstr(count);

    // copy the values into the area
    for (int i = 0; i < count; i++)
        newstr.buffer[i] = buffer[index + i];

    // return the new string
    return newstr;
}
```

The implementation of the substring operation becomes more complex if we desire the ability to use substrings on the left side of an assignment, as in the following:

```
string caroline = "caroline";
string sister = "theresa"
caroline(2,3) = sister(0,4) // caroline is now catherine
```

Two significant problems need to be overcome to provide this functionality. The value being modified should be the original base string, not a new string generated by the substring operation. Even if we can get access to the base string, the size of the value being assigned may not correspond to the size of the substring indicated by the arguments; it can be either larger or smaller.

To solve the first problem it is necessary to introduce a new data type. It is not sufficient to have the substring operator return a value of type `string`, since assignment to a `string` data value already has a well-defined meaning, and it is not this meaning we desire. Instead, we create a new class, `substring`. A `substring` value will retain a pointer back to a base string. When used on the left side of an assignment, a `substring` value will invoke a different method than that used for assignment to a `string` value, and it is in this method that we can perform the substring assignment. A class that is used to facilitate only the performance of an operation, such as our class `substring`, is often called an *auxiliary* or *facilitator* class. Users of the string abstraction should not need to know about the existence of the substring class.

The class description for `substring` is as follows. The only operations we provide are the ability to assign a value to a substring and the ability to convert a substring into an ordinary string.

```
//
// class substring
//     facilitator class to permit access to
```

```
//      portions of a string
//

class substring {
public:
     // constructors
     substring    (string & base, int start, int length);
     substring    (const substring & source);

     // assignment of string to substring
     void      operator =    (const string &) const;

     // conversion of substring to string
     operator  string        () const;

private:
     // data areas
     string &           base;
     const short int    index;
     const short int    count;
};
```

The parentheses (substring) operator in class `string` now simply returns a new substring. A complicating factor here is the necessity of using the current string as an argument in the constructor for the substring. To do this we use the pseudo-variable `this`. The variable by this name is used within a method to access a pointer to the current instance. We dereference this value since the constructor requires a reference value, not a pointer.

```
substring string::operator()(unsigned int index, unsigned int count)
{    // return substring consisting of count chars starting at index

     // if index out of range return empty string
     if (index >= length()) {
          index = 0;
          count = 0;
          }

     // convert count, if necessary
     int numberleft = length() - index;
     if (count > numberleft)
          count = numberleft;

     // make the new string, use this to be base string
     return substring(*this, index, count);
}
```

The constructor simply saves the three values in the instance data fields:

```
substring::substring(string & b, int i, int c)
    : base(b), index(i), count(c)
{   // create and initialize a substring value
    // no further initialization required
}
```

ASSIGNMENT TO SUBSTRINGS We are now finally able to return to the problem that prompted all this effort—namely, the use of subscripts on the left side of an assignment statement. To perform this operation, the assignment operator is defined as a member function in class `substring`. The subscript operator forms the new result in a local buffer, then changes the values in the base string so that they maintain these new values.

To do this, the base string is considered as three parts: the prefix, the middle, and the suffix. The prefix part consists of those elements in index positions smaller than `index`. The suffix part consists of those elements with index values larger than `index + count`. The prefix is copied into the new area, followed by the value being assigned to the substring, followed by the suffix. The following illustrates the example we used earlier, which changed the string value "caroline" into the string value "catherine."

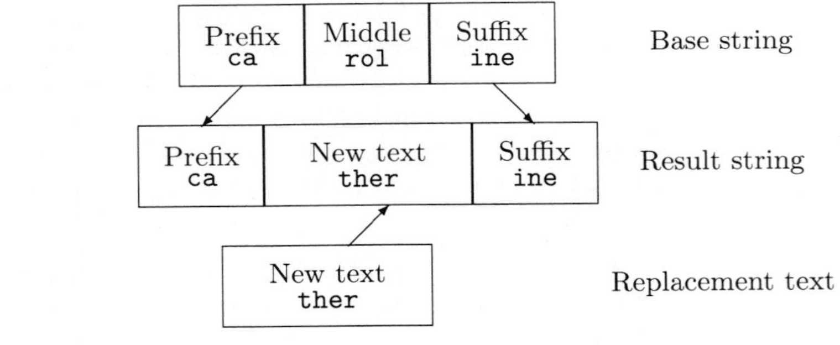


```
void substring::operator = (const string & rep) const
{   // copy a string value to a substring position
    // if lengths are equal, then no new allocation is necessary
    if (count == rep.length()) {
        for (int i = 0; i <= count; i++)
            base[index + i] = rep[i];
        return;
        }

    // otherwise compute the length of the new string
    int baselen = base.length();
    int newlen = rep.length() + baselen - count;
    char * newdata = new char[newlen+1];
```

```
    // then copy the values into the new area
    for (int i = 0; i < index; i++)
        newdata[i] = base[i];
    // catenate on the new values
    for (int j = 0; rep[j] != 0; j++)
        newdata[i++] = rep[j];
    // then catenate on the base
    for (j = index + count; base[j] != 0; j++)
        newdata[i++] = base[j];
    newdata[i] = '\0';

    // then change the base string
    delete [ ] base.buffer;
    base.bufferlength = newlen;
    base.buffer = newdata;

    return;
}
```

An example will illustrate both the use of substrings and the sequence of conversions between strings and substrings. As is common in C++ programs, a large number of functions are typically invoked "behind the scene," with no explicit user specification. The following sequence of statements will convert the string "beard" into the string "bread." Table 4.1 summarizes the functions that will be invoked during the execution of these statements.

```
string a;
string b;
a = "beard";
b = a(1, 3);
a[1] = 'r';
a(2,2) = b(0,2);
```

We will trace each statement in turn and describe the sequence of actions and conversions that take place, and the implicit functions that are being invoked.

```
string a;
string b;
```

The first two statements merely invoke constructors. These constructors create empty strings, holding no actual character values.

```
a = "beard";
```

The first statement would appear to be a simple assignment. Since the assignment operator requires a string value, a constructor is used to create a temporary string with value "beard." This temporary is then assigned to

Table 4.1 Implicit functions invoked by a sequence of statements

`string a;`	`string::string ()`
`string b;`	`string::string ()`

`a = "beard";`	`string::string (const char *)`
	`string::operator = (const string &)`
	`string::~string ()`

`b = a(1, 3);`	`string::operator() (unsigned int, unsigned int)`
	`substring::operator string ()`
	`string::operator = (const string &)`
	`string::~string ()`

`a[1] = 'r';`	`string::operator [ ] ()`

`a(2, 2) = b(0, 2);`	`string::operator() (unsigned int, unsigned int)`
	`string::operator() (unsigned int, unsigned int)`
	`substring::operator string ()`
	`substring::operator = (const string &)`
	`string::~string ()`

a, and the temporary is then deleted. Although only one operator appears in this simple statement, three methods are actually invoked: a constructor to create the temporary, the assignment operator, and a destructor. As we noted in the sidebar "Temporaries and Conversions" earlier in this chapter, the temporary and the invocation of the constructor and destructor could have been avoided by combining the declaration and the assignment, thereby changing the assignment into an initialization.

```
b = a(1,3);
```

The second statement performs a substring operation. The result produced by the substring method is a value of type substring. Since the target of the assignment is a string value, the conversion operator (to be described shortly) is invoked to create a temporary string value holding the text of the substring, a string assignment is performed, and the temporary value is deleted. Once more, some of this overhead could have been avoided by delaying the declaration of the variable `b` until this point.

Following this statement, the variable a will hold the value "beard" and the variable b will hold the value "ear."

```
a[1] = 'r';
```

The third statement is a simple character assignment, not a string assignment. The subscript operation returns a reference to the character position 1. The value stored at this location is changed into an 'r'. Thus the value held by variable a is "brard." This operation has no effect on the value held by variable b, since in the process of assignment a copy was made.

```
a(2,2) = b(0,2);
```

Five different functions are invoked during the execution of the final statement. First, the two substring operations are executed. The assignment operator for a substring value requires a string as argument. So, as before, a temporary is created for the right side using the constructor as a conversion operation from substring to string. This temporary, which holds the string value "ea," is then used in the assignment operation. Note that this assignment statement uses the substring assignment operator, which is different from the assignment operator used in the first statement. Finally, the string destructor is invoked to delete the temporary string value.

CONVERSION OF SUBSTRING TO STRING Except when it appears on the left-hand side of an assignment operator, in all other situations a substring value must be converted into a string before it can be used. As we saw when we discussed input and output operations on strings, this is done through the use of a conversion operator. The operator to be defined is the type name `string`.

```
substring::operator string () const
{   // convert a substring into a string
    // first copy the text into a temporary buffer
    char * buffer = new char[count + 1];
    assert (buffer != 0);
    for (int i = 0; i < count; i++)
        buffer[i] = base[i + index];
    buffer[count] = '\0';
    // then make it into a string, and delete the buffer
    string result(buffer);
    delete [ ] buffer;
    return result;
}
```

4.3 PATTERN MATCHING*

Pattern matching is the process of determining whether a string contains a substring matching a certain pattern, and if so the index in the text array for the substring that matches the pattern. A difficulty is the fact that there may be several instances of the pattern string that occur in the target text. If we are interested in discovering *all* matches to a pattern, it is necessary to use some sort of loop.

To solve this difficulty, we address the problem of string matching by introducing a new facilitator data structure that implements a *collection* of functions. Together these functions can be used to construct a loop that iterates over the various answers to a query. To illustrate, suppose we wish to print out the locations of the letter "`i`" in the word "`mississippi`." We could do this with the following code:

```
SimpleStringMatcher mismatch("i", "mississippi");

for (mismatch.init(); ! mismatch; mismatch++)
    cout << " letter i at position " << mismatch.position() << '\n';
```

The variable `mismatch` is declared as an instance of the class `SimpleStringMatcher`, which we will describe shortly. This class takes the pattern ("`i`") and the text for analysis ("`mississippi`") as arguments to the constructor. The `init` method means "find the first solution." The `++` operator is overloaded to mean "find the next solution." The operator `!` is defined to mean "not at the end of the solutions." The function `position` returns the position of the current solution. In addition to those shown, other functions we will use include the empty parentheses operator that returns the text of the current match.

Another example will illustrate how nontrivial problems can often be viewed simply as pattern-matching problems. Deoxyribonucleic acid, or DNA, is an exceedingly long molecule used in the nucleus of living cells to encode recipes for constructing various chemicals involved in biological processes. The elements of DNA can be viewed as consisting of four base molecules: adenine, cytosine, guanine, and thymine. These elements are combined in different forms to generate amino acids and proteins and other higher-level structures. Since DNA consists of just these four parts, we can describe a section of a DNA molecule as a pattern of the four letters `a`, `c`, `g`, and `t`; for example "`acgatactagacaga`." The question of whether a certain base or protein occurs in this section of DNA is answered by simply asking whether the pattern that corresponds to the protein occurs in the string that characterizes the DNA form. Similarly, changes in DNA can be made by cutting and splicing. A cut is performed

*Section headings followed by an asterisk indicate optional material.

by an object called a restriction enzyme. The restriction enzyme decides where to make a cut by matching the DNA strand against a specific pattern.

We will define a series of pattern matchers. These data structures will be similar, and in fact many of the details involved in implementing each of the various pattern matchers are the same from version to version. We introduce a new coding technique that will save us from having to repeatedly rewrite this code. The class `stringMatcher` (Figure 4.2) provides the bare-bones functionality of our pattern matcher. The data structure maintains three data areas: the text of the string being matched, and the position and the length of the current match. The constructor merely sets these fields:

```
stringMatcher::stringMatcher(string & t) : text(t)
{   // construct new string matcher,
    // start position at first location of text
    pos = 0;
}
```

As in the example at the start of this section, looping is performed using a combination of several operators. The `init` function sets the position pointer just before the first character, then invokes the increment operator to find the first match.

```
int stringMatcher::init ()
{   // initialize the position to start of string
    pos = -1;
    return operator ++();
}
```

We will make the convention that the position variable will be set out of range, either to a negative value or past the end of the text string, when there are no more solutions. Thus the operator we are using to control our loops (unary not symbol) simply tests for this condition.

```
int stringMatcher::operator ! () const
{   // see if there is a valid match
    return (pos >= 0) && (pos < text.length());
}
```

The empty parentheses operator returns the substring of the text at the location given by the current position and length. The position and length of the current match are provided by member functions.

```
substring stringMatcher::operator () ()
{   // return current substring match
    return text(position(), length());
}
```

```
//
// class stringMatcher
//     simple string matching operation
//

class stringMatcher {
public:
    // constructor
    stringMatcher   (string & t);

    // protocol used to generate loops
    // for (x.init(); ! x; x++)  ... x() ...

    virtual int     init            ();
    int             operator !      () const;
    virtual int     operator ++     ();
    substring       operator ()     ();

    // set or access current position
    unsigned int    position        () const;
    void            position        (unsigned int p);

    // return length of current match
    unsigned int    length          () const;

protected:
    // data areas
    string &        text;
    int             pos;
    unsigned int    patlen;
};
```

Figure 4.2 The abstract class `stringMatcher`

The only operations we have not defined is the unary operator ++ used to obtain the next solution. We will define this, and explain the meaning of the `virtual` keyword preceding the declaration of this method in the class declaration to be discussed, in the next section.

4.3.1 Simple String Matching

The first pattern matcher we will describe uses the obvious algorithm. Given a pattern and text, simply try each initial position of the text in turn, testing each character of the pattern in sequence. The heart of this algorithm, the part that returns the next valid match, therefore looks as follows:

```
int SimpleStringMatcher::operator ++ ()
{   // advance to next match of pattern
    // loop only until the last possible starting position
    int laststart = text.length() - patlen;

    // advance to next starting position
    for (pos++; pos <= laststart; pos++)

        // see if text at position matches pattern
        if (pattern == text(pos, patlen))
            return 1;

    // no further match possible, return 0
    pos = -1;
    return 0;
}
```

We can avoid having to define the remainder of the pattern-matching functions using the *subclassing* feature. Our class description for class SimpleStringMatcher asserts that instances of this class are simply a variety or kind of the earlier class stringMatcher. By stating this relationship, instances of the class SimpleStringMatcher will *inherit* the ability to perform all functions of the earlier class, without having to rewrite the code. That is, instances of the class SimpleStringMatcher will have access to data members of the class stringMatcher and to the member functions. We say that the class stringMatcher is the *parent class* for SimpleStringMatcher, and conversely that SimpleStringMatcher is a *child class* of stringMatcher. The class declaration for the child class need describe only those features that will be modified in the new structure.

```
//
// class SimpleStringMatcher
// string pattern matching using the naive brute force approach
//

class SimpleStringMatcher : public stringMatcher {
public:
    // constructor
    SimpleStringMatcher(const string & pat, string & text);

    // find the next match
    virtual int operator ++();
```

```
private:
    // data areas
    const string & pattern;
};
```

If the constructor for the parent class requires arguments, then the constructor for the child class must provide them. This is accomplished by using a syntax similar to the way data fields are initialized.

```
SimpleStringMatcher::SimpleStringMatcher(const string & p, string & t)
    : stringMatcher(t), pattern(p)
{   // create and initialize a simple string matcher
    // set length of current match to length of pattern
    patlen = p.length();
}
```

The `virtual` designation on the `init` method and the `++` operator in the parent class indicates that these methods can potentially be changed, or *overridden* in child classes. An instance of `SimpleStringMatcher` will use the definition found in the `SimpleStringMatcher` class, and not the definition found in the parent `stringMatcher` class. The `virtual` designation permits overriding; it does not require it. We have not overridden the `init` method, and thus the version in the parent class will be used. Because of the way virtual functions are implemented, they should not be defined as in-line functions. (Most compilers will permit such a definition but will generate no better code than if the functions are not declared in-line.)

We declared earlier that the data fields in class `stringMatcher` were `protected`. This designation means that the data values such as `SimpleStringMatcher` are accessible to subclasses, but they are not outside of instances of either `stringMatcher` or `SimpleStringMatcher`.

To illustrate an example of use for this class, consider the following simple loop:

```
string text = "onetwonetwone";
SimpleStringMatcher matt("one", text);

for (matt++; !matt; matt++)
    cout << "found a match at position " << matt.position() << '\n';
```

Matches for the pattern "`one`" will be found in positions 0, 5, and 10.

In order to discuss the complexity of pattern matching, consider the worst-case behavior of the `++` operation. Such behavior would occur when no successful pattern was found, but each character except the final character in the pattern needed to be tested before failure was detected. Such a situation would occur with a pattern such as "`aaaaaab`," for example, when matched against a string consisting entirely of "`a`" characters. In this case the number of comparisons performed would be roughly the size of the pattern string times the size of the text string. If we let m and n represent these two quantities, we can say that in the worst case pattern matching requires $O(nm)$ operations. In the next two sections we will investigate alternative algorithms that give significantly better performance.

4.3.2 Knuth-Morris-Pratt Pattern Matching

A major problem in the simple string matcher is that each time it increments the position value after a mismatched character, it throws away all information that may have been gained from the previous attempted match. To see how this information could be useful, suppose we are working on the problem of matching DNA sequences and our pattern is the string "`agacagata`." Notice that the beginning of the pattern ("`aga`") occurs again later in the pattern.

Position	0	1	2	3	4	5	6	7	8		
Pattern	a	g	a	c	a	g	a	t	a		
Shifted pattern					a	g	a	c	a	g	a

Let us call this a prefix pattern. We can use the existence of prefix patterns to avoid retesting characters we have already examined.

Suppose, for example, that the input is the text "`cagacagacagata`." We would initially start our pattern-matching operation under the assumption that the pattern begins in position 1. (Actually we would start in position 0, but the first character does not match so we shift over one position.) When we get to position 8, we find a mismatch. However, if we knew that the pattern in positions 5 to 7 matched the pattern in position 0 to 2, we could simply "slide over" the pattern. We would thus proceed as if we were matching the pattern under the assumption that we began the match in position 5, and were examining pattern position 3, rather than beginning in position 1, and examining pattern position 8. We can do this because we know the characters we have already seen exactly match the initial portion of the pattern (Fig. 4.3).

Assuming we can do this, an important advantage is that we never need to "back up" the input text; that is, we examine each character of the input in turn. When we are finished processing that input value, we will proceed to the next character and we will never reexamine the current character. Thus, this is known as the *Knuth-Morris-Pratt* (KMP) algorithm, named after the individuals responsible for its discovery. It is useful for *on-line* applications where input is fed into the process one character at a time. For example, this might occur if characters were being read from an external file.

In order to execute the KMP algorithm, we require an auxiliary array, which we will call the `prefix` array. This is an array of integers with a location corresponding to each character in the pattern string. A value `j` in

A mismatch occurs when matching at position 8

Position	0	1	2	3	4	5	6	7	8	9	10
Text	c	a	g	a	c	a	g	a	c	a	g . . .
Pattern		a	g	a	c	a	g	a	t	a	

so we shift the pattern right

Position	0	1	2	3	4	5	6	7	8	9	10
Text	c	a	g	a	c	a	g	a	c	a	g . . .
Pattern		a	g	a	c	a	g	a	t	a	
Shift						a	g	a	c	a	g . . .

and continue matching

Figure 4.3 Recovering from a mismatch by shifting the pattern

position `i` of the prefix array will mean that the pattern ending at position `i` is the same as the initial pattern of length `j`—that is, we can assume that `pattern(0,j) == pattern(i-(j-1),j)` and that no other value between `j` and `i` has this property.

To illustrate, assume that the pattern is the text "`agctagcagctagctg`." There are three "shifts" of the input that result in a prefix matching some portion of the input. The following diagram shows this, as well as the value of the prefix array.

Position	0	1	2	3	4	5	6	7	8	9	10	11	12	13	14	15
Prefix	0	0	0	0	1	2	3	1	2	3	4	5	6	7	4	0
Pattern	a	g	c	t	a	g	c	a	g	c	t	a	g	c	t	g
					a	g	c	t	a	g	c	a	g	c	t	a
								a	g	c	t	a	g	c	a	g
												a	g	c	t	a

The job that the prefix array is performing is to indicate how to react to a failure. Suppose we fail when we are matching the pattern at location 9. The prefix array tells us that the text we have *already* matched, in getting to position 9, could also match the pattern in positions 0 to 3. Thus, if we fail in matching the tenth character, we can legitimately shift the starting point for our match, and try the current character against the fourth character of the pattern. In this way, the prefix array tells us how to adjust the starting location of a pattern match without reexamining the previous characters.

The first task is to allocate and fill in the values for the prefix array. We do this as part of the constructor for the class `KMPstringMatcher`. As was the case with the class `SimpleStringMatcher`, the class `KMPstring-Matcher` will be declared as a subclass of `stringMatcher`, and therefore instances of the class will have access to all the fields and methods of the parent class. The description for the class is as follows:

```
//
// class KMPstringMatcher
//     a faster string pattern matcher using the
//     Knuth-Morris-Pratt pattern matching algorithm
//

class KMPstringMatcher : public stringMatcher {
public:
    // constructor and destructor
    KMPstringMatcher(const string &, string &);
    ~KMPstringMatcher();

    // override the find next match operator
    virtual int operator ++ ();
private:
    // data areas
    const string & pattern;
    int * prefix;
};
```

The prefix array is declared as a pointer since we do not know the bounds until run time, and thus the array must be dynamically allocated. This is done in the constructor, as follows:

```
KMPstringMatcher::KMPstringMatcher(const string & p, string & t) :
    stringMatcher(t), pattern(p)
{
    patlen = p.length();
    assert(patlen > 0); // make sure there is a pattern

    // allocate the prefix array
    prefix = new int[patlen];
    assert(prefix != 0);

    // now fill it in
    prefix[0] = 0;
    for (int i = 1; i < patlen; i++) {
        int k = prefix[i-1];

        // inv: pattern(0,k) == pattern(i-(k-1),k)

        while ((pattern[i] != pattern[k]) && (k != 0)) {
            k = prefix[k-1];
            }
```

```
        if (pattern[i] == pattern[k])
            prefix[i] = k+1;
        else
            prefix[i] = 0;
        }
}
```

We will argue for the correctness of this algorithm based on induction on the position `i` being filled. It is obvious that the initial position cannot have any smaller prefix, and thus the value of 0 is appropriate. The `for` loop is used to set each remaining value in the prefix array. To set value `i`, we first examine the prefix value for the previous position `i−1`. The invariant at this point is that whatever the value `k` is for this previous position, the pattern starting at position 0 and extending for `k` steps matches the pattern beginning at location `i−(k−1)`. One of two cases now occurs. Either we can continue this prefix (meaning the next character in the pattern is also the next character in the prefix) or we cannot.

Case 1: Assume we can continue the prefix. Then the while loop will terminate and the test in the following if statement will succeed and the value of prefix[i] will be one larger than the value of prefix[i−1]. Since we assumed that the prefix at location `i−1` was the largest possible and we have extended this, it must be the largest prefix possible.

Case 2: The next character does not match the next character in the prefix, and thus we cannot extend the current prefix. We need to abandon the current prefix and find a new one. But how can we find the new one? The trick to note is that to find the next prefix we can find the prefix *of the current prefix*, and we can do this using the previous value of the prefix array that we have already continued. To illustrate, let's assume we are computing the value prefix[14] in the pattern discussed earlier:

Position	0	1	2	3	4	5	6	7	8	9	10	11	12	13	14	15
Prefix	0	0	0	0	1	2	3	1	2	3	4	5	6	7	?	?
Pattern	a	g	c	t	a	g	c	a	g	c	t	a	g	c	t	g

The next character, `t`, does not match the prefix we began at location 7. But since this prefix was of length 7, if we examine prefix[6] we will find the next largest prefix. This is telling us that what we have matched up to location 14 could also have been a match of the pattern in positions 0 to 3. The `while` loop in the algorithm examines these shorter prefixes, trying to extend each in turn. The loop must terminate when a prefix of zero length is encountered, if no extensible prefix is found prior to that point.

Because the prefix array has been computed, the actual string-searching algorithm follows much the same pattern:

```
int KMPstringMatcher::operator ++ ()
{   // advance to next match of pattern
    int maxpos = text.length();
    int currentpos = pos + 1;

    // patpos will be our position in the pattern
    int patpos = 0;

    for (; currentpos < maxpos; currentpos++) {
        while ((patpos > 0) && pattern[patpos] != text[currentpos])
            patpos = prefix[patpos-1];

        if (pattern[patpos] == text[currentpos]) {
            patpos = patpos + 1;
            if (patpos == patlen) { // all done
                position(1 + currentpos - patlen);
                return 1;
                }
            }
        }

    // no more possible matches
    position(-1);
    return 0;
}
```

AMORTIZED EXECUTION TIME The algorithm examines each letter in the text string only once. Thus we would like to be able to assert that the algorithm has $O(n)$ execution performance, where n is the length of the text array. However, this fact is not obvious. To assert $O(n)$ performance, we need to be able to show that the execution time of each iteration of the outer `for` loop is bounded by a constant that is independent of the input values. Clearly, the execution time of the `while` loop depends in some complex way on the length and characters of the pattern string, and thus this assertion is simply not true.

We can, however, prove something slightly weaker but equally as good. We can show that the *average* execution time of each iteration of the `for` loop is bounded by a constant that is independent of the input size. Since we can do this, then the expected execution time of the entire searching process is still $O(n)$.

The idea behind average, or *amortized* analysis is to find a quantity, called the *potential*, that characterizes the loop you want to average. The potential should be thought of as a bank account. Like a bank account, it should never be negative. On some iterations through the outer loop, the inner `while` loop will not be executed at all, and the potential should increase. In these cases we are "saving" a bit of execution time for later use. On other executions, the `while` loop will be executed, but each step in execution reduces the potential. In these cases we are "charging" the execution time against the savings we made earlier.

The potential we wish to use in this example is the current position in the prefix array. This is an obvious choice since this value bounds the execution time of the while loop. (This is a rather loose bound, since the position value `patpos` is normally decremented exceedingly rapidly as the `while` loop executes. Nevertheless, any bound is sufficient.) Furthermore, it can be incremented by at most one each time through the outer loop. The average amount of work we will do in each iteration of the `for` loop is to execute *one* iteration of the `while` loop and increment the pattern position by one. Each time we fail to execute the `while` loop, the potential grows slightly. Eventually, we may execute the `while` loop several iterations, but the number of iterations cannot exceed the potential we have been accumulating.

This argument is sufficient to show that for any constant k, the running time of k iterations of the `for` loop is $O(k)$. Since each iteration of the `for` loop examines one new character in the input text, and thus the maximum number of iterations is bounded by the maximum length of the input text, this is sufficient to show that the asymptotic execution time of the KMP algorithm is $O(n)$.

4.3.3 Boyer-Moore Pattern Matching

It is tempting to believe that during pattern matching every character in the text string must be examined, and thus an $O(n)$ algorithm, such as the Knuth-Morris-Pratt algorithm, must certainly be optimal. To see the fallacy in this reasoning, consider the possibility of matching patterns starting from the right side of the pattern and working *backward*, instead of starting from the left side. Assume that the pattern we are seeking is the word "`perfect`," and the text being scanned is the opening lines of the Declaration of Independence.

Position	0	1	2	3	4	5	6	7	8	9	10	11	12
Text	w	e		t	h	e		p	e	o	p	l	e
Pattern	p	e	r	f	e	c	t						

The first character we try to match is the "`t`" at the end of the pattern to the blank in location 6. This fails to match, and thus we know that a correct match cannot be made by starting at location 0. But we know more; since the blank character does not occur at all in the pattern string, we know for certain that no match is possible at any location between the current point and the mismatched character. Thus we can advance the starting position by seven characters *without ever having seen or examined the intervening characters.*

Position	0	1	2	3	4	5	6	7	8	9	10	11	12
Text	w	e		t	h	e		p	e	o	p	l	e
Pattern								p	e	r	f	e	c

Suppose instead our pattern was the word "`blessings`." Our initial attempt at a match would yield a pattern like the following:

Position	0	1	2	3	4	5	6	7	8	9	10	11	12
Text	w	e		t	h	e		p	e	o	p	l	e
Pattern	b	l	e	s	s	i	n	g	s				

The mismatch occurs on the letter "`e`" in position 8. The only "`e`" present in the word "`blessings`" is the third character. Thus the only possible match would occur if we slid the pattern over so that the positions of the two "`e`" characters coincided.

Position	0	1	2	3	4	5	6	7	8	9	10	11	12	13	14	15
Text	w	e		t	h	e		p	e	o	p	l	e		o	f
Pattern							b	l	e	s	s	i	n	g	s	

Once again, we are able to skip without examination a run of characters in the input text. This insight (along with one more heuristic) is the heart of the *Boyer-Moore* pattern matching algorithm, again named after the two individuals credited with its discovery. As with the KMP algorithm, the Boyer-Moore algorithm depends upon first, during the constructor phase, building an auxiliary array of information about the pattern string. In the case of the Boyer-Moore algorithm this array is indexed by character values and contains the position of the last—that is, the rightmost—occurrence of the character value. The class description and constructor to generate this information are as follows:

```
//
// class BoyerMooreStrMatcher
//     a faster string pattern matcher using the
//     Boyer-Moore algorithm
//

class BoyerMooreStrMatcher : public stringMatcher {
public:
    // constructor
    BoyerMooreStrMatcher(const string &, string &);

    // override the find next match operator
    virtual int operator ++ ();
private:
    // data areas
```

```
    const string & pattern;
    short int positions[256];
};

BoyerMooreStrMatcher::BoyerMooreStrMatcher
    (const string & pat, string & text)
        : stringMatcher(text), pattern(pat)
{   // construct and initialize an instance of Boyer Moore pattern matcher

    // set the length field
    patlen = pattern.length();

    // first empty the positions array
    for (int i = 0; i < 256; i++)
        positions[i] = 0;

    // then record the positions of characters
    for (i = 0; pattern[i]; i++)
        positions[pattern[i]] = i;
}
```

For example, the pattern "blessings" would generate the following positions array (we show only the portion of the array corresponding to letters):

Index	a	b	c	d	e	f	g	h	i	j	k	l	m
Value	0	0	0	0	2	0	7	0	5	0	0	1	0

Index	n	o	p	q	r	s	t	u	v	w	x	y	z
Value	6	0	0	0	0	8	0	0	0	0	0	0	0

Armed with this information, pattern matching then proceeds along the following lines. We match characters from the right side of the pattern string. When a mismatch occurs, we consult the `positions` table for the rightmost position of the character in the text that caused the mismatch. Subtracting this value from the position in the pattern of the mismatch yields a shift amount that will align the mismatched character with a character in the pattern. In situations where the character that the mismatch occurred on does not appear in the pattern, the shift amount will move examination to the next unexamined location (that is, one pattern length to the right).

In the usual case, the shift amount is always positive. A negative value can occur when there are two instances of a given character in the pattern, and the character in the text that causes a mismatch happens to be the same as a character in the pattern that has already been matched successfully. The following diagram illustrates this situation:

Position	0	1	2	3	4	5	6	...
Text		g	e	e	z	e	r	...
Pattern			g	a	z	e	r	

In this case the positions heuristic actually yields a negative value to shift—one that would result in lining up the mismatched character `e` in the text with the rightmost instance of `e` in the pattern.

Position	0	1	2	3	4	5	6	...
Text		g	e	e	z	e	r	...
Pattern	g	a	z	e	r			

In order to avoid this problem, the pattern matching algorithm shifts by the maximum of the value yielded by the positions table and the value 1. This ensures that we always advance by at least one position.

```
int BoyerMooreStrMatcher::operator ++()
{   // advance to next match of pattern
    // first move on to a new position
    pos += 1;

    // the last possible starting position is lastpos
    int lastpos = text.length() - patlen;

    // now loop
    while (pos <= lastpos) {
        int j = patlen - 1;
        // loop over pattern from right side
        while ((j >= 0) && (text[pos + j] == pattern[j]))
            j -= 1;

        if (j < 0)
            return 1;    // found a match
        // else advance position pointer
        pos += max(1, j - positions[text[pos + j]]);
        }
    pos = -1;
    return 0;     // no match found
}
```

The algorithm originally described by Boyer and Moore actually includes one more heuristic that we will describe but not implement. Suppose we are matching the pattern consisting of the word "`reminiscence`," and receive a mismatch on the character "`n`" third from the end. Just as we did in the KMP algorithm, we can consider the text that we have already successfully matched against (in this case, the characters "`ce`") as a subpattern of the pattern itself, asking if that subpattern occurs at any location earlier in the pattern. In this case it does, namely at position 7, and thus we know we can shift until the characters in the text string and the characters in the pattern line up. To implement this heuristic, it is necessary to build a suffix table very much like the prefix table of the KMP algorithm, only one that considers the pattern in reverse.

Text	g	o	l	d	e	n		f	l	e	e	c	e		a	w
Pattern		r	e	m	i	n	i	s	c	e	n	c	e			
Shifted pattern					r	e	m	i	n	i	s	c	e	n	c	e

The amount to shift is then computed as the maximum of the amount given by the positions heuristic, the amount given by the suffix heuristic, plus one.

The Boyer-Moore pattern matcher is the fastest of the three when the input alphabet is large and the pattern contains relatively few different characters. This is the common situation in matching actual words of text. The KMP algorithm is often faster in cases where the alphabet is small, such as the DNA example where the alphabet consisted of only four letters.

4.4 CHAPTER SUMMARY

Key Concepts

- String literals
- Pointers
- Dynamic memory allocation, `new` and `delete`
- Destructors
- Subscript operator
- Conversion operator
- Subclassing and inheritance*
- Virtual methods*
- Amortized analysis*

The string data abstraction represents a linear array of characters. Strings are used in almost any application that must perform textual interaction with a user. We have used the development of the string type not only to illustrate the creation of a nontrivial abstract data type, but also to introduce new features of the C++ language and to reinforce understanding of the use of features introduced in earlier chapters.

Because the amount of storage used by a string must vary during the course of execution, strings maintain an internal buffer of characters that is dynamically allocated and freed. The `new` operator is used to perform dynamic allocation, and the `delete` operator is used to return dynamically allocated memory back to the run-time system.

We have seen, in earlier chapters, how *constructors* tie together variable initialization and creation, and thus ensure that proper initialization is performed whenever a new value is created. The opposite side of this is a *destructor*, which is invoked implicitly by the run-time system whenever a variable is about to be destroyed. In the case of string values, the destructor performs the task of deleting the dynamically allocated data buffer.

---

*Discussed in the optional section on pattern matching.

Member functions were defined to compute the length of a string, to access an individual character within a string, to assign one string to another, and to append the value of one string on the end of another. Operators were defined to compare two strings and to catenate two strings together to form a new string.

The substring operation introduced the idea of a *facilitator* class, a data structure that works behind the scenes and is not visible to the user of an ADT.

A series of classes were defined to perform the task of pattern matching. These examples show that even seemingly trivial operations can often have surprisingly subtle implementations. In addition, we illustrated how new classes can be created from existing classes using the mechanism of *inheritance*. We will explore this topic in more detail in the next chapter.

References

Almost all books on C++, starting from the first [Stroustrup 91], have included strings as an example of data type. The version here differs slightly from that given by Stroustrup — making copies of values on assignment and parameter passing, for example — but it is similar in most of the essential details. An alternative presentation is given by Lippman [Lippman 91]. The subscript assignment operation is adapted from Hansen [Hansen 90].

Variations on how to perform memory management in strings as well as related data structures that use dynamic memory allocation are explored in detail by Coplien [Coplien 92].

The Knuth-Morris-Pratt algorithm was invented independently by Knuth and Pratt and by Morris. Subsequently they published a joint paper [Knuth 77]. A more detailed explanation of amortized analysis, with examples drawn from many different data structures, can be found in Cormen et al. [Cormen 90].

The Boyer-Moore algorithm was developed at about the same time as the KMP algorithm [Boyer 77]. It is clear that in the worst case the execution time of the Boyer-Moore algorithm is no worse than the simple pattern-matching algorithm. Showing that expected or average execution time is better, even better than the KMP algorithm, is difficult. The analysis depends in part on discovering a good definition of "average" for word problems. A detailed analysis of both algorithms, as well as several other string matching algorithms, is given as well in Cormen [90].

The lax manner in which character values are handled by the C programming language has been used for devious purposes. In 1988 a large computer network, the Internet, was attacked by a computer worm, a form of computer virus. In part, the virus operated by copying a very carefully constructed string into a certain buffer. The string overflowed the declared size of the buffer, as a result changing the values of the locations that followed the buffer in memory. It happened that the locations that followed the buffer were occupied by machine instructions. The overflowing string replaced these instructions with new instructions that, when executed, gave the worm the ability to reproduce itself. A detailed technical discussion of the Internet worm is given in the June 1989 issue of the *Communications of the ACM* [Spafford 89]. A more general discussion of the individuals involved in the incident is presented by Hafner [Hafner 91].

Exercises

1. Implement each of the following tests for character arguments:
   a. `isLowerCase`—true if argument is a lowercase letter.
   b. `isDigit`—true if argument is a digit character.
   c. `isAlphabetic`—true if argument is either upper- or lowercase.
   d. `isAlphanumeric`—true if argument is either alphabetic or numeric.

2. Implement the procedure `toUpper`, which converts all lowercase letters in a string to uppercase.

3. Write the implementation of the remaining string comparison operators, >=, ! =, ==, <=, and <.

4. When used with a string, a possible meaning for the multiplication symbol would be to indicate repeated copies of a value. For example, the text:

```
"abc" * 4
```

would generate the result:

```
"abcabcabcabc"
```

Give an implementation of the multiplication operator that will provide this behavior.

5. When used with strings, a possible meaning for the subtraction symbol would be to indicate removal of all instances of the right string from the left string. For example, the following sequence:

```
string x = "collision";
string y = x - "lisi";
```

should result in the variable y holding the value "colon." Give an implementation of the subtraction operator that will provide this behavior.

6. Explain what functions and operators will be invoked during the execution of the following pair of statements:

```
string a;
a = 'x';
```

7. When implementation is provided for assignment of user-defined types, a common subtle error involves the possibility of self-assignment—that is, assignment of a variable to itself. This is illustrated by the following:

```
string x = "abc";
x = x;
```

Carefully review the technique used to implement assignment in Section 4.2.2. Does it work in this situation?

8. In the string comparison member function `string::compare`, the comment preceding the loop asserts that the loop continues as long as both the pointers `p` and `q` are non-null, yet the loop explicitly tests only the value of the pointer `p`. Explain how we are assured on each iteration of the loop that the value referred to by the pointer `q` is also non-null.

9. Another definition of lexicographic ordering is provided by defining three cases:
   a. A null string is smaller than any non-null string.
   b. If two non-null strings differ in the first letter, then the ordering of the strings is the same as the ordering of the letters.
   c. If two strings begin with the same letter, then the ordering of the strings is determined by comparing the remaining strings after the initial character is stripped off both strings.

   Give an argument that will demonstrate that this definition is the same as the results generated by using the `compare` function.

10. Write a conversion operator that changes a string value into an integer value. It does this by skipping blanks, searching for the first digit, then converting that digit and all subsequent digits into an integer value. Any remaining characters are ignored. Thus, each of the following strings would generate the value twelve: "12," " 12," "12abc."

11. Currently an assignment of a literal string constant to a string variable forces the creation of a temporary string value. The literal string constant is converted by a constructor into a string value. The assignment operator is then used to copy the temporary string to the target variable. Finally, the temporary string value is deleted. Find a method to fix this, by overloading the assignment operator, thus providing an alternative version that takes a character pointer argument.

12. Consider the append operator in a sequence such as the following:

```
string x("abc");
x += "def";
```

The C++ system will convert the argument into a string before performing the append. This is unnecessary because the argument is immediately converted back into a simple character pointer. Overload the append operator with a form that takes a character pointer argument and thus avoids this conversion.

13. Provide a direct implementation of the concatenation operator, +. That is, provide a description that does not simply use a combination of assignment and append.

14. The string comparison functions are inefficient when one argument is a literal character string, in that the literal character string is first converted into a temporary `string` value before invoking the relational operator function. This is clearly not necessary because the `compare` operator immediately converts the argument back into a character pointer. Provide additional overloaded versions of the relational operators that will be used when one or the other argument is a character pointer. (*Hints*: You need to overload the `compare` function as well. For the case when the left argument is a character pointer, note that each of the four comparison operators can be computed by reversing the operator and swapping the arguments.)

15. Using one of the string matching classes, write a function named `replace` that takes three string arguments:

```
void replace(string base, string pattern,
     string replacement);
```

The function should replace all instances of the pattern in the base string with the replacement string. Note that the replacement string may not be the same length as the pattern string. Instances of the pattern in the replacement should *not* be replaced. For example, if the base string is "all in good time," the pattern "good," and the replacement "very good," your procedure should avoid going into an infinite loop.

16. When used in a loop, the pattern-matching operations return all subsequences that match a certain pattern, even if they overlap. For example, if the pattern is "agaga" and the input text is "agagagagaga," matches would be reported in positions 0, 2, 4, 6, and 8. Describe what occurs if the user desires to obtain only nonoverlapping matches. (In this example that would be the matches in locations 0 and 6.)

17. Describe how many individual character comparisons the naive string matcher will make for the pattern aaag in the text aaagaaagagaaag.

18. Compute the KMP prefix function for the pattern agaggaggagaggagaggagg.

19. Experiment with different patterns and text strings to observe the actual execution time of the various pattern-matching algorithms. You may need to use a loop to repeatedly search the same text in order to obtain execution times that are not dominated by constructing the pattern-matching data value. Can you discover values for which KMP matching is faster than Boyer-Moore pattern matching?

20. Explain why the declaration of a private virtual method does not make any sense.

21. Write a program to count and report the number of words in the standard input, the number of characters in those words, and the number of vowels in those characters.

22. Write a program to compute the average length of the words in the standard input file.

23. Write a program to compute the average sentence length (number of words in a sentence) in the standard input file. You can assume that all sentences end with a period.

CHAPTER 5

Classification of Collections

It is likely that the most widely used data structures are those employed for the purpose of holding quantities of similar objects. Data abstractions that are designed for such purposes are almost always built by using variations on a few simple techniques. We will call these classic forms of data structure *collections*. In this short chapter we will characterize various types of collections, and note the type of problem each is designed to help solve. In subsequent chapters we will then examine each form of collection in more detail.

A *vector* is a fixed-length group of elements of uniform type, indexed by integer keys. Vectors are useful when the number of items to be maintained by a collection is known in advance or can at least be bounded. Vectors are also important when the ability to rapidly access arbitrary elements is important, since individual elements can be directly indexed. The elements in a vector are usually assumed to be unsequenced. In several subsequent chapters we will examine techniques for placing elements maintained in a vector into order.

v_0	v_1	v_2	…	v_{n-1}	v_n

A string can be considered to be a vector of character values. Just as the subscript operator is used to obtain individual characters within a string, in the same manner the subscript operator

is used to access individual elements within a vector.

A *list* is a data structure of choice when the number of elements in a collection cannot be bounded. Like a vector, a list maintains values of uniform type. Unlike a vector, a list can hold any number of values. Lists are not indexed. Instead, elements must be examined one by one in sequence. For this reason the amount of time required to access an element in a list depends upon the position the element holds in the list; accessing values near the head of the list is performed more rapidly than accessing elements near the end. A simple list is unordered. A variation, called an *ordered list*, maintains the values in sequence. Notice that each entry in a list has at most one immediate predecessor node, and at most one immediate successor node. The first item in a list, the single node that does not have any predecessor, is referred to as the *head* of the list. The last element in a list is referred to as the *tail* of the list.

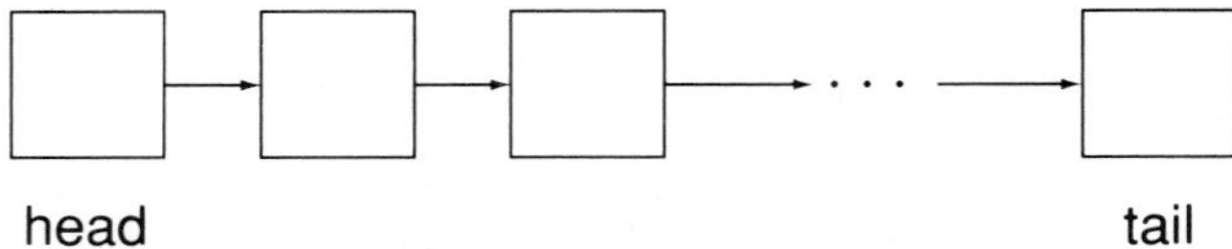

Stacks and *queues* can be thought of as specialized forms of lists (see Figure 5.1). (This is an abstract characterization, not necessarily how these data structures are implemented.) Elements in a stack obey the last-in, first-out (*LIFO*) protocol. Elements can be added and removed only from the front of a stack. Thus, an element removed from a stack is the element that has been held for the least amount of time. A queue, on the other hand, maintains the first-in, first-out (*FIFO*) protocol. Elements are inserted in the back of the queue and removed from the front. Thus, an element removed from a queue is the element that has been held by the queue for the longest amount of time. Stacks and queues are important data structures when elements in a problem need to be examined in a specific order that matches either the LIFO or FIFO properties.

Along with vectors and lists, *trees*, and in particular *binary trees*, are building blocks out of which many data structures are constructed. While vectors, lists, stacks, and queues can be thought of as linear data structures, trees are inherently two-dimensional. We saw in Chapter 1 an example tree, in the form of an inheritance hierarchy (Section 1.2.1, page 136). A tree is composed of a number of tree *nodes* (see Figure 5.2). Each node can have one or more children (a binary tree is restricted to having at most two children). The most important property of trees concerns the relationship between the depth and the number of nodes. Briefly, the number of nodes is an exponential function of the depth. By maintaining the nodes on a tree in various forms, operations such as searching for a specific element can be performed in time proportional to the depth of the tree. In

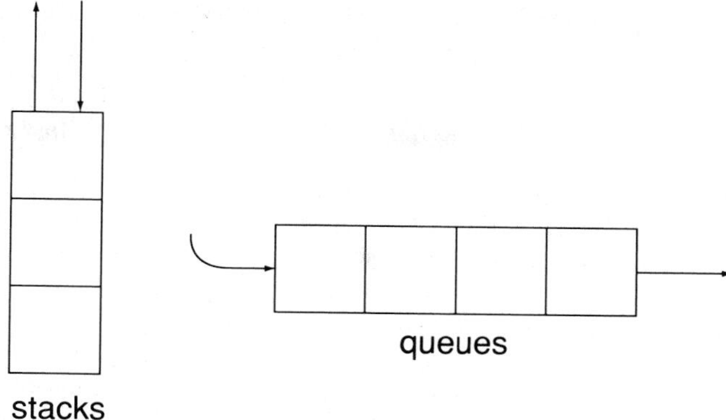

Figure 5.1 Stacks and queues

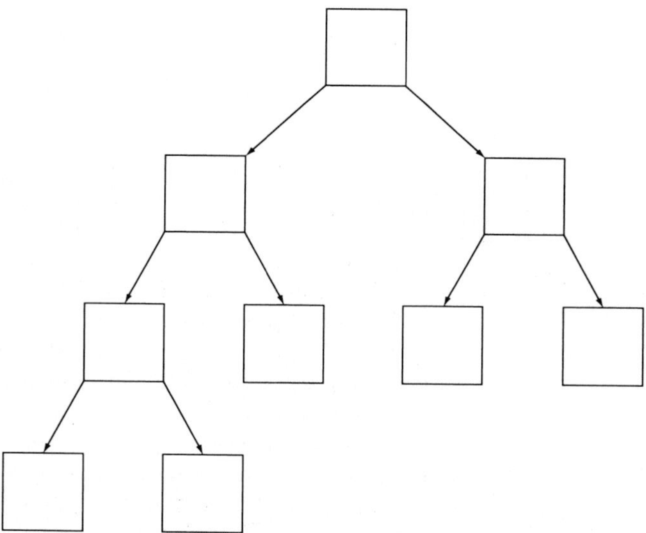

Figure 5.2 A tree structure

particular, *search trees* are a useful technique when the basic operation is to determine whether elements are or are not held in a collection. A different structuring of trees yields *priority queues,* a data abstraction that is useful when the basic operation in a problem is to repeatedly find and remove the smallest element in a collection.

Sets and *bags* are data structures that are useful in problems in which multiple collections naturally occur, and the major tasks are to form unions and intersections of different structures. A set is an unordered collection of elements in which each value is unique—that is, it appears at most once. In a bag, on the other hand, elements can be repeated multiple times.

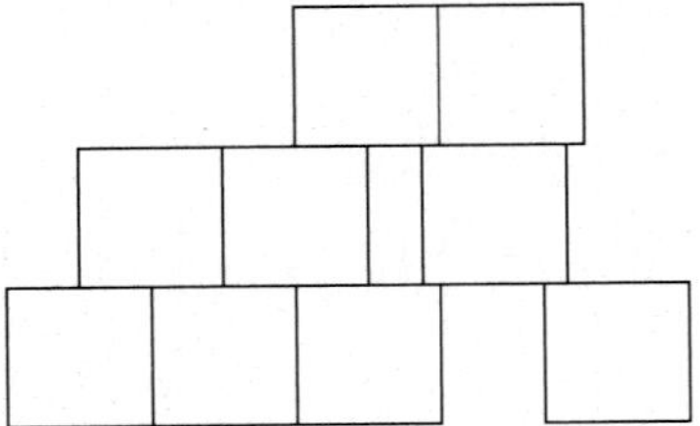

A *hash table* is a generalization of a vector. Instead of using integer indexing, the values of the elements themselves are transformed, using a function called a *hash function*, into an integer index value.

$h(v_0)$	$h(v_1)$	$h(v_2)$	$\cdots$	$h(v_{n-1})$	$h(v_n)$

The real power of hash tables is realized when the elements of the hash vector are themselves collections. Thus each entry in the hash table can be considered a bucket, potentially holding multiple values. Structures with various properties can be constructed in this fashion, depending upon the type of collection used to implement the bucket.

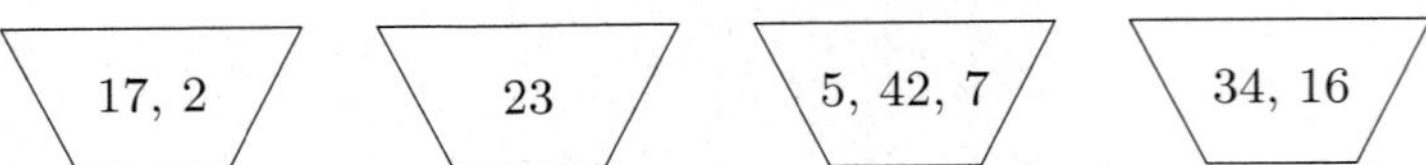

A *dictionary* (sometimes called a *table* or *mapping*) is an indexed data structure, like a vector. Instead of being restricted to integer index values, the index values in a dictionary can be of any type. Index values are stored as part of the structure itself. A dictionary can be thought of as a collection of *associations* of key and value pairs (see Figure 5.3). A dictionary is the data structure of choice in problems in which values are manipulated as a mapping between index and element values, but for which the index elements are not integers.

Finally, we will examine graphs as a data structure, where a *graph* is a collection of nodes and directed arcs connecting the nodes (see Figure 5.4). Information can be associated in the graph with either the nodes or with the arcs. Graphs naturally occur in many two-dimensional problems—for example, modeling highways, where the nodes represent cities and the arcs distances between cities.

Table 5.1 summarizes some of the properties and limitations of the data structures we will examine in this text. More detailed information about each individual data abstraction is also provided in Appendix A.

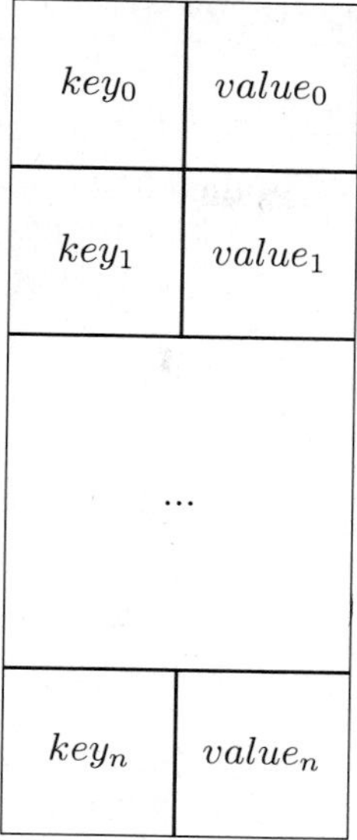

Figure 5.3 A dictionary

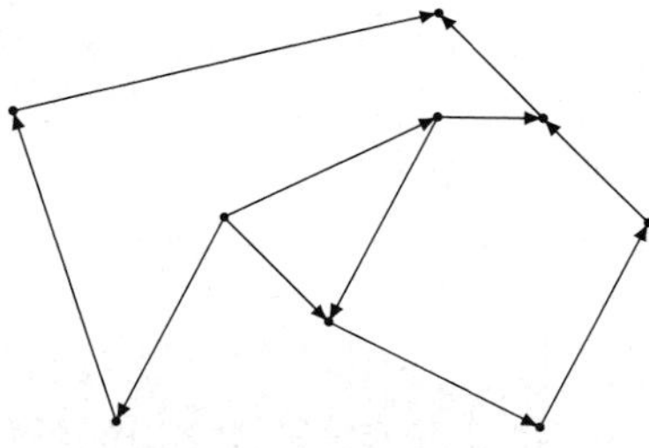

Figure 5.4 A graph

References

There are many ways in which the concepts implicit in the classic collection data structures can be organized. Knuth [Knuth 73] considers only lists and trees as major categories. The data structures book by Aho, Hopcroft, and Ullman adds chapters on sets and graphs to this division [Aho 83]. Tenenbaum et al. consider stacks as a fundamental type [Tenenbaum 90], while many other authors discuss stacks merely as a variation on lists or arrays. Schneider and Bruell [Schneider 91] divide data structures into four categories: linear (vector, list, stack, queue), hierarchical (trees), graph, and set (including hash tables).

Table 5.1 Properties and limitations of various data structures

Structure	Properties	Limitations
Vector	Direct access to each element	Fixed size
List	Arbitrary size	Sequential access, rapid access only to first element
Stack	LIFO protocol	Insertions and deletions only from front
Queue	FIFO protocol	Insertions and deletions only from ends
Tree	Rapid insertion/access	To maintain balance, requires nontrivial algorithms
AVL tree	Guaranteed log performance	Complex algorithms
Priority queue	Rapid access to smallest element	Only smallest element available at any one time
Hash tables	Rapid access to scattered storage	Requires good hash function
Set	Rapid union/intersections	Elements not maintained in order
Dictionary	Values associated with key	Complex structure
Graph	Collection of vertices and arcs	Unordered
File	Collection in external storage	Slow access

Exercises

1. Suppose that a program is designed to manage a collection of student records for a university. The appropriate data structure needed to hold the actual records might depend upon what tasks needed to be performed. For each of the following, describe briefly what data structures you think might be appropriate:

a. Adding and deleting students from different classes, eventually producing printed lists of students in each class.

b. Same as the first, but printing the students in alphabetical order.

c. Merging class lists together; for example, merging lists of students in different sections of the same class into one master list.

d. Associating grade reports with students by name; that is, an on-line system where an instructor could enter the student's name and see a report on the grades the student received in previous courses.

CHAPTER 6

Vectors and Component Reuse

In mathematics, an indexed list of values is called a vector. In C++ we can represent this abstract concept as a one-dimensional array. Recall that a one-dimensional array is a fixed-size collection of values of uniform type, indexed by integer keys. The number of elements held by the array is provided as part of the declaration. The following example creates an array of six double precision values:

```
double c[6];
```

Legal index values range from zero to one less than the size of the collection. Values are accessed using the subscript operator. A programmer can think of the elements of an array as being placed end to end in memory. The array of six elements declared above might be visualized, for example, as the following:

Element c[0]	Element c[1]	Element c[2]	Element c[3]	Element c[4]	Element c[5]

Our motivation for developing the vector as a data type mirrors the reasoning we described as prompting the creation of the string data type in the last chapter. The underlying C++ language provides only a primitive mechanism for the support of one-dimensional arrays, and this mechanism provides few safeguards. Most importantly, index values are not checked against declared bounds at run time.

This problem is compounded by the fact that arrays, unlike strings, are not "self-describing." There is no way to determine from the value of a simple C++ array the extent, or number of elements, it should contain. Furthermore, there are even fewer high level operations defined for the array type than there are for character strings. By building a new abstraction layer on top of the basic language framework, we can correct many of these deficiencies.

Vectors are the first of several fundamental "building blocks" we will encounter in this text. That is, vectors are used as a component in the construction of many structures. Other fundamental types we will subsequently investigate include lists (Chapter 8) and trees (Chapter 10). In Section 6.3 we will describe the two most common mechanisms, inheritance and composition, that are used in the creation of new structures.

Finally, in this chapter we will investigate some of the themes and variations that are possible in building vector data types. In particular, we will see that taken individually, almost all the limiting characteristic features of a vector we named in the first paragraph can be eliminated. That is, there are vectors for which the maximum size need not be known at compile time, there are vectors for which the index values need not be integer, and there are vectors for which the lower bound on index values is not required to be zero.

6.1 TEMPLATES

A vector viewed as a data abstraction is different in one very important respect from the data types we have previously investigated. As an abstract concept, the idea of a vector describes an incomplete data type. The solution of any particular problem might require a vector of integers, a vector of floating point values, or even a vector of strings. In order to abstract the concept of "vector-ness" out of these more concrete realizations, we need a facility to *parameterize* a type description with another type. That is, we need some way to describe the idea of a "vector of T," where T represents an unknown type.

A mechanism to provide this functionality will allow us to define characteristics of vectors, as long as we avoid any direct reference to operations defined on `T` values, since the type `T` is unknown. Later, we can create more specific instances of this type, by binding the unknown value `T` to another type—for example, by creating a vector of integers by binding `T` to the type `int`. The C++ construct used to express this idea is called a *template*. A template for our vector abstraction is shown in Fig. 6.1.

Three constructors are defined for the vector class. The first simply indicates the number of elements to be held by the vector. The second supplies, in addition, an initial value for each entry. The third is the copy constructor, used to create a duplicate copy of a vector. Note that within the class definition itself, the qualifier type name can be omitted on the vector type, as illustrated by the argument in the copy constructor. As was true with the string abstraction, a destructor will be used to ensure that dynamically allocated memory is released. (Note that something new has been added, in that we have declared the destructor to be `virtual`. We will postpone the explanation of this term until the next chapter.) In addition to the constructors, four additional operations are defined. These are the subscript operator, a function to return the length of the vector, and a pair of new functions called `setSize`, which we will shortly describe.

One way to think of templates is with an analogy to a function or procedure invocation. A method such as the `GCD` procedure examined in Chapter 3 provides a general framework to solve a class of problems. This problem solution is parameterized by argument values. To solve a specific problem — for example, to compute the greatest common divisor of 40902 and 24140 — the programmer supplies bindings for the arguments and executes the procedure. In the same manner a template provides a general framework for solving a class of problems (namely, creating a class of related data types). In order to use this feature in any specific situation, the programmer provides bindings (argument values) for the unknown type names. The list following the keyword `template` even looks a little like a parameter list, only it is surrounded with angle brackets instead of parentheses.

The keyword `class` in the template argument list is somewhat misleading. In fact, any legal type, not only class types, can be used as a template argument. Thus we can create vectors of integers (which are not class types) as well as vectors of strings.

Within a vector class description, the unknown parameter type (`T` in our example) can be used in any situation requiring the use of a type name. Thus we can declare instance variables as "pointer to `T`," and we can declare an operator as returning a `T` reference. In the copy constructor, we need to refer to an object of the same type as the receiver. This type is not simply a `vector`, but it must be qualified as being a vector of type `T`.

In order to use a template class as a type, we must provide bindings for the unknown argument types. This is accomplished by providing the element types in a list, again surrounded by angle brackets.[1] For example,

---

1. Various implementation schemes for templates may also require additional statements. Also, some implementations of C++ insist that the implementation of member functions for template classes appears in the interface file, while other implementations permit these function bodies to appear in an implementation file.

```
//
// class vector -
//     type safe and access safe vector data type
//     permits dynamic modification of vector length
//

template <class T> class vector {
public:
    // constructors and destructor
    vector          (unsigned int numberElements);
    vector          (unsigned int numberElements, T & initialValue);
    vector          (const vector & source);
    virtual ~vector ();

    // access to elements via subscript
    T &             operator [ ] (unsigned int index) const;

    // length of vector
    unsigned int    length       () const;

    // dynamically change size
    unsigned int    setSize      (unsigned int numberOfElements);
    unsigned int    setSize      (unsigned int numberOfElements,
                                      T & initialValue);

protected:
    // data areas
    T *             data;
    unsigned int    size;
};
```

Figure 6.1 A class declaration that uses templates

the following declares a vector of 10 integer values, each entry initialized with the value 1, a vector consisting of 30 double-precision values, each entry of which is uninitialized, and a vector of 15 strings, all initialized using the default constructor from class `string`.

```
vector<int>     a(10, 1);
vector<double>  b(30);
vector<string>  c(15);
```

The data area in the vector class is declared as `protected`. Protected fields provide for access that is between private and public. Like private fields, users of the data abstraction are not permitted access to protected fields. However, subclasses (such as the classes we will be discussing later in this chapter) are permitted to access protected fields (but not private fields).

6.2 SIMPLE VECTORS

In this section we will describe the implementation of the simple vector data type described in Fig. 6.1. The size of a vector is determined by the quantity passed as argument to the constructor, which may not be known until run time. For this reason, we must once again use dynamic allocation in the constructors to create the actual space for the vector values. The implementation of the three constructors is as follows:

```
template<class T> vector<T>::vector(unsigned int numberElements)
        : size(numberElements)
{   // create and initialize a new vector
    // allocate the space for the elements
    data = new T[size];

    // check that allocation was successful
    assert(data != 0);
}

template<class T> vector<T>::vector(unsigned int numberElements,
        T & initialValue) : size(numberElements)
{   // create and initialize a new vector
    // allocate the space for the elements
    data = new T[size];
    assert(data != 0);

    // set each element to the initial value
    for (int i = 0; i < size; i++)
        data[i] = initialValue;
}

template<class T> vector<T>::vector(const vector<T> & source)
        : size(source.size)
{   // create and initialize a new vector
    // allocate the space for the elements
    data = new T[size];
    assert(data != 0);

    // copy values from old vector
    for (int i = 0; i < size; i++)
        data[i] = source.data[i];
}
```

Recall that C++ associates closely the concepts of pointers and arrays, allowing pointer values to be indexed by using the subscripting operator. Using this power, we can store the data values as a pointer rather than as an array. The constructor uses an assertion to check that the allocation was successful. The copy constructor does the same, and then it copies the values from the argument. Both the copy constructor and the initializing constructor use loops to set the initial values in the vector. The fact that the first form of constructor does not do any explicit initialization does not mean the values stored by the elements will be totally random or uninitialized; if the type T provides a default initialization method (for example, as would occur in creating a vector of strings), then the default constructor for the element type will be automatically invoked for each position in the vector.

As was true in the string data structure, here the destructor simply frees the dynamically allocated storage. Setting the pointer field and the size to zero prevents possible errors if the same value is somehow twice deleted.

```
template <class T> vector<T>::~vector()
{   // free the dynamic memory buffer
    delete [ ] data;
    data = 0;
    size = 0;
}
```

Two of the vector operations are trivial to implement. The subscript operator takes as argument an unsigned integer value. Because the argument is unsigned, we are assured the value is positive. To check that the index is valid, it is only necessary to verify that it is smaller than the number of positions maintained by the vector. This information is stored in the data field named `size`. Having checked this condition by using an asser-

Vector Elements and Constructors

The syntax used to declare the actual elements stored in a vector places a limitation on the type of elements that can be declared with a vector. Since no constructor arguments are provided in the declaration:

```
T * data;
```

a data type defined with a class or structure declaration can only be used as a vector element if the data type provides a default (no argument) constructor. Thus we can make a vector of strings but not a vector of stringMatchers, or a vector of vectors (although we will, later in this chapter, make a vector of *pointers* to vectors).

Similarly, a reference variable can only be declared in conjunction with an initialization, which provides the value the variable refers to. Because no initialization appears in the declaration statement for the storage area in the vector, vector elements cannot be declared as reference types.

tion, the appropriate element is returned. Because this operation does not change the vector itself, the method is declared as constant.

```
template <class T> T & vector<T>::operator [ ] (unsigned int index) const
{   // subscript a vector value
    // check that index is valid
    assert(index < size);

    // return requested element
    return data[index];
}
```

The second operation is merely an accessor method, used to obtain a count of the number of elements in the vector. Once again, the method is declared as constant since it does not alter the vector itself.

```
template <class T> unsigned int vector<T>::length() const
{   // return the number of elements in the vector
    return size;
}
```

In many of the algorithms we will describe in subsequent chapters, it is difficult to know before execution begins the appropriate size to use in declaring a vector. One way around this is to provide a mechanism to permit a vector to dynamically change size. This permits a vector to grow or shrink as necessary. The user supplies a value for the new size of the vector, which can be either larger or smaller than the current size. A new data area is created to hold the values. As many as possible of the current values of the vector are copied into the new data area. If an initial value is provided, any new entries are initialized. Because this copy operation is linear in the size of the data buffer, changing the size of a vector is an expensive task. Nevertheless, we will see that the ability to perform this function will simplify the solution of many problems. The implementation of one of the `setSize` functions is shown below. The other method is similar.

```
template <class T>
unsigned int vector<T>::setSize(unsigned int numberOfElements,
        T & initialValue)
{   // dynamically alter the size of the vector

    // first create the new data area
    T * newData = new T[numberOfElements];
    assert(newData != 0);

    if (numberOfElements <= size) {
        // data area is shrinking - copy as many elements as possible
        for (int i = 0; i < numberOfElements; i++)
```

```
            newData[i] = data[i];
        }
    else {
        // data area is growing - first copy old values
        for (int i = 0; i < size; i++)
            newData[i] = data[i];
        // then initialize new values
        for (i = size; i < numberOfElements; i++)
            newData[i] = initialValue;
        }

    // delete the old data buffer
    delete [ ] data;

    // update the data member fields
    size = numberOfElements;
    data = newData;

    // return new size
    return size;
}
```

6.2.1 Application — Word Length Frequencies

Our first use of the vector data abstraction will be a simple procedure to compute the frequencies of lengths of words in the standard input. The procedure is passed an integer vector, presumably initialized to zero. (The vector can retain previous values in order to compute cumulative frequencies.) The length of this vector will be the maximum length of the words to be considered. All words longer than this length are combined into a single category, the size of which is maintained by the integer variable named *bigwords*. A loop reads in each word from the standard input. If the length of the word is smaller than the maximum length, the frequency count for the length is updated. Otherwise, if the word is longer than the number of array positions, the count of big words is incremented.

```
// tally occurrences of words by length in the standard input
//    group all words larger than maximum index of first argument
//    into bigwords category
void wordLengthFreq(vector<int> & counts, int & bigwords)
{
    const int lengthmax = counts.length();
    string word;
    // compute the word frequencies
    while (cin >> word) {
```

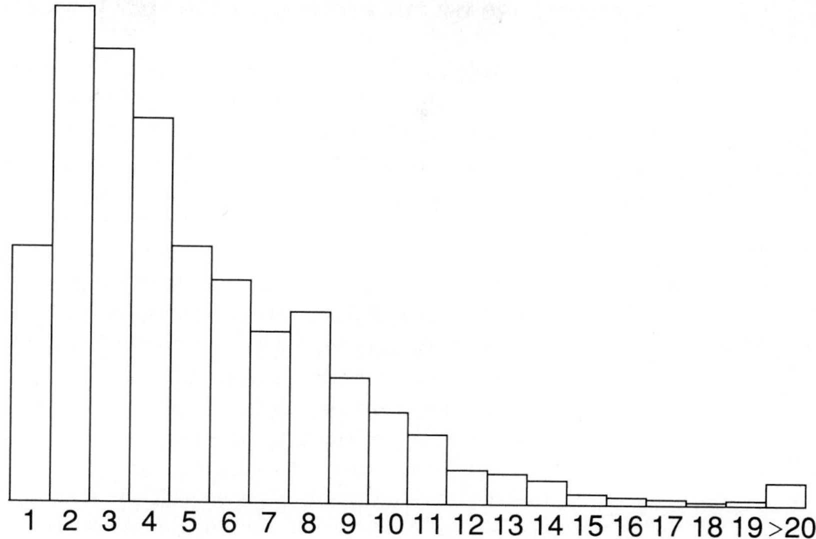

Figure 6.2 Word length frequencies

```
int wordlen = word.length();
if (wordlen < lengthmax)
    counts[wordlen]++;
else
    bigwords++;
}}
```

For example, computing the frequencies on word lengths in this chapter produces the distribution shown in Fig. 6.2.

6.3 TECHNIQUES FOR SOFTWARE REUSE

An important function of any data structure, particularly a simple data type such as our vector abstraction, is its use as a building block in the development of other components. In practice there are two common techniques used to achieve the goal of software *reuse*—that is, the utilization of existing software components in new data types: inheritance and composition. We will illustrate and contrast these mechanisms by creating two different variations on the idea of a vector. We will illustrate the use of *inheritance* in the development of a data type for a bounded vector, in which the user specifies both an upper and lower bound for index values. An alternative technique, the use of *composition*, will subsequently be illustrated by the design of the bit vector class.

6.3.1 Component Reuse by Inheritance — Bounded Vectors

Our simple vector class, like the basic C++ vectors, uses zero as the starting index value. Many problems are more naturally solved with vectors that use nonzero values as the lower bound. For example, suppose a company finds it necessary to maintain a database of figures representing the number of sales completed in the years 1976 to 1983. There are seven quantities to be maintained, so a vector of size seven should suffice. On the other hand, to use the simple vector abstraction for this purpose would require the programmer to remember that position 3, for example, corresponds to year 1979. A better solution would be to define a new vector data type that allows the programmer to set both the upper *and* lower bounds.

Many of the features of our first `vector` abstraction — for example, the `length` function or the ability to alter the number of elements held in the data area — do not depend upon the lower bound having a value of zero. By making our new abstraction, which we will call `boundedVector`, a child class of class `vector`, we inherit these abilities with no additional coding effort. That is, by the simple use of inheritance the new data type is provided with all the data areas and member functions of the parent class, with no additional coding effort required.

A class definition for our new abstraction is shown below. Constructors are provided that mirror those of the vector class. The first constructor takes as argument the lower and upper bounds. The second does the same, and in addition provides an initial value for each element. The final constructor is the copy constructor. A modified subscript operator is provided, as well as two new methods for obtaining the upper and lower bounds for the vector.

```
//
// class boundedVector
//     vectors with explicit upper and lower bounds
//

template<class T> class boundedVector : public vector<T> {
public:
    // constructors
    boundedVector  (int lowIndex, int highIndex);
    boundedVector  (int lowIndex, int highIndex, T & initialValue);
    boundedVector  (const boundedVector & source);

    // element access
    T&             operator [ ]     (int index) const;

    // structural information
    int            lowerBound       () const;
```

```
    int             upperBound      () const;

protected:
    const int       lowbound;
};
```

Because the management of the data area is performed by the parent class, the implementation of the operations in class `boundedVector` is made relatively simple. For example, consider the implementation of the constructors. There are three constructors defined. In the first two, the constructors subtract the lower bound from the higher bound then add one to obtain the number of elements to be stored. The tasks of dynamically allocating the storage areas and initializing the data values are all performed by the parent class `vector`. Note that the data field `lowbound` is declared as constant and thus must be initialized in the constructor header, not by means of an assignment statement in the constructor body. The only additional action performed by the constructor is to ensure that the lower bound on index values is less than or equal to the upper bound.

```
template <class T> boundedVector<T>::boundedVector
    (int lowIndex, int highIndex)
        : lowbound(lowIndex), vector<T>(1 + highIndex - lowIndex)
{   // create and initialize a new bounded vector
    assert(lowIndex <= highIndex);
}

template <class T> boundedVector<T>::boundedVector
    (int lowIndex, int highIndex, T & initialValue)
    : lowbound(lowIndex),
        vector<T>(1 + highIndex - lowIndex, initialValue)
{   // create and initialize a new bounded vector
    assert(lowIndex <= highIndex);
}
```

The copy constructor merely sets the value of the lower bound, then invokes the copy constructor from the parent class. No assertion is necessary since the upper and lower bounds have already been validated during the construction of the argument.

```
template <class T> boundedVector<T>::boundedVector
    (const boundedVector<T> & source)
        : lowbound(source.lowbound), vector<T>(source)
{
    // no further initialization necessary
}
```

It is unnecessary to provide a destructor for the class `boundedVector`.

The destructor for the parent class, `vector`, will automatically be invoked when an instance of `boundedVector` is destroyed.[2]

The remaining operations are easy to implement by making use of facilities provided by the parent class. For example, the subscripting operator merely subtracts the lower bound from the given index and then invokes the subscripting operator from the parent class. Note that the argument to this class is declared as integer, rather than unsigned integer, since the programmer is now free to use negative numbers as index values (as long as they legitimately lie between the lower and upper bounds). This method illustrates the *disambiguation prefix*, used to indicate that the method to be invoked inside the method is the subscripting operator from the parent class, not a recursive call on the subscripting operator in the class `boundedVector`.

```
template <class T> T & boundedVector<T>::operator [ ] (int index) const
{   // subscript operator for bounded vectors
    // subtract off lower bound
    // yielding value between 0 and size of vector
    // then use subscript from parent class
    return vector<T>::operator [ ] (index - lowbound);
}
```

The remaining two methods return the lower and upper bound. The former is simply an accessor method for the constant value stored in the structure. The latter must compute the upper bound, since the vector could conceivably change size—for example, as a result of a call on the `setSize` operation. To compute the upper bound, the size of the vector minus one, obtained by using the `length` function inherited from class `vector`, is added to the lower bound.

```
template <class T> int boundedVector<T>::lowerBound() const
{   // return smallest legal index for bounded vector
    return lowbound;
}

template <class T> int boundedVector<T>::upperBound() const
{   // return largest legal index for bounded vector
    return lowerBound() + length() - 1;
}
```

APPLICATION—LETTER FREQUENCIES Continuing the theme started by the earlier example, we illustrate the use of lower bound vectors by presenting a procedure to compute the frequencies of occurrence of

---

2. To be entirely accurate, this is only due to the fact that the destructor in class `vector` was declared as `virtual`. We will discuss the meaning of the `virtual` modifier in the next chapter.

individual letters in a text. The procedure `letterOccurrences` takes as input a string value and a lower bound vector. The range of legal index values is assumed to correspond to the range of lowercase letters. (Recall that in C++ character values are treated simply as integers.) The string is analyzed, converting uppercase letters into their corresponding lowercase values. For this purpose, the utility functions provided by the `ctype` run-time library are useful.

```
void letterOccurrences(boundedVector<int> & counts, const string & text)
{
    // make sure the upper and lower bound on counts
    // array is what we expect
    assert (counts.lowerBound() == 'a');
    assert (counts.upperBound() == 'z');

    // loop over the text string
    // considering each character in turn
    for (int i = 0; text[i] != '\0'; i++) {
        char c = text[i];
        if (isupper(c))
            c = tolower(c);
        if (islower(c))
            counts[c]++;
        }
}
```

To illustrate the declaration of a lower bound vector, the following procedure shows the invocation of the letter frequencies procedure. The program simply reads words from the standard input, accumulating cumulative frequencies until the end of input is reached. The number of occurrences of each letter is then printed.

```
void computeWordOccurrences()
{
    // declare a vector indexed from 'a' to 'z' initialized
to zero
    boundedVector<int> counts('a', 'z', 0);
    string word;

    // read and analyze the input
    while (cin >> word)
        letterOccurrences(counts, word);

    // then print the results
    for (char c = 'a'; c <= 'z'; c++)
        cout << "letter " << c << " occurrences "
            << counts[c] << '\n';
}
```

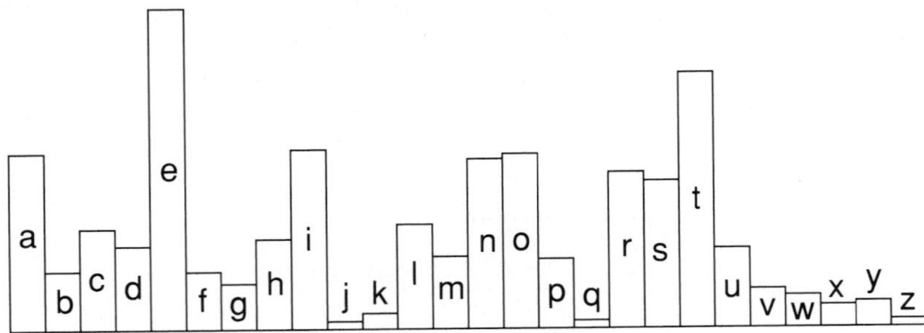

Figure 6.3 A typical character distribution

If we use as input the text of this chapter, we obtain the distribution of characters shown in Fig. 6.3.

6.3.2 Component Reuse by Composition — Bit Vectors

Inheritance is one mechanism that provides the ability to reuse existing data structures without rewriting code. Inheritance is the mechanism of choice when the entire behavior, or a substantial portion of the behavior, of the parent class is also applicable to the child class. A different form of reuse occurs when a new structure can effectively make use of an existing data structure as a component, but the behavior of the component part does not exactly match the behavior of the new structure.

An example we will use to illustrate this style of code reuse is the development of a *bit vector*. A bit vector is simply a vector of 0/1 values. Since all computer values are stored internally as bits, we can encode a bit vector in almost any data type. A convenient representation is as an array of unsigned character values. As each character represents an 8-bit quantity, 8 bit values can be stored in each character.

Bits 0-7	Bits 8-15	Bits 16-23	Bits 24-31
01101110	10011010	00101010	10110001

The class `bitVector` (Fig. 6.4) makes use of this encoding. By reusing the `vector` data structure as a field in the internal representation of the bit vector, we need not concern ourselves with issues such as dynamic memory allocation or deletion, or checking the validity of index values.

This type of component reuse is sometimes known as the *has-a* relation, in contrast to the *is-a* relation used in inheritance. Using inheritance, the child class *is-a* more specialized form of the parent class. This means that all public or protected data areas or functions defined in the parent

```
//
// class bitVector
//    a vector of binary (0 or 1) values
//    individual bits can be set or cleared, tested or flipped
//

class bitVector {
public:
    // constructors
    bitVector   (unsigned int numberOfElements);
    bitVector   (const bitVector & source);

    // number of legal index positions
    unsigned int    length   () const;

    // set, change operations
    void            set     (unsigned int index);
    void            clear   (unsigned int index);
    int             test    (unsigned int index) const;
    void            flip    (unsigned int index);

protected:
    vector<unsigned char>   bitValues;

    // position decoding functions
    unsigned int    byteNumber   (unsigned int indx) const;
    unsigned int    mask         (unsigned int indx) const;
};
```

Figure 6.4 Class definition of the bit vector class

class are also accessible in instances of the child class. With the *has-a* relationship characteristic of composition, on the other hand, the facilities provided by the component being reused can be invoked only within the new structure; they are not available to users of the new structure. For example, it is not possible to increase the size of bit vectors, since the `setSize` method is not part of the interface for the bit vector data type.

The advantages of reuse are common to both reuse by inheritance and reuse by composition. In both cases we avoid the necessity of redeveloping and recoding an existing structure. If the component being reused has been extensively tested in other situations, the potential for errors being introduced in the new structure is greatly reduced. In both cases reuse implies that the programmer can concentrate on those features that are unique to the new structure, while ignoring other aspects that are relevant only to the reused component. For example, in both the lower bound vector and the bit vector it is not necessary to be concerned about the issue of dynamic memory allocation and release, since these will automatically be handled by the `vector` data type. In neither case is it necessary to provide an explicit destructor, since the language will automatically see to the invocation of the destructor from the underlying `vector` class.

We now proceed with our exposition of the implementation of the bit vector data type. As was the case with the lower bound vector, the constructor for the bit vector does almost no work itself, instead merely serving as a conduit to invoke the constructor for the vector component that is holding the actual data values. The constructor takes an indication of the size desired for the bit vector and computes the smallest multiple of eight larger than or equal to the value. The size computation makes use of the fact that integer division will truncate any remainder values. An array of characters of the appropriate size is then allocated. By invoking the initializing form of the vector constructor, this data area can also be set to all zero values.

```
bitVector::bitVector(unsigned int numberOfElements)
    : bitValues((numberOfElements + 7)/8, 0)
{
    // no additional initialization
}
```

The copy constructor is shorter, simply invoking the copy constructor for the vector data area.

```
bitVector::bitVector(const bitVector & source) :
bitValues(source.bitValues)
{
    // no additional initialization
}
```

Since eight bits are stored in each character value, the number of legal bit positions is eight times the number of elements stored in the character vector. This value can be computed using the `length` function. (The result will always be a multiple of eight, and can potentially be larger than the value supplied to the constructor. An alternative design would be to maintain a data field in the bit vector class to hold the maximum permitted index value.)

```
unsigned int bitVector::length() const
{   // eight bits stored in every vector element
    return 8 * bitValues.length();
}
```

The four operations `set`, `clear`, `test`, and `flip` are the basic means of manipulating bit vectors. Each of these is implemented by using a pair of facilitator functions. The function `byteNumber` takes an index into the bit vector and converts it into an index into the character array. Since eight bits are stored in each character, this can be accomplished by dividing by eight. An even more efficient way to divide an unsigned integer value by eight is to shift right by three spaces. For example, suppose the index value is the number 13. The bit pattern corresponding to the value 13 is 00001101. If we shift right by three spaces, we obtain the bit pattern 00000001, which corresponds to the integer value one. Thus, the thirteenth bit in our bit vector will be stored in the character found at index position 1. The `byteNumber` function is defined as follows:

```
unsigned int bitVector::byteNumber(unsigned int index) const
{   // return index of byte containing specified value
    // byte number is index value divided by 8
    return index >> 3;
}
```

The second facilitator function computes a mask into the selected byte value, with a one bit representing the bit at the location being manipulated, and zero values in all other bit positions. To do this, the function takes the low order three bits of the index (the bits that are shifted away in the first function), and it uses this value as an amount to shift left a numeric one value. If we mask off the lower three bits of the number 13, we obtain the bit pattern 00000101, which corresponds to the number 5. Thus the value one is shifted left by five places, yielding the bit pattern 00100000. This will be the mask for each of the bit operations performed.

```
unsigned int bitVector::mask(unsigned int index) const
{   // compute the amount to shift by examining
    // the low order 3 bits of the index
    const unsigned int shiftAmount = index & 07;

    // make a mask by shifting the value "1"
    // left by the given amount
    return 1 << shiftAmount;
}
```

To set a bit, the bitwise *or* operation is used. All one bits in the array will remain one, since the bitwise *or* of one and zero is still one. The only bit that can change is the bit at the location corresponding to the one bit in the mask. This location will be turned into a one value, regardless of its original value in the array.

data	10011001
mask	00100000
result	10111001

```
void bitVector::set (unsigned int index)
{   // set the indicated bit in the data array
    bitValues[byteNumber(index)] |= mask(index); }
```

To clear a bit—that is, to set the value of the bit to zero—the bitwise *and* operation is used. First, the mask is inverted using the tilde operator. This results in a mask with one values everywhere but in the selected location. In the case of our example mask, this would yield the bit pattern 11011111. When a bitwise *and* operation is performed with the array data byte, the selected location will be turned into a zero value, regardless of its current value. Similarly all other fields will retain their previous value, regardless of their state.

data	10111001
mask	00100000
inverted mask	11011111
result	10011001

```
void bitVector::clear (unsigned int index)
{   // clear the indicated bit in the bitValues array
    bitValues[byteNumber(index)] &= ~ mask(index);
}
```

To test a bit position, the data byte is *and*-ed with the mask. If the result is nonzero, then the data byte must have had a one value in the selected location. If the result is zero, then the data type must have contained a zero bit. This is the only operation of the four that does not alter the data vector, and thus is the only function declared as constant.

data	10011001
mask	00100000
result	00000000

```
int bitVector::test (unsigned int index) const
{   // test the indicated bit in the bitValues array
    return 0 != (bitValues[byteNumber(index)] & mask(index));
}
```

Finally, to invert the value at the mask position, regardless of its current value, the *exclusive-or* bit level operation is used. The *exclusive-or* of a one and zero value is always one, while the *exclusive-or* of two one values is zero, as is the *exclusive-or* of two zero values. Thus, if the value in the location selected by the mask is one, it will become zero; if it is zero, it will become one.

data	10011001
mask	00100000
result	10111001

```
void bitVector::flip (unsigned int index)
{   // flip the indicated bit in the bitValues array
    bitValues[byteNumber(index)] ^= mask(index);
}
```

APPLICATION — SIEVE OF ERATOSTHENES We will illustrate the use of bit vectors with a classic algorithm to discover prime numbers. The technique was described by the Greek mathematician/philosopher Eratosthenes in the third century BC, and it is thus usually referred to as the *sieve of Eratosthenes*.

The basic idea behind the algorithm is to take a list of all the numbers, and strike out those that cannot possibly be prime numbers. When those that cannot be prime are removed, the remaining values must therefore be prime. Suppose we wish to discover the prime numbers less than 20. We can visualize the collection of values as follows:

2	3	4	5	6	7	8	9	10	11	12	13	14	15	16	17	18	19	20

Although we can visualize the set in this manner, we will in fact represent the set of values using a bit vector, where a one bit represents the fact that the element is in the set, and a zero bit represents the assertion that the corresponding integer is not present in the set. Since the set of values we are interested in begins with two, we will simply ignore the index positions zero and one.

The algorithm can be described as follows. A finger, or index, will move through the collection, starting from the beginning. At each step, we advance this counter to the next element that has not been eliminated. The first time we do this, we will discover the first element, namely two. We know at this point that two is in the final collection — that is, that two is a prime number. Starting from *this* position, we delete all multiples of this number. Deleting all multiples of two yields the following collection:

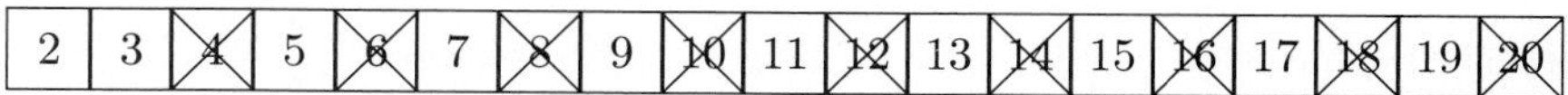

2	3	~~4~~	5	~~6~~	7	~~8~~	9	~~10~~	11	~~12~~	13	~~14~~	15	~~16~~	17	~~18~~	19	~~20~~

We next advance the finger, or counter, to the next position that has not been eliminated. In this example it is the next value, namely three. Once again we eliminate multiples of three. Note that some of these values may have already been eliminated by the previous step. The resulting collection can be visualized as follows:

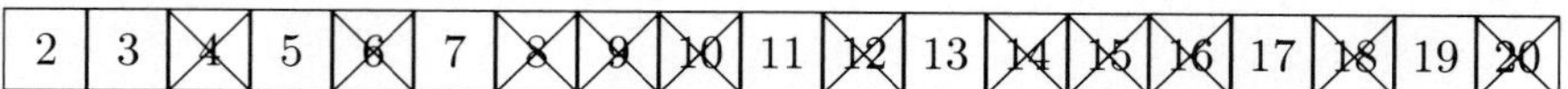

Next we consider the value five, crossing out the multiples 10, 15, and 20. We continue in this fashion until all values have been examined. Any remaining values *must* be prime. To see why, assume that there remains in the final list at least one value that is not prime. Let n be the first such value. If it is not prime, then n must have some prime factors. Let m be a prime factor of n. Since n was the first nonprime in the list, m must be on the list. But then n would have been eliminated when we deleted the multiples of m. Therefore n will not be on the final list.

The program that follows from this reasoning is shown below. The program takes as input an array of bit values. Upon return, the values indexed by prime numbers will be one, while all other values will be zero. One simplification to the algorithm previously described has been made. We can, in fact, cease examining numbers when we reach the square root of the maximum value, since any nonprime less than *max* must have at least one factor smaller than or equal to the square root. Rather than compute the square root of max, we simply cease when the square of the current value is larger than max.

```
//
// sieve of eratosthenes
//     algorithm for finding prime numbers following execution,
//     one values in bit vector represent primes
//
void sieve(bitVector & bits)
{
    const unsigned int max = bits.length();

    // first initialize to all 1 bits
    for (int i = 0; i < max; i++)
        bits.set(i);

    // now search for 1 bit positions
    for (i = 2; i*i < max; i++) {
        if (bits.test(i)) {
            // inv: i has no factors
            for (int j = i + i; j < max; j += i)
                bits.clear(j);
            // inv: all multiples of i have been cleared
            }
        // all set values smaller than i are prime
        }
    // inv: all set values are prime
}
```

6.4 OTHER VECTOR VARIATIONS*

6.4.1 Enumerated Types as Index Values

It is often convenient to use noninteger values to index a vector. This is possible if there exists a one-to-one mapping between the index values and integers between zero and the size of the array. A common situation where this occurs is when an enumerated type is used together with vector values. For example, we may have an enumerated data type defined as follows:

```
enum colors { red, orange, yellow, green, blue };
```

We would like to be able to declare a vector and use elements of type `color` as index values, rather than integers. We can do this by making use of the fact that the enumerated types are represented internally by C++ as small integers and can be converted into integer values. Thus `red` is represented internally as 0, `orange` as 1, `yellow` as 2, `green` as 3, and `blue` as 4. If `hue` is a variable of type `color` holding the value `yellow`, then the expression `int(hue)` yields the integer value 2.

The class `enumVector` makes use of this property to simplify the manipulation of vectors indexed by enumerated data values. Once again, we use the mechanism of inheritance to simplify the development of this abstraction. By inheriting from class `vector`, we can concentrate on the development of the novel aspects of the new class and simply reuse those features that are common to both classes.

```
//
// class enumVector
//      vectors using an enumerated type as index
//

template <class E, class T> class enumVector : public vector<T> {
public:
    // constructors
    enumVector  (E max);
    enumVector  (const enumVector & v);

    // operations
    T &     operator [ ]    (E index);
};
```

This class is parameterized by two values, the enumerated type used for the key values and the type of the elements being stored. Instances of this

*Section headings followed by an asterisk indicate optional material.

class are created by providing the last element of the type. (This may seem somewhat clumsy, but it is necessary in light of the fact that C++ provides no way of discovering the largest element in a list of enumerated values.) The constructors for this class are declared in the following fashion. Note that, as was the case with the lower bound vector, almost all the work is being performed by the constructor for the parent class `vector`.

```
template <class E, class T>
enumVector<E, T>::enumVector(E max) : vector<T>(1 + int(max))
{   // create and initialize a vector of enumerated values
    // no further initialization necessary
}

template <class E, class T>
enumVector<E, T>::enumVector(const enumVector<E, T> & source)
        : vector<T>(source)
{   // create and initialize a vector of enumerated values
    // no further initialization necessary
}
```

As with the lower bound vector, here the only function we need to change is the subscript operator. This merely converts the index value into an integer and invokes the subscript from the parent class.

```
template <class  E, class T> T & enumVector<E, T>::operator [ ]
     (E index)
{   // subscript operator for vector of enumerated values
    // simply invoke the subscript from class vector
    return vector<T>::operator [ ] (int(index));
}
```

The user could declare and manipulate an instance of the enumerated vector class as follows:

```
enumVector<colors, double> dat;

dat[blue] = 3.14;
dat[yellow] = 2.4;

dat[red] = dat[blue] + dat[yellow];
```

Note that since C++ does not have a "successor" function for enumerated types (that is, given a value such as `red`, we cannot determine what the "next" color should be) it is not possible to loop over all the elements in an enumerated vector. We will provide a solution to this problem in the next chapter.

6.4.2 Matrices

A matrix is conceptually simply a two-dimensional array of values. There are various ways we could implement such an idea (see the sidebar "Implementations of Matrices"). An easy approach that permits us to build on top of the vector data type is to implement a matrix as a vector of vectors. The elements of a matrix in this representation will be pointers, each pointing to another vector of data values:

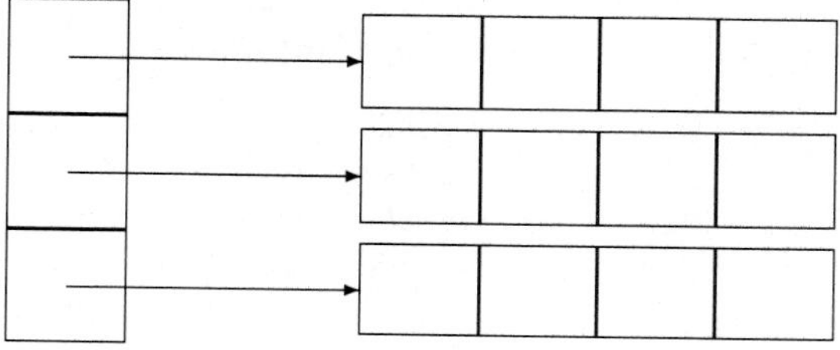

```
//
// class matrix
//     two dimensional arrays
//

template <class T> class matrix {
public:
    matrix  (unsigned int numberOfRows, unsigned int numberOfColumns);
    matrix  (unsigned int numberOfRows, unsigned int numberOfColumns,
            T & initialValue);
    ~matrix();

    vector<T> &     operator [ ]    (unsigned int index) const;

    unsigned int    numberRows      () const;
    unsigned int    numberColumns   () const;

protected:
    vector<vector<T> *> rows;
};
```

The class description for this abstraction is shown above. A protected data area holds a vector of pointers to vectors. The constructor must allocate space for each row. As we did with the vector class, we provide here two constructors, one of which will initialize each element in the matrix. The implementation of this constructor is as follows:

```
template <class T> matrix<T>::matrix(unsigned int numberOfRows,
    unsigned int numberOfColumns, T & initialValue) : rows(numberOfRows)
```

```
{
    // now allocate each row of data
    for (unsigned int i = 0; i < numberOfRows; i++) {
        rows[i] = new vector<T>(numberOfColumns, initialValue);
        // check that allocation was successful
        assert(rows[i] != 0);
        }
}
```

Because the row data are explicitly allocated, they must be explicitly freed. This is accomplished in the destructor for the class.

```
template <class T> matrix<T>::~matrix()
{   // delete all the row vectors
    unsigned int max = rows.length();
    for (unsigned int i = 0; i < max; i++) {
        // some compilers do not allow
        // subscripted variables in delete
        vector<T> * p = rows[i];
        delete p;
        rows[i] = 0;
        }
}
```

Implementations of Matrices

Although the vector of vectors is an easy way to implement matrices, it is not the only technique. Indeed, it is not the method used by the underlying C++ language to implement multidimensional arrays. Consider the following declaration of a three by four element array.

```
double d[3][4];
```

The space set aside by the compiler for this data type will consist simply of 12 double precision values. These will be placed end to end in memory and might be visualized as shown in the chart opposite.

Because elements are placed in memory in order, with the last subscript changing more quickly than the first, it is still possible to view this as a vector of vectors. That is, a singly subscripted value, such as `d[1]`, will evaluate to the address of the middle row of this structure. The placement of elements in memory for each row is exactly the same as the placement of elements in a four-element vector.

For us, the vector of vectors implementation technique has the advantage of simplicity in development. One drawback is the fact that it uses additional space, since space for the pointers themselves must be allocated in addition to space for the actual data values.

element d[0][0]	element d[0][1]	element d[0][2]	element d[0][3]
element d[1][0]	element d[1][1]	element d[1][2]	element d[1][3]
element d[2][0]	element d[2][1]	element d[2][2]	element d[2][3]

To determine the number of rows in the matrix, it is sufficient to compute the length of the `rows` vector:

```
template <class T> int matrix<T>::numberRows() const
{   // return the number of rows in the matrix
    return rows.length();
}
```

Determining the number of columns is more difficult. One way is to select any row (the row indexed by value zero will do) and compute the number of elements maintained in the vector for that row.

```
template <class T> int matrix<T>::numberColumns() const
{   // return the number of columns in the matrix
    // make sure there is a rows zero
    assert(rows[0] != 0);

    // return the number of elements in the row
    return rows[0]->length();
}
```

The C++ language permits only a single argument to be used with the subscript operator. When using multiple dimensional structures, separate subscript operations are applied for each dimension. The subscript operator for the matrix class simply returns a reference (pointer) to a vector. The vector can then be subscripted to access an individual element.

```
template <class T>
vector<T> & matrix<T>::operator [ ] (unsigned int i) const
{   // leading subscript in a matrix expression
    // check that reference is valid
    assert(rows[i] != 0);
    // return vector value, use pointer dereference to get
    // reference to actual vector
    return * rows[i];
}
```

Two-dimensional matrices are often used to describe numerical algorithms. For this purpose, the arithmetic operations are redefined to have special meaning when working with matrices. For example, the procedure shown below implements the classic algorithm for performing matrix multiplication.

```
// overload * operator to mean matrix multiplication
template <class T>
matrix<T> operator * (const matrix<T> & left, const matrix<T> & right)
{   // perform matrix multiplication of left by right
    // first get the three limiting values
    int n = left.rows();
```

```
    int m = left.columns();
    int p = right.columns();

    // check that they are compatible
    assert(m == right.rows());

    // allocate space for the result
    matrix<T> result(n, p);

    // then fill in the values
    for (int i = 0; i < n; i++)
        for (int j = 0; j < p; j++) {
            result(i, j) = 0;
            for (int k = 0; k < m; k++)
                result[i][j] += left[i][k] * right[k][j];
        }


    // return the result
    return result;
}
```

To be useful for numeric problems, we would need to define many more functions and arithmetic operators, such as assignment, matrix inversion, and the calculation of a determinant. In addition, we would have to consider the effects of round-off errors; in many cases algorithms that differ from the "classic" definitions of operations will yield more reliable results. Such topics are beyond our discussion here. A good text on numerical analysis will provide an explanation of these and many other issues.

Similarly we could provide a number of variations on the indexing schemes used to access matrix values, providing an explicit lower bound, or using enumerated data types. The techniques used to do so largely mirror those we have already seen with the vector data type, and thus we will not repeat them here.

6.5 FUNCTION TEMPLATES

Nonmember functions can also be parameterized using the `template` mechanism. For example, the following might be defined to compute the maximum of two arguments:[3]

3. As was the case with class templates, the syntax used in generating template functions for any given C++ compiler may differ slightly from that given here.

```
template <class T> T max(T a, T b)
{   // return the maximum of a and b
    if (a < b)
        return b;
    return a;
}
```

The function will work as long as the arguments are of a type that can be compared. Thus the function will work with integers, with double precision values, and even with strings.

6.5.1 Application — Bubble, Selection, and Insertion Sort

One of the most common tasks solved using a computer is the problem of *sorting*. The idea is to take a vector of values and rearrange them so that they are ordered with the smallest element appearing in position 0, the next smallest value in position 1, and so on. A sorting algorithm provides an excellent illustration of a useful and nontrivial procedure defined by using the template mechanism. Over the course of this book, we will examine several different algorithms that can be used to perform the sorting operation.

The first algorithm we will examine is perhaps the simplest, although it is far from the most efficient. The general idea behind this algorithm is to find each element of the result one at a time, starting from the largest (and therefore, last in the final result) value and moving backward. To find the largest element in the vector named `data`, we compare the first and second values, swapping them if they are out of order. Thus after one comparison we know that the largest of the first two values is stored at location `data[1]`. Next we compare the value at positions 1 and 2, again swapping them if they are out of order. We continue in this fashion. By the time we reach the end of the array, the largest value will be in the last position.

```
template <class T> void bubbleSort(vector<T> & data)
{   // sort, in place, the argument vector into ascending order
    for (int top = data.length()-1; top > 0; top--) {
        // find the largest element in position 0 .. top
        // place in data[top]
        for (unsigned int i = 0; i < top; i++) {
            // inv: data[i] is largest element in 0..i
            if (data[i+1] < data[i])
                swap(data, i+1, i);
            // inv: data[i+1] is largest element in 0..i+1
            }
        // inv: data[top..length-1] is properly ordered
        }
}
```

We have parameterized the function so that it can be used with all different types of vectors. The method used to determine if two values should be swapped is the comparison test appropriate for the template argument T. Similarly, the swap function invoked will be the swap function that has been also instantiated with the same type value as the bubble sort algorithm. The procedure to swap two values could be written as follows:

```
template <class T>
void swap(vector<T> & data, unsigned int i, unsigned int j)
{   // swap the values at positions i and j
    T temp = data[i];
    data[i] = data[j];
    data[j] = temp;
}
```

We have augmented the bubble sort algorithm with the invariants needed to prove the correctness of the outcome. The purpose of the outermost loop is to discover the largest element in the index position 0 .. `top`, and place it in position `top`. Thus at the end of this loop the values between `top` and the end of the array will all have been ordered. When the variable `top` reaches the bottom, then the entire array will have been ordered.

The inner loop performs the task of finding the largest element. The invariant maintained is that the largest element seen so far is currently being held at the top of the array positions that have been examined. That is, prior to beginning the loop, the value held in `data[i]` is the largest value in the range of index position 0 to `i`. After examining the next element, the invariant is extended to value `i + 1`. When the index value reaches `top`, the largest value will have "bubbled" up into position. Hence this sorting algorithm is called *bubble sort*.

One way to characterize the running time of sorting algorithms is by the number of comparisons they perform. To get a handle on this figure, let n represent the number of elements in the input array. Note that the first time the inner loop is executed it will perform $n-1$ comparisons. The second time it is executed it will perform $n-2$ comparisons. The last time through the loop occurs when `top` is 1, and one comparison is performed. Thus the total number of comparisons is $(n-1)+(n-2)+ \ldots +2+1$, or (n-1)n/2. We say, therefore, that bubble sort performs $O(n^2)$ comparisons.

SELECTION SORT Even a simple examination of the bubble sort algorithm shows us that it is not necessary to always exchange adjacent elements in order to find the largest element. It makes sense, then, to try to improve the algorithm by postponing the swapping until the very end. That is, we will use the inner loop to simply find the *index* of the largest element. We can then perform a single swap at the very end to move this element into place. This sorting algorithm is called *selection sort*:

```
template<class T> void selectionSort(vector<T> & data)
{   // sort, in place, the vector argument into ascending order
    for (unsigned int top = data.length()-1; top > 0; top = top - 1) {
        // find the position of the largest element
        unsigned int largeposition = 0;
        for (int j = 1; j <= top; j++) {
            // inv: data[largeposition] is largest element
            // in 0..j-1
            if (data[largeposition] < data[j])
                largeposition = j;
            // inv: data[largeposition] is largest element in 0..j
            }
        if (top != largeposition)
            swap(data, top, largeposition);
        // inv: data[top .. n] is ordered
        }
}
```

Since we have moved the call on `swap` out of the inner loop, there are at most n swap operations performed. However, counting the number of comparisons yields an arithmetic progression that is the same as the one we found in bubble sort and thus is still an $O(n^2)$ algorithm.

INSERTION SORT Like bubble sort and selection sort, the next sorting algorithm we will consider, *insertion sort*, places values one element at a time. However, rather than trying to find the last and largest value at each step, the insertion sort algorithm simply examines elements in the order they are given and inserts them into an existing ordered list. Insertion sort is similar to the way people often organize a hand of cards in a card game.

There are two key insights behind this algorithm. The first can be illustrated by the following example. Suppose we have a collection of 10 elements, and we have already ordered the first four.

1	3	5	7	2	8	9	4	6	0

To order the fifth element we need only swap the value with the next lower positions until we reach the end of the array or until we find it has moved into its correct location.

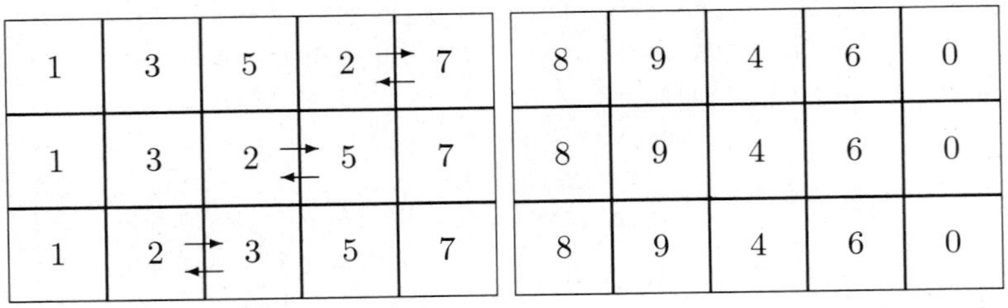

1	3	5	2 ⇄	7	8	9	4	6	0
1	3	2 ⇄	5	7	8	9	4	6	0
1	2 ⇄	3	5	7	8	9	4	6	0

The second key observation is that we always do have an initial sorted portion, as an array of zero or one element is always ordered.

In a certain sense the algorithm that proceeds naturally from these observations is similar to the bubble sort algorithm, as elements will bubble down until they are in place. Here, however, we are placing elements as we find them, and not searching at each step for the largest element. Unlike in bubble sort or selection sort, the use of a `while` loop permits the inner loop to terminate early when an element finds its proper location.

```
template <class T> void insertionSort(vector<T> & data)
{   // sort the vector argument into ascending order
    int n = data.length();
    for (int top = 1; top < n; top++) {
        // inv: data[0..top-1] is ordered
        // goal: place element data[top] in the proper position
        for(int j = top-1; j >= 0 && data[j+1] < data[j]; j--) {
            swap(data, j, j+1);
            }
        // inv: data[0..top] is ordered
        }
    // inv: data[0..n-1] is ordered
}
```

In the first two sorting algorithms, there were definite bounds on loops. This permitted us to develop precise expressions representing the number of times the comparison in the inner loop would be executed. In this algorithm, the inner loop will terminate early when an element has found its proper place. This makes our analysis somewhat more difficult.

The bad news is that in the *worst case* we will still be required to perform $O(n^2)$ comparisons and swaps. In order to see this, consider an input array that is exactly backward. Each new value to be placed will percolate all the way down to position 0. Thus the number of comparisons and swaps is once more $1 + 2 + 3 + ... + (n - 1)$. But how often will this worst case occur? If we consider the input to be randomly distributed, what is the likelihood that elements will be listed exactly backward? It is still possible to hope that an *average* input list will cause the algorithm to execute relatively quickly. Unfortunately, we can show (although the mathematics

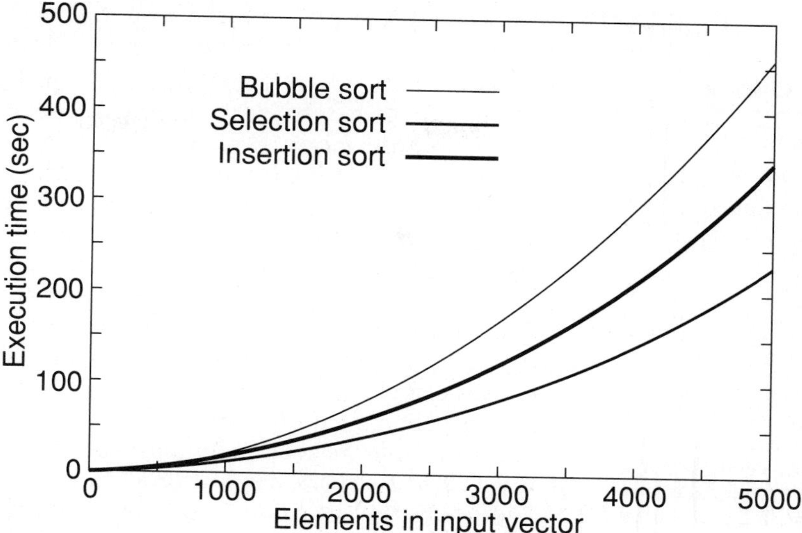

Figure 6.5 Actual execution times for sorting algorithms

are beyond our presentation here) that even the average number of comparisons performed by all three of these algorithms must be $O(n^2)$.

TIMINGS Because insertion sort always swaps adjacent elements, while selection sort swaps elements spaced farther apart, it is difficult to predict *a priori* which one will perform more rapidly on actual data. Selection sort will likely perform fewer swaps, but insertion sort will perform fewer overall comparisons. Which factor is more important?

Asymptotic analysis does not help us to answer this question, since asymptotically both algorithms have the same running time. To discover more precise information, we need to gather statistics from actual running times. Figure 6.5 diagrams the results of one such experiment. The three algorithms were executed on vectors of randomly generated integer values. The vertical axis represents actual running times in seconds, while the horizontal axis describes the length of the input vector. As expected, selection sort is always faster than bubble sort. The actual execution time for insertion sort is faster than the time for bubble sort, but it is not as fast as selection sort.

Just as asymptotic analysis has limitations as a measure of complexity, it is important to realize the limitations of actual execution timings as a measure of program behavior. Factors that can effect execution timings include the instruction set of the machine on which the algorithm is executed, the quality of the code generation algorithms used in the compiler with which the program is processed, and the processor load on the machine at the time that the statistics are gathered.

6.6 CHAPTER SUMMARY

Key Concepts

- Vector
- Template
- Inheritance
- Composition
- Disambiguation prefix
- *is-a* versus *has-a* relationship
- Variations on vectors
  - Bounded vectors
  - Bit vectors
  - Vectors indexed with enumerated values
  - Matrices
- Template functions
- Sorting techniques
  - Bubble sort
  - Selection sort
  - Insertion sort

A vector is an indexed set of similarly typed values. The underlying C++ language provides only weak support for vector values. By creating a new vector data abstraction, we can create a safer and more useful software component. In particular, our vector data type can check subscript access to ensure that index values are in bounds and can make vectors more self documenting by providing a method to determine dynamically the number of elements contained in a vector. Operations such as permitting a vector to be dynamically resized can also be provided.

The construction of a useful vector data type requires the ability to parameterize type descriptions. This is provided through the mechanism of a class template.

An important part of modern software development practices is the concept of software reuse. General software components can be reused in many different situations on several projects without needing to be rewritten for each new program. Two important techniques for software reuse are inheritance and composition. Both techniques permit the programmer to concentrate on what is new or novel in the development of a new data type and to ignore the details involved in the implementation of those features that the new data abstraction shares with the older component. Inheritance is the preferred technique when data fields and operations on the older type are also applicable to the new structure, while composition is the technique of choice when this is not the case.

Templates can be used to parameterize functions as well as classes. We have illustrated this by providing three algorithms to perform the sorting of vector values into ascending order. The examination of these procedures illustrated general techniques used in the analysis of algorithms.

References

Templates are a relatively recent addition to C++, although they have been discussed in the research literature for some time. Because they are somewhat new, not all books that describe the C++ language will mention templates. Good explanations can be found in the two books by Stroustrup [Ellis 90, Stroustrup 91] and in Lippman [Lippman 91]. All of these use vectors of one sort or another as examples.

In my introductory book on object-oriented programming [Budd 91], I discussed in more detail the techniques of inheritance and composition, and the advantages and disadvantages of each. This topic is also discussed in an article by David Taenzer et al. [Taenzer 89].

Alan Snyder [Snyder 86] suggests that inheritance adds a third face to the Janus-like face in Fig. 1.3 (page 172). The public face represents those features accessible to users of a data abstraction. The private face represents those features accessible only within the class. The protected face represents those features accessible both within the class and within subclasses but not accessible outside the class—that is, to users of the data abstraction.

Sorting is discussed extensively in volume 3 of the series by Knuth [Knuth 75]. According to Knuth, there is evidence that the first program ever developed for a stored program computer was a sorting algorithm.

The timings of the sorting algorithms given in this chapter were obtained using the g++ compiler (version 2.2) running on a 16MHz Intel 386 processor.

Exercises

1. Explain why a vector cannot be indexed using noninteger values, such as double precision numbers, rational numbers, or strings.

2. Write a template version of the `abs` procedure, which produces the absolute value of a numeric quantity.

3. Write the function `join`, with prototype definition:

```
string join(vector<string>& values,
     string & separator)
```

   The `join` function takes a vector of string values and concatenates them together to form a single string value, using the separator between each value.

4. Write methods `grow` and `shrink` for the `vector` class. These two methods take unsigned integer quantities, and they either increase or decrease the size of the vector.

5. Should it be possible to assign a vector a value that is another vector? To illustrate, consider the following declarations and assignments.

```
vector<int> x(10, 3);
vector<int> y(10);
vector<int> z(15);

y = x;
y = z;
x = x;
```

   The first would presumably copy values from the source vector to the target. Should the second statement (a) generate an error because the lengths of the two vectors do not match; (b) assign values only to the first 10 locations, leaving the remaining five locations undefined; or (c) change the size of the target vector (that is, `z`) to match the source vector. Give an argument supporting one of these alternatives, then show how your definition of assignment can be implemented. Verify that your implementation produces the expected results when a vector is assigned to itself, as in the third statement.

6. We did not define output operations for our vector data type. What should such an operation do? Modify the vector class to include a stream output operation.

7. Describe what an output method for the matrix class should do, then implement your method.

8. What is the asymptotic running time of the sieve of Eratosthenes algorithm?

9. Consider the following declaration:

```
double x[8][5];
```

   Assume it requires eight bytes in memory to represent a double precision value. Give an expression for the location, relative to the start of the array, of the value indexed by row i and column j.

10. Assume a vector has the following initial configuration:

15	88	36	9	2	95	5

Simulate the execution of all three sorting algorithms: bubble sort, selection sort, and insertion sort. For each algorithm, show the state of the vector at the end of the inner loop.

11. The following algorithm tries to combine features of bubble sort and insertion sort:

```
template <class T>
void bubbleInsertionSort(vector<T> & data)
{
    int max = data.length();
    int i = 1;

    while (i < max) {
        // inv: data[0 .. i-1] is sorted
        if ((i > 0) && (data[i] < data[i-1])) {
            swap(data, i, i-1);
            i--;
            }
        else
            i++;
        // inv: data[0 .. i-1] is sorted
        }
    // inv: data[0..max-1] is properly ordered
}
```

a. Give a proof of correctness for this algorithm.
b. Give an argument to show that the algorithm will always terminate.
c. What is the worst-case performance for this algorithm? What type of input data will cause this worst-case behavior?
d. What is the best-case performance for this algorithm? What type of input data will cause this best-case behavior?

12. A sorting algorithm is said to be stable if two values that compare equally are in the same relative ordering following the sort that they had prior to the sort. Which of the sorting algorithms we studied in this chapter are stable? *Hint*: Simulate the sort on a small vector that contains repeated values, such as the following:

15	88	15	9	88	15	2

The following three questions are repeated in part from Chapter 3.

13. It is claimed that bubble sort is an $O(n^2)$ algorithm. Appendix B gives actual timings for the bubble sort algorithm for various input values. One way to test the hypothesis that this algorithm is indeed $O(n^2)$ is to try to compute the coefficient in front of the leading term. That is, the hypothesis is that:

$$Time = c\ n^2$$

for some value of c. We can approximate c by computing the quantity $time/n^2$ for each of the data points, where n is the size of the vector input. Because its values are so small, it is convenient to scale the values and actually compute $(time \times 1000)/n^2$. Compute this value for each of the values in the column labeled `bubble` in the first table in Appendix C. Do the results seem to indicate that `bubblesort` is indeed an $O(n^2)$ algorithm? Using the value of c that you obtain, estimate how long it would take bubble sort to order a vector containing 100,000 elements.

14. Perform the same analysis as described in the previous question for the column labeled `selection`. Does the result indicate that selection sort is an $O(n^2)$ algorithm? Using the value of c that you obtain, estimate how long it would take selection sort to order a vector containing 100,000 elements.

15. Perform the same analysis as described in the previous question for the column labeled `insertion`. Does the result indicate that insertion sort is an $O(n^2)$ algorithm? Using the value of c that you obtain, estimate how long it would take insertion sort to order a vector containing 100,000 elements.

CHAPTER 7

Inheritance — Power Through Polymorphism

In Chapter 6 we introduced the concept of subclasses and inheritance. You will recall that the motivation for the technique was to facilitate the creation of new data structures that were variations on existing structures. The existing class is called the *parent class*, or *superclass*, while the new class being defined is referred to as the *child class*, or *subclass*.

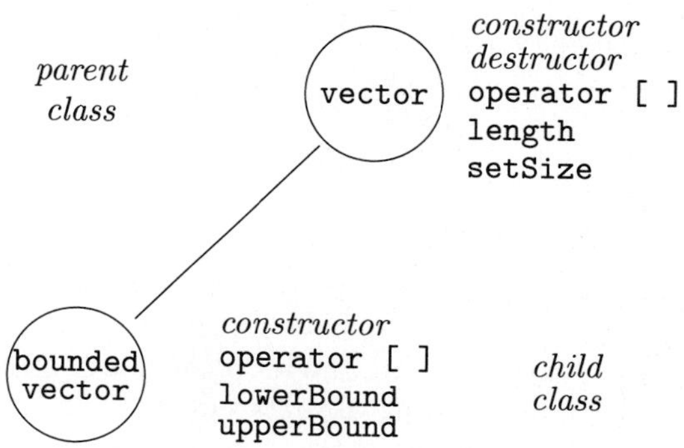

The basic idea is that by declaring a new class to be a subclass of an existing class, the new class will *inherit*, without any further actions being required, all the data values and all the behavior associated with the parent class. That is, when an instance of the child class is declared, the data areas associated with the parent class can also be used in the child class, and any behavior defined in the parent class is also applicable to the child class.

In this manner, for example, if we create an instance of the class boundedVector, which is a subclass of class vector, the methods length and setSize that are defined in class vector can also be applied to the newly created bounded vector. We often describe this by saying the child class and the parent class are bound by the *is-a* relationship, as in the sentence "a bounded vector is a vector."

7.1 STATIC AND DYNAMIC TYPES

An important consequence of the property that an instance of a subclass inherits all the data areas and behavior defined in the parent class is that an instance of a child class can often be used in situations where an instance of the parent class is expected. In C++ this almost always occurs in conjunction with call by reference parameters or pointer values. The idea is that a procedure may be expecting a value that corresponds to a type defined by a parent class, say vector. Instead, the programmer passes as a parameter value an instance of a subclass, such as boundedVector. No harm can ensue since instances of boundedVector can perform any actions defined for vector.

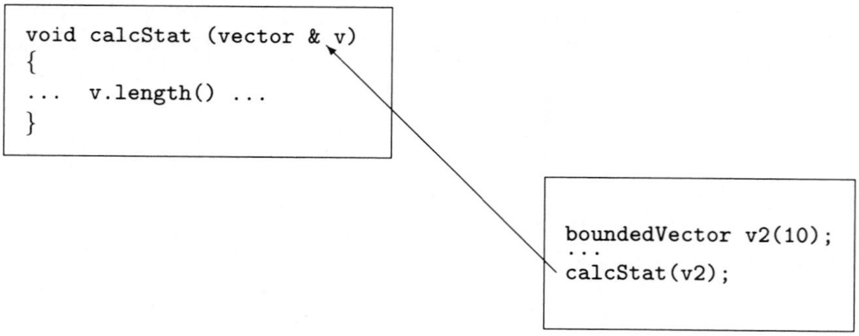

```
void calcStat (vector & v)
{
...   v.length() ...
}
```

```
boundedVector v2(10);
...
calcStat(v2);
```

The fact that the actual value manipulated by a parameter may not match the type of the declaration for the parameter leads to the introduction of two new terms. The *static* type of a parameter or pointer is the type declared (which cannot change). The *dynamic* (that is, changing) type is the type associated with the actual value. In the situation illustrated above, the static type is vector, while the dynamic type is boundedVector.

7.1.1 Polymorphism

Polymorphism is a term that is used to describe a variety of techniques employed with the purpose of creating flexible and reusable software components. The term is from the Greek, and it means roughly "many forms" (*poly* = many, *morphos* = form). You may recall the story of Morpheus in Greek mythology. Morpheus could assume the form of any human being he wished. The concept of polymorphism is found in many disciplines. In biology, a polymorphic species is a species, such as Homo sapiens, that is characterized by the occurrence of different forms or color types in individual organisms or among organisms. In chemistry, a polymorphic compound is one that can crystallize in at least two distinct forms,—for example, carbon, which can crystallize as graphite, as diamonds, or as Fullerenes.

In programming languages a polymorphic object is an entity, such as a variable or a function, that can hold or operate on values of differing types during the course of execution. Because the parameter `v` in the example program shown above can hold values of more than one type (either `vector` or `boundedVector`), we say the parameter is polymorphic. Because the procedure contains a polymorphic parameter, we say the function `calcStat` is itself polymorphic.

Much of the power obtained through the use of object-oriented programming, inheritance, and subclassing comes from polymorphism, and through the interplay between static and dynamic types. In the next few sections we will investigate these themes.

7.2 FRAMEWORKS AND VIRTUAL METHODS

The reader may have elsewhere (in programming assignments, for example) encountered the notion of a software *framework*. A framework is a class (or, in more complicated situations, a set of classes and functions) that provides the skeleton outline for the solution to some problem but does not provide any specific details. Frameworks derive their power from the use of inheritance and object-oriented techniques.

Probably the most common frameworks are those used to develop the graphical user interfaces (GUI's) used in window-based systems. In a GUI framework a library supplies a very general class—for example, a class named `application`. The behavior defined for `application` provides the ability to place a window on a display screen to move and resize the window, and to conduct other general windowing actions, but it does not implement any behavior specific to an application. A programmer creates a new application by creating a subclass of this class, supplying new behavior through methods defined in the subclass.

The principal way this is accomplished is through the ability to *override* a method in a subclass. For example, when the user of an application presses a mouse button, the framework may invoke a function, say `mouseDown`. It is likely that the application framework itself will not know how to deal with mouse buttons, and it will thus contain a method that simply returns without performing any actions. A specialized application developed by the user of a framework, however, may want to be notified of mouse actions in order to provide an application-specific response. This is accomplished by defining, in the subclass, a new method named `mouseDown`. The new method must be identical in name and argument types to the method defined in the parent class.

The software developer that makes use of an application framework is acting in the capacity of a user for a software system (namely, the framework), and it is therefore not surprising that Parnas's principles (page 178), which state that there are two sides to the software reuse process, should be applicable. There are, in fact, two views of a software framework. In a framework developer's view, an application is an instance of the parent class, `application`. In the specialized application developer's view, an application is an instance of a subclass, say, `drawingApplication` (Fig. 7.1). At run time this is reflected in the difference between the static and dynamic types. The static type within an application is the class `application`, while the dynamic type is the class `drawingApplication`.

We are now in a position to explain the central idea of this section,

An Upside-Down Library

Some people like to imagine a software framework as an upside-down library. In a normal software library, low-level routines are provided for simple operations, such as performing input/output or computing mathematical functions. The programmer writes code that sits on top of the library. Such code is *proactive*, providing overall control of the application.

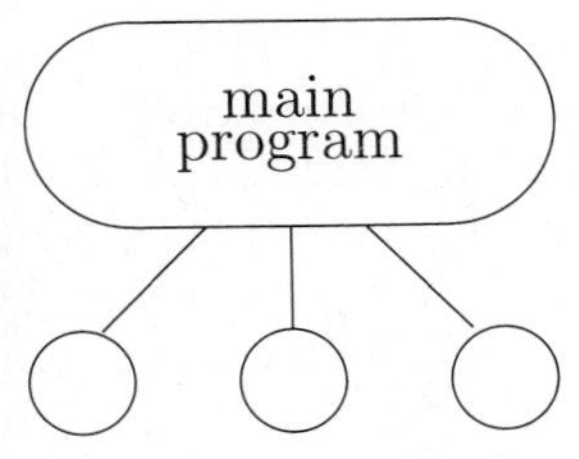

In a framework, on the other hand, the overall control of the application is provided by the framework. The programmer writes classes that, through the use of virtual functions, are invoked by the framework. Thus the code supplied by the programmer is really subordinate to the framework itself, and it is *reactive* in response to calls provided by the framework.

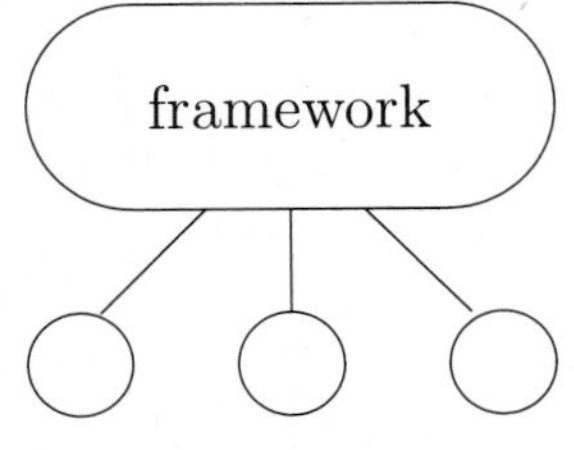

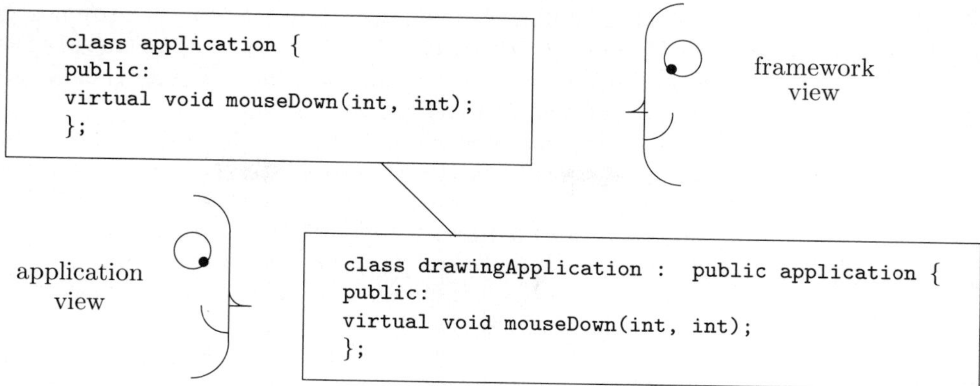

Figure 7.1 Two views of a software framework

which is the solution to the problem of deciding how to select between various versions of an overloaded function name. Recall that a subclass may override a function defined in a parent class. We see this in the framework described in Fig. 7.1, where the subclass has overridden the meaning of the method named `mouseDown`. The call on this method originates in code for the framework itself—that is, in the class `application`.

It would be natural for the code defined in the class `application` to invoke the method for `mouseDown` defined locally, within the class. How does the framework know that it should, instead, execute the method defined in the child class? The answer depends upon the difference between static and dynamic types, and upon the introduction of a new keyword, `virtual`. If a method is declared to be virtual in the class description defining the parent class, then the version of the method executed at run time will depend upon the *dynamic* class of the receiver. If a method is not declared to be virtual, then the version of the method executed will be decided by considering the *static* class of the receiver. The solution to the problem we have outlined is therefore to declare the method `mouseDown` as virtual, as shown in Fig. 7.1.

7.3 VARIETIES OF INHERITANCE

The mechanism of inheritance is used for many different purposes. Some authors have identified as many as eight or ten different forms of inheritance. In the present text we will use inheritance in only two different and distinct fashions.

The first form we have already seen in earlier examples. This is called *subclassing for specialization*. A subclass is formed because of the need to modify or specialize an existing class. The parent class is a complete, working, software component, such as the `vector` abstraction developed in Chapter 6. The child class—for example, `boundedVector`—changes some of the behavior inherited from the parent, or extends this behavior by providing new methods.

The second form, which we will see in the next section, is called *subclassing for specification*. In this form, the parent class provides a specification of behavior, but no actual implementation. The purpose of the parent class is to define *what* must be done, but not *how* the specified tasks are to be accomplished. A child class overrides the parent class methods and provides the implementation of the specified behavior.

Subclassing for specification is particularly useful in situations, such as those that we will describe in the next section, where many different subclasses will be defined, all inheriting from a single parent class. By using the same inherited protocol, we ensure that all subclasses will use the same terminology and perform in the same manner. Even more important, instances of the subclass can be used, as a dynamic type, in situations where the parent class is declared as a static type.

7.4 ITERATORS

A fundamental task of any data structure that maintains a varying number of elements, such as the collection classes that will be the principal topic of subsequent chapters, is the process of examining each value in turn. Such a process is usually performed using a loop, although recursive algorithms are also frequently useful. We have seen this already in a number of problems involving vectors.

This simple task becomes more complex when we start to consider other collection abstractions, where values are not obtained by indexing. The difficulty arises in the problem of constructing a loop in such a manner that users have access to values, but so that the inner details of the implementation of the various data structures are not exposed.

We already saw a solution to this difficulty when we considered the problem of pattern matching in Chapter 4. Recall that we constructed a loop in that situation by creating a new data structure and overloading several operators:

```
SimpleStringMatcher mismatch("i", "mississippi");
for (mismatch.init(); ! mismatch; mismatch++)
    cout << " letter i at position " << mismatch.position() << '\n';
```

The initialization method, `init`, established the initial state for the pattern matcher. The increment operator, ++, moved from one item in the collection to the next. The not operator, `!`, was used to indicate whether or not there were more values to be examined in the loop. The empty parentheses operator (not shown in our example) was used to return the current value of the collection.

```
//
// class iterator
//     define the protocol to be used by all iterators
//     subclasses must implement each of the five
//     iterator methods
//

template<class T> class iterator {
public:
     // initialization
     virtual int      init           () = 0;

     // test if there is a current element
     virtual int      operator !     () = 0;

     // current element
     virtual T        operator ()    () = 0;

     // find next element
     virtual int      operator ++    () = 0;

     // change current element
     virtual void     operator =     (T newValue) = 0;
};
```

Figure 7.2 Definition of the class `iterator`

The creation of special iterator classes that are distinct from the actual data structures themselves has several advantages. First, iteration and the holding of values are distinct responsibilities; so it is in line with our responsibility-driven design to assign these tasks to separate objects. For many data structures (trees, for example), the iteration process will require a somewhat large amount of additional storage. It would be unreasonable to require that all data structures maintain these additional values. For some data structures (again, trees are a prime example), there exists more than one style of iteration. Placing the responsibility in the class would have required selecting just one of these styles. By defining separate classes, we merely need to create a number of different iterator classes. Finally, separating the two tasks permits more than one iterator to be working simultaneously on the same structure.

We will formalize the protocol we used in the pattern-matching loop in a class structure called an `iterator`. The class definition for `iterator` is shown in Fig. 7.2. Iterators are template classes, parameterized by the element types held in the collection. We have added one new method, the assignment operator, which is typically used to change the value of the current element. The initialization and increment operators return integer values that match the value of the not operator—that is, that indicate the existence of a current element. These are ignored in the usual loop formed for iteration, but they are useful in other circumstances. A feature of this class that we have not seen previously is that there are no implementations of the member functions defined in this class. This fact is indicated by the assignment operation and the value zero in the class definitions. Such methods are known as *pure virtual* methods.[1]

The presence of pure virtual methods implies that it is not possible to generate directly an instance of class `iterator`. Instead, the class must be subclassed, and actual implementations provided for each of the pure virtual methods. Classes containing pure virtual methods are known as *abstract classes*, or as *abstract superclasses* (since they must always be a superclass of at least one additional class). The utility of abstract classes is that they provide a *protocol*, a framework for use, that is common among all the different subclasses. Furthermore, functions can be defined that are independent of the type of iterator being manipulated. We will see an example of such a function in the next section. While the value passed to such a function must always be an instance of some subclass, the function itself need know nothing more than the common iterator protocol in order to manipulate the value.

An example will illustrate how specialized implementation of iterators can be created and used. The class `vectorIterator` implements an iterator for the vector abstraction we developed in the last chapter. Instances of the class `vectorIterator` maintain a pointer to the vector being processed, and the value of the current key. The class description could be given as follows:

```
//
// class vectorIterator
//     iterator protocol used to loop over vector elements
//

template<class T> class vectorIterator : public iterator<T> {

public:
    // constructor
    vectorIterator (vector<T> & v);

    // iterator protocol
    virtual int    init         ();
    virtual int    operator !   ();
```

1. Pure virtual methods are a relatively recent addition to C++ and are not supported by all compilers. Where not supported, the method can be implemented by dummy procedure bodies, which simply return null values.

```
    virtual int       operator ++    ();
    virtual T         operator ()    ();
    virtual void      operator =     (T newValue);

    // methods specific to vector iterators
    int               operator --    ();
    unsigned int      key            ();

private:
    // data fields
    unsigned int   currentKey;
    vector<T> &    data;
};
```

The reference to the base vector, the data structure from which elements will be obtained, is set by the constructor. The constructor will also invoke the method `init`, which will set the iterator to point to the first element.

```
template <class T> vectorIterator<T>::vectorIterator(vector<T> & v)
    : data(v)
{   // create and initialize a vector iterator
    init();
}

template <class T> int vectorIterator<T>::init()
{   // set current key to first element
    currentKey = 0;
    return operator ! ();
}
```

The virtual methods providing the iterator protocol are implemented in terms of these two data values. For example, to determine if there is a current value, the value `currentKey` is compared to the size of the vector data area:

```
template <class T> int vectorIterator<T>::operator ! ()
{   // return true if there is a current element
    return currentKey < data.length();
}
```

To move the iterator to the next location is simply a matter of incrementing the index value:

```
template <class T> int vectorIterator<T>::operator ++ ()
{   // advance to the next element
    currentKey++;
    return operator ! ();
}
```

To return the current value, we index the data area with the current key value:

```
template <class T> T vectorIterator<T>::operator () ()
{   // return current value
    return data[currentKey];
}
```

Finally, the assignment operator can be used to change the value indicated by the current key:

```
template <class T> void vectorIterator<T>::operator = (T newValue)
{   // change the value indexed by current key
    data[currentKey] = newValue;
}
```

In addition, the iterator class provides two methods specific to vector iterators. The first allows an iterator to move backward as well as forward:

```
template <class T> int vectorIterator<T>::operator -- ()
{   // move current key back one element
    if (currentKey > 0)
        currentKey--;
    return operator ! ();
}
```

The second provides a method to return the current key:

```
template <class T> unsigned int vectorIterator<T>::key()
{   // return index of current value
    return currentKey;
}
```

To illustrate the use of the class `vectorIterator`, assume we have a variable `datavals` of double precision values. The following loop will output each of the values in the structure, followed by a newline.

```
vectorIterator<double> itr(datavals);
for (itr.init(); ! itr; itr++)
    cout << itr() << '\n';
```

Alternatively, the next loop computes the sum of these values:

```
double sum = 0.0;
vectorIterator<double> itr(datavals);
for (itr.init(); ! itr; itr++)
    sum += itr();
```

The assignment operator can be used to modify the value of the current element. The following, for example, doubles each element in the `datavals` array.

```
for (itr.init(); ! itr; itr++)
    itr = itr() * 2;
```

The use of vector iterators allows us to solve one problem we were unable to address in the last chapter. Recall that since we could not loop over the elements of an enumerated type, we could not construct a loop to access the elements of a vector indexed by enumerated values. By making use of the class `vectorIterator`, we can. To illustrate, assume `hue` is a vector of double precision values (saturation values, for example), indexed by colors. The following program fragment includes a loop that prints out the element values:

```
enum colors { red, blue, yellow };
enumvector<colors, double> hue(yellow);

hue[red] = 0.57;
hue[blue] = 0.63;
hue[yellow] = 0.23;

vectorIterator<double> itr(hue);

for (itr.init(); ! itr; itr++)
    cout << itr() << '\n';
```

VIRTUAL AND NONVIRTUAL OVERRIDING A careful examination of this particular example also illustrates the important but subtle distinction between virtual and nonvirtual overriding of methods. Recall that the subscript operator was defined in the class `vector` to use integer key values, and redefined in the class `enumvector` to use index values from an enumerated data type. Because the class `enumvector` is declared as a subclass of the class `vector`, we can pass the variable `hue` as argument to the constructor for class `vectorIterator`, even though the declared type of the argument is a `vector` reference. However, since internally in the `vectorIterator` class the reference to `hue` is declared as an instance of class

Prefix and Postfix ++

Given that C++ defines both prefix and postfix forms of the increment and decrement operators, you may be wondering which form is intended by the overloading of the ++ symbol. The answer is both. If only one method is provided (as here) it can be used in either a prefix or postfix manner. If it is necessary to distinguish the two uses, the prefix operator is declared with no arguments, as we have done, while the postfix operator is declared with an integer argument. This integer argument will always be passed the value zero. The following class description illustrates the declaration of both forms.

```
class X {
public:
    operator++();          // prefix ++x
    operator++(int);       // postfix x++
};
```

The prefix and postfix decrement operators are handled in the same manner.

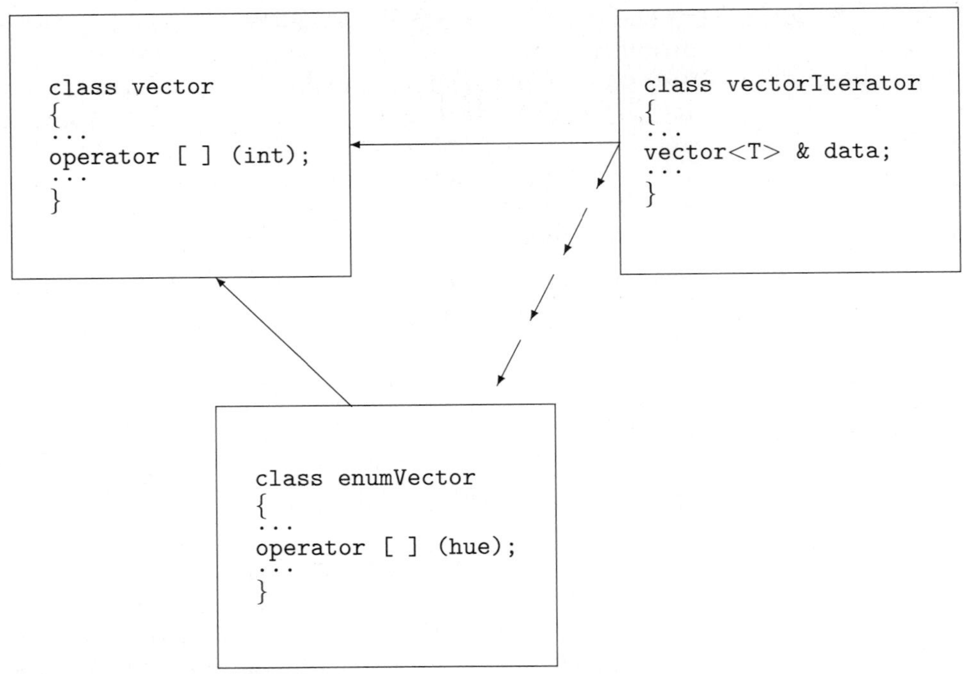

Figure 7.3 Static and dynamic types

`vector`, the subscript operation used in performing iteration will be that of the class `vector`, not the overridden operation in class `enumvector`. The `vector` operator is used despite the fact that the reference is actually pointing to an `enumvector` value.

A diagram (Fig. 7.3) will help to better illustrate this point. The field named `data` in the vector iterator class is declared as a reference to a value of type `vector`. Thus we say that class `vector` is the static type of the value. In this particular case, the actual value held by the reference is an instance of class `enumVector`. We thus say in this case that the dynamic type of the value is `enumVector`. A dynamic type must always be a subclass of the static type of a reference. The invocation of a virtual method would be bound to a procedure based on the dynamic type. When a method is *not* declared as virtual, as in this case, the binding of method to implementation is made on the basis of the static type, regardless whether or not this matches the dynamic type.

Although the fact that nonvirtual overriding was used in the subscript operator permits us to use this one abstraction with all types of vectors, it also has a consequence that the value returned by the `key` member function will always be an integer value, not the enumerated type we might expect when iterating over an enumerated type vector.

7.5 FORMS OF POLYMORPHISM*

It is perhaps appropriate that polymorphism, which means "many forms," is an idea that itself occurs in many guises. In this section we will describe some of the varieties of polymorphism found in C++.

The simplest style of polymorphism is overloading. An overloaded name, such as +, is polymorphic in the sense that it can refer to many different types of arguments. Thus the expression

$$4 + 5$$

implies an integer addition operation, while the expression

$$3.4 + 2.7$$

invokes a floating point addition. To the underlying computer, these are two entirely separate and distinct operations. We have seen, in earlier chapters, how a programmer can provide new meanings for operators when used with newly defined data types.

A second form of polymorphism is overriding, through the use of a virtual function. Here, as with overloading, the same name may result in one of a number of different function bodies being invoked. We have seen this in the overloading of the increment operation in our pattern matchers in Chapter 4, as well as in the description of iterators. The increment operator ++ will describe one of any number of different operations.

A third form is used by an algorithm defined in a parent class in a framework. Methods in a framework can work on many different types of values, depending upon the different implementations of the pure virtual methods. Unlike the virtual function situation, where there is one name and many different implementations, here there is one implementation, but many different uses. Only one method body needs to be defined as available in each of the various iterator classes.

A fourth, and in many ways the most powerful, style of polymorphism is that used when an argument value is polymorphic. We illustrated this at the beginning of this chapter with the function that could take as an argument either a vector or any subclass of a vector. The following section will describe in more detail another function that uses an argument with this property.

7.5.1 Application — Reduction

The function described in this section illustrates both the use of polymorphic parameter values and the use of our iterator abstraction. In addition,

*Section headings followed by an asterisk indicate optional material.

it also illustrates one situation where functional arguments (arguments that represent functions) are useful.

Consider the problem of reducing a vector of values to a single element. An example is computing the sum or product of an array of numbers. A sum can be viewed as a repeated application of the + operation. To compute the sum of a vector v, we evaluate the following expression:

$$(((((0 + v_0) + v_1) + v_2) + v_3) \ldots + v_n)$$

Similarly, to compute the product, we in effect evaluate the following:

$$(((((1 \times v_0) \times v_1) \times v_2) \times v_3) \ldots \times v_n)$$

We can abstract these two operations into a generalized technique, which we will implement in terms of a function that we will call `reduce`. The `reduce` function takes three arguments. The first is the iterator being manipulated. The element type of this argument is the first value in the template characterization of `reduce`. The second is an "identity" value used to initialize the loop. In the case of summation, this identity is zero; in the case of a product, this value is one. The third argument is a binary function that takes two values. Each result value is used as the left argument in the next calculation. The result of the operation is the final value generated after all the elements of the iterator have been used as the right argument in the binary function.

```
template<class T>
T reduce(iterator<T> & v, const T & identity,
     T (f)(const T &, const T &))
{    // reduce the values generated by an iterator to a single value
     // first start with the identity
     T result = identity;

     // then process each element
     for (v.init(); ! v; v++)
         result = f(result, v());

     // finally return last result
     return result;
}
```

For example, suppose the variable `datavals` holds a vector of double precision values, and that the function `dplus` returns the sum of two double precision arguments. We could compute the average of the values in the vector using the following expression:

```
double average = reduce(vectorIterator<double>(datavals), 0.0, dplus)
    / datavals.length();
```

For an example using a different data type, imagine `words` is a vector of string values. The following expression will produce a single string formed by concatenating together each element in the array. The null string is used for the identity value, and the string concatenation operator (the overloaded plus operator) is used for performing each step.

```
string concat = reduce(vectorIterator<string>(words), "", operator +);
```

If we use as our `words` array the vector containing the five strings "`this`," "`sentence`," "`has`," "`five`," and "`words`," then the result will be the string containing only the single word "`thissentencehasfivewords`."

In `reduce` it is the iterator *argument* that is polymorphic, that can take on many forms. The argument can be any type of iterator, be it an iterator for a vector, a string, a list, or any of the other types of collections we will subsequently define. Regardless of what type of object is being iterated over, the `reduce` method will cycle through and process each value. This form of polymorphism is an important mechanism to support the concept of code reuse. General purpose tools can be developed and reused in a variety of different situations.

7.6 THE SLICING PROBLEM*

We generally think of collections, such as arrays and vectors, as maintaining values that are all of the same type. It is not possible, in general, to hold a collection of values of different types in the same structure. The mechanism of inheritance, however, permits us to weaken slightly this restriction, at the cost of introducing a subtle difficulty.

Recall that the fundamental property of inheritance is the *is-a* relationship. Since a child class inherits all the data values and methods from a parent class, it can for all practical purposes be used as if it were an instance of the parent class. A consequence of this property is that *variables* declared as holding a parent class type can in fact be assigned *values* of a child class type. This feature permits a collection, such as a vector, to hold values of different types, as long as all the types are descended from a common base type. There is, however, an important limitation on the use of this technique.

To illustrate, let us consider a simple class `Shape`, with two child classes `Circle` and `Square` (Fig. 7.4). Instances of class `Shape` and subclasses all know how to compute the area they enclose. As a consequence of the *is-a* relationship, a variable declared as holding a *pointer* or a *reference* to a `Shape` value can in fact point or refer to an instance of a child class, such as a `Circle`.

---

*Section headings followed by an asterisk indicate optional material.

```
class Shape {
public:
    // compute area
    virtual double area();
};

class Circle : public Shape {
public:
    // constructor
    Circle(double radius);

    // compute area
    virtual double area();
private:
    // data area holds radius
    int r;
};

class Square : public Shape {
public:
    // constructor
    Square(double side);

    // compute area
    virtual double area();
private:
    // data area holds length of side.
    int s;
};
```

Figure 7.4 A class and two subclasses

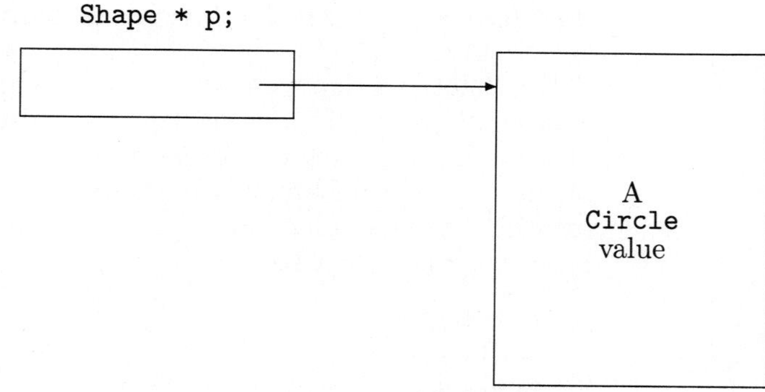

Now let us consider a value declared not as a pointer but as an actual instance of class Shape. A certain amount of storage is allocated to hold instances of this class. The amount of storage used for this purpose is only large enough to hold the data associated with the base class Shape. Instances of the child classes Square and Circle possess new fields not found in the parent class. Since there is no space for these values, the fields are simply discarded during the process of assignment. This is referred to as the *slicing problem*.

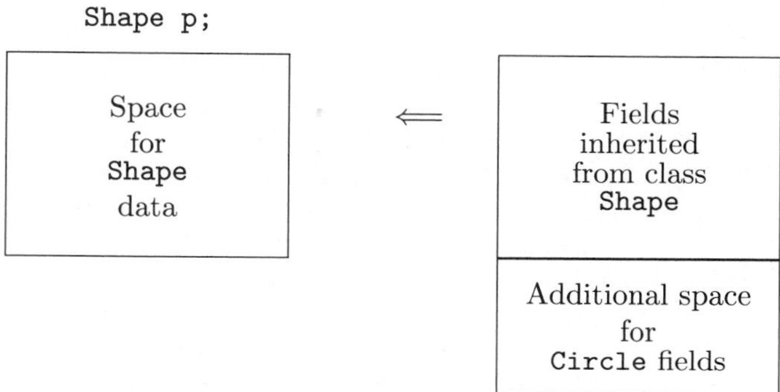

The slicing problem has an important ramification for the interpretation of virtual functions. If a variable is declared as a pointer or if a reference invokes a virtual function, the actual method used will be the function associated with the *value* held in the pointer. Thus a pointer declared as holding a Shape value may in fact, if it is holding a value of type Circle, invoke the function from a child class to compute the area associated with the shape. A variable declared as an actual class type, and not a pointer or reference, will *always* invoke the method from the base class. For although a value from a child class can be assigned to such a variable, the fields that make the value be an instance of the child class are sliced off; thus in a very important sense the value held in the variable is never of any type other than the base class.

The implication of the slicing problem for vectors is that any collection that holds values from a number of different subclasses of a given class must be defined as maintaining pointers, not actual values themselves. For example, to create a vector that will hold a number of different shapes requires code such as the following:

```
// make an array of 10 pointers to shapes
vector<Shape *> data(10);

data[0] = new Circle(5);
data[1] = new Square(7);
 ...
cout << "area of circle is " << data[0]->area() << '\n';
```

Note that the type used as a template parameter is a pointer to a shape. The function invoked when the `area` method is used in the last sentence will be the `area` method of class `Circle`, not of class `Shape`.

While the elements of a vector cannot be references, other data types we will examine in this text can hold references. For these data types, references as well as pointers can be used to avoid the slicing problem.

7.7 CHAPTER SUMMARY

Key Concepts

- Class
- Subclass and superclass
- Inheritance
- Static and dynamic types
- Polymorphism
- Framework
- Virtual method
- Iterator
- Pure virtual method
- Abstract class

In this chapter we have investigated some of the issues associated with the mechanisms of subclassing and inheritance. These techniques are some of the most powerful tools available that can be used to facilitate the reuse of existing code in new situations. Since a subclass will inherit all aspects of a parent class, an instance of a subclass can be used in situations where an instance of the parent class is expected. We therefore must draw a distinction between a declared static type of a variable, and the actual dynamic type of a value. A variable that can hold values of many different types is called a polymorphic variable. A function that makes use of at least one polymorphic argument is called a polymorphic function. Much of the power of object-oriented programming derives from the use of polymorphic functions.

Iterators are a general class of objects that are used to produce looping constructs for collection classes. By deriving iterators for different structures from a common base class, we ensure they all make use of the same protocol. This also permits functions to be defined that will work with various different types of collections, without needing to be redefined for each new form of collection.

References

There are literally hundreds of books on the market now that describe polymorphism and object-oriented programming techniques, including one by the author of this text [Budd 91]; others include [Wirfs-Brock 90], [Mullin 89], [Entsminger 90], and [Smith 91].

The description of a software framework as an upside-down library appears in Wilson [Wilson 90].

Exercises

1. Explain the meaning of the terms static type and dynamic type. Illustrate the difference by describing one situation where they would differ.

2. Explain what it means to declare a method as virtual. Illustrate the term by describing a situation in which an invocation of a method would produce one of two different results, depending

upon whether or not the method was declared as virtual. (*Hint*: The easiest way to do this is to construct a variable for which the static type and the dynamic type are different.)

3. Explain why the declaration of a private virtual method does not make any sense.
4. Using iterators, write a loop that will add one to every value in a vector of integers.
5. Using iterators, write a loop that will take a vector of strings, and prepend the word "`the`" to each of the string values.
6. Design an iterator class `stringIterator` for the `string` data type from Chapter 4.
7. Rewrite the pattern matcher class as a subclass of `iterator`. What should the template argument type be in this case?
8. Design an iterator class `bitVectorIterator` for the `bitVector` datatype from Chapter 6. Your iterator should return 0/1 values. (*Hint*: Maintain as a field in your iterator the position of the current value in the iterator. This is very similar to the `vectorIterator` class.)
9. Write a procedure that takes an iterator as argument and prints on the standard output the value of each element in the iterator collection. You can assume each element can be printed using the stream operator <<.

CHAPTER 8

Lists — A Dynamic Data Structure

The concept of a linked list is a natural data abstraction that arises in problems where a data structure must maintain a collection of elements, but the number of elements is not known in advance, or varies over a wide range. Basically, the idea of a linked list is to maintain the elements of the collection in a chain, each dynamically allocated link holding just a single value and a pointer. The pointer either contains the address of the next link, or a null value if the link is the last element in the list. The list data structure itself is simply just a placeholder, maintaining only a pointer to the first link.

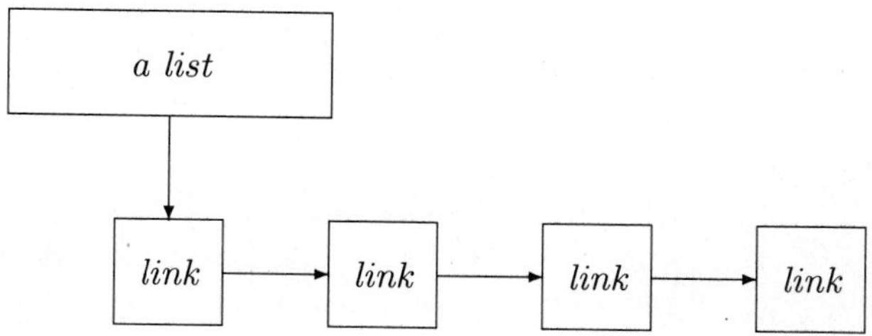

8.1 SIMPLE LISTS

There are five basic types of operations associated with the list data abstraction:

- *Insertion.* New elements can be added to the front of the list. We will provide more complex addition mechanisms when we describe the behavior of list iterators.
- *Access.* It is possible to examine the value of the initial element of the list.
- *Removal.* The first element of a list can be removed. A separate method can be used to delete all elements from a list. Again, the iterator mechanism we will subsequently describe will allow more complex removal of items.
- *Size determination.* The method `isEmpty` returns true if and only if the list contains no elements.
- *Inclusion test.* A test can be performed to determine if a particular element is present in the list. The mechanism used to test identity is the == operator, which can be overloaded by the user for any particular data type.

An operation that is *not* described is the ability to access elements randomly using the subscript operator. A characteristic of vectors is the fact that the execution time required to access any element is independent of the location of the value. Thus to access the first value requires no more work than to access the last value. This is not true of linked lists. Accessing the first value can be performed very rapidly, while access to the last value requires traversing each of the links and is thus much more costly.

A class definition for our list abstraction is shown in Fig. 8.1. In addition to the methods implementing list operations described above, we have added constructors. In line with our philosophy that costly and infrequently used functions should very clearly identify their purpose, we have called the method to remove all values from the list `deleteAllValues`.

One new syntactic concept that occurs in the `list` class definition is the declaration of the class `listIterator` as a *friend* of the class `list`. The friend mechanism permits the designer of a class to more finely tune protection policies. You will recall that public fields are accessible to any user of a software component, while private fields can only be used within a component. Protected fields are somewhere in between and can only be accessed within the component or by subclasses of the component. By declaring another class as a friend, the designer of the component is explicitly providing permission for the friend class to access the private and protected fields of the class structure. Individual functions, as well as classes, can also be declared as friends. (An example is shown in Fig. 8.3, page 214.)

```
//
// class list
//     arbitrary size lists of elements
//     permits insertion and removal only
//     from the front of the list
//

template <class T> class list {

public:
    // constructors
    list            ();
    list            (const list & source);
    virtual ~list   ();

    // operations
    virtual void    add              (T value);
    virtual void    deleteAllValues  ();
    T               firstElement     () const;
    virtual int     includes         (T value) const;
    int             isEmpty          () const;
    virtual void    removeFirst      ();

protected:
    // data field
    link<T> *       ptrToFirstLink;

    // friends
    friend class listIterator<T>;
};
```

Figure 8.1 Definition of the class `list`

This permits shared access to a common data area between two (or more) classes, or a class and a function, while restricting more widespread access. Friendship does not violate the goal of encapsulation, since friendship can be only given away, and not taken. Thus friend declarations must be part of the original design of the software component.

Operations on list values are built on top of an auxiliary class named `link`. Instances of `link` hold each value in the chain being maintained by the linked list. Thus the data areas in each link must be large enough to maintain a value and a pointer. The definition of operations in class `link` will, as well, simplify the process of constructing linked lists. The description of class `link` is given below. Note that the class `link` declares as friends both the classes `list` and `listIterator`.

```
//
// class link
//     facilitator for operations on lists
//     maintains a single element for the linked list class
//

template <class T> class link {
public:
    // insert a new element following the current value
    link *  insert  (T val);

private:
    // constructor
    link    (T linkValue, link * nextPtr);

    // duplicate
    link *  duplicate   ();

    // data areas
    T       value;
    link *  ptrToNextLink;

    // friends
    friend class list<T>;
    friend class listIterator<T>;
};
```

The class `link` is a facilitator class. Like the facilitator class used to implement the string substring operation in Chapter 4, the `link` class works behind the scenes. The user of the list abstraction is usually not even aware that the `link` class exists. By making most of the interface for class `link` private, including the constructors, we prevent users from directly manipulating link values. The classes `list` and `listIterator` are declared as friends of the `link` class and are thus able to execute the constructor in order to generate and manipulate new link values. The `insert` method, which is public, appends a new link element so as to follow the current node, setting the pointer in the new link value to refer to whatever the current node previously pointed to. It returns the pointer to the newly created link.

The constructor for the `link` class merely sets the two data fields.

```
template <class T> link<T>::link(T val, link<T> * nxt)
    : value(val), ptrToNextLink(nxt)
{   // create and initialize a new link field
}
```

The only public operation on a link structure is the insert method, used to insert a new value following a specific element.

```
template <class T> link<T> * link<T>::insert(T val)
{   // insert a new link after current node
    ptrToNextLink = new link<T>(val, ptrToNextLink);
    // check that allocation was successful
    assert(ptrToNextLink != 0);
    return ptrToNextLink;
}
```

We will postpone for the moment a discussion of the remaining operation—that is, the duplicate function.

Having provided the links with certain abilities, the implementation of the operations on a linked list are now relatively simple to define. The default constructor needs to do nothing more than initialize, to null, the pointer to the head of the list.

```
template <class T> list<T>::list() : ptrToFirstLink(0)
{
    // no further initialization
}
```

To add a new element to the front of a list requires creating a new link.

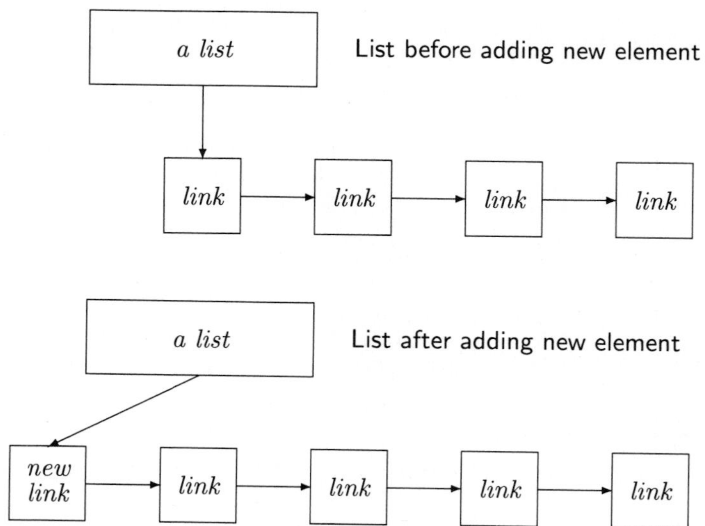

The current start of the list, held in the field named ptrToFirstLink, is used to initialize the next link field in the newly created link. The address of the new link is then stored as the new start of the list.

```
template <class T> void list<T>::add(T val)
{
    // add a new value to the front of a linked list
    ptrToFirstLink = new link<T>(val, ptrToFirstLink);
    assert(ptrToFirstLink != 0);
}
```

Because an empty list contains no elements, the pointer to the start of the chain of links will be null. A nonempty list must contain at least one field. Thus determining whether the list is empty or not simply requires an examination of the pointer to the first link. Since the method does not change the list in any way, it can be declared as constant.

```
template <class T> int list<T>::isEmpty() const
{   // test to see if the list is empty
    // list is empty if the pointer to
    // the first link is null
    return ptrToFirstLink == 0;
}
```

Accessing the first element is only possible if the list contains at least one value. An assertion checks for this condition. Once again, since this function does not change the list itself, it can be declared as constant. The method `firstElement` illustrates the use of a pointer access arrow. You will recall that the unary * operator is used to dereference the value of a pointer. The arrow is a syntactic shorthand for a combination of pointer dereference and field access. Thus the expression written as `ptrToFirstLink->value` has the same meaning as `(*ptrToFirstLink).value`. The advantage of the arrow form is that it is easier to read and less prone to error. The pointer access arrow can be used to both access data fields, as is done here, and to invoke member functions, as will be illustrated in the copy constructor to be discussed shortly.

```
template <class T> T list<T>::firstElement() const
{   // return first value in list
    // make sure there is at least one element
    assert(ptrToFirstLink != 0);
    return ptrToFirstLink->value;
}
```

Removal of the first element from a list is conceptually simply the inverse of the addition operation.

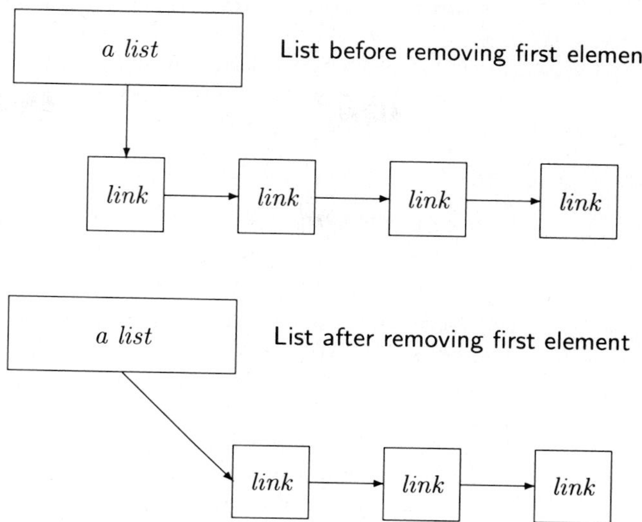

In practice, the operation is slightly more complicated. First, it must be ensured that there exists at least one element in the list, or removal is not well defined. The value of the pointer to the first link is changed to point to the next node in the sequence. Finally, the space for the link being removed is destroyed, since it is no longer required, and thus the memory it occupies can be recovered.

```
template <class T> void list<T>::removeFirst()
{
    // make sure there is a first element
    assert(ptrToFirstLink != 0);

    // save pointer to the removed node
    link<T> * p = ptrToFirstLink;

    // reassign the ptrToFirstLink node
    ptrToFirstLink = p->ptrToNextLink;

    // recover memory used by the first element
    delete p;
}
```

To test for inclusion of a value in a list requires looping over each element in the link structure, comparing each in turn against the test value. The method can be declared to be constant since it does not change the underlying list.

```
template <class T> int list<T>::includes(T v)  const
{
    // loop to test each element
    for (link<T> * p = ptrToFirstLink; p; p = p->ptrToNextLink)
        if (v == p->value)
            return 1;

    // not found
    return 0;
}
```

It is interesting to consider the running time of the searching algorithm used by the method `includes`. If the search is for an element that does not occur in the list, then, of course, the test value is compared against each existing value in the list, requiring n comparisons for a list of length n. On the other hand, let's assume the search is for a value that does occur in the list. If we assume that each element is equally likely to be sought, then the average number of comparisons performed in discovering the value is almost exactly half the cost of an unsuccessful search.

$$\frac{1}{n}(1 + 2 + \cdots + n) = \frac{n(n+1)}{2n} = \frac{n+1}{2}$$

The only action of the destructor is to invoke the method to clear all elements from the list. Note that in the class declaration (see again Fig. 8.1) the destructor is declared as virtual. Without this designation, the destructor would not be invoked when instances of *subclasses* of list are destroyed. As we will subsequently create a number of different subclasses, the virtual designation is important. Destructors should always be declared to be virtual in classes that are likely to be subclassed.

```
template <class T> list<T>::~list()
{
    // empty all elements from the list
    deleteAllValues();
}
```

The `deleteAllValues` method, like the inclusion test, iterates over the chain of link values. Each link item is deleted.

```
template <class T> void list<T>::deleteAllValues()
{
    // clear all items from the list
    link<T> * next;
    for (link<T> * p = ptrToFirstLink; p != 0; p = next) {
        // delete the element pointed to by p
        next = p->ptrToNextLink;
        p->ptrToNextLink = 0;
        delete p;
        }
```

```
    // mark that the list contains no elements
    ptrToFirstLink = 0;
}
```

The last operation we will describe is the copy constructor. The copy constructor must duplicate an entire list, including making duplicate copies of each link. If the source list contains no elements, then the pointer to the first link in the list in the new structure is simply assigned a null value. Otherwise, the copy constructor invokes the `duplicate` method from the link class.

```
template <class T> list<T>::list(const list<T> & source)
{
    // duplicate elements from source list
    if (source.isEmpty())
        ptrToFirstLink = 0;
    else {
        link<T> * firstLink = source.ptrToFirstLink;
        ptrToFirstLink = firstLink->duplicate();
        }
}
```

The `duplicate` method in the `link` class is used to create a duplicate copy of an entire linked list. It recursively duplicates all link elements until the final link is encountered.

```
template <class T> link<T> * link<T>::duplicate()
{
    link<T> * newlink;
    // if there is a next field, copy remainder of list
    if (ptrToNextLink != 0)
        newlink = new link<T>(value, ptrToNextLink->duplicate());
    else
        newlink = new link<T>(value, 0);
    // check that allocation was successful
    assert(newlink != 0);
    return newlink;
}
```

8.2 LIST ITERATORS

The functionality provided by the class `list` permits values to be inserted and removed only from the start of the list. We will use the facility of the *list iterator* to not only provide the ability to easily loop over the elements of a list, but also to provide a mechanism to remove arbitrary elements from a list, and to add elements at arbitrary locations within a list.

The natural way to implement a list iterator is to maintain a pointer to the "current" node in the linked-list structure. The increment operator can then advance this pointer to the next element.

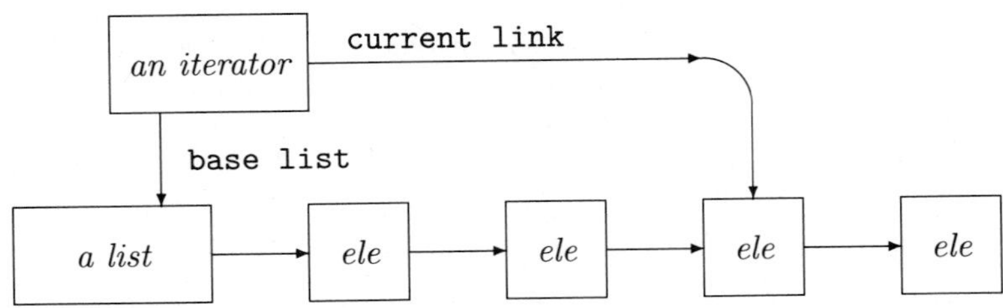

As we will see shortly, a number of algorithms are actually made more convenient if we maintain a pair of pointers. One value will refer to the current node. The second pointer will refer to the "previous" node—the node that occurs in the list immediately prior to the "current" node.

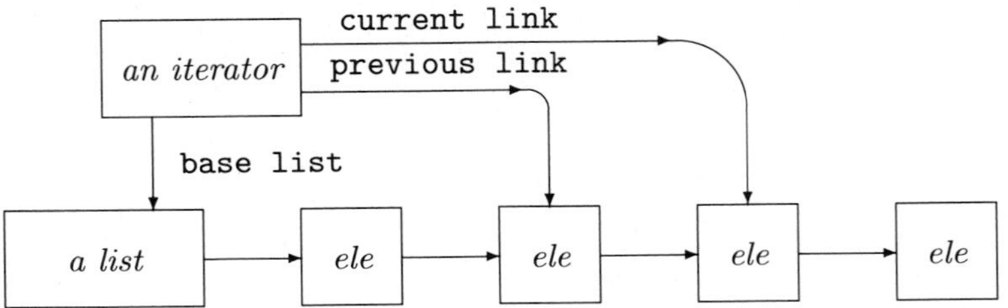

The null value, zero, is used to mark the end of iteration. Prior to commencing iteration, the previous pointer will have a null value. The pointer to the current node will naturally assume a null value when iteration is finished, as null will be the value of the link field in the last node.

Figure 8.2 gives the class definition of our iterator class for linked lists. There are three values declared in the data area: a reference to the base list, a pointer to the current element, and a pointer to the previous element. These values can be used to illustrate the difference between pointers and references. While both pointers and references provide the ability to indirectly access other data values, a reference must always refer to a specific object. A reference cannot be modified, and it cannot have a null value. A reference is tied to a specific value and is initialized either as part of a declaration or in a constructor. A pointer, on the other hand, can be modified and it can also point to nothing. The latter is indicated by the pointer being assigned a null (zero) value.

As we did with the iterator for vectors, we will define the constructor for this class so as to require a reference to a list, which is thereafter maintained as a value in the variable named `theList`. Once this value is set, the constructor performs the same actions as the initialization method. Thus to avoid duplication of code, we simply invoke the same code.

```
//
// class listIterator
//     implements iterator protocol for linked lists
//     also permits removal and addition of elements
//

template <class T> class listIterator : public iterator<T> {
public:
    // constructor
    listIterator     (list<T> & aList);

    // iterator protocol
    virtual int     init            ();
    virtual T       operator()      ();
    virtual int     operator !      ();
    virtual int     operator ++     ();
    virtual void    operator =      (T value);

    // new methods specific to list iterators
    void            removeCurrent   ();
    void            addBefore       (T newValue);
    void            addAfter        (T newValue);

protected:
    // data areas
    link<T> *       currentLink;
    link<T> *       previousLink;
    list<T> &       theList;
};
```

Figure 8.2 Definition of the class `ListIterator`

```
template <class T> listIterator<T>::listIterator(list<T> & aList)

        : theList(aList)
{   // create and initialize a new list
    init();
}

template <class T> int listIterator<T>::init()
{   // set the iterator to the first element in the list
    previousLink = 0;
    currentLink = theList.ptrToFirstLink;
    return currentLink != 0;
}
```

The value of the current element is returned by the parentheses operator. An assertion checks that the pointer to the current element actually references a legal link value.

```
template <class T> T listIterator<T>::operator()()
{   // return value of current element
    // check to see if there is a current element
    assert(currentLink != 0);
    // return value associated with current element
    return currentLink->value;
}
```

The assignment operator similarly first tests to make sure the current node is legal, before assigning the argument to the value field in the current link.

```
template <class T> void listIterator<T>::operator = (T val)
{   // modify value of current element
    assert(currentLink != 0);
    // modify the value of the current link
    currentLink->value = val;
}
```

There is an interesting and subtle interaction between the iterator protocol and the ability to remove the current element from a list. The obvious loop that we would write to test each element in a list, and to delete those that satisfy some condition, should work as expected. For example, one might write the following loop to delete all multiples of five from a list of integers.

```
listIterator<int> itr(aList);
for (itr.init(); ! itr; itr++)
    if (itr() % 5 == 0)
        itr.removeCurrent();
```

The difficulty is that subsequent to the remove operation there should be no further dangling pointers to the link node that has been deleted. One possibility would be to set the value of the "current" node to the next node in the chain. But this would have the unfortunate consequence that the increment operator would skip to the *next* element, leaving the value following the deleted node unexamined. An alternative is to, following the remove task, leave null the value of the pointer to the "current" node. Other operations must then be prepared to deal with this circumstance. (A consequence of this choice is the fact that neither the parentheses operator nor the assignment operator can be applied between a call on `removeCurrent` and a subsequent increment. This is no great problem, since the interpretation of these operators in this circumstance is not clear.)

To better understand the implementation of the remove operation, we illustrate the two cases that must be considered. The first case occurs when the element we are deleting is the first element in the list, and hence the `previousLink` pointer holds a null value. In this case the `ptrToFirstLink` field in the list header itself must be updated. The null value held in the pointer field `previousLink` remains unchanged, and the `currentLink` pointer is set to null.

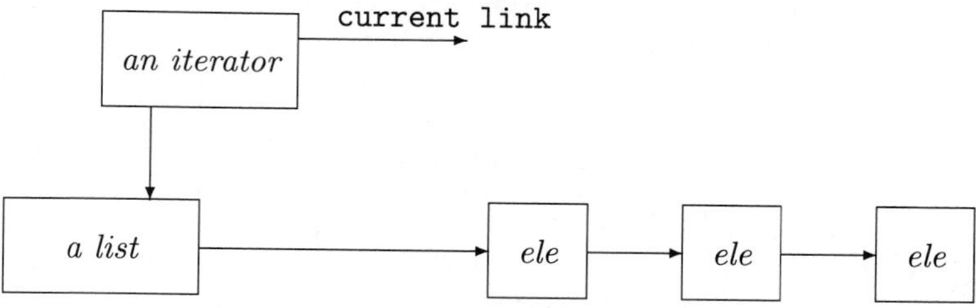

In the second, more common, case the previous link pointer references a valid link. The next link field for this link is updated, and the pointer to the current link is once again made null.

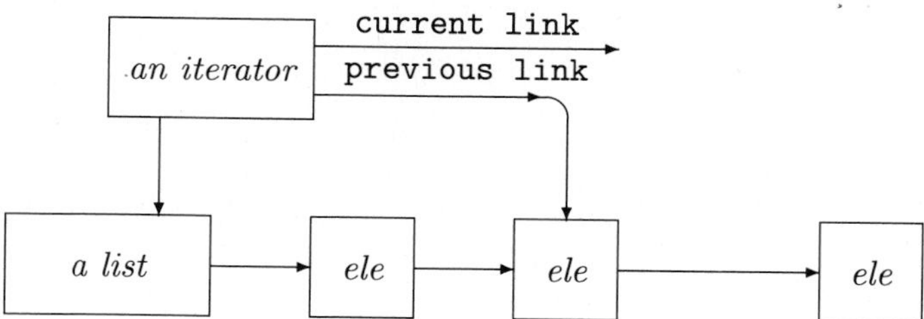

In the event that the list contains only a single element, both the value of the `currentLink` pointer and the field `ptrToFirstLink` in the list itself will be set to null. The following code is used to implement the remove operation.

```
template <class T> void listIterator<T>::removeCurrent()
{   // remove the current element from a list
    // make sure there is a current pointer
    assert(currentLink != 0);

    // case 1, removing first element
    if (previousLink == 0)
        theList.ptrToFirstLink = currentLink->ptrToNextLink;

    // case 2, not removing first element
    else
        previousLink->ptrToNextLink = currentLink->ptrToNextLink;
```

```
    // delete current node
    delete currentLink;

    // and set current pointer to null
    currentLink = 0;
}
```

We have noted that other operators must be aware of the possibility that the current element will have been deleted. The increment operator, for example, must test the potential removal of the current element by examining the value of the current link pointer. If the pointer is null, then the value is set by examining the `ptrToNextLink` field of the previous node. Only if the pointer is nonnull is the value advanced.

```
template <class T> int listIterator<T>::operator ++ ()
{   // move current pointer to next element
    // special processing if current link is deleted
    if (currentLink == 0) {
        if (previousLink == 0)
            currentLink = theList.ptrToFirstLink;
        else
            currentLink = previousLink->ptrToNextLink;
        }
    else {
        // advance pointer
        previousLink = currentLink;
        currentLink = currentLink->ptrToNextLink;
        }
    // return true if we have a valid current element
    return currentLink != 0;
}
```

Similarly, the test for end of iteration operator must check for this condition, although normally the increment operator would be invoked first before the termination test is performed.

```
template <class T> int listIterator<T>::operator ! ()
{   // test for termination of the iterator
    // if current link references a removed value,
    // update current to point to next position
    if (currentLink == 0)
        if (previousLink != 0)
            currentLink = previousLink->ptrToNextLink;

    // now see if currentLink is valid
    return currentLink != 0;
}
```

There are two new methods defined in the list iterator class that can be used to insert a new element into a list. The method `addBefore` inserts the new element immediately prior to the current node.

```
template <class T> void listIterator<T>::addBefore(T val)
{   // add a new element to list before current value
    // case 1, not at start
    if (previousLink)
        previousLink = previousLink->insert(val);

    // case 2, at start of list
    else {
        theList.list<T>::add(val);
        previousLink = theList.ptrToFirstLink;
        currentLink = previousLink->ptrToNextLink;
        }
}
```

The second method, `addAfter`, inserts a value so as to follow the current node. Both methods are simplified by the definition of the method `insert` in the class `link`. This `insert` method creates a new node, appending it to the receiver node, and returns the pointer to the new node.

```
template <class T> void listIterator<T>::addAfter(T val)
{   // add a new value to list after current value
    // case 1, not at start
    if (currentLink != 0) {
        currentLink->insert(val);
        }

    // case 2, at end of list
    else if (previousLink != 0)
        currentLink = previousLink->insert(val);

    // case 3, start of list
    else
        theList.list<T>::add(val);
}
```

As with removal, there are several special cases for both forms of insertion. In the case where we are adding an element prior to the current node, if the `previous` pointer is not null, then the new node is simply appended to the previous node, updating the value held in `previous` so as to ensure that the pointer references the node immediately before the current node. Note that this procedure works even if the "current" node is null, meaning that iteration has proceeded to the end of the list.

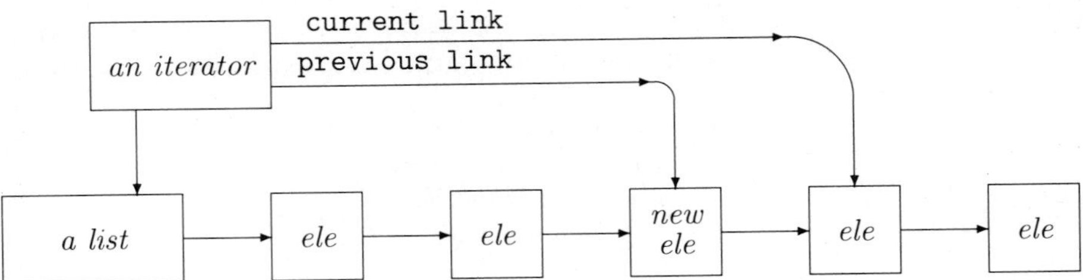

If the current node is the first element in the list, and thus the value held by the pointer `previous` is null, then the new element is added to the start of the list. A qualified name is used to ensure that the add method invoked here is the method from class `list`, not a method from a subclass. The pointer to the previous link is set to reference the new element. This method is also used if the pointer to the current link is null, as would be the case if the iteration has not begun or if the list is empty. Doing so is a reasonable response under the circumstances and avoids generating an assertion failure in this case.

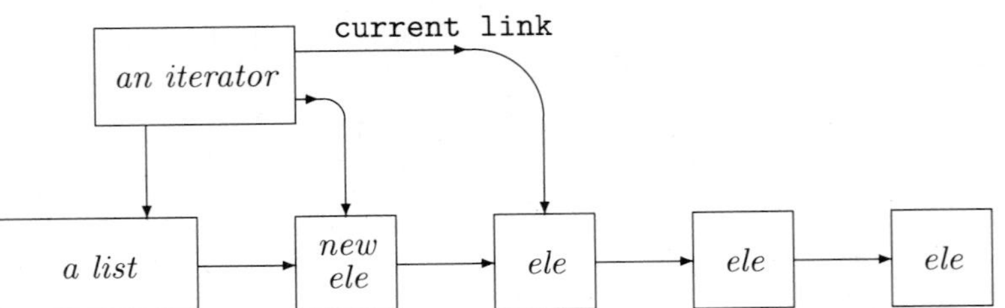

There are three cases for the method adding an element so as to follow the current node, as both the start and end of the list require special treatment. In the normal case the new element is simply appended to the current node. The current node is unchanged, and the new node will become the current node at the next iteration. Once again the add method is qualified to ensure the procedure invoked will be from the class `list`.

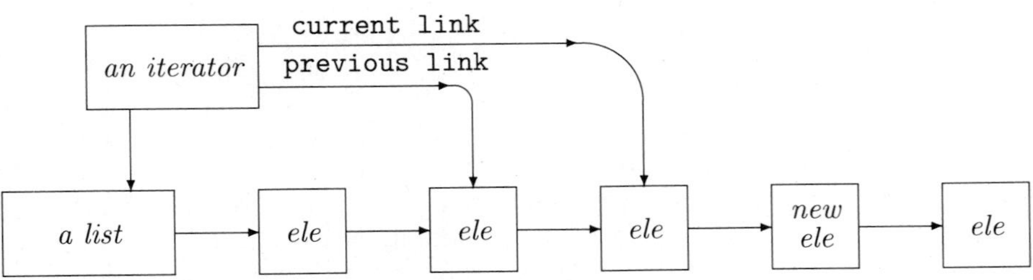

When the current node is null but the previous node is not null (indicating we have iterated to the end of the list, or the current node has been deleted), the new node is simply appended to the previous node, and becomes the current value. Strictly speaking, the new node is not inserted "after" the current node in this case, but performing a sensible action seems preferable to generating an assertion failure.

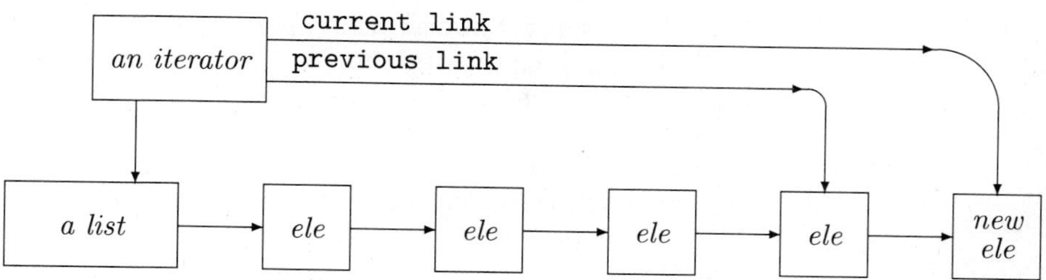

The third case occurs when iteration has not yet begun. Again, we can quibble about the meaning of the insert "after" operation in this case, but the most sensible approach would seem to be simply to insert the element at the start of the list, leaving the values of the previous link and current link pointers unchanged (both still null).

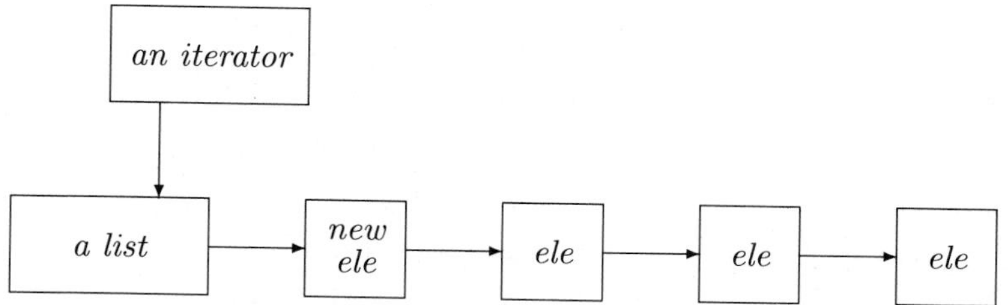

8.3 APPLICATION — POLYNOMIAL ARITHMETIC*

We will illustrate the use of our list abstraction by constructing a package for polynomial arithmetic. We can view a polynomial, such as:

$$3x^4 + 6x^2 + 4x + 5$$

as being represented by a list of terms:

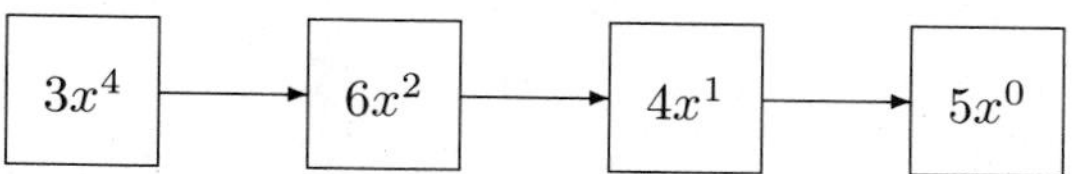

By using this representation, we can express operations on polynomials by means of operations on lists.

*Section headings followed by an asterisk indicate optional material.

Our polynomial operations will always store terms in a sequence of descending powers. For example, $10x + 3x^2 + 7$ would be stored in our representation as $3x^2 + 10x + 7$. This is the usual representation in mathematics, and by ensuring that we maintain this property we can develop simpler algorithms.

The essential information about a polynomial is contained in the coefficients and exponents, the variable element x being simply a placeholder. Hence for each term we need only record the coefficient and exponent value. It is convenient to build operations on polynomials out of operations on terms, and thus we first generate a data abstraction for the type `term`. Each term maintains an integer coefficient and exponent value. Because the power of a term will never change once it has been created, the power field can be declared as constant. Rather than providing explicit accessor functions for these data members, we instead make the data fields publicly accessible.

```
//
// class term
//     a single term in a polynomial expression
//

class term {
public:
    // constructor - set both coefficient and power
    term    (int coef, int pow);

    // data fields
    int             coefficient;
    const int       power;
};
```

When a term is multiplied by another term, the coefficients are multiplied together and the powers are added. Thus $3x^2 \times 4x^3$ is $12x^5$.

```
term operator * (const term & left, const term & right)
{   // multiple two terms together to yield a new term
    term result(left.coefficient * right.coefficient,
        left.power + right.power);
    return result;
}
```

Two terms can be added together only if they have the same power. If so, then their coefficients are added. Thus $3x^2 + 5x^2$ yields $8x^2$.

```
term operator + (const term & left, const term & right)
{   // add two terms together to yield a new term
    // check that power match
    assert(power == right.power);
    term result(left.coefficient + right.coefficient, left.power);
```

```
    return result;
}
```

Two terms are equal only if both the coefficients and powers are equal.

```
int operator == (const term & left, const term & right)
{   // see if two terms are equal
    return ((left.coefficient == right.coefficient) &&
        (left.power = right.power));
}
```

The printing of a value of type `term` is handled by the stream output operator. Since this function requires access to the data fields of the term, it must be declared as a friend. The implementation of the output operation is divided into cases. When a term with exponent zero is printed, the variable portion is omitted. When a term with exponent one is printed, the variable is displayed but the exponent itself is omitted. In all other situations both the coefficient and the exponent are printed. When a description of a problem includes multiple cases that differ depending upon the value of an integer quantity, the coding technique that most clearly describes an algorithm often makes use of a `case` statement. The code for the stream output operator illustrates this.

```
ostream & operator << (ostream & out, const term & val)
{   // output a term
    // don't print anything for zero terms
    if (val.coefficient == 0)
        return out;

    // print the coefficient
    out << val.coefficient;

    // now print the power
    switch(val.power) {
        case 0:
            break;  // do nothing

        case 1:
            out << " X";
            break;

        default:
            out << " X^" << val.power;
            break;
        }

    return out;
}
```

```
//
// class polynomial
//    represents a polynomial of a single variable
//

class polynomial {
public:
    // constructors
    polynomial  ();
    polynomial  (const polynomial & p);
    polynomial  (term & t);
    polynomial  (int one, int zero);
    polynomial  (int two, int one, int zero);

    // operations
    void    operator =      (const polynomial & right)
    void    operator +=     (const polynomial & right);
    void    operator *=     (const term &);

private:
    // data fields
    list<term>  terms;

    // friends
    friend polynomial operator *(const polynomial &, const
         polynomial &);
    friend polynomial operator +(const polynomial &, const
         polynomial);
    friend ostream & operator <<(ostream &, const polynomial &);
};
```

Figure 8.3 Definition of the class `polynomial`

The class `polynomial` (Fig. 8.3) maintains as a data value a list of terms. As with most of our data abstractions, a variety of constructors will simplify the creation and manipulation of polynomials. The default constructor creates a polynomial with no terms. The copy constructor, and the assignment operator in the operations section, use the assignment operator from the class `list` to duplicate the term values. The following sequence illustrates the declaration of several polynomials.

```
polynomial a;               // no terms
polynomial b(7);            // constant 7
polynomial c(3,0,4)         // 3x^2 + 4
polynomial d(term(4,5))     // 4x^5
```

As we have done with several other data abstractions, we will build

```
void polynomial::operator += (const polynomial & right)
{   // addition assignment of a polynomial
    // we loop over both left and right simultaneously
    listIterator<term> litr(terms);
    listIterator<term> ritr(right.terms);

    for (litr.init(), ritr.init(); !litr && !ritr; litr++) {
        // first add any leading right terms
        while (!ritr && (litr().power < ritr().power)) {
            litr.addBefore(ritr());
            ritr++;
            }
        // then combine any terms with same power
        if (!ritr && ritr().power == litr().power) {
            litr = litr() + ritr();
            ritr++;
            }
    }
    // there may be left over right terms
    while (! ritr) {
        litr.addBefore(ritr());
        ritr++;
        }
}
```

Figure 8.4 Addition assignment operator for polynomials

arithmetic operations for our polynomial data type in two steps. First, we will use a copy constructor to duplicate a value, then we will use the arithmetic assignment operator to update the value. Thus the heart of the algorithms will be the update operators.

Let us consider addition first. Assume we wish to add the two polynomials $3x^4 + 2x^2 + 3x + 7$ and $2x^3 + 4x + 5$. We can visualize this as follows:

$$\begin{array}{cccccc} & 3x^4 & & +2x^2 & +3x & +7 \\ + & & 2x^3 & & +4x & +5 \\ \hline = & 3x^4 & +2x^3 & +2x^2 & +7x & +12 \end{array}$$

As you can see, to produce the sum requires simultaneously walking down both the lists of terms from the left and right argument. Terms with powers that occur in only one list, either right or left, are simply copied to the resulting polynomial. It is only when terms of the same power occur in both lists that any combination takes place. The code to perform this can be written as shown in Fig. 8.4.

We select (more or less arbitrarily) the left argument to be the main control for the outermost loop. Within this loop a second loop detects any terms in the right argument that have powers smaller than the power of the current left element. Any such terms detected are inserted into the left (result) list. It is important for the correct functioning of this operation that the `addBefore` method does not change the value of the currently selected item for the iterator. Once any right terms less than the current power are processed, if the right and left terms have the same power, the coefficient in the left term is updated. Note that to perform the update of the polynomial term we use the assignment operator in class `list`, writing the expression as `litr = litr() + ritr()`, and not the assignment operator `litr() += ritr()`. The latter generates a copy of the left term, then modifies the copy, rather than modifying the left term directly.

The main loop terminates when either the left or right iterator becomes exhausted. If the right iterator has not become exhausted, any remaining terms are added to the end of the left list. If the main loop terminated because the right iterator, not the left, became exhausted, and it is still the case that no further processing is necessary. Since it is the left argument that is being updated, any remaining terms in the left iterator remain in the left argument.

Having implemented the addition assignment operator, the infix assignment operator is defined in the usual way, as a combination of the copy constructor and the addition assignment operator:

```
polynomial operator + (const polynomial & left, const
     polynomial & right)
{    // return the sum of two polynomial values
     // duplicate the left argument using the copy constructor
     polynomial result(left);
     // update the value using the addition assignment
     result += right;
     // return the result
     return result;
}
```

Now let us consider polynomial multiplication. Consider, for example, the problem of multiplying $2x^2 + 3x + 5$ by $4x + 3$. We can visualize the process as follows:

$$
\begin{array}{rrrrr}
 & & 2x^2 & +3x & +5 \\
\times & & & 4x & +3 \\
\hline
= 8x^3 & +12x^2 & +20x & & \\
 & +6x^2 & +9x & +15 & \\
\hline
= 8x^3 & +18x^2 & +29x & +15 &
\end{array}
$$

The result is computed in several stages. First, partial sums are created by multiplying the first polynomial by each of the terms in the second. Once each of these partial sums has been constructed, they are added together. To perform the latter we can use the addition assignment operator we have just implemented. Thus the multiplication operator can be defined in the following fashion:

```
polynomial operator * (const polynomial & left, const
     polynomial & right)
{    // compute the product of
     // two polynomial values
     // start with an empty polynomial
     polynomial result;
     listIterator<term> itr(right.terms);

     // multiply right by each left term
     // and add the partial sums
     for (itr.init(); ! itr; itr++)
         result += left * itr();

     // return the final sum
     return result;
}
```

We implement code to multiply a polynomial by a single term in the same two-step procedure we used to implement addition. First, the multiplication assignment operator is defined:

```
void polynomial::operator *= (const term & right)
{    // multiply each term of polynomial
     // by argument value
     // loop over the terms, doing the multiplication
     listIterator<term> itr(terms);
     for (itr.init(); ! itr; itr++)
         itr = itr() * right;
}
```

Again the assignment operator from the iterator class is used, so as to directly modify the value in the left polynomial. Next, infix multiplication is defined using a combination of the copy constructor and the multiplication assignment operator.

```
polynomial operator * (const polynomial & left, const term & right)
{   // multiply two polynomials
    // duplicate the left argument using the copy constructor
    polynomial result(left);
    result *= right;
    return result;
}
```

The remaining operation is output. This, too, is implemented using iterators. A flag is used to make sure that a plus sign is output between each term but that it is not preceding the first term.

```
ostream & operator << (ostream & out, const polynomial & val)
{   // output a polynomial on a stream
    int first = 1;   // used to avoid printing out initial + sign

    // iterate over terms, printing each one
    listIterator<term> itr(val.terms);
    for (itr.init(); ! itr; itr++) {
        if (! first) out << " + ";
        first = 0;
        out << itr();
        }
    return out;
}
```

8.4 ORDERED LISTS

The list data abstraction does not make any attempt to order elements as they are inserted. We can define a variation, called an ordered list, that explicitly places elements into sequence as they are inserted. Sequencing is determined by comparisons between elements using the less than operator. By subclassing this new class from the existing class `list`, we once again illustrate the power of the inheritance mechanism. The only method that needs to be redefined is the element addition method. All other behavior can be inherited directly from the base class without modification or rewriting. The class definition for our new abstraction can be given as follows:

```
//
// class orderedList
//     a list structure where each element
//     is maintained in sequence based on the
//     less-than comparison operator
//
```

```
template <class T> class orderedList : public list<T> {
public:
    // simply change the addition method
    virtual void    add (T value);
};
```

The add method uses an iterator to cycle over elements smaller than the new value. This loop terminates on either one of two conditions. If an element is found in the list that is larger than the new element, the value will be inserted and the loop (and procedure) will end via a `return` statement. Alternatively, the loop will naturally terminate if the iterator exhausts all elements in the list, indicating they are all smaller than the new value. Recalling the special behavior of the `addBefore` method in the latter case, it is clear that, following the loop, all that is necessary is to add the new element immediately behind the final value for the "current" element in the list.

Lists of References

It is often important that a single data value be held on multiple lists. For example, suppose a program is manipulating a database of student records. There is one record for every student. Each class maintains an associated list of students attending the class. However, one student can be attending multiple classes and will thus appear on more than one list. This can easily be accomplished by having each list hold a reference to the student record, and not the student record itself. A declaration for such a structure would be given as follows:

```
list<studentRec &> cs1; // list of cs1 students
list<studentRec &> cs2; // list of cs2 students
```

The use of references is largely transparent. Elements are added to the list and manipulated just as if each list held a unique record. The following illustrates the manipulation of these two lists of references.

```
studentRec sally("sally brown", 12);
studentRec fred("fred smith", 47);
studentRec alice("alice blue", 32);
studentRec sam("sam weiss", 97);

cs1.add(sally);
cs2.add(alice);
cs1.add(alice);
cs2.add(fred);
cs2.add(sam);
cs1.add(sam);

listIterator< studentRec& > x(cs1);
listIterator< studentRec& > y(cs2);

while (x.init(); !x; x++)
    cout << "cs 1 student "
         << x().name << '\n';

while (y.init(); !y; y++)
    cout << "cs 2 student "
         << y().name << '\n';

if (cs1.includes(alice))
    cout << "alice is in cs1\n";
```

```
template <class T> void orderedList<T>::add(T val)
{   // add a new value to an ordered list
    // loop over values smaller than current
    listIterator<T> itr(*this);
    for (itr.init(); ! itr; itr++)
        if (val < itr()) {
            // found location to insert value
            itr.addBefore(val);
            return;
            }

    // add to end of list if not yet inserted
    itr.addBefore(val);
}
```

The use of iterators simplifies the implementation of the addition method for this class. The disadvantage of ordered lists over their unordered counterparts, of course, is speed. In the worst case each new element added to the list will require iterating over all existing elements. Because this iteration process is proportional to the length of the list, we see that adding a new element to an ordered list requires in the worst case $O(n)$ operations, whereas adding an element to an unordered list can always be performed in constant, or $O(1)$, time. This worst case occurs if the new element being added is larger than every value already in the list. In this situation the new value will be compared to every value in the list, before finally being inserted at the end of the list.

8.4.1 Application — List Insertion Sort

The data abstraction vector does not, by itself, imply any ordering relation on the elements it contains. As we will see in Chapter 11, however, often very efficient algorithms can be discovered for some problems if we can assume the elements of a vector are maintained in an ordered sequence. In Chapter 6 we identified three algorithms that could be used to sort a vector of values. The last of these three was the insertion sorting algorithm. A surprisingly efficient variation on insertion sort can be performed using the ordered list data type.

To sort a vector of values, we create a new ordered list and simply add each element of the vector to the list. Having thus ordered the values, a list iterator loop is then used to copy the values back into the original vector. In the abstract, the sorting algorithm thus consists of two simple steps:

Step 1: Copy all values from the vector into the ordered list.
Step 2: Copy all values from the ordered list back into the vector.

```
template <class T> void listInsertionSort(vector<T> & v)
{   // sort into increasing sequence the values of the vector argument
    // declare an ordered list of the correct type
    orderedList<T> sorter;

    // copy the entire vector into the ordered list
    vectorIterator<T> vitr(v);
    for (vitr.init(); ! vitr; vitr++)
        sorter.add(vitr());

    // now copy the values back into the array
    int i = 0;
    listIterator<T> itr(sorter);
    for (itr.init(); ! itr; itr++)
        v[i++] = itr();
}
```

Figure 8.5 The list insertion sorting algorithm

The code to do this is shown in Fig. 8.5. This algorithm is called a *list insertion sort,* since it operates by inserting each value into a list structure.

To determine the worst case execution behavior for this algorithm, recall that the worst case for each insertion into an ordered list occurred when a new element was larger than any existing value held in the list. In this situation the new value would be compared to every value in the list, requiring $O(n)$ operations. The interesting consequence of this observation is therefore that the worst case behavior for this algorithm occurs when the input vector contains elements that are *already* in sorted order. The insertion of the first value requires no comparisons. To insert the second value, it must be compared against the first. The insertion of the third value requires a comparison against both the first and the second. Eventually, the insertion of the last, or n^{th}, value requires a comparison against all the existing $n - 1$ values. Thus the number of comparisons performed is equal to $1 + 2 + \cdots + (n - 1)$. This sum is equal to $(n - 1)n/2$. From this we know that in the worst case a list insertion algorithm requires $O(n^2)$ comparisons.

Despite having the same asymptotic performance as insertion sort, the list insertion sort algorithm has one definite advantage. It places elements into position using pointer manipulation, instead of swapping adjacent elements. Because of this, and despite the fact that the list insertion algorithm is performing dynamic memory allocation to create and destroy the list structure, it is still in practice roughly twice as fast as the array version of insertion sort (Fig. 8.6).

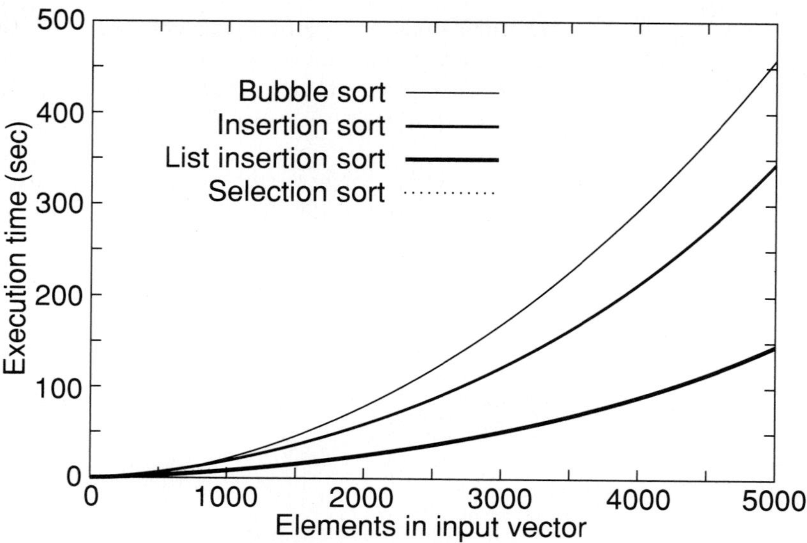

Figure 8.6 A comparison of insertion sort and list insertion sort

8.5 SELF-ORGANIZING LISTS*

Many problems using lists have the characteristic that tests to determine if a value is present in a list occur much more frequently than insertions or deletions. Furthermore, it is also often the case that once such a test has been performed, the likelihood is increased that the same element will be subsequently requested. In such situations the rather poor $O(n)$ behavior of the `includes` method can be improved by always moving an element to the front of the list on a successful search. A data structure that tries to improve *future* performance based on current usage is said to be *self-organizing*.

To create a self-organizing list we need only override the inclusion test performed by the method `includes`. For reasons we will describe in a moment, we will also add one new operation. Thus, the class description can be given as follows:

```
//
// class selfOrganizingList
//     optimize the includes test based on
//     current access patterns
//
```

*Section headings followed by an asterisk indicate optional material.

```
template <class T> class selfOrganizingList : public list<T> {
public:
    // override the includes test
    virtual int     includes     (T value);

    // method to remove arbitrary elements from a list
    void            remove       (T value);
};
```

Instead of simply looping over the values until we exhaust the list or find the requested value, the includes method in the self-organizing list will move the value on a successful search to the front of the list. Thus a subsequent search for the requested value will be performed very quickly. The task of moving the element to the front of the list can be easily accomplished as a combination of the removeCurrent iterator method and the add function in the original list.

```
template <class T> int selfOrganizingList<T>::includes(T value)
{   // determine if a value is present in the list
    // loop to see if the value is found
    listIterator<T> itr(*this);
    for (itr.init(); ! itr; itr++)
        if (itr() == value) {
            // remove the element
            itr.removeCurrent();
            // add the element to the front
            add(value);
            // return success
            return 1;
            }
    // not found
    return 0;
}
```

Since elements are moved to the front, we can now provide a method to remove an arbitrary value from a list, an operation we did not provide as part of our basic list data structure. Such an operation is a simple combination of an includes test and a removal from the front.

```
template<class T> void selfOrganizingList<T>::remove(T value)
{   // remove the argument value from the list
    if (includes(val))
        removeFirst();
}
```

To illustrate the effectiveness of the self-organizing concept, consider a list containing the numbers 1 to 9, initially in order. Assume that a sequence of requests is performed as shown in Table 8.1. We have here constructed the request sequence so that requests for the values 4 and 7 are more frequently performed than requests for the other values. The table indicates the position of the request in the current list, which is thus the number of comparisons performed to find the given element. The table also shows the self-organized list following each search. After 30 searches, the self-organizing list will have performed only 129 comparisons, while the non–self-organizing list would have required 154 comparisons.

8.6 DOUBLE ENDED LISTS*

In the list structures we have seen up to this point, insertions and deletions can only be performed to or from the start of the list (with the exception of additions or removal performed using an iterator, of course). As part of the process of solving many problems, it is often necessary to make use of linear lists in which insertions can be performed either at the front or the back of a list.

We could, of course, implement the ability to add an element to the end of a list by each time looping over all elements in the list to find the last element, and then appending the new value to the last element. Such an algorithm would require $O(n)$ steps to insert each new value. We can reduce the cost of insertion to a constant time operation independent of the size of the list by maintaining two pointers. The `ptrToFirstLink` field will continue to point to the start of the list. A new field, `ptrToLastLink`, will point to the end of the list.

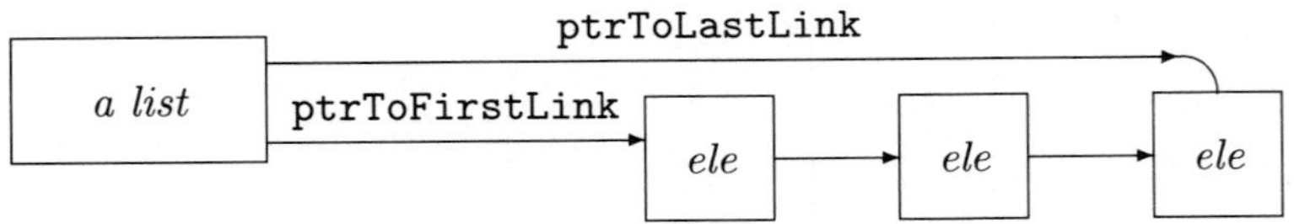

As we did with ordered lists, we can reduce the amount of code we need to write for our new class `doubleEndedList` by subclassing from the existing class `list`. The only operations we need to modify are those involved in insertion and removal of elements.

```
//
// class doubleEndedList
//     a variation on lists - can add elements to end
//     as well as to front

template <class T> class doubleEndedList<T> : public list<T> {
```

*Section headings followed by an asterisk indicate optional material.

Table 8.1 The execution of a self-organizing list

Request	Position	New list
7	7	7 1 2 3 4 5 6 8 9
4	5	4 7 1 2 3 5 6 8 9
4	1	4 7 1 2 3 5 6 8 9
7	2	7 4 1 2 3 5 6 8 9
3	5	3 7 4 1 2 5 6 8 9
7	2	7 3 4 1 2 5 6 8 9
8	8	8 7 3 4 1 2 5 6 9
6	8	6 8 7 3 4 1 2 5 9
4	5	4 6 8 7 3 1 2 5 9
3	5	3 4 6 8 7 1 2 5 9
4	2	4 3 6 8 7 1 2 5 9
3	2	3 4 6 8 7 1 2 5 9
5	8	5 3 4 6 8 7 1 2 9
9	9	9 5 3 4 6 8 7 1 2
5	2	5 9 3 4 6 8 7 1 2
4	4	4 5 9 3 6 8 7 1 2
2	9	2 4 5 9 3 6 8 7 1
4	2	4 2 5 9 3 6 8 7 1
5	3	5 4 2 9 3 6 8 7 1
7	8	7 5 4 2 9 3 6 8 1
6	7	6 7 5 4 2 9 3 8 1
6	1	6 7 5 4 2 9 3 8 1
7	2	7 6 5 4 2 9 3 8 1
4	4	4 7 6 5 2 9 3 8 1
2	5	2 4 7 6 5 9 3 8 1
4	2	4 2 7 6 5 9 3 8 1
7	3	7 4 2 6 5 9 3 8 1
4	2	4 7 2 6 5 9 3 8 1
7	2	7 4 2 6 5 9 3 8 1
6	4	6 7 4 2 5 9 3 8 1
154	129	Total number of comparisons

```
public:
    // constructor
    doubleEndedList ();
    doubleEndedList (const doubleEndedList & v);

    // override the following methods from class list
    virtual void    add             (T value);
    virtual void    deleteAllValues ();
    virtual void    removeFirst     ();

    // add a new element to the end of the list
    void            addToEnd        (T value);

protected:
    // data area
    link<T> * ptrToLastLink;
};
```

The constructor must be redefined so as to initialize, to zero, the value of the last link pointer. The copy constructor must be similarly redefined.

```
template <class T> doubleEndedList<T>::doubleEndedList() : list<T>()
{   // create and initialize a new double ended list
    ptrToLastLink = 0;
}
```

The only change to the add method is to check for the one special case when the first element is added to an empty list. In this case both the pointer to the first link and the pointer to the last link must be set to point to the new element. The `ptrToFirstLink` field will be set automatically by the method in class `list`, and thus by using this method we need only set the `ptrToLastLink` pointer.

```
template <class T> void doubleEndedList<T>::add(T val)
{   // add an element to the front of a double ended list
    // only need to handle addition to empty list
    if (isEmpty()) {
        list<T>::add(val);
        ptrToLastLink = ptrToFirstLink;
        }
    else
        list<T>::add(val);
}
```

Adding an element to the end of a list is as simple as appending the value to the final link. The only exception occurs if an attempt is made to insert into an empty list. In this case calling the add method ensures that both the pointer to the first link and the pointer to the last link will be correctly set.

```
template <class T> void doubleEndedList<T>::addToEnd(T val)
{   // add a new element to the end of a double ended
list
    // if there is an end, add to it
    if (ptrToLastLink != 0)
        ptrToLastLink = ptrToLastLink->insert(val);

    // otherwise, just add to front
    else
        add(val);
}
```

When all elements are deleted from the list, we must also ensure the pointer to the last element is set to null.

```
template <class T> void doubleEndedList<T>::deleteAllValues()
{   // delete all values from collection
    // invoke the list method to do the actual work
    list<T>::deleteAllValues();
    // then set the pointer to last element to zero
    ptrToLastLink = 0;
}
```

Finally, the only special case that must be handled during the removal of the first element occurs when the last element is removed, in which case the `ptrToLastLink` must be zeroed as well.

```
template <class T> void doubleEndedList<T>::removeFirst()
{   // remove first element from double ended list
    // invoke the method from list to do the work
    list<T>::removeFirst();

    // only do something different if we removed last element
    if (isEmpty())
        ptrToLastLink = 0;
}
```

In the next chapter we will present an application of double-ended lists.

8.7 OTHER COMMON VARIATIONS

Some of the more common variations on linear list structures that we have not discussed include circular lists and doubly linked lists.

In a circular list, sometimes called a *ring buffer*, the link on the last element is set to point to the first, thus completing a circle of pointers. Care must be taken when inserting the first element into such a list, (making sure the node points to itself) and in removing the last element from the list.

Since a circular list has no ending element, care must also be taken during iteration to avoid infinite loops. Two common solutions to this problem are employed. The first is to maintain a count of the number of list entries and to control the loop by measuring the number of values scanned. The second approach is to use a special, recognizable node in the list as a *sentinel*. The sentinel is never removed from the list. Iteration will check at each increment, and halt when the sentinel node is encountered.

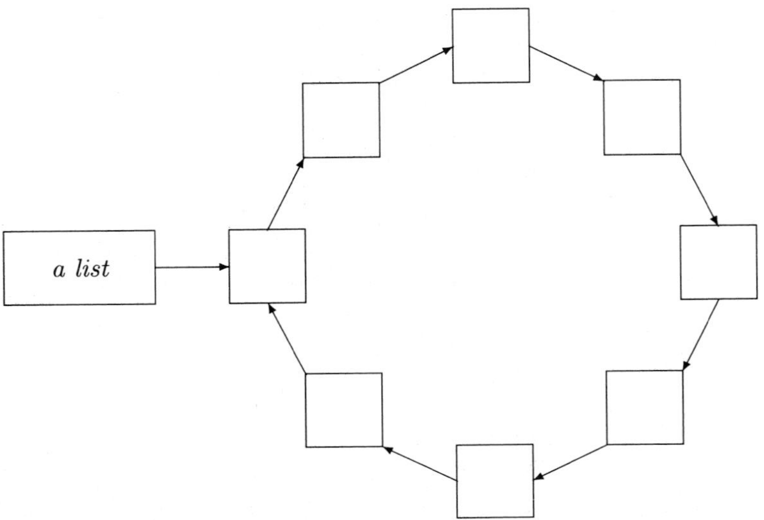

The second major class of variations involves maintaining links at each node that point both forward and backward. Such an arrangement is known as a *doubly linked* list. The maintenance of two links makes it easier to discover both the predecessor and successor of any node, making insertions and removals possible with only a pointer to a single node, instead of the two pointers we required when we defined operations using iterators. Often doubly linked lists are combined with circular structures, to form doubly linked circular lists.

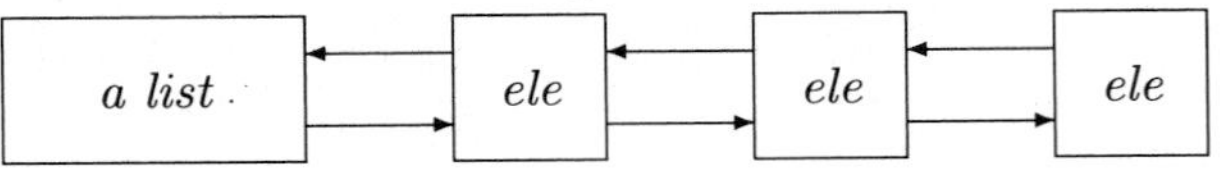

8.8 APPLICATION—FREE LISTS*

Consider for the moment how the built-in procedures `new` and `delete` might be implemented. The major difficulty arises from the fact that

*Section headings followed by an asterisk indicate optional material.

memory is a fixed resource, and thus to avoid premature termination of a program because of insufficient memory space the locations returned to the system via a `delete` statement must be remembered and recycled for later use. To accomplish this, the system requires a data structure that can maintain an arbitrary number of elements and has the ability to grow and shrink as necessary. The obvious solution is to employ a linked list. Such a list used for memory management purposes is often called a *free list*.

The basic idea is the following. Initially, there is a large block of contiguous free memory to be used for memory allocation. As requests are made for data values, small pieces of this large block are sliced off and given to the user.

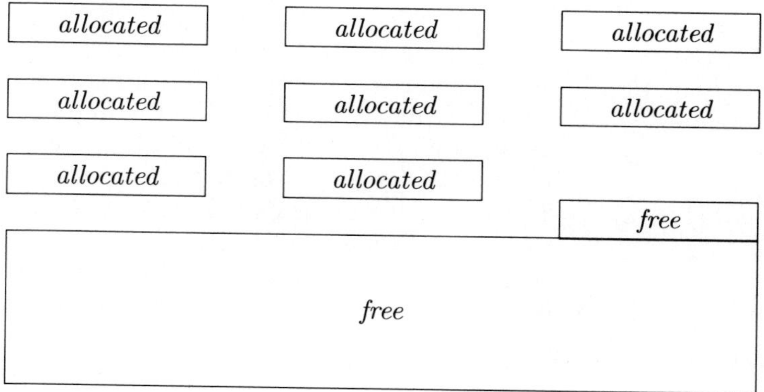

At some point, the user will start to return memory to the system using the `delete` statement. The difficulty for the memory management system is that these deletions can arrive in random order, and they are not guaranteed (or even likely) to be adjacent to the remaining large block of free storage. Instead, deleted memory areas are placed at the front of a linked list of free storage areas. The head of this free list thus points to the most recently deleted node. This node, in turn, will point to the next free area, and so on.

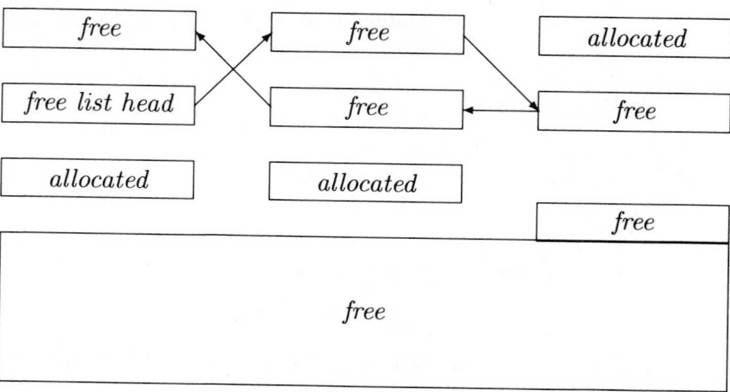

Now when a request is made for new dynamic memory, the free list is first examined. If there is a value on the free list that can be reutilized, the value is removed from the free list and returned to the user. Only if no appropriate value is found on the free list is a new value sliced from the original memory block.

The algorithm would be relatively straightforward were it not for various complicating factors. Foremost of these is the fact that memory requests are not all the same size. A solution to this is to maintain two values in each memory structure on the free list. These two values are the link to the next node and a figure representing the size of the memory structure. Thus an allocation from the free list cannot simply take the first node, but may require searching the list for a value that is sufficiently large.

There are various approaches to deciding which node to allocate. Suppose we are attempting to allocate a block of memory 12 bytes long. The first sufficiently large item on the free list is 30 bytes in length. Should we break this value into two smaller pieces? Alternatively, should we continue searching for a value that more closely matches the requested size? The first heuristic is called the *first-fit* strategy, while the second is called the *best-fit* approach. While the first-fit technique is clearly faster at allocation, it has the disadvantage that over time large blocks of memory are broken down into small units, and memory is divided almost entirely into small blocks. This difficulty is known as *fragmentation*.

A technique that tries to avoid fragmentation is to maintain not a single free list, but a vector of free lists. The first element in this vector might hold the free lists for blocks of size 8 or less, the second for blocks of size 9 to 16, the third for blocks of size 17 to 24, and so on. Thus an allocation is always made from a block that is close to the appropriate size.

The implementation of the `delete` operation can be similarly complex. Should an attempt be made to combine two adjacent free memory blocks into a single larger block? Clearly, this would be useful in responding to a subsequent request for the larger block, but it might not be beneficial if subsequent requests were for blocks similar to those being returned. These and other issues make memory allocation an exceedingly subtle and complex issue. Further information can be found in some of the references cited at the end of this chapter.

To illustrate the use of free lists, we might envision the construction of a class named `memoryManagedList` that provides its own version of a free list. It is only necessary to override the addition and removal methods from the class `list`.

```
template <class T> class memoryManagedList : public list<T> {
public:
    // constructor
    memoryManagedList();

    // override the methods to add or remove an entry
```

```
    virtual void     add            (T value);
    virtual void     removeFirst    ();

protected:
    // data area
    link<T> *        freeList;
};
```

To see how the free list is constructed, we describe the removal method first. As before, the remove method disassociates the head of the list from the remainder of the links. Now, rather than deleting the value, it places it on the free list.

```
template <class T> void memoryManagedList<T>::removeFirst()
{   // remove first element and place on to free list
    // make sure there is a first node to remove
    assert(ptrToFirstLink);

    // take it off the list
    link<T> * p = ptrToFirstLink;
    ptrToFirstLink = p->ptrToNextLink;

    // add it to the free list
    p->ptrToNextLink = freeList;
    freeList = p;
}
```

The add operation first tries to remove a node from the free list. Only if no node is available on the free list is the system memory allocation routine invoked.

```
template <class T> void memoryManagedList<T>::add(T val)
{   // add a new element to a list
    if (freeList) {
        // take node off the free list
        link<T> * p = freeList;
        freeList = p->ptrToNextLink;

        // fill the fields of the new node
        p->value = val;
        p->ptrToNextLink = ptrToFirstLink;
        ptrToFirstLink = p;
        }
    else {
        // allocate the node
        ptrToFirstLink = new link<T>(val, ptrToFirstLink);
        // make sure allocation worked
        assert(ptrToFirstLink != 0);
        }
}
```

8.9 CHAPTER SUMMARY

Key Concepts

- List
- Links
- Friends
- Variations on lists
  - Ordered lists
  - Self-organizing lists
  - Double-ended lists
  - Circular lists
  - Doubly linked lists
- List insertion sort
- Self-organizing data structures
- Memory allocation
  - First fit
  - Best fit
  - Fragmentation

In this chapter we have examined the concept of a linked list. A list is an unordered collection of values. Unlike a vector, a list has no fixed size but instead grows or shrinks as elements are added or removed from the structure. In the basic list structure, elements can be added or removed only from the front of the list.

We have seen several variations on the concept of a list:

- ▲ A list iterator not only permits the programmer to easily write a loop that iterates over the values contained in a list but also permits elements to be added or removed from arbitrary positions in the list.
- ▲ An ordered list maintains the elements of the list in sequence. The implementation of the ordered list data type is simplified by the use of inheritance. By implementing the class `orderedList` using inheritance from the class `list`, almost all behavior is made available to the new structure without the need to write any new code.

  Ordered lists also make possible a new sorting technique, the list insertion sort algorithm.
- ▲ Self-organizing lists optimize repeated searches for the same element. Each time that an element is accessed, it is moved to the front of the list. Thus a second search for the same element will be performed in fewer steps than the first search.
- ▲ A double-ended list permits insertions to be made either at the front of the list or at the end of a list.
- ▲ A circular list, or ring buffer, maintains values in a circular structure. There is no front or end of this list; each element simply points to the next in sequence.
- ▲ In a doubly linked list each link maintains two pointers. The first points forward to the next link; the second points backward to the previous link.
- ▲ A free list is a linked list used to maintain pointers to unused memory blocks.

A new C++ mechanism introduced in this chapter is the concept of a friend. A class declaration can specify other classes, or individual functions, as friends. Friend classes or functions are permitted access to the private and protected fields of the class structure. Without the friend declaration, these fields would otherwise be inaccessible.

References

As with almost all data structures we will consider, the classic description of algorithms on linked lists is provided by Knuth in volume 1 of his series on the art of computer programming [Knuth 73]. Knuth also discusses polynomial arithmetic in volume 3 [Knuth 75]. A number of algorithms for memory allocation are discussed by Knuth in volume 1, as well as in the book by Aho, Hopcroft, and Ullman [Aho 83]. A good analysis of self-organizing lists is presented by Gonnet and Baeza-Yates [Gonnet 91].

A relatively recent change to the C++ language permits the nesting of class definitions one within another. This mechanism allows facilitator classes, such as our class `link`, to be entirely and effectively hidden from users of the list abstraction. Such a style is advocated by Coplien [Coplien 92], as well as others. I have here avoided the use of nested classes for two reasons. First, the explanation of this feature would be yet one more little bit of syntax, an unnecessary addition in a text already brimming with explanations of syntax. Second, since this is a relatively new change to C++, not all compilers can be expected to support this feature.

In order to keep the list data abstraction as simple as possible, I have also avoided discussing the meaning of the assignment statement when used with lists. This is more serious, since the compiler will automatically generate an implementation for the assignment operator that is typically, for user-defined types, not what the programmer wishes. There are two common solutions to this problem. The first is to explicitly define the assignment operator for each data structure. Such implementations typically end up sharing much of the same logic used by a copy constructor, since they are doing much the same task. Unfortunately, this operator then needs to be redefined in each of the various forms of the structure (list, orderedList, and so on). The second approach is to define an assignment operator, but place it in a private section of the class description. This effectively makes assignments to instances of the class illegal. It is not even necessary to provide anything more than a simple null statement for the body of this method.

Exercises

1. Write a method for the class `list` that, given an integer value n, returns the nth item in the list. What is the execution time of your operation? How does this compare to the execution time for the corresponding operation on a vector?

2. Write a function that takes a list as an argument and returns a new list in which the order of the elements is the exact reversal of the argument list. (*Hint*: This is easier than it seems.)

3. Write a procedure named `append` that takes as arguments two lists and returns a new list containing elements from both arguments, in which all the elements of the second list appear after all the elements from the first list. Would it be easier to write this function using doubled-ended lists? Would it be easier to write as a method?

4. Write the code for polynomial subtraction. Implement both the assignment operator and the infix operator.

5. Propose a definition for polynomial division, and implement this operation.

6. It can happen that a term with a coefficient of zero can occur as a result of the addition of two polynomials. One would think that such a term could be eliminated from the polynomial, using the `remove` instruction. Explain why this is not

so. (*Hint*: Trace carefully the value of the `previous` and `current` pointers during the iteration of the main loop in the addition assignment operator.)

7. Design a stream input routine for polynomials. How do you know when you have reached the end of a polynomial?

8. Design a method that can be used to raise a polynomial to a positive integer power. What is the complexity of your solution? (*Hint*: Recall the discussion of integer powers from Chapter 3.)

9. How would you change the polynomial representation to accommodate polynomials of two or more variables. How would the definition of the various operations change?

10. The `removeFirst` method in class `list` could have alternatively been defined so as to perform no action on an empty list, as in the following:

```
void list<T>::removeFirst()
{
    if (ptrToFirstLink) {
        link<T> * p = ptrToFirstLink;
        ptrToFirstLink = p->next;
        delete p;
        }
}
```

Describe the advantages and disadvantages of the two approaches. Which would likely lead to the earliest detection of programming errors?

11. Suppose for a certain application it was important to always know the number of elements in a list. To discover this value, we could use the method `size`. But as defined, this method employs a loop, and thus has $O(n)$ execution time. Using subclassing, write a new class named `countedList` that maintains an explicit count on the number of values held in the list and can thus respond to the `size` method in constant time. For this problem you can ignore insertions and deletions performed using iterators.

12. Carefully verify that the addition method for ordered lists works correctly (a) when inserting into an empty list; (b) when inserting to the beginning of a nonempty list; (c) when inserting into the middle of a nonempty list; and (d) when inserting to the end of a nonempty list.

13. Using the techniques described in Exercise 15, Chapter 3 (page 234), test the hypothesis that list insertion sort is an $O(n^2)$ algorithm. Using the value of c that you compute, estimate for the list insertion algorithm how long it would take to sort a vector of 100,000 elements.

14. Imagine you have two ordered lists, L_1 and L_2. Write a procedure to efficiently yield a new ordered list that is the union of the two lists (you can assume that values in either list are unique). Write a procedure to efficiently yield the intersection of the two lists. Write the same procedures for unordered lists, and compare the efficiency of your two approaches.

15. When used with ordered lists, insertions and deletions performed using the list iterator do not maintain the ordering property, since the `addBefore` and `addAfter` methods can insert elements at arbitrary locations. Write a new iterator that implements all the features of the class `listIterator` and also maintains the ordering property.

16. When used with double-ended lists, insertions and deletions performed using the list iterator do not maintain the invariant that the `ptrToLastLink` always references the last element. Write a new iterator that implements all the features of the class `listIterator` and also maintains this property.

17. Another technique for making lists self-organizing is the transpose method. Using this technique, whenever a search is successful in finding a value, the element is swapped with the value that immediately precedes it in the list (provided, of course, it is not already at the front of the list). Describe the `includes` method for a self-organizing list using this approach.

18. Describe insertion and removal algorithms for circular linked lists. Take care to make sure you cover the exceptional cases of inserting into an empty list, or removing the last element from a list.

19. Describe insertion and removal algorithms for doubly linked lists. Take care to make sure you cover all the exceptional cases, such as inserting or removing from the beginning or end of a list, inserting into an empty list or removing the last element from a list.

20. Is the list insertion sort algorithm stable? (See Chapter 5, Exercise 12, page 234).

CHAPTER 9

Stacks and Queues — Higher-Level Abstractions

MOST PEOPLE have a good intuitive understanding of the stack and queue data abstractions, based on experience with everyday objects. An excellent example of a stack is a pile of papers on a desk, or a stack of dishes in a cupboard. In both cases the important characteristic is that it is the item on the top that is most easily accessed. New items are similarly added most easily to the collection by placing them above all the current items in the stack. In this manner, an item removed from a stack is the element that has been most recently inserted into a stack.

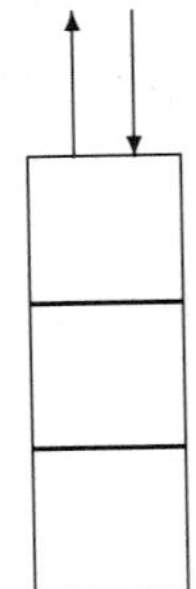

An everyday example of a queue, on the other hand, is a line of people waiting to enter a theater. Here new additions are made to the back of the queue, as new people enter the line, while items are removed from the front of the structure, as patrons enter the theater. The removal order for a queue is the opposite of that for a stack. In a queue, the item that is removed is the element that has been present in the queue for the longest period of time.

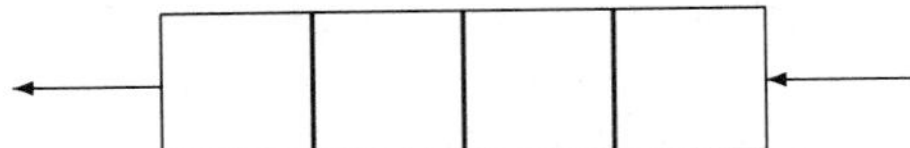

A stack is sometimes referred to as a *LIFO* structure, and a queue is called a *FIFO* structure. The abbreviation *LIFO* stands for *L*ast *I*n, *F*irst *O*ut. This means the first entry removed from a stack is the last entry that was inserted. The term *FIFO*, on the other hand, is short for *F*irst *I*n, *F*irst *O*ut. This means the first element removed from a queue is the first element that was inserted into the queue.

We have already, in fact, encountered at least one use of stacks in the examples discussed in earlier chapters. In Chapter 2, Fig. 2.5 (page 50) we noted the method `putback` used with input streams. The `putback` method "returns" a character to an input stream. A subsequent character read operation will first yield the pushed-back character, before continuing with the remainder of input from the file.

The stream data structure maintains two data areas. It must hold a pointer to the file from which the raw characters are obtained. It must maintain a stack of characters that have been pushed back into the input. Suppose, for example, the stream is returning the text of this chapter. Imagine the words "Most people have a good" have been read, and subsequently the four characters of the word "good" are pushed back into the input. We could visualize this as follows:

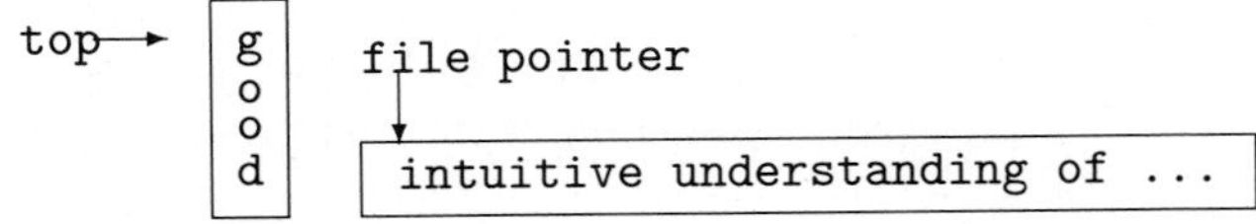

A two-step process is used to read a character from a stream. First, the stack of pushed-back characters is examined. If it is not empty, the topmost character from the stack is popped and returned. Only if the push-back stack is empty is the next character read from an input file.

Stacks are used at the heart of the most common implementation technique for programming languages. Space for parameters and local variables is created internally within the computer using a stack. Using for our example the rational number abstraction developed in Chapter 2, recall the steps used to print instances of the class `rational` on an output stream. The stream output (<<) operator for class rational calls the stream output operator for the integer numerator. The integer stream output operator invokes the stream output method for unsigned integers (Fig. 2.4, page 49), which recursively calls itself once for each digit in the number. Finally, each digit value is printed by calling the stream output function with a character argument.

For each function call, a memory stack is incremented to create space for the parameters and local variables associated with the function. This space for local variables and parameters is known as the *activation record* for the function call. The use of a stack to perform memory allocation has many advantages. It allows recursive procedures, such as the recursive routine to print unsigned integers, to possess in each iteration a unique data area for local variables. The release of memory simply means decrementing the stack, and invoking destructors for any values that define destructors. This can be performed very rapidly. Finally, no more memory is required for the stack than is necessary for the local variables and parameters in use at any one time.

Top →	Local variables and parameters for ostream << char
	Local variables and parameters for ostream << unsigned
	Local variables and parameters for ostream << unsigned
	Local variables and parameters for ostream << integer
	Local variables and parameters for ostream << rational

Queues are also extensively used in the internal functioning of computer systems. When output is submitted to a printer, for example, it is typically placed in a queue with several other tasks. This permits the printer system to receive output requests even when the printer is busy responding to a previous job. Since a queue is used to hold pending tasks, rather than a stack, output will be produced in the order the requests are received.

9.1 THE ABSTRACT CLASSES `stack` AND `queue`

As we did with iterators in Chapter 5, we will define the protocol for our stack and queue abstractions as an *abstract class*. An abstract class describes the names and argument types for each of the operations on the stack and queue data structure, but it does not provide any implementation. In subsequent sections we will outline various implementation techniques.

Traditionally, the stack data type is characterized by four operations. New items can be inserted at the top of the stack using the method `push`. The function `isEmpty` returns a Boolean true value if and only if the stack contains no elements. Because this operation does not alter the stack, it is declared as constant. The function `top` returns the topmost element of the stack but does not remove it from the stack. It, too, can be declared as constant. The function `pop`, on the other hand, removes and returns the topmost item from a stack. We will add a fifth operation, `deleteAllValues`, which will empty all values from the stack.

```
//
// class stack
//     abstract class - simply defines protocol for stack operations
//

template <class T> class stack {
public:
    virtual void    deleteAllValues  () = 0;
    virtual int     isEmpty          () const = 0;
    virtual T       pop              () = 0;
    virtual void    push             (T value) = 0;
    virtual T       top              () const = 0;
};
```

The queue data type is similar, also traditionally characterized by four operations. New values are added to the back of the queue using the message `enqueue`. Elements are removed from the front of the queue via the function `dequeue`. The first element of the queue can be obtained using the method `front`. As with stacks, the function `isEmpty` will return a true value in the event there are no elements in the queue. Also as with the stack, we will add one more operation to delete all items from the queue.

```
//
// class queue
//     abstract class - simply defines protocol for queue operations
//

template <class T> class queue {
public:
    virtual void    deleteAllValues    () = 0;
    virtual T       dequeue            () = 0;
    virtual void    enqueue            (T value) = 0;
    virtual T       front              () = 0;
    virtual int     isEmpty            () const = 0;
};
```

Because the only valid extraction operations on the stack and queue data type provide access to only the first element, we do not define iterator data structures for the stack and queue data abstractions.

9.2 STACKS

There are two major techniques used to implement stacks. The first of these uses a vector as the underlying data structure to hold the stack elements, while the second uses a list. We will describe the benefits and disadvantages of each, in the following sections.

9.2.1 Vector Implementation

As the name would suggest, the `stackVector` data structure uses a vector to hold the actual data items.

```
//
// stackVector
//     stack implemented using vector
//     vector will grow as necessary to avoid overflow
//

template <class T> class stackVector : public stack<T> {
public:
    // constructor requires a starting size
    stackVector     (unsigned int size);
    stackVector     (const stackVector & v);

    // stack operations
    virtual void    deleteAllValues  ();
    virtual int     isEmpty          () const;
```

```
    virtual T       pop             ();
    virtual void    push            (T value);
    virtual T       top             () const;

protected:
    // data fields
    vector<T>       data;
    unsigned int    nextSlot;
};
```

The initial size of this vector is determined by an argument passed to the constructor.

```
template <class T> stackVector<T>::stackVector(unsigned int size)
        : data(size)
{   // create and initialize a stack based on vectors
    // make sure stack is initially empty
    deleteAllValues();
}
```

The copy constructor simply duplicates the fields held by the argument stack. By making use of the copy constructor for the class `vector`, this operation becomes trivial to implement.

There is no need to define a destructor for the class `stackVector`. If no other destructor is defined, a *default destructor* will automatically be generated. This destructor will simply invoke destructors for each of the data fields in the class. Thus the destructor for the class `vector` will automatically be invoked when an instance of class `stackVector` is destroyed.

```
template <class T> stackVector<T>::stackVector(const stackVector<T> & v)
    : data(v.data), nextSlot(v.nextSlot)
{
    // no further initialization
}
```

The data field named `nextSlot` is used to determine the number of elements currently being held by the stack. Items are stored in the stack starting from the first field of the vector. The value of `nextSlot` is the position in the vector that will be filled by the next `push` operation.

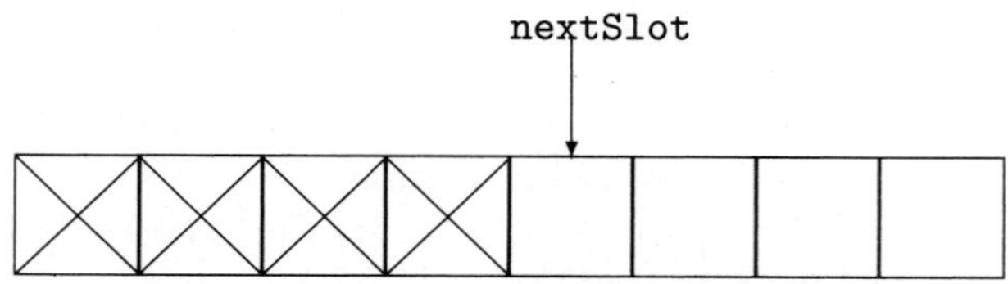

To clear the stack, we simply reset this pointer to the bottom of the data vector. No items are actually removed from the stack; the space is simply marked as empty and the locations will be overwritten when the next push operation is performed.

```
template <class T> void stackVector<T>::deleteAllValues()
{   // clear all elements from stack, by setting
    // index to bottom of stack
    nextSlot = 0;
}
```

Since `nextSlot` points to the next empty slot, to return the top of the stack requires returning the data item held at index position `nextSlot - 1`. An assertion checks to make sure we are not attempting to remove an item from an empty stack.

```
template <class T> T stackVector<T>::top() const
{   // return the topmost element in the stack
    assert(! isEmpty());
    return data[nextSlot-1];
}
```

Popping the top element involves first decrementing the `nextSlot` pointer and then returning the value at the updated index position. Either `top` or `pop` will fail with an assertion error if there are no elements being held by the stack. This is known as a *stack underflow* condition.

```
template <class T> T stackVector<T>::pop()
{   // return and remove the topmost element in the stack
    assert(! isEmpty());
    return data[--nextSlot];
}
```

The test to determine whether the stack is empty or not can be performed by simply testing whether the `nextSlot` value is zero.

```
template <class T> int stackVector<T>::isEmpty() const
{   // return true if stack is empty
    // if nextSlot points to bottom of stack
    // then there are no elements
    return nextSlot == 0;
}
```

Another potentially erroneous condition occurs if an attempt is made to insert a value when the stack is full—that is, when all elements of the underlying vector have been assigned. This is known as a *stack overflow* condition. One possibility here would have been to generate an assertion error, just as we did for the stack underflow condition. Another solution to this problem is to use the ability of vectors to increase their size using the setSize instruction. When a potential stack overflow occurs, we increase the size of the data vector. Overflow errors will never occur with this design.

```
template <class T> void stackVector<T>::push(T val)
{   // push new value on to stack
    // if stack is too small, then increase the size
    if (nextSlot >= data.length())
        data.setSize(data.length() + 5);
    data[nextSlot++] = val;
}
```

Since stack operations are implemented using only assignment and integer increments or decrements, they are executed very quickly. On the other hand, the size of the stack must be known in advance, or at least roughly estimated. As we noted in Chapter 6, the setSize operation is relatively costly, and we do not want to be incrementing the size of the stack very frequently. The major advantage of the alternative implementation technique we will describe next is the fact that it does not place any limitation on the number of elements held in the stack.

9.2.2 List Implementation

Recall that the list data type developed in Chapter 8 permitted elements to be inserted and removed from the front of a list. These are the basic operations for our stack data abstraction, only known by different names. In light of this fact, it is relatively easy to create a class, stackList, built on top of the list abstraction.

```
//
// class stackList
//     stack implemented using list operations
//

template <class T> class stackList : public stack<T> {
public:
    // constructors
    stackList       ();
    stackList       (const stackList & v);

    // stack operations
    virtual void    deleteAllValues  ();
    virtual int     isEmpty          () const;
    virtual T       pop              ();
    virtual void    push             (T value);
    virtual T       top              () const;
```

```
protected:
    // data fields
    list<T>        data;
};
```

Both the default constructor and the copy constructor have trivial implementations, since the majority of the work can be performed by invoking the constructor from the `list` class.

```
template <class T> stackList<T>::stackList() : data()
{
    // create and initialize a new stackList
}

template <class T> stackList<T>::stackList(const stackList<T> & v)
    : data(v.data)
{
    // create and initialize a new stackList
}
```

No destructor is necessary. As we saw in the `stackVector` data abstraction, if no destructor is defined, a default destructor will automatically be generated, which will invoke destructors for each field of the structure. Thus the `list` destructor will be executed when instances of `stackList` are destroyed.

A `push` corresponds to a list `add`, while returning the topmost element of the stack corresponds to performing a `firstElement` operation on the stack. A test for an empty stack is translated into a test for an empty list. To clear all elements from the stack, we simply perform the list operation `deleteAllValues`.

All operations but one are implemented by a trivial one-line function that simply invokes the relevant operation on the underlying list. The sole exception is the function used to pop an element from the stack. This operation is built out of a combination of the list operations `firstElement` and `removeFirst`.

```
template <class T> T stackList<T>::pop()
{   // pop and return topmost element in list
    // get first element in list
    T result = data.firstElement();
    // remove element from list
    data.removeFirst();
    // return value
    return result;
}
```

A stack underflow error will be manifest as an assertion error from the `first` method; an alternative would have been to check the empty status of the stack in the pop method and report an error directly. Since lists are not limited in size (except by the total amount of computer memory), stack overflow conditions cannot occur.

You will recall that a considerable amount of effort was consumed in the development of the list abstraction with questions of memory management. We needed to check not only that dynamic memory allocations were successful but also that dynamic memory consumed by the links was freed when it was no longer needed. This could occur either as a result of deleting a single element, or through the release of an entire list. By building the stack abstraction on top of the existing list data structure, we avoid having to once again and independently solve these same problems, since the solution is already contained in the list class. Deletion of single elements is actually performed by the list deletion method. Furthermore, the default destructor generated by the C++ language will automatically invoke the destructor for the list field when an instance of the stack class is destroyed.

We have already noted that the major advantage of the list implementation over the vector implementation technique concerns size. There is one additional relatively minor technical advantage. As we noted in Chapter 6, vectors cannot hold reference values, while as we saw in Chapter 8, there is no such restriction on list data structures. Thus a stack formed by using vectors cannot hold references, while instances of `stackList` do not have this restriction.

9.3 APPLICATION — RPN CALCULATOR*

The classic application of a stack is in the simulation of a calculator. Operands, such as integer constants, are pushed on a stack of values. As operators are encountered, the appropriate number of operands are popped off the stack, the operation is performed, and the result is pushed back on the stack.

We can divide the development of our stack simulation into two parts. A calculator engine is concerned with the actual work involved in the simulation, but it does not perform and direct input or output operations. The name is intended to suggest an analogy to a car engine, or a computer processor — a mechanism that performs the actual work but with which the user does not normally directly interact. Wrapped around this, the calculator simulator will interact with the user, passing appropriate instructions to the calculator engine. By dividing responsibilities in this manner, our design can offer greater flexibility than would be possible if the two tasks

*Section headings followed by an asterisk indicate optional material.

were combined; for example, the calculator engine component will not change even if we make changes to the user interface.

A class definition for the calculator engine can be given as follows. Inside the class declaration we define an enumerated list of values to represent each of the possible operators the calculator is prepared to accept. We have made two simplifying assumptions: All operands will be integer values, and we will handle only binary operators.

```
//
// class calculatorEngine
//     simulate the behavior of a simple integer calculator
//

class calculatorEngine {
public:
    enum  binaryOperator {plus, minus, times, divide};

    int   currentMemory    ();
    void  pushOperand      (int value);
    void  doOperator       (binaryOperator theOp);

protected:
    stackList<int> data;
};
```

An integer stack is used to hold the actual data values. To push an operand into the calculator memory, the value is simply pushed on to the data stack:

```
void calculatorEngine::pushOperand(int value)
{        // push a new operand on to the operand stack
    data.push(value);
}
```

To view current memory value for the calculator, we simply return the topmost element in the stack.

```
int calculatorEngine::currentMemory()
{        // return topmost item in operand stack
    return data.top();
}
```

To perform an operation, the arguments are popped from the stack (notice the right argument is on top of the left argument), the appropriate operation is executed, and the result is pushed back on the stack.

```
void calculatorEngine::doOperator(binaryOperator theOp)
{   // perform a binary operation on stack values
    int right = data.pop();
```

```
        int left = data.pop();
        int result;
        switch(theOp) { // do the operation
            case plus:
                result = left + right;
                break;
            case minus:
                result = left - right;
                break;
            case times:
                result = left * right;
                break;
            case divide:
                result = left / right;
                break;
            }

        // push the result back on the stack
        data.push(result);
}
```

In developing the second component in our simulation, we will again make a simplifying assumption. We will assume the input is presented in *postfix polish notation* (sometimes called *reverse* polish notation, or RPN). Polish notation was named for its inventor, the logician Jan Lukasiewicz, who lived in the early part of this century.[1] The major virtue of the form is that it can be processed one symbol at a time reading left to right, and it does not require parentheses. For example, an expression such as $(17 + 23 * 42) + 55$ would be written in postfix polish notation as 17 23 42 $*$ $+$ 55 $+$. Input is composed either of operators (such as $+$ or $-$) or operands (only integers in our simple example). Operands are pushed on a stack as they are encountered. By the time an operator is encountered, all operands will have been seen already and pushed on the stack. The appropriate number of operands for the operator are popped from the stack, the operation performed, and the result pushed back on the stack.

The procedure given below is our reverse polish calculator program. In addition to the arithmetic operators, the letters "p" and "q" are used as operators. The letter "p" prints, but does not remove, the current top of the stack. The letter "q" is used to halt the program. Notice the handling of digits. A digit character may represent the first character in a multi-character number, such as 132. The character is pushed back into the in-

---

1. So then why isn't polish notation referred to as Lukasiewicz notation?

put, making use of the stack of characters used by the stream I/O package, and the entire number is reread using the stream operator with an integer argument. Notice also the use of the disambiguation prefix used to clearly indicate the value of the binary operator enumerated values declared in the calculator engine class.

```
void calculator()
{   int intval;
    calculatorEngine calc;
    char c;

    while (cin >> c) {
        switch(c) {
            case '0': case '1': case '2': case '3': case '4':
            case '5': case '6': case '7': case '8': case '9':
                cin.putback(c);
                cin >> intval;
                calc.pushOperand(intval);
                break;

            case '+':
                calc.doOperator(calculatorEngine::plus);
                break;

            case '-':
                calc.doOperator(calculatorEngine::minus);
                break;

            case '*':
                calc.doOperator(calculatorEngine::times);
                break;

            case '/':
                calc.doOperator(calculatorEngine::divide);
                break;

            case 'p':
                cout << calc.currentMemory() << '\n';
                break;

            case 'q':
                return; // quit calculator
            }
        }
}
```

9.4 APPLICATION — CONVERSION OF INFIX TO POSTFIX*

Another classic application for a stack is the conversion of standard, or *infix*, expressions into postfix form. Factors that complicate infix notation are parentheses and the different precedence of operators. An expression written in infix format as:

$$5 * (27 + 3 * 7) + 22$$

would be translated into postfix as:

$$5\ 27\ 3\ 7\ *\ +\ *\ 22\ +$$

When an operand (such as a constant) is read, it is immediately appended to the output. Operators, such as + and $*$, cannot be output until both their arguments have been processed. Thus they must be saved on a stack. If an operator being pushed on a stack has a lower precedence than the current top of a stack, then the top of the stack is popped and output. This occurs, for example, in the expression $4 * 6 + 5$. When the + is encountered, the output contains the symbols 4 and 6, and the top of the stack holds the $*$ operator. Since the precedence of multiplication is higher than that of addition, the multiplication symbol is output and the addition symbol placed on the stack.

A left parenthesis is immediately pushed on the stack, regardless of the precedence of the current top of stack. Left parentheses will be considered to have "precedence" lower than any other symbol, and thus will never be popped off the stack by the rule described in the preceding paragraph. Instead, right parentheses will cause the stack to be popped and output until the corresponding left parenthesis is found. The left parenthesis is popped, but not output.

Finally, when the end of input is encountered, the stack is popped until empty, appending symbols to the output.

We need a way to encode the precedence of operators. An easy way to do this is to use the ordering of an enumerated data type, listing operators from lowest precedence to highest:

```
// operators listed in precedence order
enum operators { leftparen, plus, minus, times, divide };
```

In order to display a visual representation of the operators, we need a way to convert from their enumerated type to a string. An easy way to do this is to write a function, as follows:

```
string opString(operators theOp)
{   // return a textual representation of an operator
    switch (theOp) {
```

*Section headings followed by an asterisk indicate optional material.

```
        case plus:   return " + ";
        case minus:  return " - ";
        case times:  return " * ";
        case divide: return " / ";
    }
}
```

The procedure to implement the infix to prefix converter is shown in Fig. 9.1. As with the calculator application, a main loop reads new tokens. Constants are immediately appended to the result string. The processing of parentheses is as described earlier. Operators must test their precedence value against the current stack contents. This is accomplished using the following short routine:

```
void processOp
    (operators theOp, stackList<operators> & opStack, string & result)
{
    // pop stack while operators have higher precedence
    while ((! opStack.isEmpty()) && (theOp < opStack.top()))
        result += opString(opStack.pop());
    // then push current operator
    opStack.push(theOp);
}
```

An important property to note is that the infix to postfix conversion requires only one pass through the input.

9.5 QUEUES

As was the case with the implementation of stacks, there are two major techniques used to implement the queue data structure. The first is built out of vectors, while the second is based on lists. A third variation, also built using list elements, tries to combine the best features of both the vector and list techniques.

9.5.1 Vector Implementation

The vector implementation of a queue uses a vector of fixed length to store the data items. The length of the vector is provided as an argument in the constructor for the queue. The following is a class description of our `queueVector` data type:

```
//
// class queueVector
//     queue implemented using a fixed length vector
//
```

```
void infixToPrefix(string & infixStr)
{   stackList<operators> opStack;
    string result("");
    int i = 0;

    while (infixStr[i] != '\0') {
        if (isdigit(infixStr[i])) { // process constants
            while (isdigit(infixStr[i]))
                result += infixStr[i++];
            result += " ";   // add separator
            }
        else
            switch(infixStr[i++]) { // process other characters
                case '(':
                    opStack.push(leftparen);
                    break;
                case ')':
                    while (opStack.top() != leftparen)
                        result += opString(opStack.pop());
                    opStack.pop();   // pop off left paren
                    break;
                case '+':
                    processOp(plus, opStack, result);
                    break;
                case '-':
                    processOp(minus, opStack, result);
                    break;
                case '*':
                    processOp(times, opStack, result);
                    break;
                case '/':
                    processOp(divide, opStack, result);
                    break;
                }
        }
    while (! opStack.isEmpty()) // empty the stack on end of input
        result += opString(opStack.pop());

    infixStr = result; // copy result back into argument string
}
```

Figure 9.1 Infix to postfix conversion program

```
template <class T> class queueVector : public queue<T> {
public:
    // constructor requires size of vector
    queueVector     (unsigned int size);
    queueVector     (const queueVector & v);

    // implement queue protocol
    virtual void    deleteAllValues  ();
    virtual T       dequeue          ();
    virtual void    enqueue          (T value);
    virtual T       front            ();
    virtual int     isEmpty          () const;

protected:
    vector<T>              data;
    const unsigned int     max;
    unsigned int           nextSlot;
    unsigned int           nextUse;
};
```

The `queueVector` data structure maintains two pointers into the data area. The first, `nextSlot`, indicates the location that will be filled by the next value inserted into the queue. The second, `nextUse`, points to the location that holds the next value to be removed from the queue. Initially these point to the same locations, a situation that indicates the queue is empty.

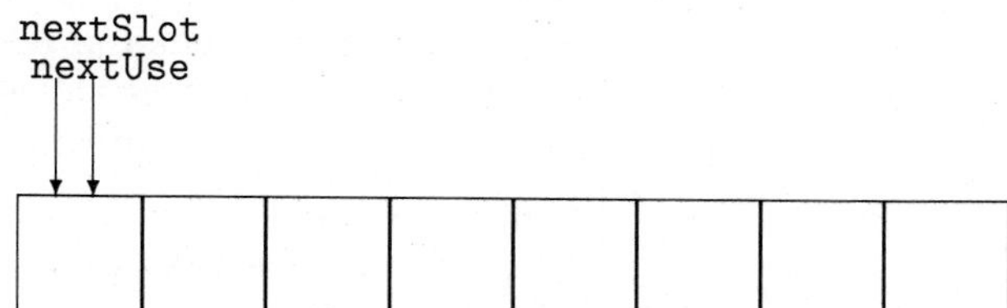


```
template <class T> queueVector<T>::queueVector(unsigned int size)
        : max(size), data(size)
{   // constructor for queue based on vectors
    // make sure queue is initially empty
    deleteAllValues();
}

template <class T> void queueVector<T>::deleteAllValues()
{   // clear all items from queue
    nextSlot = 0;
    nextUse = 0;
}
```

```
template <class T> int queueVector<T>::isEmpty() const
{   // return true if queue is empty
    // queue is empty if next slot is
    // pointing to same location as next use
    return nextSlot == nextUse;
}
```

As values are added to the back of the queue, the `nextSlot` pointer is incremented.

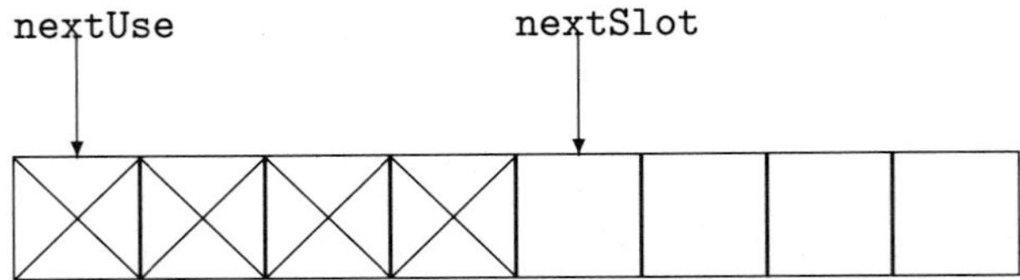

As values are removed from the head of the queue, the `nextUse` pointer is also incremented.

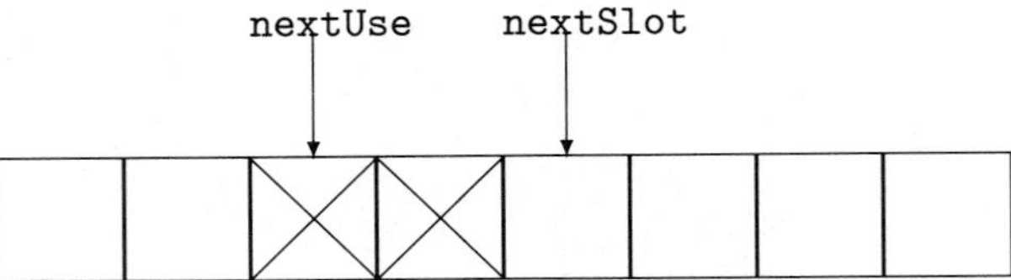

Eventually, the `nextSlot` pointer will reach the maximum position in the data area. When this occurs, the `nextSlot` pointer wraps around, starting again from zero. The `nextUse` pointer will also similarly wrap around when it reaches the maximum position in the data vector.

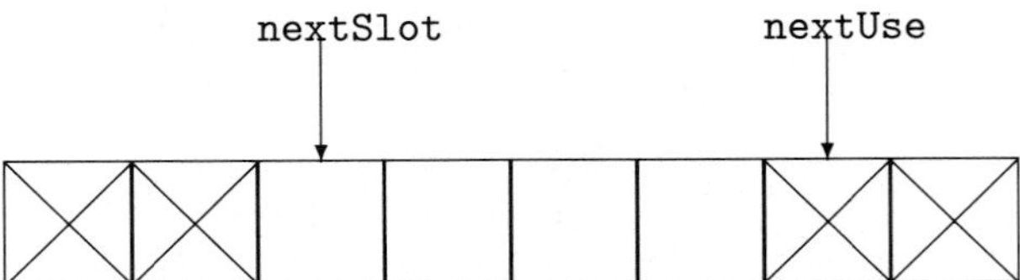

A collision occurs if the `nextSlot` pointer is incremented and as a consequence runs into the `nextUse` pointer. In this case a *queue overflow* error has occurred, as the queue can hold no more elements (see Exercise 7 at the end of this chapter). A similar error occurs if an attempt is made to remove, or dequeue, an item when the two pointers refer to the same location. This indicates an attempt to remove an item from an empty queue.

```
template <class T> void queueVector<T>::enqueue(T val)
{   // add a new element to end of queue, and advance index to next slot
    data[nextSlot++] = val;
    if (nextSlot >= max)     // wrap around
        nextSlot = 0;
    // make sure queue has not overflowed
    assert(nextSlot != nextUse);
}

template <class T> T queueVector<T>::dequeue()
{   // remove element from front of queue
    // can not dequeue from an empty queue
    assert(! isEmpty());
    int dataloc = nextUse;
    nextUse++;
    if (nextUse >= max)      // wrap around
        nextUse = 0;
    return data[dataloc];
}
```

The advantages of the vector implementation are simplicity and speed. Adding and removing elements require only simple index increments. The space requirements for the queue are fixed, and no dynamic memory allocations are necessary to create and destroy linked list nodes. The major disadvantage of the vector implementation of a queue is the fact that the maximum size of the queue must be known in advance. Unlike the stack, it is not possible for the queue to be increased to a new size once it has been created.

9.5.2 List Implementation

The list implementation of queues is based on the `doubleEndedList` data type described in Chapter 8. You will recall that the `doubleEndedList` type was designed specifically to permit values to be added to the end of a list. The `enqueue` operation is mapped directly on to an `addToEnd`, and a `dequeue` operation corresponds to removing an item from the front of a list.

```
template <class T> void queueList<T>::enqueue(T value)
{   // insert by adding to end of data list
    data.addToEnd(value);
}

template <class T> T queueList<T>::dequeue()
{   // remove first item from front of list
    T result = data.firstElement();
```

```
    data.removeFirst();
    return result;
}
```

The test for an empty queue is answered by testing the underlying list of data items. Unlike the vector implementation, the list implementation of a queue has no fixed size. It is thus suitable for problems in which the number of items to be maintained by the queue cannot be determined in advance. On the other hand, the list implementation is inherently slower, since dynamic memory allocation and deallocation must be performed as values are inserted and removed from the list.

As we noted when discussing the stack abstraction, a relatively minor technical difference involves the use of a reference value as an element. As we saw in Chapter 6, it is not possible to use references as elements in vectors. Hence it is not possible to use a reference type as the template argument in the `queueVector` class. Because no such restriction applies to lists, nothing prevents the user from supplying a reference type as the argument to our other major implementation technique.

9.5.3 Ring Buffer Implementation

A third implementation technique tries to realize the best features of both the vector and list implementations of a queue. This technique is built around the concept of a ring buffer, introduced earlier in Section 8.7. As with the list implementation of the queue, the elements will be maintained in instances of class `link`. However, unlike the list implementation, these will not be dynamically allocated and released when elements are added or removed from the queue. Instead, a collection of links is simply allocated when the data structure is created. These links are reused over and over again, thus saving the expense of dynamic memory management.

As with the vector implementation, a pair of pointers are maintained into the data area. These differ slightly from the pointers used by the array data structure. The `lastFilled` pointer references the element that was last filled by an `enqueue` operation, while the `lastFree` pointer refers to the last position in the free section of the list (Fig. 9.2).

To remove an element from the queue, we simply advance the last free pointer to the next position, which must be the first filled position.

```
template <class T> T queueRingBuffer<T>::dequeue()
{   // remove element from front of queue
    // cannot dequeue from empty queue
    assert(! isEmpty());
    // advance last free position
    lastFree = lastFree->ptrToNextLink;
```

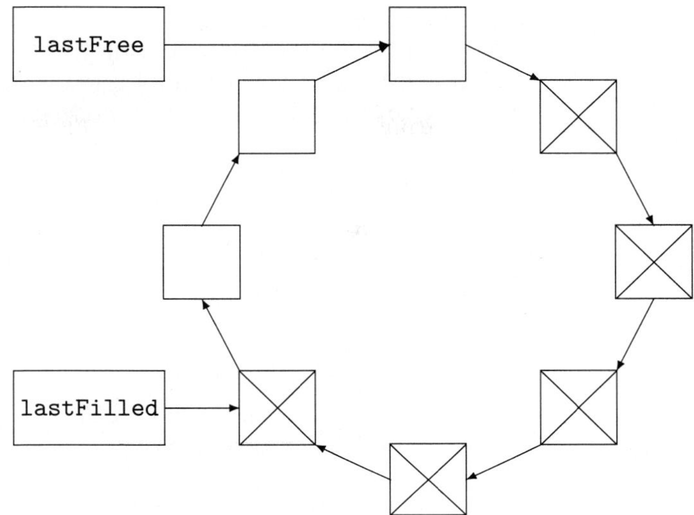

Figure 9.2 Snapshot of a ring buffer queue

```
    // return value stored in last free position
    return lastFree->value;
}
```

The `front` method returns the same element, without advancing the last free pointer.

The `enqueue` method advances the last filled pointer. However, when the queue becomes full, rather than issuing an error message, a new link will be created and inserted into the structure. Queue overflow conditions can never occur with this structure.

```
template <class T> void queueRingBuffer<T>::enqueue(T val)
{   // add new element to end of queue buffer
    // first check for potential overflow
    if (lastFilled->ptrToNextLink == lastFree)
        lastFilled = lastFilled->insert(val);
    else {
        // simply advance the last filled pointer
        lastFilled = lastFilled->ptrToNextLink;
        lastFilled->value = val;
        }
}
```

Since the ring buffer can dynamically grow as new elements are needed, it is not necessary to have a fixed size known in advance of execution. On the other hand, since dynamic memory allocation occurs only at the beginning, and when queue overflow occurs, the efficiency penalty of the simple list implementation is minimized.

The constructor for the class queueRingBuffer takes a count of the number of elements to initially allocate in the ring buffer.

```
queueRingBuffer<T>::queueRingBuffer(unsigned int max)
{   // constructor for queues based on ring buffers
    // create the first link
    T initialvalue;
    lastFree = new link<T>(initialvalue, 0);
    assert(lastFree != 0);
    lastFilled = lastFree;
    // make value point to itself
    lastFilled->ptrToNextLink = lastFilled;
    // now add the remainder of the elements
    while (max-- > 0)
        lastFilled->insert(initialvalue);
}
```

The destructor must cycle around the buffer and delete all links.

```
template <class T> queueRingBuffer<T>::~queueRingBuffer()
{   // delete all memory associated with ring buffer
    link<T> * p = lastFree;
    link<T> * next;

    // walk around the circle deleting nodes
    while (p->ptrToNextLink != lastFree) {
        next = p->ptrToNextLink;
        delete p;
        p = next;
        }
}
```

9.6 APPLICATION — BREADTH-FIRST SEARCH

A common situation where queues are utilized is in the solution of problems involving searching a nonlinear collection of states. We will use as an example of this genre the classic "farmer, wolf, goat, and cabbage" problem.

A farmer finds himself on the south side of the Thames River holding a wolf, a goat, and a cabbage. Somehow he must transport all four to the north side of the river. Unfortunately, he has only one very small boat. So small, in fact, that in addition to himself it can hold only one other occupant.[2] Only the farmer can row the boat. He cannot leave the goat alone with the cabbage, nor can he leave the wolf alone with the goat. The wolf, fortunately, is a committed carnivore and will not eat the cabbage. What are the crossings the farmer must perform to carry all four to the north side of the Thames?

To solve this problem, we first need a way of encoding the positions of the various players. A convenient representation is to use numbers between 0 and 15, interpreting the four binary digits in each number as four bit values. We can use a 0 to represent south, and a 1 value to represent north. The four bits in each number will represent the locations of the farmer, the wolf, the cabbage, and the goat, respectively. Thus the number 5 will be interpreted as representing the fact that the farmer and the cabbage are on the south side of the Thames, while the wolf and goat are on the north side. (A most unsafe position, and one that will probably quickly change to 4 when the wolf eats the goat.)

$$5 = \boxed{0101} = \text{SNSN}$$

Farmer and cabbage on south side
Wolf and goat on north side

In order to hide the representation of positions, we can use a set of four functions, one for each of the four protagonists. Each function will take a position and return the location of the associated player.

```
int farmer  (int location) { return 0 != (location & 0x08); }
int wolf    (int location) { return 0 != (location & 0x04); }
int cabbage (int location) { return 0 != (location & 0x02); }
int goat    (int location) { return 0 != (location & 0x01); }
```

The first step is then to describe what sets of states are `safe` for all of the characters in the story. According to the problem description, a state is unsafe if the cabbage and the goat are on the same bank and the farmer is not present, or if the goat and the wolf are on the same bank and the farmer is not present. We can encode this information in a function that takes a location and determines whether or not it is safe.

```
int safe(int location)
{   // return true if situation is safe
    // goat eats cabbage
    if ((goat(location) == cabbage(location)) &&
        (goat(location) != farmer(location)))
            return 0;

    // wolf eats goat
```

2. It is a very large cabbage.

```
    if ((goat(location) == wolf(location)) &&
        (goat(location) != farmer(location)))
            return 0;

    // everything else is safe
    return 1;
}
```

With these, we are now ready to begin the solution of the problem. The overriding idea is that at each step we will enumerate all the possible moves the farmer can make that will take the players into a new arrangement that is safe, and that has not been previously explored. For example, from the initial state (0000, or all on the south bank) there is really only one move the farmer can make. He must carry the goat across the river, leaving the wolf and cabbage behind. Similarly, once across the river there is really only one further safe move that can be made, which is to return alone. At this point, however, there are *two* legal and safe moves the farmer can try. He can either carry the wolf across the river (returning with the goat), or carry the cabbage across the river (and again return with the goat).

If we step back and view the problem slightly more abstractly, we see that the solution really involves finding a path through a graph, such as that shown below. Nodes (or vertices) in the graph represent safe states, and arcs represent the ability to move from one state to another. A solution to the problem is thus no more than a path that leads from the start state (SSSS) to the final state (NNNN).

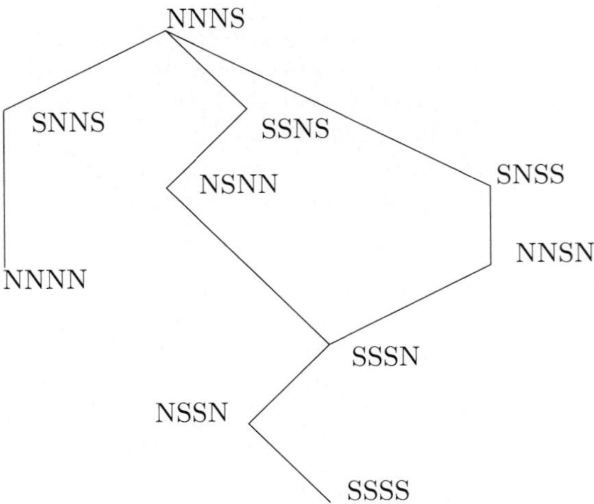

There are two major categories of graph-searching algorithms, differentiated by the way in which they respond to the situation where there is a choice of alternatives to pursue. When faced with a choice, we must select one possibility for immediate investigation and somehow remember the alternatives for later examination should the choice prove incorrect. The variety of data structures that we use to hold the alternatives will determine which of the two different styles of search is performed. The data structure we will use first is the queue, and the style of search that naturally follows from this choice is called *breadth-first search*.

The term breadth-first is meant to convey the idea that we are exploring *all* possible alternatives at once, across the entire breadth of possibilities. A good intuitive visualization is to imagine pouring a bottle of ink at the starting node. The ink moves in all directions at once, exploring many alternative paths in parallel. In practice, this is achieved by enumerating all the states that can be reached in one step and placing them in a queue. (In our problem, we have already observed, there is only one such possibility, but in other problems there may be more.)

Front	1	1	1

We pull out the first possible new state, and enumerate all the possible locations that can be reached from *this* state, and thus can be reached in two steps from the origin. These are placed at the end of the queue.

Front	1	1	2	2	2

Because elements are always added to the end of the queue and removed from the beginning, before investigating *any* of the states reachable in two steps, we will investigate *all* of the states that can be reached in one step.

We return now to the problem of the farmer and the goat. In addition to a queue, we need as well a method to remember which states have already been investigated, and a way of recording each step of the proper path should a solution be found. We solve both difficulties by constructing a vector, which we will call `route`. The vector is initialized with all -1 values. Each time we place a new state in the queue, we mark the `route` vector with the location from which the new state can be reached. A non-negative value in `route` therefore means that the state has been or is scheduled to be considered, and in the end we can use the values in the `route` table to reconstruct the proper path.

A program to solve the farmer, wolf, goat, and cabbage problem is shown in Fig. 9.3. Initially, the starting state represented by 0 (all on the south side) is placed in the queue. As long as the queue is not empty, a value is removed. This represents a safe location that can be reached via some sequence of steps from the starting point. A `for` loop is used

```
void farmerProblem() {
    queueVector<int> moves(5);
    vector<int> route(16, -1);

    // all start out of south side of the Thames
    moves.enqueue(0x00);

    // now make moves
    while (! moves.isEmpty()) {
        // get our current location
        int location = moves.dequeue();
        for (int movers = 1; movers <= 8; movers <<= 1 ) {
            // farmer always moves
            int newLocation = location ^ (0x08 | movers);
            if (safe(newLocation) && (route[newLocation] == -1))
                {
                route[newLocation] = location;
                moves.enqueue(newLocation);
                }
            }
        }

    // now print out route
    cout << "Path: ";
    for (int location = 15; location > 0; location = route[location])
        cout << " " << location;
    cout << '\n';
}
```

Figure 9.3 Solution to the farmer, wolf, goat, and cabbage problem

to enumerate all the possible characters that could be moved, including the farmer himself. Notice that the `for` loop uses a left shift in the increment portion and will thus enumerate the values 1, 2, 4, and 8, indicating the transport of the goat, cabbage, wolf, and farmer, respectively. Since in each move the farmer must change state (he is the only one who can row the boat), the value of the variables `movers` is or'ed with the binary value 0x08, to yield a mask where the 1 bit represents the items that will be in the boat. Performing an exclusive or with the current location will yield the new state that will be reached if the farmer makes the given move. This new location is tested to see if it is safe, and if it has not yet been explored. If both conditions are satisfied, it is placed into the queue.

Figure 9.4 diagrams the locations and the order they are investigated by the searching algorithm. As we have already noted, there is only one safe move for the first two steps. At step 3, there are two possibilities. Notice

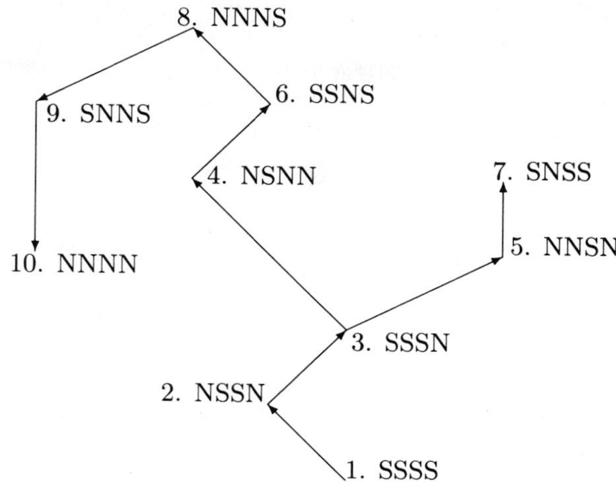

Figure 9.4 Search path followed by a breadth-first search

how the breadth-first search algorithm jumps back and forth between the two choices. An investigation of location number 4 indicates there is one safe move that can be made, leading to node 6. Before this new location is investigated, however, we jump back to the alternative, which was the node labeled 5. Here, too, there is one safe state that can be reached. But before we investigate this new state the algorithm jumps back to the first path, discovering and placing node 8 into the queue. Node 7 is then removed from the queue, but all further successor locations are either unsafe or have already been investigated. An investigation of node 8, on the other hand, yields node 9, and node 9 yields node 10.

Retracing the path using the `route` vector yields the following seven-step solution:

```
farmer carries goat to north side
returns to south bank alone
farmer carries cabbage to north side
returns with goat to south side
farmer carries wolf to north side
returns alone
farmer carries goat to north side
all are now on north bank of river
```

9.6.1 Depth-First Search

If we imagine a breadth-first search as a bottle of ink being poured at the start node and running in parallel directions until the target node is

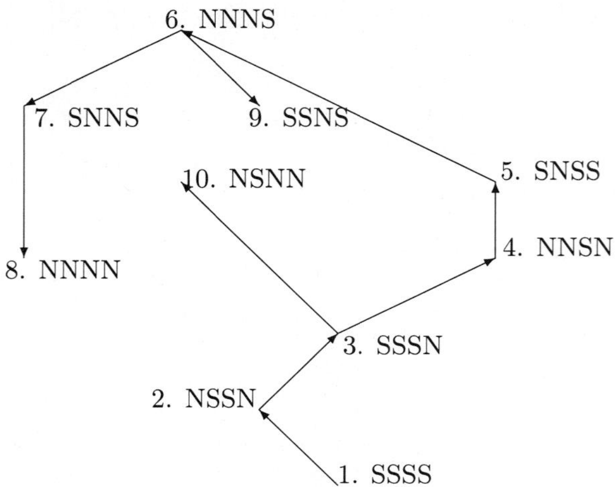

Figure 9.5 Search path followed by depth-first search

reached, then a *depth-first search* might be envisioned as a single individual walking through a maze. Only one path at a time can be explored, and so the explorer simply remembers those locations where an alternative presented itself. One path is traced completely from beginning to end before any alternatives are explored.

We noted earlier that changing the data structure used to hold the alternatives changes the nature of the search performed. If we substitute a stack for the queue in the program in Figure 9.3, changing the `enqueue` messages into `push` and the `dequeue` instructions into pop, the program is still correct and a solution will still be discovered, but the style of search performed is changed to depth-first search. The characteristic nature of depth-first search follows directly from the use of a stack to maintain alternatives rather than a queue. If two alternatives are placed on the stack, the first will not be removed until the path derived from the second has been completely mapped out. This is shown in Fig. 9.5, which illustrates the sequence of states investigated by the depth-first search algorithm. Notice that at steps 3 and 6 there were alternatives, but these alternatives were not investigated until after one path had been completely traced to the end.

The solution discovered by the depth-first search algorithm is different from the solution discovered by the breadth-first algorithm, having transposed the positions of the goat and the cabbage.

```
farmer carries goat to north side
returns to south bank alone
farmer carries wolf to north side
returns with goat to south side
```

```
farmer carries cabbage to north side
returns alone
farmer carries goat to north side
all are now on north bank of river
```

The following differences can be noted in comparing breadth-first and depth-first searching:

▲ Since all paths of length one are investigated before examining paths of length two, and all paths of length two before examining paths of length three, a breadth-first search is guaranteed to always discover a path from start to goal containing fewest steps.

▲ Since one path is investigated before any alternatives are examined, a depth-first search *may*, if it is lucky, discover a solution more quickly than the equivalent breadth-first algorithm. Notice this occurs here, where the goal is encountered after examining only eight locations in the depth-first algorithm, while the goal is only reached after 10 iterations in the breadth-first algorithm. But this benefit is not certain, and a bad selection of alternatives to pursue can lead to many dead-end searches before the proper path to the goal is revealed.

▲ In particular, suppose for a particular problem that some but not all paths are infinite, and there exists at least one path from start to goal that is finite. Breadth-first search is guaranteed to find a finite solution. Depth-first search may have the unfortunate luck to pursue a never-ending path, and it can hence fail to find a solution.

9.7 APPLICATION — A FRAMEWORK FOR BACKTRACKING*

A classic use of stacks in computer science is the application of a problem-solving technique called *backtracking*. To use backtracking, a problem must have the characteristic that a solution is discovered as a sequence of steps. At some of these steps there may be multiple alternative choices for the next step, and insufficient information to decide which alternative will ultimately be the correct choice. A stack is then used to record the state of the computation at the point of choice, permitting the program to subsequently "restart" the calculation from that point and pursue a different alternative. Thus backtracking is nothing more than one form of depth-first search.

To illustrate the idea of backtracking, we will use a classic puzzle involving the knight chess-piece. In chess, a knight can legally move in an L-shaped pattern, either one forward or backward and two left or right, or

*Section headings followed by an asterisk indicate optional material.

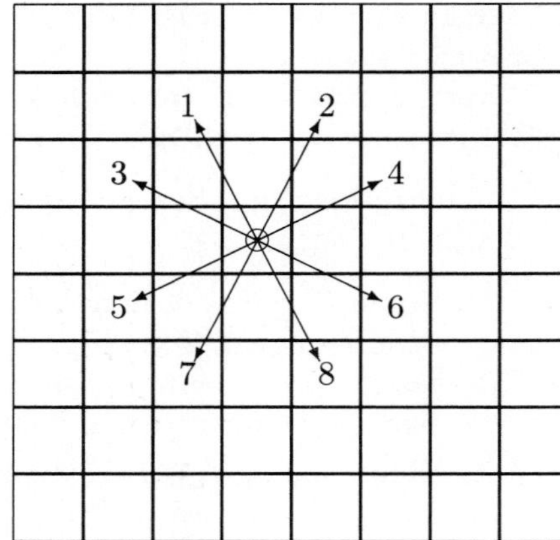

Figure 9.6 Legal knight moves

1	10	31	64	33	26	53	62
12	7	28	25	30	63	34	51
9	2	11	32	27	52	61	54
6	13	8	29	24	35	50	41
3	18	5	36	49	40	55	60
14	21	16	23	46	57	42	39
17	4	19	48	37	44	59	56
20	15	22	45	58	47	38	43

Figure 9.7 A solution to the knight's tour problem

two forward or backward and one left or right. Figure 9.6 illustrates the legal moves for a knight starting in the given position on a conventional eight-square chess board. A piece may not move off the board, so near the edges of the board the number of legal moves may be less than eight.

A *knight's tour* is a sequence of 64 moves in which a knight visits, using only legal moves, each and every square on the board once. The classic knight's-tour problem is to discover a knight's tour starting from a specific location. For example, Figure 9.7 shows the steps in a complete knight's tour, starting from the upper left corner.

As an illustration of backtracking, consider the following state (Fig. 9.8) in which our program finds itself rather early in the search for a solution

1	10	31		33	26	57	42
12	7	28	25	30	43	50	
9	2	11	32	27	34	41	56
6	13	8	29	24	49	44	51
3	18	5	38	35	40	55	
14	21	16	23	48	37	52	45
17	4	19	36	39	46		54
20	15	22	47		53		

Figure 9.8 Backtracking in knight's tour

after having successfully performed 57 moves. There is no legal unvisited location to which the piece at move 57 can advance. The program will "back-up" to move 56, and try a different alternative. But in fact there is no other alternative possible at move 56, and so the program will back up to move 55, and then to 54, 53, and 52. It is only at move 52 that a new untried legal alternative is discovered, namely to move to the bottom left corner. This move is tried, but then immediately abandoned since there is no successor. No further alternative is possible for move 52, or for move 51 or 50. We must backtrack all the way to move 49 before we can find another possibility, which is to make the new move 50 be the now vacant location of the previous move 52.

Nonrecursive programs that solve a problem using backtracking generally have a very similar structure. We can use this observation to develop a generic *framework* for such problems. A framework is a class (or, in more complicated situations, a set of classes and functions), that together provide the skeleton outline for the solution to some problem but do not provide any specific details. The most common frameworks are associated with graphical user interfaces, but many other types of frameworks are possible. To generate a solution to a specific problem, the programmer specializes the framework, generally using inheritance.

A generic backtracking problem can be described as follows:

```
template <class T> int backtrackFramework<T>::run()
{
    // initialize the problem
    initialize();
    done = ! theStack.isEmpty();

    // do the main loop
```

```
    while (! done) {
        // if we can't advance from current state
        // then pop the stack
        if (! advance(theStack.top()))
            theStack.pop();
        // if stack is empty then we can't continue
        if (theStack.isEmpty())
            done = 1;
        }

    // return true if stack is not empty
    return ! theStack.isEmpty();
}
```

A procedure `initialize` is used to establish whatever conditions need to be set to start the problem, including pushing the first state on the stack. A Boolean variable `done` indicates when the problem is finished. It will be set automatically if the stack becomes exhausted, but it may be set by other conditions as well. The heart of the algorithm is a simple loop. At each step, a procedure called `advance` is called, passing as argument the current state. If it is possible to advance to a new state, then execution continues; if it is not possible, the topmost state is popped off the stack, and execution backtracks to a previous point.

The method just given is from a class called `backtrackFramework`. The template parameter is the class used to encode state information. The complete class description is as follows:

```
//
// class backtrackFramework
//     general framework for solving problems
//     involving backtracking
//

template <class T> class backtrackFramework {
public:
    // protocol for backtrack problems
    virtual void    initialize     ();
    virtual int     advance        (T newstate) = 0;
    virtual int     run            ();

protected:
    stackList<T>    theStack;
    int             done;
};
```

In order to specialize this general approach to make a solution to the knight's-tour problem, we first need to describe how we record information concerning the current position. We then need to subclass the `backtrackFramework` class and describe how to advance, and how to determine when we have a solution.

The encapsulation for the "state" of the search at any point will be an instance of a class we will call `Position`. A `Position` corresponds to a location on the chessboard. A position will maintain a pair of `x` and `y` values corresponding to coordinates on the board, a variable `moveNumber` that will record the sequence of moves in the solution, and a fourth integer variable, named `visited`, that will indicate what subsequent moves have been attempted. To encode this last value, we will simply try, at each step, the moves in order and numbered as they were in Fig. 9.6. A zero stored in the `visited` variable indicates the position has not yet been used on the knight's tour, while a nonzero value indicates the position has been used on the knight's tour, and furthermore the type of move that was used to generate the next step.

The following is the class description for `Position`. The output operator is used to print the final result.

```
//
// class Position
//     record a position in the knight's move tour
//

class Position {      // position in chessboard
public:
    void          init          (int, int);
    Position *   nextPosition ();

private:
    // data fields
    // x and y are coordinate positions
    int    x, y;
    // moveNumber records the sequence of steps
    int    moveNumber;
    // visited is a bit vector marking what positions have been visited
    int    visited;

    // private method used to find the next move
    Position * findMove(int visitedPosition);

    // friends
    friend class knightsTour;
    friend ostream & operator << (ostream & out, Position & v);
};
```

The chessboard itself will simply be declared as a two-dimensional matrix of positions, named `board`. Because the matrix constructor does not permit the initialization of each position individually, initialization of each element is performed with a loop that simply invokes the `init` method for each value. We see this shortly in the initialization portion of the program.

A hallmark of object-oriented programming and the responsibility-driven design technique we outlined in Chapter 1 is the concept of making data structures responsible for their own operation. The `Position` data structure illustrates this idea. Each position is responsible for finding the next potential move in the solution. The process of finding the solution is performed by the method `nextPosition`. This method returns a pointer to a position, returning a null pointer if no legal alternative exists. In order to discover a position, the method increments the value held in the variable `visited`, using the facilitator method `findMove` to perform the encoding of the number into a position value. If the incremented value of the `visited` variable denotes a position that is legal and not yet visited, it is returned. Otherwise the loop continues. If all eight possible moves have been examined, then no alternative exists and a null value is returned. Before returning in this case we zero the variable `visited`, so that the position can be revisited along a different path. We saw this in the earlier example of backtracking, where position 52 was first abandoned but later reached from a different direction.

```
Position * Position::nextPosition()
{
    while (++visited < 9) {
        Position * next = findMove(visited);
        // if there is a neighbor not visited then return it
        if ((next != 0) && (next->visited == 0))
            return next;
        }
    // can't move to any neighbor, report failure
    visited = 0;
    return 0;
}
```

The method `findMove` simply translates a value between 1 and 8 into a position, filtering out moves that are not on the board.

```
Position * Position::findMove(int typ)
{   int nx, ny;

    switch(typ) {
        case 1: nx = x - 1; ny = y - 2; break;
        case 2: nx = x + 1; ny = y - 2; break;
        case 3: nx = x - 2; ny = y - 1; break;
```

```
        case 4: nx = x + 2; ny = y - 1; break;
        case 5: nx = x - 2; ny = y + 1; break;
        case 6: nx = x + 2; ny = y + 1; break;
        case 7: nx = x - 1; ny = y + 2; break;
        case 8: nx = x + 1; ny = y + 2; break;
        }

    // return null value on illegal positions
    if ((nx < 0) || (ny < 0))
        return 0;
    if ((nx >= board.numberRows()) || (ny >= board.numberColumns()))
        return 0;

    // return address of new position
    return & board[nx][ny];
}
```

To create a solution to the knight's-tour problem, we simply need to tie the `Position` data structure into our backtracking framework. We create a subclass, called `knightsTour`, to specialize the framework. The class indicates which methods in the framework we need to modify. In the present case there are two methods: the initialization method and the method to advance to the next state. The complete class description is as follows:

```
//
// class knightsTour
//     solve the n by n knight's tour problem
//

class knightsTour : public backtrackFramework<Position &> {
public:

    // redefine the backtracking protocol
    virtual void    initialize      ();
    virtual int     advance         (Position &);

    // new method
    void            solve           ();
};
```

The initialization method loops over each board position to establish the initial conditions for each value. It then pushes the starting location, board position 0:0, onto the stack. This board position is our initial state.

```
matrix<Position> board(8, 8);

void knightsTour::initialize()
{
    // initialize the parent class
    backtrackFramework<Position &>::initialize();

    // initialize chessboard
    for (int i = 0; i < board.numberRows(); i++)
        for (int j = 0; j < board.numberColumns(); j++)
            board[i][j].init(i, j);

    // set move number on first position
    board[0][0].moveNumber = 1;

    // push initial position
    theStack.push(board[0][0]);
}
```

To complete the framework, we need only describe how to discover the next move from any given position. This is performed by the method `advance`. The `advance` method is given, in the argument, the current state. It asks a position to try to find a next position in sequence. It does this by invoking the `nextMove` method we described earlier. The `advance` function returns a true value if advancement is possible from the current position, and a false value if no advancement can be made. An additional responsibility is to test to see if the solution to the problem has been found. If so, then the `done` flag must be set.

```
int knightsTour::advance(Position & currentPosition)
{   // try to advance from a given position
    Position * newPosition = currentPosition.nextPosition();
    if (newPosition) {
        // move forward
        newPosition->moveNumber = currentPosition.moveNumber + 1;
        theStack.push(*newPosition);
        // if we have filled all squares we are done
        if (newPosition->moveNumber ==
            board.numberRows() * board.numberColumns())
                done = 1;
        // return success
        return 1;
        }
    else
        return 0;    // can't move forward
}
```

The final method to describe is the one new method added by class knightsTour to the framework protocol. This method simply starts the framework running. If success is reported, then the stack is popped in order to print the result.

```
void knightsTour::solve()
{
    // start framework
    if (run()) {     // print solution
        cout << "solution is:\n";
        while (! theStack.isEmpty())
            cout << theStack.pop() << '\n';
        }
    else
        cout << "no solution ";
}
```

9.8 CHAPTER SUMMARY

Key Concepts

- Stack and queue operations
- LIFO and FIFO
- Underflow and overflow
- Vector implementation
- List implementation
- Ring buffer implementation
- Depth-first search
- Breadth-first search
- Framework

In this chapter we introduced the abstract concepts of a stack and a queue. Both structures maintain collections of values in a linear sequence. In a stack items are inserted and removed from one end:

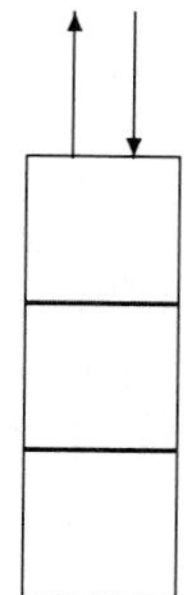

In a queue, on the other hand, values are inserted at one end and removed from the other:

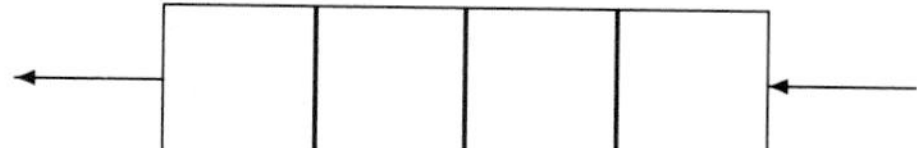

The protocol for the use of the stack and queue data structures was described using abstract classes. An abstract class provides a specification of behavior, but it does not provide any implementation. An abstract class must always be subclassed in order to implement the necessary behavior.

We have explored different approaches to the implementation of each data structure. Both stacks and queues can be built on top of fixed-length vectors, or on top of list structures. Generally the advantage of a vector implementation is improved performance, while the advantage of a list implementation is greater flexibility, since the number of elements need not be known in advance. In addition to the vector and list implementation techniques for a queue, we have described a third implementation approach using a ring buffer. The ring buffer provides both speed and flexibility.

To illustrate the use of the stack data type, we have described a program to simulate a reverse polish calculator, and a program to convert infix expressions into reverse polish (postfix) notation.

To illustrate the use of the queue data type, we have described a program to solve a simple searching problem, the classic farmer, wolf, goat, and cabbage puzzle.

In the optional last section we introduce the use of stacks in the creation of a framework for the solution of problems involving backtracking. A framework is a class, or set of classes, that together provide the outline for the solution of a set of problems but do not provide specific details of any single problem. Using inheritance, a programmer can then specialize the framework for use in a new situation. A framework thus provides reuse not only for code but also for the reuse of an idea or approach to solving a class of similar problems.

References

Stacks and queues are discussed extensively by Knuth [Knuth 73]. The terms LIFO and FIFO, which were first used by accountants, can also be illustrated by the following hypothetical example. In March, Mr. Jones purchases 10 shares of stock at $70; in April, he purchases 20 more shares at $90. Now imagine that in July Mr. Jones sells 10 shares of stock at $80. Should the shares be considered to be those purchased in March (first in, first out), or should they be considered to be the ones purchased in April (last in, first out). Under the first assumption the investment will have shown a profit, while under the other the investment will have lost money.

Because polish notation simplifies so many notation problems, it is actually surprising that it was not discovered before 1929. The original source is [Lukasiewicz 29].

Exercises

1. Explain the terms LIFO and FIFO.

2. Explain the terms underflow and overflow as they are used in conjunction with stacks and queues.

3. What is the polish notation representation of the following expression?

$$(a * (b + c)) + (b/d) * a$$

4. Add the following instructions to the reverse polish notation calculator.

Letter	Meaning
c	clear all values from stack
d	double top value on stack

5. The reverse polish notation calculator produces an assertion error and halts if an operation is attempted with too few values—for example, in the input 23 − +. Change the program so that it will produce a more helpful error message and recover gracefully from such errors.

6. How does the infix to prefix conversion routine described in Fig. 9.1 handle runs of operators of the same precedence, such as $a + b + c$? For some operators, the normal rules associate to the left, so $a + b + c$ is properly interpreted as $(a + b) + c$, while other operators associate to the right. Describe how the conversion algorithm must be modified to be able to handle both situations.

7. Explain why in the vector implementation of a queue, a queue declared as size n can only hold at most $n - 1$ values. (*Hint*: Insert n elements and then try to perform a dequeue operation.)

8. Write a program to check for balanced curly braces { } in the input.

9. Expand upon the program for the last exercise so that it will check for properly nested parentheses, curly braces, and square brackets. (*Hint*: Use a stack to store the most recent unmatched left symbol.)

10. Explain how it is possible to implement two stacks using one array. Your stacks should not generate an overflow condition unless the sum of the number of elements held in the stacks exceeds the size of the array.

11. Explain the difference between a depth-first and breadth-first search.

12. Consider the following graph. Starting from node A, list the vertices as they might be visited in a breadth-first search, and as they might be visited in a depth-first search. Note that there are many different sequences for both forms of search.

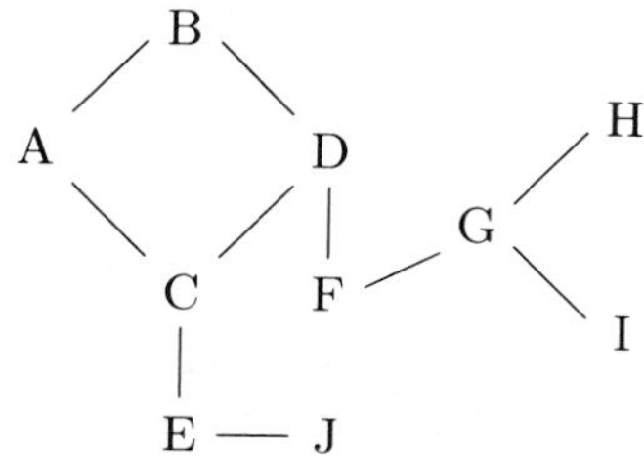

13. In discussing the partial solution to the knight's-tour problem presented on page 264, we note that the move to the lower right corner will also soon be abandoned in failure, and describe how the next few steps will be found. How many more moves will the program make from this new state before it again finds itself without a legal next move? How far back will it then have to backtrack to find an alternative?

14. A maze can be described as a matrix of true/false values, where true indicates that it is possible to move in a given direction and false indicates a barrier. There is a designated starting square for the maze, and a designated ending square. An example is the following, which also illustrates the solution to the maze.

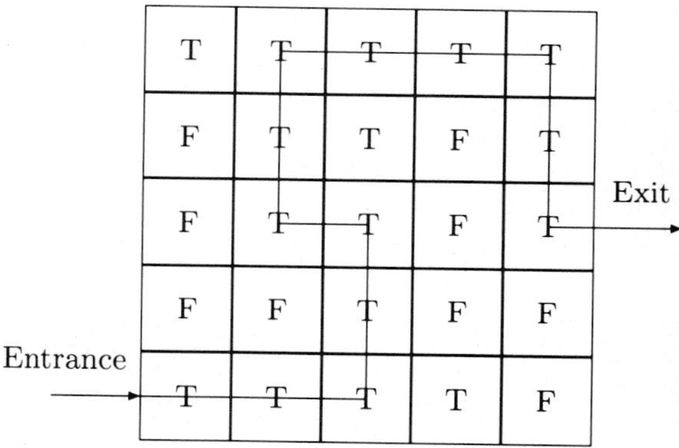

Write a program that reads a description of a maze from the input, then prints a solution, as a sequence of squares that represents a path through the maze. Print "no solution" if no solution is possible.

15. A *deque* (pronounced either "deck" or "DQ") is a data structure that maintains a linear collection of values and supports addition or removal from either end. A deque can thus logically be said to be a combination of a stack and queue. Describe how a deque can be implemented using the vector approach.

16. Instead of coding the deque entirely from scratch, it could be created using inheritance. Would it make more sense to inherit from a stack or from a queue? Explain why, then implement the data structure in this fashion.

CHAPTER 10

Trees — A Nonlinear Data Structure

JUST AS THE INTUITIVE CONCEPTS of a stack or a queue can be based on everyday experience with similar structures, so too is the idea of a tree — and not just the arboreal variety — found frequently in everyday life. For example, sports events are often organized using trees, where each node represents a pairing of contestants, the winner of each pairing advancing to the next level. The winner of the last pairing, the root of the tree, is declared the winner of the tournament.

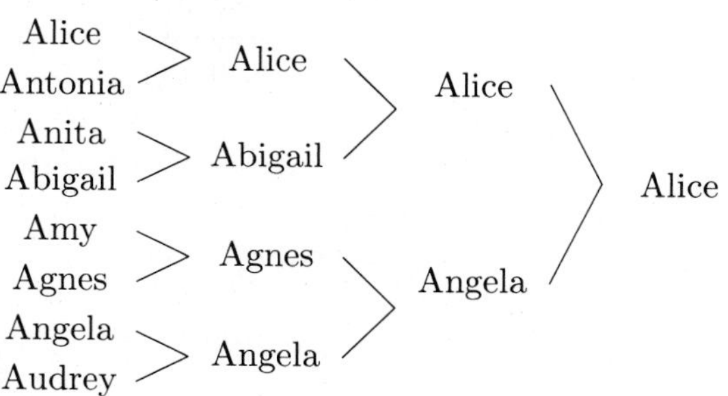

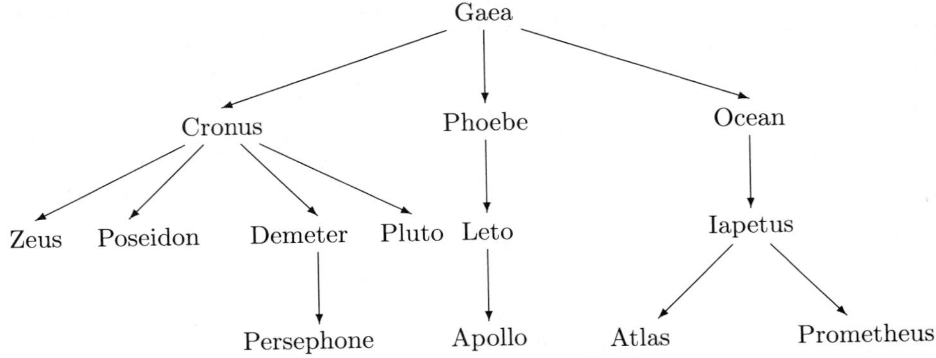

Figure 10.1 A typical family tree

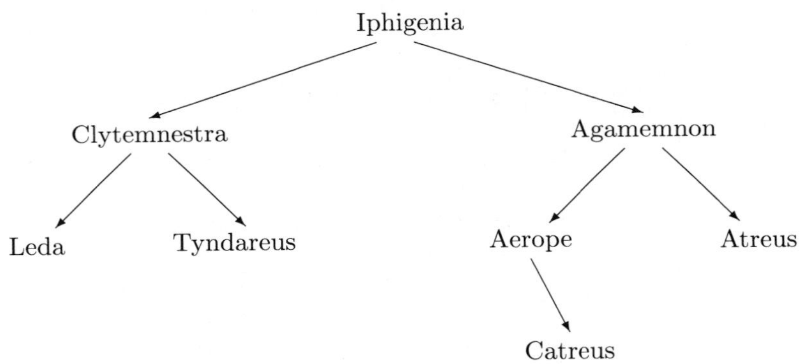

Figure 10.2 A typical ancestor tree

Similarly, information about ancestors and descendants is often organized into a tree structure. A typical family tree is shown in Fig. 10.1. An arrow emanating from a node indicates the individuals represented by the targets of the arrows are children of the individual described by the source node. For example, Persephone is the daughter of Demeter, and Zeus and Poseidon are both children of Cronus. As we will see, much of the terminology used in computer science to discuss trees is derived from such usage. For example, "child nodes" correspond to children in the family tree.

The inverse, in a sense, of a family tree is an ancestor tree. While a family tree traces the descendants from a single individual, an ancestor tree records the ancestors of an individual. An example ancestor tree is shown in Fig. 10.2. We could infer from this tree, for example, that Iphigenia is the child of Clytemnestra and Agamemnon, and Clytemnestra is in turn the child of Leda and Tyndareus. We will shortly have more to say about the characteristics of trees typified by these two forms.

After vectors and lists, trees are perhaps the data structure most frequently encountered in computer algorithms. Algorithms on trees illustrate many of the most important concepts in data structures and the analysis of algorithms. For example, a tree is a natural representation for information that is organized in a hierarchical fashion. We have seen this already in the description of classes based on inheritance, in Section 1.2.1 (page 23). The table of contents of this book provides another example of a hierarchical structure.

The general characteristics of trees can be seen by looking again at Fig. 10.1. A tree consists of a collection of *nodes*, connected by directed arcs. A tree is headed by a single *root* which, in contradiction to nature, appears at the top of the structure.[1] A node that points to other nodes is said to be the *parent* of the nodes pointed to, which in turn are referred to as the *children* of the first node. Continuing the familial metaphor, the term *descendants* is used to describe the children of a node, and the children of those nodes, and their children, and so on. A characterization of the root node is, therefore, that the root is the single node in the structure that does not possess a parent, and from which all other nodes are descended. At the other end, nodes that do not have children are called *leaf nodes*. A node that does possess children is often called an *interior node*. Information is associated with both leaf and interior nodes.

An important characteristic of trees is the fact that there is a single unique path along arcs from the root to any particular node. That is, arcs do not join together. Figure 10.3 illustrates various trees, and various non-trees. The length of the longest path from root to any node is known as the *depth* of the tree.

Note that in a valid tree any node can itself be considered to be a root of the tree formed by considering only the descendants of the node (Fig. 10.4). We call this second tree the *subtree* rooted at the node. This recursive nature of trees leads naturally to an alternative, recursive, characterization of trees.

- A node with no children is a tree. Such a node is called a *leaf*. A leaf node has *depth* one.
- A node with a nonempty collection of trees is a tree. The trees in the collection are known as the *children* of the node. The tree so constructed is in turn called the *parent* to the children trees. A tree with a nonempty set of children is called an *interior* node. The depth of an interior node is one greater than the maximum depth of any child.
- A single node with no parent is called the *root* of the tree.

---

1. Donald Knuth claims the convention of writing the root of the tree at the top stems from handwritten drawings, where naturally it is easier to begin with the fixed root and proceed down the page.

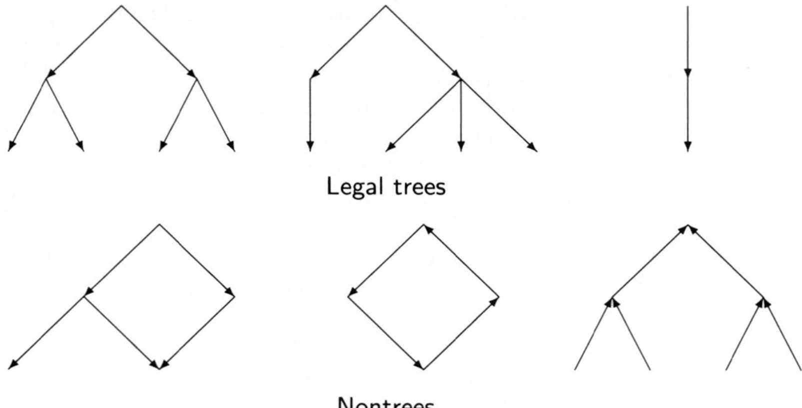

Figure 10.3 Various trees and nontrees

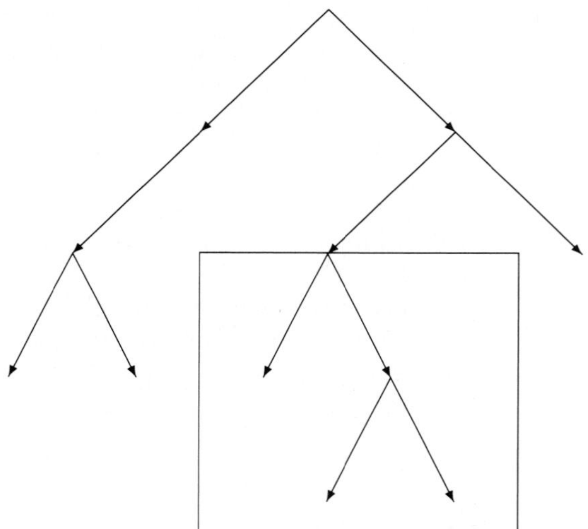

Figure 10.4 A subtree is also a tree

Trees appear in computer science in various forms. A common example is the *parse tree*. Computer languages, including C++, are defined in part using a grammar. Grammars provide rules that explain how the tokens in the language can be put together. A portion of the grammar for C++ could be given as follows:

```
<statement>        ::= <select-statement> | <expr>
<select-statement> ::= if ( <expr> ) <statement> else <statement>
<expr>             ::= <relational-expr> | <assign-expr> | identifier
```

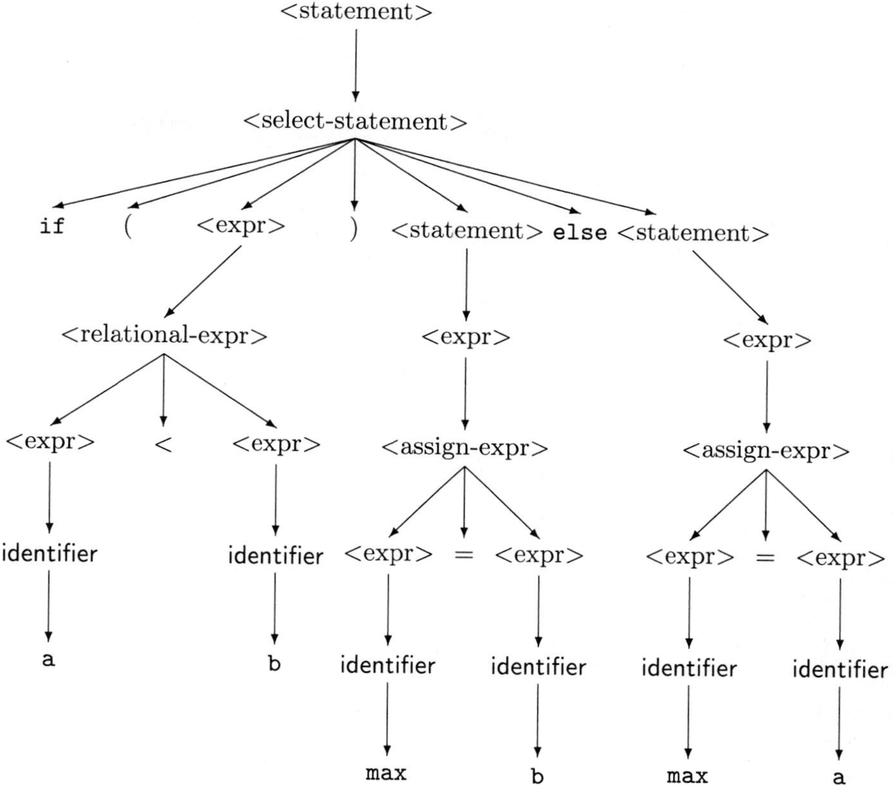

Figure 10.5 A typical parse tree

```
<relational-expr>  ::= <expr> < <expr>
<assign-expr>      ::= <expr> = <expr>
```

A C++ statement, such as:

```
if (a < b) max = b else max = a
```

is analyzed by constructing a tree (Fig. 10.5). Leaf nodes represent the tokens, or symbols, used in the statement. Interior nodes represent syntactic categories. A major task of a compiler is to construct a parse tree for an input program, then to associate information, such as types, with every node in the tree. As a last step in the compilation process, code is produced for the program by traversing the tree—that is, by visiting each node in the tree in sequence. At each node encountered during this traversal, code is generated that will, when executed, perform the operation being described.

A slightly different form of tree is an *expression tree*. As the name suggests, an expression tree (sometimes called an *abstract syntax tree*)

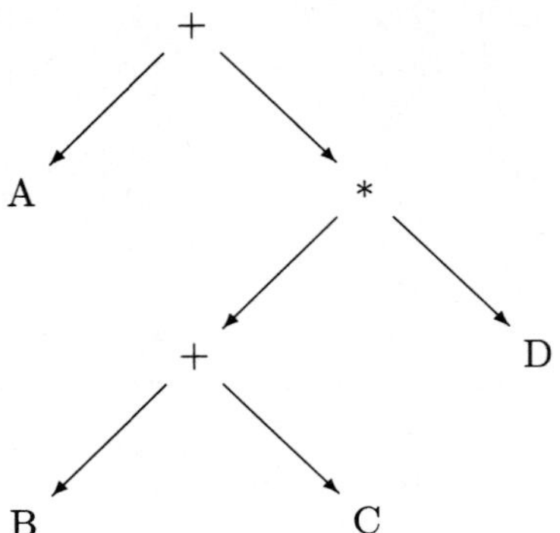

Figure 10.6 A typical expression tree

is used to describe expressions. The two-dimensional nature of the tree eliminates the need for features such as parentheses or precedence. An expression tree for $A + (B + C) * D$ is shown in Fig. 10.6.

Given our characterization of trees, there is an obvious implementation in which a tree is defined as a recursive structure, or tree node. Each tree node maintains some information, and a list of children tree nodes (as shown below). It turns out, however, that almost all trees used in computer algorithms are of a specialized form, called a binary tree, and for this form we can develop much more efficient algorithms.

```
template <class T> class treeNode {
public:
    ...
private:
    // data fields
    T value;
    list< treeNode & > children;
};
```

10.1 BINARY TREES

The defining characteristics of a binary tree can be illustrated by comparing the trees shown in Figs. 10.1 and 10.2. An important characteristic of the tree shown in Fig. 10.2 is the fact that no node has more than two children. Furthermore, we have ordered the nodes; the mother is always represented by the left child arc, and the father by the right child arc. Since no individual can have more than two parents,[2] every node can be thought

2. At least prior to the advent of modern surrogate techniques.

of as possessing exactly two child fields. In some situations the field may be empty, indicating in this example that the information is not known. A node can have only one subtree (indicating that only one of the parents is known) but it must be made clear whether the subtree represents a left or right child. For example, the information that Catreus is the father of Aerope is conveyed by the fact that the node Catreus is the right subtree of the node Aerope, not the left subtree. A tree with these characteristics is known as a *binary tree*. The importance of binary trees stems from their frequency (they occur often in algorithms), and from the fact that they can be very efficiently manipulated.

The most important properties of trees, and in particular binary trees, are related to the ratio of the number of nodes to the depth of the tree. Thus we first investigate this value:

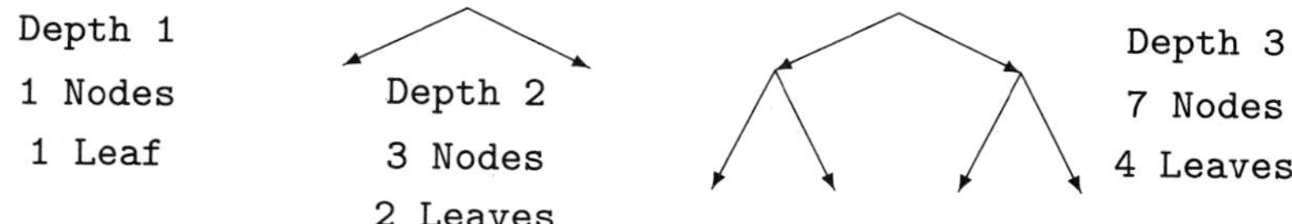

A binary tree with depth one can hold one node, which must be a leaf. A full binary tree with depth two holds three nodes, two of which are leaves. A full binary tree of depth three holds seven nodes, including four leaves. It is not difficult to see that at each new level, the number of leaves will be twice the number of leaves of the preceding level.

Theorem 10.1 A full binary tree of depth n will have 2^{n-1} leaves.

The proof is by induction. We have the base case of zero, and 2^0 or 1. Assume a tree of depth n has 2^{n-1} leaves. To form a full tree of depth $n+1$, we create a new root with subtrees of depth n. The number of leaf nodes is thus $2 \times 2^{n-1}$, or 2^n.

Theorem 10.2 The number of nodes in a full binary tree of depth n is $2^n - 1$.

This theorem is validated by noting that the number of nodes in a full binary tree is $1 + 2 + ... + 2^{n-1}$. The fact that this sum is $2^n - 1$ can be easily verified by induction. An alternative illustration of this fact should also be obvious to computer scientists. The binary representation of 2^n is a 1 followed by n zeros. Thus 2^5 is represented in binary as 100000. The sum $1 + 2 + ...2^{n-1}$ is therefore represented in binary as a sequence of $n - 1$ one bits. Adding one additional value will force a carry in each position, yielding as a result a one followed by n zeros, or 2^n.

We have been careful in the preceding discussion to describe the trees as "full" binary trees. Without this property, the results do not hold. Consider a tree with four nodes, all linked down the right child arc (Fig. 10.7). The tree has depth four, yet only four nodes, instead of the 16 nodes predicted by the theorem. The reason is obvious; the tree is "thin" since most

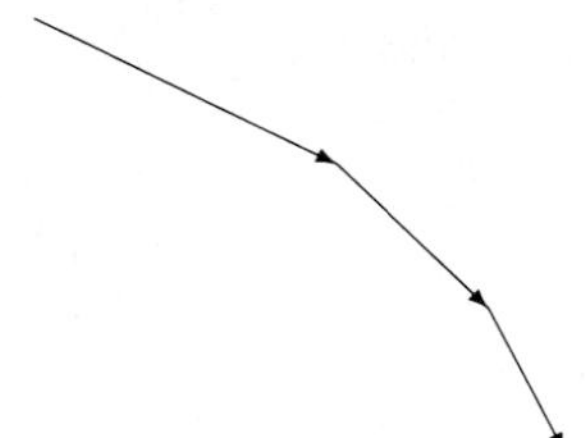

Figure 10.7 A thin and unbalanced tree

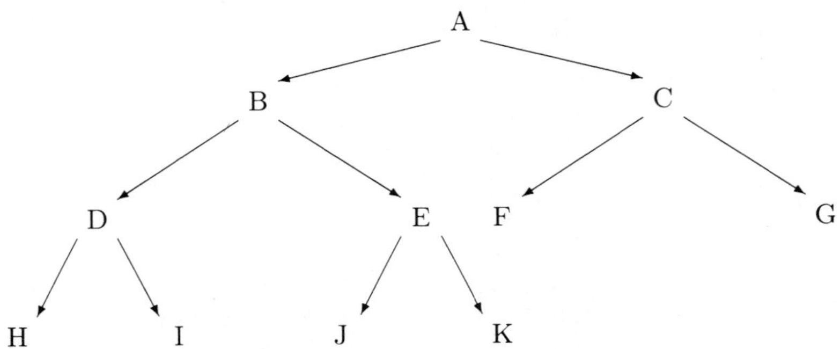

Figure 10.8 A complete binary tree

of the nodes have only one child. Most of the algorithms associated with trees possess a running time proportional to the height of the tree. Thus attaining good performance will require ensuring that long thin trees do not occur. One approach is to require trees to maintain a certain form. A common requirement is that every node have exactly two children, except on the bottommost two levels. A binary tree that is completely filled, with the possible exception of the bottom level, and is filled from left to right, is known as a *complete binary tree*. Figure 10.8 gives an example of such a tree.

It is easy to see that a complete binary tree of height h has between 2^h and 2^{h+1} nodes. Inverting this shows that a complete binary tree containing n nodes must have a depth greater than $\lfloor \log n \rfloor$, and less than $\lceil \log n \rceil$. From this we see that the longest path from root to leaf in a complete binary tree is $O(\log n)$.

Complete binary trees provide the maximal number of leaves with the minimal path length. This observation is behind a pair of theorems we will use to obtain lower bound values in later chapters.

Theorem 10.3 A binary tree containing n nodes must have at least one path of length $\lceil \log n \rceil$.

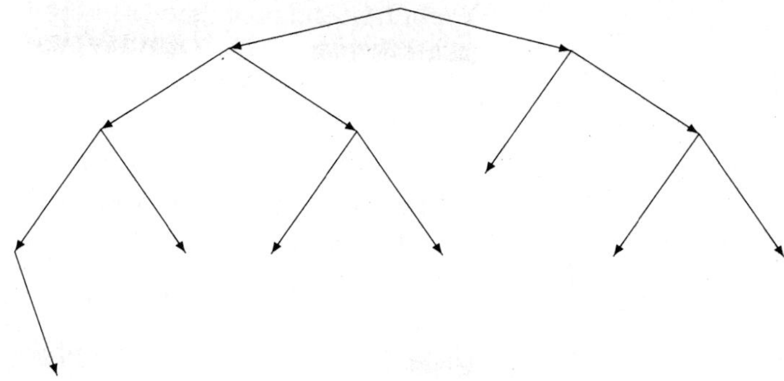

Figure 10.9 A height-balanced binary tree

Theorem 10.4 In a complete binary tree containing n nodes the longest path traverses $\lceil \log n \rceil$ nodes.

Another type of tree we will study in Chapter 11 uses a slightly different structural property in order to guarantee that trees do not get too far out of balance. A *height-balanced* binary tree has the property that for each node the *difference* in the heights of the right and left child is no larger than one. This property ensures that locally, at each node, the balance is roughly maintained, although globally over the entire tree differences in path lengths can be somewhat larger. Figure 10.9 shows an example of a height-balanced binary tree.

Clearly, a complete balanced binary tree is also height balanced. Thus the *largest* number of nodes in a balanced binary tree of depth n is 2^{n-1}. An interesting question is to discover the *smallest* number of nodes in a height-balanced binary tree. For depth zero, there is clearly only one tree. For depth one, there are three trees:

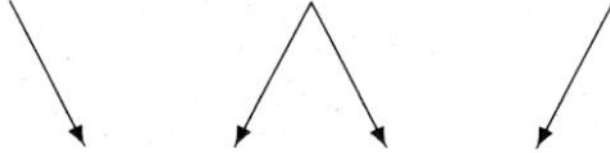

The smallest of these has two nodes. In general, for a tree of depth n the smallest number of nodes is found by connecting the smallest tree of depths $n-1$ and $n-2$.

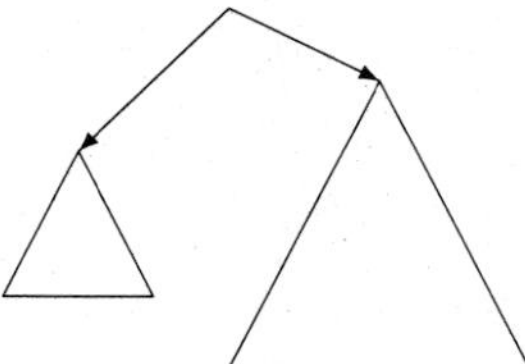

If we let M_n represent the function yielding the minimum number of nodes for a height-balanced tree of depth n, we obtain the following equations:

$$M_0 = 1$$
$$M_1 = 2$$
$$M_{n+1} = M_{n-1} + M_n + 1$$

These equations are very similar to the famous *Fibonacci numbers* defined by the formula $f_0 = 0, f_1 = 1, f_{n+1} = f_{n-1} + f_n$. In fact it is easy to see that each value of M_n is one larger than the corresponding Fibonacci number. We know from Chapter 3 that we can bound the Fibonacci numbers by 2^n. In fact, it is possible to establish an even tighter bounding value. Although the details need not concern us here, the Fibonacci numbers have a closed form solution—that is, a solution defined without using recursion (see Exercise 7 at the end of this chapter). Using this information, we can show that the function M also has an approximate closed form solution:

$$M_n \approx \frac{1}{\sqrt{5}}\left[\frac{1+\sqrt{5}}{2}\right]^n - 1$$

By taking the logarithm of both sides and discarding all but the most significant terms, we obtain the result that $n \approx 1.44 \log M_n$. This tells us that the longest path in a height-balanced binary tree with n nodes is at worst only 44 percent larger than the $\log n$ minimum length. Hence algorithms on height-balanced binary trees that run in time proportional to the length of the path are still $O(\log n)$.

We have only touched the surface in describing the known properties of binary trees. Many other interesting characteristics are described in the literature. However, these few properties will be sufficient for our purposes for the remainder of this book.

10.1.1 Vector Implementation

Because a complete binary tree possesses such a regular structure, it can be easily represented by a vector, to hold the data, and an associated collection of rules to access the data. Just as the vector implementations of stacks and queues were more efficient than the linked list versions, because they avoided the necessity of dynamic memory allocation, so too is the vector implementation of a tree very efficient.

To represent a tree in a vector, we will store the root of the tree in position 0. The children of the node stored at position i will be stored in position $2 \times i + 1$ and $2 \times i + 2$. In this manner the complete binary tree shown in Fig. 10.8 would be stored as follows:

0	1	2	3	4	5	6	7	8	9	10
A	B	C	D	E	F	G	H	I	J	K

Accessing the parents is similarly trivial. The parents of the node stored at position i will be found at position $(i-1)/2$. Thus not only is the storage for pointers not required in this representation but the operations used to move up and down the tree are simple arithmetic operations and can be performed very rapidly. We will use the vector representation of complete binary trees when we discuss the *heap* data structure in Chapter 12.

The difficulty with this representation, of course, is the requirement that the trees be complete. To represent the thin unbalanced tree in Figure 10.7 would require a vector of 15 elements, the same as for the complete and full binary tree of depth three. Yet most of these would be "unused." Some indication would need to be maintained in order to know which elements in the vector are valid, and which represent "holes." Such a scheme is occasionally encountered, but in most cases where the complete binary tree structural property cannot be easily maintained the more general dynamic memory implementation described in the next section will be used to implement operations on trees.

0	1	2	3	4	5	6	7	8	9	10	11	12	13	14
A	ϵ	B	ϵ	ϵ	ϵ	C	ϵ	ϵ	ϵ	ϵ	ϵ	ϵ	ϵ	D

10.1.2 Dynamic Memory Implementation

The obvious representation for a node in a binary tree is a structure containing a value field, and pointers to right and left children. Such a class description is shown below. Constructors permit the creation of a node with no children, or the creation of a node with both the children and the value specified. The comparison operator is defined so as to indicate that two nodes are equal if their values are the same.

```
//
// class node
//     a single node from a binary tree
//

template <class T> class node {
public:
    // constructors
    node     (T value);
    node     (T value, node * left, node * right);

    // public data area for value field
    T              value;

    // duplicate tree rooted at this node
```

```
    node *          copy            () const;

    // release entire tree rooted at this node
    void            release         ();

    // accessing, changing child nodes
    node *          left            () const;
    void            left            (node<T> * l);
    node *          right           () const;
    void            right           (node<T> * r);

protected:
    // data areas
    node<T> *       leftptr;
    node<T> *       rightptr;
};
```

Accessor functions `left` and `right` are defined to set and retrieve the left and right child nodes. These simply return or set the value of the appropriate data fields.

The `copy` method is used to duplicate an entire tree rooted at a given node. The procedure first recursively duplicates the child subtrees, then creates a new root node. Because this operation does not change the original tree, the method is declared as constant.

```
template <class T> node<T> * node<T>::copy() const
{   // return copy of tree rooted at node
    node<T> * newLeft;
    node<T> * newRight;

    // duplicate left child
    if (leftptr != 0)
        newLeft = leftptr->copy();
    else
        newLeft = 0;

    // duplicate right child
    if (rightptr != 0)
        newRight = rightptr->copy();
    else
        newRight = 0;

    // duplicate node, check that allocation worked
    node<T> * newptr =  new node<T>(value, newLeft, newRight);
    assert (newptr != 0);
```

```
    // return new node
    return newptr;
}
```

The `release` method frees the memory associated with the children of a node. The `copy` and `release` methods will be used in subsequent chapters in building new data structures that make use of binary trees.

```
template <class T> void node<T>::release()
{   // release memory associated with children
    if (leftptr) {
        // release left child
        leftptr->release();
        delete leftptr;
        leftptr = 0;
        }
    if (rightptr) {
        // release right child
        rightptr->release();
        delete rightptr;
        rightptr = 0;
        }
}
```

10.1.3 Application — Guess the Animal Game

We will illustrate the use of binary trees with a program that plays a simple interactive game, called "guess the animal." The player thinks of an animal. The computer then poses a number of questions, attempting

Pointers Versus References

In earlier chapters we have usually used references when we wished to indirectly refer to another object. The tree data type is the first time we have made extensive use of pointers instead of references. Why?

The reason for the difference is the importance of null pointers in manipulating trees. A reference should always be understood to be an indirect means of obtaining access to a valid object. That is, the concept of a "null reference" is meaningless (although some compilers will accept such constructs). On the other hand, null pointers are exceedingly common. A leaf node is simply represented as an instance of class `node` that happens to have null values in the pointers to left and right children. An interior node, on the other hand, holds non-null values.

The use of pointers is not without dangers. Attempting to use a null pointer as though it referred to a valid item is perhaps the most common source of programming errors when dynamic structures are manipulated. For this reason, we almost always will test a pointer value before using it. Such tests are not necessary when references are employed.

to discover the animal the player has in mind. An example session might look as follows:

```
Does it live in water?
no
Does it bark?
no
I know.  Is it a cat?
yes
I won!
Try again?
```

The database of animal facts is stored in a binary tree of strings. Interior nodes represent questions, and leaf nodes represent answers (animals). Initially the game database has very little information. In our game, we start with simply one answer, namely the animal "cat." When the computer fails to match the animal the player has in mind, it "learns" by asking for the name of the user's animal, and a distinguishing question to differentiate the animal from some known animal. An example session might look as follows:

```
Does it live in water?
yes
I know.  Is it a fish?
no
What is the animal you had in mind?
a duck
What is a yes/no question that I can use to tell a fish from a
duck?
Does it have webbed feet?
For a duck is the answer yes or no?
yes
Try again?
```

The main program stores the database of animal facts in the tree held by the variable `root`, although this is used only during reinitialization of the game. The current node is referred to by the variable `current`, which travels down the tree asking questions.

```
void animalGame() {
    // initialize the database with one animal
    root = new node<string> ("cat");
    node<string> * current = root;
    // now start the game
    cout << "let's play guess the animal.\n";
    while (current != 0) {
        // if current node has children it is a question
        if (current->left() != 0) {
```

```
            cout << current->value << '\n';
            if (answer() != 0)
                current = current->left();
            else
                current = current->right();
            }
        // if no children it is an answer
        else {
            cout << "I know.  Is it a " << current->value << "?\n";
            if (answer() != 0)
                cout << "I won.\n";
            else {
                // we didn't get it.
                // time to learn something
                learnNewAnimal(current);
                }
            cout << "Try again?\n";
            if (answer() != 0)
                current = root;
            else
                return;
            }
        }
}
```

The majority of questions are designed to have simple yes/no answers. The decoding of the user responses is performed by the routine named `answer`, as follows:

```
int answer() {
    // get yes no answer
    string ans(100);
    ans.getline(cin);
    if ((ans[0] == 'y') || (ans[0] == 'Y'))
        return 1;
    else if ((ans[0] == 'n') || (ans[0] == 'N'))
        return 0;
    cout << "please answer yes or no.\n";
    return answer();
}
```

The only other procedure is the code used to learn about a new animal when the computer makes a wrong guess. This is performed by the procedure `learnNewAnimal`. The procedure asks for the name of the new animal and the distinguishing question. The current node, which must be a leaf node, is then changed into a question node, and the two animals are installed as child nodes.

```
void learnNewAnimal(node<string> * current)
{   // learn about a new animal type

    string currentAnimal = current->value;
    cout << "what is your animal?\n";
    string newAnimal(200);
    newAnimal.getline(cin);
    cout << "What is a yes/no question that I can use to tell a "
        << current->value << " from a " << newAnimal << " ?\n";
    string newQuestion(200);
    node<string> * node1 = new node<string>(newAnimal);
    node<string> * node2 = new node<string>(currentAnimal);
    // make sure allocation worked
    assert ((node1 != 0) && (node2 != 0));

    newQuestion.getline(cin);
    cout << "For a " << newAnimal << " is the answer yes or no?\n";
    if (answer() != 0) {
        current->left(node1);
        current->right(node2);
        }
    else {
        current->left(node2);
        current->right(node1);
        }
    current->value = newQuestion;
}
```

10.2 OPERATOR PRECEDENCE PARSING*

In Section 9.4 (page 290), we described an algorithm to convert an infix string into a postfix polish representation. The basic technique employed by that algorithm, called *operator precedence parsing*, can be used as well to convert a string representation of an expression into an expression tree. In this section we will describe the details of this transformation.

The first step is to describe the representation for the expression tree. As before, we will simplify the task somewhat by dealing only with binary operators. In addition, we will also assume the only operands are one-character identifier names. (The exercises explore the removal of some of these simplifying assumptions.) We will represent nodes in the expression tree with a class named `expressionInformation`, represented as follows:

*Section headings followed by an asterisk indicate optional material.

```
enum operators {identifier, leftparen, plus, minus, times, divide};

class expressionInformation {
public:
    // data areas, type, other information
    operators type;
    string name;

    // constructors
    expressionInformation(char n);
    expressionInformation(operators);
};
```

The global type `operators` describes the set of tokens in our language. Instances of `expressionInformation` hold an operator type. If the node represents an identifier, the name of the identifier will be stored in a string. The name field is otherwise unused.

The infix to postfix conversion routine required a single stack, which held pending operators that had not yet been processed. The expression parsing algorithm will use a *pair* of stacks. The first is the operand stack, similar to the earlier algorithm. The second stack contains expressions trees, representing expressions that have *already* been processed.

We will illustrate the operation of this algorithm by working through the recognition of the expression `a * b + c * d`. The various steps involved in the creation of the expression tree are shown in Fig. 10.10.

Operators are always immediately made into nodes and pushed on to the operand stack. This is shown in the first step in Fig. 10.10. The multiplication operand is, as in the earlier infix to postfix algorithm, immediately pushed on the operator stack. By the time the addition operator is read, two values have been pushed on to the operand stack. Since the addition operator has lower precedence than the multiplication operator, already on the operator stack, the multiplication operator is popped from the stack. In this algorithm, unlike in the infix to postfix conversion algorithm, when a binary operator is popped from the operator stack, the two arguments for the operator are also popped from the operand stack. A new tree is formed by creating a new node for the binary operator and by using the two popped operands as the left and right child.

Execution proceeds following this pattern. When the end of input is encountered, the operator stack contains two values, and the operand stack three. As in the earlier algorithm, the final step is to simply empty the operator stack, by repeatedly popping and processing operators. When the stack is empty, there will be one remaining value in the operand stack, which is the desired expression tree.

The following procedure implements the popping of a binary operator from the operator stack. The two operands are popped from the operand

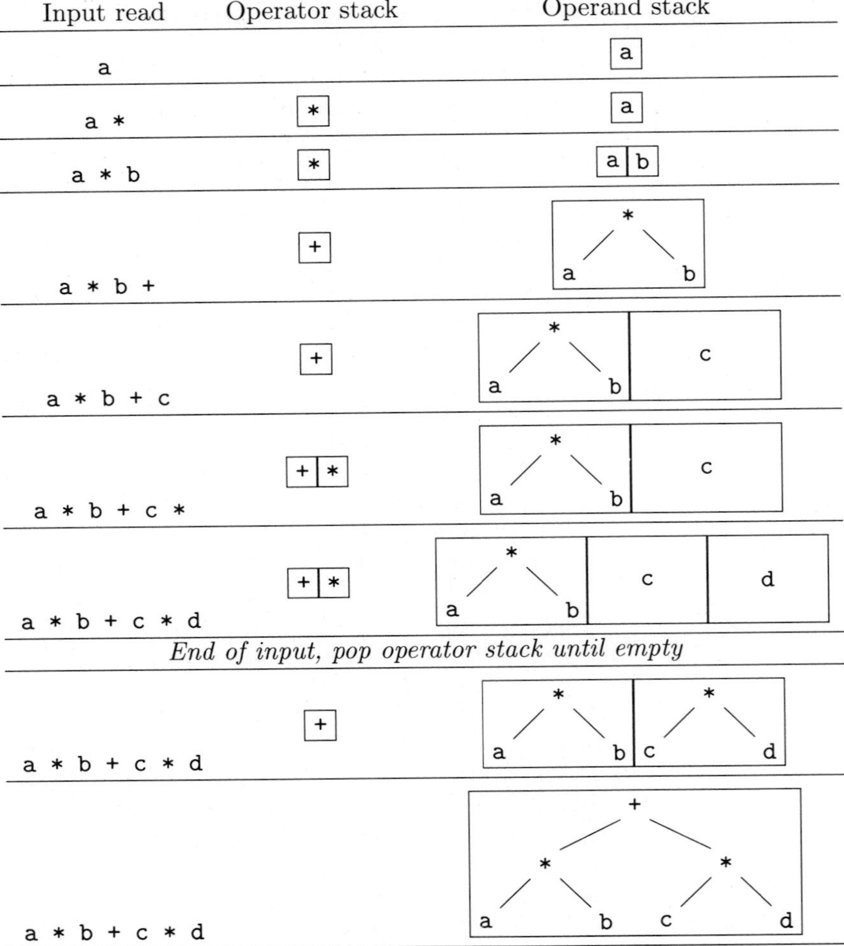

Figure 10.10 Execution of an operator precedence parsing algorithm

stack, a new node is created, and the new expression pushed back on to the operand stack.

```
void doBinary(operators theOp,
  stackList<node<expressionInformation> *> & operandStack)
{   // build a binary operator node by combining child nodes
    // pop the argument expressions
    node<expressionInformation> * right = operandStack.pop();
    node<expressionInformation> * left = operandStack.pop();
    // build the new binary operator node
    node<expressionInformation> * newNode =
```

```
            new node<expressionInformation>(theOp, left, right);
        assert(newNode != 0);
        // push new expression back on stack
        operandStack.push(newNode);
}
```

As in the earlier algorithm, a function named `processOp` is used to compare a newly encountered operator to the existing binary operators on the operator stack. Operators on the stack are popped and processed as long as they have higher priority than the argument operator.

```
void processOp(operators theOp, stackList<operators> & operatorStack,
            stackList<node<expressionInformation> *> & operandStack)
{
    // pop stack while operators have higher precedence
    while ((! operatorStack.isEmpty()) && (theOp < operatorStack.top()))
        doBinary(operatorStack.pop(), operandStack);

    // then push operator
    operatorStack.push(theOp);
}
```

The following procedure is the main program for the parsing process. The structure of the program is almost identical to the structure of the infix to postfix conversion routine that was shown in Fig. 9.1 (page 250).

```
node<expressionInformation> * parse(const string & inputString)
{
    // stacks for both operators and operands
    stackList<operators> operatorStack;
    stackList<node<expressionInformation> *> operandStack;

    int i = 0;
    while (inputString[i] != '\0')
        if (isAlphabetic(inputString[i])) {
            // create an operand node for an identifier
            node<expressionInformation> * newNode =
                new node<expressionInformation>
                    (expressionInformation(inputString[i++]));
            assert(newNode != 0);
            operandStack.push(newNode);
            }
        else
            switch(inputString[i++]) {
                case '(':
                    operatorStack.push(leftparen);
                    break;
```

```
                case ')':
                    while (operatorStack.top() != leftparen)
                        doBinary(operatorStack.pop(), operandStack);
                    // pop the right parenthesis
                    operandStack.pop();
                    break;
                case '+':
                    processOp(plus, operatorStack, operandStack);
                    break;
                case '-':
                    processOp(minus, operatorStack, operandStack);
                    break;
                case '*':
                    processOp(times, operatorStack, operandStack);
                    break;
                case '/':
                    processOp(divide, operatorStack, operandStack);
                    break;
            }

        // pop all operators remaining on the stack
        while (! operatorStack.isEmpty())
            doBinary(operatorStack.pop(), operandStack);

        // return the final expression
        return operandStack.pop();
}
```

10.3 TREE TRAVERSALS

Just as it is often necessary to examine each node of a linked list in sequence, it is frequently necessary to examine every node in a binary tree. But while a list has an obvious linear ordering, no single ordering is the obvious "correct" way to iterate over the elements of a tree. If we consider each of the n nodes of a binary tree as independent, then there are $n!$ different orderings, or sequences in which one could visit every node. ($n!$ is n factorial, or $n \times (n-1) \times \ldots \times 1$). Of course, most of these sequences have little regularity and are thus of dubious use in practice. Generally, traversal algorithms are defined recursively out of three steps:

- Process a node.
- Recursively visit and process the left child.
- Recursively visit and process the right child.

But even within this framework, there are six possible ways to arrange these tasks:

- ▲ Process value, then left child, then right child
- ▲ Process left child, then value, then right child
- ▲ Process left child, then right child, then value
- ▲ Process value, then right child, then left child
- ▲ Process right child, then value, then left child
- ▲ Process right child, then left child, then value

In almost all cases of interest, the subtrees are analyzed left to right. Thus the six possibilities are reduced to the first three, each of which is given a name. Visiting the node first, followed by the left child and then the right child is called *preorder traversal*. Visiting the left child first, followed by processing the node, followed by visiting the right child is called *inorder traversal*. Finally, visiting the left child first, then the right child, and lastly processing the node is known as *postorder traversal*.

Just as the "post" in postfix polish notation implied that we viewed the arguments before encountering the operator in an arithmetic expression, here the "post" means we will process the child nodes prior to processing the parent. In fact, there is a simple relationship between these tree traversals and pre- and postfix polish notation. Consider a tree traversal of the expression tree that was shown in Fig. 10.6, printing out the value of each node when it is processed. A prefix traversal will result in the following output:

$$+ a * + b c d$$

This is simply the prefix polish form of the tree, where operators are written first and then followed by their operands. An inorder traversal results in the following:

$$a + b + c * d$$

This is close to the infix form of the expression, minus the parentheses (see Exercise 12 at the end of this chapter). A postfix traversal, as you might expect, produces the postfix polish expression:

$$a b c + d * +$$

The translation of these into recursive functions that operate on instances of class node is relatively simple, as illustrated by the following:

```
// preorder processing of tree rooted at current
void preorder(node<T> * current)
{   // visit node, left child, right child
    if (current) {
        // process current node
```

```
        process(current->value);
        // then visit children
        preorder(current->left());
        preorder(current->right());
        }
}

// inorder processing of tree rooted at current
void inorder(node<T> * current)
{   // visit left child, node, right child
    if (current) {
        inorder(current->left());
        process(current->value);
        inorder(current->right());
        }
}

// postorder processing of tree rooted at current
void postorder(node<T> * current)
{   // visit left child, right child, node
    if (current) {
        postorder(current->left());
        postorder(current->right());
        process(current->value);
    } }
```

Each function is performing only a constant amount of work at each node. Thus iterating over all n elements in a tree can be performed in $O(n)$ steps, regardless of the order used.

Unfortunately, these functions suffer from the same problems that motivated the development of iterators in Chapter 5. The functions must be rewritten for each task to be performed. Furthermore, the writing of these methods exposes the internal representation details of the structure. To avoid this, we define a family of iterator classes for traversing trees. By means of these, a normal iterator loop can be used to access each element of the tree.

10.3.1 Postorder Tree Traversal Iterator

The first traversal algorithm we examine is the postorder traversal. The postorder traversal examines the left child first, then the right child, and finally processes a node. The following picture numbers the nodes in the order they would be processed by a postorder traversal.

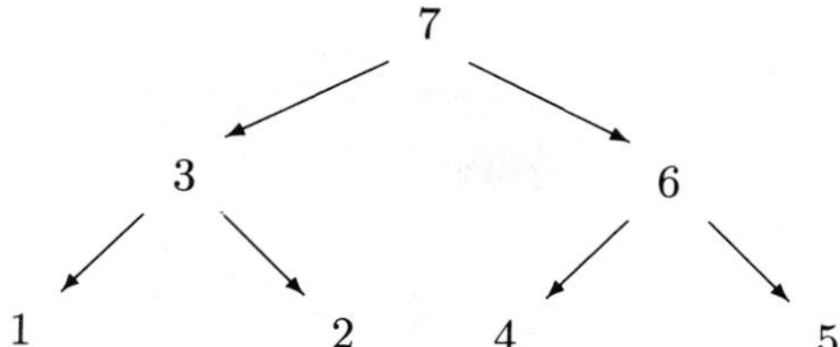

We examine this traversal first not because it is the easiest, but in fact because it is the most difficult; thus a naïve brute-force approach is about the best we can do. The basic idea is to use a stack, from Chapter 9, to hold the nodes in the opposite order they are to be visited. The constructor is provided with the root for the stack.

```
//
// class postorderTreeTraversal
//     perform a post order traversal of a binary tree
//

template <class T> class postorderTreeTraversal : public iterator<T> {
public:
    // constructor
    postorderTreeTraversal          (node<T> * root);

    // reimplement iterator protocol
    virtual int     init            ();
    virtual int     operator !      ();
    virtual T       operator ()     ();
    virtual void    operator =      (T val);
    virtual int     operator ++     ();

    // also permit changing the root
    void            setRoot         (node<T> * root);
private:
    // data areas
    node<T> *       root;
    stackList<node<T> *> itrstack;

    // internal method used to stack children of a node
    void            stackChildren   (node<T> *);
};
```

The initialization routine fills the stack, and thereafter the iterator protocol simply removes items from the stack.

```
template <class T> int postorderTreeTraversal<T>::init ()
{
    // clear out the stack
    itrstack.deleteAllValues();

    // then initialize it
    stackChildren(root);
    return ! itrstack.isEmpty();
}
```

The stack must be filled in the opposite order from that used to iterate over the elements. To do this, we stack first the current node, followed by the right children and then the left children.

```
template <class T>
void postorderTreeTraversal<T>::stackChildren(node<T> * n)
{   // stack all the children of the current node
    itrstack.push(n);
    node<T> * next = n->right();
    if (next)
        stackChildren(next);
    next = n->left();
    if (next)
        stackChildren(next);
}
```

To see if there are any more nodes to generate, we simply test the stack. The same technique will be used in all the tree traversal iterators.

```
template <class T> int postorderTreeTraversal<T>::operator ! ()
{   // we are done when stack is empty
    return ! itrstack.isEmpty();
}
```

The current value of the iterator is simply the value associated with the current top of stack. This, too, will be similar in all the tree traversal iterators.

```
template <class T> T postorderTreeTraversal<T>::operator() ()
{   // return value of current node
    node<T> * n = itrstack.top();
    return n->value;
}
```

To move to the next value in sequence, it is sufficient to simply pop the stack.

```
template <class T> int postorderTreeTraversal<T>::operator ++ ()
{   // move to the next item in sequence
    // pop current node from stack
    itrstack.pop();
    // return false if stack is empty, and hence there are no more items
    return ! itrstack.isEmpty();
}
```

Clearly, the initialization of the stack requires $O(n)$ steps. Thereafter, each step can be performed very quickly, in constant time. Iterating over all n elements therefore requires $O(n)$ time. However, the stack requires as much space as the list itself. Thus we say that postorder iteration also requires $O(n)$ space. We will see that other traversal algorithms can be performed using much less space.

10.3.2 Preorder Tree Traversal Iterator

A preorder traversal visits first the current node, then visits nodes associated with the left child, and finally nodes associated with the right child. The following figures indicate the sequence in which nodes would be visited using a preorder traversal.

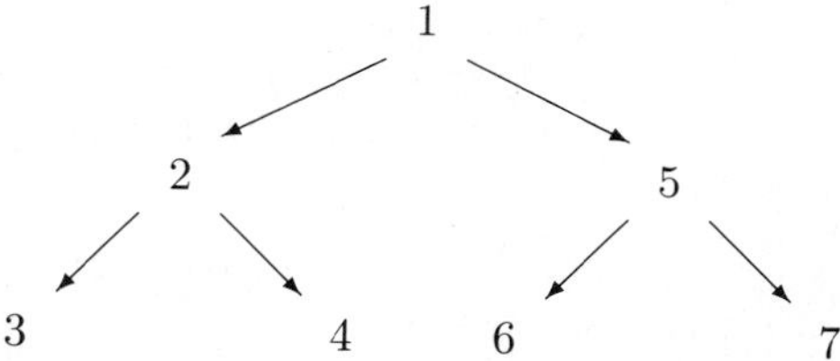

The preorder tree iterator also uses a stack, but it stacks only those elements along the path from the root to the current node.

```
//
// class preorderTreeTraversal
//     perform a preorder traversal of a binary tree
//

template <class T> class preorderTreeTraversal : public iterator<T> {
public:
    // constructor
    preorderTreeTraversal          (node<T> * root);

    // iterator protocol
    virtual int     init           ();
    virtual int     operator !     ();
```

```
    virtual T        operator ()     ();
    virtual void     operator =      (T val);
    virtual int      operator ++     ();

    // in addition, permit user to set new root
    void             setRoot         (node<T> * root);

private:
    // data areas
    node<T> *        root;
    stackList<node<T> *>   itrstack;
};
```

Initialization consists of simply pushing the root on the stack.

In this manner the root node will be the first node returned as a result of iteration.

```
template <class T> int preorderTreeTraversal<T>::init ()
{   // initialize a preorder traversal of a tree
    // first initialize the stack
    itrstack.deleteAllValues();

    // first time out, just push the root
    if (root != 0)
        itrstack.push(root);
    return ! itrstack.isEmpty();
}
```

To perform the iterator increment operation, we maintain the invariant that for each node on the stack except the top all left children are in the process of being investigated, and for each node on the stack including the top no right child has been examined. Thus, to continue the preorder traversal, we first try to push on the stack the left child of the current node. It is only if the current node does not have a left child that the next step is undertaken.

```
int preorderTreeTraversal<T>::operator ++ ()
{
    // inv - for each node on stack except top
    // left children are being investigated
    // for all including top no right children
    // have been visited
    node<T> * current = itrstack.top();
    node<T> * next = current->left();
    if (next) {
        itrstack.push(next);
        return 1;
        }
```

```
        // no more left nodes,
        // find unexplored right child
        while (! itrstack.isEmpty()) {
            current = itrstack.pop();
            next = current->right();
            if (next) {
                // note parent is not on stack,
                // preserving invariant
                itrstack.push(next);
                return 1;
                }
            }
        return 0;
}
```

If the current node does not have a left child, then we must start to examine right subtrees. The stack is popped until we find a node that possesses a right child. This node is popped, and the right child pushed on the stack. Note that by popping the parent node, we preserve the invariant we noted earlier. Leaving the parent node on the stack would have destroyed the invariant, since for that node it would not be true that right children had not yet been investigated.

It is easy to see that the maximum depth of the stack is the maximum length of any path from root to leaf. In fact, this figure is overly large, since only on all left-sided paths will all nodes ever be present at the same time in the stack.

The running time of the increment operator is less easy to characterize. The presence of the loop implies that the running time cannot be guaranteed to be constant, as it could with the postorder iterator. Indeed, we cannot make any guarantees less than $O(n)$ about the running time of any one invocation of the increment operator. However, just as we did with the pattern-matching iterators of Chapter 4, we can use an *amortized analysis* to bound the complete iteration loop over the entire tree. To do this, we note that we can "save" the cost of unstacking each time we insert a new element into the stack. The "cost" of the loop is proportional to the number of items on the stack. Thus the cost of each iteration can be "charged" to a previous savings. This is sufficient to show that, even if we cannot bound the running time of any single increment operation, the cost of iterating over all elements of a tree is still $O(n)$.

10.3.3 Inorder Tree Traversal Iterator

An inorder traversal visits the left child first, then the current node, and finally the right child. The following diagram illustrates the order in which nodes would be processed using an inorder traversal.

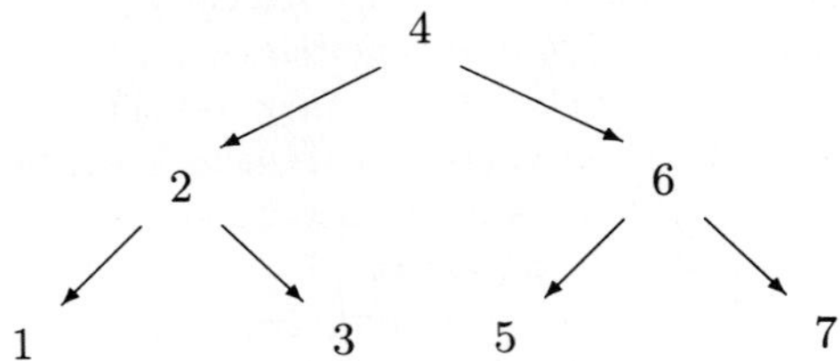

Inorder traversal also uses a stack. As with preorder traversal, the maximum depth of the stack is limited by the longest path from root to leaf. The first value yielded by the iteration process is, however, the leftmost child node, not the root. To reach this node, the method **slideLeft** loops down the left links, using the stack to remember the path that has been followed.

```
// class inorderTreeTraversal
//     perform an inorder traversal of a binary tree

template <class T> class inorderTreeTraversal : public iterator<T> {
public:
    // reimplement iterator protocol
    virtual int     init            ();
    virtual int     operator !      ();
    virtual T       operator ()     ();
    virtual void    operator =      (T val);
    virtual int     operator ++     ();

    // also permit changing the root
    void            setRoot         (node<T> * root);
private:
    // data ares
    node<T> *       root;
    stackList<node<T> *>   itrstack;

    // internal method to slide down left subtree
    void            slideLeft       (node<T> *);
};

int inorderTreeTraversal<T>::init ()
{   // initialize inorder tree traversal
    // clear out the stack
    itrstack.deleteAllValues();

    // then reinitialize it
    slideLeft(root);
```

```
    return ! itrstack.isEmpty();
}

void inorderTreeTraversal<T>::slideLeft(node<T> * current)
{   // slide left from the current node
    while (current) {
        itrstack.push(current);
        current = current->left();
        }
}
```

The invariant being maintained by the increment operator is again expressed in terms of the stack. Namely, for all nodes except the topmost node on the stack, left children are being explored and right children have not yet been examined. For the topmost node, the left children have all been processed and the right children have not. Thus, to find the next node, we first pop the current node. If the current node has right children, we process them (starting, as we did with the root, by sliding down the left links). If the node that was popped did not have a right child, then both right and left children have been processed and the next lower node on the stack is the next node that will be examined.

```
int inorderTreeTraversal<T>::operator ++ ()
{
    // inv - for each node on stack, left children
    // have been explored, right children have not
    if (! itrstack.isEmpty()) {
        node<T> * n = itrstack.pop();
        node<T> * next = n->right();
        if (next)
            slideLeft(next);
        }
    // if stack isn't empty we have nodes
    return ! itrstack.isEmpty();
}
```

The running time of the increment operator is constant, with the exception of the slide left operation. The run-time analysis of the slide left process here is in some sense the opposite of the analysis for preorder traversal. We can associate, or "charge," each step in the loop to a future pop. Since the number of pop operations is $O(n)$, the total running time of an inorder tree traversal iteration loop is $O(n)$, despite the fact that we cannot bound the execution of any single instance of the increment operator.

10.3.4 Level-Order Tree Traversal Iterator

We will examine a fourth type of tree iterator, a form that is encountered occasionally, although less frequently than the previous three. It does, however, provide yet another example of the use of the queue data type. A *level-order* traversal of a tree examines all nodes at level 1 (namely, the root) before examining nodes at level 2. Next all nodes of level 2 are examined. In general, all nodes of level i are examined before any node of level $i+1$. A level-order traversal would visit nodes of a complete binary tree of depth three in the following order:

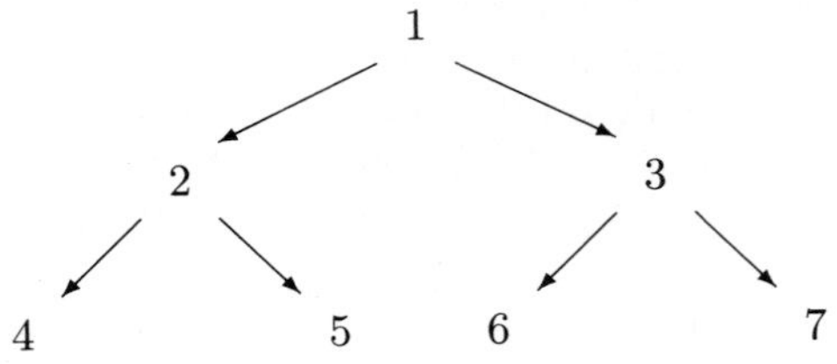

```
                1
          2           3
       4     5     6     7
```

```
//
// class levelorderTreeTraversal
//     perform a level order traversal of a binary tree
//

template <class T> class levelorderTreeTraversal : public iterator<T> {
public:
    // constructor
    levelorderTreeTraversal         (node<T> * root);

    // reimplement iterator protocol
    virtual int     init            ();
    virtual int     operator !      ();
    virtual T       operator ()     ();
    virtual void    operator =      (T val);
    virtual int     operator ++     ();

    // also permit changing the root
    void            setRoot         (node<T> * root);

private:
    // data areas
    node<T> *       root;
    queueList<node<T> *>   itrqueue;
};
```

To initialize the level-order traversal, the root node is inserted into an empty queue. To increment each step, a node is removed from the front of the queue, and the children of the removed node are inserted into the end of the queue. The nature of the queue will ensure the level-order property.

```
int levelorderTreeTraversal<T>::operator ++ ()
{ // queue children of current node
    if (! itrqueue.isEmpty() ) {
        node<T> * n = itrqueue.dequeue();
        node<T> * next;
        next = n->left();
        if (next)
            itrqueue.enqueue(next);
        next = n->right();
        if (next)
            itrqueue.enqueue(next);
        }
    return ! itrqueue.isEmpty();
}
```

The execution time of the increment operator can be bounded by a constant, and thus the total execution time is $O(n)$. The maximum number of elements in the queue is bounded by the maximum number of elements at any one level. Unfortunately, as an examination of a complete full binary tree will show, this value can be as large as $n/2$.

10.4 BINARY TREE REPRESENTATION OF GENERAL TREES

It is interesting to note that the binary tree abstract data type is actually sufficient to represent any tree structure. To illustrate this, consider a general tree such as the following:

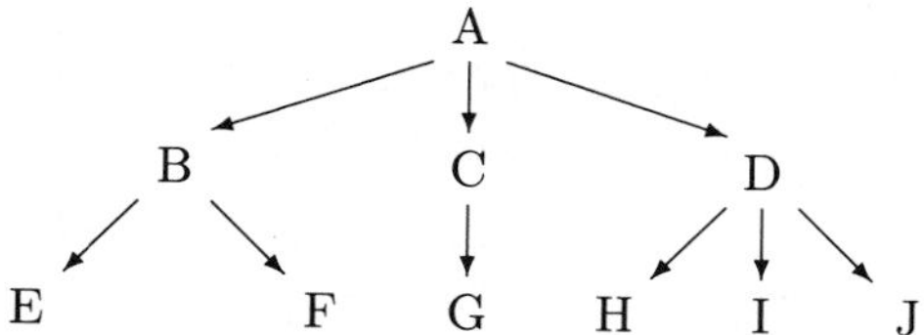

In a general case of this type, the concept of an inorder traversal is not well defined. However, preorder and postorder traversals can be described. For this example, these two traversal algorithms would visit the nodes in the following orders:

Preorder   A B E F C G D H I J
Postorder   E F B G C H I J D A

To represent this tree using binary nodes, let us use the left pointer on each node to indicate the first child of the current node. Let us use the right pointer to indicate a "sibling," a child with the same parents as the current node. The tree would thus be represented as follows:

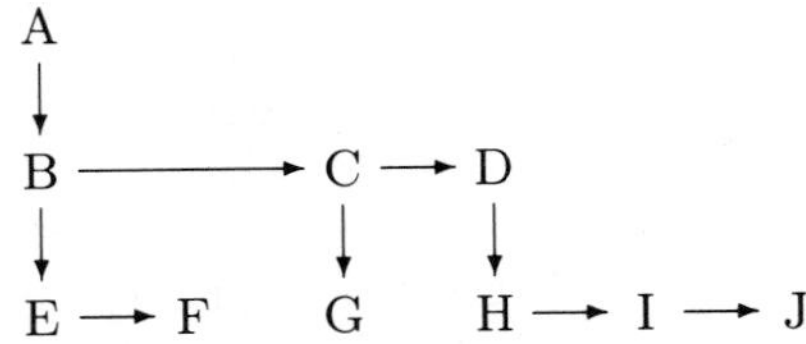

Turning the tree 45 degrees makes the representation look more like the binary trees we have been examining in earlier parts of this chapter.

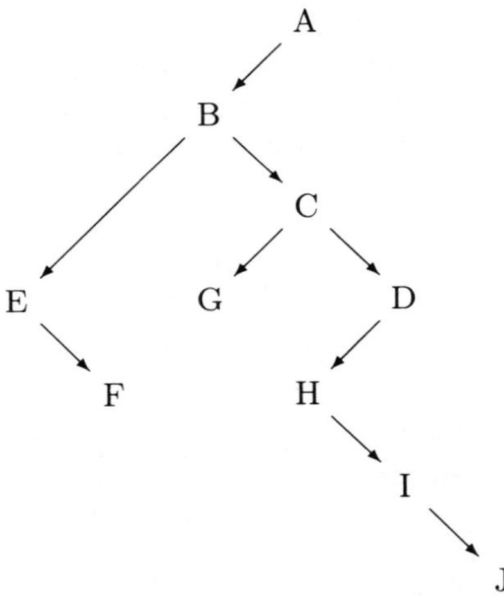

Now let us note the order that nodes would be examined in the various traversal strategies:

Preorder   A B E F C G D H I J
Inorder   E F B G C H I J D A
Postorder   F E G J I H D C B A

An interesting fact to observe is that a preorder traversal of the binary tree representation corresponds to the preorder traversal of the original tree. Even more surprising, a postorder traversal of the original tree corresponds to an inorder traversal of the binary tree representation.

10.5 CHAPTER SUMMARY

Key Concepts

- Tree
  - Node
  - Root
  - Arc
  - Parent
  - Child
  - Leaf
  - Interior node
  - Subtree
  - Depth
- Binary tree
- Vector implementation of complete binary tree
- Operator precedence parsing
- Tree traversals
  - Preorder
  - Inorder
  - Postorder
  - level-order

In this chapter we have introduced the concept of a binary tree. Along with vectors and lists, trees are a fundamental building block for many important data structures. The importance of trees stems from the fact that they can hold a great deal of information and yet access the information very quickly; in a balanced tree the longest path from a root to any node is approximately proportional to the logarithm of the number of elements held by the tree.

In a binary tree, each node has at most two children. The children of a tree are themselves trees. We have examined two implementation techniques for binary trees: an encoding that packs elements of a binary tree into a vector and a more general technique that uses pointers and dynamically allocated nodes.

One use of trees is in the representation of expressions. We have presented an algorithm, called operator precedence parsing, that can be used to convert an expression from a textual representation into a tree form.

There is no obvious linear order for the elements in a tree. We have examined four different traversal strategies for a binary tree. The differences are characterized by the order in which each node is processed relative to the processing of the nodes in the subtrees associated with the left and right children.

- ▲ A preorder traversal visits each node, followed by a preorder traversal of the left child, and finally a preorder traversal of the right child.
- ▲ An inorder traversal performs an inorder traversal of the left child, followed by visiting the node, and finally an inorder traversal of the right child.
- ▲ A postorder traversal performs a postorder traversal of the left and right children, then visits the node.
- ▲ A level-order traversal visits all nodes of a specific depth from the root, before considering any nodes of a further depth.

Finally, we noted how arbitrary trees with any number of children per node can be encoded using binary trees. Since algorithms making use of binary trees are common and easy to use, this encoding makes it easy to extend these processes to general tree structures.

Exercises

1. What are some of the ways that trees are used as descriptive devices in non-computer science applications?

2. Write the expression tree for $(a + b) * (c + d * e)$.

3. Write the prefix and postfix representations of the expression given in the previous question.

4. Write the parse tree for the statement

```
if (x < y) then a = x else if (y < z) then a =
z else z = y
```

5. A common variation in binary trees is to have each node maintain a pointer to its parent node. Modify the declaration of the node data structure so as to maintain this information. How should this field be set? (*Hint*: Do not add any new method to class node to set this field. Instead, it should be maintained as part of the actions of methods that are already defined for the class.)

6. Would the presence of pointers to parent nodes, described in the previous question, simplify any of the algorithms described in this chapter?

7. Prove that the following formula describes the Fibonacci numbers. (The first three parts of this question are repeated from Chapter 3.)

$$\mathrm{Fib}_n = \frac{1}{\sqrt{5}}\left[\left(\frac{1+\sqrt{5}}{2}\right)^n - \left(\frac{1-\sqrt{5}}{2}\right)^n\right]$$

a. Verify that the formula works for values 0, 1, and 2.
b. Show that $(\frac{1+\sqrt{5}}{2})^2$ is the same as $1 + \frac{1+\sqrt{5}}{2}$, and similarly $(\frac{1-\sqrt{5}}{2})^2$ is the same as $1 + \frac{1-\sqrt{5}}{2}$.
c. By substituting the formula, verify that $\mathrm{Fib}_{n+1} = \mathrm{Fib}_{n-1} + \mathrm{Fib}_n$. (*Hint*: Rewrite $(\frac{1+\sqrt{5}}{2})^{n+1}$ as $(\frac{1+\sqrt{5}}{2})^{n-1} \times (\frac{1+\sqrt{5}}{2})^2$, then use the property you verified in the previous step.)
d. Argue why as n gets larger the second term in the subtraction contributes less and less to the result. (*Hint*: Consider the values of the second term as n increases.)
e. From (d), we know that, for large values of n, the value of Fib_n is approximately $\frac{1}{\sqrt{5}}\left(\frac{1+\sqrt{5}}{2}\right)^n$. Let c represent the constant value $\frac{1+\sqrt{5}}{2}$. Compute the decimal approximation to c, giving at least two digits to the right of the decimal point.
f. Taking the logarithm of both sides, we obtain $\log \mathrm{Fib}_n \approx \log \frac{1}{\sqrt{5}} + n \log c$. We can ignore the left argument to the addition as insignificant. Compute the value of $\log c$.
g. Dividing both sides by $\log c$, we obtain the final result, which is that $n \approx \frac{1}{\log c} \log \mathrm{Fib}_n$. Compute the value of $\frac{1}{\log c}$.

8. Modify the `expressionInformation` data structure so as to also accommodate integer values. Then modify the parsing algorithm so that it will recognize integer constants.

9. Modify the expression tree parsing algorithm so that it will recognize identifiers of more than one character in length.

10. The following is a complete binary tree of depth four.

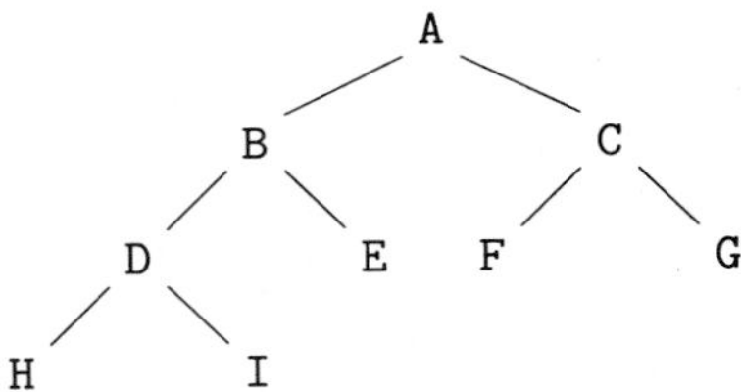

For each of the traversal algorithms we have described (preorder, inorder, postorder, and level-order), describe the sequence in which nodes would be processed.

11. Describe the sequence of index values used in the various tree traversals of the complete binary tree shown in Fig. 10.8 stored in the vector implementation of Section 10.1.1. Propose a general algorithm for each type of traversal.

12. Recall that the inorder traversal of an expression tree did not yield the original expression, since parentheses grouping was lost. One possible solution to this problem is to print out an opening parenthesis prior to visiting every child node, and a close parenthesis after visiting each child. This, however, results in far too many parentheses. For the expression tree shown in Figure 10.6, the result would be $((a) + (((b) + (c)) * (d)))$. Describe a recursive algorithm that prints out the minimal number of parentheses necessary. For this example expression tree, it should produce the original expression $a + (b + c) * d$.

13. Investigate empirically the relative execution speeds of the various iteration techniques. Do this by constructing a somewhat large tree, then iterating over the nodes several times. Make several timings of the program execution using the different iteration techniques.

14. Threaded lists: Notice that left nodes in binary trees do not use their child pointer fields, although space is allocated for these. The late Alan J. Perlis described an ingenious algorithm to make use of this otherwise wasted space

[Perlis 60]. Suppose we have a means of distinguishing two types of pointers; one possibility is to maintain a one-bit field with each pointer, another possibility is to use positive and negative values for pointers. One type of pointer will be used for ordinary purposes. The second type, called a *thread*, will be used in child nodes, in which case the pointer will refer to the next node in the inorder traversal of the list.

a. Describe an inorder iterator for these lists, and show that this data structure need maintain no more than a single pointer field.

b. (Harder) Describe the new insertion algorithm for this data structure that maintains the threads.

c. (Harder still) Describe the removal algorithm for this data structure.

15. Rewrite the family tree shown in Fig. 10.1 (page 276) using the binary tree representation of general trees described in Section 10.4 (page 305). What is the depth of the resulting tree?

16. In Section 10.4 we described how general trees could be represented as binary trees, but we did not produce working code for the data abstraction. Create a class definition that implements this technique for representing general tree structures. What methods should your class provide?

CHAPTER 11

Searching

IN THIS CHAPTER we will investigate data structures that are useful when a predominate task in a problem is discovering whether a certain element is contained in a collection. We have seen techniques that can be used to answer such queries in at least one of the data structures we have previously developed. The `list` data type provides the function `includes`, which will indicate whether or not an element is contained in a list. In this case, however, the operation is performed by searching linearly through the collection, thus in the worst case requiring n comparisons. This is true even if we maintain the list in sequence, using the `orderedList` data type. If a test for inclusion is a common operation, then alternative data structures must be used to obtain more efficient execution.

11.1 DIVIDE AND CONQUER

To see how this might be possible, consider a vector that contains elements in sorted order. An example is the following list of names. We have seen already, in Section 8.4.1, one algorithm that could be used to generate such a list from an unorganized vector of values. We will see another algorithm later in this chapter.

0	1	2	3	4	5	6	7	8	9	10
Abigail	Abner	Adam	Adela	Agnes	Alex	Alice	Allen	Angela	Arthur	Audrey

Imagine we are attempting to discover whether the name "Amanda" occurs in the list. We could just walk through the list in turn, as is done by the `includes` method in the class `list`. This would require 11 comparisons before we could say for certain the name was not present.[1] An alternative strategy is to compare the element we are searching for with the *middle* element of the vector. In our case this is element number 5, which holds the value "Alex." With a single comparison of "Alex" to "Amanda," we can tell (since "Alex" is lexicographically smaller than "Amanda") that the value "Amanda" cannot occur in the first six elements. Thus in one stroke we have eliminated more than half the possibilities for a match and thus reduced the size of the problem by half.

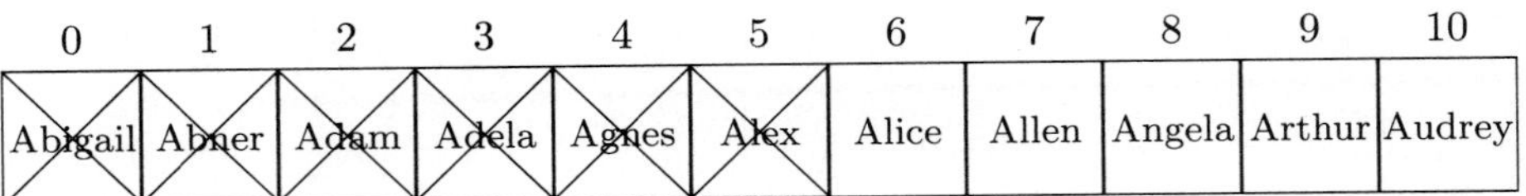

This is an example of the general problem-solving heuristic *divide and conquer* that was first introduced in Chapter 1. The basic idea of divide and conquer is to choose an initial step that divides the problem roughly in half. The greatest benefit of the heuristic occurs when we apply the technique recursively. We know now that "Amanda" must occur, if it occurs at all, in the latter half of the list. Thus our second query attempts to divide this in half, by comparing "Amanda" to position 8, which contains "Angela." Since "Amanda" is less than "Angela," we know the name does not occur any later than position 8.

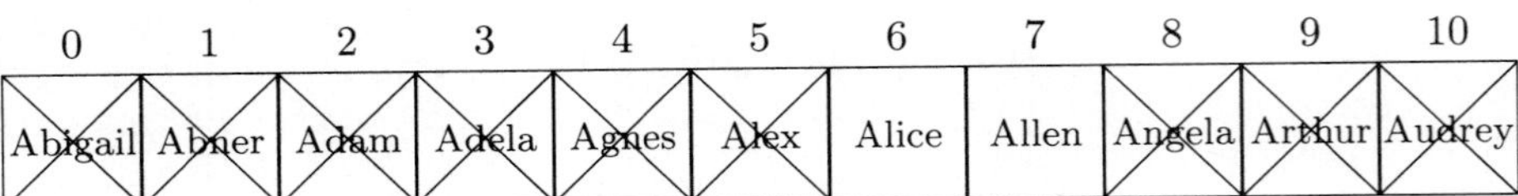

The next comparison is to position 6. When no match occurs, we know the only possibility is position 7. This comparison is then sufficient to tell us that the name "Amanda" does not occur in the list. The most important feature is that we have been able to discover this fact with only four comparisons, instead of the 11 comparisons required for the brute-force approach.

1. To be totally accurate, the search could actually be abandoned after nine comparisons if we remembered that the list was ordered.

```
template<class VecType, class EleType>
unsigned int binarySearch(VecType data, EleType value, unsigned int max)
{   // perform binary search on data, seeking index of value
    unsigned int low = 0;
    unsigned int high = max;

    while (low < high) {

        // inv: data[0..low-1] are all less than value
        // data[high..max] are all greater than value
        unsigned int mid = (low + high) / 2;
        if (data[mid] < value)
            low = mid + 1;
        else
            high = mid;
        }

    // return element for which data[0..low-1] less than value
    // and value less than or equal to data[low]
    return low;
}
```

Figure 11.1 The binary search algorithm

11.2 BINARY SEARCH

The technique illustrated by the example in the last section is known as *binary search*. We can formalize the technique in the procedure shown in Fig. 11.1. The procedure takes three arguments: the data structure to be searched, the element being searched for, and the number of values in the collection. We parameterize the template definition by two classes, rather than simply the element type, so that it can be used both with instances of class `vector` and with conventional C++ vectors.

If the element being tested is smaller than the largest (and last) value in the vector, the algorithm will return the position i such that all values $data[j], j < i$ are smaller than $data[i]$, and the tested element is less than or equal to $data[i]$. If the element being searched for is larger than the largest element in the array, then the value `max` will be returned. One way to picture this is to imagine that the next data position, $data[max]$, contains an infinitely large value. Then the first description of the result holds for all values.

The algorithm proceeds by manipulating two values. The variable `low` is the smallest index value that could possibly match the element being tested. The variable `high` is the first position that is definitely known to be larger than the element. The invariant for the loop simply preserves these properties. The values `low` and `high` are initially 0 and the vector size, which is one larger than the maximum index value. In each iteration of the loop, we examine the midpoint. For the purposes of showing correctness, it is only necessary that the midpoint be larger than or equal to `low` and smaller than or equal to `high`. If the data item at `mid` is smaller than the test element, then all values smaller than the midpoint must be smaller than the element, and thus we can make `low`, which represents the lowest value that could possibly match the element, be `mid + 1`. On the other hand, if the data value is larger than or equal to the test element, then we can set the value of `high` to the midpoint with the certainty that all elements associated with index values high or greater are larger than the test element.

To prove termination, we must ensure that either `low` or `high` is changed on each iteration of the loop. This in fact depends upon a property of integer division, which is that for non-negative values, division rounds *down* to the next lower value in cases where a fractional value would result. Thus, if $low < high$ then $(low + high)/2$ must be strictly smaller than $high$ (although it could be the same as low). With this assumption, we then know that either `low` is being set to `mid` + 1, in which case it is clearly increasing in value, or `high` is being set to `mid`, in which case it is decreasing.

11.2.1 Application — Root Finding

The idea behind the binary search technique can be used in many applications, not simply in searching vectors of values. We illustrate this by

Comparisons

It almost goes without saying that in order for binary search, search trees, or almost any other searching algorithm to work, we need the ability to compare two elements. Note that this was not true for the `list` data structure. The only operator we used in developing lists was the equality test operator, ==, used to determine if two values were equal. Here we require in addition the relational operator, <, to determine if one value is less than another. As always, when a new data type is created, these can be overridden by programmers to have any desired meaning. Usually, when comparisons are overridden, programmers will want to define the four relational operators (<, <=, >=, and >) as well as the two equality testing operators (== and ! =). It is also important that whatever meaning is attached to these operators satisfy the transitivity relation, which is if $x < y$ and $y < z$ then $x < z$, and the inverse relation, which is if $x < y$ is true then $y < x$ is false.

The algorithms we develop will only use the operators < and ==. Thus a minimal data type need only define these two in order to be used with the data structures described in this book.

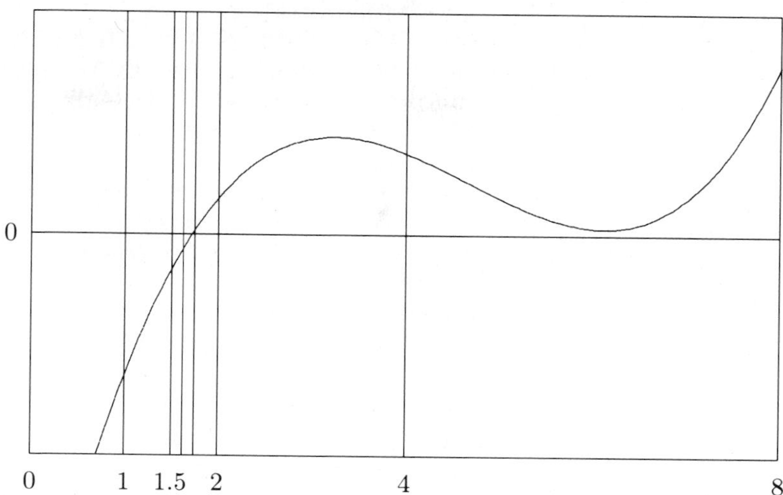

Figure 11.2 Steps in discovering a root of a function

describing how binary search can be used to discover a root of a function. (A root is the point where the function has value zero.) Figure 11.2 shows a portion of the graph for the function $x^3 - 14x^2 + 59x - 65$. If we evaluate the function at 0, and again at 8, we can readily see that the *signs* of the two results are different; that is, one value is positive and the other is negative. Therefore the function must cross the zero axis somewhere in between. The invariant maintained by our root-finding algorithm will be to preserve this property; that is, at each step we compute the midpoint value. Either the low or high value is changed to this midpoint value so as to maintain the property that the sign of the function at the low value is different from the sign of the function at the high value. When the low and high positions are sufficiently close (a condition determined by a factor provided by the user), we return the result, which is presumably close to the root value.

A procedure that implements this idea is shown in Fig. 11.3. To determine if two quantities have different signs, the values are multiplied together. If the result is less than or equal to zero, then the quantities must have different signs; otherwise they have the same sign. When applied to the function shown in Fig. 11.2, the algorithm first examines location 4. Since the value of the function at 4 is also positive, we know the root must be between 0 and 4. Thus location 2 is examined next, with the same result. The value of the function at location 1 is negative, so the lower bound can be changed to that value. The sequence of values examined next continues in this fashion, examining 1.5, 1.75, 1.625, 1.71875, and so on. Within 10 iterations the root can be determined to within 0.01.

```
double rootSearch
    (double (&f)(double), double low, double high, double epsilon)
{   // search the function argument for a root between low and high
    // make sure there is a root in the range
    assert(f(low) * f(high) <= 0);

    // search while range is larger than epsilon
    while (epsilon < (high - low)) {
        // inv: f(low) and f(high) have different signs
        // examine mid point
        double mid = (high + low) / 2.0;
        // replace either high or low
        if (f(mid) * f(high) <= 0)
            low = mid;
        else
            high = mid;
        // inv: f(low) and f(high) have different signs
        }

    // return midpoint of last region
    return (high + low) / 2.0;
}
```

Figure 11.3 A binary search root-finding algorithm

11.3 ORDERED VECTORS

We can use the ability to perform binary search, add it to the ability of our vector data structure to dynamically change size, and from these create a variety of vector that can be very efficiently searched to determine if it contains a specific element. The class declaration for our new data structure can be given as follows:

```
//
// class orderedVector
//     vector maintained in sorted order
//

template <class T> class orderedVector {
public:
    // constructors
    orderedVector();
    orderedVector(const orderedVector & v);

    // subscript
```

```
    T &        operator [ ]        (unsigned int index) const;

    // protocol for searching
    void       add                 (T value);
    void       deleteAllValues     ();
    int        includes            (T value) const;
    int        isEmpty             () const;
    void       remove              (T value);

private:
    // data area is vector for values
    vector<T> data;

    friend class orderedVectorIterator<T>;
};
```

The actual data values are stored in a vector, declared as a private data field in the structure. As we will see when we describe the insertion algorithm, the values will be maintained in order. The default constructor initializes the size of the vector to zero, while the copy constructor copies values from the data area in the argument vector. A few of the other methods are similarly trivial. To delete all values, the size of the data vector is once again made zero. Testing to see if the collection is empty is simply a way of seeing if the length of the data area is zero.

The remaining operations all use binary search. To see if a particular value is present in the collection, we perform a binary search on the data vector. If the index returned by the search represents a valid position (remember, the index could be the size of the array, should the element being searched for be larger than any value held by the array), then if the index value corresponds to the requested value it is present in the collection, otherwise it is not present in the collection.

```
template <class T> int orderedVector<T>::includes(T value) const
{   // see if vector includes given element
    unsigned int max = data.length();
    unsigned int index = binarySearch(data, value, max);
    // if value is the right element, return 1
    if (index < max)
        if (value == data[index])
            return 1;
    // not found
    return 0;
}
```

Using this procedure, we can search for a collection of n elements in $O(\log n)$ steps.

To add a value to the collection is more difficult. To illustrate the procedure, consider adding the value *Adam* to the following collection:

0	1	2	3	4	5
Abigail	Adela	Agnes	Alex	Alice	Audrey

To insert a new value, we first make the collection one element larger; creating a "hole" at the end.

0	1	2	3	4	5	6
Abigail	Adela	Agnes	Alex	Alice	Audrey	

Next, all the elements in index positions larger than the location for the new element are moved over one location, thereby moving the "hole" down to the desired location.

0	1	2	3	4	5	6
Abigail		Adela	Agnes	Alex	Alice	Audrey

Finally, the new value is placed into the hole.

0	1	2	3	4	5	6
Abigail	Adam	Adela	Agnes	Alex	Alice	Audrey

The code to perform this insertion operation is as follows:

```
template <class T> void orderedVector<T>::add(T value)
{   // add a new element to an ordered vector collection
    // get the current length of the vector
    unsigned int max = data.length();

    // perform binary search to find proper location for element
    unsigned int index = binarySearch(data, value, max);

    // grow vector to new size
    data.setSize(max + 1);

    // move everything up to make space
```

```
    for (unsigned int i = max; i > index; i--)
        data[i] = data[i-1];

    // place element in location
    data[index] = value;
}
```

Unfortunately, asymptotic analysis of this procedure is not encouraging. Although the binary search can be performed very quickly, the `setSize` operation requires, in the worst case, $O(n)$ steps for a vector of n elements. Even without the change in size, the loop to shift elements right by one position can still require $O(n)$ iterations. Thus insertions are considerably slower than lookup for this data structure. Later in this chapter we will explore several data structures that have both efficient lookup and efficient insertion.

Although these subsequent structures will be faster, they have the disadvantage of also requiring more space. Thus the ordered vector data structure is preferable in situations where space is important, or where lookup operations are performed much more frequently than additions or removal of elements.

The implementation of the remaining method, `remove`, is left as an exercise. A final note on the ordered vector data type is the observation that an iterator for this data structure is trivial to implement using inheritance, by building on top of the vector iterator class.

```
template <class T>
class orderedVectorIterator : public vectorIterator<T>
{
public:
    orderedVectorIterator(orderedVector<T> & x);
}
```

No operations need to be defined. The constructor merely invokes the constructor for the vector iterator class. All the iterator operations will be inherited from the vector iterator class.

```
template <class T>
orderedVectorIterator<T>::orderedVectorIterator(orderedVector<T> & x)
    : vectorIterator<T>(x.data)
{
    // no further initialization
}
```

11.4 BINARY SEARCH TREES

Binary search over a vector of values is an appropriate technique for the problem of *static* searching, where the data values are known in advance

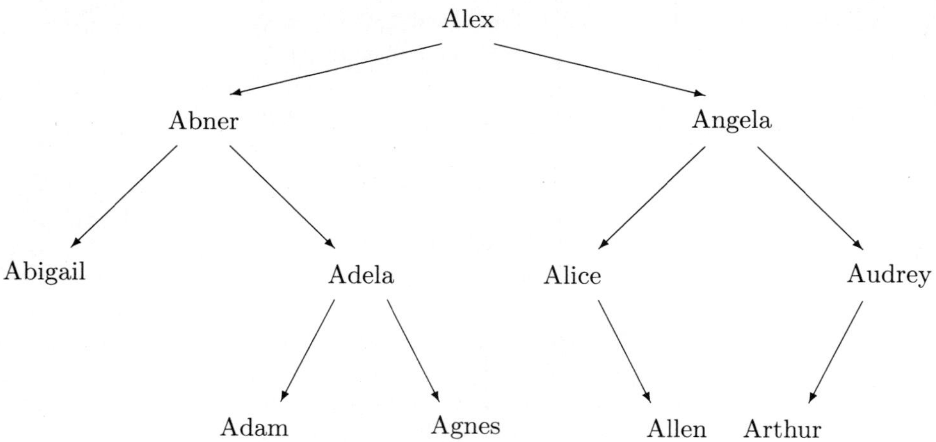

Figure 11.4 A binary search tree

and it is not possible to add or delete elements from the collection (or where addition and removal of elements is very infrequent). In the more general *dynamic* search problem, additions and deletions to the collection are permitted. In these cases a vector may not be an appropriate structure. As we noted in the last section, both addition and deletion to an ordered vector require, in the worst case, the movement of all elements with index values larger than the affected position and are thus $O(n)$ operations. Using alternative data structures, we can reduce this complexity significantly. One such data structure is the *binary search tree*.

A binary search tree is a binary tree with the following additional property: at each node, all the values associated with the descendants of the left child are less than or equal to the value of the node, and all the values associated with descendants of the right child are greater than the value of the node. An example of a binary search tree is shown in Fig. 11.4.

Determining whether a node is present in a binary search tree is relatively easy. All that is necessary is to follow a single path from the root to the leaf, checking at each node to determine whether the right or left child links should be recursively pursued. Since only one path needs to be traversed, the running time of the procedure is proportional to the length of the path, not the number of nodes in the tree. The following illustrates this search procedure:

```
int searchTree<T>::includes(T val) const
{   // see if argument value occurs in tree
    if (root) {
        node<T> * current = root;
        while (current) {
            if (current->value == val)
```

```
                return  1;
            if (current->value < val)
                current = current->right();
            else
                current = current->left();
            }
        }
    // not found
    return 0;
}
```

The method is from the class searchTree. The class definition is shown below. Adding a new element to the tree is similar to the inclusion test. The path that would lead to the element were it already in the tree is traced out; when the bottom of the tree is encountered, the new element is inserted. Thus the running time is again proportional to the length of the path from the root to the point of insertion, not to the total number of nodes in the tree.

```
//
// class searchTree
//     collection designed for fast insertion, test and
//     removal operations
//
template <class T> class searchTree {
public:
    // constructor
    searchTree     ();
    searchTree     (const searchTree &);
    ~searchTree    ();

    // protocol for search trees
    virtual void  add              (T value);
    void          deleteAllValues  ();
    int           includes         (T value) const;
    int           isEmpty          () const;
    virtual void  remove           (T value);

protected:
    // data areas
    node<T> *  root;
    friend class searchTreeIterator<T>;

    // method used internally to delete top node
    node<T> *  removeTop        (node<T> *);
};
```

The instructions used to perform insertion of a new element are as follows:

```
void searchTree<T>::add(T val)
{   // add value to binary search tree
    if (root) {
        node<T> * current = root;
        node<T> * child;
        while (current) {
            if (current->value < val) {
                // add to right subtree
                child = current->right();
                if (! child) {
                    current->right(new node<T>(val));
                    return;
                    }
                }
            else {
                // add to left subtree
                child = current->left();
                if (! child) {
                    current->left(new node<T>(val));
                    return;
                    }
                }
            current = child;
            }

        }
    else
        root = new node<T>(val);
}
```

The copy constructor for this class will use the add method to add values from the argument collection. Doing so permits us to use this same method for both search trees and for the class avlTree, which will be described later in this section.

```
template <class T> searchTree<T>::searchTree(const searchTree<T> & v)
{   // initialize tree by adding all the elements from argument
    searchTreeIterator<T> itr(v);
    for (itr.init(); ! itr; itr++)
        add(itr());
}
```

As is the case with many data structures, the removal of an item is the most complex task. The problem is divided into two steps. The first step is to discover the node that needs to be deleted. Here the algorithm is much the same as for the addition and inclusion test, and it is again proportional to the length of the path from root to node. Once the node is found, it must be removed. We cannot simply leave a hole in the data structure, so instead another node must be found to take the place of the eliminated value. The most important factor is to ensure the maintenance of the search tree property. There is one node that will satisfy this condition. The leftmost child of the right subtree rooted at the eliminated node is guaranteed to be both larger than the deleted value and smaller than all other values in the right side. Thus we remove this value and use it to replace the deleted node.

For example, suppose we wish to remove the value 5 from the following tree. Having found the node containing the value 5, we examine the right child, and search for the leftmost descendant of this right child. This yields the value 6, which is both larger than 5 and the smallest value in the right subtree. Thus the value 6 is removed from the right subtree, and it replaces the position of the deleted node 5. The `remove` method using this technique is shown in Fig. 11.5.

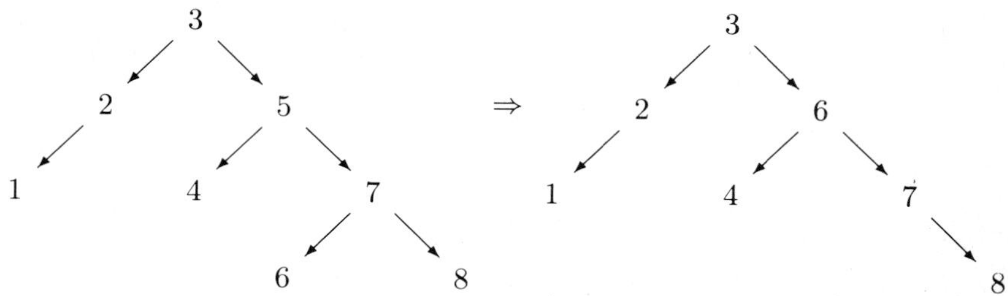

The `removeTop` procedure (Fig. 11.6) is passed the subtree rooted at the node that is to be deleted. It has four special cases. If the node to be deleted

Duplicate Keys

One source of variation in problems involving binary search trees is the question of whether duplicate keys are permitted. When trees are used to implement set-type structures (which we will be discussing in Chapter 14), duplicate keys are not permitted. In many other problems they cause no difficulty. In the case where duplicate keys are not permitted, there are again two possible techniques for resolving the problem when they occur. Most commonly, the new value replaces the old value in the tree. Alternatively, an error message can simply be produced.

The data structures discussed in this chapter make no attempt to prevent duplicate values from being inserted into collections.

```
void searchTree<T>::remove(T val)
{   // remove value from a binary search tree
    // no root, just quit
    if (! root)
        return;

    // deleting root
    if (root->value == val) {
        node<T> * newroot = removeTop(root);
        delete root;
        root = newroot;
        return;
        }

    // otherwise some other node
    node<T> * parent = root;
    while (parent != 0) {
        node<T> * child;
        if (parent->value < val) {
            // search right subtree
            child = parent->right();
            if (child && (child->value == val)) {
                parent->right(removeTop(child));
                delete child;
                child = 0;
                }
            }
        else {
            // search left subtree
            child = parent->left();
            if (child && (child->value == val)) {
                parent->left(removeTop(child));
                delete child;
                child = 0;
                }
            }
        parent = child;
        }
}
```

Figure 11.5 Removing an element from a binary search tree

```
node<T> * searchTree<T>::removeTop(node<T> * topNode)
{   // remove topmost node from
    //  a binary search tree
    node<T> * left = topNode->left();
    node<T> * right = topNode->right();

    // case 1, no left node
    if (left == 0)
        return right;

    // case 2, no right node
    if (right == 0)
        return left;

    // case 3, right node has no left node
    node<T> * n = right->left();
    if (n == 0) {
        right->left(left);
        return right;
        }

    // case 4, slide down left tree
    node<T> * parent = right;
    while (n->left() != 0) {
        parent = n;
        n = n->left();
        }
    // now parent point to n,
    // n has no left child
    // disconnect and move to top
    parent->left(n->right());
    n->left(left);
    n->right(right);
    return n;
}
```

Figure 11.6 Method to return a tree after removing the root node

does not have a left child, the right child can be simply returned. This requires only a constant amount of time. This would occur, for example, if we were to remove the value 7 from the tree from which we earlier removed to value 5. Alternatively, if the node to be deleted does not have a right child, then the left child can be returned. Again, this requires only a constant amount of time. An example here would be the removal of the value 2 from the earlier tree.

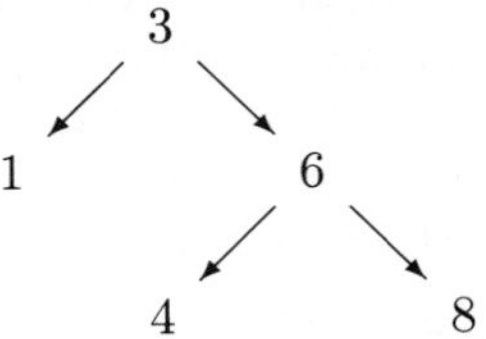

Let's assume that the node being eliminated has both left and right children, but the right child does not have a left child. Then since the left child of the root must by the search tree ordering property be less than the right child, the left child can be made the left child of the right node and the right node can be returned. This would occur if we were to now delete the value 6.

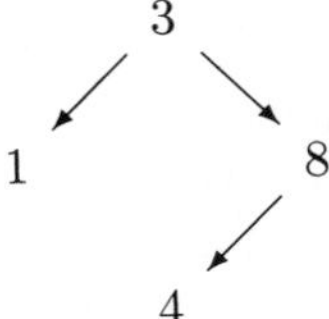

The most general case occurs if the eliminated node contains both a left child and a right child, and the right child in turn possesses a left child. An example would be the node containing the value 3. A loop iterates down the left children of the right node, finding the smallest element along the right side. This loop runs in time proportional to the length of the path from root to smallest child. This element can be easily removed from the right subtree, since the removal of this element is simply case 1 from above. This smallest element from the right side is then made the new root, with the former left subtree as its left child and the newly reformed right subtree as right child.

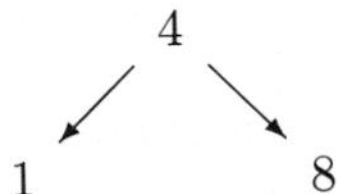

The removal of all elements from a search tree is accomplished by using the `release` method on the root node, then deleting the root. This method is also invoked by the destructor.

```
template <class T> void searchTree<T>::deleteAllValues()
{   // remove all values from tree
    if (root != 0) {
        root->release();
        delete root;
        root = 0;
        }
}
```

To list the elements of a search tree in order requires an inorder traversal of the search tree. Since the user does not have direct access to the nodes of the tree (because the `root` field is private), we define a simple iterator class that merely subclasses from the inorder traversal class. The only method that needs to be redefined is that used for initialization; all other methods are inherited directly from the tree traversal class.

```
template <class T>
class searchTreeIterator : public inorderTreeTraversal<T> {
public:
    // constructor
    searchTreeIterator     (searchTree<T> & tree);

    // initialize iteration, find first element
    virtual int      init  ();
private:
    // store reference to the entire tree
    searchTree<T> &  base;
};
```

The initialization method needs to set the root, then perform the initialization method from the inorder traversal class.

```
template <class T> int searchTreeIterator<T>::init()
{
    // first set root for the iterator
    setRoot(base.root);
    // then do inorder iterator initialization
    return inorderTreeTraversal<T>::init();
}
```

11.5 AVL TREES

We have been careful to note that the asymptotic complexity of each of the operations performed on search trees is proportional to the length of the path from the root to the node being manipulated. The major problem with search trees is that this value can be quite large. In a well-balanced tree, such as that shown in Fig. 11.4, the length of the longest path is roughly $\log n$. On the other hand, if we happen to insert elements into the tree in order, we can easily create the tree shown in Fig. 11.7. This is still a search tree, but the time to perform any operation will be $O(n)$, or linear in the number of nodes. This is simply a very expensive way to implement a linked list. In order to avoid this difficulty, we require a method to ensure that our search trees remain balanced. In this section we will investigate one simple technique to preserve this property.

An *AVL tree* attempts to guarantee efficient performance by maintaining the height-balanced characteristic discussed in the last chapter. That

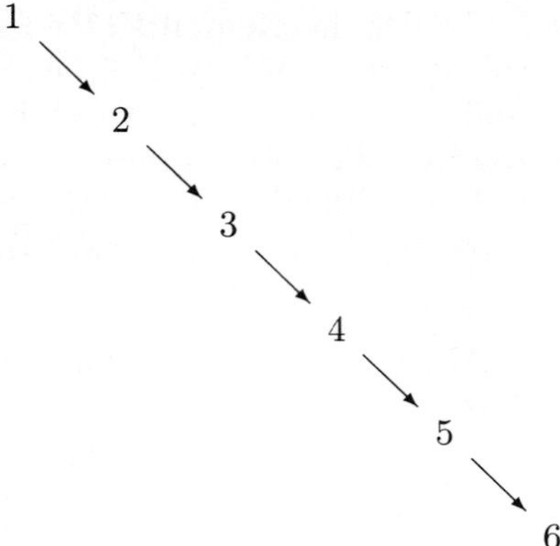

Figure 11.7 A very unbalanced search tree

is, for each node we maintain the property that the difference in heights between the left and right subtrees is no larger than one. The method for doing this was first described in 1962 by two Russian mathematicians, G. M. Adel'son-Vel'skiĭ and E. M. Landis, and the resulting binary search trees are named in their honor.

As we noted in the last chapter, in a height-balanced binary tree containing n nodes, the longest path cannot exceed roughly $1.5 \log n$. In order to maintain the height-balanced property, it is actually not necessary to know the height of each subtree. We can get by with only maintaining at each node a *balance factor* that indicates the difference in heights of the left and right subtrees. A value of -1 indicates the left child is "heavier";

Casts

There are two primary methods for changing the types associated with a particular value. We have seen, in earlier chapters, how constructors with a single argument can be used as conversion operators. A second technique used to change type is the *cast*. A cast is written as a type expression, enclosed in parentheses, preceding the expression to be changed. In our AVL node class, casts are used in the functions `left` and `right` to change the type of the value returned by the methods of the same name in the base class `node` from being a pointer to a `node`, instead of being a pointer to an `avlNode`.

Cast expressions, and in particular cast expressions involving pointers, should *always* be treated with suspicion. In converting from one pointer type to another, no actual data transformation is taking place. It is only the type the compiler associates with a value that is being altered. The run-time system cannot, in general, guarantee the legitimacy of the conversion. Thus extra care must be applied to ensure that no error can occur. In our particular case, the addition of new nodes is only accomplished by using the methods `left` and `right`. Since these can take only AVL nodes as arguments, we know that every node in an AVL tree must be an AVL node. Thus the conversion of the type is permissible.

that is, there is a path from root to leaf in the left child subtree of length n, for some value of n, whereas the longest path in the right child subtree is length $n - 1$. (It cannot be any smaller than $n - 1$ and still maintain the height-balanced property.) A balance factor of 0 will indicate that the longest paths in the two child subtrees are equal, while a value of 1 will indicate that the right child possesses the longest path.

The class definition for a node in our AVL tree is shown in Fig. 11.8. We subclass from the earlier class `node`. This permits us to use features of the earlier class, such as iterators. The binary search tree iterator will work as well for AVL trees. The AVL node class defines a large number of private facilitator methods, which we will shortly describe. More importantly, the methods `right` and `left` are overridden so as to require and return instances of `avlNode`, instead of simply `node`.

The class `avlTree` is similarly declared as a type of `searchTree`. Doing so permits us to inherit, without writing any additional code, those methods, such as the inclusion test, that do not depend upon the height-balanced property. Thus the only methods we need to describe are the techniques used to insert and remove an item from an AVL tree.

```
//
// class avlTree
//     a form of binary search tree that maintains
//     the height balance property
//     thus ensuring efficient operation
//

template <class T> class avlTree : public searchTree<T> {
public:
    // insertion procedure
    virtual void    add      (T value);

    // removal procedure
    virtual void    remove   (T value);

private:
    avlNode<T> *   rootptr();
};
```

We will consider first the problem posed by the addition of a new node to an AVL tree, and how transformations must be applied to maintain the height-balanced property. We will do so by working through a simple example, and then abstracting the general algorithm from the specific problems we encounter. Consider inserting the integer values 1 to 7 in order into an empty tree. Of course, inserting 1 into an empty tree causes no difficulty. An insertion of 2 yields the following structure.

```
//
// class avlNode
//     a single node in an avl tree
//

template <class T> class avlNode : public node<T> {
public:
    // constructor
    avlNode(T value);

    // redefine access to left and right children
    void            left    (avlNode * v);
    avlNode *       left    () const;
    void            right   (avlNode * v);
    avlNode *       right   () const;

    // insert a new node into tree
    avlNode *       add     (T value);

    // remove an item from tree, setting reference to containing node
    avlNode *       remove  (T , avlNode * &);

    // duplicate tree
    avlNode *       copy    () const;

private:
    short  balanceFactor;    // balance factor, either -1, 0 or 1

    avlNode *       singleRotateLeft        ();
    avlNode *       singleRotateRight       ();
    avlNode *       restoreLeftBalance      (int);
    avlNode *       restoreRightBalance     (int);
    avlNode *       balance                 ();
    avlNode *       removeLeftChild         (avlNode * &);
};
```

Figure 11.8 Class definition of an AVL tree node

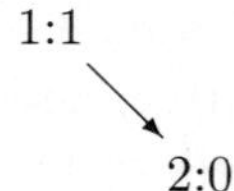

As with the earlier binary search trees, we first walk down the path until we discover a leaf node or interior node with only one child where the value can be inserted. The insertion is either along a left link or along a right link. In the case of the addition of 2, the insertion is along the right link. The number following the colon indicates the balance factors of each node.

There are actually two cases that can occur at the leaf. The situation we have seen occurs when the leaf node was balanced and thus becomes unbalanced. On the other hand, the leaf could have a child along the other branch. For example, suppose we were to now insert the value 0. The root would now become balanced.

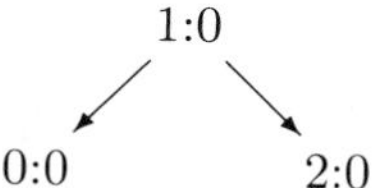

Instead of inserting 0, imagine now we continue the addition of ascending numbers. When we try to insert the value 3, we run into our first problem. The child node 2 has balance factor 1, and as a consequence the balance factor on the root is increased to 2. To rectify this, we perform a *rotation* to the left, making the node 2 into the new root.

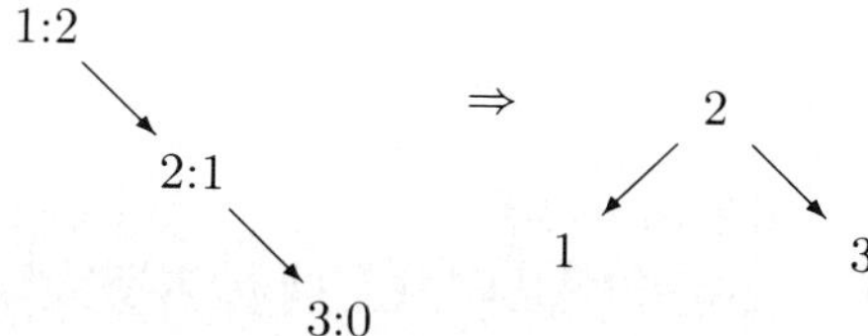

The question then becomes what the new balance factors should be for the node following the rotation. Rather than simply answering the question for this specific case, let us investigate the solution to the more general problem. Assume we are performing a rotation on a node A with right child B. Let the maximum height of the right subtree for A be n. If we let A_{bf} represent the balance factor for A, then the height of the left subtree must be $n - A_{bf}$. The heights of the child subtrees of B depend upon the balance factor for node B. If B_{bf} is positive, then we know the right subtree of node B must be $n - 1$ (since the right subtree is larger than the left, and with the addition of one more node the length of the subtree rooted at B must be n). Thus the height of the left subtree must be $(n - 1) - B_{bf}$. If B_{bf} is negative, the reverse argument can be given.

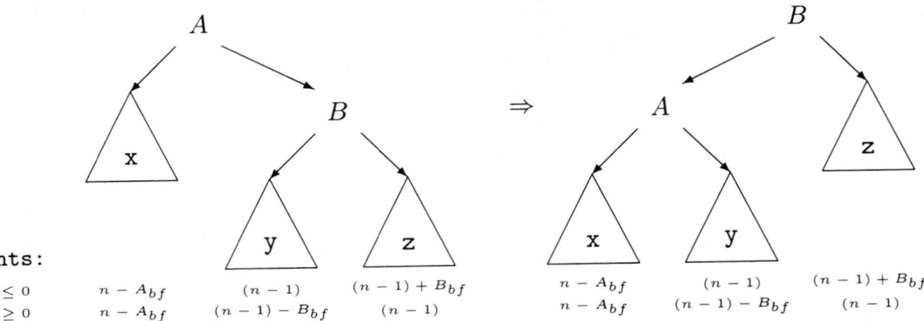

Suppose now we perform a left rotation, moving node A to a subordinate position and elevating node B to the root. The rotation preserves the search tree property, since all values in the left subtree of B (labeled y in our diagram) must be both greater than the value associated with A and less than the value associated with B. Since we know the heights of the two children, it is a simple matter to discover the balance factor for the new node A, expressed in terms of the balance factors A_{bf} and B_{bf}.

Condition	Balance Factor for A
$B_{bf} \le 0$	$(n-1) - (n - A_{bf}) = A_{bf} - 1$
$B_{bf} \ge 0$	$((n-1) - B_{bf}) - (n - A_{bf}) = A_{bf} - B_{bf} - 1$

Discovering the balance factor for B involves knowing the height of the new subtree rooted at A. Unfortunately, we don't know which of the children for A is the larger. Thus the previous two cases must each be further subdivided, yielding four cases. In the case where the balance factor of B is less than or equal to zero, the right subtree of A is larger if the balance factor of A is greater than or equal to 1; otherwise the left subtree is larger. Similarly, if the balance factor of B is greater than or equal to zero, the right subtree is larger if the balance factor of A is less than or equal to that of B; otherwise the left subtree is the larger of the two.

Condition	Height of A
$B_{bf} \le 0 \wedge A_{bf} \ge 1$	n
$B_{bf} \le 0 \wedge A_{bf} < 1$	$(n+1) - A_{bf}$
$B_{bf} \ge 0 \wedge A_{bf} \le B_{bf}$	$(n+1) - A_{bf}$
$B_{bf} \ge 0 \wedge A_{bf} > B_{bf}$	$n - B_{bf}$

Knowing the size of the subtree rooted at node A provides all the information we need to compute the new balance factor for B.

Condition	Balance Factor for B
$B_{bf} \leq 0 \wedge A_{bf} \geq 1$	$(n-1) + B_{bf} - n = B_{bf} - 1$
$B_{bf} \leq 0 \wedge A_{bf} < 1$	$(n-1) + B_{bf} - ((n+1) - A_{bf}) = A_{bf} + B_{bf} - 2$
$B_{bf} \geq 0 \wedge A_{bf} \leq B_{bf}$	$(n-1) - ((n+1) - A_{bf}) = A_{bf} - 2$
$B_{bf} \geq 0 \wedge A_{bf} > B_{bf}$	$(n-1) - (n - B_{bf}) = B_{bf} - 1$

In the situation that prompted our investigation of rotations, we had initially $A_{bf} = 2$ and $B_{bf} = 1$. Following the rotation all balance factors were zero. The reader should verify that the equations we developed will also yield the value zero.

The code used to perform a right or a left rotation on a node is given below. Both procedures return the new balanced root and update the balance factors according to the equations we have developed. The verification of the equations for the right rotation is left as an exercise.

```
avlNode<T> * avlNode<T>::singleRotateLeft()
{   // perform a single left rotation of the current node
    avlNode * nodeA = this;
    avlNode * nodeB = nodeA->right();
    // make reconnections
    nodeA->right(nodeB->left());
    nodeB->left(nodeA);
    // now update the balance factors
    int Abf = nodeA->balFac;
    int Bbf = nodeB->balFac;
    if (Bbf <= 0) {
        if (Abf >= 1)
            nodeB->balFac = Bbf - 1;
        else
            nodeB->balFac = Abf + Bbf - 2;
        nodeA->balFac = Abf - 1;
        }
    else {
        if (Abf <= Bbf)
            nodeB->balFac = Abf - 2;
        else
            nodeB->balFac = Bbf - 1;
        nodeA->balFac = (Abf - Bbf) - 1;
        }
    return nodeB;
}

avlNode<T> * avlNode<T>::singleRotateRight()
{   // make a single right rotation of current node
    avlNode * nodeA = this;
    avlNode * nodeB = nodeA->left();
```

```
    // make reconnections
    nodeA->left(nodeB->right());
    nodeB->right(nodeA);

    // now update the balance factors
    int Abf = nodeA->balFac;
    int Bbf = nodeB->balFac;
    if (Bbf <= 0) {
        if (Bbf > Abf)
            nodeB->balFac = Bbf + 1;
        else
            nodeB->balFac = Abf + 2;
        nodeA->balFac = 1 + Abf - Bbf;
        }
    else {
        if (Abf <= -1)
            nodeB->balFac = Bbf + 1;
        else
            nodeB->balFac = Abf + Bbf + 2;
        nodeA->balFac = 1 + Abf;
        }
    return nodeB;
}
```

Returning to our example, the insertion of the value 4 causes no difficulty. The insertion of the value 5 forces another left rotation, this time rooted at the right child node.

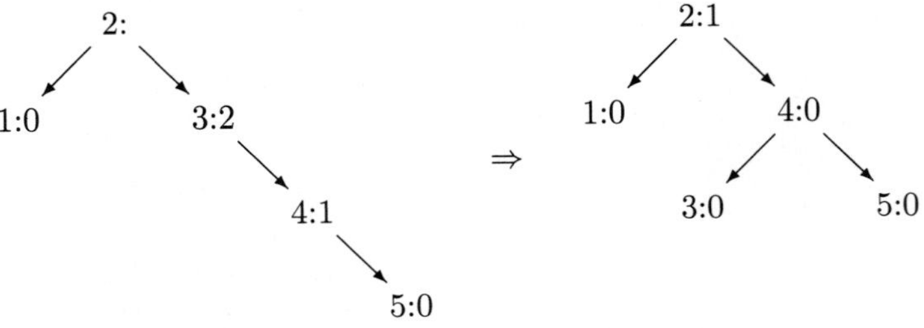

The insertion of 6 does not cause a balance problem for the child subtrees, but it does generate a problem for the root, since the left subtree has height 0 but the right subtree would have height 2. A single rotation restores the correct balance, by making the previous root, 2, a child of the new root 4. The insertion of 7 causes one last rotation, leaving us with a balanced tree.

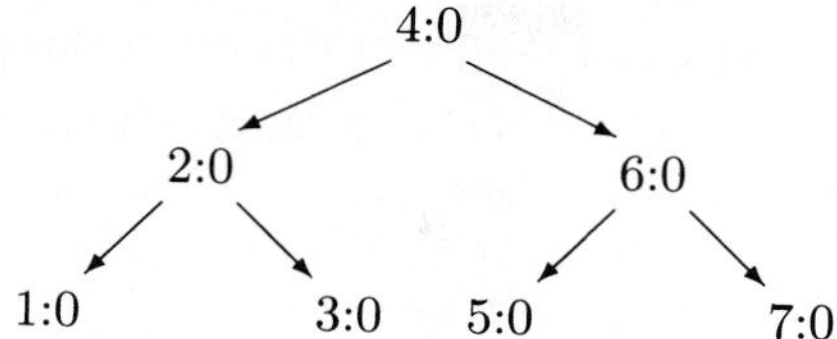

Occasionally, single rotations are not sufficient. To see this, let us continue inserting the values 15 and 16 in reverse order. The insertion of 16 is simple, but the insertion of 15 causes a height imbalance. Unlike the earlier cases, a single rotation is not sufficient to restore the height-balanced property.

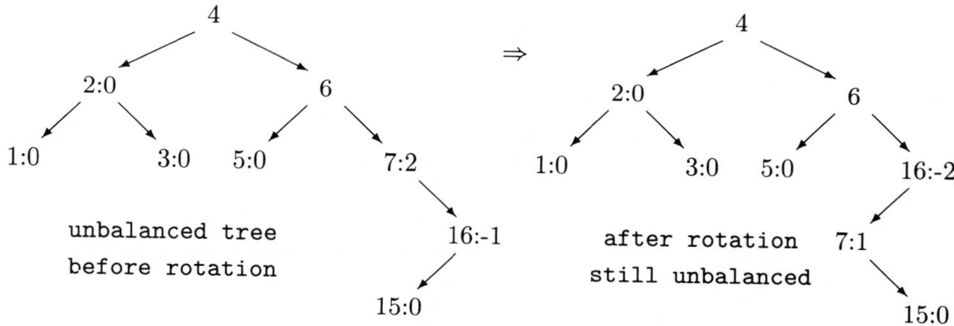

The problem arises when an insertion is made into the left child, causing the left child to become heavy, of a node that is itself a heavy right child. Using the equations we derived earlier, the reader can verify that this case, and the symmetric case for right child insertions, are the only two instances where a single rotation will produce a value that is not balanced. Fortunately, this situation is both easy to recognize and easy to handle. The solution is a combination of *two* single rotations, and it is thus called a *double* rotation. First, we perform a right rotation on the right child. This is followed by a left rotation at the point of the earlier imbalance.

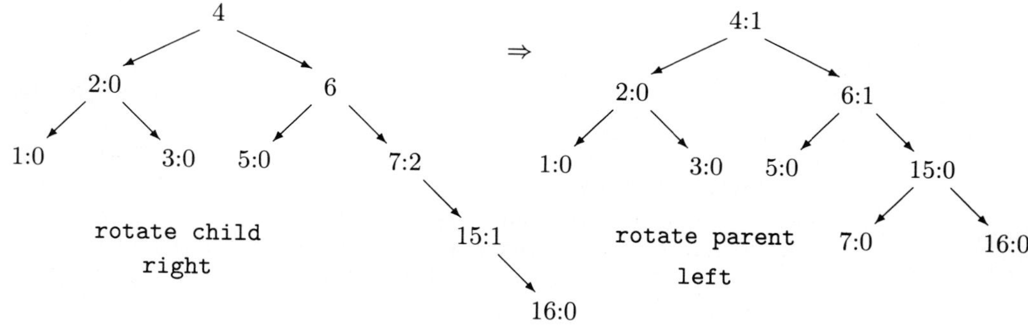

We may use the following procedure to rebalance a subtree, selecting either a single or double rotation as necessary.

```
avlNode<T> * avlNode<T>::balance()
{   // balance tree rooted at node
    // using single or double rotations as appropriate
    if (balFac < 0) {
        if (left()->balFac <= 0)
            // perform single rotation
            return singleRotateRight();
        else {
            // perform double rotation
            left(left()->singleRotateLeft());
            return singleRotateRight();
            }
        }
    else {
        if (right()->balFac >= 0)
            return singleRotateLeft();
        else {
            // perform double rotation
            right(right()->singleRotateRight());
            return singleRotateLeft();
            }
        }
}
```

Using this, we are finally in a position to present the code for insertion into an AVL tree: The method in class `avlTree` either creates a new root (if the tree is empty) or passes the request for insertion on to an existing node.

```
avlNode<T> * avlNode<T>::add(T val)
{   // add new element into balanced avl tree
    if (val < value) { // insert into left subtree
        if (left()) {
            int oldbf = left()->balFac;
            left(left()->add(val));
            // check to see if tree grew
            if ((left()->balFac != oldbf) && left()->balFac)
                balFac--;
            }
        else {
            left(new avlNode(val));
            // 0 becomes -1, 1 becomes 0
            balFac--;
            }
```

```
        }
    else {  // insert into right subtree
        if (right()) {
            int oldbf = right()->balFac;
            right(right()->add(val));
            // check to see if tree grew
            if ((right()->balFac != oldbf) && right()->balFac)
                balFac++;
            }
        else {
            right(new avlNode(val));
            // 0 becomes 1, -1 becomes 0
            balFac++;
            }
        }

    // check if we are now out of balance, if so balance
    if ((balFac < -1) || (balFac > 1))
        return balance();
    return this;
}
```

The method is class avlNode and it inserts into either the left or right subtree, updates the balance factors, and then rebalances if necessary.

```
void avlTree<T>::add(T val)
{   // add new value into balanced AVL tree
    if (root)
        root = rootptr()->add(val);
    else
        root = new avlNode<T>(val);
}
```

Both single and double rotations can be performed in constant time independent of the size of the subtrees they are manipulating. Insertion basically walks a path from root to leaf, then performs insertions when returning; thus when coupled with the observation concerning the longest path in a height-balanced tree, this is sufficient to show that insertion can be performed in $O(\log n)$ time. In fact, rotations are relatively rare. It can be shown that a single rotation is the most that is ever required to bring a height-balanced tree back into form following an insertion. This follows from the observation that a single or double rotation always results in a balanced subtree.

Removal of a node is similar to removal of a node from an ordinary search tree. A path is traced from the root to the node being removed. The first task is to find a new node to *replace* the deleted node. As we saw with search trees, the one candidate that preserves the search tree property is the leftmost descendant of the right child. A special case occurs if there is no right child, but this is easily handled. Once the leftmost descendant is found, we walk back up the tree, rebalancing as necessary. The leftmost descendant then replaces the deleted node, and we walk back to the root, rebalancing as necessary. Unlike the situation in insertion, during deletion several rotations may be necessary to bring the tree back into balance.

There are thus actually two removal algorithms. The first is used to find and remove a leftmost descendant. This algorithm is shown in

$O(\text{Log } n)$ Not a Lower Bound on Searching

It is tempting to conjecture that the $O(\log n)$ performance of the AVL tree is asymptotically the best that is possible for the searching problem. An argument to this effect might be made somewhat along the following lines. The element being matched could be any one of the n values in the collection, or it might not appear in the collection. Thus there are $n+1$ possible outcomes. We can represent the execution of the program itself as a tree, with leaves representing the final result and interior nodes representing statements where a choice is made. Since we know there are $n+1$ different outcomes, there must be at least $n+1$ leaves in this tree. But then we know there must be at least one path of length $\lceil \log n \rceil$ in this tree. Hence traversing the tree—that is, executing the program—requires at least $O(\log n)$ steps.

This argument is reasonably valid if the only operations permitted are comparisons of elements in the collection to the item being examined. The fallacy is to assume that this is the only possibility. Just as we used binary search to rule out large numbers of elements in the beginning of this chapter, we can use an alternative technique, `hashing`, to avoid many comparisons. Recall from Chapter 6 that a hash function was a mapping from element values on to the integers. In Chapters 14 and 17 we will see how hash functions can be used to implement very efficient data structures, called hash tables. By making use of an appropriate hash function, we can reduce the complexity of searching to almost constant time.

Is It Worth the Effort?

The AVL tree algorithms are surely nontrivial. Although their asymptotic performance is impressive, a real practical question is whether they are worth the effort. The answer, unfortunately, is not clear. If the values being added to a tree arrive in a relatively random fashion, and if deletions from the tree are infrequent, then a search tree would "likely" not get far out of balance even if we used the simple search tree algorithms and made no effort to rebalance the tree. On the other hand, if the values arrive in a nonrandom fashion (for example, in order) then the simple scheme would rapidly break down, and a tree such as that shown in Fig. 11.7 could easily be produced.

Since the interface for the class `searchTree` is identical to the interface for the class `AVLtree`, a simple solution is to try both. To change a program from using a search tree to using an AVL tree requires at most altering a few declaration statements. We must experiment with small but realistic test cases, and perform actual timings using both algorithms.

Fig. 11.9, which also shows the procedure used to rebalance a tree after deletion. There is a symmetric `restoreRightBalance` procedure, which is not shown. An interesting feature of the `removeLeftmostDescendant` method is the use of a reference to a pointer argument. This permits the value of a pointer variable to be modified in the subroutine and accessed in the method `remove`. Removal of a node is accomplished by the procedure shown in Fig. 11.10. A similar reference to pointer is used in the method `remove` to return a pointer to the eliminated node, so that it can be deleted properly by the method in the class `avlTree`, as follows:

```
void avlTree<T>::remove(T val)
{   // remove an element from an AVL Tree
    avlNode<T> * eliminatedNode = 0;
    if (root)
        root = rootptr()->remove(val, eliminatedNode);
    if (eliminatedNode)
        delete eliminatedNode;
}
```

11.6 APPLICATION — TREE SORT

Just as the ordered list data structure led naturally to the list insertion sorting algorithm (Section 8.4.1), so, too, does the search tree data structure naturally suggest a sorting algorithm. The basic idea behind the tree sort algorithm is the same as the basic idea underlying the list insertion sort. Elements of a vector are added, one by one, into a search tree. The addition process will naturally order the elements. Once all the elements have been ordered, an iterator is constructed to remove the elements and place them back into the vector.

```
template <class T> void treeSort(vector<T> & v)
{
    // declare a search tree of the correct type
    avlTree<T> sorter;

    // copy the entire vector into the tree
    vectorIterator<T> vitr(v);
    for (vitr.init(); ! vitr; vitr++)
        sorter.add(vitr());

    // now copy the values back into the array
    int i = 0;
    searchTreeIterator<T> itr(sorter);
    for (itr.init(); ! itr; itr++)
        v[i++] = itr();
}
```

```
avlNode<T> * avlNode<T>::removeLeftmostDescendant
    (avlNode * & childptr)
{   // find and remove the leftmost descendant of a node
    // first see if we are the left child
    avlNode * leftchild = left();
    if (! leftchild) {  // we are
        childptr = this;
        return right(); // remove self
        }

    // else save old bal factor of left child
    int oldbf = leftchild->balFac;

    // do the deletion
    left(leftchild->removeLeftmostDescendant(childptr));

    // fix up our balance factors
    return restoreLeftBalance(oldbf);
}

avlNode<T> * avlNode<T>::restoreLeftBalance(int oldbf)
{
    avlNode * leftchild = left();

    // fix up our balance factors
    if (! leftchild)
        balFac++;
    else if ((leftchild->balFac != oldbf) &&
         (leftchild->balFac == 0))
        balFac++;

    // rebalance if necessary
    if (balFac > 1)
        return balance();
    return this;
}
```

Figure 11.9 Finding and removing the leftmost descendant

```
avlNode<T> * avlNode<T>::remove(T val, avlNode * & junk)
{   // remove indicated node, returning node in variable junk
    if (val == value) { // we're it
        junk = this;
        // if no right child, return left
        if (! right())
            return left();
        // else find and remove smallest left
        // child of the right child
        int oldbf = right()->balFac;
        avlNode * newroot;
        right(right()->removeLeftmostDescendant(newroot));
        // connect new root
        newroot->left(left());
        newroot->right(right());
        newroot->balFac = balFac;
        return newroot->restoreRightBalance(oldbf);
        }
    else if (val < value) { // remove from left child
        if (! left())
            return this;     // no left child
        // do the deletion
        int oldbf = left()->balFac;
        left(left()->remove(val, junk));
        return restoreLeftBalance(oldbf);
        }
    else {  // remove from right child
        if (! right())
            return this;
        // do the deletion
        int oldbf = right()->balFac;
        right(right()->remove(val, junk));
        return restoreRightBalance(oldbf);
        }
}
```

Figure 11.10 Removal of a node from an AVL tree

The advantage of the tree sort algorithm over the list insertion sort is that the addition operation can be performed much more rapidly using a search tree than using an ordered list. In particular, the addition of all n elements of the vector input into the search tree can be performed in $O(n \log n)$ steps. Since the traversal to copy the values back into the vector is linear, this means the total asymptotic running time of the algorithm is $O(n \log n)$.

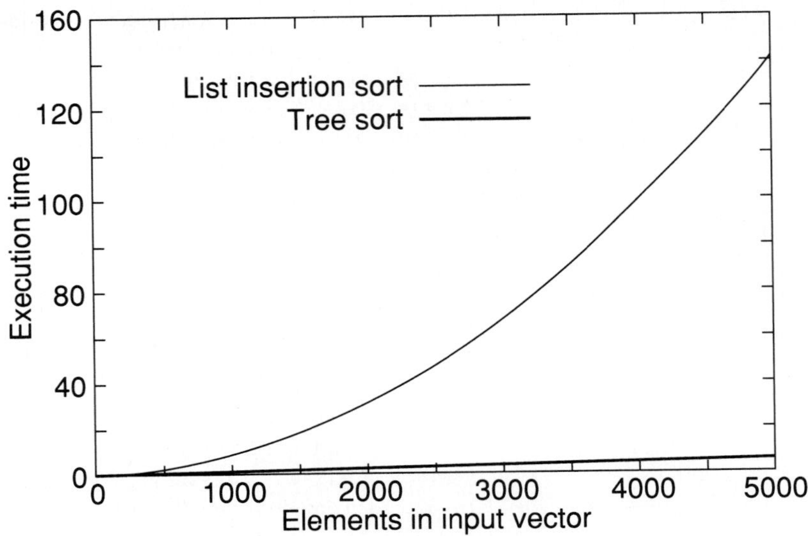

Figure 11.11 A comparison of list insertion sort and tree sort

To better understand the difference between an $O(n^2)$ algorithm and an $O(n \log n)$ algorithm, consider the graph shown in Fig. 11.11. This graph compares the running time of list insertion sort, which is the best sorting procedure we have seen up to this point, with the tree sort algorithm. At the far right side of the graph, where list insertion sort requires approximately 150 seconds to sort an array of 5000 elements, the tree sort algorithm requires only about 5 seconds.

In fact, to get an impression of the asymptotic growth in the running time for the tree sort algorithm, we need to consider far larger values (Fig. 11.12). For a 7000-element vector, the list insertion sort requires over four minutes. The running time of the tree sort algorithm is hardly noticeable. In fact, the tree sort algorithm can sort vectors 10 times this size in only slightly over two minutes, and sort a vector of 100,000 elements in less than four minutes. To sort a vector of this size would require more than 16 hours using list insertion sort. To sort a vector of this size using bubble sort would require 185,000 seconds, or approximately two days.

11.7 FINDING THE N^{TH} LARGEST

In this section we will consider a slightly different searching problem, which is to find the Nth largest element in a vector of values. To simplify matters, we will match N to the range of valid vector index positions. Thus the smallest element will be discovered by asking for element 0, the next smallest by asking for element 1, the median (midpoint) by asking for element $n/2$ (where n is the length of the vector), and so on.

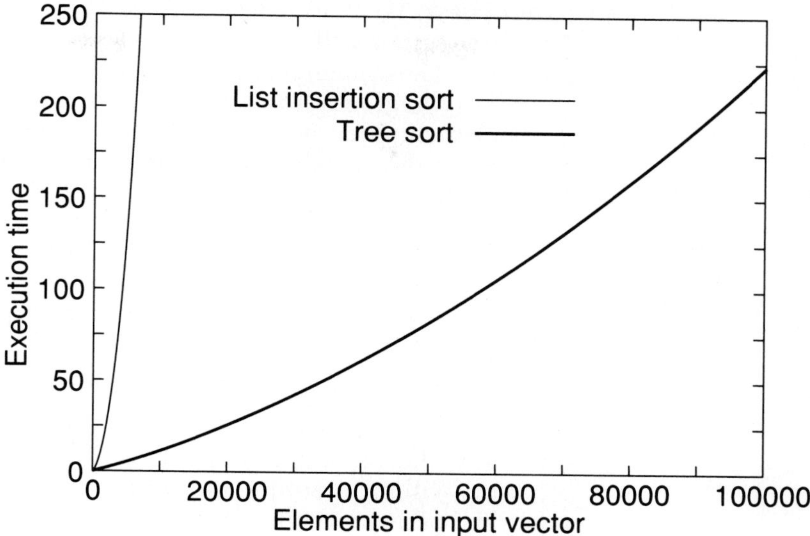

Figure 11.12 The asymptotic execution time of tree sort

A simple and obvious algorithm is to first sort the vector. The Nth largest value would then be the value contained at index position N. Using the tree sort algorithm we just encountered, the sorting process can be performed in $O(n \log n)$ operations. Since indexing of a vector can be performed in constant time, we see that we can discover the Nth largest value in a vector of n elements in no more than $O(n \log n)$ steps.

But sorting is doing much more work than is necessary. The sorted vector will tell us the position of each value in the ordered array, not simply the single value we are seeking. If we are interested in only *one* position (the median, for example), then we might think there is a better (that is, faster) algorithm that can be employed. In fact, there is a faster algorithm. Even more interesting, an investigation of this new algorithm will lead to the development of an elegant sorting algorithm.

The key step in the improved searching algorithm will be to *partition* the vector into two components. Suppose, for example, we have the following vector of eleven values. Imagine that we wish to discover the median value, which would be the element in index position 5 of the sorted vector.

2	97	17	37	12	46	10	55	80	42	39

To start, we will simply guess an answer. Let us guess that the value found in index position 3—that is, 37—is the answer. To see if we are correct, we will systematically compare every element in the collection to our guess. We rearrange the elements of the vector into two sections. The first section will be those elements that are smaller than or equal to the guess. Those elements in the second section will be the elements that are strictly larger than the guess. When we are finished, we will put the guess element back between the two groups, and return the new index position for the guess element (which may or may not be the position we are seeking).

<= pivot   pivot ↓   > pivot

12	10	17	2	37	97	46	55	80	42	39

An algorithm to perform this partition step is shown in Fig. 11.13. Traditionally, the value of the "guess" is known as the *pivot*, since all other elements will pivot around the value. The first step in the algorithm is to move the pivot to the beginning of the array, by swapping the pivot position with the first element. The index values `low` and `high` then move toward each other. The invariant to be preserved is that those values in positions smaller than `low` contain values smaller than or equal to the pivot, while those values in positions greater than `high` contain values that are larger than the pivot. Values held in positions between `low` and `high` are unexamined, and hence unknown. A typical snapshot in the middle of execution might be described by the following diagram:

During each step through the loop, either the value `low` is incremented, if the next position in sequence is smaller than the pivot, or the value `high` is decremented, if the value pointed to by `high` is greater than the pivot. If neither of these two conditions is satisfied, then two elements are out of place and can be swapped. When the index values `low` and `high` have met and passed each other, then all values will have been examined.

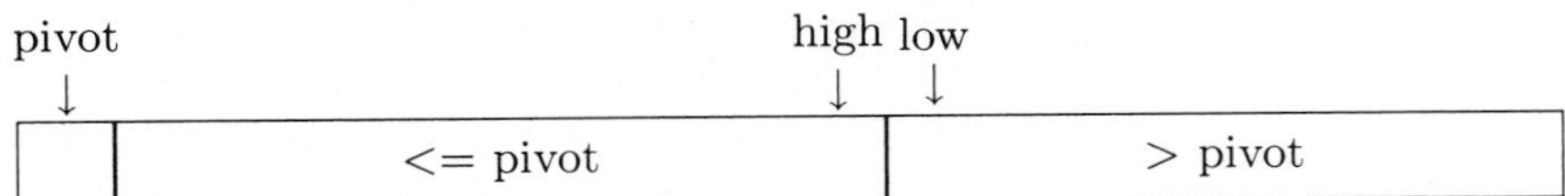

The final step is to move the pivot element between the two groups. Since the index value contained in `high` points to the last value is definitely known to be smaller than or equal to the pivot, we can swap this value with the pivot value.

```
template <class T>
unsigned int partition(vector<T> & v, unsigned int low,
    unsigned int high, unsigned int pivotIndex)
{
    // move the pivot value to the bottom of the vector
    if (pivotIndex != low)
        swap(vec, low, pivotIndex);
    pivotIndex = low;
    low++;

    // invariant:
    //  v[i] for i less than low are less than or equal to pivot
    //  v[i] for i greater than high are greater than pivot

    // move elements into place
    while (low <= high) {
        if (v[low] <= v[pivotIndex])
            low++;
        else if (v[high] > v[pivotIndex])
            high--;
        else
            swap(v, low, high);
        }

    // put pivot back between two groups
    if (high != pivotIndex)
        swap(v, pivotIndex, high);
    return high;
}
```

Figure 11.13 The vector partition algorithm

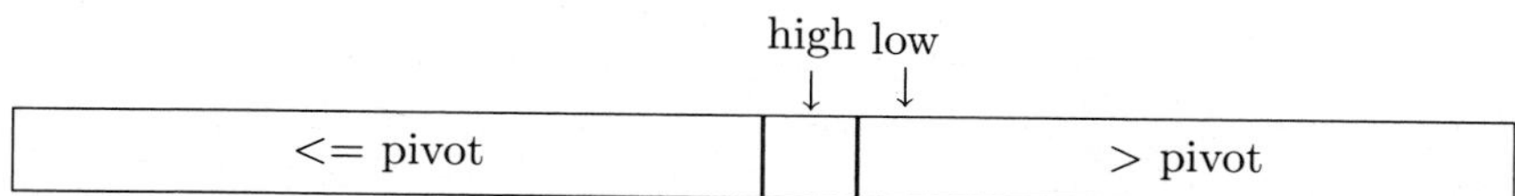

The resulting new position for the pivot following partitioning is either the index value we were seeking, or it is not. If it is, then we are finished. If it is not, then it might at first appear that little information has been gained. But this is not necessarily the case. We have, in fact, divided the vector into two portions. Just as with binary search, we can in one step immediately rule out a large number of possible answers. By comparing the resulting index position for the pivot to the position we are seeking, we can recursively search either the lower or the upper portion of the transformed vector. The algorithm that results from this insight is as follows:

```
template <class T>
T findElement(vector<T> & v, unsigned int N,
        unsigned int low, unsigned int high)
{
    // first select a pivot
    unsigned int pivotIndex = (high + low)/2;

    // partition the vector
    pivotIndex = partition(v, low, high, pivotIndex);

    // see if we are done
    if (pivotIndex == N)
        return v[N];

    // else try again
    if (N < pivotIndex)
        return findElement(v, N, low, pivotIndex);
    else
        return findElement(v, N, pivotIndex, high);
}
```

How fast is this algorithm? It is relatively easy to see that the partition step will run in time proportional to the section of the vector it is processing. (To see this, note that each element in this section is examined only once.) The worst case running time of the `findElement` algorithm, however, depends upon how lucky we are in finding good pivot positions. The best case occurs if we just happen to stumble upon the answer before we have recursed very many times. The next best case occurs when the algorithm recursively calls itself until a partition consisting of just a single element is found, but the algorithm is fortunate in the selection of pivot elements. This happens when every pivot divides the vector roughly in half.

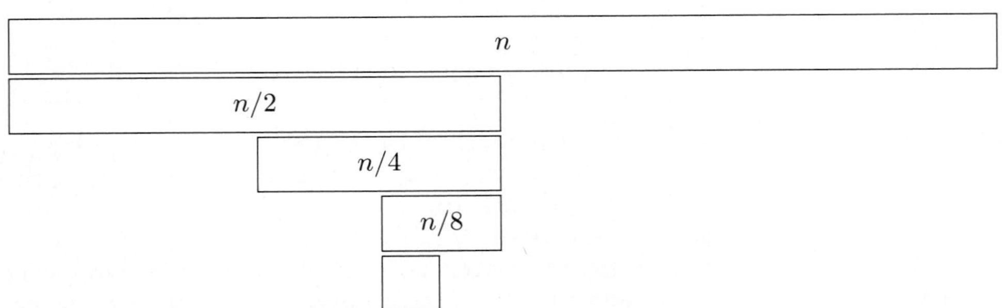

Execution time in this case is proportional to the sum $n + \frac{n}{2} + \frac{n}{4} + \cdots + 1$. If we factor out the common n term, the remaining sum can be expressed as $1 + \frac{1}{2} + \frac{1}{4} + \cdots$. The infinite series given by this pattern is bounded by the value 2, and thus any finite initial portion of the series must be similarly bounded. This is sufficient to show that in the best case the `findElement` algorithm will run in $O(n)$ steps.

But what if we make a series of bad choices for the pivot value? The worst choice for a pivot would be one that represents either the largest or the smallest element in the collection. In this situation one or the other of the vectors will be empty, and with $O(n)$ work we will have succeeded in eliminating only *one* element.

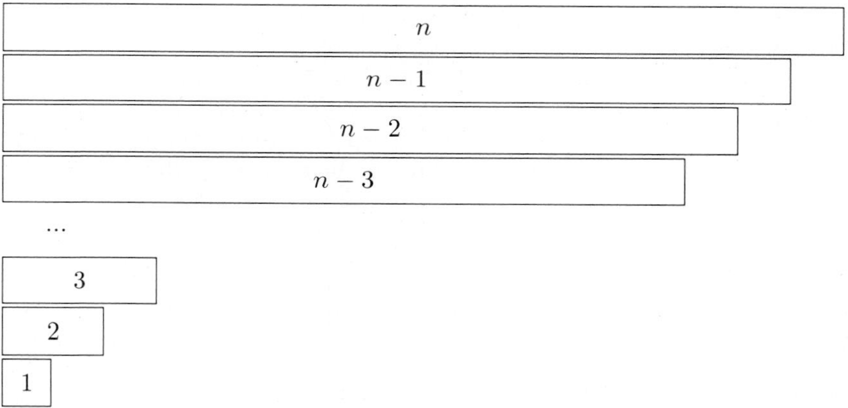

The series that results from this string of poor choices is $n + (n-1) + (n-2) + \cdots + 1$. As we have seen in earlier chapters, this series characterizes an algorithm with $O(n^2)$ operations. This is even worse than our naive approach which first sorted the vector.

So `findElement` is an algorithm that has terrific best case performance and terrible worst case performance. How does it perform in the "average" case? Are there techniques that can be used to ensure the worst case performance is relatively rare? The answer to the first question is that on average the `findElement` algorithm performs very quickly. Unfortunately, the mathematics necessary to formally prove this is beyond our presentation here.

The key to positively ensuring fast performance is to try to intelligently select the pivot value. Various authors have proposed different strategies to do this, including the following:

- ▲ Simply use the first element as the pivot value. This avoids the need for the initial swap, but it is a relatively poor choice if the vector is somewhat, but not completely, ordered.

- Select the pivot at random from the range of values.
- Select the pivot as the value in the midpoint of the range of elements. (This is the option used in our version of the algorithm.)
- Select three values from the range, and compute the median (middle) value from these three.

Readers interested in more complete analysis of these, and many other, possibilities can investigate the references cited at the end of this chapter.

11.7.1 Application — Quicksort

The partition algorithm shown in Fig. 11.13 is at the heart of one of the smallest, fastest, most elegant and interesting sorting algorithms known. The algorithm was named *quicksort* by its originator, Tony Hoare, now of Oxford University. The idea behind quicksort is simple. After one partition step, we have not entirely sorted a vector, but we have made some progress. For example, following the partitioning of the 11-element vector we described in the last section, the vector held the following values:

<= pivot				pivot ↓		> pivot				
2	17	12	10	37	97	46	55	80	42	39

Although the elements are not sorted, they are at least closer to their final destination. To obtain a full sorting, we simply recursively call the quicksort procedure, in order to sort each of the two subvectors resulting from the partition. This algorithm can be given as follows:

```
template <class T>
void quickSort(vector<T> & v, unsigned int low, unsigned int high)
{
    // no need to sort a vector of zero or one elements
    if (low >= high)
        return;

    // select the pivot value
    unsigned int pivotIndex = (low + high) / 2;

    // partition the vector
    pivotIndex = partition(v, low, high, pivotIndex);

    // sort the two sub arrays
    if (low < pivotIndex)
        quickSort(v, low, pivotIndex - 1);
```

```
    if (pivotIndex < high)
        quickSort(v, pivotIndex + 1, high);
}
```

To make an algorithm that takes only a single vector argument, matching the format for the other sorting algorithms we have seen, we can overload the function name and create an alternative procedure that merely invokes the recursive routine.

```
template <class T> void quickSort(vector<T> & v)
{
    unsigned int numberElements = v.length();
    if (numberElements > 1)
        quickSort(v, 0, numberElements - 1);
}
```

As with the `findElement` algorithm, the asymptotic execution time of the `quickSort` algorithm depends in part on how lucky we are in selecting a pivot position. The best case occurs when the pivot breaks the vector exactly in half. The recursive calls then sort two arrays of approximately $n/2$ elements. Similarly each of these is divided roughly in half, resulting in four arrays of approximately $n/4$ elements. The number of times that a vector of size n can be divided in half is approximately $\log n$. Since each partition step executes in time proportional to the length of the array, the total time is $O(n \log n)$.

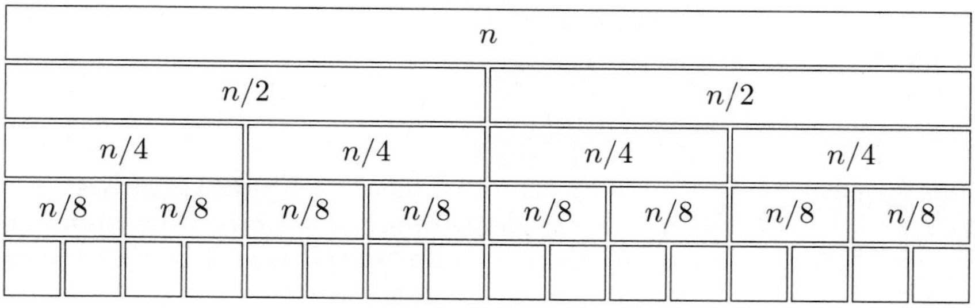

n

$n/2$ $n/2$

$n/4$ $n/4$ $n/4$ $n/4$

$n/8$ $n/8$ $n/8$ $n/8$ $n/8$ $n/8$ $n/8$ $n/8$

The other extreme occurs when the pivot is always either the smallest or the largest element. One partition is then empty, and the other contains $n - 1$ elements. In this case, n recursive calls will be performed, and the total execution time will be proportional to $n + (n - 1) + (n - 2) + \cdots + 1$. As we have seen, this is $O(n^2)$.

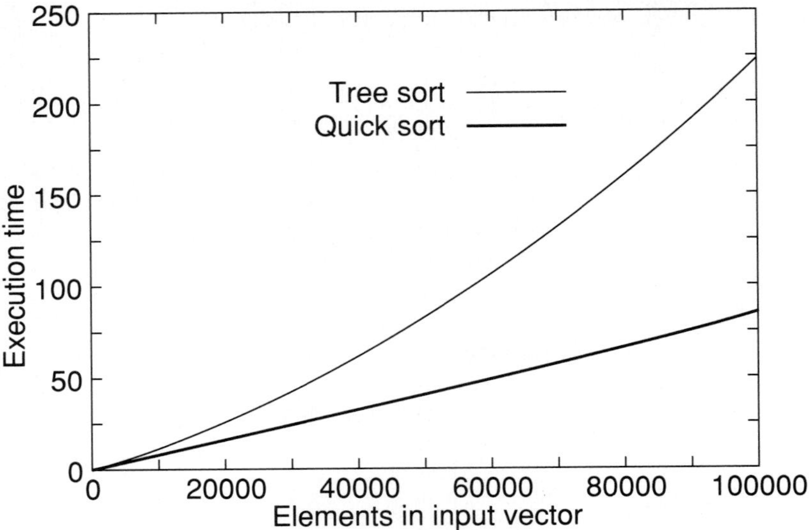

Figure 11.14 Execution time of quicksort versus treesort

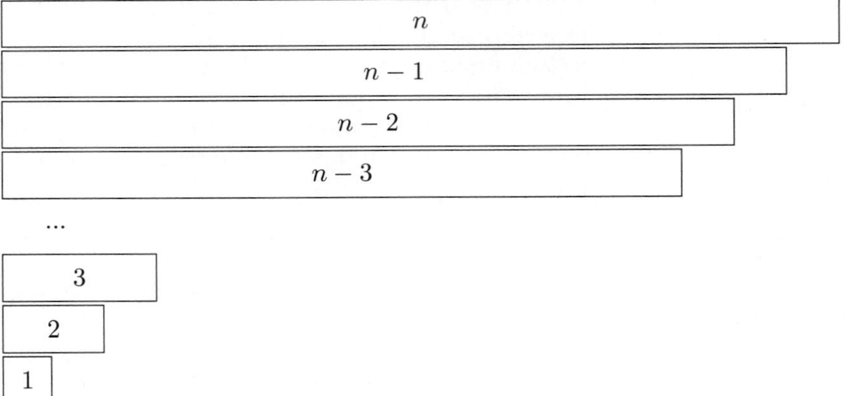

Once again we have vastly different best and worst case execution behavior. To determine the average execution time, we can either resort to sophisticated mathematics (see the references at the end of this section), or perform empirical timings.

EXECUTION TIMINGS FOR QUICKSORT In actual timings on random input values, the quicksort algorithm lives up to its name. Fig. 11.14 graphs execution time in comparison to tree sort over the same range used in Fig. 11.12 (page 343). For vectors of 100,000 elements, quicksort is almost three times faster than tree sort.

Empirical timings are, in a certain sense, almost as coarse a measuring device as is asymptotic analysis. As we noted in Chapter 6, factors that can alter the actual timing of an algorithm include the quality of the code generation for the compiler in use, the hardware and operating system for the computer on which the program is run, and the load balance (that is, other processes also in execution) of the computer at the time the measurements are taken. In addition, the quicksort algorithm is influenced very profoundly by the algorithm used to select the pivot value, and by the degree to which the input values are ordered or random. Thus execution timings of the algorithm on random values may or may not be a good predictor for the execution time of the algorithm in any particular circumstance.

11.8 CHAPTER SUMMARY

Key Concepts

- Divide and conquer
- Binary search
- Ordered vectors
- Search trees
- AVL trees
- Tree sort
- Partition, FindElement
- Quicksort

The solution of many problems involves searching a collection of values to find a specific element. In this chapter we have explored techniques that can be used to permit this operation to be performed quickly. In all cases, the speed is obtained by maintaining values in some sort of order.

If a vector of values is maintained in order, then binary search can be used to quickly locate a specific value. At each step in a binary search, the middle element is compared to the test value, and half the values in the collection are thereby eliminated from consideration.

Binary search of a vector is efficient if the data values are fixed, and insertions and removal of items are infrequent or do not occur at all. To insert or remove an item into or from an ordered vector requires, in the worst case, the movement of every value in the collection. In the more general dynamic search situation, these operations can be performed more rapidly using a search tree.

A search tree is a binary tree that maintains the property that, for every node, all the values associated with the descendant of the left child are less than or equal to the value of the node, and the values associated with each descendants of the right child are greater than the value of the node. By maintaining this property, it is possible to very quickly search for an item, and insertions and deletions can be performed rapidly as well, as long as the tree does not become too unbalanced.

To ensure that a search tree remains balanced, an additional requirement is necessary. We have explored one form of tree, the AVL tree, that maintains the height-balanced property. This guarantees that the difference in heights between the left and right child of any node is never larger than one. This property is then sufficient to guarantee efficient tree operations.

A slightly different variation on the searching problem is finding a single value in an ordered collection without ordering the entire collection—for example, finding the median (middle) value. Using the technique of partitioning, we can create an algorithm that will very rapidly discover this single value from a vector of elements. This same partitioning process is the key idea behind quicksort, an elegant and fast recursive sorting algorithm.

References

Searching large quantities of data was one of the first applications for modern digital computers. Thus trees and search trees have been extensively studied, and have a large associated literature. Most of the classic algorithms are examined in volumes 1 and 3 of Knuth [Knuth 73, Knuth 75]. The book by Weiss [Weiss 92] also provides an extensive bibliography.

AVL trees were first proposed by Adel'son-Vel'skiĭ and Landis in 1962 [Velskii 62]. The tree sort algorithm was first described by Robert Floyd in 1964 [Floyd 64]. The partition, findElement, and quicksort algorithms were first described by Tony Hoare [Hoare 61, Hoare 62]. In his ACM Turing Award lecture published in [Ashenhurst 87], Hoare recounts how the algorithm was first developed in a nonrecursive form. The nonrecursive version was extremely difficult to code or understand. It was only with the introduction of recursion in the language Algol-60 that the elegance of the algorithm became clear. Sedgewick [Sedgewick 78] provides an extremely thorough analysis of the quicksort algorithm. A slightly more accessible discussion of the relative merits of various techniques for selecting the pivot element is provided by Weiss [Weiss 92]. Several variations are described by Gonnet and Baeza-Yates [Gonnet 91].

Exercises

1. Trace the values of `low` and `high` in Algorithm 11.1 during the course of a binary search for element 7 in the following vector:

   2 4 5 7 8 12 24 37 40 41 42 43 50 68 67

2. How many elements will be examined in performing a binary search on a vector of 10,000 values?

3. The binary search algorithm shown in Fig. 11.1 will continue searching until the values `low` and `high` meet, even if by chance the element being targeted is discovered sooner. For example, if we were searching the vector of names for the value "Alex," we would discover the element on the first comparison. Modify the algorithm so that it will halt if the element is discovered.

4. Write the method `remove` for the ordered vector data structure. First perform a binary search to find the location of the argument. Test this location to make sure the value is actually contained in the collection. If so, then shift the values with larger index positions down one position, thereby removing the element. Finally, set the size of the collection to be one fewer than it was before the remove operation.

5. Instead of constantly changing the size of the ordered vector data structure, we could instead maintain both a "logical" size of the data vector (the number of values in use) and a "physical"

size (the size of the actual data area). Deleting a value would change the logical size, but not the physical size. Similarly adding a value would only require changing the size of the data area if the logical size became larger than the physical size. Would implementing the ordered vector data structure in this fashion change the asymptotic running time of any operation?

6. In Exercise 5 in the last chapter (page 308) we discussed the possibility of adding to each node in a tree a pointer to its parent node. Would such values simplify any of the algorithms discussed in this chapter?

7. Modify the way the new element insertion routine for binary search trees handles duplicate elements:
   a. The detection of duplicate elements produces an error message.
   b. A duplicate value inserted into a tree replaces the existing value.

8. Verify the formulas used in the single right rotation algorithm.

9. Assume a node has a balance factor of 2. Assuming this is the first such unbalanced node encountered in a walk back up a path from leaf to root, there are nine possible values for the child subtrees (−1, 0, or 1 in each). Verify that for each of these nine values the method `balance` will restore the height-balanced property of the search tree.

10. Is the tree sort algorithm stable? (See Chapter 6, Exercise 12, page 174.)

11. Using the techniques described in Exercise 15, Chapter 3 (page 84), test the hypothesis that tree sort is an $O(n \log n)$ algorithm. Using the coefficient c that you compute, estimate for the tree sort algorithm how long it would take to sort a vector of 100,000 elements. Is your value in agreement with the actual time presented in the second table in Appendix C? What factors do you think contribute to the discrepancy? (See "Asymptotic Analysis—Grains of Salt," on page 72.)

12. Trace the series of recursive calls performed by quicksort during the process of sorting the following vector: 3, 1, 4, 1, 5, 9, 2, 6, 5, 3, 5.

13. Is the quicksort algorithm stable? (See Exercise 10.)

14. What is the execution time of the quicksort algorithm when all elements in a collection are equal? Compare this to the execution time for tree sort in the same situation.

15. What is the execution time of the quicksort algorithm when the input is already sorted? How would this be different if instead of the midpoint we selected the first element as the pivot value?

16. Construct a vector of 10 elements that makes quicksort exhibit the worst-case $O(n^2)$ behavior when we use the pivot selection strategy presented in this chapter.

CHAPTER 12

Priority Queues

A PRIORITY QUEUE is a data structure useful in problems where it is important to be able to rapidly and repeatedly find and remove the smallest element from a collection of values. An everyday example of a priority queue is the "to do" list of tasks waiting to be performed that most of us maintain to keep ourselves organized. Some jobs, such as "clean desktop," are not imperative and can be postponed arbitrarily. Other tasks, such as "finish report by Monday" or "buy flowers for anniversary," are time crucial and must be addressed more rapidly. Thus we sort the tasks waiting to be accomplished in order of their importance (or perhaps based on a combination of their critical importance, their long-term benefit, and the fun we will have doing them) and choose the most pressing.

For a more computer-related example, an operating system might use a priority queue to maintain a list of pending processes, where the value associated with each element is the priority of the job. It may be necessary to respond rapidly to a key pressed at a terminal, for example, before the data are lost when the next key is pressed. The task of copying a listing to a queue of similar output waiting to be processed by a printer is something that can be postponed for a short period, as long as it is eventually handled. Thus those jobs with urgent priority will be executed prior to any jobs with less urgent requirements.

Another example might be listings waiting to be output on a computer printer. It would be a reasonable policy to print several one-page listings before a single hundred-page job, even if the larger task was submitted earlier than the smaller ones. Thus a queue would maintain files to be printed in order of size, or a combination of size and other factors, and not simply on time of submission.

A simulation, such as the one we will describe in Section 12.3, can use a priority queue of "future events," where the value is associated with the time at which an event is to take place. The element in this collection with the smallest time value is the next event that should be simulated. These are only a few instances of the types of problems for which a priority queue is a useful tool.

In terms of abstract operations, a priority queue is a data structure that takes elements of type T and implements the operations `isEmpty`, which indicates whether there are elements in the collection; `add`, which adds a value to the collection; and `deleteMin`, which returns and removes the smallest element from the queue. While these three operations represent the traditional definition of priority queue, in practice it is useful to divide the last operation, `deleteMin`, into two components. The function `min` returns the smallest element but does not remove it. The procedure `removeMin` removes the smallest element but does not return it. The procedure `deleteMin` is a trivial combination of these two functions, but each of the functions is also often useful on its own.

```
template <class T> T priorityQueue<T>::deleteMin()
{   // remove and return smallest element
    T result = min();
    removeMin();
    return result;
}
```

Figure 12.1 defines an abstract class for our priority queue data structure. Since priority queues are unordered, it is generally not important to examine any value in a queue other than the smallest. Thus we will not provide iterators for our priority queue structures, although it would be relatively straightforward to do so.

Note that the name priority *queue* is a misnomer in that the data structure is not a queue, in the sense we used the term in Chapter 9, since it does not return elements in a strict first-in first-out sequence. Nevertheless, the name is now firmly associated with this particular data type.

There are at least three obvious, but inefficient, ways to implement a priority queue. One approach would be to insert new elements at the front of a list, thus requiring only constant time for addition. To delete the smallest element would involve traversing the list to discover the minimum, requiring $O(n)$ time. Using an ordered list instead of a simple list would make for rapid discovery of the minimum, but necessitate $O(n)$ time for insertion. A declaration for such a class is shown in Fig. 12.2.

Another approach to implementing a priority queue is to take the list of items in a collection and sort them. From the sorted list, we can obtain not only the smallest element, but the next smallest, and the next, and so on.

```
//
// class priorityQueue
//     ordered collection of values permitting
//     rapid removal of smallest value
//

template <class T> class priorityQueue {
public:
    virtual void    add          (T value) = 0;
    T               deleteMin    ();
    virtual int     isEmpty      () const = 0;
    virtual T       min          () const = 0;
    virtual void    removeMin    () = 0;
};
```

Figure 12.1 Definition of the abstract class `priorityQueue`

But as we have seen, sorting is a relatively expensive operation. Furthermore, it is difficult to insert new values into a sorted list. (As we noted in the description of the ordered vector data structure, insertion can require $O(n)$ assignments — that is, a number of assignment operations that is proportional to the number of elements maintained in the collection.) Since we are interested only in finding the smallest element in the collection, we can employ techniques that are much more efficient. In particular, we will develop data structures in which we can find the smallest element in a collection of n elements in constant time, and we can find and remove the smallest element in time proportional to $\log n$.

There is one more method that is obvious, and not obviously inefficient. In Chapter 11 we examined balanced binary search trees. Recall that a new element could be added to a search tree, such as an AVL tree, in $O(\log n)$ steps. While removing the minimum element was not an explicit operation provided by such trees, we did provide the ability to construct an iterator, which has the ability to cycle over the values in order. To discover the minimum, we merely create an iterator and return the first value yielded. A careful examination of the iterator procedure will show that this requires no more than $O(\log n)$ steps. Thus, using a balanced binary search tree, we can perform both insertions and removals in logarithmic time.

The reason for rejecting the balanced binary search tree solution is inefficiency — not asymptotic inefficiency, but practical realistic inefficiency. A search tree is maintaining more information than we need. With all the rebalancing required, a search tree is simply doing too much work. We can develop alternative data structures that, while they have no better asymptotic efficiency — they are still $O(\log n)$ — generally yield execution times much better than would be possible using AVL trees.

```
//
// class priorityQueueList
//     implement priority queue protocol
//     using a linked list structure
//

template <class T> class priorityQueueList : public priorityQueue<T> {
public:
    // constructors
    priorityQueueList   ();
    priorityQueueList   (const priorityQueueList & v);

    // priority queue protocol
    virtual void    add             (T value);
    virtual int     isEmpty         () const;
    virtual T       min             () const;
    virtual void    removeMin       ();

private:
    orderedList<T>  lst;
};

template <class T> void priorityQueueList<T>::add(T value)
{   // add item to queue by adding to list
    lst.add(value);
}

template <class T> int priorityQueueList<T>::isEmpty() const
{   // queue is empty if list is empty
    return lst.isEmpty();
}

template <class T> T priorityQueueList<T>::min() const
{   // smallest item is first element in list
    return lst.firstElement();
}
```

Figure 12.2 Building a priority queue out of an ordered list

We will investigate two data structures that can be used to implement priority queues. The first, called a *heap*, maintains the values of the collection in an array. The operations to add or remove an element to or from the heap are relatively efficient. However, the heap suffers from the problem common to many array-based algorithms: It is necessary to declare a maximum size for the heap when it is created. Declaring too large a maximum value will waste space; declaring too small a value means that a heap will need to grow when an attempt is made to insert a new item. The second data structure, a *skew heap*, avoids the maximum size restriction by maintaining the heap values in a binary tree. But solving one problem comes only at the cost of introducing another—namely, the difficulty of keeping the tree relatively well balanced. Skew heaps are interesting in that the worst case cost for insertions and deletions is a relatively slow $O(n)$, but we can show that this worst case behavior does not occur frequently and cannot be sustained. In particular, the occurrence of a worst case situation must necessarily be followed by several insertions and deletions that are much faster. Thus, amortized over a number of insertions and deletions, the average cost of operation is still relatively good. Yet another advantage of the skew heap will be that it provides a fast implementation of yet another operation—namely, merging two priority-queue heaps to form a new queue.

12.1 HEAPS

A *heap* is a binary tree in which every node possesses the property that the value associated with the node is smaller than or equal to the value associated with either child node. This is referred to as the *heap order property*. It follows from this property that the smallest element in a heap will always be held by the root node. This is unlike a search tree, where the smallest element is always held by the leftmost child. Thus discovering the minimum value in a heap is a trivial operation.

Recall from Chapter 10 that a *complete binary tree* is a binary tree that is completely filled (in which every node has two children), with the exception of the bottom level, which is filled from left to right. Figure 12.3 shows a complete binary tree that is also a heap. The key insight behind the heap data structure is the observation, which we noted in Chapter 10, that because a complete binary tree is so regular, it can be represented efficiently in an array. The root of the tree will be maintained in position 0 of the array. The two children of node n will be held in positions $2n+1$ and $2n+2$. Thus the array corresponding to the tree in Fig. 12.3 is the following:

0	1	2	3	4	5	6	7	8	9	10
2	3	5	9	10	7	8	14	12	11	16

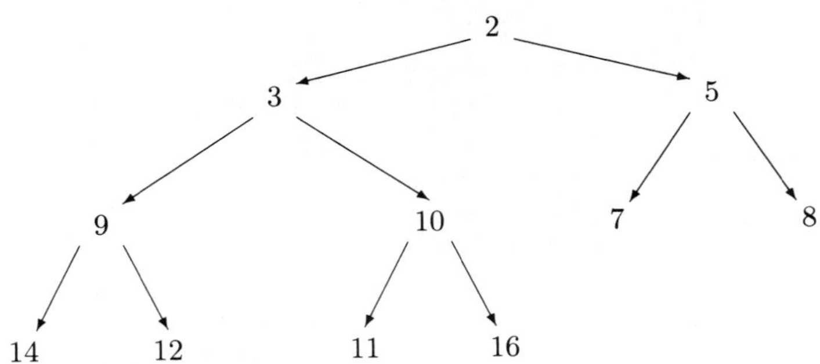

Figure 12.3 A complete binary tree in heap form

Given the index to a node, discovering either the parents or the children of that node is a simple matter of division or multiplication. (Even better, traversal is accomplished by multiplication or division of an unsigned quantity by 2; as we noted when discussing the bit vector data structure, such operations can be simulated by shift instructions, which on many machines are faster than multiplications and divisions.) Thus no explicit pointers need be maintained in the array structure, and traversals of the heap can be performed very efficiently. Notice that the property of completeness is important to ensure there are no "gaps" in the array representation. A more serious problem with this representation is that it requires the allocation of the array before any heap operations are performed. Thus the programmer must supply a maximum heap size in advance, prior to starting to perform insertions or deletions.

Figure 12.4 gives the declaration for our `Heap` datatype. The constructor for the heap requires that the programmer supply an integer value used to indicate the maximum size of the heap. The public interface provides the declarations of the four operations we left unimplemented in the abstract class. The `heapmax` and `heapsize` fields contain the maximum and current size of the heap, respectively.

The only nontrivial operations are insertion and deletion. We will deal with insertion first. When a new element is added to the priority queue, it is obvious that *some* value must be moved to the end of the array, to maintain the complete binary tree property. However, it is likely that the new element cannot be placed there without violating the heap order property. This violation will occur if the new element is smaller than the parent element for the location. Conceptually, a solution is to place the new element in the last location, then move it into place by repeatedly exchanging the node with its parent node until the heap order property is restored (that is, until the new node either rises to the top, or until we find a parent node that is smaller than the new node). The swapping operation requires three assignment statements. A more efficient algorithm is obtained if we maintain the last position as a "hole," since a hole can be filled with a

```
//
// class heap
//    a priority queue managed as a vector heap
//

template <class T> class heap : public priorityQueue<T> {
public:
    // constructors
    heap    (unsigned int maxsize);
    heap    (const heap &);

    // priority queue protocol
    virtual void    add             (T value);
    virtual int     isEmpty         () const;
    virtual T       min             () const;
    virtual void    removeMin       ();

    void            deleteAllValues ();
private:
    // data areas
    vector<T>       data;
    unsigned int    heapmax;
    unsigned int    heapsize;
};
```

Figure 12.4 Declaration for the class `heap`

single assignment. We then move the "hole" up the tree until we find the location of the new element. One step in this process is illustrated in Fig. 12.5. Here the element 8 has been moved to the end of the heap, and the element 5 has been moved to the former position of the element 8. The "hole" is now occupying the location of the former element 5. Since the new element, 4, is smaller than the parent for this position (the current smallest element, 2), the new value will be inserted into the hole. Since the new element rises until it finds a correct location, this process is

Heaps and Heaps

The term *heap* is used for two very different concepts in computer science. The heap *data structure* is an abstract data type used to implement priority queues; it is also used in a sorting algorithm we will discuss later in this chapter. The terms *heap*, *heap allocation*, and so on are also frequently used to describe memory that is allocated and released directly by the user, using the `new` and `delete` operators. You should not confuse the two uses of the same term.

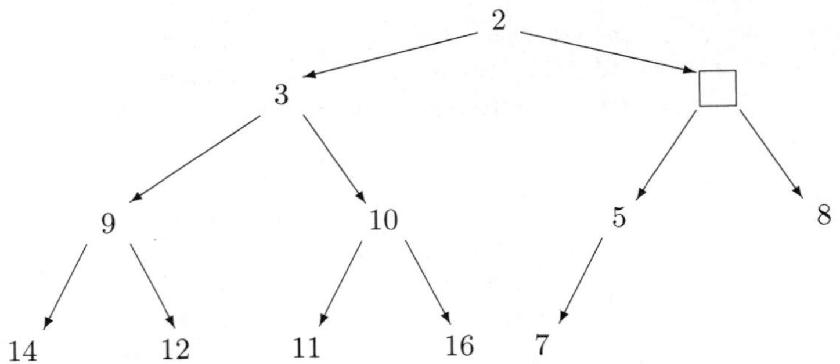

Figure 12.5 One step in percolating element 4 into place

generally known as a *percolate up*. The insertion method for percolating a value into place is shown in Fig. 12.6. Note that an attempt to add an element to a completely full heap results in the heap growing by five new locations. (There is nothing magic in the number 5; we have selected it arbitrarily.) We have added the invariants required to prove the correctness of the procedure. Basically, these invariants assert that each time we fill the hole, the subtree rooted at the newly occupied position satisfies the heap property. Since the `while` loop moves up one level of the tree during each cycle, it is obvious that it can iterate no more than $\log n$ times. Thus the running time of the insertion procedure, assuming the data vector does not need to grow, is $O(\log n)$. If the vector must be increased in size to accommodate a new element, the running time, of course, will be $O(n)$. Thus it is important for the performance of this data type that the user select an appropriate size for the data vector heap.

The deletion procedure is handled in a manner similar to insertion. We swap the last position into the first location. Since this may destroy the heap order property, the element must percolate down to its proper position by exchanging places with the smaller of its children. For reasons that will become clear shortly, we invoke another routine named `buildHeap` to do this task. Once again, we can improve efficiency by avoiding actual swaps, and instead treat the current position as a hole until we find the proper location for the element to be inserted, in the meantime holding the new value in a temporary variable. Figure 12.7 shows an intermediate step in this process. The value 3 has been promoted to the root position, where it now represents the smallest element. The hole has moved down to the position formerly occupied by the element 3. The temporary variable is holding the former last element in the heap, namely 7. Since this value is smaller than the smallest child of the hole position (9 in this case), the value will be moved into the hole. Otherwise the smallest child would have been promoted to the hole position, and the hole would have moved down one further level. If the hole reaches the bottom level with-

```
template <class T>
void heap<T>::add(T newele)
{   // add a new element to the heap
    // make sure there is room for new element
    if (heapsize + 1 >= heapmax) {
        data.setSize(data.length() + 5);
        heapmax += 5;
        }

    // value starts out in last position
    unsigned int position = heapsize++;
    // inv: position not equal to 0 and less than heapmax

    // now percolate up
    while (position > 0 && newele < data[(position-1)/2]) {
        data[position] = data[(position-1)/2];
        // inv: tree rooted at "position" is a heap
        position = (position-1)/2;
        }

    // found location, add new element
    data[position] = newele;
    // inv: tree rooted at position is a heap
    // inv: data holds a heap
}
```

Figure 12.6 Method for insertion into a heap

out finding a location for the value, the element is simply copied to the hole location. The code to perform deletion is shown in Fig. 12.8.

Since at most three comparisons of data values are performed at each level, and the while loop traces out a path from the root of the tree to the leaf, the asymptotic complexity of the deletion procedure is also $O(\log n)$.

12.1.1 Application — Heap Sort

The heap data structure provides an elegant technique for sorting an array. The basic idea is to first form the array into a heap. To sort the array, the top of the heap (the smallest element) is swapped with the last element of the array, and the size of the heap is reduced by one. The effect of the swap, however, may be to destroy the heap property. But this is exactly the same condition we encountered in deleting an element from the heap. And, not surprisingly, we can use the same solution. Heap order is restored by invoking the `buildHeap` procedure. (Note that this technique produces

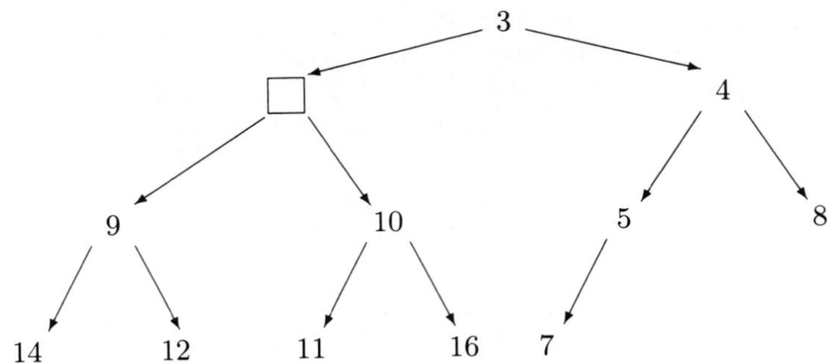

Figure 12.7 Filling a hole left by the deletion of the smallest element

a list sorted in *decreasing* order, while the previous sorting algorithms we have seen produced lists in *increasing* sequence.)

Slightly more surprising is the fact that we can use the `buildHeap` procedure to generate the initial heap. To see this, note that a subtree consisting of a leaf node by itself satisfies the heap order property. To build the initial heap, we start with the smallest subtree containing interior nodes, which corresponds to the middle of the data array. Invoking the `buildHeap` method for this value will ensure that the subtree satisfies the heap order property. Walking back toward the root of the tree, we repeatedly invoke the `buildHeap`, thereby ensuring all subtrees are themselves heaps. When we finally reach the root, the entire tree will have been made into a heap.

The heap sort algorithm can be given as follows:

```
template <class T>
void heapSort(vector<T> & data)
{   // sort the vector argument using a heap algorithm
    unsigned int max = data.length();

    // first build the initial heap
    for (int i = max/2; i >= 0; i--)
        buildHeap(data, max, i);

    // now swap the smallest element to the last position
    for (i = max - 1; i > 0; i--) {
        swap(data, i, 0);
        // and rebuild the heap again
        buildHeap(data, i, 0);
        }
}
```

To derive the asymptotic running time for this algorithm, recall that we noted that the `buildHeap` procedure requires $O(\log n)$ steps. There are n executions of `buildHeap` to generate the initial heap and n further

```
template <class T> void heap<T>::removeMin()
{   // remove the smallest element from a heap
    // move the last element into the first position
    data[0] = data[--heapsize];

    // then move into position
    buildHeap(data, heapsize, 0);
}

template <class T> void buildHeap
    (vector<T> & data, unsigned int heapsize, unsigned int position)
{   // rebuild the heap
    T value  = data[position];

    while (position < heapsize) {
        // replace position with the smaller of the
        // two children, or the last element
        unsigned int childpos = position * 2 + 1;
        if (childpos < heapsize) {
            if ((childpos + 1 < heapsize) &&
                data[childpos + 1] < data[childpos])
                    childpos += 1;
            // inv: childpos is smaller of two children
            if (value < data[childpos]) {
                // found right location
                data[position] = value;
                return;
                }
            else {
                data[position] = data[childpos];
                position = childpos;
                // recur and keep moving down
                }
            }
        else {  // no children
            data[position] = value;
            return;
            }
        }
}
```

Figure 12.8 Method for deletion from a heap

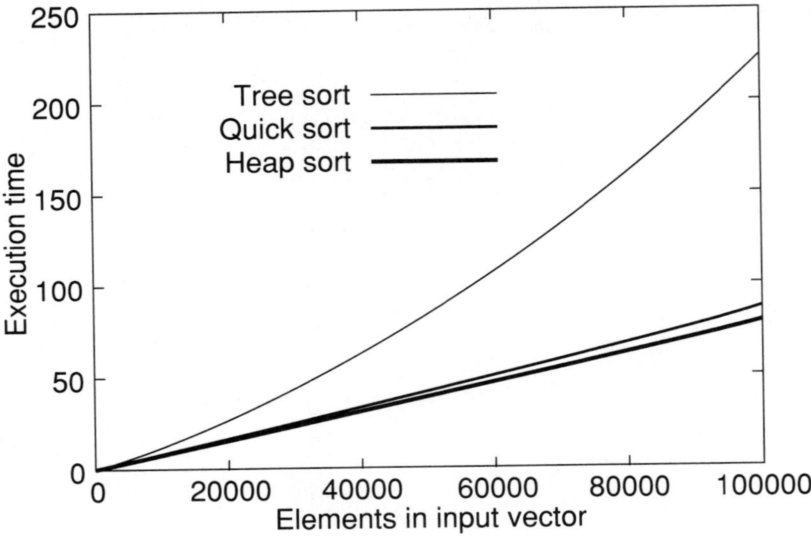

Figure 12.9 Empirical timing of heap sort

executions to reheap values during the sorting operation. Thus the total running time is $O(n \log n)$. This matches that of the tree sort algorithm (Section 11.6), and it is better than the $O(n^2)$ list insertion sort algorithms (Section 8.4.1).

Of a more practical benefit, note that the heap sort algorithm does not require any additional space, since it constructs the heap directly in the vector input value. This was not true of the previous sorting algorithms we have seen. Those algorithms must pay the cost not only of the sorting itself but of the allocation and deallocation of the data structures formed during the process of ordering the elements.

An empirical analysis of the running time of the heap sort algorithm is illustrated in Fig. 12.9. As we see here, for almost all vector sizes heapsort is comparable in speed, if not faster, to quicksort. An advantage of heap sort over quicksort is that the heap sort algorithm is less influenced by the initial distribution of the input values. You will recall that a poor distribution of values can make quicksort exhibit $O(n^2)$ behavior, while heap sort is $O(n \log n)$ in all circumstances.

12.2 SKEW HEAPS*

The obvious method to avoid the bounded-size problem of heaps is to use a tree representation. This is not, however, quite as simple as it might seem.

---

*Section headings followed by an asterisk indicate optional material.

The key to obtaining logarithmic performance in the heap data structure is the fact that at each step we were able to guarantee that the tree was completely balanced. Finding the next location to be filled in an array representation of a completely balanced binary tree is trivial; it is simply the next location following the current top of the array. In a tree form this is not quite as easy. Consider again the tree that was shown in Fig. 12.3. Knowing the location of the last element (16) is of no help in discovering where the next element should be inserted in order to maintain the balanced binary tree property. In fact, the next element is part of an entirely different subtree than that containing the current last element.

A *skew heap* avoids this problem by making no attempt to maintain the heap as a completely balanced binary tree. As we saw when we examined search trees, this means that a tree can potentially become almost linear, and we can place no guarantee on logarithmic performance for any individual operation. But there is another critical observation we can make concerning heaps, which is that the order of the left and right children for any node is essentially arbitrary. We can exchange the left and right children of any node in a heap without destroying the heap order property. We can make use of this observation by systematically swapping the left and right children of a node as we perform insertions and deletions. A badly unbalanced tree can affect the performance of one operation, but it can be shown that subsequent insertions and deletions must as a consequence be very rapid. In fact, if m insertions or deletions are performed, it can be shown (although the details are beyond the discussion here) that the total time to perform all m operations is bounded by $O(m \log n)$. Thus, *amortized* over time, each operation is no worse than $O(\log n)$.

The second observation critical to the implementation of skew heaps is that both insertions and deletions can be considered as special cases of merging two trees into a single heap. This is obvious in the case of the deletion process. Removing the root of the tree results in two subtrees. The new heap can be constructed by simply merging these two child trees.

```
template <class T> void  skewHeap<T>::removeMin()
{   // remove the miminum element from a skew heap
    assert (! isEmpty());
    node<T> * top = root;
    root = merge(root->right(), root->left());
    delete top;
}
```

Similarly insertion can be considered a merge of the existing heap and a new heap containing a single element.

```
template <class T> void skewHeap<T>::add(T val)
{   // to add a new value, simply merge with
    // a tree containing one node

    // create the new tree with one node
```

```
    node<T> * newnode = new node<T>(val);
    assert(newnode != 0);

    // merge with current tree
    root = merge(root, newnode);
}
```

The skewHeap data structure, shown in Fig. 12.10, implements both insertions and deletions using an internal method merge. The recursive merge operation is shown below. If either argument is empty, then the result of a merge is simply the other tree. Otherwise we will assume the smallest value is the root of the first tree, by returning the merge of the arguments reversed if this is not the case. To perform the merge, we move the current left child of the left argument to the right child of the result, and recursively merge the right argument with the old right child.

```
template <class T>
node<T> * skewHeap<T>::merge(node<T> * h1, node<T> * h2)
{   // merge two skew heaps to form a new heap
    // if either tree is empty, return the other
    if (! h1) return h2;
    if (! h2) return h1;

    // assume smallest is root of h1
    if (h2->value < h1->value)
        return merge(h2, h1);

    // reverse children and recur
    node<T> * lchild = h1->left();
    if (lchild) {
        h1->left(merge(h1->right(), h2));
        h1->right(lchild);
        }
    else    // no left child
        h1->left(h2);
    return h1;
}
```

For example, suppose we are merging a heap containing the elements 2, 5, and 7 with a heap containing the two elements 4 and 6. Since the element at the top of the left heap, 2, is smaller, it becomes the new root. At the same time the old left child of the root becomes the new right child. To form the new right child, we recursively merge the old right child and the original right argument.

```
//
// class skewHeap
//     heap priority queue implemented using skew heap merge
//     operations
//

template <class T> class skewHeap : public priorityQueue<T> {
public:
    // constructors
    skewHeap        ();
    skewHeap        (const skewHeap & v);
    ~skewHeap       ();

    // priority queue protocol
    virtual void    add         (T value);
    virtual int     isEmpty     () const;
    virtual T       min         () const;
    virtual void    removeMin   ();

    // delete all values
    void            deleteAllValues ();

    // merge two heaps together
    void            add         (skewHeap & secondHeap);

private:
    // root of heap
    node<T> *       root;

    // private method to merge two heaps
    node<T> *       merge       (node<T> *, node<T> *);
};
```

Figure 12.10 The skewHeap class declaration

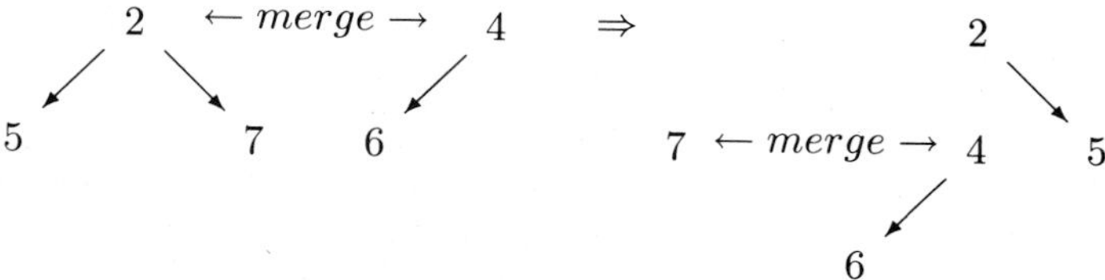

The first step in the recursive call is to flip the arguments, so that the smallest element is held in the first argument. The top element of this heap then becomes the new root. As before, the old left child of this value becomes the new right child. A recursive call is made to insert the right argument, 7, into the now empty former right child of the node 4. This results in the node 7 being returned, and the final result produced.

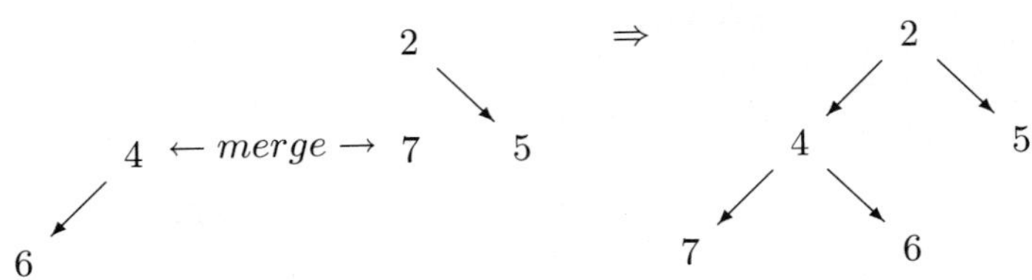

To illustrate why the amortized analysis of skew heaps can be so good, note that the worst case situation occurs when the left subtree contains a long path along the right child links. For example consider the merging of the singleton 10 into such a tree.

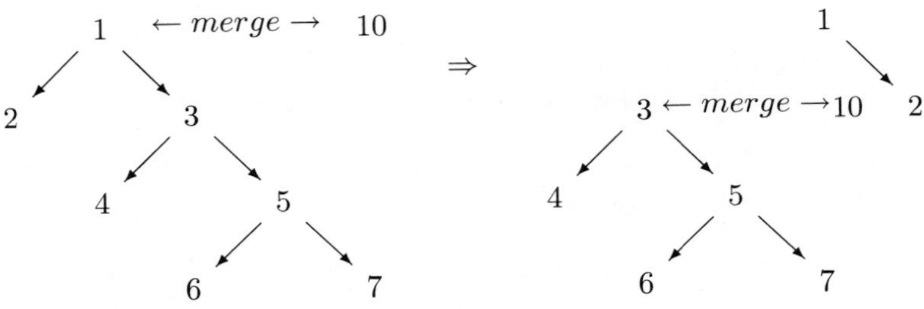

The merge requires four steps. However, note that now the long right path has been converted into a long left path.

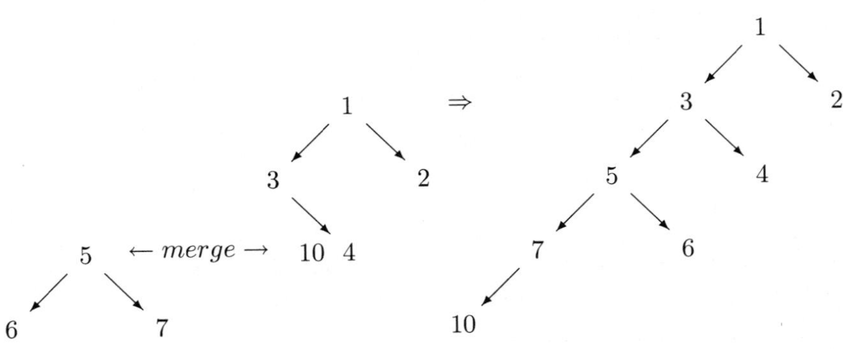

Thus the next insertion will be relatively quick. For example, assume that we now insert the single element 11.

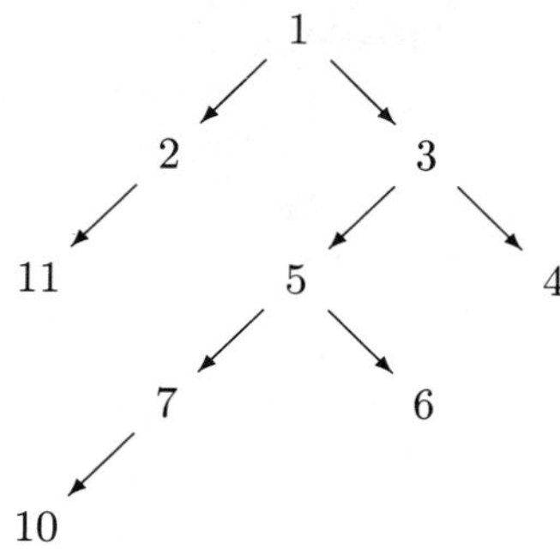

It is tempting to conjecture that after two insertions we would be back to the original poor configuration. But note that this has not occurred. The longest path is still a left path, although it is now on the right side. It will be quite a few steps before the situation can arise where a long right path can slow insertions.

Merging Heaps

The fact that skew heaps basically operate by merging two heaps to form a new heap means that it is relatively easy to combine together two instances of the data structure. We have taken advantage of this by providing an additional add method, one that takes another instance of skew heap as argument.

```
template <class T> void skewHeap<T>::add
        (skewHeap<T> & secondHeap)
{   // merge elements from a second heap
    // into current heap
    root = merge(root, secondHeap.root);
    // empty values from second heap
    secondHeap.root = 0;
}
```

The merge procedure used is the same as the merge used in implementing the addition and removal methods, and it can thus be expected to run very rapidly, in a time proportional to the longest path in the largest heap, not the number of elements in the argument heap, as would be the case if the values were simply added one by one.

An important feature to note, however, is that this operation effectively empties the argument heap by setting its root value to zero. The reason why this is necessary has to do with the way in which our data structures are performing memory management. In our scheme, each node in a tree must be "owned" by one and only one data structure. This data structure is responsible for performing a deletion to free up the memory used by the node when it is no longer being used as part of the structure. If a single node were to be used in two different structures, it is possible, indeed inevitable, that it would be deleted at two different times by two different structures.

We will encounter this situation again when we describe set union and set intersection problems in Chapter 14.

12.3 APPLICATION — DISCRETE EVENT-DRIVEN SIMULATION

Imagine you are thinking about opening an ice cream store on a popular beach location. You need to decide how large the store should be, how many seats you should have and so on. If you plan too small, customers will be turned away when there is insufficient space and you will lose profits. On the other hand, if you plan too large, most of the seats will be unused and you will be paying useless rent on the space, and hence losing profits. So you need to choose approximately the right number — but how do you decide?

One approach would be to perform a simulation. You first examine similar operations in comparable locations, and form a model that includes, among other factors, an estimation of the number of customers you can expect to arrive in any period of time, the length of time they will take to decide upon an order, and the length of time they will stay after having been served. Based on this, you can design a simulation.

A *discrete event-driven simulation* is a popular simulation technique. Objects in the simulation are modeled after objects in the real world, and they are programmed to react as much as possible as the real objects would react. A priority queue is used to store a representation of "events" that are waiting to happen. This queue is stored in an order based on the time the event should occur; thus the smallest element will always be the next event to be modeled. As an event occurs, it can spawn other events. These subsequent events are placed into the queue as well. Execution continues until all events have occurred, or until a preset time for the simulation is exceeded.

To see how we might design a simulation of our ice cream store, consider a typical scenario. A group of customers arrive at the ice cream store. From our measurements of similar stores, we derive a probability that indicates how frequently this occurs. For example, suppose we assume that groups will consist of from one to five people, selected uniformly over that range. (In actual simulations the distribution would seldom be uniform. For example groups of size two and three might predominate, with groups of size one and groups larger than three being relatively less frequent. The mathematics involved in forming nonuniform distributions is subtle, and not particularly relevant to our discussion. Thus we will use uniform distributions throughout.) These groups will arrive at times spaced from 1 to 10 minutes apart, again selected uniformly. Once they arrive, a group will either be seated, or see that there are no seats and leave. If seated, they will take from 2 to 10 minutes to order, and once they order they will remain from 15 to 35 minutes in the store. We know that every customer will order from one to three scoops of ice cream, and that the store makes a profit of $0.35 on each scoop.

```
extern random randgen; // a random number generator

class CustomerGroup {
public:
    const int groupsize;

    // constructor
    CustomerGroup       ();

    // method to order number of scoops
    int     orderSize    ();
};

CustomerGroup::CustomerGroup() : groupsize(randgen.between(1,5))
{     // create and initialize a new customer group
}

int CustomerGroup::orderSize()
{   // decide how many scoops group will order
    int scoops = 0;
    // each member of the group orders between 1 and 3 scoops
    for (int i = 0; i < groupsize; i++)
        scoops += randgen.between(1, 3);
    return scoops;
}
```

Figure 12.11 Description of the class `CustomerGroup`

From this description we can abstract the components of the simulation. The most obvious component is a customer. But in actual fact customers are never treated as individuals, merely as members of a group. Thus a more useful unit of abstraction is a customer group. A customer group must have a fixed size (number of people), and must be able to say how many scoops of ice cream they will order. The class definition shown in Fig. 12.11 is sufficient to describe this behavior. Note that the `groupsize` is part of the public interface for the class `CustomerGroup`, but the `const` declaration prevents it from being modified once it has been set. The value of the constant is set as part of the construction process.

To provide the implementation of the customer group, it is necessary to describe how to compute random numbers. We will defer for the moment a fuller description of the details, and for now we will simply assume that there exists a global variable `randgen` that is an instance of class `random`. The class `random` provides an operation `int between(int,int)` which returns an integer value uniformly distributed between the two bounds. Thus, the implementation of the customer group can be provided as shown in Fig. 12.11.

The next object in the simulation is the store itself. It might seem odd to provide "behavior" for an inanimate object such as a store; however, we can think of the store as a useful abstraction for the servers and managers who work in the store. The store manages two data items: the number of available seats and the amount of profit generated. The behavior of the store can be described by the following list:

- ▲ When a customer group arrives, the size of the group is compared to the number of seats. If insufficient seats are available, the group leaves. Otherwise the group is seated (and thus the number of seats decreased) and an "order event" is scheduled.
- ▲ When a customer group orders and is served, the amount of profit is computed and a "leave event" is scheduled.
- ▲ When a customer group leaves, the seats are released for another customer group.

A FRAMEWORK FOR SIMULATIONS Rather than simply code a simulation of this one problem, we will generalize the problem and first produce a generic *framework* for simulations. This is similar to the framework for backtracking problems we presented in Chapter 9.

At the heart of a simulation is the concept of an *event*. An event will be represented by an instance of class event. The only value held by the class will be the time the event is to occur. The method processEvent will be invoked to "execute" the event when the appropriate time is reached.

```
//
// class event
//     execution event in a discrete event driven simulation
//

class event {
public:
    // constructor uses time of event
    event (unsigned int time);

    // time is a public data field
    const unsigned int time;

    // execute event by invoking this method
    virtual void processEvent() = 0;
};
```

The constructor for the class merely sets the time field. Two events can be compared, and the ordering is determined by their time fields. By means of this ordering, a priority queue will automatically maintain events in the sequence they are to be executed.

```
int operator < (const event & left, const event & right)
{   // compare times for two events
    return left.time < right.time;
}
```

The simulation itself will be controlled by the class `simulation`. The major purpose of this class is simply to manage a queue of pending events. A method is provided to insert new events into the queue and to return the current time (which is the time of the last event executed). Since the priority queue will actually hold not events, but instances of subclasses of events, in order to avoid the slicing problem (Chapter 7) we must declare the template class for the skew heap as either a pointer or a reference. Declaring the heap as holding pointer values would be a poor choice, since then comparison between items would be based on pointer comparisons. Thus, the priority queue is declared as holding references to events.

```
//
// class simulation
//     framework for discrete event-driven simulations
//

class simulation {
public:
    // constructor
    simulation    ();

    // start and run simulation
    void            run            ();

    // return current time
    unsigned int    currentTime    ();

    // schedule a new future event
    void            scheduleEvent  (event &);

    // flag to set when simulation is finished
    int             done;

protected:
    skewHeap<event &> eventQueue;
    unsigned int    time;
};
```

The method to insert a new event into the queue takes a pointer to an event, which is assumed to be dynamically allocated. The pointer value is dereferenced to obtain a reference, which is then inserted into the priority queue.

```
void simulation::scheduleEvent(event * newEvent)
{
    // make sure pointer is non-null
    assert(newEvent != 0);
    // then insert reference into queue
    eventQueue.add(* newEvent);
}
```

The heart of the simulation is the method named run. This method repeatedly pulls events from the event queue and executes them. As with the backtrack framework, a variable done is used to control execution of the loop. This variable will be set when the priority queue is empty, but it may also be set by the programmer to signal other conditions (for example, if the simulation should stop after a fixed period of time). After the event is processed the event record is deleted. Notice that to do this the reference must be changed back into a pointer value, using the address operator.

```
void simulation::run()
{   // execute as long as event queue is not empty
    done = eventQueue.isEmpty();

    while (! done) {
        event & nextEvent = eventQueue.deleteMin();
        time = nextEvent.time;
        nextEvent.processEvent();

        // then delete event record
        delete & nextEvent;

        // if there are no more events, we are done
        if (eventQueue.isEmpty())
            done = 1;
        }
}
```

ICE CREAM STORE SIMULATION Having created a framework for simulations in general, we now return to the specific simulation in hand, the ice cream store. The principal class for the simulation will be a subclass of simulation called storeSimulation. A global variable named store will hold an instance of this class. The major task of the store simulation is to keep track of the number of free chairs, and the amount of profit generated. Methods are provided to signal an order and to print a final report of profits. The constructor initializes the profits to zero and the number of free chairs to however many are indicated in the simulation design.

```
class storeSimulation : public simulation {
public:
        storeSimulation();
        void   order          (unsigned int numberOfScoops);
        void   printProfits   ();

private:
    // data areas
        unsigned int freeChairs;
        double profits;

    // events that alter number of chars
    friend class arriveEvent;
    friend class leaveEvent;
};
```

As we have noted already, there are three types of events in our simulation. Each event is indicated by a separate subclass of the class `event`. The arrival event is described by the following class:

```
class arriveEvent : public event
{
public:
    arriveEvent(unsigned int, CustomerGroup *);
    virtual void processEvent();

private:
    CustomerGroup * group;
};
```

The constructor for the arrival event merely sets the time and the group value. When the execution of the event is signaled, the customer group decides if there is space. If there is, the group then schedules the next event, which is ordering.

```
void arriveEvent::processEvent()
{   // simulate a group of customers arriving

    cout << "customer group of size " << group->groupsize
        << " arrives at time " << time << '\n';

    // if there is space, schedule order, otherwise leave
    if (group->groupsize < store.freeChairs) {
        store.freeChairs -= group->groupsize;
        event * oe = new orderEvent(time, group);
```

```
        assert(oe != 0);
        store.scheduleEvent(oe);
        }
    else
        cout << "no space, group leaves\n";
}
```

The order event is similar. When executed, it schedules the leaving event:

```
void orderEvent::processEvent()
{   // simulate a group of customers ordering

    int scoops = group->orderSize();
    cout << "customer group of size " << group->groupsize
        << " orders " << scoops << " scoops of ice cream at time "
        << time << '\n';
    store.order(scoops);
    event * le = new leaveEvent(time, group);
    assert (le != 0);
    store.scheduleEvent(* le);
}
```

Finally, the leave event frees the chairs occupied by the group:

```
void leaveEvent::processEvent()
{   // simulate a group of customers leaving

    cout << "customer group size " << group->groupsize
        << " leaves at time " << time << '\n';
    store.freeChairs += group->groupsize;
}
```

The main program simply creates a certain number of initial events, then sets the simulation in motion. In our case we will simulate two hours of operation, with groups arriving with random distribution between two and five minutes apart.

```
void iceCreamStoreSimulation()
{
    // first create a number of arrival events,
    // simulate two hours of operation
    for (unsigned int time = 0; time < 120;
          time += randgen.between(2,5)) {
        CustomerGroup * group = new CustomerGroup;
        assert (group != 0);
        event * ae = new arriveEvent(time, group);
        assert (ae != 0);
```

```
        store.scheduleEvent(* ae);
        }

    // then run the simulation
    store.run();
}
```

An example execution might produce a log such as the following:

```
customer group of size 4 arrives at time 11
customer group of size 4 orders 5 scoops of ice cream at time 13
customer group size 4 leaves at time 15
customer group of size 2 arrives at time 16
customer group of size 1 arrives at time 17
customer group of size 2 orders 2 scoops of ice cream at time 19
customer group of size 1 orders 1 scoop of ice cream at time 19
customer group size 1 leaves at time 22
    .
    .
    .
customer group of size 2 orders 3 scoops of ice cream at time 136
customer group size 2 leaves at time 143
total profits are 26.95
```

12.3.1 Random Numbers*

An important part of the simulation described in this chapter was the ability to generate random numbers with certain characteristics. An algorithm that can generate truly random numbers is almost a contradiction in terms. As we noted in Chapter 3, each step of an algorithm must be clearly defined. An algorithm must therefore be deterministic; if started in the same initial conditions, it must always generate the same result. Without resorting to complex tricks (for example, an input device that is measuring cosmic rays), the best that we can attain using a computer is a series of *pseudo-random* numbers.

A pseudo-random number generator is a function that will produce a series of numbers that appear to be random but in fact are created using an algorithm. One of the easiest algorithms is known as the *linear congruential* method. The algorithm actually generates a series of unsigned integer values, called *seed* values. Each seed value is used to generate the next, by a combination of a multiplication and an addition by constant values:

```
newseed = multiplier * seed + adder;
```

*Section headings followed by an asterisk indicate optional material.

In order to keep the seed from growing infinitely large, the result must then be truncated. On most machines we can eliminate the truncation step by simply noting that multiplications and additions that cause a computation to exceed the fundamental machine word size will be silently truncated automatically, and the excess digit values ignored.

The effectiveness of the algorithm depends upon finding good values for the initial seed, and for the multiplier and the adder. Further information can be obtained by consulting some of the references cited at the end of this chapter.

Our random numbers will be generated by instances of the class `random`, which is described as follows:

```
//
// class random
//     random numbers generated using
//     linear congruential algorithm
//     assumes 16-bit short values
//

class random {
public:
    // constructor
    random              ();
    random              (unsigned short initialSeed);

    // methods used to get values
    unsigned short   randomInteger   ();
    double           randomReal      ();
    double           between         (double low, double high);
    int              between         (int low, int high);

private:
    unsigned short   seed;
};
```

The constructor initializes the seed value with a number known to have good properties. (The second constructor allows the programmer to select a different initial seed.)

```
random::random()
{   // start seed with an odd prime value
    seed = 44449;
}
```

To compute a new random integer number, the seed is modified as we described earlier.

```
unsigned short random::randomInteger()
{   // return a new random positive short value
    const int multiplier = 15625;
    const int adder = 22221;

    // modify seed, assume overflow quietly truncated
    seed = multiplier * seed + adder;

    // return new seed
    return seed;
}
```

In many cases it is more useful to have a random number represent a floating point value between 0 and 1. This can easily be produced by dividing the seed by its maximum size. The value 1 will itself never be generated, but values close to 1 will be produced.

```
double random::randomReal()
{   // return a random floating point value between 0 and 1
    double dseed = randomInteger();
    // divide by 2^16 - 1
    return dseed / 65535.0;
}
```

To return a random double precision value with a different range, it is a simple matter to scale the value. If X is a random number between 0 and 1, then $low + (high - low) \times X$ is a random value between low and high. Note that the interval is open on the high end; the value *high* will never be generated, but values close to it will be produced.

```
double random::between(double low, double high)
{   // return a random real between low and high
    return low + (high - low) * randomReal();
}
```

Finally, we describe the method used in our simulation, which generated a random integer between two values. Here we do want all values, including both the low and high value, to be potential elements. For this reason, we generate a random floating point value between the low bound and one larger than the high bound, then truncate the result to obtain an integer value.

```
int random::between(int low, int high)
{   // return random integer between low and high

    double dlow = low;
    double dhigh = high + 1;
```

```
    // return random real, then truncate
    double result = between(dlow, dhigh);
    return int(result);
}
```

12.4 CHAPTER SUMMARY

Key Concepts

- Priority queue
- Heap
- Heap order property
- Heap sort
- Skew heap
- Discrete event-driven simulation
- Pseudo-random number
- Linear congruential method

A priority queue is not a queue at all but rather a data structure designed to permit rapid access and removal of the smallest element in a collection. Priority queues can be structured by building them on top of lists, trees, or vectors. The vector structure is called a heap.

The heap structure forms the basis of a very efficient sorting algorithm.

A skew heap is a form of heap that does not have the fixed-size characteristic of the vector heap. The skew heap data structure is interesting in that it can potentially have a very poor worst case performance. However, it can be shown that the worst case performance cannot be maintained, and following any occurrence the next several operations of insertion or removal must be very rapid. Thus, when measured over several operations, the performance of a skew heap is very impressive.

A common problem addressed using priority queues is the discrete event-driven simulation. We have illustrated the use of heaps in an example simulation of an ice cream store.

We ended the chapter by presenting an algorithm for the generation of pseudo-random numbers using a computer.

References

The binary heap was first proposed by John Williams in conjunction with the heap sort algorithm [Williams 64]. Although heap sort is now considered to be one of the standard classic algorithms, a thorough theoretical analysis of the algorithm has proven to be surprisingly difficult. It was only in 1991 that the best case and average case execution time analysis of heap sort was reported [Schaffer 91].

Skew heaps were first described by Robert Tarjan and D. Sleator in [Sleator 86]. An explanation of the amortized analysis of skew heaps is presented in [Weiss 92]. The ice cream store simulation is derived from a similar simulation in my earlier book on Smalltalk [Budd 87].

The linear congruential algorithm for generating random numbers is discussed in volume 2 of Knuth [Knuth 81]. The constant values used in the random number generator described in this chapter were suggested by Naps [Naps 92].

Exercises

1. Why is a priority queue not a true queue type of data structure?
2. While it is possible to implement iterators for the heap data structure, argue why it makes little sense to do so.
3. Give an example of a priority queue that occurs in a non–computer science situation.
4. It should be obvious that while in this chapter we have used heaps to find the smallest elements in a collection, we could equally well define data structures used to find the largest elements. Explain how the `Heap` and `skewHeap` data structures would need to be changed in order to use them to find maximum values.
5. Show what a heap data structure looks like subsequent to insertions of each of the following values:

   4 2 5 8 3 6 1 10 14

6. Show what a skew heap data structure looks like subsequent to insertions of each of the following values:

   4 2 5 8 3 6 1 10 14

7. Consider the following alternative implementation of the add method for the class `heap`:

```
void heap<T>::add(T newele)
{
    // make sure there is room for the new element
    if (heapsize + 1 >= heapmax) {
        data.setSize(data.length() + 5);
        heapmax += 5;
        }

    // value starts out in last position
    int position = heapsize;
    data[position] = newele;
    heapsize++;

    // now restore the possibly lost heap property
    while (position > 0) {
        // reheap our parent
        buildHeap(data, heapsize,
              (position-1)/2);
        // move up the tree
        position = (position-1)/2;
        }
}
```

   a. Prove that this algorithm will in fact successfully add a new element to the heap.
   b. Explain why as a practical matter this algorithm is less desirable than the algorithm presented in the text.

8. The following simple recursive algorithm can be used to yield a pointer to a node in a binary tree from the index value of the node.

```
node<T> * getNode(unsigned int n,
     node<T> * root)
{
    // if n is zero then we are done
    if (n == 0)
        return root;

    // otherwise find the parent
    node<T> * parent = getNode((n - 1) >> 1,
         root);

    // then return either right or left child
    if (odd(n))
        return parent->left();
    return
        parent->right();
}
```

   Using this, we can create a simple alternative to skew heaps. The `treeHeap` class, like the class `heap`, maintains a count on the number of elements in the heap and a pointer to the root of the heap. Using the count and the `getNode` function just described, implement the remaining operations in the class `treeHeap` in a manner analogous to the way we implemented the class `heap`.

9. Using the techniques described in Exercise 15, Chapter 3 (page 84), test the hypothesis that heap sort is an $O(n \log n)$ algorithm. Using the coefficient c that you compute, estimate for the heap sort algorithm how long it would take to sort a vector of 100,000 elements. Is your value in agreement with the actual time presented in the second table in Appendix C? Why do you think the values computed for small vectors represent a better predictor of performance for heap sort than did the equivalent analysis performed for tree sort?
10. Another heap-based sorting algorithm can be constructed using skew heaps. The idea is to simply copy the values from a vector into a skew

heap, then copy the values one-by-one back out of the heap using `deleteMin`. Write the C++ procedure to do this.

11. Perform empirical timings on the algorithm you wrote for the previous question. Use as input vectors of various sizes containing random numbers. Compare the running time of this algorithm to that of tree sort and heap sort.

12. In exercise 5 in Chapter 10 (page 384) we discussed the possibility of adding to each node in a tree a pointer to its parent node. Would such values simplify any of the algorithms discussed in this chapter?

13. Design a simulation of an airport. The airport has two runways. Planes arrive from the air and request permission to land, and independently planes on the ground request permission to take off.

14. Design a simulation of a bank teller line. Customers arrive periodically, and stand in a common queue. When a teller is free the first customer in the queue is serviced.

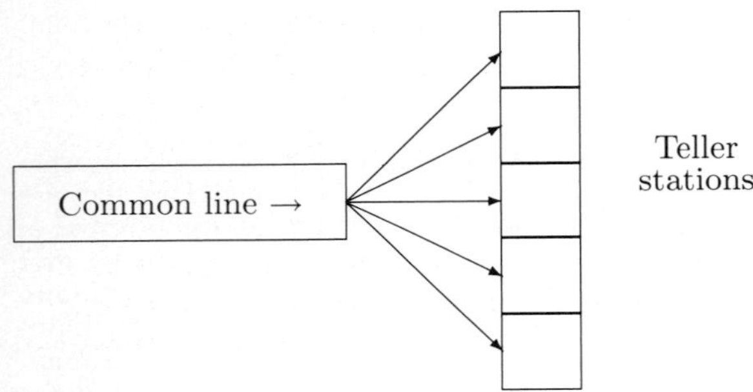

How might such a simulation be used to decide the number of tellers to hire for a certain period of the day?

15. Why is it difficult to generate truly random numbers using a computer?

16. One alternative to the use of uniform distributions is the idea of a weighted discrete probability. Suppose we observe a real store and note that 65% of the time customers order one scoop, 25% of the time they order two scoops, and only 10% of the time they order three scoops. This is certainly a far different distribution from the uniform distribution we used in the simulation. In order to simulate this behavior, we can add a new method to our class `random`.

a. Add a method named `weightedDiscrete` to the class `random`. This method will take as an argument a vector of unsigned integer values. For example, to generate the distribution above, the programmer would pass the method a vector of three elements, containing 65, 25, and 10.

b. The method first sums the values in the array, resulting in a maximum value. In this case the value would be 100. A random number between 1 and this maximum value is then generated.

c. The method then decides in which category the number belongs. This can be discovered by looping through the values. In our example, if the number is less than 65, then the method should return 0 (remember, index values start at 0), if less than or equal to 90, return 1, and otherwise return 2.

17. Modify the ice cream store simulation so that it uses the weighted discrete random number generated function implemented in the previous question. Select reasonable numbers for the weights. Compare a run of the resulting program to a run of the program using the uniform distribution.

CHAPTER 13

Hash Tables

IN CHAPTER 6 we developed the enumerated vector data structure. You may recall that the enumerated vector could be indexed not by integer values but by instances of an enumerated type. The creation of the enumerated vector data structure is an example of a special case for a more general programming technique. The only requirement we used in the definition of the `enumVector` data type was the ability to *convert* the enumerated index values into small integers. We present now a somewhat contrived but illustrative example of another data structure that employs this idea in a slightly different manner. A generalization from this example will then lead us to the development of a very practical and powerful data structuring technique.

Suppose there are six friends, *Alfred, Alex, Alice, Amy, Andy*, and *Anne*, who have started a club and wish to maintain a database containing the amount of club dues they each have paid. Dues are paid each time a member attends a meeting, but not all members attend all meetings, nor do they pay the same amount each time they meet. The club programmer, Amy, is in charge of writing programs to do the bookkeeping. Initially, Amy used the integer values 0 to 5 to represent each of the individual members. After the last meeting, Amy discovers an interesting system. She takes the third letter of each member's name and treats the letter as representing an integer by letting *a* represent the value 0, *b* represent the value 1, and so on up to *z*, which represents 25. She then computes the remainder yielded after dividing each value by 6. The result is that each name returns a different integer value between 0 and 5.

	Name		Value	Remainder
Al	f	red	5	5
Al	e	x	4	4
Al	i	ce	8	2
Am	y		24	0
An	d	y	3	3
An	n	e	13	1

What Amy has discovered is called a perfect hash function. A *hash function* is a function that takes as input an element from some set of index values and returns an unsigned integer result. The term "to hash" evokes an image of random mixing and shuffling. This is appropriate, since hash functions are permitted wide latitude in the sort of transformations they may employ. We will have much more to say about hash functions in our subsequent discussion. A *perfect hash function* is a hash function that in addition yields a one-to-one mapping from the index elements to the integers starting at zero and extending to the number of elements in the set.

Having discovered a hash function, we can define a new type of vector which we will call class `hashVector`. Instances of `hashVector` maintain one additional field, a pointer to a perfect hash function. The class is parameterized by two types: the type of the index values and the type of value held by the vector.

```
//
// class hashVector
//     vector indexed using hashed key values
//     template types are type of key
//     and type of value stored in vector

template<class H, class T> class hashVector : public vector<T> {
public:
    // constructors
    hashVector  (int max, int (*f)(const H*));
    hashVector  (int max, int (*f)(const H*), T & initialValue);
    hashVector  (const hashVector & v);

    // subscript operation
    T & operator [ ] (const H * idx);

private:
    // store pointer to the hash function
    int (*hashfun)(const H*);
};
```

Just as we used a cast to convert the enumerated index type in the `enumVector` data type, we here invoke the hash function to convert a subscript value into a small integer before invoking the subscript operator from class `vector`. Since only a pointer to the function is stored in the data structure, the value must be dereferenced before the function can be invoked. We will move the remainder division operation from the hash function into the data structure itself, so as to ensure that the index is always referring to a valid position.

```
template <class H, class T>
T & hashVector<H, T>::operator [ ] (const H& index)
{   // subscript a hash vector
    // hash the index value before indexing vector
    return vector<T>::operator [ ] (hashfun(index) % tablesize);
}
```

To illustrate the use of hash vectors, Amy has written a program (Fig. 13.1) that reads from the standard input a list of names and amounts (recall that members pay a certain amount at each meeting that they attend). An input file such as the following is given:

```
Alfred 2.32
Alex 1.76
Alice 4.87
Alfred 3.71
Amy 0.51
Andy 7.59
Alex 2.63
Anne 3.62
```

The output of the program would be the following:

```
Dues paid:
  Alfred: $6.03
  Alex: $4.39
  Alice: $4.87
  Amy: $0.51
  Andy: $7.59
  Anne: $3.62
total dues paid: $27.01
```

Of course, Amy's carefully worked out system falls apart when the set of index values changes. Suppose, for example, that *Alan* wishes to join the club. The `namehash` calculation for Alan will yield 0, the same value as for Amy. Two values that have the same hash value are said to have *collided*.[1] Although it would seem that collisions would preempt the use

---

1. Therefore another definition of a perfect hash function is a hash function that operates on a set of n elements, generating result values between 0 and $n - 1$, and for which no two values cause a collision.

```
//
// Amy's program to compute club finances
//

unsigned int namehash(const string & name)
{   // perfect hash function for
    // Alfred, Alex, Alice, Amy, Andy and Anne
    return name[2] - 'a';
}

void clubFinances() {
    hashVector<string &, double> data(6, namehash, 0.0);

    string name;
    double amount;
    double totalDues = 0;    // total dues paid

    // loop while there are records
    while (cin >> name >> amount) {
        // add the new amount to the data record
        data[name] += amount;
        // add to the total dues paid
        totalDues += amount;
        }

    // report the result
    cout << "Dues paid:\n";
    cout << "  Alfred: $" << data["Alfred"] << '\n';
    cout << "  Alex: $" << data["Alex"] << '\n';
    cout << "  Alice: $" << data["Alice"] << '\n';
    cout << "  Amy: $" << data["Amy"] << '\n';
    cout << "  Andy: $" << data["Andy"] << '\n';
    cout << "  Anne: $" << data["Anne"] << '\n';
    cout << "total dues paid: $" << totalDues << '\n';
}
```

Figure 13.1 Amy's program to compute club finances

of a hash vector, we will see in the next section how this difficulty can be overcome.

It might appear at this point that the discovery of a hash function, and in particular a pure hash function, is simply a matter of blind luck. This is in part true, and in part not true. It is true that there is no known systematic procedure that can be used to generate a perfect hash function from an arbitrary set of values. However, there are techniques that can be used in the majority of cases of practical interest. The reference section at the end of this chapter will point the interested reader to some of the related literature. We will postpone a further discussion on techniques used to create hash functions until after we have discussed a more general use of hash vectors.

13.1 COLLISION RESOLUTION USING BUCKETS

The true power of the hashing technique comes when each element in the hash vector is itself a collection. Basically stated, the idea is to separate the elements to be maintained into one of several *buckets*. Each bucket can hold an arbitrary number of elements. Thus, for example, the addition of a new element is a two-step process: First choose the bucket into which the element is to be inserted, then place the element into the bucket. The inclusion test and removal of an element from the collection are handled similarly. Since buckets can hold multiple elements, the problem of collisions effectively goes away.

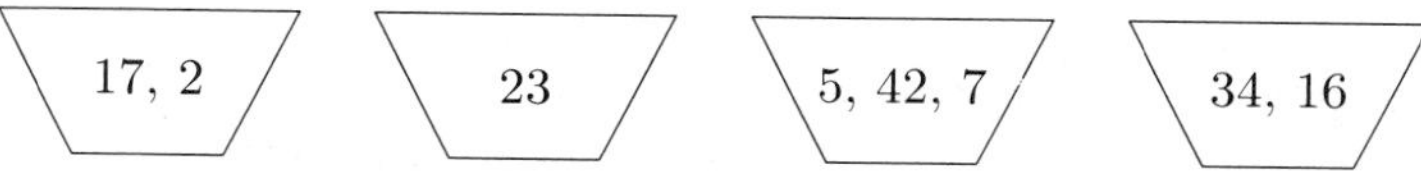

To bring this idea to realization, we will build on the `hashVector` data structure. The class `hashTable` (Fig. 13.2), is the starting point for our development. The hash table template is characterized by three types. The class type `B` represents the type for the buckets, which is left unspecified for now. The class type `H` is the type of the elements processed by the hash function. The type `T` is the type associated with the values used by the iterator for the hash table. Often, but not always, the second and third types will be the same. Like the hash vector, the hash table maintains a vector of values, indexed by the hashed values of the element type for our table, and holding bucket values. Only the operations of testing whether the table is empty and clearing the buckets are handled by the hash table itself. All other tasks will be performed by subclasses.

The two public methods perform their tasks by looping over the buckets. To clear all items from the table requires deleting all elements from the individual buckets.

```
template <class H, class T>
void hashTable<B, T>::deleteAllValues()
{   // delete all values from a hash table
    // clear the elements from each of the buckets
    for (int i = 0; i < tablesize; i++)
        buckets[i].deleteAllValues();
}
```

```
//
// class hashTable
//     collection of buckets indexed by hashed key values
//     template types
//     B - bucket type
//     H - key value
//     T - elements held in buckets
//

template <class B, class H, class T> class hashTable {
public:
    // constructors
    hashTable  (unsigned int max, unsigned int (&f)(const H&));

    // test if the set is empty
    virtual int    isEmpty           ();

    // clear the elements of the set
    virtual void   deleteAllValues   ();

protected:
    friend class hashTableIterator<B, H, T>;

    // the actual table itself is a vector of buckets
    const unsigned int tablesize;
    vector<B> buckets;
    unsigned int (&hashfun)(const H&);

    // convert key into unsigned integer value in range
    unsigned int    hash    (const H& key) const;

    // make iterator for given position in table
    virtual iterator<T> *  makeIterator  (unsigned int) = 0;
};
```

Figure 13.2 Definition of the class `hashTable`

Similarly, to test whether the collection contains any elements potentially requires testing each bucket. If any bucket contains an element, then so does the collection. Only if all buckets are empty is it reported that the collection is empty.

```
template <class H, class T>
int hashTable<B, T>::isEmpty()
{   // if any table is non-empty, return 0
    for (int i = 0; i < tablesize; i++)
```

```
        if (! buckets[i].isEmpty())
            return 0;
    // all empty
    return 1;
}
```

We will postpone for the moment a discussion of iterators for hash tables. To compute the hash value of any key we use the protected method `hash`. Because this method does not alter the table, it is declared as constant.

```
template <class B, class H, class T>
unsigned int hashTable<B, H, T>::hash(const H& key) const
{   // return hashed value of key
    return (*hashfun)(key) % tablesize;
}
```

To use the hash table data structure, we must supply a type for the buckets. This is most easily accomplished by creating a subclass. The subclass must provide a constructor method and indicate how to generate an iterator for the individual buckets. In addition, new functionality can also be provided. Figure 13.3 illustrates this by showing the definition of the class `hashTree`. In this class each bucket is an instance of the class `avlTree` studied in Chapter 11.

Methods are provided to add and remove elements from the collection, as well as to test to see if an element is contained in the collection. Each of these operations simply uses the hash function to select the appropriate bucket, then uses the method from the underlying data structure. The following example illustrates this technique:

```
template <class T> void hashTree<T>::add(T newele)
{   // find the right bucket, then add the element
    buckets[hash(newele)].add(newele);
}
```

Note that the class `hashTree` is parameterized by only one type, the type of elements held in each bucket. A similar class could be constructed using lists or ordered lists for the bucket type (see the exercises at the end of the chapter).

13.2 ASYMPTOTIC ANALYSIS OF HASH TABLE OPERATIONS

A major motivation for using hash tables is the speed with which operations can be performed. To illustrate this, let us consider the asymptotic complexity of performing a lookup operation on a hash table, using the `includes` method.

An analysis of the asymptotic running time of hash table operations is complicated by the uncertainty involved in the hash function. The worst

```
//
// class hashTree
//     hash table implemented using trees for buckets
//

template <class T> class hashTree : public hashTable<avlTree<T>, T, T> {
public:
    // constructor
    hashTree  (unsigned int max, unsigned int (&f)(const T &));

    // add an element to the collection
    void      add        (T newele);

    // test to see if the collect includes an element
    int       includes  (T ele) const;

    // remove an element
    void      remove    (T ele);

protected:
    virtual iterator<T> * makeIterator(unsigned int i);
};
```

Figure 13.3 Definition of the class `hashTree`

case hash function would be one that always returned a single value—for example, zero. While this behavior is certainly permissible under our definition of a hash function, the effect would be to place all elements into a single bucket. This does imply, however, that our worst case complexity is certainly no slower than the execution behavior of the underlying data structure. In the case of our hash table built on top of the AVL tree data type, this means that in the worst case the asymptotic complexity of lookup is $O(\log n)$.

The best possible hash function would be one that uniformly distributes elements over the range of hash values—that is, a function that has the effect of maintaining approximately the same number of elements in each bucket. Discovering such a function is not always easy, but it is the key to obtaining the best performance from a hash table. We will present the asymptotic run-time analysis of our hash table assuming this case.

If we let m represent the size of our hash table, then there are approximately n/m elements in each bucket. If we assume the time to compute the hash function itself is constant, and the time to discover which bucket an element corresponds to is essentially simply a division statement (see again Fig. 13.2), then the time to add an element is the addition time for an underlying table of size n/m. Since the addition of an element to an

AVL tree can be performed in $O(\log n)$ steps, this means the addition of an element to the hash table can be performed in $O(\log(n/m))$ steps.

We next assume that the number of hash table entries is roughly *proportional* to the total number of elements. That is, that the number of elements in the table will never exceed, say $m * 10$. Thus n/m is no larger than $\frac{10m}{m}$ or 10. Hence $O(\log(n/m))$ is $O(\log 10)$. The logarithm of any constant is itself a constant, so we can simply say that the asymptotic complexity of insertion is $O(1)$.

Hence, we see that the worst case performance for a hash table is essentially the worst case performance of the underlying bucket data structure. The best case performance permits operations to be performed in constant time. Analysis of the "average" case is complicated, in part because of the uncertainty involved in defining the meaning of the term "average" for various hash functions and distributions of key values. Nevertheless, in practice when used with a reasonable hash function the performance of hash tables is quite good.

13.3 HASH TABLE ITERATORS

The iterator for the hash table data type is one of the most complex data structures we will describe in this book. To iterate over each element in the hash table, we must iterate over each bucket in turn. To do this, the hash table iterator maintains two values: the index of the bucket currently being generated and a pointer to a dynamically allocated iterator for that bucket.

Fast Searching Using Buckets

In Chapter 11 we noted that hash tables would, in theory, provide us with a means to perform searches for elements in faster than $O(\log n)$ time, but only under certain conditions. Having described the hash table technique, the idea is obvious. To determine if a certain element is contained in a collection, it is only necessary to select the appropriate bucket to which the element would be assigned if it were present, and search just the one bucket. The hash operation is typically fast, and if the element is present it must be in only one bucket. Thus the time to search for a single element is the time to search just a single bucket, which is potentially much faster than the time to search the entire collection.

For this to be a nontrivial gain in execution time, the requirement is that the number of buckets be a significant percentage of the number of elements being maintained (so that each bucket contains only a few elements), and that the hash function distributes elements from the collection relatively uniformly to each of the buckets. Because it is frequently difficult to discover a hash function having these characteristics, using an asymptotically less efficient data structure, such as an AVL tree, will often be more practical.

```
//
// class hashTableIterator
//     iterator protocol for hash tables
//

template <class B, class H, class T>
class hashTableIterator : public iterator<T> {
public:
    // constructor
    hashTableIterator  (hashTable<B, H, T> & v);

    // iterator protocol
    virtual int     init          ();
    virtual T       operator()    ();
    virtual int     operator !    ();
    virtual int     operator ++   ();
    virtual void    operator =    (T value);

protected:
    hashTable<B, H, T> &  base;
    unsigned int          currentIndex;
    iterator<T> *         itr;

    // getNextIterator used to set internal iterator pointer
    int             getNextIterator();
};
```

To initialize iteration, it is necessary to create an iterator for the first bucket. However, this bucket may have no elements, in which case it is necessary to examine each bucket in turn until we find a bucket that contains at least one element. The latter task is performed by a method named `getNextIterator`.

```
template <class B, class H, class T>
        int hashTableIterator<B, H, T>::init()
{   // initialize iterator,
    // start search with first bucket
    currentIndex = 0;
    itr = 0;
    return getNextIterator();
}

template <class B, class H, class T>
int hashTableIterator<B, H, T>::getNextIterator()
{
    // if there is an old iterator, delete it
```

```
    if (itr != 0)
        delete itr;

    // now search for a new one
    for (; currentIndex < base.tablesize; currentIndex++) {
        // generate a new iterator at the current point
        itr = base.makeIterator(currentIndex);
        assert(itr != 0);
        // if it has at least one element, we're done
        if (itr->init())
            return 1;
        // otherwise delete it, try again
        delete itr;
        }

    // all out of iterators, can quit
    itr = 0;
    return 0;
}
```

A similar situation occurs with the increment operator. If the current iteration can be advanced, then the element yielded by that iterator is used as the current value. Otherwise, the method `getNextIterator` is once more invoked to find the value from the next bucket.

```
template <class B, class H, class T>
int hashTableIterator<B, T>::operator ++ ()
{
    // see if current iterator can be advanced
    if (itr && (*itr)++)
        return 1;
    // if not, get next iterator
    currentIndex++;
    return getNextIterator();
}
```

Just as subclasses of `hashTable` simply added information to the template description of the parent class and provided almost no new methods themselves, so too are subclasses of `hashTableIterator` simply a renaming of the parent class. Here is the class description of the hash tree data structure iterator.

```
//
// class hashTreeIterator
//     iterator implementation for hash tree structures
//
```

```
template <class T>
class hashTreeIterator : public hashTableIterator<avlTree<T>, T, T> {
public:
    hashTreeIterator(hashTree<T> & x);
};

template <class T>
hashTreeIterator<T>::hashTreeIterator(hashTree<T> & x)
        : hashTableIterator<avlTree<T>, T, T>(x)
{
    // no further initialization
}
```

13.4 APPLICATION—BUCKET SORTING

We have seen in earlier chapters how the data structures ordered lists, trees, and heaps each naturally suggested an associated sorting algorithm. In the same way, the hash table data structure suggests a novel approach to sorting, at least under certain conditions.

As with all hash table based algorithms, the general idea will be to separate elements into the different buckets, sort each of the buckets, then append the sorted elements together to form the final answer. For this to be effective, it must be possible to merge very efficiently into the final list the results of sorting each of the buckets individually. One way to ensure this is to insist that the hash function supplied by the user has the property that all values assigned to the first bucket be smaller than any values assigned to the other buckets, and that all values assigned to the second bucket be smaller than the values in subsequent buckets, and so on. Thus to form the final list it is sufficient to merely append end-to-end the sorted lists from each of the separate buckets.

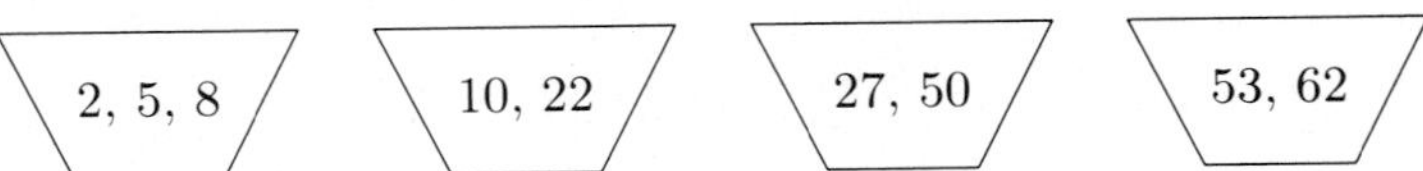

The *bucket sort* algorithm shown in Fig. 13.4 utilizes this idea. Compare this function to the list insertion sort algorithm in Section 8.4.1 (page 220) and the tree sort algorithm in Section 11.6 (page 396). The user is required to supply an appropriate size and function for the hash table that satisfies the properties we have outlined.

Because we are using so little of the general functionality provided by the hash table data structure, we can improve efficiency by using the idea of a hash table, but implementing it using slightly less complex structures. In particular, we can avoid the overhead involved in the dynamic allocation of iterators required to loop over all the elements of a general hash

```
template <class T>
void bucketSort(vector<T> & data, unsigned int tablesize,
     unsigned int (&f)(const T &))
{
    unsigned int max = data.length():
    hashTree<T> table(tablesize, f);

    // put each element into the appropriate bucket
    for (unsigned int i = 0; i < max; i++)
        table.add(data[i]);

    // now put elements back into vector
    hashTreeIterator<T> itr(table);
    int j = 0;
    for (itr.init(); ! itr; itr++)
        data[j++] = itr();
}
```

Figure 13.4 The bucket sort algorithm (version 1)

table. This version is shown in Fig. 13.5. Here the buckets are formed by simply declaring a vector of ordered lists. Elements are added to the lists, invoking the hashing function directly in the bucket sort algorithm rather than in the hash table data structure. Once all the elements have been ordered, they are copied back into the array.

An analysis of the actual timings of bucket sort is made difficult by the fact that there are now two independent variables: the size of the input vector and the number of buckets. Our initial analysis will use a hash table with 1000 buckets. Input values will be randomly distributed between 0 and 16,000. The hash function will simply shift the input value right by four places (effectively dividing by 16). This test program is shown in Fig. 13.6.

We would expect the bucket sort algorithm to operate very rapidly for small vector inputs. Indeed, for input vectors with less than 1000 elements we would expect less than one value per bucket. Even after the size of the input vector exceeds the number of buckets, the rate of change in the graph mapping the execution time for the bucket sort algorithm is almost linear up until about 4000 elements, where it starts to curve upward slightly (see Fig. 13.7). At 10,000 elements, where each bucket holds on average 10 elements, the execution time of the bucket sort algorithm is still approximately twice as fast as any algorithm we have yet seen.

As the input vector size increases, the ratio of the number of vector elements to the number of buckets becomes larger, and bucket sort loses the linear growth pattern. After the point where each bucket holds approxi-

```
template <class T>
void bucketSort(vector<T> & data, unsigned int tablesize,
    unsigned int (*hashfun)(const T &))
{
    unsigned int max = data.length();
    vector< orderedList<T> >  buckets[tablesize];

    // put each element into the appropriate bucket
    for (unsigned int i = 0; i < max; i++)
        buckets[(*hashfun)(data[i])].add(data[i]);

    // now put elements back into vector
    int j = 0;
    for (i = 0; i < tablesize; i++) {
        // empty the elements from the bucket
        listIterator<T> itr(buckets[i]);
        for (itr.init(); ! itr; itr++)
            data[j++] = itr();
        }
}
```

Figure 13.5 The bucket sort algorithm (version 2)

mately 25 elements, the heap sort algorithm starts to be faster in execution, and this trend becomes more pronounced as the input vector size is increased (Fig. 13.8).

In order to assess the effect of the number of buckets on the execution time for the bucket sort algorithm, we executed the text program shown in Fig. 13.6 with 1000 buckets, then again with 2000 buckets. The results are shown in Fig. 13.9. As expected, increasing the number of buckets improved the performance of the procedure, but it did not change the overall asymptotic behavior. Once a sufficiently large number of elements is being maintained in each bucket, the benefits of using buckets are diminished.

13.5 HASH FUNCTIONS

The application of a hash function is almost always a two-step process:

1. Transform the key into an integer value.
2. Map the resulting integer into a valid index for the hash table.

To accomplish the first task, there are a number of well-known methods. Often these are used in combination.

- *Mapping.* Integer values that occur in the key can be transformed or mapped into other integer values. This is the technique Amy used in

```
// hf is the hash function for the bucket sort test
unsigned int hf(const int x)
{
    return x >> 4;
}

main() {
const int max = 100000;

vector<int> vec(max);

for (int i = 0; i < max; i++)
    vec[i] = rand.between(0,16000);

bucketSort(vec, (unsigned int) 1000, hf);
}
```

Figure 13.6 The bucket sort test program

her hash function. The character 'a' was mapped on to 0, the character 'b' on to 1, and so on. Often more complex maps are defined using an array. The elements of the array are specified ahead of time, when the program is compiled. To hash a value is simply a matter of indexing into the array. This idea is the basis for the most commonly used algorithm for generating a perfect hash function from a known set of identifiers.

- *Folding.* Using folding, the key is partitioned into several parts, and the (perhaps hashed) integer values for the individual parts are combined. The combination is usually accomplished using an efficient operation, such as addition, multiplication, or the logical exclusive or operation. For example, the following loop converts a string into an integer value by summing the integers corresponding to each character.

```
unsigned int hashval = 0;
int i = str.length();
while (i > 0)
    hashval += str[--i];
```

- *Shifting.* Often the application of these methods results in values for which the low order bits are not random. For example, printable character values are only a small range of the total integer values. In these situations a shift operation can be used to eliminate these bits.

  Shifting can also be used to avoid a problem that occurs when

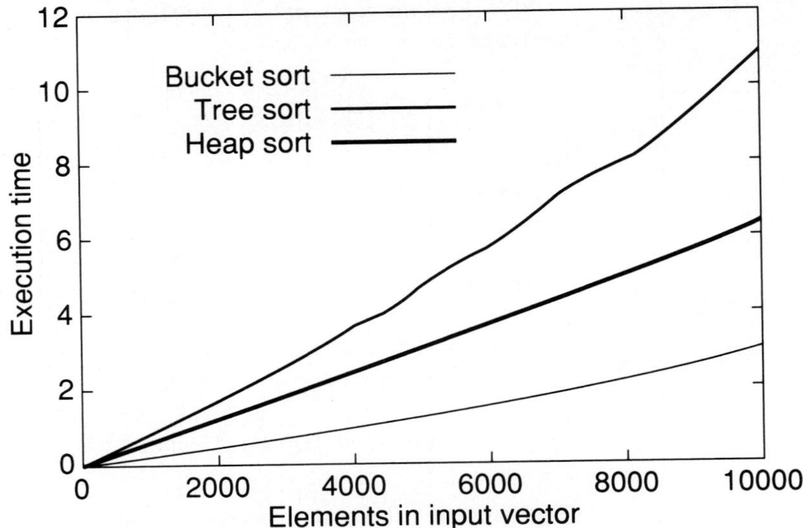

Figure 13.7 Execution timings of bucket sort on small inputs

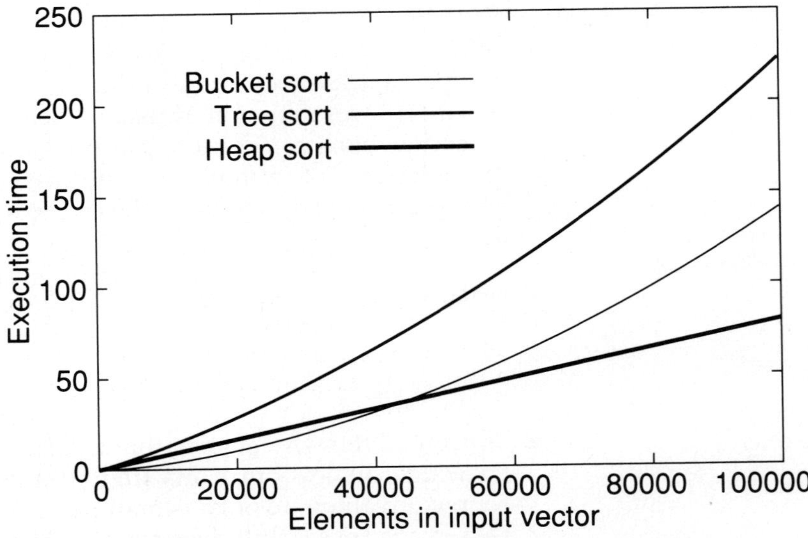

Figure 13.8 Execution timings of bucket sort on large inputs

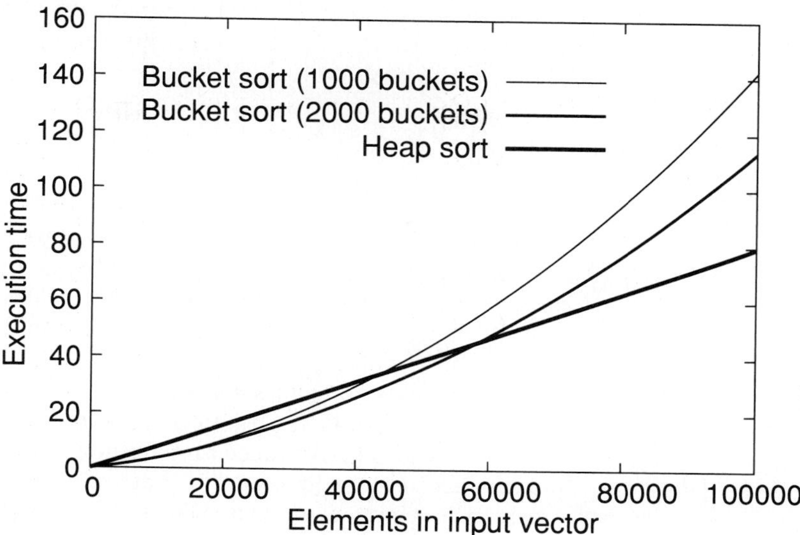

Figure 13.9 Execution timings of bucket sort with differing numbers of buckets

folding is performed using a commutative operator, such as addition. This problem is the fact that a commutative operator will produce the same hash value for permutations of the arguments. Thus the loop just given will produce the same hash value for the strings "apt," "tap," and "pat." By shifting the results of the previous calculation before performing the addition, we can eliminate this difficulty.

```
unsigned int hashval = 0;
int i = str.length();
while (i > 0)
    hashval = (hashval << 1) + str[--i];
```

- *Casts.* A cast can be used to convert almost any type into an integer. Most frequently this is used when the location of an object in memory—that is, its pointer address—is used as a hash value. A cast is applied to convert this pointer value into an integer.

Almost always the second step, transforming the hashed key value into a legal index, is accomplished simply by taking the remainder (or mod) after dividing by the table size. While this is easy, it is not the only possibility. In the bucket sort algorithm in Fig. 13.5, we used a shift instruction. Shift instructions have a speed advantage over divisions, but they can be used only in situations where the number of buckets is a power of two. Another alternative is to use bit-wise operations to select just a few binary digits from an integer key.

If division is used, the only source of variation is the size of the table. Let us consider the effect of a computation to take the remainder by dividing by n, the hash table size:

$$index = key \bmod n$$

Some values of n are much better than others in shuffling the key values. If n is even, for example, then the index will be even for even key values and odd for odd key values. In many cases this is unacceptable. For example, on most machines pointer addresses are always even, and always multiples of four. If the key is simply an address, this would result in the odd-numbered buckets being totally unused.

If n is a power of two, then the mod is simply the low order bits of the key value. Not only is the mod instruction an inefficient way to obtain this value, but usually these bits are not as random as we would like.

Empirical evidence suggests that better scattering is achieved in cases where n is a prime number. Thus if one wants a hash table of "about" 1000 elements, then a size of 997 or 1009 is preferable.

The Birthday Paradox

The frequency of collisions when performing hashing is related to a well-known mathematical puzzle. How many randomly chosen people need be in a room before it becomes likely that two people will have the same birth date? Most people would guess the answer would be in the hundreds, since there are 365 possible birthdays (excluding leap years). In fact, the answer is only 24 people.

To see why, consider the opposite question. With n randomly chosen people in a room, what is the probability that no two have the same birth date? Imagine we take a calendar, and mark off each individual's birth date in turn. The probability that the second person has a different birthday from the first is 364/365, since there are 364 different possibilities not already marked. Similarly the probability that the third person has a different birthday from the first two is 363/365. Since these two probabilities are independent of each other, the probability that they are *both* true is their product. If we continue in this fashion, if we have $n-1$ people all with different birthdays, the probability that individual n has a different birthday is:

$$\frac{364}{365} \times \frac{363}{365} \times \frac{362}{365} \times \cdots \times \frac{365-n+1}{365}$$

When $n \geq 24$, this expression becomes less than 0.5. This means that if 24 or more people are gathered in a room the odds are better than even that two individuals have the same birthday.

The implication of the birthday paradox for hashing is to tell us that for any problem of reasonable size we are almost certain to have some collisions. Functions that avoid duplicate values are surprisingly rare, even with a relatively large table.

13.6 CHAPTER SUMMARY

Key Concepts

- Hashing
- Collisions
- Hash vectors and hash tables
- Buckets
- Asymptotic analysis of hash tables
- Bucket sorting

To *hash* a value means simply to apply a function that transforms a noninteger key into an integer value. This simple idea is the basis for a very powerful data structuring technique. If it is possible to discover a function that transforms a set of keys via a one-to-one mapping on to a set of integer index values, then it is possible to construct a vector using noninteger keys. More commonly, several key values will map on to the same integer index. Two keys that map on to the same value are said to have *collided*. The problem of multiple key values for each index can be accommodated by maintaining a *bucket* for each possible key value. The bucket will hold all values with the same hash value. Such a structure is known as a hash table.

The process of hashing permits access and testing operations that potentially are the fastest of any data structure we have considered. Unfortunately, this potential depends upon the wise choice of a hash function. A good hash function must uniformly distribute key values over each of the different buckets. Discovering a good hash function is the most difficult part of using the hash table technique.

References

The hash table technique described here—technically known as *collision resolution by chaining*—is but one of a great number of hash table techniques. Probably the most important technique that is not discussed in this book is *open table hashing*, or *open addressing*, where the actual element values are stored in the hash table, instead of the table being an array of buckets. A practical disadvantage of the open table technique (and the reason why we do not present it here) is the requirement that it be possible to tell whether a position has been filled or not. Despite this, for hashing values for which this is no difficulty (for example, pointers or integers), open addressing is an acceptable approach that does have the merit of using less space. We will discuss a simple version of open addressing in Chapter 17.

Another topic we do not address is *extendible hashing*, which occurs when the hash table is maintained in memory but the data items themselves are maintained on disk. Here the main consideration is to reduce the number of disk accesses. Again, we will discuss a simple external hashed data structure in Chapter 17.

As with most data structures, the exposition by Knuth [Knuth 75] provides a wealth of information on hashing. Good analysis of the average time complexity of hashing is found in Cormen et. al [Cormen 90], and in

Gonnet and Baeza-Yates [Gonnet 91]. Other explanations can be found in Aho et al. [Aho 83], and Weiss [Weiss 92]. The merits of various hash functions in a practical setting (namely, compiler symbol tables) is discussed in Aho et al. [Aho 86].

Exercises

1. Give an explanation of each of the following terms: hashing, collision, bucket.

2. When Alan wishes to join the circle of six friends, why can't Amy simply use the `grow` operation on the data vector to increase its size?

3. Will the class `vectorIterator` work with Amy's hash table vector? Explain how. What values will be returned by the `key` member function?

4. Give a class definition for a hash table, similar to that shown in Fig. 13.3, that uses lists for the individual bucket elements.

5. Give a class definition for a hash table that uses ordered lists for the individual bucket elements.

6. Design a variation of the bucket sorting algorithm shown in Fig. 13.5 that uses search trees, rather than ordered lists. Empirically compare the running time of the two algorithms on various vectors.

7. Amy's club has grown, and now includes the following members:

Abel	Abigail	Abraham	Ada
Adam	Adrian	Adrienne	Agnes
Albert	Alex	Alfred	Alice
Amanda	Amy	Andrew	Andy
Angela	Anita	Anne	Antonia
Arnold	Arthur	Audrey	

a. Find what value would be computed by Amy's hash function for each member of the group.

b. Assume we use Amy's hash function and assign each member to a bucket by simply dividing the hash value by the number of buckets. Determine how many elements would be assigned to each bucket for a hash table of size 5. Do the same for a hash table of size 11.

8. Using the techniques described in Exercise 15, Chapter 3 (page 84), test the hypothesis that tree sort is an $O(n)$ algorithm for small values of n. Use the data presented in the first table in Appendix C. Then use the same techniques, but use the data from the second table.

9. Is the bucket sort algorithm shown in Fig. 13.4 stable? (See Chapter 11, Exercise 10, page 353.)

10. Is the bucket sort algorithm shown in Fig. 13.5 stable? (See Chapter 8, Exercise 20, page 234.)

11. Another variation on the bucket sort algorithm shown in Figure 13.5 (page 398) uses an array of skew heaps. Elements are first inserted into the different heaps. Then elements are taken out of the heaps, using the `deleteMin` function. Write the C++ procedure that implements this algorithm.

12. Using empirical timings, compare the execution time of the algorithm you constructed for the last question against the execution time of the bucket sort algorithm shown in Figure 13.5.

CHAPTER 14

Sets and Bags — Unordered Collections

THE CONCEPT of a *set* underlies much of mathematics and is as well an integral part of many algorithms. Basically stated, a set is an unordered collection of values. The fundamental operations involved in the set abstraction include adding and removing elements, testing for the inclusion of an element, and forming unions, intersections, and differences with another set. It is the latter operations that are particularly characteristic of the idea of a set. Within this framework, there are, however, many possible variations.

- Some types of sets maintain actual data values, while other formulations of the set data type merely maintain an indication of the presence or absence of an element. A set containing elements that are characters or small integers, for example, need to maintain only enough information to determine whether an element is present in the set, since it can be easily regenerated if necessary. On the other hand, a set containing employee records, or floating point numbers, must carry around the actual data values themselves, since they are not easily reconstructed.

- In most formulations of the abstract concept of a set, an element is not permitted to appear more than once. A *multiset* or *bag* is a set-like data structure that permits elements to be repeated. In practice, whether the implementation of a set data structure has a similar bag counterpart is related to the first point—namely, those implementations that maintain only presence information generally can be used only for sets, while those that maintain entire values can be used (with slight modification) for either sets or bags. We will describe only the set forms of those data structures that can be used for both sets and bags. It is conventionally assumed that no harm comes from attempting to include an element in a set multiple times, and all additions of the same element after the first are ignored.
- The definition of a set explicitly states that the elements are unordered, and the only comparison required of all values is a test for equality. Nevertheless, for the sake of a gain in efficiency some set implementations will use the ability to compare ordering between elements. Thus when selecting a set implementation for a particular problem, an important question to be addressed is whether elements can or cannot be placed in order.

14.1 SET OPERATIONS

The characteristic new feature of a set is the inclusion of operations that act on entire collections of values. These operations are the following:

- *Union*. A union of two sets is formed by adding to one set all values from a second set that do not already appear in the first set.

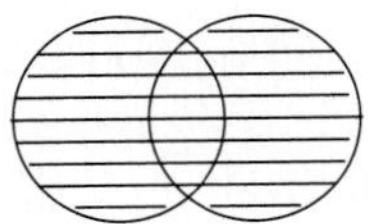

- *Intersection*. The intersection of two sets is the collection of values that appears in both sets. An intersection of one set from another can be formed by removing from the first set all values that do not appear in the second.

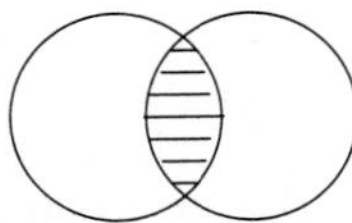

- *Difference*. The difference of two sets is the opposite of the intersection; it is the set of values from one set that do not appear in a second set.

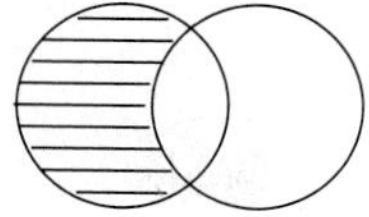

▲ *Subset.* A set is said to be a subset of another set if all values from the first set appear also in the second set.

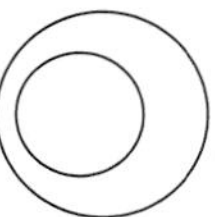

▲ *Equality.* Two sets are equal if all values from the first set appear in the second, and all values from the second also appear in the first. Another way to state this is to say that two sets are equal if they are both subsets of each other.

14.2 BIT VECTOR SETS

In Chapter 6 we introduced the bit vector data structure. A bit vector was implemented using an array of character values, which were in turn simply viewed as eight-bit integer quantities. Just as the C++ language allows the programmer to think about integer values as both arithmetic and logical quantities, the programmer can think of a binary vector as a representation for a set of integer values. A one bit stored at a given index location will indicate that the corresponding value is contained in the set, while a zero value will indicate that the value is not part of the set. The actual values themselves are not stored as part of the set.

It is relatively easy to add set operations to the `bitvector` data structure we developed earlier. Each step of the operation simply loops over the underlying data vector, performing operations on the pair-wise grouping of elements. The operations are well-defined only if the argument vector contains the same number of data values as the receiver vector.

To generate the union of one bit vector set with another, the bitwise *or* operation is used.

Data	10011001
Argument	00111000
Result	10111001

```
void bitVector::unionWith(bitVector& right)
{   // form the union of set with argument set
    // only works if we're both same size
    assert(length() == right.length());
```

```
    const int asize = data.length();
    for (int i = 0; i < asize; i++)
        data[i] |= right.data[i];
}
```

The intersection of one set with a second consists of those values from the first set that are also found in the second. This can be discovered using the bitwise *and* operation:

Data	10011001
Argument	00111000
Result	00011000

```
void bitVector::intersectWith(bitVector& right)
{   // form the intersection of set with argument set
    // only works if we're both same size
    assert(length() == right.length());

    const int asize = data.length();
    for (int i = 0; i < asize; i++)
        data[i] &= right.data[i];
}
```

The difference between one set and a second is the set of values that appears in the first but does not appear in the second. This can be discovered using a bitwise *and* on the inverse of the argument value.

Data	10011001
Argument	00111000
Inverse argument	11000111
Result	10000001

```
void bitVector::differenceWith(bitVector& right)
{   // form the difference of set from argument set
    // only works if we're both same size
    assert(length() == right.length());

    const int asize = data.length();
    for (int i = 0; i < asize; i++)
        data[i] &= ~ right.data[i];
}
```

Two operations are used to compare one set against another. The equality testing operator will determine if two sets are identically equal, while the subset function will return a true value if the argument is a subset of the receiver set. For the former operation, we simply compare the corresponding values in the two arrays.

```
int bitVector::operator == (bitVector& right)
{   // test to see if two sets are the same
    // only works if we're both same size
    assert(length() == right.length());

    // test to see if every position is equal to the argument
    const int asize = data.length();
    for (int i = 0; i < asize; i++)
        if (data[i] != right.data[i])
            return 0;

    // all equal, two sets the same
    return 1;
}
```

For the latter, we first form the intersection, using the bitwise *and* operation, and then compare the argument to the intersection. If the argument value is equal to the intersection, then every value in the argument is also present in the receiver. If not, then the argument must contain at least one value that is not present in the receiver, and thus the subset test is false.

```
int bitVector::subset(bitVector& right)
{   // return true if set is subset of argument
    // only works if we're both same size
    assert(length() == right.length());

    // test to see if every position of the argument
    // is a subset of the corresponding receiver position
    const int asize = data.length();
    for (int i = 0; i < asize; i++)
        if (right.data[i] != (data[i] & right.data[i]))
            return 0;

    return 1;
}
```

Note that the running time of each of these operations is proportional to the size of the set but independent of the number of items (one bits) held in the set. This is not true of the other data structures we have considered in this text.

14.2.1 Character Sets

A common special case of bit sets involves forming sets of characters. Recall that in C++ characters are implemented simply as small integers. Shown below is the class declaration for a datatype `charSet`, which is short for character set.

```
//
// class charSet
//     set indexed by character values
//

class charSet : public bitvector {
public:
    // constructors
    charSet ();
    charSet (char *);
    charSet (const charSet &);

    // set protocol
    void    add             (char ele);
    void    deleteAllValues ();
    int     includes        (char ele) const;
    void    remove          (char ele);
};
```

We have provided for our character sets a constructor that can be used to initialize a `charSet` using a literal character string.

```
charSet::charSet(char * initstr) : bitvector(256)
{   // initialize the set with character from string
    while (*initstr)
        add(*initstr++);
}
```

The addition, inclusion test, and removal operations are all redefined in order to ensure the arguments are characters. A *cast* is used to convert the argument value into an integer, which is then used in the execution of the method inherited from the parent class.

```
void charSet::add(char ele)
{   // simply invoke method from bit vector class
    set((unsigned int) ele);
}

int charSet::includes(char ele) const
{   // return true if set includes argument character
    return test((unsigned int) ele);
}

void charSet::remove(char ele)
{   // remove argument character from set
    clear((unsigned int) ele);
}
```

Because character sets inherit from the class `bitVector`, the remaining set operations (union, intersection, equality test) can all be used as they can with bit vectors.

14.2.2 Application — Splitting a String into Words

We will illustrate the use of character sets by providing a function that will split a string into individual words. Before we define that function, however, we first create a number of useful utility routines. The first of these routines takes as arguments a string, a position, and a character set of "skip characters." The position is assumed to be a valid index into the text. The position is incremented as long as the character indexed belongs to the set of skip characters — hence the name of the procedure, since the purpose is to skip over instances of characters represented in the set. The procedure terminates either when a character is found that is not in the set of skip characters or when the end of the string is reached.

```
unsigned int skipOver
    (string & text, unsigned int position, const charSet & skipchars)
{   // loop as long as we see characters from charSet
    while ((text[position] != '\0') &&
        skipchars.includes(text[position]))
```

Operator Functions or Methods

As we have seen throughout this book, operators can be defined either by using ordinary functions or by using methods (member function). Only a few operators, such as assignment, are restricted to only one form. Up until this chapter, we have consistently defined the equality testing operator as an ordinary function. In the `bitVector` class we instead elected to define equality testing as a member function. We can therefore use this opportunity to describe some of the advantages and disadvantages of the two approaches, and to give some guidelines on how to choose between the two implementation techniques.

The major advantage of defining operators as ordinary functions is the fact that implicit conversions will be applied to both arguments equally. When an operator is defined as a member function, conversions will be applied only to the argument value for the method — that is, to the right argument of the operator. This factor is usually most important in the implementation of arithmetic or relational operators.

The major advantage of defining operators as member functions is the fact that the operator has legitimate access to the internal data areas of the data structure. This was the reason for electing to use a member function to implement the equality testing operator in the class `bitVector`, which allowed us to access the base vector of character values directly. (Admittedly, we could also have provided this access by declaring the equality testing operator to be a friend of the `bitVector` class.)

In general there are no hard and fast rules that fully explain the circumstances under which one technique is preferable to the other. Consequently, this is one area where experience and intuition must be guiding principles.

```
            position = position + 1;

    // return updated position, which may be null character
    // if we ran off end of string
    return position;
}
```

The second procedure is the opposite; it skips characters that are *not* found in the argument set. It returns a position that corresponds either to a character from the set or to the null character if the end of the text string is reached.

```
unsigned int skipTo
    (string & text, unsigned int position, const charSet & haltset)
{   // loop as long as we fail to see characters from halt set
    while ((text[position] != '\0') &&
        ! haltset.includes(text[position]))
            position = position + 1;

    // return updated position, which may be null character
    // if we ran off end of string
    return position;
}
```

We will use these procedures to solve the problem of breaking a string into words. We will approach the problem in two steps. In the first phase, we determine the starting position and length of each word. These will be maintained in a vector, each entry of which is an instance of a simple class that holds two data values and defines no behavior:

```
class wordPosition {
public:
    int startingPos;
    int length;
};
```

The procedure `findSplitPositions` takes as argument a string, a character set of separators, and a vector of words. The last value is resized if necessary. The value returned is the number of words.

```
int findSplitPositions
    (string & text, const charSet & separators,
         vector<wordPosition> & splits)
{   // find the start and length of each word in the argument text
    int lastpos = text.length();
    int numberOfWords = 0;

    // now loop over the text, looking for new words
```

```
    int position = 0;
    while (position < lastpos) {
        // first skip any leading separators
        position = skipOver(text, position, separators);

        // either we are at end of text
        if (position < lastpos) {
            // or at beginning of a word
            if (numberOfWords >= splits.length())
                splits.setSize(splits.length() + 5);
            splits[numberOfWords].startingPos = position;

            // now skip over non-separator characters
            position = skipTo(text, position, separators);

            // length is current position - start
            splits[numberOfWords].length =
                position - splits[numberOfWords].startingPos;
            numberOfWords += 1;
            }
        }

    // return the number of words in words array
    return numberOfWords;
}
```

The procedure `split`, which solves the problem we originally posed, merely invokes `findSplitPositions` to discover the start and length of each word, then uses the substring operation to extract each word from the argument text.

```
void split
    (string & text, const charSet & separators, vector<string> & words)
{
    // invoke procedure to compute word starting positions and lengths.
    // the size of the words array is unimportant, as
    // the vector will grow if necessary
    vector<wordPosition>  splitPos(2);
    int numberOfWords = findSplitPositions(text, separators, splitPos);

    // we now have an array of all the starting positions and lengths
    // simply loop over vector to break string
    words.setSize(numberOfWords, "");
    for (int i = 0; i < numberOfWords; i++)
         words[i] = text(splitPos[i].startingPos, splitPos[i].length);
}
```

14.3 THE ABSTRACT SET OPERATIONS

It is clear that some set operations can be defined in terms of the operations of addition, testing for inclusion, and removal of elements. By making use of iterators and templates, we can write generic polymorphic procedures to implement these operations. For example, the union of one set with another could be implemented in the following fashion:

```
template <class ST, class T>
void setUnionWith(ST & set, iterator<T> & itr)
{
    // simply add every element from the argument iterator
    for (itr.init(); ! itr; itr++)
        set.add(itr());
}
```

The procedure simply uses the iterator passed as the second argument to cycle over elements. Each element is added to the first argument. The only requirement necessary is that the first argument provide a method for add.

The difference between two sets could be similarly defined. Every element in the argument set (represented by an iterator) is tested. If it is found in the first argument set, it is then removed. The elements that remain represent the difference.

```
template <class ST, class T>
void setDifferenceFrom(ST & set, iterator<T> & itr)
{
    // test every element to see if it is in the receiver
    for (itr.init(); ! itr; itr++)
        // if current set has it
        if (set.includes(itr()))
            // then remove it
            set.remove(itr());
}
```

To test whether a set is a subset of another set, it is sufficient to merely test each element of the smaller set and to make sure it is included as an element in the larger set.

```
template <class ST, class T>
int setSubset(ST & set, iterator<T> & itr)
{
    // every element of right must also be in receiver
    for (itr.init(); ! itr; itr++)
        // if set does not have it
        if (! set.includes(itr()))
            // then can't be a subset
```

```
            return 0;

    // everything checks out, must be a subset
    return 1;
}
```

To form the intersection of two sets is a more difficult operation. Our notion of an iterator is not guaranteed to access all elements if some values are deleted from the collection during the process of iteration. Thus to form the intersection of two sets, we first compute the difference, collecting those values that appear in the set but are not in the argument set. Once these values have been computed, they are then removed from the set.

```
template <class ST, class T>
void setIntersectWith(ST & set, iterator<T> & itr)
{
    // make a list of elements in the difference
    list<T> difference;

    // for each element in iterator
    for (itr.init(); ! itr; itr++)
        // if it is not in set
        if (! set.includes(itr()))
            // then save it
            difference.add(itr());

    // now remove elements from the difference
    listIterator<T> litr(intersect);
    for (litr.init(); ! litr; litr++)
        set.remove(litr());
}
```

From these simple implementations we can obtain an upper bound on the running time of various operations in terms of the running times of addition, test for inclusion, and removal. If we let `A`, `I`, and `R` represent these three times and if we let n represent the number of elements in the argument set, the union of two sets can be performed in $O(An)$ time, the intersection and subset tests in $O(In)$, and the intersection in the maximum of $O(In)$ and $O(An)$. The latter form is sometimes written as $O(In + An)$.

For example, an obvious and simple way to implement a set would be to use the `List` data structure from Chapter 8, as shown in Fig. 14.1. Before adding an element to the set, we see if it is already present in the list, as follows:

```
//
// class setList
//     set protocol built on top of list implementation
//

template <class T> class setList : public list<T> {
public:
    // add an item to the set
    virtual void add(T val);

    // removal test
    virtual void remove( T );

    // union formation
    void unionWith(setList<T> &);

    // intersection
    void intersectWith(setList<T> &);

    // difference between sets
    void differenceFrom(setList<T> &);

    // subset test
    int subset(setList<T> &);
};
```

Figure 14.1 Defining sets using lists

```
template <class T> void setList<T>::add(T val)
{   // only add if it is not already in the set
    if (! includes(val))
        list<T>::add(val);
}
```

Recalling that operations on lists execute in linear time (the addition of a new element also requires linear time, since it involves testing to see whether the element is already present in the list), we can see that the operations inherited from class Set will run in $O(n^2)$ time.

Recall also that to remove an arbitrary item from a list required a list iterator. An iterator is also constructed for each of the set operations inherited from class set. Thus the argument to the union operation—for example, in class setList—is a value of the same type, while the argument in class set is an iterator.

```
template <class T> void setList<T>::remove(T val)
{
    listIterator<T> itr(data);
    for (itr.init(); ! itr; itr++)
        if (itr() == val) {
            itr.remove();
            return;
            }
}

template <class T> void setList<T>::unionWith(setList<T> & right)
{
    // simply make an iterator and then use the generic method
    setListIterator<T> itr(right);
    setUnionWith(*this, itr);
}

template <class T> int setList<T>::subset(setList<T> & right)
{
    setListIterator<T> itr(right);
    return setSubset(*this, itr);
}
```

The equality testing operator is implemented using two invocations of the subset test.

```
template <class T>
int operator == (setList<T> & left, setList<T> & right)
{
    // two sets are equal if both are subsets of each other
    return left.subset(right) && right.subset(left);
}
```

Since a `setList` is a `list`, we can use the class `listIterator` to generate the individual values. The exercises explore how a similar, and asymptotically more efficient, set implementation can be built out of the search tree data structure.

Table 14.1 summarizes information on the obvious implementations of sets that build upon data structures we have encountered previously, as well as the new implementation technique we will describe shortly in this chapter. A set produced using lists is trivial to implement and does not require the elements to provide comparison operations, but it has relatively poor performance for anything but simple insertions and deletions. As we will investigate in some of the exercises, using an ordered list (which, of course, requires that elements can be compared against each other) somewhat improves the efficiency of unions and intersections; however, search

Table 14.1 Asymptotic execution of various set operations

	List	Ordered list	Search tree	Bit vector	Hash table
Holds element	yes	yes	yes	no	yes
Bag version	yes	yes	yes	no	yes
Requires comparison	no	yes	yes	no	no
Addition	$O(n)$	$O(n)$	$O(\log n)$	$O(1)$	$O(1)$
Inclusion test	$O(n)$	$O(n)$	$O(\log n)$	$O(1)$	$O(1)$
Removal	$O(n)$	$O(n)$	$O(\log n)$	$O(1)$	$O(1)$
Union	$O(n^2)$	$O(n)$	$O(n \log n)$	$O(n)$	$O(n)$
Intersection	$O(n^2)$	$O(n)$	$O(n \log n)$	$O(n)$	$O(n)$
Subset test	$O(n^2)$	$O(n)$	$O(n \log n)$	$O(n)$	$O(n)$
Equality test	$O(n^2)$	$O(n)$	$O(n \log n)$	$O(n)$	$O(n)$

trees provide an even more efficient technique. Bit vectors, as we have seen, can implement set operations very efficiently. The technique we will investigate in the next section, hash tables, provides dramatically better performance but only by imposing additional restrictions. Using the hash table data structure, optimal performance is guaranteed only if it is possible to provide a hash function that uniformly distributes the elements.

14.4 BUILDING SETS FROM HASH TABLES

One reason the bit vector representation of a set operates so efficiently is that the set operations that deal with an entire vector, such as the union of two bit vectors, can be performed element by element in the underlying array. The next data structure we will investigate builds on this insight, extending the idea to general set structures and not simply bit vectors. Basically stated, the idea is to build on the hash table data type we investigated in the last chapter. You will recall that with hash tables the elements in a collection are separated into a number of buckets. Each bucket can itself hold an arbitrary number of elements. To add a new element to the collection, we first discover the bucket into which it should be placed, then insert the element in the bucket.

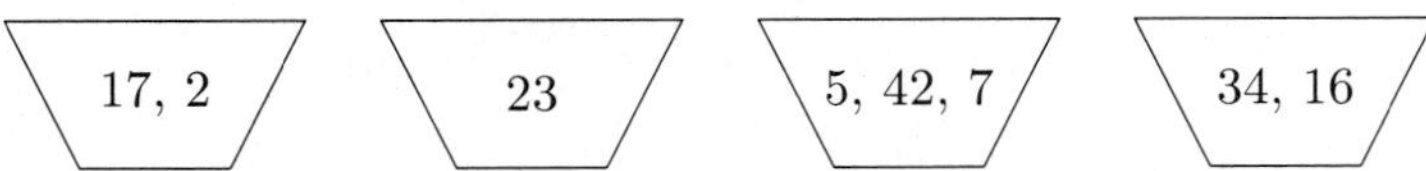

The real power of the technique comes in implementing the set operations, such as union and intersection. Just as we did with the bit vector set data structure, we will perform these operations by pairing corresponding buckets. That is, imagine that our set data type is represented by a set of four buckets. To form the union of this set with another set that is similarly represented by four buckets, we simply combine the elements of the argument set's first bucket with the first bucket from the receiver, the values held in the argument set's second bucket with the second bucket, and so on.

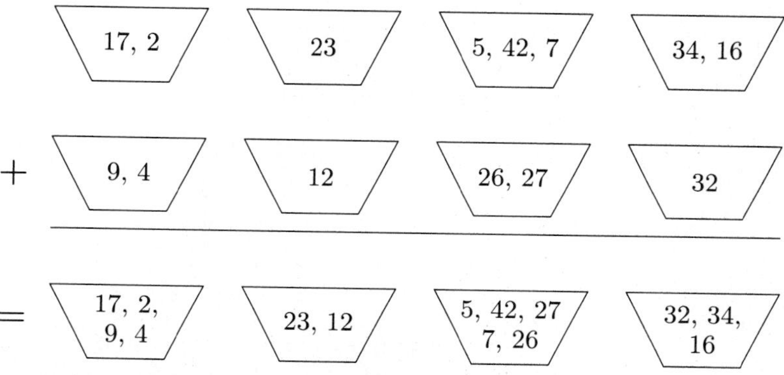

To bring to realization this idea, we will build on the `hashTable` data structure we studied in Chapter 13. Recall that instances of `hashTable` maintained a function, called the *hash function*, that mapped element values into integer indices that were then used to access values from a vector. The class `setTable` illustrates the construction of the set operations on top of the hash table abstraction. Insertion, removal, and the inclusion test are performed by simply hashing the argument into the correct bucket, then performing the operation using the bucket value.

```
//
// class setTable
//      set protocol built out of hash tables
//

template <class T> class setTable : public hashTable<setList<T>, T, T> {
public:
    // constructor
    setTable(unsigned int max, unsigned int (&f)(const T &));

    // implement set protocol
    void    add            (T val);
    void    differenceFrom (setTable<T> &);
    int     includes       (T val) const;
    void    intersectWith  (setTable<T> &);
```

```
    void    remove          (T val);
    void    unionWith       (setTable<T> &);
    int     subset          (setTable<T> &) const;
    int     operator ==     (setTable<T> & ) const;

protected:
    // make an iterator
    iterator<T> * makeIterator(unsigned int i);
};

template <class T> void setTable<T>::add(T val)
{   // compute bucket, then add element
    buckets[hash(val)].add(val);
}

template <class T> int setTable<T>::includes(T val) const
{   // compute bucket, then see if it includes element
    return buckets[hash(val)].includes(val);
}
```

Set operations, such as union and intersection, are performed by looping over the vector of buckets and performing each operation bucket by bucket.

```
template <class T> void setTable<T>::unionWith(setTable<T> & right)
{
    assert(tablesize == right.tablesize);

    // form the union of each bucket independently
    for (int i = 0; i < tablesize; i++)
        buckets[i].unionWith(right.buckets[i]);
}

template <class T>
int setTable<T>::subset(setTable<T> & right)
{
    assert(tablesize == right.tablesize);

    // test subset of each bucket independently
    for (int i = 0; i < tablesize; i++)
        if (! buckets[i].subset(right.buckets[i]))
            return 0;
    // all bucket subsets smaller than corresponding buckets
    return 1;
}
```

14.4.1 Application — Spelling Checker

As an application of the use of sets we will present a very simple spelling checker. The basic idea behind the spelling checker is to maintain, using a hash table, a dictionary of correctly spelled words. To check the spelling of words in the input document, each word is examined and tested with the dictionary. Any word that is not found in the dictionary is added to a set of misspelled words. Thus two sets are used by the algorithm: the set holding the dictionary and the set holding misspelled words. (Using a set for the latter ensures that misspelled words will be reported only once.)

We will use the `setTable` data structure to hold the dictionary. To use this structure, we first need a hashing function. A simple hash function for words is to use the letter values of the first and second character, multiplying the first by 26 and adding the second. The dictionary is read using a simple stream loop. The input file, unlike the dictionary, can be assumed to contain punctuation characters. For this reason, the text file is read line by line, rather than word by word. The function `split` is then invoked to both separate the line into individual words and strip off punctuation characters.

```
unsigned int wordhash(const string & word)
{   // compute hash value from word
    int len = word.length();
    unsigned int result = 0;
    if (len > 0) {
        result = word[0] - 'a';
        if (len > 1)
            result = result * 26 + (word[1] - 'b');
        }
    return result;
}

void spellcheck(istream & dictionary, istream & infile, ostream &
     outfile)
{   string word(120);
    string line(120);
    setTable<string> theDict(676, wordhash);
    setList<string> misspelled;

    // first read the dictionary into the table of words
    while (dictionary >> word)
        theDict.add(word);

    // then read the input file
    // read line by line and use split to both separate into words
```

```
        // and strip off punctuation
        while (line.getline(infile)) }
            // translate into lower case
            toLower(line);
            // split into individual words
            vector<string> words(10);
            split(line, " .;?!:", words);
            // now loop over each word
            // if it is not in the dictionary then it may be wrong
            vectorIterator<string> itr(words);
            for (itr.init(); ! itr; itr++)
                if (! theDict.includes(itr()))
                    misspelled.add(itr());
            }
        // then output the list of misspelled words
        listIterator<string> itr(misspelled);
        for (itr.init(); ! itr; itr++)
            outfile << itr() << '\n';
}
```

The spelling checker algorithm is divided into three steps. In the first step the dictionary to correctly spelled words is read from a file into the hash table data structure. In the second phase the input is processed one word at a time and the list of misspelled words is gathered. In the final phase a loop is used to print out the list of misspelled words.

14.5 CHAPTER SUMMARY

Key Concepts

- Set operations:
  - Union
  - Intersection
  - Difference
  - Subset
- Set implementations
  - Using lists
  - Using trees
  - Using hash tables

The key idea behind the set data structure is the ability to perform operations that affect entire collections at one time. The basic set operations are union, intersection, difference, subset, and equality testing. We have seen various implementations of the set protocol. The class `bitVector` can be used to produce sets of bit values. A special case of this are sets of character values, which are described by class `charSet`. Two other set implementations we have examined are sets built on top of lists and sets built on top of hash tables. The latter requires the user to supply a hash function to convert elements into integer keys. As with all hash table techniques, the efficiency of the resulting data structure will depend upon the degree to which the hash function uniformly distributes key values.

References

A good introduction to the use of sets in mathematics is provided by Ross and Wright [Ross 85]. Since sets form such an integral part of mathematics, it is somewhat surprising that sets are used relatively little in programming, at least in comparison to more basic types such as vectors, lists, and trees. The likely reason is that sets are almost by definition dynamic data structures, and the implementation of sets can be easily constructed out of lists, which are relatively common. One interesting computer language in which sets are a fundamental data type is the language SETL [Schwartz 86, Baxter 89].

Exercises

1. Describe the union, intersection, and differences for the following two sets:

Set A: 1, 2, 5, 7, 12

Set B: 1, 5, 12, 36, 52

2. Explain why it is not possible (or, at least, not easy) to generate a bag version of a set that is implemented using bit vectors.

3. How would you implement a character bag—a bag version of the character set?

4. Prove that a set A is a subset of a set B if and only if the intersection of A and B is equal to A. Would this be a very good way to implement the subset test? Why or why not?

5. Prove that a set A is a subset of a set B if and only if the union of A and B is equal to B. Would this be a very good way to implement the subset test? Why or why not?

6. Describe an `orderedSetList` data structure that is similar to the `setList` data type but in addition maintains the values in sequence.

7. Describe the `setSearchTree` data structure that makes use of the `searchTree` class from Chapter 11 to implement sets.

8. Describe the bag versions of `setList` and `setSearchTree`.

9. Using the skew heap data structure described in Chapter 12, we can implement union very quickly (see page 423). Explain why this would nevertheless not be a good data structure on which to base an implementation of sets. (*Hint*: Consider the asymptotic complexity of other operations.)

10. Explain how using ordered lists instead of lists can reduce the running time for the subset tests and set equality tests from $O(n^2)$ to $O(n)$.

11. Explain how using ordered lists instead of lists can reduce the running time for the union, intersection, and difference operations from $O(n^2)$ to $O(n)$. (*Hint*: Recall the methods ADDBEFORE and ADDAFTER for list abstractions.)

CHAPTER 15

Dictionaries and Tables

LET US RECONSIDER THE PROBLEM Amy faced in Chapter 13 in writing a program to manage her club's finances. The data structure she wanted for her program in Fig. 13.1 (page 425) was similar to an array, a structure to hold as values the dues that each member had paid. She would like to index this structure with the name of the club member. Thus, unlike an array, the index type for this data structure would not be an integer. In Chapter 13 we explored one approach, which was the utilization of a pure hash function on top of the vector data type. The difficulty with this solution was that the range of recognized index values could not easily be enlarged. When new members joined the club, the entire data structure needed to be redesigned. In this chapter we will explore an entirely different data structure that can be used to solve Amy's difficulty with the program in Fig. 13.1.

Abstractly, a *dictionary* (sometimes called a *table*, *mapping*, or *associative array*) is an indexed structure, similar to a vector. In a dictionary, unlike in a vector, the index values, as well as the elements, can be any type. Elements are accessed by making use of the subscript operator. One other difference between a dictionary and a vector is that the dictionary does not limit the size, or the number of elements, that can be held in the structure.

```
//
// class association
//     A single key/value pair,
//     usually maintained in a dictionary
//

template <class K, class V> class association  {
public:
    // value field is publicly accessible
    V           valueField;

    // constructor
    association  (K initialKey, V initialValue);

    // assignment can be either to association or value
    void        operator =    (association<K, V> &);
    void        operator =    (V val);

    // accessor methods for key and value
    K           key           () const;
    V           value         () const;

protected:
    // key field cannot be altered
    const K     keyField;
};
```

Figure 15.1 Definition of the class `association`

15.1 ASSOCIATIONS

Internally, a dictionary will maintain items as pairs of values. Both the key and the element value are stored as part of the data structure. This differs from the vector data type, where only the element values, not the indices, were explicitly stored. The data type we will use for this purpose is the class `association`, shown in Fig. 15.1.

The index value for an association is called the *key*. The key field in an association is fixed; once set, it cannot be altered. The value field, on the other hand, is public and can be changed. An association can be compared to another association, and the two associations are equal if they have the same key value. An association can also be compared to a key value alone, and returns true if the key matches. Similarly, an association can be assigned the value of another association, or a value, but only the value field is changed. Finally, a pair of accessor functions permits the manipulation of the key and value fields.

15.2 DICTIONARIES AS LISTS OF ASSOCIATIONS

The first implementation technique we will use for building a dictionary is to represent the data as a list of associations. This is shown in Fig. 15.2.

A number of the methods, such as the function to clear all values from the collection and the test for emptiness, are easily mapped onto similar tests for the list structure. The programmer has the ability to specify an initial value for each new entry, either with the constructor or with the method `setInitial`.

In addition to those we just named, there are only three new public operations. The first is the subscript operator, used both to create and to modify associations. The second is the method used to remove an association from the collection. The third tests to see if a particular key is in the database. A fourth private method, `associatedWith`, is used in the implementation of the public interface.

The principal method used to interact with a dictionary is the subscripting operator. This operator, however, is built first out of a method used to find an association corresponding to a given key. The `associatedWith` method returns a pointer. This value is nil if no appropriate association exists.

```
template <class K, class V>
association<K, V> * dictionary<K, V>::associatedWith(K key)
{   // return the association with the given key
    // or the null pointer if no association yet exists
    listIterator<association<K, V> *> itr(data);

    // loop over the elements, looking for a match
    for (itr.init(); ! itr; itr++)
        if (itr() == key)
            // return the pointer
            return itr();

    // not found, return null pointer
    return 0;
}
```

To see if the dictionary contains an entry with a given key, the `includes` method simply seeks an association; if successful, then the entry exists.

```
template <class K, class V> int dictionary<K, V>::includesKey(K key)
{   // if there is an association, then element is in the dictionary
    return associatedWith(key) != 0;
}
```

```
//
// class dictionary
//     A collection of key/value pairs
//     implemented as a list of associations
//

template <class K, class V> class dictionary {
public:
    // constructors
    dictionary  ();
    dictionary  (V initialValue);
    dictionary  (const dictionary & v);

    // dictionary protocol
    V &             operator [ ]    (K key);
    void            deleteAllValues ();
    int             includesKey     (K key);
    int             isEmpty         () const;
    void            removeKey       (K key);
    void            setInitial      (V initialValue);

private:
    // data is maintained in a list of associations
    list<association<K, V> *> data;
    V               initialValue;

    // friends
    friend class dictionaryIterator<K, V>;
    friend class table<K, V>;

    // find association with given key
    association<K, V> *     associatedWith  (K key);
};
```

Figure 15.2 Definition of the class `dictionary`

The subscript operator will always return the value field from a legitimate association. If no association is currently matched to the key, a new association is created.

```
template <class K, class V>
V & dictionary<K, V>::operator [ ] (K key)
{   // return value of association specified by key
    // first look to see if association is there already
    association<K, V> * newassoc = associatedWith(key);
```

```
        // if not there, make a new one
        if (! newassoc) {
            newassoc = new association<K, V>(key, initialValue);
            assert(newassoc != 0);
            data.add(newassoc);
            }

        // return reference to value field
        return newassoc->valueField;
}
```

To remove an item from a collection, the user specifies a key. A search is performed to find the matching association. Once found, it is removed from the data list.

```
template <class K, class V>
void dictionary<K, V>::removeKey(K key)
{
    // loop over the elements looking for key
    listIterator<association<K, V> *> itr(data);
    for (itr.init(); ! itr; itr++)
        if (itr()->key() == key)
            itr.removeCurrent();
}
```

15.2.1 Dictionary Iterators

An iterator for the dictionary data structure can be quickly formed using the iterator for the underlying list data type. By making the `dictionaryIterator` class inherit from the `listIterator` class, the only method that needs to be defined is a new constructor. All other functionality is provided by the list iterator. Notice the iterator returns associations. The user can use the methods `key` and `value` to break these into their component parts.

```
//
// class dictionaryIterator
//     implementation of iterator protocol for dictionaries
//

template <class K, class V>
class dictionaryIterator : public listIterator<association<K, V> *> {
public:
    // constructor
    dictionaryIterator(dictionary<K, V> & dict);
};
```

```
template <class K, class V>
dictionaryIterator<K, V>::dictionaryIterator(dictionary<K, V> & dict)
    : listIterator<association<K, V> *>(dict.data)
{
    // no further initialization
}
```

Amy's revised program uses a dictionary rather than the hash vector. Not only is the program shorter, but since it is not limited by the number of members in the club it is more robust.

```
//
// Amy's program to maintain club finances
//

void clubFinances() {
    dictionary<string,double> data(0.0);

    string name;
    double amount;
    double totalDues = 0;     // total dues paid

    // loop while there are records
    while (cin >> name >> amount) {
        // add the new amount to the data record
        data[name] += amount;
        // add to the total dues paid
        totalDues += amount;
        }

    // report the result
    cout << "Dues paid:\n";
    dictionaryIterator<string,double> itr(data);
    for (itr.init(); ! itr; itr++)
        cout << itr().key() << ": $" << itr().value() << '\n';
    cout << "total dues paid: $" << totalDues << '\n';
}
```

15.2.2 Application — Sparse Matrices

In Chapter 6 we introduced the `matrix` data structure, which was used to maintain two dimensional collections of values accessed through a double pair of subscripts. In many applications that use matrices, almost all values in the matrix may be empty — that is, may have a default value (often zero). Such a matrix is called *sparse*. If a matrix is sufficiently sparse, then a considerable amount of storage may be wasted in storing these values. A better scheme would store only those values that possess a nonzero value.

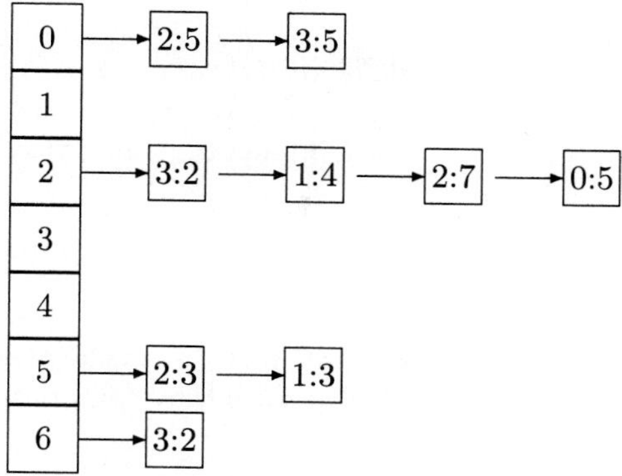

We will present two implementations of the sparse matrix data type, both built on top of the dictionary data structure. The first approach uses a vector of dictionaries. The first subscript is used to index the vector, yielding a dictionary. The second subscript is used to index the dictionary, which stores integer and value pairs. In the preceding diagram we have illustrated the fact that in the dictionary, unlike in the vector or matrix data structures, the elements need not be stored in sequence.

The class declaration of the sparse matrix data type implements only constructors and the subscript operation.

```
//
// class sparseMatrix
//     two dimensional matrix using dictionaries to store rows
//

template <class T> class sparseMatrix {
public:
    // constructors
    sparseMatrix    (unsigned int n, unsigned int m);
    sparseMatrix    (unsigned int n, unsigned int m, T initial);

    // only operation is subscript
    dictionary<int, T> & operator [ ]   (unsigned int n);

private:
    vector< dictionary<int,T> > data;
};
```

The constructor ignores the second argument, and uses the first argument to allocate the vector and the third argument (if given) to set the initial value for the dictionaries.

```
template <class T>
sparseMatrix<T>::sparseMatrix<T>(unsigned int n, unsigned int m,
     T initial): data(n)

{    // set the initial value for each dictionary
     for (unsigned int i = 0; i < n; i++)
         data[i].setInitial(initial);
}
```

The subscript operator simply returns the selected dictionary.

```
template <class T>
dictionary<int,T> & sparseMatrix<T>::operator [ ] (unsigned int n)
{    // simply return the appropriate dictionary
     return data[n];
}
```

To index a specific element, a pair of subscript operators are used. In the expression `smat[i][j]`, for example, the first operator is handled by the sparse matrix subscript operator, which will yield a dictionary. The second operator is then handled by the dictionary, and yields the final value.

If one dictionary is good, two may be even better. If it happens that entire rows are empty, then there is no reason to store even a dictionary for that row. A second approach uses two dictionaries. The first is a dictionary with integer keys that maintains as values the dictionary of rows. By this scheme, only rows that contain at least one value will be maintained.

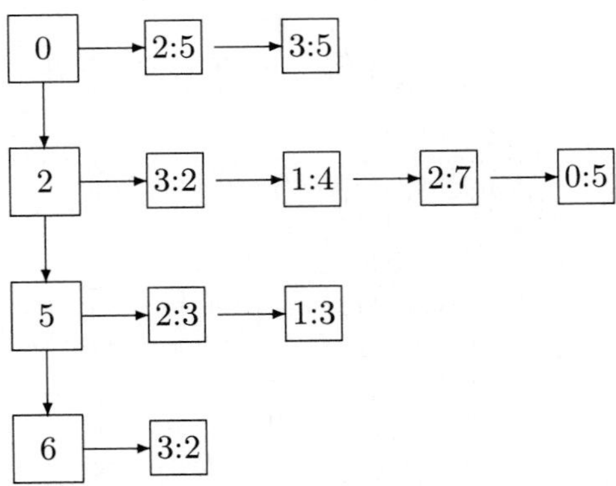

The class declaration that implements this form of sparse matrix is the following:

```
//
// class sparseMatrix2
//     second form of sparse matrix,
//     uses dictionaries for both rows and columns
//
```

```
template <class T> class sparseMatrix2 {
public:
    // constructors
    sparseMatrix2   (unsigned int n, unsigned int m) {}
    sparseMatrix2   (unsigned int n, unsigned int m, T init);

    dictionary<int,T> & operator [ ] (unsigned int n);

private:
    // data areas
    T initialValue;
    dictionary<int, dictionary<int, T> > data;
};
```

The subscript operator for the second form of sparse matrix must first check to see if the accessed row exists; if not it must be initialized.

```
template <class T>
dictionary<int, T> & sparseMatrix2<T>::operator [ ] (unsigned int n)
{   // subscript operator for sparse matrices
    // if we already have a row, just return it
    if (data.includesKey(n))
        return data[n];

    // else make a new entry and set initial value
    data[n].setInitial(initialValue);
    return data[n];
}
```

One problem with both of these implementations of sparse matrices is that simply requesting an element will bring the requested entry into existence, even if only the value of the entry is needed. That is, a loop such as the following, which is typical of matrix algorithms, will force the creation of every entry in the matrix.

```
sum = 0;
for (i = 0; i < numberRows; i++)
    for (j = 0; j < numberColumns; j++)
        sum += mat[i][j];
```

One solution to this problem is to implement a method `includesKey`, similar to the method in class dictionary. This method would take as argument a pair of indices, and return true if the indices represented a valid entry. Using this, the loop above would be rewritten as the following:

```
sum = 0;
for (i = 0; i < numberRows; i++)
    for (j = 0; j < numberColumns; j++)
        if (mat.includesKey(i, j))
            sum += mat[i][j];
```

In the exercises we will investigate the implementation of the method `includesKey`.

15.3 ORDERED DICTIONARIES

The `dictionary` data structure makes no attempt to keep in sequence the entries contained in the collection. A variation, called an `ordered-Dictionary`, maintains values in an order based on the sequencing of key values. To construct this sequence requires just two simple changes to the `dictionary` class. The first change is to maintain the data values using an `orderedList`, rather than a simple (unordered) `list`. The second change is to maintain as values instances of the class `cAssociation`, which is a form of association that permits two values to be compared on the basis of their keys. The class declaration for cASSOCIATION is as follows:

```
//
// class cAssociation
//     a form of association that allows elements to be compared
//

template <class K, class V>
class cAssociation : public association<K, V> {
public:
    // constructor
    cAssociation(K initialKey, V initialValue);
};
```

All behavior, and the data areas, are inherited from the class `association`. The new functions permit only two associations to be compared, or a single association to be compared to a key value. (We show only the former.)

```
template <class K, class V>
int operator < (cAssociation<K, V> & left, cAssociation<K, V> & right)
{   // compare the key values for two associations
    return left.key() < right.key();
}
```

15.3.1 Application — A Concordance

A concordance is an alphabetical list of words in a text, that shows the line numbers on which each word occurs. We will use the development of a concordance to illustrate the use of the ordered dictionary data structure.

The creation of the concordance is divided into two steps: First the concordance is generated (by reading lines from an input stream), and then the result is printed. The main procedure for our concordance application illustrates this separation. The concordance itself is maintained in an ordered dictionary that uses strings as the keys and sets of integers as values. The set data type is used since a word may appear more than once on a line, and we wish to record only the first occurrence.

```
void generateConcordance(istream & in)
{   // generate a concordance for the text given by the input stream
    orderedDictionary<string, setList<int> > concordance;
    // first make the concordance
    makeConcordance(in, concordance);
    // then print it out
    printConcordance(concordance);
}
```

To generate the concordance, each line of the input stream is read in turn, using the method `getline`. A local variable maintains the line number. The line of text is split into words, using the `split` procedure we encountered in Chapter 14 (in addition to spaces, punctuation characters are also considered to be separators). Iterating over the list of words, the subscript operator will enter a new word into the dictionary of words, if it is not there already. Using the add operation from the `setList` data type, the line number is added to the set of lines on which the word appears. The entire procedure is remarkably concise.

```
void makeConcordance(istream & in,
    orderedDictionary<string, setList<int> > & concordance)
{   // read from the indicated input stream, making a concordance
    string line(256);
    vector<string> words(10);

    for (int lineNumber = 1; line.getline(in); lineNumber++) {
        split(line, " .;:?,", words);
        vectorIterator<string> witr(words);
        for (witr.init(); ! witr; witr++)
            concordance[witr()].add(lineNumber);
        }
}
```

To print the concordance requires a nested pair of iterators. The outer iterator loops over the dictionary, while the inner iterator generates the set of line numbers. Each word is printed on a separate line.

```
void printConcordance
    (orderedDictionary<string, setList<int> > & concordance)
{   // print out the values in a concordance
    orderedDictionaryIterator<string, setList<int> > ditr(concordance);
```

```
    for (ditr.init(); ! ditr; ditr++) {
        cout << ditr().key() << ": ";
        setList<int> slist(ditr().value());
        listIterator<int> litr(slist);
        for (litr.init(); ! litr; litr++)
            cout << litr() << " ";
        cout << '\n';
        }
}
```

For example, the input might be as follows:

```
it was the best of times,
it was the worst of times.
```

Then the output, from `best` to `worst`, would be:

```
best: 1
it: 2 1
of: 2 1
the: 2 1
times: 2 1
was: 2 1
worst: 2
```

15.4 DICTIONARIES AS HASH TABLES

The problem with the `dictionary` data structure is fundamental to the use of lists; to perform almost any operation, it may be necessary to examine every entry in the collection. For large collections of values, this may be much too inefficient. One approach to reducing this complexity would be to use trees. This technique is investigated in the exercises. Asymptotically, an even better solution is to make use of the hash table data structure developed in Chapter 13.

The declaration for the `table` data structure is shown in Fig. 15.3. While the technique of composition was used to build the `dictionary` data structure out of the `list` type, here we use the technique of inheritance to build the `table` data type from the `hashTable` class. Because behavior is inherited from the parent class, despite the appearance, the interface for the two data structures is identical (except for constructors).

The constructor for the `table` class requires a hash function, a table size, and an initial value for new entries. The first two are simply passed to the constructor for the underlying hash table. The same operations are implemented in the `table` class as were implemented in the `dictionary` class. Since the interfaces are the same (except for the constructor), one can be used anywhere the other is used.

```
//
// class table
//     dictionary collection of key/value pairs
//     implemented using hash tables
//

template <class K, class V>
class table : public hashTable<dictionary<K, V>, K,
     association<K, V> *> {
public:
    // constructors
    table   (unsigned int max, unsigned int (*f)(const K &));
    table   (unsigned int max, unsigned int (*f)(const K &), V &);

    // new table operators
    V &     operator [ ]    (K key);
    void    removeKey       (K key);
    void    setInitial      (V initialValue);

protected:
    iterator<association<K, V> *> * makeIterator(unsigned int i);
};
```

Figure 15.3 Declaration of the `table` data structure

Each bucket in the `table` type is declared, by the template argument, as an instance of class `dictionary`. The constructor for the class must explicitly set the initial value in each `dictionary`, since the `vector` data type uses the default (no-initialization) constructor for the bucket class. To do so, the method uses the function `setInitial`:

```
template <class K, class V>
table<K, V>::table(unsigned int max, unsigned int (&f)(const K &), V & v)
        : hashTable<dictionary<K, V>, K, association<K, V> *>(max, f)
{   // set the initial value in each bucket
    setInitial(v);
}

template <class K, class V> void table<K, V>::setInitial(V val)
{   // set the initial value in each bucket
    for (int i = 0; i < tablesize; i++)
        buckets[i].initialValue = val;
}
```

The implementation of the subscript and `removeKey` methods simply hashes the argument to find the correct bucket, then invokes the same method on the bucket data value.

```
template <class K, class V>
V & table<K, V>::operator [ ] (K key)
{   // find right dictionary, then subscript dictionary
    return buckets[hash(key)][key];
}

template <class K, class V>
void table<K, V>::removeKey(K key)
{   // find the right bucket, then remove the key
    buckets[hash(key)].removeKey(key);
}
```

Note that, unlike the classes in the last two chapters, in the class `table` the second and third template arguments are different. We hash on the key type, but iterators return references to associations.

15.4.1 Table Iterators

Just as the dictionary iterator was easily formed by subclassing from the list iterator, in a similar manner the table iterator is quickly formed by subclassing from the hash table iterator.

```
//
// class tableIterator
//     iterator protocol for tables
//

template <class K, class V> class tableIterator
    : public hashTableIterator<dictionary<K, V>, K, association<K, V> *>
{
public:
    // constructor
    tableIterator(table<K, V> & v);
};

template <class K, class V>
tableIterator<K, V>::tableIterator(table<K, V> & v)
        : hashTableIterator<dictionary<K, V>, K, association<K, V> *>(v)
{
    // no further initialization
}
```

15.5 CHAPTER SUMMARY

Key Concepts

- Associations, both ordered and unordered.
- Dictionary or table
  - Built using lists of associations
  - Built using tables
  - Built using hash tables

A dictionary is an indexed collection, similar to a vector. Unlike a vector, the index keys can be any type, as can the element values. In this chapter we have explored various implementation techniques that can be used in the realization of the dictionary abstraction.

A high level data structure, such as a dictionary, can simplify the solution of many problems. An illustration of this is the concordance constructed in Section 15.3.1. To generate the concordance requires only five lines of code. Nevertheless, in these five lines the program makes use of no less than fourteen different data structures:

- ▲ The input consists of an input stream, `istream`, and an ordered dictionary of values.
- ▲ The `orderedDictionary` data type is built on top of the `orderedList` form, which is again built on top of the `list` data abstraction.
- ▲ Elements in the ordered dictionary are instances of `cAssociation`, which is in turn built on top of the class `association`.
- ▲ The template arguments for the ordered dictionary are the types `string`, and a `setList` of `integers`. The `setList` is again built on top of the `list` data abstraction.
- ▲ The `split` procedure requires as arguments a `string`, a `vector` of strings, and a set of characters. Internally, the procedure uses a `vector` of words.
- ▲ The class `charSet` is built on top of the `bitVector` class, which is in turn built on top of a `vector` of character types.

We have not even counted facilitator classes, such as `link`, or the iterator classes used in printing the final results.

References

While dictionaries and tables are not basic to C and C++, they are found in a number of other programming languages. They are one of the fundamental data structures in the string processing language SNOBOL [Griswold 71], and in Icon, the more recent language by the same author [Griswold 90]. The dictionary type is also a basic part of the Smalltalk standard library [Goldberg 83].

Exercises

1. Add a method `size` to the `dictionary` data structure described in Fig. 15.2. This method should return the number of elements held by the collection.

2. Add a method `index` to the `dictionary` data structure described in Fig. 15.2. This method should return the pointer to the association containing the first key associated with an argument value. Return a null pointer if no such association exists. Why can we not simply return a key value?

3. One way to avoid the linear lookup cost of the list implementation of dictionaries is to use a tree. Create a data structure similar to the `dictionary` definition shown in Fig. 15.2 that uses a search tree to store the underlying data. To do this, you will need to use the form of association that allows comparisons based on key values.

4. Rewrite the `dictionary` data structure to use inheritance, rather than composition. That is, change the class `dictionary` to inherit from the class `list`. What other changes do you need to make? Does this simplify the implementation? Does it introduce any new capabilities that were not present in the first implementation?

5. Rewrite Amy's program to use the `table` data type. Use the hash function Amy originally proposed in Fig. 13.1 (page 389). Assume a table size of 7.

6. Amy's club has become popular, and now includes the following members.

Abel	Abigail	Abraham	Ada
Adam	Adrian	Adrienne	Agnes
Albert	Alex	Alfred	Alice
Amanda	Amy	Andrew	Andy
Angela	Anita	Anne	Antonia
Arnold	Arthur	Audrey	

Assuming that the changes to the program from the previous question have been made, how many entries will there be in each bucket?

7. Add the method `includesKey` to the first sparse matrix class described on page 430 in Section 15.2.2.

8. Add the method `includesKey` to the second sparse matrix class described in Section 15.2.2. Note that the entry can fail to exist either because the first dictionary does not include the row or because the row exists but the row dictionary does not include the column value.

9. Add a method `size` to the `table` data structure described in Fig. 15.3. This method should return the number of elements held by the collection. You can assume the same method has been added to the `dictionary` data structure.

10. Add a method `index` to the `table` data structure described in Fig. 15.3. This method should return the pointer to the association containing the first key associated with an argument value. Return a null pointer if no such association exists. You can assume the same method has been added to the `dictionary` data structure. Why can we not simply return a key value?

11. Add the method `includesKey` to the `table` data structure described in Fig. 15.3. The method should return true if the argument is a valid key for the table.

12. Write a procedure that scans an input stream and produces an alphabetized list of the words in the input along with their frequency of occurrence.

13. Individuals unfamiliar with a foreign language will often translate a sentence from one language to another using a dictionary and word-for-word substitution. While this does not produce the most elegant translation, it is usually adequate for short sentences, such as "Where is the train station?" Write a program that will read from two files. The first file contains a series of word-for-word pairs for a pair of languages. The second file contains text written in the first language. Examine each word in the text, and output the corresponding value of the dictionary entry.

CHAPTER 16

Graphs

IN THIS CHAPTER we will explore the idea of a graph as it is realized using a number of different data structures. Our purpose is not to summarize the field of graph theory, which is a rich and complex cross between mathematics and computer science; rather, the objective of this chapter is simply to illustrate the use of many of the data structures we have been developing in earlier chapters in the solution of realistic nontrivial problems.

A graph can be considered to be composed of *vertices* and *arcs* (Fig. 16.1). Either may carry additional information. If the graph is being used to model real world objects — for example, a map — then the value of a vertex might represent the population of a city, whereas the value associated with an arc might represent the distance from one city to the next.

There are a number of variations on the basic idea of a graph. A graph is said to be *directed* if the arcs have a designated beginning and ending side; otherwise a graph is said to be undirected. We will restrict our discussion in this chapter to directed graphs. This is, in fact, no restriction at all since an undirected graph can always be simulated by a directed graph, where each arc is represented by two arcs traveling in opposite directions:

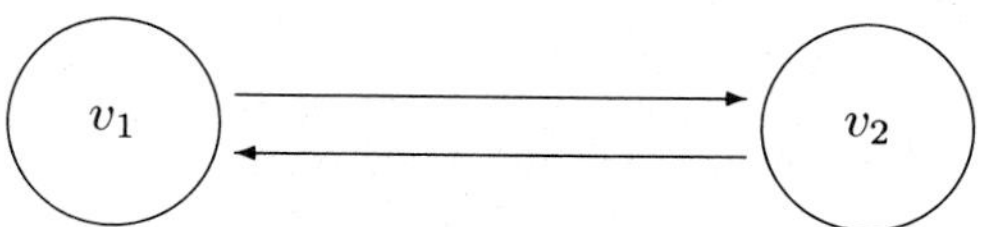

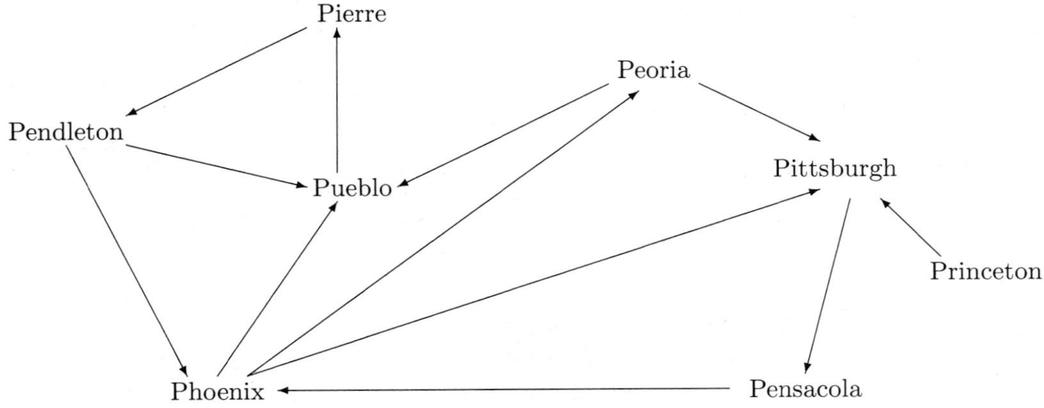

Figure 16.1 A typical graph

A second source of variation in the idea of a graph is the distinction between a *weighted* or *labeled* graph and an *unweighted* graph. In a weighted graph each arc is given a numerical value. For example, the value might represent the distance of the highway connecting two cities, or the cost of the fare between two points. An unweighted graph carries no information. We will begin by considering algorithms for unweighted graphs. This discussion will then be followed by a pair of algorithms that operate on the weighted forms.

16.1 ADJACENCY MATRIX REPRESENTATION

One of the most common ways of representing a graph is to use a matrix, such as those studied in Chapter 6. The vertices in the graph are used as index values for the matrix. This means the vertices must either be numbered in the original graph, or some mechanism must be provided to associate each vertex with an integer value. To represent the graph shown in Fig. 16.1, we could simply list the cities in alphabetical order, and number the list. Entries in the matrix are Boolean values, represented by 0 and 1. A one value in the position indexed by i and j in the matrix indicates the fact that there is an arc between vertices i and j, while a zero value indicates there is no such connection. By convention, a node is always considered to be connected to itself; thus all positions in the major diagonal (that is, positions with the same row and column index value) are set to 1. The adjacency matrix representation for the graph in Fig. 16.1 is as follows:

City	0.	1.	2.	3.	4.	5.	6.	7.
0. Pendleton	1	0	0	1	0	0	0	1
1. Pensacola	0	1	0	1	0	0	0	0
2. Peoria	0	0	1	0	0	1	0	1
3. Phoenix	0	0	1	1	0	1	0	1
4. Pierre	1	0	0	0	1	0	0	0
5. Pittsburgh	0	1	0	0	0	1	0	0
6. Princeton	0	0	0	0	0	1	1	0
7. Pueblo	0	0	0	0	1	0	0	1

There are a number of questions we could ask concerning any particular graph. One of the fundamental problems is the question of *reachability*. That is, what is the set of vertices that can be reached by starting from a particular vertex and moving only along the given arcs in the graph? Conversely, are there any vertices that cannot be reached by traveling in such a fashion?

There are two basic variations on this question. The *single source* question poses a specific initial starting vertex and requests the set of vertices reachable from this vertex. The *all pairs* question seeks to generate this information simultaneously for all possible vertices. Of course, a solution to the all pairs question will answer the single source question as well. For this reason, we would expect that an algorithm that solves the all pairs problem will require at least as much effort as any algorithm for the single source problem. In the next section we will present a solution to the all pairs reachability problem. A solution to the single source reachability problem will subsequently be presented in Section 16.2.

16.1.1 Warshall's Algorithm

The algorithm we will describe to illustrate the use of the adjacency matrix representation of graphs (Fig. 16.2) is known as Warshall's algorithm, named after the computer scientist credited with its discovery. The heart of Warshall's algorithm is a trio of loops, which operate very much like the loops in the classic algorithm for matrix multiplication. The key idea is that at each iteration through the outermost loop (index `k`), we add to the graph any path of length 2 that has node `k` as its center.

The process of adding information to the graph is performed through a combination of bitwise logical operations. The expression `a[i][k] & a[k][j]` is true if there is a path from node `i` to node `k`, and if there is a path from node `k` to node `j`. By using the bitwise or-assignment operator,

```
// warshall - adjacency matrix
// solve the all pairs reachability problem
//
void warshall(matrix<int> & a)
{
    // find the limit, make sure matrix is square
    int n = a.numberRows();
    assert(n == a.numberColumns());

    // each step through the outer loop
    // see if it is possible to make a connection
    // from vertex i to vertex j through vertex k
    for (int k = 0; k < n; k++)
        for (int i = 0; i < n; i++)
            for (int j = 0; j < n; j++)
                a[i][j] |= a[i][k] & a[k][j];
}
```

Figure 16.2 Warshall's algorithm

we add this to position a[i][j]. The use of bitwise-or ensures that if there was a one bit already in the position, indicating we had already discovered a previous path, then the earlier information will not be erased. Figure 16.3 gives the intermediate values of the matrix a as we execute Warshall's algorithm on the adjacency matrix from the graph of Fig. 16.1.

The easiest way to understand Warshall's algorithm is to simulate a few iterations through the outer loop. In the first iteration we are looking for paths that flow through node 0, which represents Pendleton. Since Pierre has the only arc flowing into Pendleton, it is the source of the only possible new paths. In this case there are two new paths discovered, one that links Pierre with Phoenix and another that links Pierre with Pueblo.

In the second iteration we investigate paths that travel through node 1, Pensacola. We discover one new arc, which links Pittsburgh with Phoenix. It turns out in the next step that there are no new paths that flow through Peoria, and thus we have omitted this table from Fig. 16.3.

The next step is to discover paths through Phoenix, and it is here that we can see how Warshall's algorithm really operates. From the original graph we can derive the arcs from Pendleton to Peoria, and Pendleton to Pittsburgh, just as we did in the earlier steps. But now we can do more. From the previous steps we now know that we can travel from Pierre to Phoenix and from Pueblo to Phoenix. Thus, by extending paths we have earlier encountered, we can now say that it is possible to travel from Pierre to Peoria and Pittsburgh, and from Pueblo to the same two destinations. Even though at each step we consider only paths of length

1	0	0	1	0	0	0	1	1	0	0	1	0	0	0	1
0	1	0	1	0	0	0	0	0	1	0	1	0	0	0	0
0	0	1	0	0	1	0	1	0	0	1	0	0	1	0	1
0	0	1	1	0	1	0	1	0	0	1	1	0	1	0	1
1	0	0	0	1	0	0	0	1	0	0	1	1	0	0	1
0	1	0	0	0	1	0	0	0	1	0	0	0	1	0	0
0	0	0	0	0	1	1	0	0	0	0	0	0	1	1	0
0	0	0	0	1	0	0	1	0	0	0	0	1	0	0	1

1	0	0	1	0	0	0	1	1	0	1	1	0	1	0	1
0	1	0	1	0	0	0	0	0	1	1	1	0	1	0	1
0	0	1	0	0	1	0	1	0	0	1	0	0	1	0	1
0	0	1	1	0	1	0	1	0	0	1	1	0	1	0	1
1	0	0	1	1	0	0	1	1	0	1	1	1	1	0	1
0	1	0	1	0	1	0	0	0	1	1	1	0	1	0	1
0	0	0	0	0	1	1	0	0	0	0	0	0	1	1	0
0	0	0	0	1	0	0	1	0	0	0	0	1	0	0	1

1	0	1	1	0	1	0	1	1	1	1	1	0	1	0	1
0	1	1	1	0	1	0	1	0	1	1	1	0	1	0	1
0	0	1	0	0	1	0	1	0	1	1	1	0	1	0	1
0	0	1	1	0	1	0	1	0	1	1	1	0	1	0	1
1	0	1	1	1	1	0	1	1	1	1	1	1	1	0	1
0	1	1	1	0	1	0	1	0	1	1	1	0	1	0	1
0	0	0	0	0	1	1	0	0	1	1	1	0	1	1	1
1	0	1	1	1	1	0	1	1	1	1	1	1	1	0	1

1	1	1	1	0	1	0	1	1	1	1	1	1	1	0	1
0	1	1	1	0	1	0	1	1	1	1	1	1	1	0	1
0	1	1	1	0	1	0	1	1	1	1	1	1	1	0	1
0	1	1	1	0	1	0	1	1	1	1	1	1	1	0	1
1	1	1	1	1	1	0	1	1	1	1	1	1	1	0	1
0	1	1	1	0	1	0	1	1	1	1	1	1	1	0	1
0	1	1	1	0	1	1	1	1	1	1	1	1	1	1	1
1	1	1	1	1	1	0	1	1	1	1	1	1	1	0	1

Figure 16.3 Some intermediate graphs obtained while executing Warshall's algorithm

two, by repeatedly extending existing arcs the algorithm discovers paths of arbitrary length.

It is easy to see that Warshall's algorithm is $O(n^3)$, where n is the number of nodes in the graph. It is less easy to give a formal proof of correctness for the algorithm. To do so is beyond the purpose of the text here; however, suggestions on how such a proof could be developed are presented in the exercises at the end of the chapter.

16.2 EDGE LIST REPRESENTATION

The adjacency matrix representation has the disadvantage that it always requires $O(n^2)$ space to store a matrix with n vertices, regardless of the number of arcs. An alternative representation stores only the arcs, and it is thus advantageous if the graph is relatively sparse.

The basic idea is for each vertex to maintain both a value and a list of those vertices to which it is connected. This is accomplished by the following class declaration:

```
//
// class vertex
//     a simple unweighted graph vertex
//
template <class T> class vertex {
public:
    // data value and arcs are publicly accessible
    T   value;
    setList<vertex &>  arcs;

    // constructor
    vertex();
    vertex(T init);

    // add a new arc
    void addArc(vertex &);
};
```

Instances of the class `vertex` can be compared to each other and are equal if their values match. The method `addArc` can be used to create a new arc that originates at the vertex. For example, the graph in Fig. 16.1 could be created by the following sequence of statements:

```
// make the initial vertices
vertex<string> pendleton("pendleton");
vertex<string> pensacola("pensacola");
vertex<string> peoria("peoria");
vertex<string> phoenix("phoenix");
```

```
vertex<string> pierre("pierre");
vertex<string> pittsburgh("pittsburgh");
vertex<string> princeton("princeton");
vertex<string> pueblo("pueblo");

// create the initial links
pendleton.addArc(phoenix); pendleton.addArc(pueblo);
pensacola.addArc(phoenix);
peoria.addArc(pittsburgh); peoria.addArc(pueblo);
phoenix.addArc(peoria); phoenix.addArc(pittsburgh);
     phoenix.addArc(pueblo);
pierre.addArc(pendleton);
pittsburgh.addArc(pensacola);
princeton.addArc(pittsburgh);
pueblo.addArc(pierre);
```

16.2.1 Reachability Using Depth-First Search

We will illustrate the use of the `vector` data type by presenting an algorithm for the single-source reachability problem—that is, a procedure to discover which vertices may be reached by a sequence of arcs starting from a single-source vertex.

The procedure used to compute this is shown in Fig. 16.4. The algorithm uses depth-first search, a technique that we encountered previously in Chapter 12. You will recall that the depth-first search algorithm utilizes a stack of vertices that are known to be reachable, and through which other vertices may be reachable. Initially, the stack contains simply the source vertex.

At each step of processing, one node is removed from the stack. If it is a node that has not previously been reported as reachable, then the neighbors of the node are pushed on the stack. When the stack is finally empty, then all nodes that can be reached will have been investigated.

For example, executing the following instructions will reveal that in our example graph it is possible to get from Pierre to any city except Princeton.

```
// find which cites are reachable from pierre
setList<vertex<string> &> reachable;
findReachable(pierre, reachable);

// print them out
listIterator<vertex<string> &> itr(reachable);
for (itr.init(); ! itr; itr++)
    cout << itr().value << '\n';
```

```
void findReachable
    (vertex<string> & source, setList<vertex<string> &> & reachable)
{   // find all the vertices that are reachable from a given source
    // use depth first search algorithm
    stackList<vertex<string> &> pendingVertices;
    pendingVertices.push(source);

    // while not empty, pull an item from the stack and process it
    while (! pendingVertices.isEmpty()) {
        vertex<string> & vertx = pendingVertices.pop();
        // if we haven't visited it yet, then do so now
        if (! reachable.includes(vertx)) {
            reachable.add(vertx);
            // now record that neighbors are reachable
            listIterator<vertex<string> &> itr(vertx.arcs);
            for (itr.init(); ! itr; itr++)
                pendingVertices.push(itr());
            }
        }
}
```

Figure 16.4 Single-source reachability algorithm

16.3 WEIGHTED ADJACENCY MATRIX

Just as important as the question of what cities can be reached by starting at a given location is the question of how much the trip will cost. But to determine this, we must somehow encode the "cost" of traversing an arc. To accommodate this, we have the notion of a *weighted graph*, in which every arc has an associated value. For example, we might weight the arcs in Fig. 16.1, producing a graph such as that shown in Fig. 16.5.

Just as there were two major representations of unweighted graphs, so, too, are there two main techniques of encoding weighted graphs. These are the weighted adjacency matrix, and the labeled edge list representation. We will explore each of these in turn.

The weighted adjacency matrix is a two-dimensional matrix, just like the unweighted form. Instead of simply using 0/1 values, now the value in each position is the cost of moving from the vertex associated with the row to the vertex associated with the column. There are two special cases. The cost to move from any vertex to itself is zero, and the cost to move from any vertex to a vertex to which it is not connected is infinity (by convention, written ∞). In practice any value larger than any quantity expected to arise during computation can be used to represent infinity. The weighted adjacency matrix representation of the graph shown in Fig. 16.5 is as follows:

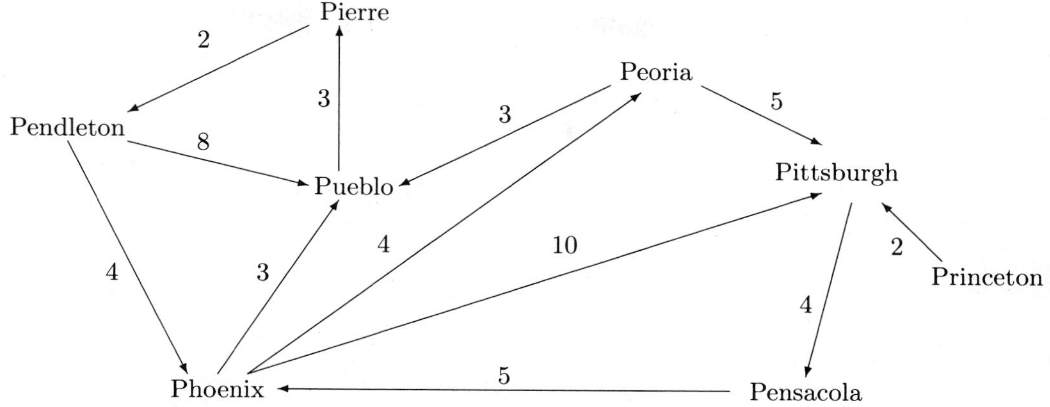

Figure 16.5 A weighted graph

City	0.	1.	2.	3.	4.	5.	6.	7.
0. Pendleton	0	∞	∞	4	∞	∞	∞	8
1. Pensacola	∞	0	∞	5	∞	∞	∞	∞
2. Peoria	∞	∞	0	∞	∞	5	∞	3
3. Phoenix	∞	∞	4	0	∞	10	∞	3
4. Pierre	2	∞	∞	∞	0	∞	∞	∞
5. Pittsburgh	∞	4	∞	∞	∞	0	∞	∞
6. Princeton	∞	∞	∞	∞	∞	2	0	∞
7. Pueblo	∞	∞	∞	∞	3	∞	∞	0

16.3.1 Floyd's Algorithm

The weighted adjacency matrix version of Warshall's algorithm is called Floyd's algorithm, again, named for the computer scientist credited with its discovery. (The same Robert Floyd was the first to describe the tree sort algorithm we presented in Chapter 11.) The procedure is shown in Fig. 16.6. In place of the bitwise-and operation in Warshall's algorithm, an addition is used in Floyd's; and in place of the bitwise-or used to update the path matrix, Floyd's algorithm uses a maximum value calculation.

If we apply this algorithm to the data in our sample graph, we obtain the intermediate values shown in Fig. 16.7. These can be contrasted with the similar output from Warshall's algorithm. Note that each time a value is changed in Warshall's matrix, the same value is being modified here. Now, however, the value held in the matrix is not simply an indication that there is a path, but it is the lowest known cost of the path.

```
//
// floyd - all pairs shortest path algorithm
//
void floyd(matrix<int> & a)
{
    int max = a.numberRows();

    for (int k = 0; k < max; k++)
        for (int i = 0; i < max; i++)
            for (int j = 0; j < max; j++) {
                int newPathLength = a[i][k] + a[k][j];
                if (newPathLength < a[i][j])
                    a[i][j] = newPathLength;
                }
}
```

Figure 16.6 Floyd's algorithm

16.4 LABELED EDGE LIST REPRESENTATION

In the unweighted graph, each vertex maintains a set of nodes to which it is connected. We can use the same general idea in the representation of graphs with labeled (and weighted) arcs. In place of a set, each vertex will maintain a dictionary structure. The key fields in this dictionary will represent the neighbor vertices to which the vertex is connected. The value fields will represent the edge label, or weight for the connecting arcs. Adding the same utility methods that we used in the class `vertex`, the description of the class `labeledVertex` can be given as follows:

```
//
// class labeledVertex
//    vertex maintaining arcs with edge labels
//    type T is vertex label, type A is arc label
//

template <class T, class A> class labeledVertex {
public:
    // value and arcs are both public
    T value;
    dictionary<labeledVertex &, A>  arcs;

    // constructors
    labeledVertex();
    labeledVertex(T init);
```

0	∞	∞	4	∞	∞	∞	8	0	∞	∞	4	∞	∞	∞	8
∞	0	∞	5	∞	∞	∞	∞	∞	0	∞	5	∞	∞	∞	∞
∞	∞	0	∞	∞	5	∞	3	∞	∞	0	∞	∞	5	∞	3
∞	∞	4	0	∞	10	∞	3	∞	∞	4	0	∞	10	∞	3
2	∞	∞	∞	0	∞	∞	∞	2	∞	∞	6	0	∞	∞	10
∞	4	∞	∞	∞	0	∞	∞	∞	4	∞	∞	∞	0	∞	∞
∞	∞	∞	∞	∞	2	0	∞	∞	∞	∞	∞	∞	2	0	∞
∞	∞	∞	∞	3	∞	∞	0	∞	∞	∞	∞	3	∞	∞	0

0	∞	∞	4	∞	∞	∞	8	0	∞	8	4	∞	13	∞	7
∞	0	∞	5	∞	∞	∞	∞	∞	0	9	5	∞	14	∞	8
∞	∞	0	∞	∞	5	∞	3	∞	∞	0	∞	∞	5	∞	3
∞	∞	4	0	∞	10	∞	3	∞	∞	4	0	∞	9	∞	3
2	∞	∞	6	0	∞	∞	10	2	∞	10	6	0	15	∞	9
∞	4	∞	9	∞	0	∞	∞	∞	4	13	9	∞	0	∞	12
∞	∞	∞	∞	∞	2	0	∞	∞	∞	∞	∞	∞	2	0	∞
∞	∞	∞	∞	3	∞	∞	0	∞	∞	∞	∞	3	∞	∞	0

0	∞	8	4	∞	13	∞	7	0	17	8	4	∞	13	∞	7
∞	0	9	5	∞	14	∞	8	∞	0	9	5	∞	14	∞	8
∞	∞	0	∞	∞	5	∞	3	∞	9	0	14	∞	5	∞	3
∞	∞	4	0	∞	9	∞	3	∞	13	4	0	∞	9	∞	3
2	∞	10	6	0	15	∞	9	2	19	10	6	0	15	∞	9
∞	4	13	9	∞	0	∞	12	∞	4	13	9	∞	0	∞	12
∞	∞	∞	∞	∞	2	0	∞	∞	6	15	11	∞	2	0	14
5	∞	13	9	3	18	∞	0	5	22	13	9	3	18	∞	0

0	17	8	4	∞	13	∞	7	0	17	8	4	10	13	∞	7
∞	0	9	5	∞	14	∞	8	13	0	9	5	11	14	∞	8
∞	9	0	14	∞	5	∞	3	8	9	0	12	6	5	∞	3
∞	13	4	0	∞	9	∞	3	8	13	4	0	6	9	∞	3
2	19	10	6	0	15	∞	9	2	19	10	6	0	15	∞	9
∞	4	13	9	∞	0	∞	12	17	4	13	9	15	0	∞	12
∞	6	15	11	∞	2	0	14	19	6	15	11	17	2	0	14
5	22	13	9	3	18	∞	0	5	22	13	9	3	18	∞	0

Figure 16.7 Intermediate steps in Floyd's algorithm

```
    // add an arc
    void addArc(labeledVertex & to, A label);
};
```

To create the graph shown in Fig. 16.5, we could use the following sequence of statements:

```
// make the initial vertices
labeledVertex<string, double> pendleton("pendleton");
labeledVertex<string, double> pensacola("pensacola");
labeledVertex<string, double> peoria("peoria");
labeledVertex<string, double> phoenix("phoenix");
labeledVertex<string, double> pierre("pierre");
labeledVertex<string, double> pittsburgh("pittsburgh");
labeledVertex<string, double> princeton("princeton");
labeledVertex<string, double> pueblo("pueblo");

// create the initial links
pendleton.addArc(phoenix, 4); pendleton.addArc(pueblo, 8);
pensacola.addArc(phoenix, 5);
peoria.addArc(pittsburgh, 5); peoria.addArc(pueblo, 3);
phoenix.addArc(peoria, 4); phoenix.addArc(pittsburgh, 10);
    phoenix.addArc(pueblo,3);
pierre.addArc(pendleton, 2);
pittsburgh.addArc(pensacola, 4);
princeton.addArc(pittsburgh, 2);
pueblo.addArc(pierre, 3);
```

16.4.1 Dijkstra's Algorithm

We illustrate the use of the weighted graph data structure by describing a solution to the *single source shortest path* problem. As the name suggests, the problem consists of discovering the shortest distance from a specific starting vertex to all other reachable nodes in a graph. The program, named `dijkstra` in honor of the computer scientist credited with discovering the algorithm, is shown in Fig. 16.8. Two `typedef` statements are used to simplify the presentation of the algorithm. We will refer to weighted vertices of string values and double precision edge labels using the shorter name `node`, and use the term `arc` to refer to an association of a weight and node pair.

The input to the procedure is the starting node, the "single source" named in the problem description. The output is returned in the second argument, which is a dictionary keyed by vertices and holding distance values. The algorithm is a form of breadth-first search centered around a priority queue, and it is thus similar to the simulations we examined in Chapter 12. The elements in the priority queue represent vertices and

```
typedef labeledVertex<string, double> node;
typedef cAssociation<double, node &> arc;

void dijkstra(node & start, dictionary<node &, double> & distances)
{
    // make sure distances dictionary is empty
    distances.clear();

    // process a priority queue of distances to nodes
    priorityQueueList<arc> que;
    que.add(arc(0.0, start));

    // continually remove smallest element from queue
    while (! que.isEmpty()) {
        arc neighbor = que.deleteMin();
        node & neighborNode = neighbor.value();
        // if neighbor has not already been seen,
        // process it
        if (! distances.includesKey(neighborNode)) {
            double dist = neighbor.key();
            distances[neighborNode] = dist;
            dictionaryIterator<node &, double> itr(neighborNode.arcs);
            for (itr.init(); ! itr; itr++)
                que.add(arc(dist + itr().value(), itr().key()));
            }
        }
}
```

Figure 16.8 Dijkstra's single source shortest path algorithm

distances. Initially the priority queue contains only the source vertex and the distance value zero.

Figure 16.9 illustrates the changes, to both the priority queue and the result dictionary of distances, as the program is executed on our example graph. Initially the distance collection is empty and the queue contains the starting vertex, Pierre. At each step the smallest element in the priority queue is removed. If the vertex removed from the queue is not yet present in the distances collection, then we have found the length of the shortest path to a new node. The newly discovered node is added to the distances collection. Knowing the shortest distance to this node, and knowing the distance to each neighbor of the node, we can compute the distances to each of the neighbor nodes.

In the first step we discover the distance to the starting node is zero. The distances to its only neighbor, namely the city Pendleton, is 2. This

```
distances          priority queue

                   Pierre: 0
Pierre: 0          Pendleton: 2
Pendleton: 2       Phoenix: 6, Pueblo: 10
Phoenix: 6         Pueblo: 9, Peoria : 10, Pueblo: 10, Pittsburgh: 16
Pueblo: 9          Peoria: 10, Pueblo: 10, Pierre: 12, Pittsburgh: 16
Peoria: 10         Pueblo: 10, Pierre: 12, Pueblo: 13, Pittsburgh: 15,
                   Pittsburgh: 16
                   Pierre: 12, Pueblo: 13, Pittsburgh: 15, Pittsburgh: 16
                   Pueblo: 13, Pittsburgh: 15, Pittsburgh: 16
                   Pittsburgh: 15, Pittsburgh: 16
Pittsburgh: 15     Pittsburgh: 16, Pensacola: 19
                   Pensacola: 19
Pensacola: 19      Phoenix: 24
                   empty
```

Figure 16.9 Trace of execution of Dijkstra's algorithm

value is computed and placed into the queue, where it is immediately removed.

Next, the destination Pendleton is removed. Adding the distance to Pendleton to the distance from Pendleton to its neighbors, Phoenix and Pueblo, we discover two new paths and place them into the priority queue. Note that the queue maintains values in an order based on their distance, so the entry representing Phoenix will be in front of the entry representing Pueblo.

The processing of the entry for Phoenix illustrates the importance for this algorithm of the use of a priority queue, rather than a stack, as in depth-first search, or a simple queue, as in breadth-first search. From Phoenix we discover paths to Peoria, Pittsburgh, and Pueblo. The latter is, in fact, a shorter path than the entry placed earlier into the queue that represented the arc from Pendleton. Because the priority queue maintains values in order of their least cost, it will be the shortest path to Pueblo, the path through Phoenix, that will be removed first from the queue. Subsequent deletion from the queue of cities that have already been processed will simply be ignored. In this manner the shortest distance to each city will be discovered.

16.5 FINITE AUTOMATA

Another common use of graphs is in the representation of *finite automata*. Finite automata are very simple models of computing devices. Like a labeled graph, an automata consists of a sequence of vertices, called *states*,

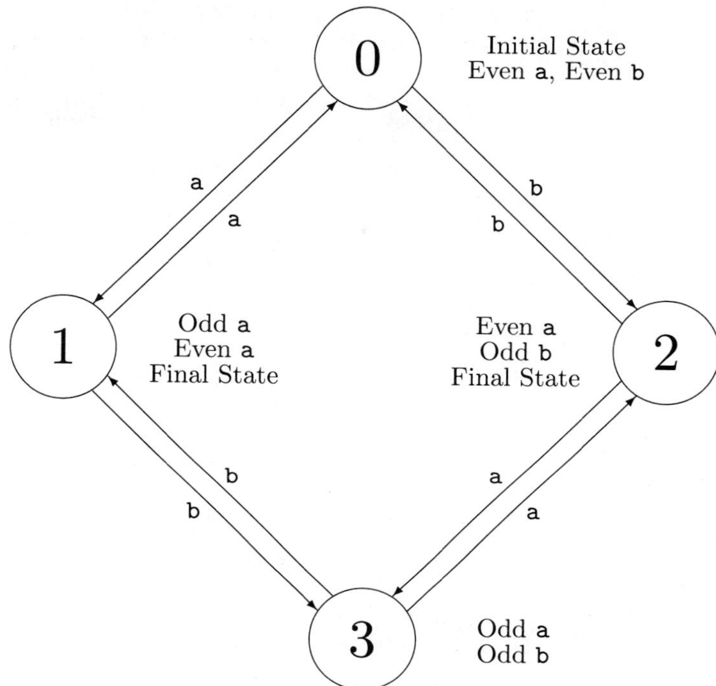

Figure 16.10 A typical finite automata

and a series of labeled arcs connecting the states. One state is special and is designated the *initial state*. Other states may be designated as *final states*.

Finite automata are devices used to recognize sequences of symbols with certain properties. For example, the finite automata shown in Fig. 16.10 processes strings of a and b symbols, and recognizes those strings with either an odd number of a symbols or of b symbols, but not an odd number of both.

The automata consists of four states, labeled 0, 1, 2, and 3. State 0 is the initial state. To understand how the automata operates, we can give alternative descriptions for each of the states. State 0, the initial state, corresponds to having already processed an even number of a symbols and an even number of b symbols. If the automata is in this state and the next symbol is an a, then we will move from having seen an even number of a symbols to the state that corresponds to having seen an odd number of a symbols. This is state 1. Similarly, state 2 corresponds to the situation where there is an even number of a symbols but an odd number of b symbols.

Once in state 1, if the next symbol is another a, then we can move back into state 0 since the two a symbols balance out, and we have thus once more seen an even number of a's. If, however, the next symbol is a b, then the automata must move into a state that records the fact that we have seen both an odd number of a symbols and an odd number of b symbols. This is state 3. Any symbol read in this state will return the automata to either state 1 or state 2.

We can simulate a finite automata using a data structure such as the following:

```
//
// class fa
//     finite automata

template <class V, class A> class fa {
public:
    // constructor - takes start state
    fa   (labeledVertex<V, A> & start);

    // add state to final state
    void addFinal            (labeledVertex<V, A> &);

    // methods to move current state
    labeledVertex<V, A> * currentState;
    void setCurrentToStart  ();
    int  advance             (A arcvalue);
    int  inFinal             () const;
    int  accept              (iterator<A> &);

private:
    labeledVertex<V, A> &   startState;
    setList<labeledVertex<V, A> &> finalStates;
};
```

The constructor for the class requires a start symbol, which is placed into a local data area. The data area also maintains a set of final states. New states can be added to this set using the method addFinal.

To simulate the execution of the finite automata, the data structure maintains a pointer to a state, called the "current" state. The method setCurrentToStart sets this pointer to the start state. Thereafter, the method advance can be used to move the automata from one state to the next.

```
template <class V, class A> int fa<V, A>::advance(A arcValue)
{   // see if any entry in the dictionary matches arc
    // can't advance if we aren't anywhere to start with
    if (currentState == 0)
        return 0;
```

```
        dictionaryIterator<labeledVertex<V, A> &, A>
             ditr(currentState->arcs);
        for (ditr.init(); ! ditr; ditr++)
            if (ditr().value() == arcValue) {
                // found arc - advance current state
                currentState = & ditr().key();
                return 1;
                }
        // can't advance on that symbol
        currentState = 0;
        return 0;
}
```

The advance method searches the dictionary for arcs labeled with the argument token. If one is found, the current state is changed to the associated vertex, and a value of 1 is returned. If no appropriately labeled arc is found, the current state is changed to the null pointer and a value of zero is returned.

In order to simplify moving the finite automata through a sequence of steps, a method accept is defined that takes as argument an iterator of tokens. The finite automata is started in the initial state and the iterator used to direct the movement through the various states. If, when the iterator is finally exhausted, the current state is one of the designated final states, then the sequence of moves generated by the iterator is recognized as a legal value.

```
template <class V, class A> int dfa<V, A>::accept(iterator<A> & itr)
{    // see if automata will accept string represented by iterator
     // start in initial state
     setCurrentToStart();

     // run through all the transitions
     for (itr.init(); ! itr; itr++)
         advance(itr());

     // return true if we are in a final state
     return inFinal();
}
```

The following sequence of statements can be used to generate a data structure that will simulate the finite automata shown in Fig. 16.10:

```
// make the states
labeledVertex<int, char> zero(0);
labeledVertex<int, char> one(1);
labeledVertex<int, char> two(2);
labeledVertex<int, char> three(3);
```

```
zero.addArc(one, 'a'); zero.addArc(two, 'b');
one.addArc(zero, 'a'); one.addArc(three, 'b');
two.addArc(zero, 'b'); two.addArc(three, 'a');
three.addArc(two, 'a'); three.addArc(one, 'b');

// create the finite automata
fa<int, char> rec(zero);
rec.addFinal(one); rec.addFinal(two);
```

To see if the finite automata will accept various strings, we can create a string iterator as an argument for the `accept` method:

```
if (rec.accept(stringIterator("ababa")))
    cout << "accepted\n";
else
    cout << "not accepted\n";
```

16.6 CHAPTER SUMMARY

Key Concepts

- Graphs, vertices, and arcs
- Adjacency matrix representation, weighted and unweighted
- Edge list representation, unweighted and weighted (or labeled)
- Warshall's algorithm — all pairs reachability
- Depth-first search used to compute single source reachability
- Floyd's algorithm — all pairs shortest distance
- Dijkstra's algorithms — single source shortest path
- Finite automata

The major theme of this chapter has been to demonstrate the utilization of many of the data structures we have described in this text in the solution of realistic problems. Graphs are ubiquitous, and the processing of graphs is a common occurrence. By making use of some of the data structures that we have developed here, algorithms on graphs can be succinctly and elegantly described.

Consider the data structures used in Dijkstra's algorithm (Fig. 16.8).

- ▲ The input to the algorithm is a `labeledVertex`, and a `dictionary` of weighted vertices and `double` precision values.
- ▲ Each weighted vertex maintains a `string` value as well as a dictionary of weighted vertices and arcs.
- ▲ The dictionary data type is built on top of a `list` of `associations`.
- ▲ The algorithm makes use of a `priorityQueueList`, a data type that inherits from the class `priorityQueue` and uses an instance of the class `orderedList` to hold data values. The class `orderedList`, in turn, inherits the majority of its behavior from the class `List`.
- ▲ The template argument for the priority queue is the class `cAssociation`, which is a form of association that permits elements to be compared against each other. The class `cAssociation` inherits behavior from the class `association`.
- ▲ The class `dictionaryIterator` is used to generate a loop that enumerates the elements of a dictionary. This class inherits behavior from class `listIterator`, which is in turn subclassed from class `iterator`.

In total, more than 14 different data types have been used in the execution of this algorithm.

Finally, in this chapter we introduced the notion of a finite automata. Finite automata are among the simplest and most basic models of computation. They are extensively used in both theoretical computer science and in practical applications.

References

Algorithms on graphs are described in a number of books dealing with algorithms. Examples include [Aho 83], [Cormen 90], [Sedgewick 92], and [Weiss 92]. Further information on graph theory as a discipline in itself can be found in the book by Hartsfield and Ringel [Hartsfield 90].

Dijkstra's algorithm was first described in 1959 [Dijkstra 59]. Floyd's and Warshall's algorithms both appeared in 1962 [Floyd 62, Warshall 62]. The concept of a finite automata was first described in the 1940s [McCulloch 43].

More complete information on finite automata can be found in a book by Hopcroft and Ullman [Hopcroft 69]. The use of finite automata in compiler construction is described by Aho, Sethi, and Ullman [Aho 86]. The use of automata in other areas of computer science has been described by Wulf et al. [Wulf 81].

Exercises

1. Construct the adjacency matrix representation for the following graph:

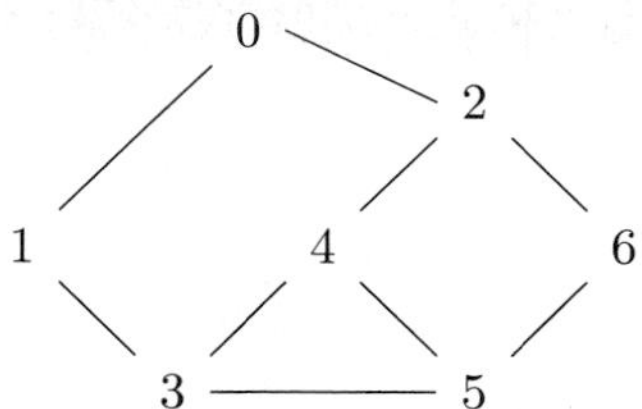

2. Suppose there is a path from some vertex v_i to some other vertex v_j in a graph. Argue why there must then be a path that never travels through any vertex more than once. (*Hint*: Assuming a path does travel through some vertex two or more times, show how the path can be shortened to eliminate one of the visits.)

3. The proof of correctness for Warshall's algorithm is established by proving the following invariant: At the end of the outermost `for` loop (the loop controlling the variable `k`), if there exists a path from vertex `i` to vertex `j` that does not go through any vertex numbered higher than `k`, then the matrix position indexed by `i` and `j` will have a 1 value.

a. Establish the base case by simulating the loop execution one and verifying the induction hypothesis.

b. Establish the induction step. Assume you are on some iteration `k` of the loop, and the induction hypothesis holds for values up to `k-1`. Show that the induction hypothesis must now hold for values up to `k`.

c. Show how this loop invariant can then be tied to a proof of correctness for the algorithm.

4. Trace the depth-first search path followed by the algorithm given in Fig. 16.4 through the graph given in Fig. 16.1, numbering the vertices in the order they are visited by the algorithm.

5. An induction proof of correctness for Floyd's algorithm is very similar to the induction proof of correctness for Warshall's algorithm. Following the steps outlined above for Warshall's algorithm, provide a proof of correctness for Floyd's algorithm.

6. Redraw the graph shown in Fig. 16.5, and number the vertices in the order they are visited by Dijkstra's algorithm.

7. Using the graph below as an illustration, argue why Dijkstra's algorithm requires the input graph to have non-negative arc weights.

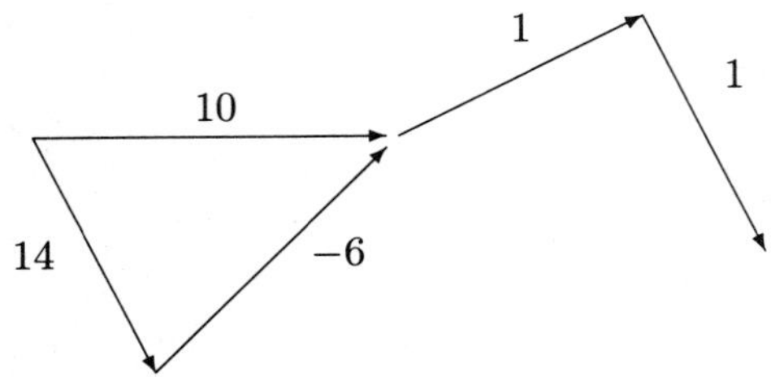

8. A proof of correctness for Dijkstra's algorithm is most easily presented using the technique of proof-by-contradiction.
   a. First argue that the values associated with elements as they are *removed* from the priority queue must always increase or stay constant, never decrease. (This observation requires the assumption of non-negative arcs discussed in the previous question.)
   b. Assume there exists a vertex x and Dijkstra's algorithm discovers the shortest cost path from source to x has cost c. Assume this path comes through vertex v_1.

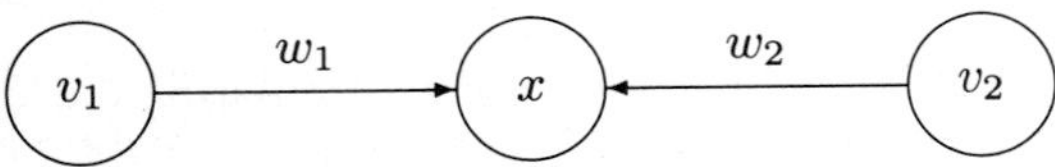

   To give a proof by contradiction establishing the correctness of Dijkstra's algorithm, assume this is not the shortest path but there exists, in fact, another path through vertex v_2 with lower cost. There are then a series of cases depending upon the relative costs of reaching nodes v_1 and v_2, and the weight of the arcs from each of these to x. For each case, you must argue that x could not possibly have been removed from the priority queue prior to the lower cost path having been discovered.

9. Which of the following strings are accepted by the finite automata shown in Fig. 16.10?
   a. ababa
   b. aaaaa
   c. aabbaba
   d. bababba

10. Give a sequence of tokens that will cause the finite automata in Fig. 16.10 to move in the following patterns:
   a. First left, then right, then left, then right.
   b. In a clockwise direction, moving twice through each state.
   c. In a counterclockwise direction, moving twice through each state.
   d. Clockwise once through all four states, then counterclockwise once through all four states.

11. Construct a finite automata that will accept a sequence of a symbols if and only if the length of the input is a multiple of 3. Valid strings include aaa and aaaaaaaaa. Invalid strings include a, aaaa, and aaaaaaaa.

12. Construct a finite automata that will accept a string consisting of two a symbols and one b symbol, in any order.

13. In practice, finite automata differ from labeled graphs representing maps in one very important manner. It is common for a finite automata to have more than one arc from a given vertex to another given vertex. For example, the following figure indicates that the automata will move from state 1 to state 2 if *either* an a token or a b token is observed:

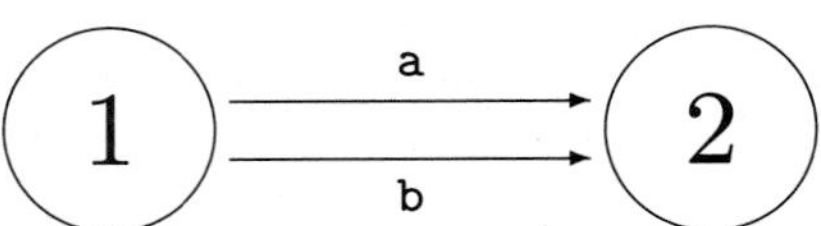

   Explain why such graphs cannot be represented using the structures we have described in this chapter.

14. There are two different solutions to the problem described in the last question.
   a. Change the order of the key and value pairs in the dictionary that maintains the arc information. That is, use the arc label as the key and the destination state as the value.
   b. Instead of a simple value for the arc label information, store a set of values (representing the set of values which will cause the automata to move into the indicated state).

Select one of these alternatives and rewrite the finite automata classes, and whatever other classes also need modification, so as to permit the form of graphs we are discussing.

15. Using either depth-first search or breadth-first search, generate an iterator for a graph represented in an unweighted edge-list representation. Your data structure should return vertex values, it must not return the same vertex twice, and it must be guaranteed to terminate for any finite graph.

CHAPTER 17

Files — External Collections

THE DATA STRUCTURES discussed in this book have all been designed to reside in local or global memory. Such abstractions are known as *internal* data structures. Although these are by far the most common form of data structures, there are nevertheless two major drawbacks with this arrangement:

- ▲ Memory is always a fixed resource. Given enough items to hold, a data structure may grow so large it cannot be maintained in memory.
- ▲ The data held by the structure exists only as long as a program is running. As soon as a program exits, any internal data structures are lost.

To circumvent these problems, a programmer can use an *external* storage device, such as a file. At the most fundamental level, a file is simply a sequence of character values. The advantage of a file is that it is not held in memory. It is thus not limited in size by the amount of available memory, and it can exist even after a program has finished execution.

In Chapter 2 we introduced streams, and we have been using stream operations ever since throughout this book. Streams are the principal means of access to files in C++. In the next section we will discuss some additional operations on streams.

17.1 CHARACTER STREAM OPERATIONS

As we noted in Chapter 2, stream input is accomplished using instances of the class `istream`, and stream output using instances of the class `ostream`. Two subclasses of these data structures can be used to attach a stream to a file. These classes are `ifstream`, for input file streams, and `ofstream`, for output file streams. The constructor for both classes takes a string representing the name of the file, and during initialization tries to open the file. The success of the initialization operation can be tested using the unary not operator. For example, the following program simply copies words from one file (named "infile") to another (named "outfile"). If a failure is encountered while opening either file, then an error message is printed on the standard output.

```
ifstream ifile("infile");
ofstream ofile("outfile");
string word(120);

if (! ifile)
    cout << "cannot open input file\n";
else if (! ofile)
    cout << "cannot open output file\n";
else while (ifile >> word)
    ofile << word << '\n';
```

In addition to the stream operator >>, the following operations can be used with input streams:

`get()`: The get operation returns the next character. Unlike the >> operator, white space is not ignored. The operation returns the symbolic value EOF at end of input. On most systems the value of EOF is −1, which does not correspond to any character value. For this reason, the return type for the `get` operation is declared as integer, not character.

`peek()`: The peek operation "peeks" at the next character, returning the character value but not processing the operation as a read. A subsequent read operation will then yield the value of the peeked character. We will examine a use for this operation in the next section.

`putback(c)`: The putback operation pushes a character back into the input stream. The next input operation will then yield the value of the pushed back character. A simple implementation of `peek` can be constructed using a combination of `get` and `putback`. We encountered this operation both in Chapter 2 and in Chapter 9. When streaming over a file, it has no actual effect on the external file, merely changing the sequence of characters read from the file.

`getline(buffer, size)`: This operation reads a line of input into the buffer. A line is a sequence of characters terminated with a newline character. The buffer must be able to hold at least as many characters as indicated by the second argument. No more than this number of characters will be read.

`read(buffer, size)`: This operation reads the indicated number of characters into the buffer, if sufficient characters remain in the input stream. The actual number of characters input (which may be less than the requested size if the end of the input stream was encountered) can be determined by invoking the function `gcount()`.

Conversely, in addition to the stream operator <<, the following operations can be used with output streams:

`put(c)`: The put operation places a single character into the output stream.

`write(buffer, size)`: This operation writes the indicated number of characters from the buffer into the output stream.

17.1.1 Application—Lexical Analysis

A compiler is typically structured in many layers, or phases. One of the first phases is devoted to the task of reading the sequence of characters from an input file and converting the characters into a sequence of tokens, such as identifiers and integers. This task is known as *lexical analysis.* A description of a class that can be used to perform lexical analysis will serve to illustrate the use of some of the stream functions described in the previous section.

In response to a call on the method `nextToken`, the lexical analysis class will read characters from an input stream and form a single token. The method returns a Boolean value that is true if a token is found and false when the end of input is reached and no more tokens can be formed. The text of the token itself will be contained in a string data area. The class description of the lexical analysis data structure can be given as follows:

```
//
// class lexicalAnalyzer
//     transform a sequence of characters into tokens
//     return next token on each call to nextToken
//

class lexicalAnalyzer {
public:
    lexicalAnalyzer(istream & is);

    // operations
    int nextToken();
```

```
    // data area for result
    string token;

private:
    istream & input;
};
```

The structure of the `nextToken` method is rather simple; an `if` statement finds the next input character, automatically skipping white space. If the end of input is reached, then a false value is returned from the function. This function is shown in Fig. 17.1.

If the character is a letter, then it must be the beginning of an identifier. A loop is used to read the remaining characters of the identifier. The `peek` facility is used to peek at the next character; if the character is an alphabetic or numeric character, then it must be part of the current identifier. If so, then the character is appended to the token string. Note that the `get` function returns an integer. For the append function to work, this must first be cast into a character value (the previous peek has assured us the conversion is proper). This character value will then be converted into a string and appended to the token.

```
if (isLetter(c)) {  // read identifier
    while (isAlphaNumeric(input.peek()))
        token += char(input.get());
    }
```

A similar loop is used to read integer values. A complicating factor is the fact that integer and floating point constants both begin in the same fashion. If a period follows an integer number, then the token is a floating point constant.

```
if (isDigit(c)) {    // read number
    while (isDigit(input.peek()))
        token += char(input.get());
    if (input.peek() == '.') {
        // read fractional part
        token += char(input.get());
        while (isDigit(input.peek()))
            token += char(input.get());
        }
    if ((input.peek() == 'e') || (input.peek() == 'E')) {
        // read exponent part
        token += char(input.get());
        // optional sign
        if ((input.peek() == '+') || (input.peek() == '-'))
            token += char(input.get());
```

```
int lexicalAnalyzer::nextToken()
{   // read the next lexical token
    char c;
    token = "";
    // try to read the next character
    if (input >> c) {
        token = c;
        // switch on the type of character
        if (isLetter(c)) {  // read identifier
            while (isAlphaNumeric(input.peek()))
                token += char(input.get());
            }
        else if (isDigit(c)) {  // read digit
            while (isDigit(input.peek())) {
                token += char(input.get());
                }
            }
        else            // read some other character
            switch(c) {
                // characterize next token
                case '*': // * or *=
                    ...

                case '+': // +, ++ or +=
                    ...

                ...
                }
        return 1;
        }
    else       // can't read character, return failure
        return 0;
}
```

Figure 17.1 Skeleton outline for lexical analyzer function

```
        // read exponent digits
        while (isDigit(input.peek()))
            token += char(input.get());
        }
    }
```

The remaining characters are processed using a large switch statement. Many characters simply represent themselves:

```
case ';': case '(': case ')': case '[': case ']':
    // nothing more to add to token
    break;
```

Some characters may be the start of several different tokens. The * character, for example, may represent the multiplication symbol or it may represent the multiplication assignment operator, *=. To select between these alternatives, the algorithm peeks at the next symbol. If it is an equal character, the symbol is added to the current token.

```
case '*':   // * or *=
    if (input.peek() == '=')
        token += char(input.get());
    break;
```

Similarly the + symbol can be any one of three tokens, +, ++, or += :

```
case '+':   // + or ++ or +=
    if ((input.peek() == '+') || (input.peek() == '='))
        token += char(input.get());
    break;
```

The backslash character is slightly more complex. If it is followed by another backslash, it represents a comment, and all characters up to the newline character should be read. Comments are typically ignored by a compiler, and thus the token returned should be the next token that follows the comment. This is easily accomplished by having the routine `nextToken` recursively call itself in this situation.

```
case '/':   // comment or / or /=
    if (input.peek() == '/') {  // comment
        while (input.get() != '\n')
            ; // do nothing
        return nextToken();
        }
    else if (input.peek() == '=')
        token += char(input.get());
    break;
```

Using variations on these simple patterns, all lexical tokens can be similarly processed.

17.1.2 Application — Merge Sort

The second application we will examine in this chapter is yet another sorting algorithm. Unlike previous sorting algorithms, this sorting algorithm is not limited by memory size, and it can thus be used to sort very large files. A sorting algorithm that works with external storage devices is called an *external sorting algorithm*. The algorithms we have studied in previous chapters are technically known as *internal sorting algorithms*.

Both input and output for the merge sort algorithm are specified using streams. The basic idea behind the algorithm is quite simple. The input stream is divided into small pieces, each piece small enough to be sorted using an internal sorting algorithm. The sorted portion of the input is then written to a temporary file. When this first phase is finished, there will be some number of temporary files, each holding a sorted portion of the input:

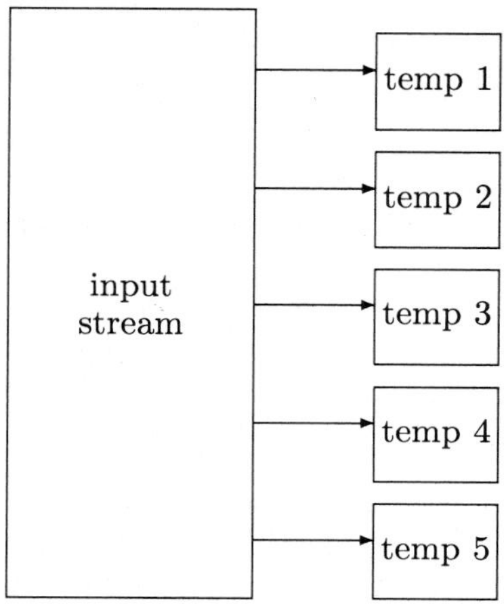

The next phase is the *merge* step. It is based on the premise that it is relatively easy to merge two sorted streams together to form a new sorted file. At each step of merging, it is necessary to compare only the current element from each stream and to output the smaller of the two. In this manner the first two temporary files are merged to form a new temporary file, which is added to the end of the list.

This process is repeated again and again. At each step, two temporary files are deleted and one new temporary file created. The process halts when only one temporary file exists. This temporary file is then copied to the output stream (see Fig. 17.2).

The first step in the realization of this program is a means to create a temporary file. We will number these files consecutively, temp1, temp2, and so on. Using this scheme, we can uniquely describe a file using an integer index. The following procedure converts an integer value into a file name. The low-order digits are stripped off the number and appended to the string. Since digits are discovered right to left, the concatenation operator is used to build up the string representation of the number.

```
string tempFileName(int i)
{   // create a temporary file name from integer i
    string name = "temp";
    string num = "";
    // first convert i into a string name
```

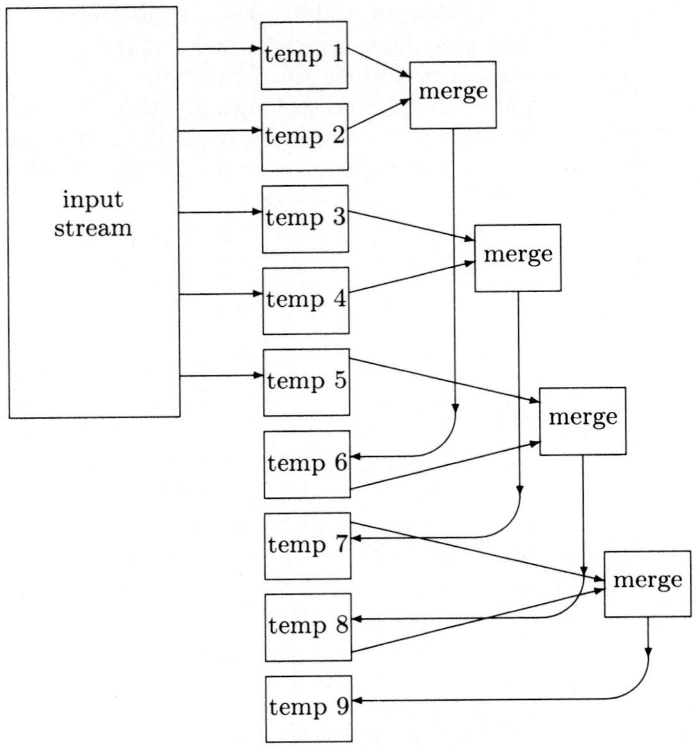

Figure 17.2 Steps in merge sort

```
    while (i > 0) {
        char val = (i % 10) + '0';
        num = string(val) + num;
        i = i / 10;
        }
    // then append the string version of i to name
    name += num;
    return name;
}
```

The utility procedure now takes a vector of strings, sorts them, then writes the sorted vector to a temporary file. A global variable named `topFile` keeps track of the number of temporary files that have been created.

```
int topFile = 0;

void copyToTemporary(vector<string> & words)
{    // copy the sorted list of words to a new temporary file
```

```
    // first sort the list of words
    treeSort(words);

    // then copy to temporary file
    topFile = topFile + 1;
    string t1(tempFileName(topFile));
    ofstream tempfile((const char *) t1);
    vectorIterator<string> witr(words);
    for (witr.init(); ! witr; witr++)
        tempfile << witr() << '\n';
}
```

This procedure is used in the first phase of the merge sort algorithm. You will recall that this first phase consisted of reading the input stream and dividing it up into sorted components.

```
void phase1(istream & infile)
{   // phase 1 of heap sort
    // read all lines from input file,
    // and separate into temporary files
    string buffer(200);
    const int wordVectorSize = 1000;
    vector<string> words(wordVectorSize);
    int wordcount;

    // read words and put them into temporary files
    wordcount = 0;
    while (buffer.getline(infile)) {
        words[wordcount++] = buffer;
        if (wordcount >= wordVectorSize) {
            copyToTemporary(words);
            wordcount = 0;
            }
        }
    // if wordcount is greater than zero, it means
    // there are leftover words
    if (wordcount > 0) {
        words.setSize(wordcount);
        copyToTemporary(words);
        }
}
```

The heart of the second phase is a procedure that takes two input streams and one output stream, and merges the input files into the output file. The major complicating factor here occurs with the handling of the end of input. When one of the input streams is terminated, the remaining values from the other stream should then be copied to the output.

Thus the procedure can be viewed as being divided into two parts; the first portion is active when there is a value from both input streams, while the second portion is active when one or the other input stream has been exhausted.

```
void mergeFiles(istream & in1, istream & in2, ostream & out)
{   // merge two sorted input streams into one output stream
    string word1(200);
    string word2(200);
    int flag1 = 0;
    int flag2 = 0;

    // get first words
    if (word1.getline(in1))
        flag1 = 1;
    if (word2.getline(in2))
        flag2 = 1;

    while ((flag1 != 0) && (flag2 != 0)) {
        // write out smallest word and refill buffer
        if (word1 < word2) {
            out << word1 << '\n';
            if (! (word1.getline(in1)))
                flag1 = 0;
            }
        else {
            out << word2 << '\n';
            if (! (word2.getline(in2)))
                flag2 = 0;
            }
        }

    // copy remainder from files
    while (flag1 != 0) {
        out << word1 << '\n';
        if (! (word1.getline(in1)))
            flag1 = 0;
        }

    while (flag2 != 0) {
        out << word2 << '\n';
        if (! (word2.getline(in2)))
            flag2 = 0;
        }
}
```

The following is the main program that ties these procedures together. The merge sort procedure takes two stream arguments. It invokes the `phase1` procedure to divide the input into sorted pieces. It then merges the pieces together until only one file remains. This file is then copied to the output stream.

```
void mergeSort(istream & infile, ostream & outfile)
{   // sort input stream, placing result on output stream
    topFile = 0;

    // phase 1, break input into temporary files
    phase1(infile);

    // phase 2, merge files back together
    int i = 1;
    while (i < topFile) {
        // open input files
        ifstream temp1((const char *) tempFileName(i));
        i++;
        ifstream temp2((const char *) tempFileName(i));
        i++;

        // open output file
        topFile++;
        ofstream temp3((const char *) tempFileName(topFile));

        // merge files together
        mergeFiles(temp1, temp2, temp3);
        }

    // phase 3, copy from final temporary file to output file
    ifstream from((const char *) tempFileName(topFile));
    char ch;
    while (from.get(ch))
        outfile.put(ch);
}
```

17.2 BINARY FILES

A file is in many ways similar to a vector of characters. The analogy can be made even closer using two new features. The first feature is the `fstream` data type, which permits the creation of file streams that can be used simultaneously for both input and output. The second feature is the `seekg` method, which permits a stream to be positioned at an arbitrary location within a file. Using the latter, we can perform random access operations on a file, just as a vector permits random access to any data element.

Using these features, we can design a class that will permit a programmer to think of a file as a vector of arbitrary types of elements. The only restriction we require is that the elements held by the vector have a fixed size, known at compile time. While this rules out elements represented by dynamic data structures, such as strings and lists, in practice the limitation is not generally a problem.

We will call the data structure a random access stream, or `rstream`. Instances of `rstream` can be used as vectors, assigning values to specific locations using the method `put`, and retrieving the value of specific locations using the method `get`. The class description for this method is as follows:

```
//
// class rstream
//     randomly accessible streams of elements
//

template <class T> class rstream {
public:
    // constructor
    rstream      (const string & name);

    // access to element
    int            get     (unsigned int index, T & value);

    // placement of element
    void           put     (unsigned int index, const T & value);

    // number of elements
    unsigned int   length  ();

private:
    fstream        theStream;
};
```

The actual data values will be accessed using an instance of `fstream`. The constructor for our class establishes the connection to the file stream. To do this, the method uses the function `open`. This function takes as argument a name and an access mode. There are three access modes, defined in a parent class named `ios`. These three modes are `ios::in`, for input, `ios::out`, for output, and `ios::app`, for appending new values to the end of an existing file. Modes can be combined using the bitwise or operator. In this case we wish to open the file for both input and output.

```
template <class T> rstream<T>::rstream(const string & name)
{   // construct an instance of rstream
    // convert string into C-style pointer variable
    const char * cName = name;
    // open the file for both input and output
    theStream.open(cName, ios::in | ios::out);
}
```

To write to the stream we use the method put. This method uses the function seekg to position the file pointer at a given location. Since index values are given in terms of the element values, (instances of class T), and the seekg function requires a byte position, we multiply the index value by the size of an element of type T. The latter quantity can be determined using the built-in function sizeof, which is the only function in C++ that takes a type name as argument. For historical reasons, the type of the argument used by the write procedure is a pointer to a character; we must therefore cast the argument value into this form before writing.

```
template <class T>
void rstream<T>::put(unsigned int index, const T & value)
{   // place a value into a random access stream
    // first position the stream
    theStream.seekg(sizeof( T ) * index);

    // then write the value
    const char * valuePtr = (const char *) & value;
    theStream.write(valuePtr, sizeof( T ));
}
```

The get method is similar. It must first position the stream, then read the value found at the given location. Whereas a write can be used to extend a file, a read operation will never work past the end of the file. The number of characters processed by a read can be determined by invoking the function gcount. We can use this to determine if the read operation was successful. The integer value returned as a result of this function will be nonzero if the read operation worked, and zero if the operation was unsuccessful.

```
template <class T> int rstream<T>::get(unsigned int index, T & value)
{   // read a value from a random access stream
    // first position the stream
    theStream.seekg(sizeof( T ) * index);
    // then read the value
    char * valuePtr = (char *) & value;
    theStream.read(valuePtr, sizeof( T ));
    // return the number of characters read
    return theStream.gcount();
}
```

The final operation we will provide is a method to determine the number of elements contained in a random access file. To compute the length of the file, we first move the file pointer to the end of the file. This can be accomplished by using the `seekg` function with a second argument, which indicates we want to measure starting from the end of the file. Moving zero bytes from the end will position the file at the end of the file. The function `tellg` then returns the byte position in the file. By dividing this by the size of each entry, we can determine the number of elements held by the collection.

```
template <class T> unsigned int rstream<T>::length()
{    // return number of elements held in collection.
     // first, seek to end
     theStream.seekg(0, ios::end);
     // then divide current byte offset by size of elements
     return theStream.tellg() / sizeof( T );
}
```

To construct an iterator for the random access stream data structure, we merely maintain an index for the current element. The increment operator simply increments this value. If the read operation for this index is successful, then the element exists. If the read operation fails, then we have reached the end of the collection.

17.2.1 Open Table Hashing

We will illustrate the use of the random access stream data abstraction by developing a data structure that uses another form of hashing, called open table hashing. Like the hash table data structure we examined in Chapter 13, open table hashing uses a hash function to try to uniformly distribute elements over a range of values. Unlike the hash table structures we examined earlier, with open table hashing all values are stored in the table itself, which is actually an external file. Thus the size of the hash table strictly limits the number of elements that can be maintained by the data structure.

As an example of the use of open table hashing, let's assume again that we are placing string values containing the names of Amy's club from Chapter 13, using again the hash function that took the third character of a name and converted the value into an integer between 0 and 25 (and, of course, using the remainder when the result is divided by the size of the collection). Let us insert in order the names *Alex*, *Amanda*, *Albert*, *Alice*, *Amy*, *Anne*, *Alfred*, *Andy*, *Arthur*, and *Abraham* into a 10-element collection.

Inserting the names *Alex*, *Amanda*, *Albert* and *Alice* causes no difficulty. They each hash into a distinct location in the collection. Following the insertion of the last, we can visualize the collection as follows:

0	1	2	3	4	5	6	7	8	9
Amanda hash: 0	Albert hash: 1			Alex hash: 4				Alice hash: 8	

Now let us insert the name *Amy*. You will recall that the difficulty with the hash table mechanism occurred when two names hashed to the same location, which is called a collision. We see this here, since *Amy* hashes to the same location, 4, currently occupied by *Alex*. To avoid having two values at the same location, we will simply examine succeeding positions, in order, until we find an empty location. Doing this, we find that position 5 is currently empty, and we place the record for *Amy* at that location.

0	1	2	3	4	5	6	7	8	9
Amanda hash: 0	Albert hash: 1			Alex hash: 4	Amy hash: 4			Alice hash: 8	

The value *Anne* hashes to location 3, which is unoccupied and is thus easily inserted. The value *Alfred*, on the other hand, hashes to location 5, which is now occupied by *Amy*. The next empty position is location 6, which is where the record for *Alfred* is stored. The table now looks like the following:

0	1	2	3	4	5	6	7	8	9
Amanda hash: 0	Albert hash: 1		Anne hash: 3	Alex hash: 4	Amy hash: 4	Alfred hash: 5		Alice hash: 8	

The entry for *Andy* hashes to location 3. Unfortunately, that position is already occupied, by the value *Anne*. Similarly positions 4, 5, and 6 are also occupied. The value *Andy* can finally be inserted into location 7.

0	1	2	3	4	5	6	7	8	9
Amanda hash: 0	Albert hash: 1		Anne hash: 3	Alex hash: 4	Amy hash: 4	Alfred hash: 5	Andy hash: 3	Alice hash: 8	

The entry for *Arthur* can be inserted with no difficulty into location 9. The final entry, *Abraham*, hashes to index value 7. Values 7, 8, and 9 are all filled. To find the next position, we cycle the index values around to the beginning of the collection, to test position 0. Positions 0 and 1 are also filled. We finally find the last empty position at position 2. The final collection is as follows:

0	1	2	3	4	5	6	7	8	9
Amanda hash: 0	Albert hash: 1	Abraham hash: 7	Anne hash: 3	Alex hash: 4	Amy hash: 4	Alfred hash: 5	Andy hash: 3	Alice hash: 8	Arthur hash: 9

To better understand the advantage gained by using the hashing technique, consider the number of file accesses required to find a given record. If the file was totally unorganized, a linear search would be required to determine if a specific record was contained in the file. If the record was not found in the file, then all ten records would need to be searched, and this is the same for the open hash table.

But consider the situation when searching for a record that *is* found in the database. If the file was unorganized, then on average half the entries, or 5 values, would be examined until we found the correct element. But over half the elements in the open hash table (namely, the records for *Amanda*, *Albert*, *Anne*, *Alex*, *Alice* and *Arthur*) hash immediately to the location where the values are stored and thus can be located with a single access. Two more values, the records for *Amy* and *Alfred*, require only two file access operations.

As is often the case, the elements inserted into an almost full hash table require more operations. To recover the record for *Andy* requires five operations, and to read the record for the last inserted value, *Abraham*, uses six file operations.

Nevertheless, on average to recover a record for an element that is contained in the database requires only slightly more than two file operations, which is less than half the work that would be required if hashing were not employed.

THE OPEN HASH TABLE DATA STRUCTURE We will implement this idea in a data structure called an `openHashTable`. The class declaration for this structure can be given as follows:

```
//
// class openHashTable
//     extern hash table
//     template type must supply equality test
//     and function isEmpty

template <class T> class openHashTable {
public:
    // constructor
    openHashTable(const string & name, unsigned int (&f)(const T &));

    // operations
    void      create     (unsigned int size);
```

```
    int        add        (const T & value);
    int        includes   (T & value);

private:
    // data areas - hash function, random access stream, and size
    unsigned int  (&hashfun)(const T &);
    rstream<T>    rfile;
    unsigned int  size;
};
```

The data areas maintained by the structure include a reference to the hash function, the size of the collection, and a random access stream that will contain the actual values. Since values are not stored in memory but are instead maintained using an external file, the structure can hold a large number of elements.

The constructor takes as an argument the name of the file associated with the random access stream, and the name of the hash function. The length of the file is used to determine the size of the collection. If the file does not exist, then the length function will return a zero value.

```
template <class T> openHashTable<T>::openHashTable
    (const string & name, unsigned int (&f)(const T &))
        : hashfun(f), rfile(name)
{   // set size to length of stream
    size = rfile.length();
}
```

The `create` method is used to initially create a collection with a fixed number of entries. The size is stored in the appropriate data area, and a number of elements are placed into the data file. It is assumed that the default constructor for the template type creates a value that will test as being null.

```
template <class T> void openHashTable<T>::create(unsigned int sz)
{   // create a new open hash table with sz records
    size = sz;

    // assume default constructor creates an empty value
    T initialValue;
    for (unsigned int i = 0; i < sz; i++)
        rfile.put(i, initialValue);
}
```

New elements are added to the collection using the method `add`. The function first computes the hash value for the new element. It must then examine, or *probe*, the collection until an empty location is found. If no empty location is found, the method does nothing and returns a false value (zero). Otherwise, the value is placed into the collection and a true (one) value returned. To determine if a position has been assigned a value, the function `isEmpty` is invoked. Each template type used with the open hash table abstraction must provide a definition for this function.

```
template <class T> int openHashTable<T>::add(const T & value)
{   // add record to an open hash table

    // find initial hash value
    unsigned int hashValue = hashfun(value) % size;
    unsigned int index = hashValue;

    // see if occupied
    T currentValue;
    rfile.get(index, currentValue);
    while (! isEmpty(currentValue)) {
        // it's filled, see if next record is empty
        index = index + 1;
        if (index >= size)
            index = 0;
        if (index == hashValue)
            return 0;
        rfile.get(index, currentValue);
        }
    // found an empty position, place argument value
    rfile.put(index, value);
    return 1;
}
```

Elements can be extracted from an open hash table in one of two ways. In the exercises we will develop an iterator that will permit a loop to cycle over all the values of a collection. The alternative mechanism is a method, `includes`, that will determine if an element matching the argument is contained in the collection.

```
template <class T> int openHashTable<T>::includes(T & value)
{   // see if the hash table includes a value matching argument
    unsigned int hashValue = hashfun(value) % size;
    unsigned int index = hashValue;
    T currentValue;
    rfile.get(index, currentValue);
    // loop as long as we don't see value
    while (! (currentValue == value)) {
        index = index + 1;
        if (index >= size)
            index = 0;
        if (index == hashValue)
            return 0;
```

```
        rfile.get(index, currentValue);
        }

    // found it, set value
    rfile.get(index, value);
    return 1;
}
```

If a matching element is found, the value is twice read: once to establish the value for the purposes of comparison, and the second time to copy the value into the argument variable. (Usually, the equality testing operator will examine only a few fields, and the remaining fields will contain useful information.)

17.2.2 Application — A Simple Database

We will illustrate the use of the open hash table data structure by describing a simple database. This database will be used by Amy's club to keep track of each member's favorite flavor of ice cream. Because each record in an external file must be a fixed length, we cannot use our `string` abstraction directly. Instead, the actual information in the file is stored using a simple C-style array of characters. Nevertheless, for ease of use, methods are defined that convert this information both to and from string values. The class description for the record structure is as follows:

```
class iceCreamRecord {
public:

    // constructors
    iceCreamRecord();
    iceCreamRecord(const string & namestr, const string & flavorstr);

    // field access
    string name() const;
    string flavor() const;

private:
    // data fields for name and flavor
    char nameField[20];
    char flavorField[20];
};
```

The equality operator, used by the add method and by the `includes` method, tests only the name field. We can search for a record matching a given name, and the remaining field will be set as a side effect by the `includes` method. Following a successful search, the argument record will be replaced by the value found in the file, which will include the remaining fields.

```
int operator == (const iceCreamRecord & left,
        const iceCreamRecord & right)
{   // equality between records based only on name
    return left.name() == right.name();
}
```

A program to create the database might be written as follows:

```
unsigned int hf(const iceCreamRecord & x)
{   // hash function for ice cream database
    string name(x.name());
    return name[2] - 'a';
}

void createIceCreamDatabase()
{
    openHashTable<iceCreamRecord> hashtab("iceCreamDatabase", hf);
    hashtab.create(10);

    hashtab.add(iceCreamRecord("Alex", "vanilla"));
    hashtab.add(iceCreamRecord("Amanda", "strawberry"));
    hashtab.add(iceCreamRecord("Albert", "bubblegum"));
    hashtab.add(iceCreamRecord("Alice", "peach"));
    hashtab.add(iceCreamRecord("Amy", "marionberry"));
    hashtab.add(iceCreamRecord("Anne", "chocolate"));
    hashtab.add(iceCreamRecord("Alfred", "blueberry"));
    hashtab.add(iceCreamRecord("Andy", "chocolate"));
    hashtab.add(iceCreamRecord("Arthur", "vanilla"));
    hashtab.add(iceCreamRecord("Abraham", "strawberry"));
}
```

A subsequent program can be written to recover and print the values held in the ice cream database. The following procedure, for example, takes a name and returns the ice cream flavor associated with the name. To discover the value, the procedure first makes a new record entry with only the name field filled in. The `includes` method is then invoked. If the inclusion test is successful, then the flavor field of the record will have been filled in by the `includes` method. If not, then the name given by the argument is not present in the database and the string "not in database" is returned.

```
string iceCreamFlavor(const string name)
{   // find the flavor favored by the named individual
    // make a new record with name but not known flavor
    iceCreamRecord rec(name, " ");
```

```
    // read the database
    if (hashtab.includes(rec))
        return rec.flavor();
    // not in database
    return "not in database";
}
```

17.3 CHAPTER SUMMARY

Key Concepts

- Character stream operations
  - get
  - put
  - peek
  - putback
  - getline
  - read
  - write
- Merge sort
- Direct access files and streams
- Open table hashing

In this chapter we have explored the use of external files, which are accessed using stream operations, as a mechanism for developing data structures. At the most fundamental level, a file is simply a stream of characters. Many applications, such as lexical analysis, can process a file character by character. Since files are not limited in size by the amount of available memory, it is possible to store and process vast amounts of data using a file. We illustrated this by developing the merge sort algorithm, which can operate on collections even if they are larger than will fit in available memory. Finally, using the ability to position a file at any location, we showed how a file could be considered to be a vector of fixed-size elements. Building on this view, we created a new form of hash table, called an open hash table. If provided with a sufficiently good hash function, open hash tables can give very efficient access to large amounts of information.

References

More information on streams can be found in the books by Stroustrup [Stroustrup 91] and Lippman [Lippman 91]. Lexical analysis is discussed extensively by Aho, Sethi, and Ullman in [Aho 86].

External sorting and hashing are both discussed in volume 3 of Knuth [Knuth 75]. The merge sort algorithm presented here is adapted from the version described by Brian Kernighan and Peter Plauger [Kernighan 76].

There are many variations on open table hashing. Knuth discusses several of these; careful analysis of running times for various algorithms is presented by Gonnet [Gonnet 91].

Exercises

1. The technique used to read a floating point value in the lexical analysis data abstraction does not check to make sure there is at least one decimal number value following the exponent indication (that is, the character `e` or E). Modify the procedure to check for this condition, pushing the extraneous character back into the input if a number is not found.
2. Comments can be written using either two slash characters, or a slash followed by a star. In the

latter form, comments extend (possibly over many lines) until a matching star-slash pair is found.

```
/*
    this example comment extends over
    many lines
*/
```

Revise the code for the slash character so as to recognize both types of comments.

3. Simulate the merge sort algorithm using the following data values. Assume that initially a maximum of five values is inserted into each temporary file. Show the contents of each temporary file.

Abel	Abigail	Abraham	Ada
Angela	Anita	Anne	Antonia
Albert	Alex	Alfred	Alice
Adam	Adrian	Adrienne	Agnes
Amanda	Amy	Andrew	Andy
Arnold	Arthur	Audrey	

4. Complete the design of an iterator class for the random access stream data abstraction.

5. We purposely did not include a method to remove an entry from the open table hashing data structure described in Section 17.2.1. To see some of the problems involved with deletion, assume first that when an entry is deleted we simply copy a new blank (uninitialized) value into the emptied location. Delete the value for *Amy* from the full table. Now simulate the execution of the `includes` method with value *Alfred*. What happens? What other values have now "disappeared" from the collection?

6. A solution to the problem uncovered in the previous question is to have two types of empty values. Initially, all entries have true empty values. When an entry is deleted, it is replaced by a special record that indicates "deleted" but not "empty." A function `isDeleted` can be used to check for this condition.

   a. Write a `delete` method that will create such entries.

   b. Modify the `includes` method so that it will skip deleted entries in searching for a match to the argument value.

   c. Modify the `add` method so that it will reuse a deleted entry position if it finds either an empty location or a deleted entry during the process of insertion.

7. It is important that the same hash function used to create the entries is used to examine entries in a hash table. To see why, assume that the hash table for Amy's club is saved before all locations have been filled—for example at the point where eight of the ten positions have been filled (as shown on page 484). Now assume that a subsequent program tries to use the table but hashes using the second, rather than the third, character in each name. How many entries can be successfully recovered by the `includes` method? How does this situation change if we use the final, completely full hash table?

8. Develop an iterator for the open hash table data abstraction. Like the iterator for the random access stream, the iterator for the hash table need maintain only the index of the current position. When incrementing, the iterator should skip empty or deleted positions. (You will likely want to make the iterator class a friend of the hash table class.)

9. Write a program that allows members of Amy's club to change the value held in the ice cream database. Your program should prompt for the member name, verify that the member is included in the club (by making sure an entry already exists in the database), then prompt for the type of ice cream preferred. With this information, your program should then alter the value held in the database.

10. Write a procedure to sort a file represented by a random access stream.

11. Write a procedure to perform a binary search on a sorted random access stream.

APPENDIX A

Catalogue of Data Structures

THE FOLLOWING SECTIONS summarize each of the different data structures we have introduced in this book. The description of each data type is divided into four sections:

- *Description*—a short description of the data structure and its intended use.
- *Constructors*—a description of the format used in declaring instances of the data type.
- *Behavior*—a listing of the functions that can be invoked when using instances of the data type. In classes that are implemented using inheritance, this list includes not only methods defined by the class itself but also any useful behavior inherited from parent classes.
- *Iteration*—for those data types that maintain collections of values, a description of the most common technique used to iterate over the elements in the collection.

We do not list facilitator classes, such as the `link` class used in the implementation of linked lists, or the `node` class used in the development of search trees, since the end-user programmer need not be aware of these structures.

A.1 association—A KEY AND VALUE PAIR

An association is simply a data structure used to maintain a key and value pair as a single entity. The key field is fixed and cannot be altered once the association is created. The value is accessible and can be modified.

A.1.1 Constructors

The constructor requires an initial value for both the key and value field. The copy constructor takes both values from the argument value.

```
association<string, int> assoc("abc", 27);
association<string, int> assocDup(assoc);
```

A.1.2 Behavior

`assoc == x`: An association can be compared to another association, or to a key value. In both cases only the key field is tested.

`assoc = x`: An association can be assigned a value using another association, or simply a value. In both cases, only the value field is modified.

`assoc.key()`: Returns the key as a constant value. This value cannot be modified.

`assoc.value()`: Returns the value of the association. The value field can also be accessed directly using the name `valueField`.

A.1.3 See Also

The class `cAssociation` defines a form of association that can be used in situations where it is necessary to compare one association with another. Associations are used in the implementation of the `dictionary` and `table` data structures.

A.2 AVLtree—SEARCH TREE WITH GUARANTEED PERFORMANCE

An AVL tree is a binary search tree that, in addition, guarantees logarithmic performance of access, insertion, and removal of elements. (See the `searchTree` data structure for an alternative.)

A.2.1 Constructor

The default constructor requires no arguments. The copy constructor initializes the collection with duplicates of values from the argument tree.

```
AVLtree<int> tree;
AVLtree<int> treeTwo(tree);
```

A.2.2 Behavior

`tree.add(value)`: Adds a new value to the collection held by the search tree.

`tree.deleteAllValues()`: Deletes all items held in the search tree.

`tree.includes(value)`: Returns true if the tree holds a value matching the argument. The equality operator, ==, is used to determine the match.

`tree.isEmpty()`: Returns true if the collection maintained by the tree holds no values.

`tree.remove(value)`: Removes a value from the collection held by the tree. The equality operator, ==, is used to determine the match. No action is performed if no matching element is found.

A.2.3 Iteration

Instances of the class `searchTreeIterator` can be used to loop over the values maintained by an AVL tree.

```
searchTreeIterator<int> itr(tree);
for (itr.init(); ! itr; itr++)
    ... itr() ...
```

A.3 `bitVector` — VECTOR OF BINARY DIGITS

A bit vector is an indexed collection of bit (binary digit) values. Individual bit values can be set or cleared, tested or inverted. Set operations can also be used with bit vectors.

A.3.1 Constructors

The most common form of constructor requires a count of the number of binary positions to be maintained by the collection. The copy constructor can be used to initialize the values of one bit vector with a copy of values from another.

```
bitVector vec(75);
bitVector vec2(vec);
```

The number of bit values maintained by a bit vector is always a multiple of 8. The value given in the constructor is rounded up to the next largest multiple of 8 to determine the size of the collection.

A.3.2 Behavior

`vec == vec2`: Returns true if the two sets of values are equal.

`vec.clear(i)`: Sets to zero the value of the bit indicated by the argument index. Argument value must be between zero and the number of bits declared in the constructor.

`vec.deleteAllValues()`: Clears all values from the set.

`vec.differenceFrom(vec2)`: Forms the set difference with the argument set. Deletes any value in the set that occurs as well in the argument set.

`vec.flip(i)`: Inverts the value of the bit indicated by the argument index. If the previous value of the bit was zero, it is made one. If the previous value was one, it is made zero.

`vec.intersectWith(vec2)`: Forms an intersection with the argument set. Deletes any value in the set that does not occur in the argument set.

`vec.length()`: Returns the number of bit values maintained by the collection.

`vec.set(i)`: Sets (to one) the value of the bit indicated by the argument index.

`vec.subset(vec2)`: Returns true if the set is a subset of the argument set—that is, if all values in the set are also present in the argument set.

`vec.test(i)`: Returns as result the value of the bit indicated by the argument index.

`vec.unionWith(vec2)`: Generates the union of the set with the argument set; adds to the set any value from the argument set that does not appear in the vector.

A.3.3 Iteration

To iterate over the values of a bit vector, an integer loop is constructed so as to cycle over the index values. Individual bit values are then accessed using the `test` function.

```
const int max = vec.length();
for (int i = 0; i < max; i++) {
    ... vec.test(i) ...
    }
```

A.3.4 See Also

See also the data structure `charSet`.

A.4 `boundedVector` — VECTOR WITH ARBITRARY LOWER BOUND

A `boundedVector` is a form of vector. Unlike the basic vector class, the boundedVector class permits the programmer to specify both the upper and lower index values.

A.4.1 Constructors

In normal use the first two arguments to the constructor are the lower and upper bounds on indexing. An assertion error is generated if the upper bound is less than the lower bound. An optional third argument provides an initial value for each entry. A copy constructor can be used to initialize the values of one vector with the values from another.

```
boundedVector<int> bvec(13,19);
vector<double> bvecTwo(-7,-5,3.14159);
vector<int> bvecThree(bvec);
```

A.4.2 Behavior

`bvec[i]`: Subscription is used to access individual elements. Legal subscript values must be between the lower bound and the upper bound. An assertion error is generated for illegal index values

`bvec.length()`: Returns a count of the number of elements in the vector.

`bvec.lowerBound()`: Returns the smallest legal index value that can be used with the vector.

`bvec.setSize(newSize)`: Changes the size of the vector to the new value. Where possible, the previous values stored in the vector are retained.

`bvec.setSize(newSize, initial)`: Changes the size of the vector to the new value. Where possible, the previous values stored in the vector are retained. Any new values allocated are initialized with the value of the second argument.

`bvec.upperBound()`: Returns the largest legal index value that can be used with the vector.

A.4.3 Iteration

There are two common techniques for looping over the elements in a bounded vector. The first form explicitly computes the lower and upper index values, using the functions `lowerBound` and `upperBound`. An integer loop then cycles over the legal index values, and the subscript operator is used to access the actual items.

```
const int max = bvec.upperBound();
for (int i = bvec.lowerBound(); i <= max; i++) {
    ... bvec[i] ...
    }
```

Since the class `boundedVector` is a subclass of class `vector`, it is also possible to use vector iterators to access the individual elements in the collection. The current value of the iterator is returned using the parentheses operator.

```
vectorIterator<int> itr(bvec);
for (itr.init(); ! itr; itr++) {
    ... itr() ...
    }
```

A.4.4 See Also

See also the `vector` data type.

A.5 `cAssociation`—A COMPARABLE KEY AND VALUE PAIR

A `cAssociation` is a form of association that, in addition to the behavior provided by the class `association`, also permits values to be compared relationally against each other using the less than relation.

A.5.1 Constructors

The constructor requires an initial value for both the key and value field. The copy constructor takes both values from the argument value.

```
cAssociation<string, int> assoc("abc", 27);
cAssociation<string, int> assocDup(assoc);
```

A.5.2 Behavior

`assoc < x`: An association can be compared to another association, or to a key value. Only the key fields are compared.

`assoc == x`: An association can be compared to another association, or to a key value. In both cases only the key field is tested.

`assoc = x`: An association can be assigned a value using another association, or simply a value. In both cases, only the value field is modified.

`assoc.key()`: Returns the key as a constant value. This value cannot be modified.

`assoc.value()`: Returns the value of the association. Value field can also be accessed directly using the name `valueField`.

A.6 charSet — SETS OF CHARACTER VALUES

A `charSet` is simply a set of character values. Each value is unique and can appear at most once in a set.

A.6.1 Constructors

In addition to the default constructor, a second constructor can take as argument a literal string; characters from the string are then initially placed into the set. The copy constructor copies values from the argument set.

```
charSet cset;
charSet vowels("aeiou");
charSet csetTwo(vowels);
```

A.6.2 Behavior

`cset.add(c)`: Adds the indicated character to the set; has no effect if the character is already present in the set.

`cset.deleteAllValues()`: Clears all values from the set.

`cset.differenceFrom(csetTwo)`: Forms the set difference with the argument set. Deletes any value in the set that occurs as well in the argument set.

`cset.includes(c)`: Returns true if the set includes the indicated character.

`cset.intersectWith(csetTwo)`: Forms an intersection with the argument set. Deletes any value in the set that does not occur in the argument set.

`cset.subset(csetTwo)`: Returns true if the set is a subset of the argument set — that is, if all values in the set are also present in the argument set.

`cset.remove(c)`: Removes the indicated character from the set; has no effect if the character was not present in the set.

`cset.unionWith(cset2)`: Generate the union of the set with the argument set; add to the set any value from the argument set that does not appear in the vector.

A.6.3 Iterators

The most common form of loop used with a character set is a simple arithmetic for loop using character values.

```
for (char c = 'a'; c <= 'z'; c++)
    ... cset.test(c) ...
```

A.7 dictionary—COLLECTION OF KEY/VALUE PAIRS

A dictionary is a collection of key and value pairs. Neither key nor value are restricted in their type. Access to values is provided through the subscript operator.

A.7.1 Constructors

In addition to the default constructor, a dictionary can also be created with an optional initial value. If the initial value is provided, any new entry created as a result of the subscripting operator will have the indicated initial value. The copy constructor copies both values and the initial value of the argument dictionary.

```
dictionary<string, int> dict;
dictionary<string, int> dict2(0);
dictionary<string, int> dictDup(dict2);
```

The default initial value for dictionary entries can also be specified using the method `setInitial`.

A.7.2 Behavior

`dict["xyz"]`: A dictionary can be subscripted and returns a reference to the associated value. If no entry existed with the given key, a new entry is created. In situations where the programmer wishes to avoid the creation of such entries, the method `includesKey` (below) should be used to test positions prior to the subscript operation.

`dict.deleteAllValues()`: Removes all entries from the dictionary. Following this operation, the dictionary is empty.

`dict.includesKey("xyz")`: Returns true if the dictionary includes a key with the given value; returns false if no such entry is present in the dictionary.

`dict.isEmpty()`: Returns true if the dictionary contains no entries.

`dict.removeKey("xyz")`: Removes the entry with the indicated key value.

`dict.setInitial(37)`: Specifies an initial value to be used for each new entry created in response to the subscript operator.

A.7.3 Iteration

To enumerate values held in a dictionary, the programmer constructs an instance of the class `dictionaryIterator`.

```
dictionaryIterator<string, int> itr(dict);
for (itr.init(); ! itr; itr++)
    ... itr() ...
```

Note that the iterator returns associations. To access the individual fields in the dictionary entry, the programmer must use the methods `key` and `value` from the association data type.

A.7.4 See Also

The `orderedDictionary` data structure is a type of dictionary that in addition maintains elements in sequence based on the ordering of the key values.

The `table` data abstraction implements the same methods as the `dictionary`.

A.8 `doubleEndedList`—LISTS WITH INSERTION AT EITHER END

A double ended list is a variation on the list data structure. Elements can be added to either the front or the back of the structure. Elements can be removed only from the front.

A.8.1 Constructors

The most common form of the constructor requires no arguments. A copy constructor can be used to form a duplicate copy of a list.

```
doubleEndedList<int> dlst;
doubleEndedList<int> dupdList(dlst);
```

A.8.2 Behavior

`dlst.add(val)`: Adds a new item to the front of the list.

`dlst.addToEnd(val)`: Adds a new item to the back of the list.

`dlst.deleteAllValues()`: Deletes all values from the list. Following this operation the list is empty.

`dlst.firstElement()`: Returns the first element from the list. The element is not removed from the list.

`dlst.includes(val)`: Returns a true value if the list includes the given value; returns false if otherwise. The element is not removed from the list.

`dlst.isEmpty()`: Returns true if the list contains no elements; returns false if otherwise.

`dlst.removeFirst()`: Removes the first element from the list.

A.8.3 Iteration

Because a double ended list is a form of list, iteration over list elements is accomplished with the aid of a list iterator.

```
listIterator<int> itr(dlst);
for (itr.init(); ! itr; itr++) {
    ... itr() ...
    }
```

The list iterator methods `removeCurrent`, `addBefore`, and `addAfter` can also be used with double ended lists.

A.8.4 See Also

See the description of the `list` data type.

A.9 `enumVector` — VECTOR INDEXED BY ENUMERATED VALUES

The `enumVector` class is a variation on the `vector` type, permitting index values to be taken from an enumerated data type.

A.9.1 Constructors

We will use as our example of enumerated values the following type:

```
enum colors {red, blue, yellow, white, green};
```

The most common form of constructor takes as argument the largest (last) value in the enumerated list of index values. The copy constructor can be used to initialize an enumerated vector with values from another enumerated vector.

```
enumVector<colors, int> evec(green);
enumVector<colors, int> evecToo(a);
```

A.9.2 Behavior

evec[i]: Subscription is used to access individual elements. Legal subscript values are enumerated types smaller than the value listed in the constructor. An assertion error is generated when the argument represents an illegal index value.

evec.length(): Returns a count of the number of elements in the vector.

A.9.3 Iteration

Since an enumerated vector is a subclass of class vector, vector iterators can be used to loop over the values of the collection.

```
vectorIterator<int> itr(vec);
for (itr.init(); ! itr; itr++) {
    ... itr() ...
    }
```

A.9.4 See Also

See also the description of the vector data type.

A.10 hashTree—HASH TABLE WITH TREES FOR BUCKETS

A hash tree is a form of hash table in which AVL trees are used to maintain buckets. Key values are translated using a function, called a *hash function*, into indices. Values that are transformed into the same index locations are maintained together as a single tree.

A.10.1 Constructors

The constructor for the hash tree data type requires an integer representing the number of buckets to create for the data structure and a function that will map key values into integer indices. No copy constructor is provided for the hash tree data structure.

```
hashTree<string> hashTab(30, hf);
```

A.10.2 Behavior

`hashTab.add(val)`: Adds a new item to the collection.

`hashTab.deleteAllValues()`: Deletes all values from the collection. Following this operation, the table is empty.

`hashTab.includes(val)`: Returns a true value if the collection includes the given value; returns false if otherwise. The element is not removed from the table.

`hashTab.isEmpty()`: Returns true if the collection contains no elements; returns false if otherwise.

A.10.3 Iteration

The class `hashTreeIterator` is used to loop over values held in a hash table.

```
hashTreeIterator<string> itr(hashTab);
for (itr.init(); ! itr; itr++)
    ... itr() ...
```

A.11 `hashVector` — VECTOR WITH NONINTEGER KEYS

A hashVector is a form of vector in which key values are translated using a function, called a *hash function*, into indices. The hash function must be *pure*, which means it must translate key values by a one-to-one mapping on to integer index values.

A.11.1 Constructors

The hash vector data type template is parameterized by two types: the type of the index values and the type of the elements. The user must supply a hash function, as well as the maximum size of the table. Additionally, the user can supply an initial value that will be assigned to each element in the collection. The copy constructor simply copies the hash function from the argument.

```
hashVector<string, int> vec(20, hf);
hashVector<double, int> vecToo(30, hf2, 3.14);
hashVector<string, int> vecCopy(vec);
```

A.11.2 Behavior

`vec[i]`: Subscription is used to access individual elements. The key value is transformed using the hash function, and the value stored at the corresponding location is accessed.

`vec.length()`: Returns a count of the number of elements in the vector.

A.11.3 Iteration

Since the hash vector is a subclass of class vector, a `vectorIterator` can be used to loop over the elements of a hash vector.

A.12 `heap`—PRIORITY QUEUE BASED ON TREES

A heap is a priority queue based on the vector implementation of a complete binary tree. Besides the use of heaps as a priority queue, the data structure is also the basis for a very efficient sorting algorithm.

A.12.1 Constructors

The constructor for the heap must be given an initial estimate of the number of elements to be maintained by the collection. The size of the heap is first determined from this value, but it may be increased as necessary. The copy constructor duplicates elements held in the argument collection.

```
heap<int> que(15);
heap<int> queTwo(que);
```

A.12.2 Behavior

`que.add(value)`: Inserts a new value into the collection of values maintained by the priority queue.

`que.deleteMin()`: Removes, and then returns the smallest element in the queue.

`que.isEmpty()`: Returns true if the queue contains no elements.

`que.min()`: Returns, but does not remove, the smallest element maintained in the collection.

`que.removeMin()`: Removes the smallest element in the collection.

A.12.3 See Also

The skewHeap data structure implements another type of priority queue.

A.13 list — ARBITRARY LENGTH LINKED LISTS

A list is an arbitrary length collection of values. Elements can be added or removed only from the front of the list.

A.13.1 Constructors

The most common form of the constructor requires no arguments. A copy constructor can be used to form a duplicate copy of a list.

```
list<int> lst;
list<int> dupList(lst);
```

A.13.2 Behavior

lst.add(val): Adds a new item to the front of the list.

lst.deleteAllValues(): Deletes all values from the list. Following this operation, the list is empty.

lst.firstElement(): Returns the first element from the list. The element is not removed from the list.

lst.includes(val): Returns a true value if the list includes the given value; returns false if otherwise. The element is not removed from the list.

lst.isEmpty(): Returns true if the list contains no elements; returns false if otherwise.

lst.removeFirst(): Remove the first element from the list.

A.13.3 Iteration

Iteration over list elements is accomplished with the aid of a list iterator.

```
listIterator<int> itr(lst);
for (itr.init(); ! itr; itr++) {
    ... itr() ...
    }
```

In addition to the normal iterator protocol, the method removeCurrent can be used to remove the current element. For example, the following will remove all multiples of 7 from a list.

```
for (itr.init(); ! itr; itr++) {
    if (itr() % 7 == 0)
        itr.removeCurrent();
    }
```

The iterator methods addBefore and addAfter can be used to add elements before or after the current value of the iterator.

A.13.4 See Also

See also the data structure orderedList.

A.14 matrix — TWO-DIMENSIONAL ARRAY OF VALUES

A matrix is a two-dimensional collection of values. Individual items are retrieved or modified using a double application of the subscript operator. The range of legal index values is provided to the constructor when the matrix is declared.

A.14.1 Constructors

The first two arguments for the matrix constructor represent the number of rows and the number of columns. An optional third argument represents the initial value to be assigned to each position. A copy constructor is not provided.

```
matrix<int>     mat(4, 5);
matrix<double>  matTwo(7, 6, 3.14159);
```

A.14.2 Behavior

mat[i][j]: Returns the value from row i and column j of the indicated matrix. An assertion error is generated for index values that are out of range.

mat.numberRows(): Returns the number of rows being maintained by the matrix.

mat.numberColumns(): Returns the number of columns being maintained by the matrix.

A.15 `orderedDictionary`—ORDERED KEY/VALUE PAIRS

An ordered dictionary is a variation on the dictionary type that maintains the collection of key and value pairs in order, based on comparisons between key values. Neither key nor value are restricted in their type. Access to values is provided through the subscript operator.

A.15.1 Constructors

In addition to the default constructor, an ordered dictionary can also be created with an optional initial value. If the initial value is provided, any new entry created as a result of the subscripting operator will have the indicated initial value. The copy constructor copies both the values and the initial value of the argument dictionary.

```
orderedDictionary<string, int> dict;
orderedDictionary<string, int> dict2(0);
orderedDictionary<string, int> dictDup(dict2);
```

The default initial value for ordered dictionary entries can also be specified using the method `setInitial`.

A.15.2 Behavior

`dict["xyz"]`: A dictionary can be subscripted, and returns a reference to the associated value. If no entry existed with the given key, a new entry is created. In situations where the programmer wishes to avoid the creation of such entries, the method `includesKey` (below) should be used to test positions prior to the subscript operation.

`dict.deleteAllValues()`: Removes all entries from the dictionary. Following this operation, the dictionary is empty.

`dict.includesKey("xyz")`: Returns true if the dictionary includes a key with the given value; returns false if no such entry is present in the dictionary.

`dict.isEmpty()`: Returns true if the dictionary contains no entries.

`dict.removeKey("xyz")`: Removes the entry with the indicated key value.

`dict.setInitial(37)`: Specifies an initial value to be used for each new entry created in response to the subscript operator.

A.15.3 Iteration

To enumerate values held in a dictionary, the programmer constructs an instance of the class `dictionaryIterator`.

```
dictionaryIterator<string, int> itr(dict);
for (itr.init(); ! itr; itr++)
    ... itr() ...
```

Note that the iterator returns associations. To access the individual fields in the dictionary entry, the programmer must use the methods `key` and `value` from the association data type.

A.16 `orderedList`—LIST VALUES IN ORDER

An ordered list is a form of list in which elements are maintained in sequence. To determine sequencing, comparisons are performed using the less than relation.

A.16.1 Constructors

The most common form of the constructor requires no arguments. A copy constructor can be used to form a duplicate copy of a list.

```
list<int> lst;
list<int> dupList(lst);
```

A.16.2 Behavior

`lst.add(val)`: Adds a new item to the list. Elements will be inserted in the appropriate location so as to preserve sequencing.

`lst.deleteAllValues()`: Deletes all values from the list. Following this operation, the list is empty.

`lst.firstElement()`: Returns the first element from the list. The element is not removed from the list.

`lst.includes(val)`: Returns a true value if the list includes the given value; returns false if otherwise. The element is not removed from the list.

`lst.isEmpty()`: Returns true if the list contains no elements; returns false if otherwise.

`lst.removeFirst()`: Removes the first element from the list.

A.16.3 Iteration

Since an ordered list is a form of list, iteration over list elements is accomplished with the aid of a list iterator.

```
listIterator<int> itr(lst);
for (itr.init(); ! itr; itr++) {
    ... itr() ...
    }
```

A.17 orderedVector — VECTOR VALUES IN ORDER

An ordered vector is a data structure that maintains values in a sorted vector. Binary search is used to provide a very efficient lookup operation. Insertions and removals are somewhat slower. Thus an ordered vector should be used only when lookup operations occur much more frequently than insertions or deletions.

A.17.1 Constructors

Only the default constructor and the copy constructor are provided.

```
orderedVector<string> vec;
orderedVector<string> vecCopy(vec);
```

A.17.2 Behavior

`vec.add(val)`: Adds a new value to the ordered vector. The position of the value will be determined by comparing the element to existing values in the collection.

`vec.deleteAllValues()`: Removes all values from the collection. Following this operation, the collection will be empty.

`vec.includes(val)`: Returns true if the collection contains the indicated value; returns false if the value is not held in the collection.

`vec.isEmpty()`: Returns true if the collection is empty — that is, if it contains no elements.

`vec.remove(val)`: Removes the indicated value from the collection; has no effect if the value is not contained in the collection.

A.17.3 Iteration

The class `orderedVectorIterator` can be used to generate a loop that will iterate over the values contained in an ordered vector.

```
orderedVectorIterator<string> itr(vec);
for (itr.init(); ! itr; itr++)
    ... itr() ...
```

A.17.4 See Also

The `orderedList` data structure provides slower access, but it is not limited in size. If it is necessary to access only the smallest element of a collection, then one of the several varieties of a priority queue can be used.

A.18 `priorityQueue` — EFFICIENT ACCESS TO SMALLEST ELEMENT

A priority queue is a structure designed to maintain a collection of values and provide fast access to the smallest element. The class `priorityQueue` is an abstract class. It provides a definition of the protocol used to manipulate priority queues, but it does not provide any implementation. See the data structures `priorityQueueList`, `heap`, and `skewHeap` for three different implementations.

A.18.1 Behavior

`que.add(value)`: Inserts a new value into the collection of values maintained by the priority queue.

`que.deleteMin()`: Removes and returns as result the smallest element in the queue.

`que.isEmpty()`: Returns true if the queue contains no elements.

`que.min()`: Returns, but does not remove, the smallest element maintained in the collection.

`que.removeMin()`: Removes the smallest element in the collection.

A.18.2 Iteration

Iteration is not supported by the priority queue data structure. At any time, it is only possible to access the smallest element of a queue.

A.19 `priorityQueueList` — PRIORITY QUEUE USING LISTS

The class `priorityQueueList` implements the protocol for priority queues using a linked list data structure. Although this is a general technique and provides few size restrictions, it is not the most efficient implementation approach for priority queues. This class should thus be used only for very small queue structures.

A.19.1 Constructors

The default constructor creates an initially empty queue. The copy constructor duplicates the values held by the argument queue.

```
priorityQueueList<int> que;
priorityQueueList<int> queTwo(que);
```

A.19.2 Behavior

`que.add(value)`: Inserts a new value into the collection of values maintained by the priority queue.

`que.deleteMin()`: Removes and returns as result the smallest element in the queue.

`que.isEmpty()`: Returns true if the queue contains no elements.

`que.min()`: Returns, but does not remove, the smallest element maintained in the collection.

`que.removeMin()`: Removes the smallest element in the collection.

A.20 `queue`—FIFO COLLECTION

A queue is a *FIFO*, or First In, First Out, data structure. This means that when an element is removed from the queue, the value returned is the first value that was inserted into the stack.

The class `queue` is an abstract class. It provides a definition of the protocol used to manipulate a queue, but it does not provide any implementation. See the data structures `queueVector`, `queueList`, and `queueRingbuffer` for three different implementations.

A.20.1 Iteration

Iteration over queue structures is not provided.

A.21 `queueList`—QUEUE IMPLEMENTED USING A LIST

The class `queueList` implements queue operations using a double ended list. This is not as fast as the vector implementation (see `queueVector`), but it does not impose any restrictions on the size of the queue. A queue list can also maintain a collection of references, which a queue vector cannot.

A.21.1 Constructor

The default constructor takes no arguments. The copy constructor duplicates the values held by the argument queue.

```
queueList<int> que;
queueList<int> queTwo(que);
```

A.21.2 Behavior

`que.deleteAllValues()`: Empties all items from the queue.

`que.dequeue()`: Returns and removes the first value in the queue. An assertion error is generated if the queue is empty when this operation is performed.

`que.enqueue(value)`: Places a new value at the end of the queue.

`que.front()`: Returns, but does not remove, the first value in the queue. An assertion error is generated if the queue is empty when this operation is performed.

`que.isEmpty()`: Returns true if the queue is empty—that is, if it contains no elements.

A.22 `queueRingBuffer`—QUEUE IMPLEMENTED USING A RING BUFFER

The class `queueRingBuffer` implements queue operations using a ring buffer. This has the speed advantage of the queue implemented using a vector, and the ability to grow as necessary, like the queue list.

A.22.1 Constructor

The constructor must be provided with an initial estimate for the size of the ring buffer. The indicated number of links is initially allocated. If more links are subsequently necessary, they are created as needed.

```
queueRingBuffer<double> que(15);
```

A.22.2 Behavior

`que.deleteAllValues()`: Empties all items from the queue.

`que.dequeue()`: Returns and removes the first value in the queue. An assertion error is generated if the queue is empty when this operation is performed.

`que.enqueue(value)`: Places a new value at the end of the queue.

`que.front()`: Returns, but does not remove, the first value in the queue. An assertion error is generated if the queue is empty when this operation is performed.

`que.isEmpty()`: Returns true if the queue is empty—that is, if it contains no elements.

A.23 `queueVector`—QUEUE IMPLEMENTED USING A VECTOR

The class `queueVector` implements queue operations using a fixed size vector. Vector operations are fast, but the size of the data area is fixed when the queue is constructed and cannot be increased.

A.23.1 Constructor

The constructor must be provided with the size of the queue data area. The copy constructor duplicates values from the argument queue.

```
queueVector<double> que(15);
queueVector<double> queTwo(que);
```

A.23.2 Behavior

`que.deleteAllValues()`: Empties all items from the queue.

`que.dequeue()`: Returns and removes the first value in the queue. An assertion error is generated if the queue is empty when this operation is performed.

`que.enqueue(value)`: Places a new value at the end of the queue. An assertion error is generated if the queue is full at the time this operation is performed.

`que.front()`: Returns, but does not remove, the first value in the queue. An assertion error is generated if the queue is empty when this operation is performed.

`que.isEmpty()`: Returns true if the queue is empty—that is, if it contains no elements.

A.24 `rstream`—POSITIONABLE STREAMS

An rstream builds on top of the simple stream data abstraction to create a random access data structure, similar to a vector. Since values are stored in an external file, they persist even after execution of a program, and they are not limited by memory size.

A.24.1 Constructors

The constructor for the data type requires as argument the name of the file in which the values will be held. The template argument for an rstream must be a fixed length structure, with no dynamic (pointer) fields.

```
rstream<double> rstr("figures");
```

A.24.2 Behavior

`rstr.get(index, val)`: Reads the element stored at the given index, placing the value into the second argument. An integer true value is returned as a result of this operation if the read was successful, while a false value is returned if no element exists at the given index position. (Generally this occurs because the index value extends beyond the limit of the file.)

`rstr.length()`: Return the length (number of elements) of the file.

`rstr.put(index, val)`: Place the value of the second argument into the file at the position specified by the first argument.

A.25 `searchTree`—RAPID ACCESS, INSERTION, AND REMOVAL

A search tree maintains an ordered collection of values and permits rapid access, insertion, and removal of values. Elements in a search tree must be able to be compared using the equality testing operator, ==, and the less-than relational operator, <.

A search tree may become unbalanced, resulting in a loss of efficiency, if additions or deletions are made following a nonrandom distribution. In this case better performance can be obtained using AVL trees.

A.25.1 Constructor

The default constructor requires no arguments. The copy constructor duplicates each value held by the collection. As this duplication can be very expensive, search trees should be passed by reference, not by value, whenever possible.

```
searchTree<int> tree;
searchTree<int> treeTwo(tre);
```

A.25.2 Behavior

`tree.add(value)`: Adds a new value to the collection held by the search tree.

`tree.deleteAllValues()`: Deletes all items held in the search tree.

`tree.includes(value)`: Returns true if the tree holds a value matching the argument. The equality operator, ==, is used to determine the match.

`tree.isEmpty()`: Returns true if the collection maintained by the tree holds no values.

`tree.remove(value)`: Removes a value from the collection held by the tree. The equality operator, ==, is used to determine the match. No action is performed if no matching element is found.

A.25.3 Iteration

Instances of the class `searchTreeIterator` can be used to loop over the values maintained by a search tree.

```
searchTreeIterator<int> itr(tree);
for (itr.init(); ! itr; itr++)
    ... itr() ...
```

A.26 setList—SET OPERATIONS BUILT WITH LISTS

A set list is built on top of the list data structure but in addition provides an implementation of set operations.

A.26.1 Constructors

The default constructor creates a set with no values. The copy constructor initializes the set with copies of values from the argument set.

```
setList<int> set;
setList<int> settwo(aset);
```

`set == settwo`: Returns true if the set is equal to the argument set—that is, if both sets are subsets of each other.

`set.add(val)`: Adds a new item to the set; has no effect if the value is already present in the set.

`set.deleteAllValues()`: Deletes all values from the set. Following this operation, the set is empty.

`set.differenceFrom(settwo)`: Computes the difference from the argument set. Every value from the set that occurs as well in the argument set will be removed.

`set.includes(val)`: Returns true if the set includes the given value; returns false if otherwise. The element is not removed from the list.

`set.intersectWith(settwo)`: Computes the intersection with the argument set. Every value that does not occur as well in the argument set will be removed.

`set.isEmpty()`: Returns true if the set contains no elements; returns false if otherwise.

`set.remove(val)`: Removes a value from the set; has no effect if the value is not present in the set.

`set.subset(settwo)`: Returns true if the set is a subset of the argument set—that is, if every value from the set occurs as well in the argument set.

`set.unionWith(settwo)`: Computes the union of the set and the argument set. Adds to the set any value from the argument set that is not already present.

A.26.2 Iteration

Since a set list is a list, the class `listIterator` can be used to loop over the values contained in the collection.

```
listIterator<int> itr(aset);
for (itr.init(); ! itr; itr++)
    ... itr() ...
```

A.27 `setTable`—SETS BUILT FROM HASH TABLES

A set table is a set structure built on top of the hash table abstraction. Like all hash tables, the user must supply a hash function to be used to convert element values into integer keys. The efficiency of the structure will depend upon the degree to which the hash function uniformly distributes element values.

A.27.1 Constructors

The programmer must supply the size of the hash table to be created and a function that maps the element values into integers. No copy constructor is provided for this data structure.

```
setTable<int> tab(20, hf);
```

A.27.2 Behavior

`tab == tabtwo`: Returns true if the set is equal to the argument set — that is, if both sets are subsets of each other.

`tab.add(val)`: Adds a single value to the set; has no effect if the value is already present in the set.

`tab.deleteAllValues()`: Removes all values from the set. Following this operation, the set is empty.

`tab.differenceFrom(tabtwo)`: Computes the difference between the set and the argument set. Removes all values from the set that occur as well in the argument set.

`tab.includes(value)`: Returns true if the set includes the indicated value.

`tab.intersectWith(tabtwo)`: Computes the intersection of the set with the argument set. Removes any value from the set that does not occur as well in the argument.

`tab.remove(value)`: Removes the item from the set. This operation has no effect if the value is not present in the set.

`tab.subset(tabtwo)`: Returns true if the set is a subset of the argument set — that is, if every value from the set is present as well in the argument set.

`tab.unionwith(tabtwo)`: Computes the union of the set with the argument set. Adds to the set any value from the argument set that is not already present.

A.27.3 Iteration

To iterate over instances of this type, the programmer creates an instance of the class `setTableIterator`.

```
setTableIterator itr(tab);
for (tab.init(); ! itr; itr++)
    ... itr() ...
```

A.28 `skewHeap` — TREE-BASED PRIORITY QUEUES

A skew heap is a priority queue implemented using binary trees.

A.28.1 Constructors

```
skewHeap<int> que;
skewHeap<int> queTwo(que);
```

A.28.2 Behavior

`que.add(value)`: Inserts a new value into the collection of values maintained by the priority queue.

`que.deleteMin()`: Removes and returns as result the smallest element in the queue.

`que.isEmpty()`: Returns true if the queue contains no elements.

`que.min()`: Returns, but does not remove, the smallest element maintained in the collection.

`que.removeMin()`: Removes the smallest element in the collection.

A.28.3 See Also

The `heap` data structure is another implementation of the priority queue protocol.

A.29 `stack`—LIFO COLLECTION

A stack is a *LIFO*, or *L*ast *I*n, First *O*ut, data structure. This means that when an element is removed from the stack, the value returned is the last value that was inserted into the stack.

The class `stack` is an abstract class. It provides a definition of the protocol used to manipulate a stack, but it does not provide any implementation. See the data structures `stackVector` and `stackList` for two different implementations.

A.29.1 Iteration

Iteration over stack structures is not provided.

A.30 `stackList`—STACK IMPLEMENTED USING A LIST

The `stackList` class implements the stack data abstraction using a list. While this is not as efficient as the vector implementation (see `stackVector`), it does not place any restriction on the size of the stack. A stack list can also hold reference values, while a stack vector cannot.

A.30.1 Constructor

The default constructor requires no arguments. The copy constructor duplicates values from the argument stack.

```
stackList<double> stk;
stackList<double> stkTwo(stk);
```

A.30.2 Behavior

`stk.deleteAllValues();`: Empties all values from the stack.

`stk.isEmpty`: Returns true if the stack is empty—that is, if it contains no values.

`stk.pop()`: Returns and removes the topmost item from the stack. An assertion error is given if the stack is empty at the time that the operation is performed.

`stk.push(value)`: Pushes a new value onto the stack.

`stk.top()`: Returns, but does not remove, the topmost item from the stack. An assertion error is given if the stack is empty at the time the operation is performed.

A.31 `stackVector`—STACK IMPLEMENTED USING A VECTOR

The `stackList` class implements the stack data abstraction using a vector. This is slightly more efficient than the implementation using lists (see `stackList`), but it requires knowing in advance an initial size for the stack. A stack vector cannot hold reference values, while a stack list can.

A.31.1 Constructor

The constructor must be given an initial size for the stack. The copy constructor duplicates this information from the argument stack.

```
stackVector<double> stk(10);
stackVector<double> stkTwo(stk);
```

A.31.2 Behavior

`stk.deleteAllValues();`: Empties all values from the stack.

`stk.isEmpty`: Returns true if the stack is empty—that is, if it contains no values.

`stk.pop()`: Returns and removes the topmost item from the stack. An assertion error is given if the stack is empty at the time the operation is performed.

`stk.push(value)`: Pushes a new value onto the stack. The size of the underlying data buffer will be increased as necessary to accommodate push operations.

`stk.top()`: Returns, but does not remove, the topmost item from the stack. An assertion error is given if the stack is empty at the time the operation is performed.

A.32 `string`—TEXTUAL STRING VALUES

A string is a linear array of character values. Strings are most commonly used in input and output operations.

A.32.1 Constructors

Strings can be initialized with either an integer representing the maximum length of the string, a literal string value, or a character value. The copy constructor can be used to initialize a string with the value of another string.

```
string a;
string b = "abc";
string c = 'c';
string d = b;
string e(14);
string f("abc");
string g('x');
string h(c);
```

A.32.2 Behavior

Let `str` and `rstr` represent two string values.

`str[i]`: Returns the character value at the given position and returns the null character for out-of-range index values; can be used as the target of an assignment.

`str(index, count)`: Returns the substring of the string formed by starting at the given index position and extending for the indicated number of characters.

`str += rstr`: Appends the value of the right-hand side to the left-hand string.

`str + rstr`: Returns the string formed by catenating the right string to the left. Argument strings are unchanged.

`str < rstr`: Returns true if the left string is lexicographically smaller than the right. Other relational operators are similarly defined.

`istream >> str`: Reads a white-space separated word from the input stream, copying the value to the indicated string.

`ostream << str`: Writes a string to the output stream.

`str.getline(istream)`: Reads a line of text from the indicated input stream.

`str.length()`: Returns the number of non-null characters in the string.

String values can in addition be converted into ordinary C type character pointers. Stream output, for example, is implemented in this fashion.

A.33 `table`—COLLECTION OF KEY/VALUE PAIRS

A table is a collection of key and value pairs, similar to a dictionary. Neither key nor value are restricted in their type. Access to values is provided through the subscript operator. The table data structure can be more efficiently accessed than the dictionary, but it requires the programmer to supply a hash function for key values.

A.33.1 Constructors

As arguments to the table constructor, the user must supply the number of buckets to be used in the hash table, and a hash function that maps key values into integer indices. A second form of constructor permits, in addition, the specification of an initial value to be used in conjunction with the creation of any new entry created as a result of the subscripting operator. There is no copy constructor provided with the table data structure.

```
table<string, double> dict(20, hf);
table<string, double> dict2(20, hf, 0.0);
```

The default initial value for dictionary entries can also be specified using the method `setInitial`.

A.33.2 Behavior

`dict["xyz"]`: A dictionary can be subscripted and will return a reference to the associated value. If no entry existed with the given key, a new entry is created. In situations where the programmer wishes to avoid the creation of such entries, the method `includesKey` (below) should be used to test positions prior to the subscript operation.

`dict.deleteAllValues()`: Removes all entries from the dictionary. Following this operation, the dictionary is empty.

`dict.includesKey("xyz")`: Returns true if the dictionary includes a key with the given value; returns false if no such entry is present in the dictionary.

`dict.isEmpty()`: Returns true if the dictionary contains no entries.

`dict.removeKey("xyz")`: Removes the entry with the indicated key value.

`dict.setInitial(37)`: Specifies an initial value to be used for each new entry created in response to the subscript operator.

A.33.3 Iteration

To enumerate values held in a table, the programmer constructs an instance of the class `tableIterator`.

```
tableIterator<string, double> itr(dict);
for (itr.init(); ! itr; itr++)
    ... itr() ...
```

A.33.4 See Also

The `dictionary` data structure implements the same protocol.

A.34 `vector`—INDEXED COLLECTION

A `vector` is an indexed collection of values. Individual items are retrieved or modified using the subscript operator. Legal index values range from zero to one less than the number of entries in the collection.

A.34.1 Constructors

```
vector<int> vec(10);        // a vector of 10 elements
vector<double> b(5,3.14159);      // explicit initial value
vector<int> c(vec); // copy constructor
```

A.34.2 Behavior

`vec[i]`: Subscription is used to access individual elements. Legal subscript values are between zero and one less than the number of elements in the vector. An assertion error is generated when the argument represents an illegal index value.

`vec.length()`: Returns a count of the number of elements in the vector.

`vec.setSize(newSize)`: Changes the size of the vector to the new value. Where possible, the previous values stored in the vector are retained.

`vec.setSize(newSize, initial)`: Changes the size of the vector to the new value. Where possible, the previous values stored in the vector are retained. Any new values allocated are initialized with the value of the second argument.

A.34.3 Iteration

There are two common techniques for looping over the elements in a vector. In the first form the `length` function is used to determine the number of items in the vector. The subscript operation is then used to retrieve the actual data values.

```
const int max = vec.length();
for (int i = 0; i < max; i++) {
    ... vec[i] ...
    }
```

The second technique uses a vector iterator and the normal iterator loop. The current value of the iterator is returned using the parentheses operator.

```
vectorIterator<int> itr(vec);
for (itr.init(); ! itr; itr++) {
    ... itr() ...
    }
```

A.34.4 See Also

See also the data structures `boundedVector`, `enumVector`, and `matrix` for variations on the vector data structure.

APPENDIX B

If C++ Is the Solution, Then What Is the Problem?

C++ IS A PROGRAMMING LANGUAGE that is rich in a variety of mechanisms used to overcome various difficulties encountered during software development. The language is so rich, in fact, that a programmer first starting to create software using C++ is often hard-pressed to understand the utility or importance of a particular feature, simply because he or she may not understand the problem that the feature is designed to help solve.

In this appendix we will briefly overview the most commonly used programming mechanisms encountered in C++ programs, and we will outline the major problem addressed by each feature. These are presented in roughly the same order they have been introduced in the main body of the text.

B.1 CLASS DEFINITIONS

There are two major benefits provided by the class mechanism;

- ▲ Encapsulation
- ▲ Instansiation

The term *encapsulation* refers to the fact that the class definition can bring together, in a single unit, functions and data areas that are linked by a common purpose. This allows the programmer to think of a class structure as a single conceptual object, not simply a collection of separate functions.

A related aspect of this encapsulation is a reduction in name space congestion. Classes allow a fine degree of control over the exposure or access to names (see Sections B3 and B12). Without classes, most data areas that would need to retain values between function invocations would be declared global. This practice results in a large increase in global names, which causes both conceptual and practical problems when names from separate programming units are similar or identical.

The term *instansiation* refers to the ability to create multiple instances of a class. That is, once a class has been defined, it is no more difficult to create 10 independent instances of the class than it is to create a single instance. Without the class mechanism, a similar sort of functionality is usually provided using global variables; however, with global variables the creation of multiple independent instances is considerably more difficult.

Classes are introduced in Chapter 2 (page 31).

B.2 MEMBER FUNCTIONS

Member functions are the primary mechanism used to associate behavior (that is, functionality) with classes. Unlike an ordinary function, a member function is always associated with a specific class. To invoke a member function, an instance of the class must be specified. The syntax of member functions reflects this (except where operators are defined as member functions; see Section B8). The instance being manipulated (called the *receiver* for the function invocation) is described first, followed by a period, followed by the member function name. The following illustrates the member function `length` being applied to a vector named `data`:

```
data.length()
```

The code that implements a member function must name both the member function being implemented and the class in which the function is defined. Different classes can, and often do, implement member functions with a common name.

Within a member function, the value of the receiver is available through a pointer variable named `this`.

When a member function is invoked from within another member function, the receiver does not need to be named if it is the same as the receiver for the initial invocation.

Member functions are introduced in Chapter 2 (page 31).

B.3 ACCESS CONTROLS (PUBLIC, PRIVATE, AND PROTECTED)

A class can be envisioned as a software component that is designed to provide a specific service. In a software development team composed of several programmers, for any individual class we can divide the team into *users* of the software service and *implementers* of the service. These two different subgroups require different levels of information concerning the class.

Features defined in the *public* portion of a class describe elements of interest to users of the data abstraction provided by the class. Features defined in the *private* portion of a class outline functions and data values of interest only to the implementers of the class, and they are not necessary for users of the class. Access control is enforced by the compiler. Private fields can be manipulated only from within member functions associated with the class, or by explicitly designated friends (see Section B12).

Fields described as *protected* are slightly more accessible than private fields, but they are not public. They can be manipulated by member functions associated with the class, or by member functions associated with subclasses (see Section B13).

Private and public access control was described in Chapter 2 (page 31). Protected access control was introduced in Chapter 6 (page 141).

B.4 REFERENCES AND POINTERS

A *reference* is an alias, a mechanism to permit access to a single data value under two (or more) different names. The most common use of references is in the implementation of pass-by-reference parameter passing (see Section B5). References are also used to permit a field in one class to refer to another class or to an individual data value held by another class. This occurs in many iterator structures, where a field in the iterator refers to the structure over which iteration is being performed.

In most cases the implementation mechanism used to simulate references is the same as the technique used to implement pointers. That is, the value stored in memory is the address of the object referred to by the alias. Thus a reference can in one sense be envisioned as simply a form of pointer. References differ from pointers in three important respects:

- ▲ A reference can never be null; it must always refer to a legitimate object.
- ▲ Once established, a reference can never be changed so as to make it point to a different object.
- ▲ A reference does not require any explicit mechanism to dereference the memory address and access data values.

With the exception of pass-by-reference parameter passing, which is introduced in Chapter 2, references are first encountered in Chapter 4.

B.5 REFERENCE PARAMETERS

The semantics of the C++ programming language requires that, unless the programmer specifies otherwise, a *copy* of a data value must be generated whenever a value is passed as an argument. This default parameter passing mechanism is known as *call-by-value.* An alternative mechanism, *call-by-reference,* is indicated by placing an ampersand in the parameter list, as in the following example function definition:

```
double sqrt(complex & value)
{
    .
    .
    .
}
```

To implement a call-by-reference parameter, only a reference (that is, a pointer) is passed to the function. This eliminates the necessity of making a copy of the argument. For almost all data types, this results in much more rapid execution. Thus reference parameters are extensively used in the parameter passing of large structures.

Since a reference parameter is simply an alias for the associated argument value, changes to the reference made within a function will be reflected in subsequent changes to the argument value following execution of the procedure. This is not true with call-by-value semantics, since changes to the parameter merely change a copy of the argument value.

Protection of the argument value from undesired modification can be ensured by declaring the parameter as *constant*. This is accomplished by prepending the keyword `const` to the parameter declaration. The resulting parameter passing mechanism is sometimes then referred to as call-by-constant reference.

Parameter passing mechanisms are introduced in Chapter 2.

B.6 CONSTRUCTORS

A *constructor* is a function used to ensure that newly created instances of a class are properly initialized. A constructor is characterized as a member function having the same name as the class. Constructors are never explicitly invoked by the user; instead, constructors are invoked as part of the processing of a declaration statement. Where needed, arguments to a constructor are provided using the same syntax as a function call.

```
rational x;         // invoke constructor with no arguments
rational y(2, 3);   // invoke constructor with two arguments
```

Note that no parentheses are used in a declaration statement that invokes a constructor with no arguments. The use of parentheses in this situation is a common programming error.

The implementation of a constructor differs from a normal member function implementation in that the return type is not named, and the function heading can be followed by a sequence of initializers. Initializers either provide initial values for class data fields, arguments for constructors of class data fields, or arguments for constructors for parent classes from which the class definition inherits.

```
rational::rational(int numerator, int denominator)
    : top(numerator), bottom(denominator)
{
    normalize();
}
```

Constructors are also one of two mechanisms used by C++ to define conversion operations. A constructor with a single argument implicitly defines how conversions are to be performed from the argument type to the type associated with the class of the constructor. For example, the following constructor defines the conversion from integer to rational number. Conversions will be performed automatically by the C++ compiler to ensure compatibility between the left and right sides of an assignment statement, or between parameters and argument values.

```
rational::rational (int numerator) : top(numerator), bottom(1)
{
    // no further actions needed
}
```

Explicit conversion operators (see Section B9) provide the second method used to define conversions from one type to another.

Constructors are discussed in Chapter 2.

B.7 COPY CONSTRUCTORS

Copy constructors are characterized as constructors that take as argument a constant call-by-reference parameter of the same type as the class in which the constructor is defined. The following illustrates the copy constructor for the class `rational` defined in Chapter 2.

```
rational::rational(const rational & value)
    : top(value.numerator()), bottom(value.denominator())
{
    // no further initialization required
}
```

As the name implies, copy constructors are invoked by the C++ compiler whenever it is necessary to form a duplicate copy of a value. Most often this occurs when instances of a class are passed by value to a function or procedure. Copy constructors should therefore do whatever is necessary to form a duplicate copy of a value.

Copy constructors are discussed in Chapter 2.

B.8 OPERATORS AS FUNCTIONS AND OPERATORS AS MEMBERS

Operators (built-in, nonalphabetic functions, such as + and *) are unique in that they can be implemented either as ordinary functions or as member functions associated with a particular class. Differences between these two are as follows:

- When defined as an ordinary function, all arguments to the operator are described in the argument list. When defined as a member function, the leftmost argument is treated as the receiver, and it is not described in the argument list.
- When used as a member function, the leftmost argument can only be an instance of the class in which the member function is defined.
- When defined as an ordinary function, automatic conversion will be applied to all arguments in order to match argument types to declared function types. When used as a member function, such conversions will not be applied to the receiver.
- Operators defined as member functions are, like all member functions, permitted access to the private components of the class definition in which they appear. Such access is denied to nonmember functions.

Note that the number of operators, the number of arguments they take, and their precedence is fixed by the language definition and cannot be changed by the programmer.

Operators are discussed in Chapter 2.

B.9 CONVERSION OPERATORS

Data types can be defined as member function operators. Such a function is then invoked when an instance of the class in which the member function appears is to be converted into the type specified by the operator. For example, the following member function appears in the class `rational`. It is invoked when it is desired to convert a rational number into a double precision floating point value.

```
rational::operator double ()
{
    return double(top) / double(bottom);
}
```

Notice that no return type is specified for the conversion operator.

Conversion operators were introduced in conjunction with the `string` data abstraction described in Chapter 4.

B.10 DYNAMIC ALLOCATION

Most variables are declared, implicitly, as *automatic*. This means that storage for the variable is allocated when the procedure containing the declaration of the variable is entered, and freed (again, automatically) when the procedure exits. At the other extreme are global variables, which are created when the program begins and destroyed when the program exits.

The dynamic allocation mechanism permits the programmer to allocate and initialize storage that can outlive the scope in which the storage is created. Most often, this is done for one of three reasons:

- ▲ The lifetime of a variable is neither local or global, but in-between. Using dynamic allocation, the programmer controls when values come into existence and when they are deleted. This occurs with the allocation of nodes in a linked list. Nodes are created when elements are added to the list, and they are deleted when values are removed from the list.
- ▲ The size of a data value is not known at compile time, but it is determined at run time. This occurs in both the string and vector data abstractions, where operations (catenation, setSize) may alter the number of elements held by the data value.
- ▲ Polymorphism. True dynamic polymorphic behavior is possible in C++ only when pointer values (either true pointers are references) are used (see Section B.15). Sometimes dynamic allocation is used simply to make use of this feature.

Dynamic values are created using the operator `new`. This operator is followed by a type name, which is then optionally followed by arguments used in a constructor to initialize the new value. The following illustrates the dynamic allocation of an instance of `rational`, the class discussed in Chapter 2. Note that the `new` operator always returns a pointer.

```
rational * ratptr = new rational(2, 3);
```

An array of values can also be allocated using the operator `new`. The size of the array is specified after the type name. The following illustrates the allocation of an array of 25 integer values.

```
int * intarray = new int[25];
```

Note that memory that is allocated dynamically must be explicitly freed by the programmer. This is accomplished using the `delete` operator.

```
delete ratptr;
delete [ ] intarray;
```

The second illustrates the form used to delete a vector of values.

Dynamic allocation is used extensively in the string data type described in Chapter 4, the vector data abstraction described in Chapter 6, and the list data structure described in Chapter 8.

B.11 DESTRUCTORS

A destructor is simply a function that is invoked implicitly when an instance of a class is destroyed. Values are destroyed when local variables go out of scope, when dynamically allocated values are deleted, or when a value containing data fields is destroyed (in which case every field is individually destroyed). A destructor, if defined, is executed immediately before the data area occupied by the value is recovered.

A destructor is characterized as a member function named by a tilde followed by the name of the class in which it is defined. Destructors take no arguments, return no values, and are never directly invoked by the programmer. The following illustrates the definition of the destructor for the class `string`.

```
string::~string()
{
    // recover the memory used by the string
    delete [ ] buffer;
}
```

Destructors are defined for the string class described in Chapter 4, for the vector class described in Chapter 6, and for the list class described in Chapter 8.

B.12 FRIENDS

A class definition can specify one or more *friends*. A friend can be either another class or an individual function. By specifying a friend, the designer of a class explicitly permits the friend to access the private and protected fields of the class. The friend mechanism provides the programmer with very precise control over access to features of a class.

Friend classes where introduced in Chapter 8, where the classes `list` and `link` were mutual friends of each other.

B.13 SUBCLASSES — INHERITANCE

Two major mechanisms for software reuse are composition and inheritance. Composition refers to simply using an instance of one class as a data field in a larger structure. Inheritance is used when a new data abstraction is a variation or simplification of an existing data structure. Inheritance permits instances of the new class to access member functions and data areas from the older class without requiring any new code to be written.

For example, in Chapter 6 we defined the class `vector`, and followed this by creating a new class `boundedVector`. Through the use of inheritance, instances of the class `boundedVector` were easily defined and provided with functionality.

Inheritance is also used when a parent class provides specification for actions but no implementation. This was illustrated by the class `iterator` (Chapter 7), and the classes `stack` and `queue` (Chapter 9). Such a class is known as an *abstract* class.

B.14 TEMPLATES

The *template* mechanism is a facility used to parameterize a class description or a function. By use of templates, one or more types can be left unspecified in the class description. Using templates we can create, for example, a list data abstraction without specifying a type for the elements to be held by the list. Without the template facility, each new type of list would require the development of a new data structure.

Templates were introduced in Chapter 6. Since the majority of classes used in this text are collections of elements, templates are used extensively throughout.

B.15 POLYMORPHISM — VIRTUAL FUNCTIONS

A *polymorphic* variable is one that can hold values of different types. In C++ only references and pointers to class instances can be truly polymorphic. These can refer to instances of the class with which they have been declared, or instances of any *subclass* of that class (see Section B.13). The term *static type* is used to describe the declared type of such a variable, while the term *dynamic type* describes the type of the actual value (which may vary at different times during execution).

A member function invoked using such a value can either be matched to a function body in the class associated with the static type or the class associated with the dynamic type. If the member function has been declared to be *virtual* in the parent class, then the member function associated with the class of the dynamic type will be executed. Otherwise the member function associated with the class of the static type will be executed.

It is important to note that polymorphism occurs only through the use of pointers or references. An instance of a subclass that is assigned to a simple variable declared as holding values associated with a parent class will be *converted* into the parent class. This is the so-called "slicing problem."

Polymorphism is introduced in Chapter 7.

APPENDIX C

Timing Data for Sorting Algorithms

THE TWO TABLES IN THIS APPENDIX provide raw data on execution timings for various sorting algorithms. These figures were used to generate the graphs in the text. Note that values should be used only for comparisons, as timings will vary on different machines using different compilers. These timings were generated using the Gnu G++ compiler running on a 16MHz Intel 386. The elements for sorting were randomly selected integers between 0 and 16,000. In the first table the bucket sort algorithm was performed using 1000 buckets. Figures are in seconds, with a clock resolution of roughly 1/10 second. In the second table, the last column provides timings for the bucket sort algorithm with 2000 buckets.

Size				**Algorithm**				
	Bubble	**Selection**	**Insertion**	**List**	**Tree**	**Quick**	**Heap**	**Bucket**
500	4.7	2.3	3.5	1.5	0.3	0.2	0.2	0.1
1000	18.6	9.3	14.0	5.9	0.7	0.5	0.5	0.2
1500	42.1	21.1	31.6	13.4	1.2	0.8	0.7	0.3
2000	74.6	37.4	55.8	23.4	1.6	1.0	1.0	0.4

Size	Algorithm							
	Bubble	**Selection**	**Insertion**	**List**	**Tree**	**Quick**	**Heap**	**Bucket**
2500	115.2	58.5	85.1	35.7	2.1	1.4	1.3	0.5
3000	166.1	84.2	122.8	51.6	2.6	1.6	1.6	0.6
3500	227.5	114.6	169.3	71.1	3.1	2.0	2.0	0.8
4000	297.7	149.7	222.1	94.1	3.6	2.3	2.3	0.9
4500	375.8	189.4	279.4	118.8	4.0	2.6	2.6	1.0
5000	466.1	233.8	348.2	147.9	4.7	3.0	3.0	1.1

Size	Algorithm				
	Tree	**Quick**	**Heap**	**Bucket**	**Bucket-2000**
1000	0.7	0.5	0.5	0.2	0.2
2000	1.6	1.0	1.0	0.4	0.4
3000	2.5	1.7	1.6	0.6	0.7
4000	3.6	2.3	2.3	0.9	0.9
5000	4.6	3.0	3.0	1.2	1.1
6000	5.7	3.7	3.6	1.5	1.5
7000	7.1	4.3	4.3	1.8	1.7
8000	8.0	4.9	5.0	2.2	2.0
9000	9.4	6.0	5.7	2.7	2.5
10000	11.0	6.5	6.4	3.1	2.8
20000	25.1	14.2	13.9	9.2	7.9
30000	42.5	22.7	21.7	18.9	14.9
40000	61.9	31.0	29.7	30.1	23.6
50000	83.9	39.8	38.1	42.6	33.9
60000	108.5	49.1	46.5	58.3	47.2
70000	134.2	56.7	54.8	75.5	62.5
80000	163.5	67.3	63.8	98.3	77.6
90000	192.9	76.2	72.4	119.7	95.7
100000	226.5	87.7	81.0	143.8	114.0

APPENDIX

D

Table of Various Functions

The table in this appendix supply approximate values for several functions. Each line provides values for $\log n$, $\sqrt{n}$, n, $n \log n$, and n^2. These values are used in the solution of various exercises throughout the text.

$\log n$	$\sqrt{n}$	n	$n \log n$	n^2
0.0	1.0	1	0.0	1.0
1.0	1.4	2	2.0	4.0
1.6	1.7	3	4.8	9.0
2.0	2.0	4	8.0	16.0
2.3	2.2	5	11.6	25.0
2.6	2.4	6	15.5	36.0
2.8	2.6	7	19.7	49.0
3.0	2.8	8	24.0	64.0
3.2	3.0	9	28.5	81.0
3.3	3.2	10	33.2	100.0
4.3	4.5	20	86.4	400.0
4.9	5.5	30	147.2	900.0
5.3	6.3	40	212.9	1600.0

$\log n$	$\sqrt{n}$	n	$n \log n$	n^2
5.6	7.0	50	282.2	2500.0
5.9	7.7	60	354.4	3600.0
6.1	8.4	70	429.1	4900.0
6.3	8.9	80	505.8	6400.0
6.5	9.5	90	584.2	8100.0
6.6	10.0	100	664.4	10000.0
6.6	10.0	100	664.4	10000.0
7.6	14.1	200	1528.8	40000.0
8.2	17.3	300	2468.6	90000.0
8.6	20.0	400	3457.5	160000.0
8.9	22.4	500	4482.9	250000.0
9.2	24.5	600	5537.3	360000.0
9.4	26.5	700	6615.9	490000.0
9.6	28.3	800	7715.1	640000.0
9.8	30.0	900	8832.4	810000.0
9.9	31.7	1000	9965.8	1.0×10^6
10.6	38.7	1500	15826.1	2.2×10^6
10.9	44.7	2000	21931.6	4.0×10^6
11.3	50.0	2500	28219.3	6.2×10^6
11.6	54.8	3000	34652.2	9.0×10^6
11.8	59.2	3500	41206.0	1.2×10^7
11.9	63.2	4000	47863.1	1.6×10^7
12.1	67.1	4500	54610.7	2.0×10^7
12.3	70.7	5000	61438.6	2.5×10^7
12.6	77.5	6000	75304.5	3.6×10^7
12.8	83.7	7000	89412.0	4.9×10^7
12.9	89.4	8000	103726.0	6.4×10^7
13.1	94.9	9000	118221.0	8.1×10^7
13.3	100.0	10000	132877.0	1.0×10^8
14.3	141.4	20000	285754.0	4.0×10^8
14.9	173.2	30000	446180.0	9.0×10^8
15.3	200.0	40000	611508.0	1.6×10^9
15.6	223.6	50000	780482.0	2.5×10^9

$\log n$	$\sqrt{n}$	n	$n \log n$	n^2
15.9	244.9	60000	952360.0	3.6×10^9
16.1	264.6	70000	1.1×10^6	4.9×10^9
16.3	282.8	80000	1.3×10^6	6.4×10^9
16.5	300.0	90000	1.5×10^6	8.1×10^9
16.6	316.2	100000	1.7×10^6	1.0×10^{10}

BIBLIOGRAPHY

[Aho 83] Aho, Alfred V., John E. Hopcroft, and Jeffrey D. Ullman. *Data Structures and Algorithms*. Reading, Mass.: Addison-Wesley, 1983.

[Aho 86] Aho, Alfred V., Ravi Sethi, and Jeffrey D. Ullman. *Compilers: Principles, Techniques, and Tools*. Reading, Mass.: Addison-Wesley, 1986.

[Ashenhurst 87] Ashenhurst, Robert L., ed. *ACM Turing Award Lectures, the First Twenty Years*. Reading, Mass.: Addison-Wesley, 1987.

[Baxter 89] Baxter, Nancy, Ed Dubinsky, and Gary Levin. *Learning Discrete Mathematics with ISETL*. New York: Springer-Verlag, 1989.

[Beck 89] Beck, Kent, and Ward Cunningham. "A Laboratory for Teaching Object-Oriented Thinking." *Proceedings of the 1989 OOPSLA — Conference on Object-Oriented Programming Systems, Languages and Applications*; reprinted in *Sigplan Notices*, 24(10):1–6, 1989.

[Birtwistle 79] Birtwistle, Graham M., Ole-Johan Dahl, Bjørn Myhrhaug, and Kristen Nygaard. *Simula Begin*. Lund, Sweden: Studentlitteratur, 1979.

[Boyer 77] Boyer, Robert S., and J. Strother Moore. "A Fast String-searching Algorithm. " *Communications of the ACM* 20(10):762–72, 1977.

[Budd 87] Budd, Timothy A. *A Little Smalltalk*. Reading, Mass.: Addison-Wesley, 1987.

[Budd 91] Budd, Timothy A. *An Introduction to Object-Oriented Programming*. Reading, Mass.: Addison-Wesley, 1991.

[Cargill 92] Cargill, Tom. *C++ Programming Style*. Reading, Mass.: Addison-Wesley, 1992.

[Coad 90] Coad, Peter, and Edward Yourdon. *Object-Oriented Analysis*. Englewood Cliffs, N. J.: Prentice-Hall, 1990.

[Coad 91] Coad, Peter, and Edward Yourdon, *Object-Oriented Design*. Englewood Cliffs, N. J.: Prentice-Hall, 1990.

[Coplien 92] Coplien, James O. *Advanced C++ Programming Styles and Idioms*. Reading, Mass.: Addison-Wesley, 1992.

[Cormen 90] Cormen, Thomas H., Charles E. Leiserson, and Ronald L. Rivest. *Introduction to Algorithms*. Cambridge: MIT Press, 1990.

[Cox 90] Cox, Brad J. "Planning the Software Industrial Revolution." *IEEE Software*. 7(6):25–35, November 1990.

[Cox 91] Cox, Brad J., and Andrew J. Novobilski. *Object-Oriented Programming: An Evolutionary Approach*, 2d ed. Reading, Mass.: Addison-Wesley, 1991.

[Dahl 72] Dahl, Ole-Johan, Edsger W. Dijkstra, and C. A. R. Hoare. *Structured Programming*. New York: Academic Press, 1972.

[Dijkstra 59] Dijkstra, Edsger W. "A Note on Two Problems in Connection with Graphs." *Numerische Mathematik* 1:269–71, 1959.

[Dijkstra 76] Dijkstra, Edsger W. *A Discipline of Programming*. Englewood Cliffs, N. J.: Prentice-Hall, 1976.

[Ellis 90] Ellis, Margaret A., and Bjarne Stroustrup. *The Annotated C++ Reference Manual*. Reading, Mass.: Addison-Wesley, 1990.

[Entsminger 90] Entsminger, Gary. *The Tao of Objects*. Redwood City, Calif.: M & T Books, 1990.

[Floyd 62] Floyd, Robert W. "Algorithm 97: Shortest Path." *Communications of the ACM*. 5(6):345, 1962.

[Floyd 64] Floyd, Robert W. "Algorithm 245: Treesort." *Communications of the ACM* 7:701, 1964.

[Goldberg 83] Goldberg, Adele, and David Robson. *Smalltalk-80: The Language and Its Implementation*. Reading, Mass.: Addison-Wesley, 1983.

[Gonnet 91] Gonnet, Gaston H., and Ricardo Baeza-Yates. *Handbook of Algorithms and Data Structures in Pascal and C*. Reading, Mass.: Addison-Wesley, 1991.

[Gries 81] Gries, David. *The Science of Programming*. New York: Springer- Verlag, 1981.

[Griswold 71] Griswold, Ralph E., James F. Poage, and Ivan P. Polonsky. *The Snobol4 Programming Language*. 2d ed. Englewood Cliffs, N. J.: Prentice- Hall, 1971.

[Griswold 90] Griswold, Ralph E., and Madge T. Griswold. *The Icon Programming Language*, 2d ed. Englewood Cliffs, N. J.: Prentice-Hall, 1990.

[Hafner 91] Hafner, Katie, and John Markoff. *Cyberpunk — Outlaws and Hackers on the Computer Frontier*. New York: Simon & Schuster, 1991.

[Hansen 90] Hansen, Tony L. *The C++ Answer Book*. Reading, Mass.: Addison-Wesley, 1990.

[Harel 92] Harel, David. *Algorithmics: The Spirit of Computing*, 2d ed. Reading, Mass.: Addison-Wesley, 1992.

[Hartsfield 90] Hartsfield, Nora, and Gerhard Ringel. *Pearls in Graph Theory*. Boston: Academic Press, 1990.

[Hoare 61] Hoare, Charles Antony Richard. "Algorithm 63: Partition; Algorithm 64: Quicksort; Algorithm 65: Find." *Communications of the ACM* 4(7):1059–62, 1961.

[Hoare 62] Hoare, Charles Antony Richard. "Quicksort," *The Computer Journal* 5:10–15, 1962.

[Hopcroft 69] Hopcroft, John E., and Jeffrey D. Ullman, *Formal Languages and Their Relation to Automata*. Reading, Mass.: Addison-Wesley, 1969.

[Kay 77] Kay, Alan. "Microelectronics and the Personal Computer." *Scientific American* 237(3):230–44, 1977.

[Keller 90] Keller, Daniel. "A Guide to Natural Naming," *Sigplan Notices* 25(5):95–102, 1990.

[Kernighan 76] Kernighan, Brian W., and Peter J. Plauger. *Software Tools*. Reading, Mass.: Addison-Wesley, 1976.

[Kirkerud 89] Kirkerud, Bjørn. *Object-Oriented Programming with Simula*. Reading, Mass.: Addison-Wesley, 1989.

[Knuth 73] Knuth, Donald E. *The Art of Computer Programming, Vol. 1: Fundamental Algorithms*, 2d ed. Reading, Mass.: Addison-Wesley, 1973.

[Knuth 75] Knuth, Donald E. *The Art of Computer Programming, Vol. 3: Sorting and Algorithms*. Reading, Mass.: Addison-Wesley, 1975.

[Knuth 77] Knuth, Donald E., James H. Morris, Jr., and Vaughan R. Pratt. "Fast Pattern Matching in Strings." *SIAM Journal on Computing*. 6(2):323–50, 1977.

[Knuth 81] Knuth, Donald E. *The Art of Computer Programming, Vol. 2: Seminumerical Algorithms* 2d ed. Reading, Mass.: Addison-Wesley, 1981.

[Lukasiewicz 29] Lukasiewicz, Jan. *Elementy Logiki Matematyczny*. Warsaw, 1929; English translation: *Elements of Mathematical Logic*. London: Pergamon Press, 1963.

[Lippman 91] Lippman, Stanley B. *The C++ Primer*. Reading, Mass.: Addison-Wesley, 1991.

[McCulloch 43] McCulloch, William S., and William Pitts, "A Logical Calculus of the Ideas Immanent in Nervous Activity." *Bulletin Mathematical Biophysics* 5:115–33, 1943.

[Meyers 92] Meyers, Scott. *Effective C++*. Reading, Mass.: Addison-Wesley, 1992.

[Mullin 89] Mullin, Mark. *Object-Oriented Program Design, with Examples in C++*. Reading, Mass.: Addison-Wesley, 1989.

[Naps 92] Naps, Thomas L. *Introduction to Data Structures and Algorithm Analysis*. St. Paul, Minn.: West Publishing, 1992.

[Parnas 72] Parnas, David L. "On the Criteria to be Used in Decomposing Systems into Modules." *Communications of the ACM* 15(12):1059–62, 1972.

[Perlis 60] Perlis, Alan J., and Charles Thornton. "Symbol Manipulation by Threaded Lists." *Communications of the ACM* 3(4):195–204, 1960.

[Ross 85] Ross, Kenneth A., and Charles R. B. Wright. *Discrete Mathematics*. Englewood Cliffs, N. J.: Prentice-Hall, 1985.

[Rumbaugh 91] Rumbaugh, James, Michael Blaha, William Premerlani, Frederick Eddy and William Lorensen, *Object-Oriented Modeling and Design*, Prentice- Hall, Englewood Cliffs, N. J., 1991.

[Schaffer 91] Schaffer, Russell, and Robert Sedgewick. "The Analysis of Heapsort." Technical Report Number CS-TR-330-91, Department of Computer Science, Princeton University, January 1991.

[Schneider 91] Schneider, G. Michael, and Steven C. Bruell. *Concepts in Data Structures & Software Development*. St. Paul, Minn.: West Publishing Company, 1991.

[Schwartz 86] Schwartz, Jacob T., Robert B. K. Dewar, Edward Dubinsky, and Edward Schonberg. *Programming With Sets, an Introduction to SETL*. New York: Springer-Verlag, 1986.

[Sedgewick 78] Sedgewick, Robert. *Quicksort*. New York: Garland Publishing, 1978.

[Sedgewick 92] Sedgewick, Robert. *Algorithms in C++*. Reading, Mass.: Addison-Wesley, 1992.

[Sleator 86] Sleator, Donald D., and Robert E. Tarjan. "Self-adjusting Heaps." *SIAM Journal on Computing*, 15:52–69, 1986.

[Smith 91] Smith, David N. *Concepts of Object-Oriented Programming*. New York: McGraw-Hill, 1991.

[Spafford 89] Spafford, Eugene H. "The Internet Worm: Crisis and Aftermath." *Communications of the ACM* 32(6):678–88, June 1989.

[Stevens 81] Stevens, William, Gilford Myers, and Larry Constantine. "Structured Design," *IBM Systems Journal*, 12(2), 1974; reprinted in Edward Yourdon, ed. *Classics in Software Engineering*. Englewood Cliffs, N.J.: Prentice-Hall, 1979.

[Stroustrup 91] Stroustrup, Bjarne. *The C++ Programming Language*. 2d ed. Reading, Mass.: Addison-Wesley, 1991.

[Snyder 86] Snyder, Alan. "Encapsulation and Inheritance in Object-Oriented Programming Languages." *Proceedings of the 1986 OOPSLA — Conference on Object-Oriented Programming Systems, Languages and Applications*; reprinted in *Sigplan Notices* 21(11):38–45, 1986.

[Taenzer 89] Taenzer, David, Murthy Ganti, and Sunil Podar. "Object-

Oriented Software Reuse: The Yoyo Problem," *Journal of Object-Oriented Programming* 2(3):30–35, 1989.

[Tenenbaum 90] Tenenbaum, Aaron M., Yedidyah Langsam, and Moshe J. Augenstein. *Data Structures Using C*. Englewood Cliffs, N. J.: Prentice-Hall, 1990.

[Van Wyk 91] Van Wyk, Christopher J. *Data Structures and C Programs*. Reading, Mass.: Addison-Wesley, 1991.

[Velskii 62] Adel'son-Vel'skiĭ, Georgii M., and Evgeniĭ Mikhaĭlovich Landis, "An Algorithm for the Organization of Information." *Soviet Mathematics Doklady* 3:1259–63, 1962.

[Warshall 62] Warshall, Stephen. "A Theorem on Boolean Matrices." *Journal of the ACM* 9(1):11–12, 1962.

[Wegner 86] Wegner, Peter. "Classification in Object-Oriented Systems." *Sigplan Notices* 21(10):173–82, October 1986.

[Weiss 92] Weiss, Mark Allen. *Data Structures and Algorithm Analysis*. Redwood City, Calif.: Benjamin Cummings, 1992.

[Williams 64] Williams, John W. J. "Algorithm 232: Heapsort." *Communications of the ACM* 7:347–48, 1964.

[Wilson 90] Wilson, David A., Rosenstein, Larry S. and Shafer, Dan. *Programming with MacApp*. Reading, Mass.: Addison-Wesley, 1990.

[Winder 91] Winder, Russel. *Developing C++ Software*. New York: Wiley, 1991.

[Wirfs-Brock 89] Wirfs-Brock, Rebecca, and Brian Wilkerson. "Object-Oriented Design: A Responsibility-Driven Approach," *Proceedings of the 1989 OOPSLA — Conference on Object-Oriented Programming Systems, Languages and Applications*; reprinted in *Sigplan Notices*. 24(10):71–76, October 1989.

[Wirfs-Brock 90] Wirfs-Brock, Rebecca, Brian Wilkerson, and Lauren Wiener. *Designing Object-Oriented Software*. Englewood Cliffs, N.J.: Prentice-Hall, 1990.

[Wulf 81] Wulf, William A., Mary Shaw, Paul N. Hilfinger, and Lawrence Flon. *Fundamental Structures of Computer Science*. Reading, Mass.: Addison-Wesley, 1981.

INDEX